OTHER BOOKS BY THE AUTHOR:

Priests of a Century: Commemorating the Centenary of the Diocese of Wilmington, Delaware, 1868-1968

Cooke Publishing Company of Devon
Pennsylvania, 1970

The Cutting Edge: A Biography of Thomas A. Becker, First Bishop of Wilmington, Delaware, and Sixth Bishop of Savannah, Georgia

Cooke Publishing Company of Devon
Pennsylvania, 1982

Catholics in Colonial Delmarva

Cooke Publishing Company of Devon
Pennsylvania, 1996

Catholic Priests of the Diocese of Wilmington, A Jubilee Year 2000 Commemoration

Cooke Publishing Company of Devon
Pennsylvania, 2000

Dear Anne,

Enjoy Reading,

Father Bateman

BOHEMIA

1704 – 2004

A HISTORY OF

ST. FRANCIS XAVIER CATHOLIC SHRINE

IN CECIL COUNTY, MARYLAND

By

Rev. Thomas J. Peterman
A Priest of the Diocese of Wilmington

Copyright ©2004 by Thomas Joseph Peterman
All rights reserved
ISBN: 0-9758749-0-X
Library of Congress Control Number: 2004110911

Published by: William T. Cooke Publishing, Inc.
            Devon, Pennsylvania

✺ TABLE OF CONTENTS ✺

PORTRAIT OF POPE JOHN PAUL II 5
Portrait and Letter of Most Reverend Michael Saltarelli, D.D.,
    Bishop of Wilmington 6
AUTHOR'S INTRODUCTION 8
PASTORS OF ST. Francis XAVIER SHRINE 12

CHAPTER ONE 13
JESUIT MISSION IN COLONIAL MARYLAND (1704-1789)
FIRST PERMANENT CATHOLIC ESTABLISHMENT ON DELMARVA (1704-1726) ...13
    English Jesuit, Rev. Thomas Mansell, S.J.
    English Jesuit, Rev. Thomas Hodgson, S.J.
JESUITS REACH OUT FROM BOHEMIA (1726-1742) 19
    English Jesuit, Rev. Peter Attwood
    English Jesuit, Rev. James Quinn
    The Jesuit Academy at Bohemia
    English Jesuit, Rev. Thomas Poulton, S.J.
    English Jesuit, Rev. John Kingdom, S.J.
EXPANSION, SUPPRESSION, AND REVOLUTION (1764-1788) 35
    English Jesuit, Rev. Joseph Greaton, S.J.
    English Jesuit, Rev. John Lewis, S.J.
    English Jesuit, Rev. Matthias Manners, S.J.
    English Jesuit, Rev. John Lewis, S.J.

CHAPTER TWO 79
THE EPISCOPATE OF JOHN CARROLL (1789-1815)
NEW NATION, NEW BISHOP 79
    English Former Jesuit, Rev. Robert Molyneux
    English Former Jesuit, Rev. Francis Beeston
    French Sulpician, Rev. Ambrose Maréchal
    Irish Augustinian, Rev. George Staunton
    Irish Capuchin, Rev. Lawrence Phelan
    French Secular Priest, Rev. William Pasquet

CHAPTER THREE 129
THE NEXT FOUR ARCHBISHOPS OF BALTIMORE (1815-1852)
The Episcopate of Leonard Neale (1815-1817 129
    Irish Secular Priest, Rev. James Moynihan
    Belgian Jesuit, Rev. John Henry
The Episcopate of Ambrose Maréchal (1817-1828) 135
    Belgian Jesuit, Rev. Michael J. Cousinne
    American Jesuit, Rev. John Francis Hickey
    French Jesuit, Rev. Peter Epinette
The Episcopate of James Whitfield (1828-1834) 143
    American Jesuit, Rev. Richard B. Hardey
    German Secular, Rev. Francis Varin
The Episcopate of Samuel Eccleston (1834-1852) 152
    German Secular, Rev. Francis Varin (continued)
    American Jesuit, Rev. George King French Jesuit, Rev. James F. M. Lucas
    Swiss Jesuit, Rev. George Villiger
    French Jesuit, Rev. John Baptist Carey
    German Jesuit, Rev. Michael Tuffer

German Jesuit, Rev. Nicholas Steinbacher
American Jesuit, Rev. William F. Clarke
American Jesuit, Rev. James Powers
Irish Jesuit Brothers, Rev. John and James O'Sullivan

CHAPTER FOUR ...187
THE AMERICAN CIVIL WAR AND RECONSTRUCTION (1853-1868)
The Episcopate of Francis P. Kenrick (1852-1863) ...187
   American Jesuit, Rev. James Powers (continued)
   Dutch Jesuit, Rev. Matthew F. Sanders
   Swiss Jesuit, Rev. George Villiger
The Episcopate of Martin J. Spalding (1863-1872) ...193
   Swiss Jesuit, Rev. George Villiger (continued)

CHAPTER FIVE ...233
JESUIT MISSION IN THE DIOCESE OF WILMINGTON (1868-1898)
The Episcopate of Thomas A. Becker (1868-1886) ...233
   Swiss Jesuit, Rev. George Villiger (continued)
   Bavarian Jesuit, Rev. Charles H. Heichemer
   American Jesuit, Rev. John B. Gaffney
The Episcopate of Alfred A. Curtis (1886-1896) ...240
   French Jesuit, Rev. John M. Giraud
   French Jesuit, Rev. Joseph Desribes
   American Jesuit, Rev. Daniel F. Haugh
The Episcopate of John J. Monaghan (1896-1925) ...245
   American Jesuit, Rev. Daniel F. Haugh (continued)

CHAPTER SIX ...269
DIOCESAN PASTORS (1898-2004)
The Episcopate of John J. Monaghan (1896-1925) (continued) ...269
   Rev. John Daly
   Rev. Charles P. McGoldrick
   Rev. Charles Crowley
The Episcopate of Edmond J. Fitz Maurice (1925-1960) ...273
   Rev. John H. Walsh
The Episcopate of Michael W. Hyle (1960-1968) ...283
   Rev. Herbert T. Rimlinger
   Rev. John H. Dewson
   Rev. John P. McLaughlin
The Episcopate of Thomas J. Mardaga (1968-1984) ...287
   Rev. Russell H. Perkins
   Rev. Patrick Brady
   Rev. Carmen Vignola
The Episcopate of Robert E. Mulvee (1984-1995) ...292
   Rev. Philip L. Siry
   Rev. Thomas Flowers
The Episcopate of Michael A. Saltarelli (1995-____) ...297
   Rev. Thomas Flowers (continued)
   Rev. Steven Giuliano

INDEX ...338
PATRONS ...381
ABOUT THE AUTHOR ...383

**His Holiness
Pope John Paul II**

**Most Reverend Michael A. Saltarelli
Bishop of the Diocese of Wilmington**

DIOCESE OF WILMINGTON

POST OFFICE BOX 2030
WILMINGTON, DE 19899-2030
(302) 573-3100

OFFICE OF THE BISHOP

Dear Friends in Christ,

The Jesuit missionaries who came to Cecil County, Maryland in 1704 brought with them the iron cross which had been brought over on the Ark and Dove in 1634 when the English colony of Maryland was founded. Father Thomas Mansell, who established the mission at Bohemia, named the church in honor of Saint Francis Xavier, a great Jesuit missionary who carried the message of the cross to India, Ceylon, Mozambique and Japan, and who died of exhaustion off the coast of China 152 years before the church at Bohemia was named in his honor. In the spirit of that great missionary the Jesuit Fathers centered at Bohemia labored to plant the cross in Pennsylvania, Delaware and on the Eastern Shore of Maryland for the next two hundred years. Our first expression of gratitude on this landmark occasion of the Tercentenary of the Bohemia Mission, therefore, is extended deservedly to those members of the Society of Jesus who labored long and hard from the mission center at Bohemia to plant the Catholic faith in the territory of the present Diocese of Wilmington.

Since 1898, when because of population shifts and the needs of their own Order the Jesuits turned the mission over to the care of the Bishops of Wilmington, one diocesan pastor after another has struggled to maintain and preserve this ancient shrine. Our heartfelt gratitude goes out to those pastors who worked with their people to guarantee the continuance of this cradle of Catholicity on the Delmarva Peninsula.

The Old Bohemia Historical Society, formed in 1953, has succeeded in restoring and perpetuating the entire complex of church, rectory, grounds, cemetery and farm museum. Up to the present moment the board and members of that Society continue to support and promote interest in this hallowed spot. With the greatest joy on this occasion, therefore, I send congratulations on behalf of the whole Diocese and impart my Episcopal blessing to all associated with this endeavor to perpetuate and celebrate this monument to early Catholicity as well as to Catholic education in colonial America. Old Bohemia stands proudly as a dramatic reminder of the missionary task assigned to each of us in the church today.

Sincerely yours in Christ,

✝ Michael A. Saltarelli

Most Reverend Michael A. Saltarelli
Bishop of Wilmington

❧ AUTHOR'S INTRODUCTION ❧

The first Catholic priest to live on the Delmarva peninsula was Father John Gravenor "alias" Altham, an English Jesuit, who celebrated Mass on Kent Island in an Indian hut as early as 1635. He died shortly thereafter as the result of an accident and was not replaced. By 1662 the Wye River Basin had become a safe haven for the largest and most flourishing Catholic population on the Eastern Shore. The Wye Chapel built around 1675, was the first structure dedicated exclusively to Catholic worship on the Delmarva Peninsula. Jesuit Father Nicholas Gulick was resident priest there until the chapel was closed in 1689. It's foundations today, are under the eroding waters of the Wye River.

The Bohemia Mission became the earliest permanent Catholic establishment on the Delmarva Peninsula and one of the earliest in the English colonies. Its Academy founded in 1745 was attended by Charles Carroll of Carrollton, a signer of the Declaration of Independence, and his cousin John Carroll, first Catholic Bishop in the United States. Its story then is of prime importance not only locally but nationally. Bohemia played a critical role in the faith's growth in the English Colonies, enabling Jesuit priests to minister to Catholics during a period of religious intolerance. Many parishes on Maryland's Eastern Shore and in Delaware can trace their roots there. For three centuries it has survived fire, disarray, and neglect. Bohemia is too important locally not to have a complete history compiled. Therefore, I am grateful to the Old Bohemia Historical Society for the invitation to author this history as part of the tercentennial observance. A committee appointed for the production of the book included Father Steven Giuliano, George Barczewski, Donn Devine, Esq., Helen Dugan, Mary Maloney, Joseph Chaika, Geoffrey Gamble, Esq., and Margaret Matyniak, president. I am grateful to this committee for their helpful guidance. I also wish to thank Donn Devine, Wilmington Diocesan Archivist, and his assistant, Deacon John G. Parisi, for invaluable help in researching local church records.

A special word of thanks too, must be given to the staff at the Jesuit Provincial Archives, housed at Georgetown University, Washington, D.C., particularly to Lynn Conway, archivist in charge of the special collections division. A great debt of gratitude is owed as well to the staff at Associated Archives at St. Mary's Seminary and University, where the Baltimore archdiocesan records are kept, and where Tricia Pyne is director.

Finally, a sincere expression of gratitude is extended to the staff of the Philadelphia Archdiocesan Historical Research Center, especially to Lois Wilson who always had time to be of expert assistance.

This work, of course, could never have reached completion without the reliable and consistent skill of the typists, Loretta Edwards and Peg Tillinghast.

Rev. Thomas J. Peterman

Rev. Thomas J. Peterman
Galena, Maryland
November 9, 2004

ST. FRANCIS XAVIER SHRINE

The mother Church of the Catholic Diocese of Wilmington sits majestically on a hilltop just north of Warwick, Maryland. It was named for St. Xaverius, (1502-1552), one of the great Jesuit missionaries of the Catholic Church, canonized in 1622. It is not to be confused with *Bohemia Manor*, the estate granted to Augustine Herman in 1662, located on the main waterway which Herman named The Bohemia River after his native country. *Bohemia Plantation*, which the Jesuits called simply *Bohemia*, was so named because of its location between the two upper branches of the Bohemia River. Warwick, a couple of miles south of the church became a village 40 years after the establishment of the mission.

St. Francis Xavier stands today as a testament to three centuries of Catholic faith and two centuries of religious liberty. From this small but significant beginning the Catholic Diocese of Wilmington, as we know it today, has grown to encompass a 5300 square mile area which includes 57 parishes with a Catholic population 205,000.

Old Bohemia can be reached from Wilmington via Route 13, or Rt. 1, South to Exit 36, take Rt. 299 West through Middletown to Warwick where a historical marker will point the way to St. Francis Xavier Church. From Elkton South on 213 over Bohemia River Bridge and just north of Cecilton, turn left onto Bohemia Church Road.

MAP OF SURROUNDING AREA

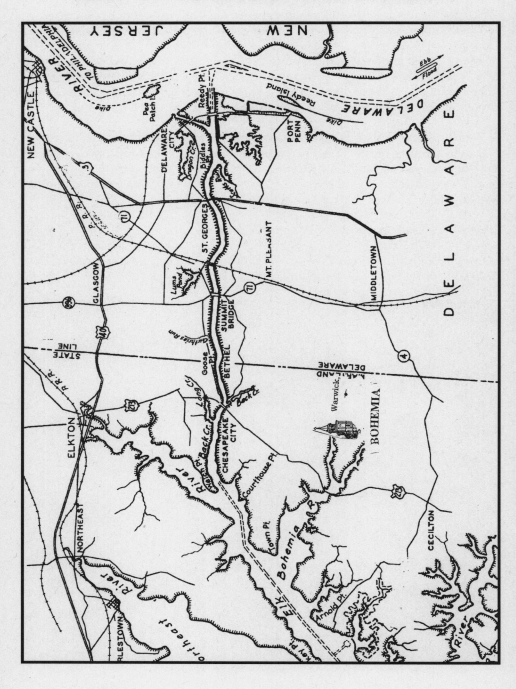

Introduction 11

The following listed priests are buried under the ancient boxwood pictured above at the rear of the church:

	Date and Country of Birth	Date of Death
Thomas Hodgson (Hudson), S.J.	1682, England	18 Dec. 1726
Thomas Poulton (Poulton), S.J.	1697, England	23 Jan. 1749
Joseph Greaton, S.J.	1679, England	19 Aug. 1753
Matthias Manners, S.J. (Sittensberger)	1719, Germany	15 June 1775
John Lewis, S.J.	1721, England	24 Mar. 1788
Stephen Faure	1761, France	21 Aug. 1798
Charles Whelan, O.S.F.	1741, Ireland	21 Mar. 1806
Michael J. Cousinne, S.J.	1767, Belgium	31 July 1810
Peter Epinette, S.J.	1760, France	8 Jan. 1832
John Baptist, Carey S.J.	1772, France	20 May 1843

PASTORS OF ST. FRANCIS XAVIER SHRINE
(OLD BOHEMIA)

1704-1712	Rev. Thomas Mansell, S.J., Founder.
1712-1726	Rev. Thomas Hodgson, S.J.
1726-1742	
1742-1749	Rev. Thomas Poulton, S.J., Founder of BohemiaAcademy 1745.
1749-	Rev. John Kingdon, S.J.
-1753	Rev. Joseph Greaton, S.J., Founder of Old St. Joseph's Church, Willings' Alley, Philadelphia – 1733.
1753-1764	Rev. John Lewis, S.J.
1764-1775	Rev. Matthias Manners, S.J., Founder of First Catholic Church in Delaware at Coffee Run – 1772.
1775-1788	Rev. John Lewis, S.J., served as Vicar General during Revolutionary War Period.
1788-1790	Rev. Robert Molyneaux, S.J.
1790-1793	Rev. Francis Beeston, S.J.
1793-1799	Rev. Ambrose Maréchal, Antoine Garnier
	Rev. Jean Tessier, Sulpicians
1799-	Rev. Lawrence S. Phelan
1806-1815	Rev. William Pasquet
1815-1817	Rev. James Moynahan
1817-1818	Rev. John Henry, S.J.
1818-1819	Rev. Michael J. Cousinne, S.J.
1820-1832	Rev. Peter Epinette, S.J.
1833-1838	Rev. Francis Varin
1838-1851	Rev. George King, S.J.
1852-	Rev. James Power, S.J.
1852-1856	Rev. Matthew Sanders, S.J.
1856-1878	Rev. George Villiger, S.J.
1878-1881	Rev. Charles H. Heichemer, S.J.
1881-1886	Rev. John B. Gaffney, S.J.
1886-1890	Rev. John M. Giraud, S.J.
1890-1894	Rev. Daniel F. Haugh, S.J.
1894-1895	Rev. Joseph Desribes, S.J.
1895-1898	Re. Daniel F. Haugh, S.J., Last Jesuit Pastor at Old Bohemia.
1898-1901	Rev. John A. Daly
1901-1904	Rev. Charles P. McGoldrick
1904-1929	Rev. Charles A. Crowley
1929-1956	Rev. John H. Walsh
1956-1962	Rev. Herbert T. Rimlinger,
1962-1964	Rev. John H. Dewson,
1964-1968	Rev. John P. McLaughlin
1968-1978	Rev. Russell H. Perkins
1978-1985	Rev. Patrick Brady
1985-1987	Rev. Carmen Vignola
1987-1992	Rev. Philip L. Siry
1992-2002	Rev. Thomas Flowers
2002-	Rev. Steven Giuliano

CHAPTER ONE

Jesuit Mission in Colonial Maryland 1704-1789

First Permanent Catholic Establishment On Delmarva

*I*n early 1704, Governor John Seymour arrived in Maryland to commence a tenure of slightly more than five years. He had a military background and supported unequivocally the cause of the Anglican Church. Any moderate toleration for Catholics, who had founded the Maryland colony, had ended. The Jesuits were compelled to distance themselves from the seat of government and to take refuge in Cecil County near Pennsylvania, founding St. Xaverius, the oldest and, for more than 60 years, the only missionary headquarters for the entire Delmarva Peninsula. The Jesuits used the plantation and its buildings to skirt Maryland laws that for most of the 18th century, banned the public celebration of the Mass. Private citizens could have a shrine or chapel in or attached to their homes and under what was known as Queen Anne's Law could invite friends to worship with them. The Jesuits invited Catholics to visit them at Bohemia and sent circuit-riding priests to Catholic homes to celebrate Mass and administer sacraments. Until the guarantees of religious freedom in the new American Constitution, the missionaries did not make any record of sacraments given at Bohemia. Such a record could have been used as a basis for arrest and fines under the Maryland law of the time.

After 1702, Catholics provided the strongest opposition to the Anglican establishment in Maryland. Quakers suffered a numerical decline as more and more of their fold were attracted to the established church. The only other sizable dissenting group, the Presbyterians, were confined mainly to the lower Eastern Shore, where their denomination prospered.

With eight priests and three brothers actively officiating for more than 2,000 communicants, and large numbers added each year in a swelling stream of migrating "Irish Papists," the Catholics caused enough alarm to the new and intolerant governor to provoke a major crackdown.

In 1704, the most restrictive and intolerant anti-Catholic legislation passed the Maryland Assembly. entitled: "An Act to Prevent the Increase of Popery in the

Province, "it was aimed primarily at education. Bishops and priests were prohibited from publicly celebrating the liturgy, from exercising the spiritual functions of their ministry, or endeavoring to gain converts, (although Catholics were still allowed to hear Mass with their own families and on their own property.) With regard to orphaned children the new law stated that:

> If a Protestant shall die and leave widow and children and such widow shall intermarry with any person of the Romish Communion, or be herself of the opinion or profession, it shall and may be lawful for his Majesty's Governor and Council, within this Province, upon application made to them, to remove such child or children out of the custody of such parents, and place them where they may be securely educated in the Protestant religion."

On September 11, 1704, Governor Seymour had two Jesuits brought before him and the Council. Father William Hunter was accused of consecrating a new chapel of St. Inigoe near St. Mary's City. The newly built chapel, which exists to this day, replaced the original chapel blown up by one Coode in 1689, a year after the last Catholic King of England, James II, was swept from the throne by his Dutch son-in-law. Hunter apologized for any public annoyance but explained that since only a bishop could consecrate a Catholic church, he could not be guilty of the charge. He admitted, however, to wearing priestly vestments in the new chapel, but not before a congregation, and that was before Seymour's arrival in Maryland. Father Robert Brooke was explicitly accused of saying Mass in the new chapel, and he acknowledged that he had, as priests always had done in St. Mary's chapel. The two were reprimanded by the governor, who said among other things in a long tirade:

> You might methinks be content to let the exercize of your superstitious vanities be confined to yourselves without proclaiming them at publick times and in publick places, unless you expect by your gaudy shows and serpentine policy to amuse the multitude and beguile the unthinking weakest part of them.[1]

The priests had as their lawyer Charles Carroll, grandfather of Charles Carroll of Carrollton. When Carroll presented himself before the governor, he was denied any hearing. Fathers Hunter and Brooke were allowed to leave after Seymour ended his harangue with a threat:

> You are the first that have given any disturbance to my government, and if it were not for the hopes of your better demeanor, you should be the first that should feel the effects of doing so. Pray take notice that I am an English Protestant Gentleman and can never equivocate.[2]

This outburst so pleased the members of the Maryland lower house that they sent the governor a message of congratulations, saying in part:

> As all your actions, so this in particular gives us satisfaction. We advise and desire his Excellency to give immediate orders for shutting up the Popish

chapel, and that no person presume to make use thereof under any pretense whatsoever.³

Accordingly, on September 19, 1704, Governor Seymour ordered the St. Mary's County sheriff to lock up St. Inigoe's Chapel and keep the key.⁴

The following month, Seymour induced the Assembly to enact legislation "To Prevent the Growth of Popery" by prohibiting any Catholic services at all in the province, whether for baptism, marriage, or the ordinary performance of the Mass. No priest could participate in any Catholic rite, publicly or privately. The Jesuit school at Newtown was closed, as were all chapels in the province. In an effort to restrict immigration of Catholics, a tax of 20 shillings was imposed on "Irish servants."⁵

With the support of other elements in the population, Maryland's Catholic leaders petitioned the Assembly to suspend the Anti-Popery Act and were granted a temporary suspension to allow time for the Maryland government to consult with the English government. Priests were temporarily allowed to officiate, but for private services only.⁶

The Catholic Proprietor of Maryland, Lord Baltimore, was summoned to the place of Whitehall in London and asked to account for the "continued irregularities" of his coreligionists in Maryland. He made the point that all other dissenters from the state church in Maryland had won toleration. Queen Anne, the Protestant daughter of James II, was persuaded that Catholics should be allowed to continue their private services, but she instructed Lord Baltimore to write the colony's Jesuits to cease their proselytization and to be more discreet in their activities.⁷ Privately, Lord Baltimore encouraged the Maryland Catholic Mission by instructing Charles Carroll, his agent in Maryland, to pay 1,000 pounds of tobacco from his own funds annually to each of the Maryland priests.⁸

Irish immigration continued, nonetheless, largely through the efforts of Charles Carroll. By 1703 Carroll had settled 200 Irishmen at the head of the Chesapeake Bay on land in Baltimore County near George Talbot's Susquehanna Manor in Cecil County.⁹ This action was a source of great distress to Governor Seymour, who declared to the Assembly that the "root of the evil" was the fact that the owner of the soil was "Lord Baltimore whose agents give great encouragement to their seating here." Seymour informed the Lords of Trade in England that Charles Carroll had promised the Irish "good tracts of land at the head of the Bay and free toleration and exercise of their superstitious worship."¹⁰

By 1705 Carroll patented more than 15,000 acres in Baltimore County (which included a portion of what is now upper Cecil County), furnishing the 50 acres per servant himself, or with Lord Baltimore's authority, as a headright in this frontier area. As a result, great numbers of immigrants poured into the upper-bay area, where land was fertile and cheap, and where Catholics might take refuge away from the public eye.¹¹

With their chapels and school now closed on the Western Shore, the Jesuits decided to establish a new mission that would be fairly central to the Catholics at the head of the bay and convenient for ministering to the increasing numbers of Catholics in Pennsylvania. The area's proximity to William Penn's tolerant colony also was a factor in selecting the site should the need for refuge arise. Prominent

Catholics had died in the Wye area, where the Catholic chapel had been closed and was kept under surveillance. They decided against reviving this first missionary center and, instead, chose to relocate farther north, in Cecil County.

Father Thomas Mansell had been attracted regularly since his 1700 arrival in Maryland to minister to the Catholic families in the upper bay area. In 1704 he began negotiations to acquire land for a new mission center.[12]

A Cecil County tract named Morris O'Daniell's Rest, containing 300 acres situated on Little Bohemia Creek, Middle Neck, had been surveyed on March 18, 1683, by a special warrant for sisters Marian and Margaret O'Daniell. In 1704, as Margaret was dying, Marian O'Daniell promised the tract to Thomas Mansell and to one William Douglass. Mansell later purchased Douglass' portion, and, since no record of the 1683 survey could be found, a resurvey revealed the extent of the tract to be 458 acres.[13] The grant was satisfied and the land conveyed to Thomas Mansell by Lord Baltimore on July 10, 1706. Henry Darnall, keeper of the Great Seal in Maryland, witnessed the grant for 488 acres, including adjacent vacant contiguous lands.[14]

Father Mansell named the new mission St. Xaverius, for the famed Jesuit missionary of India and Japan, canonized in 1622. The first building was a log structure, part of it set aside as a chapel. However, none of the earliest buildings have survived. The first brick structure was built in 1720.[15] Father Mansell brought with him a wrought-iron cross thought to have been transported by the first Marylanders to America on their ships "Ark and the Dove" in 1634. This cross is now in the Georgetown University archives, as are a ledger and a daybook begun

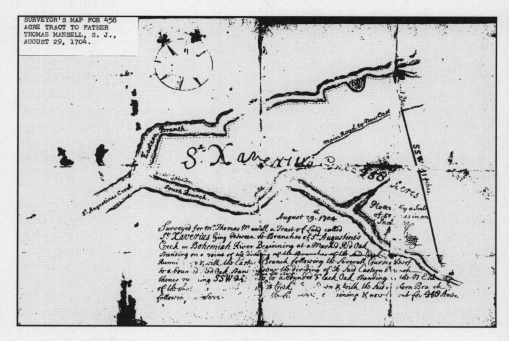

Surveyor's map for forty-eight acre tract to Father Mansell, August 29, 1704.

Jesuit Mission in Colonial Maryland 17

Aerial view taken in 1956 of same territory covered in Surveyor's map of August 29, 1704.

Boundary stone set by Father Mansell in 1704

Wrought Iron Cross from Bohemia Manor Mission 1704.

Historical Marker of Old Bohemia on Rt. 213

Historical Marker of Worsall Manor

in 1735. The earlier records of St. Xaverius no longer survive. Following the purchase of the original tract, the Jesuits at St. Xaverius over the years acquired a total of 1,700 acres.[16]

Not far from where the first log structure was built lay Bohemia Landing, shown as Priests' Landing on later maps. The landing included a trading post, where supplies from Europe could be directly received and tobacco shipped in return. Nearby was Augustine Herman's cart road, or "The Delaware Path," which was an artery for traffic between the Chesapeake and Delaware bays. Thus, from the new mission site, the Jesuit priests could readily make periodic visits to Catholics across the Pennsylvania border and to places in what is today the state of Delaware. *Bohemia Mission* was never a large congregation, but it was important as a base for serving an extensive mission area.

Forty-nine Catholics lived in Cecil County in 1708. Near St. Xaverius Mission is Worsell Manor, granted first to Peter Sayer in 1683. At Sayer's death, it passed to his nephew Charles Blake, who never lived there. In 1709 Blake exchanged the property with James Heath, on even terms, for a parcel of land called Heath's Wold on Corsica Creek near Centreville, in Queen Anne's County. James Heath had married Martha Blake of Worsell Manor, Peter Sayer's niece, of Worsell in

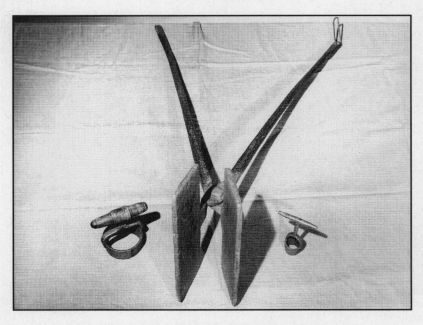

Mold for pressing hosts may date back to Fr. Mansell

Yorkshire, England. In 1710 Martha died, with no surviving children. A year later, James Heath married Mary Drake. They had several children, but only James Paul Heath, born at Worsell Manor in 1712, survived his father.[17]

In 1711 the senior James Heath, whose family kept a secret Catholic chapel during the 1700s at Mount Harmon on the Sassafras in Cecil County, patented 336 acres adjoining the St. Xaverius tract under the name of St. Ignatius.[18] He later sold it to Father Mansell, who was appointed superior of the Maryland Mission in 1712. He was succeeded at the Bohemia mission by Father Thomas Hodgson, who, like Father Mansell, was a native of Yorkshire, England. Father Hodgson would serve the Cecil County mission for the next 14 years.[19]

The Jesuits had begun to reach out toward Pennsylvania, establishing the Appoquinimink mission in what is now Delaware in 1706. The effort did not last, however, and the mission was closed within several years. No records survived, but John Gilmary Shea refers to the mission in his early history of Old Bohemia Mission.[20]

Lord Baltimore renewed his support of the Maryland Catholic mission in 1712 by ordering his agent, Charles Carroll, to pay 1,000 pounds of tobacco to the Jesuit superior and to the "the rest of his brethren being in all eight persons," with a further thousand pounds to be paid to James Haddock, superior of the Franciscan mission.[21] The mission, so long sustained from England, was bearing fruit. Robert Brooke, the first native Marylander to become a Jesuit, died in 1714.[22]

In a petition to Queen Anne, Lord Baltimore made a final effort to secure the Delaware part of the peninsula, but the division that had been officially confirmed in 1683 was sustained.[23] Queen Anne died in August 1714, putting an end to Penn's plan to sell all his interests in America and to Baltimore's hope to secure them.

Jesuits Reach Out Into Eastern Shore

A decade and more of peace settled on Maryland during the last days of summer in 1720, after Governor John Hart's departure for England. The next two governors, Charles Calvert (Lord Baltimore's cousin) and Benedict Leonard Calvert (Lord Baltimore's younger brother), pursued a policy of greater leniency towards Catholics.

Governor Charles Calvert began his conciliatory administration with a statement of assurance to the Maryland Assembly, declaring that "those little heats which lately disturbed you are now happily at an end."[24] Lord Baltimore himself aroused a vigorous protest in the lower house when he issued a proclamation that he wished the Assembly to understand that the statutes of England had no force of law in Maryland; that is to say, the strict laws discriminating against Catholics in England did not apply in the Maryland province.[25] The Jesuits were relatively free to carry on their work.

For the next 12 years, provincial energies were channeled into interests other than religious. For instance, legislation was passed to improve the quality of Maryland's tobacco, still its chief export. In 1723 an act was passed to establish one good school in each county, and legislators attempted in 1724 to restrict evils resulting from the importation of convict labor.

One good reason for this period of tranquility for Catholics was the absence of any war with France or Spain during the decade. The Stuart cause had come to a temporary halt with James Edward Stuart's loss of interest in ever gaining the English crown. With the birth of the son of James II, Charles Edward Stuart, "Bonnie Prince Charlie," in 1720, the Jacobites postponed their activities until Charles should reach maturity. A second son, Henry, born in 1725, and later Cardinal of York, gave Stuart supporters further reason to bide their time.[26]

Thomas Brooke, as president of the Maryland Assembly, served as acting governor from Hart's departure until Charles Calvert's arrival a year later. Brooke had been reared a Catholic and had three brothers who were Jesuit priests: Robert, Ignatius, and Matthew. However, Thomas Brooke professed Anglicanism at the time of its establishment in Maryland. His son, Clement, had married Jane Sewall, a staunch Catholic and daughter of Colonel Nicholas Sewall, who remained a strong Catholic influence in the colony until his death in 1737.[27]

The Jesuits were the only priests ministering to the increasing number of Catholics in Maryland, Delaware, and Pennsylvania. With the death of Father James Haddock in 1720, the Franciscan mission to Maryland had come to an end.[28] Maryland's population soared from 50,200 in 1715 to an estimated 80,000 in 1728. Irish immigrants poured in through New Castle, Philadelphia, and the ports of entry on the Chesapeake Bay. Between 1729 and 1735, the port of New Castle alone received 3,667 Irish immigrants, mostly Scotch-Irish Presbyterians, but among them a good number of Catholics. Germans also arrived in increasing numbers through the port of Philadelphia, where they were required to register and take an oath of loyalty to the British government.[29] The new immigrants formed small Catholic congregations here and there who looked to the priests from St. Xaverius for spiritual ministration.

Father James Hodgson (Hudson), S.J., had been superior of the Cecil County mission since 1712. In 1720 he saw to the building of the first brick structure to replace the original wooden chapel and residence there.[30] A plantation of many acres was needed to support the missionaries and their work. In 1721 Father Thomas Mansell, superior of the entire Maryland mission, acquired additional acreage with the purchase of a large tract from James Heath, a prominent Catholic who lived nearby at "The Holt." The tract, for which Father Mansell paid £20, was called St. Ignatius (100 acres) and lay just across St. Augustine Creek.[31] He further purchased from the same James Heath part of Worsell Manor (165 acres) and part of Woodbridge (70 acres), both adjoining the St. Ignatius tract. Old Bohemia mission now comprised 793 acres. In 1722 Father Mansell bequeathed all this property to Father Hodgson. Mansell, the founder of St. Xaverius, died and was buried at St. Inigoe's in St. Mary's County on March 18,1724.[32]

The Jesuit priests had received by John Simms' bequest further acreage, on Fairlee Creek in Kent County, Maryland, on September 10, 1714. This tract, called Simms' Prime Choice (75 acres), had been part of Heath's Longlands, and an additional 40 acres of Heath's Longlands was conveyed by Heath himself.[33] On October 10, 1722, Henry Darnall II transferred to the Jesuits an additional 300-acre farm on Fairlee Creek.[34]

These lands were cultivated as extensive tobacco farms and required many workhands. Some of these were indentured Europeans while others were African slaves. The Black population in Maryland by 1720 had reached 25,000. The Jesuits

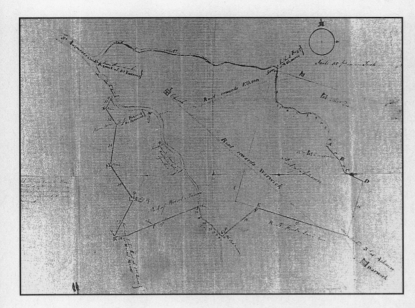

Plat showing St. Xaverius' Church and Road to Warwick and Elkton (c. 1800)

acquired these workhands in line with the economic structure of the day, and many of them became Catholic. For Catholics earning their living from the land, the nearly 30 holy days of obligation then established each year proved a real problem. On December 21, 1722, accordingly, the Jesuits secured Rome's approval of a regulation that permitted farm hands to do servile work between May and October, except on the feasts of the Ascension, Whitmonday, Corpus Christi, and the Assumption of Mary.[35]

Father Nicholas Gulick, who had served earlier in the Wye River area, died in 1718 and was buried on the Western Shore, where he had spent his last years.[36] Father William Hunter also died and was buried on the Western Shore in 1723. Father Thomas Hodgson died at Bohemia on December 18, 1726. His unmarked grave is the first under the huge boxwoods that once grew over the priests' plot at St. Xavier Church cemetery.[37]

Father Hodgson bequeathed the properties to Father John Bennett, who was stationed for a time at Old Bohemia. His name disappears from the list of Maryland missionaries in 1729, when he returned to England. On April 9, 1728, Father Bennett transferred the land to Father Peter Attwood, who added considerably to the acreage of Bohemia. He appears as a principal in some transactions concerning the lands of Bohemia in 1731 and 1732 and became involved in a land dispute with one Joseph George, who had purchased "Little Bohemia" from Ephraim Herman.

After the purchase, George obtained a warrant to have his property surveyed. The survey took in all of St. Xaverius, and there was a possibility that the Jesuits would be put off their land. Father Attwood was compelled to compromise by paying George £35 for a deed of release of all claim he might have to "any or all lands I hold between the two branches of St. Augustine Creek." Father Attwood was superior of the entire Maryland mission at the time of his death in 1734. As superior he resided at Newtown on the Western Shore.[38]

Two years before his death, Father Peter Attwood acquired another large tract of land, called Askmore, adjacent to St. Xaverius plantation in Cecil County. The 550-acre tract was purchased on April 20, 1732, from Vachel Denton for £200 current money.[39] With this acquisition, the Jesuit lands at Bohemia comprised 1,343 acres and would never exceed it. A boundary stone bearing the words "3rd of Askmore" (third stone, third corner) still stands in Warwick at the intersection of Water Street and Bethel-Warwick Road. The Jesuits today own some 700 acres of their St. Xaverius properties.

A set of old manuscript sermons delivered by the Cecil County Jesuits, the earliest dated 1726, is now preserved in the archives of Georgetown University. Locations of their delivery are noted and include Chestertown, Georgetown, and Head of Bohemia on the Eastern Shore. No earlier records of the Jesuit mission at Bohemia survive. A log and account book, begun in 1731, provides the first written record of the missionary activity from St. Xaverius.[40]

Jesuits Reach Out Into Delaware And Pennsylvania

Beginning again in 1731, the question of the Maryland-Pennsylvania boundary was continually disputed until its final adjustment by survey more than three decades later. The people along the Delaware would remain under the executive control of Pennsylvania until the adoption of a state constitution in 1776. In 1733, Fr. Joseph Greaton left Bohemia's Mission at Ivy Mills to found Old St. Joseph's, the first catholic church in Philadelphia.

The Quakers in Pennsylvania gave no trouble to Catholics in the public exercise of their religion. As early as 1720, a Jesuit was assigned to visit the Catholics in Philadelphia and offer Mass in their homes. Father Joseph Greaton, S.J., was residing in Philadelphia by 1729. His congregation, consisting mainly of Irish and Germans, had grown to 50 by the early 1730s. He purchased property on Willings Alley in 1733 and completed the first public chapel in Pennsylvania by 1734, dedicating it to Saint Joseph.[41]

The sacramental records of Saint Joseph's Church prior to 1758 have been lost, but with regular business trips and shopping jaunts to Philadelphia by ship from New Castle or down the coast, Catholics could avail themselves at least periodically of Mass and sacraments at the chapel in Philadelphia. There were sufficient numbers of Catholics in New Castle and Dover to warrant systematic ministry of a priest traveling overland on horseback from Bohemia by the 1730s.[42] From the time it was laid out in 1717, Dover grew steadily. A new courthouse was built in 1722 (where the present State House stands today). A letter written from Dover by a Mr. Bluett to the Anglican Society for the Propagation of the Gospel attests to the presence of Roman Catholics in the area.[43]

There were three or four Catholic families near Lewes in Sussex County, according to another letter written by one William Beckett to the Anglican Society for the Propagation of the Gospel on September 1, 1722.[44]

The set of old Jesuit manuscript sermons names localities where these sermons were delivered, such as Taylor's Bridge (near Dover), Duck Creek (Smyrna), Appoquinimink (Odessa-Middletown), and New Castle. Father Peter Attwood was superior of the entire Maryland-Pennsylvania mission until his death in 1734.

By that time, 19 Jesuits were ministering to an estimated 3,000 Catholics under their care. In 1735 Father James Farrar began a record of missionary journeys from the Cecil County mission. The record was continued by Father James Quin in February and March 1736 and by Father Vincent Philips from March 1736 to February 1740.[45]

One of the mission stations along the route from Cecil County to Philadelphia was at Concord, a small village originally settled by Quakers in 1683. Thomas Willcox, a Quaker, settled there in 1718 and opened a paper mill in Concord (now called Ivy Mills) in 1729. He married Elizabeth Cole, an Irish Catholic, at Old Swedes' Church in Wilmington on June 3,1727, and became a Catholic. Ten children were born to the couple. The Willcoxes kept a chapel in their residence, where Mass was celebrated for more than a century from 1727 to 1837.[46] Catholics who settled in upper New Castle County could travel just over the line to attend Mass at Concord, by way of the Concord Pike, which was opened in 1720 for travel to and from Delaware.

The beginnings of the first Catholic church in Delaware took place in Mill Creek Hundred, New Castle County at Cuba Rock on Red Clay Creek about seven miles northeast of Wilmington (near Hockessin today). In 1730 Mass was offered at the home of Cornelius "Con" Hollahan, an Irish Catholic farmer and blacksmith, who with his wife, Margaret Kelly, reared a family on a 148-acre tract purchased from Letitia, a daughter of William Penn. Con Hollahan and his wife had five children: John (born 1748). David (born 1750), James (born 1753), Margaret (date of birth unknown), and Mary (date of birth unknown). The family moved from Mt. Cuba to Coffee Run, in the same county, where Cornelius owned land as early as 1771. Cornelius left Mt. Cuba to his children in his will; it passed out of family hands on January 12, 1773[47] Con Hollahan sold property to Father Manners in 1772 as the site of the first church in Delaware.[48]

In lower New Castle County, Joseph Weldon, a farmer and progenitor of a large Catholic family in Appoquinimink Hundred, had been granted 203 acres on the upper reaches of Duck Creek by William Penn in 1701.[49] Nearby, in the area of the disputed Maryland-Delaware border, lived John Reynolds, an able farmer, born in 1666 and imported as a bondsman with his brother William. After serving his indenture, John acquired a tract called "Sarah's Joynture," which lay on Sandy Branch, a stream that flows into the Bohemia River. When the state boundaries were finally set years later, part of his tract fell into what is now the state of Delaware. John Reynolds died in 1731 and was buried at St. Xaverius Cemetery.[50]

Nicholas Reynolds, John's son, married Grace Lowber, daughter of a Catholic, Michael Lowber, who lived in Kent County, Delaware. Nicholas inherited 125 acres of Sarah's Joynture and lived there with his wife until 1736. He obtained from the Penn government an additional 212 acres on Black Stallion Creek.[51] In his will, Philip Edwards, a Catholic neighbor of Nicholas Reynolds, requested Father Mansell to look after his son.[52] Another Catholic neighbor, Richard McWilliams, received a grant of land between Sandy Branch and Tanyard Branch before the year 1740.[53]

While attending Sunday Mass at Meekins Neck in Dorchester County in 1712, Thomas Heverin met Hannah, a housekeeper at a Catholic home. They were married at Meekins Neck, and in 1714 their son William was born. When William was

18, both his parents died, but he continued to operate the plantation. At a Mass at Meekins Neck in 1739, William met Father James Quin, who told him about Appoquinimink Forest and invited him to visit Old Bohemia Mission.[54]

The period of calm enjoyed by Catholics in the decade of the 1730s allowed relatively free exercise of their religion and growth in numbers throughout the small congregations scattered over the peninsula. The decade ended, however, with an ominous hint of worse things to come for Catholics. War was soon to develop between England and Spain and to explode into an all-out struggle with France for dominance in North America. Governor George Thomas of Pennsylvania, in his 1738 inaugural address, grouped Quakers with the whole body of Protestants as moved by a common opposition to "the bloody Religion of France and Spain."[55]

The Mission At Appoquinimink

In the southwestern corner of New Castle County in Delaware is a largely rural area that from earliest times has been called "The Forest of Appoquinimink." In the 1740s it was settled gradually by many Catholic families from Maryland, a good number of whom were of Irish extraction. Since their chapel and school were only a dozen miles from St. Xaverius Mission, they received regular ministry from the Jesuits in Cecil County, Maryland.

Charles Calvert, Fifth Baron Baltimore, had every opportunity to inform himself before signing an agreement, in May 1732, with the heirs of William Penn to a plan that set the southern boundary of what is now Delaware as a line running westward from Cape Henlopen. But the Penns misled Calvert by using an old map that showed Cape Henlopen where Fenwick Island is now. By that mistake, the Penns gained for Delaware an additional 20 miles down the Atlantic coast.[56]

In the winter of 1732. the new Lord Baltimore arrived in Annapolis amid fireworks and pageantry, only to be quickly informed of the extent of the territory he had thus sacrificed. Angrily, Lord Baltimore announced that he would not honor the terms stipulated in the agreement.[57] So the boundary confusion dragged on until the English Court of Chancery in 1750 upheld the Penns' claims against Lord Baltimore. Before the necessary survey project was delayed once again, at least the southern boundary of Delaware as agreed on in 1732 was confirmed, in 1751, and so it stands today.[58]

Neither was the entire western boundary of Delaware settled by the mid-18th century. A tract on Black Stallion Branch, for instance, now in New Castle County, Delaware, was then on the Maryland rent rolls. It was named "Eleanor's Delight," for the wife of Nicholas Reynolds, Eleanor, who had inherited the land. In 1736 Nicholas and his wife moved to Eleanor's Delight, giving then and always their address as Kent County, Maryland.[59]

The Reynolds were Catholics, descending from John Reynolds, a former indentured servant, who had settled near Millington, Maryland, on land surveyed in 1680 for Richard Peacock. Nicholas and Eleanor Reynolds reared a large Catholic family and, after a long life, were buried in what became a large Catholic cemetery at Eleanor's Delight. It was more than a family burial place, as is indicated by an 1830 map of Delaware that designates it as "Catholic Community Cemetery." The plot is still called "The Graveyard Field" today.[60]

Only in 1764, after Charles Mason and Jeremiah Dixon ran the north-south Delaware-Maryland boundary, was Eleanor's Delight found to be in Delaware. A son, James Reynolds, born in 1731, lived on Eleanor's Delight until his death in 1787. Nicholas Reynolds applied in 1738 to the Pennsylvania authorities for a grant of vacant land that was adjacent to Eleanor's Delight. He received it, and a survey made in 1739 listed it as in New Castle County in "The Forest of Appoquinimink."[61]

Appoquinimink Forest had remained unsettled up to the year 1710. In that year Edward Mitchell, a land speculator, was granted by Maryland a tract of 1,650 acres along Cypress Creek. He began to settle farmers on the land, which he named "Mitchell's Park," located on the northwest side of Cypress Creek Bridge.[62]

In 1730 Daniel Dulany, a close friend of Lord Baltimore and then attorney-general of Maryland, bought all the Mitchell holdings.[63] Dulany had married Henrietta Maria Lloyd II, half-niece of Richard Bennett III and first cousin of Dorothy Blake, wife of Dr. Charles Carroll of Annapolis. In 1735 Daniel Dulany's daughter, Rebecca, married James Paul Heath, a Catholic, of Worsell Manor near Old Bohemia Mission in Cecil County. Heath's father, James, had died in 1731 and was buried first at "Warren" and reinterred in 1959 in the cemetery at St. Xaverius. His tombstone reads, "Here lyes the body of James Heath who was born at Warwick (England) on the 27th day of July 1658, died 10th day of November 1731, in the seventy-fourth year of his age."[64] This James Heath had planned the town of Warwick in Cecil County. James Paul Heath, his son and heir, carried out the plan and is regarded as the town's founder.[65] Like his father, James Paul Heath continued to ship large quantities of produce to the West Indies from his wharves on the Sassafras River.

Besides Worsell Manor, James Paul Heath inherited "Mount Harmon," a prospering tobacco plantation on the Sassafras. The manor house at Mount Harmon was built in 1731, and the Heaths also built a Catholic chapel there in what is called Shinai Woods, on the upper reaches of McGill Creek.[66] The site of this early chapel is now accessible through a 3/4-mile nature trail from the Mount Harmon driveway.

In 1741 James Paul Heath's sister-in-law, Rachel Dulany, married William Knight, another prominent Cecil County Catholic and parishioner of St. Xaverius Mission.[67] William Knight was grandfather of the celebrated Catherine "Kitty" Knight, a local heroine of the War of 1812. William and Kitty Knight are both buried at St. Xaverius Cemetery.

Daniel Dulany considered all his lands to be in Maryland. Still, Penn's sons continued to offer land in the disputed area to any who would pay the surveyor's fee. Gradually, the territory was settled, largely by Catholics of Irish extraction. Among them are found the names of Weldon, Cole, Clayton, Lyons, Heverin, Crouch, Pryor, Beck, Wright, McWilliams, McMurphy, McKay, McCool, O'Neill, Jones, Francis, O'Conner, Harris, Linkhorn, and Cartwright.[68]

Produce and furs were bartered at a trading post at the nearby community called Head of Sassafras (now Sassafras). The first road to be laid from there to Duck Creek (Smyrna), a distance of about 10 miles, was called Sassafras Road. For generations it was the most important road through the Forest community.[69] The

Appoquinimink Catholic chapel and schoolhouse, first referred to in the Bohemia records in 1750, were located on this road (today County Road #147) at what is now called Coldwell Corners (not Caldwell as on modern maps, but for the cold well available to travelers there), right on the Delaware-Maryland line.[70] James Heath's original property, "The Holt" (400 acres), was located there. From his residence James Heath reserved an 8-foot-wide pathway through the woods to Old Bohemia Mission to facilitate travel over the 12 miles.[71] The Appoquinimink Mission became one of the largest served by the Jesuits from Cecil County.

Another road connected Sassafras Road to Cypress Creek, and another ran along the east bank of Cypress Creek to the town of Chester Bridge, or Head of Chester. Patrick Lyons dammed the creek and operated the first of several gristmills at Chester Bridge, which soon came to be known as Millington, Maryland. Patrick Lyons' first wife, Catherine, was the widow of James Murphy, the local blacksmith and horse doctor. Ira E. Lyons, son of Patrick Lyons, inherited the mill property. In 1937 a heavy rain washed out the old mill dam.[72]

The only village that developed in "The Forest" was given the name Blackbird. Earliest settlers had called the whole vicinity by that name because large migrating flocks congregated there to rest and feed. Blackbird appears on Augustine Herman's 1670 map, designating the area.[73] The village exists today, as it formed, at the intersection of Sassafras-Smyrna Road and King's Road (today the DuPont Highway, Route 13), then the only overland route that ran from New Castle down the peninsula through Dover.

The Weldon family lived for several generations near Blackbird. On the northern side of Sassafras-Smyrna road was the home and farm of John Weldon, son of Joseph Weldon, who had settled there in 1701, and William Weldon acquired a farm located on King's Road near Blackbird.[74] Isaac Weldon received 203-1/4 acres in the area west of Linkhorn Park near the grant given to his father.[75] Isaac's wife was Ann Hollett. also a Catholic. Their children were Joseph, William, Isaac, and Josiah. Abraham Weldon lived on 50 acres he inherited from his father, Joseph.[76] His children were Rowland, Verate, Benjamin, Elizabeth (who married Peregrine Cole) and Milly (who married Elisha Crouch).[77]

An interesting development in American constitutional law involving Blackbird, Delaware, occurred in 1829, when the United States Supreme Court dealt with the Blackbird Creek Marsh Company versus a merchant named Willson. In that case, the company had sued Willson for damage done by his ship to a dam across the navigable tidal creek. The company won in state court, and the decision was upheld by Chief Justice John Marshall in this, his last commerce case.[78]

Patrick Lyons became a leader in the local Catholic group. He had received a fair education, most likely in the Appoquinimink Mission school. Benjamin Donoho built a hotel on the east side of King's Road as a depot for stage coaches traveling up and down the peninsula. Edward FitzRandolph ran a store on the opposite side of the road.[79]

In 1739 at Bohemia Chapel, Father James Quin introduced William Heverin to William Hill, who lived in the Appoquinimink Forest. Hill told Heverin that a tract of land in The Forest east of his land was unclaimed and invited Heverin to return home with him. Heverin liked what he saw and rode to New Castle to request the land from the county land office. In 1740 Heverin received a grant of 183 acres, which he named "Crispin Ramble," after Saint Crispin, patron of cobblers.[80] Heverin then sold his farm in Dorchester County, Maryland. and moved his farm equipment to his new property in New Castle County.

Father James Quin performed the ceremony when William Heverin married William Hill's daughter Matilda Ann. Six years later, Heverin heard during a Mass at Old Bohemia that Father Quin had been killed in an accident while leaving a ferry on the Choptank River on his way to Dorchester County.[81] Heverin and his wife cleared the new land, built a log house, and reared 10 children: William, Hannah, Ann, Barbara, Charles, Robert, Benjamin, Thomas, James, and Sarah. Matilda and the elder William Heverin were buried at Old Bohemia Mission. Sacramental entries in the Old Bohemia records for the Heverins were the largest numerically. A Heverin family graveyard near Reynolds Corners was plowed up many years ago.[82]

Samuel Beck, a Catholic, was brought to America as an indentured servant by the Dulany family. Joseph and Jacob Clayton, Catholics, lived on Dulany land. John Cole, another Catholic farmer of Appoquinimink Forest, lived on a 75-acre tract that was part of the 203 acres granted to Joseph Weldon by William Penn in 1701. John Cole was survived by five sons (Lambert, Isaac, Archibald, Peter, and Peregrine) and one daughter (Mary, who married a Reynolds).[83]

Adjacent to Mitchell's Park in Maryland was the extensive property owned by Thomas Collins, a Catholic, who had been granted three tracts in 1680. They were London Bridge (near Millington), Kilkenny, and Killmainam (an Irish name).[84] Contiguous to these properties were two of the five tracts (altogether 4,200 acres) granted to John Londey, another Catholic, possibly a priest. He had willed one-half to the Jesuits and the other half to Madam Henrietta Maria Lloyd in 1694.[85]

These many families in the area around Warwick, Middletown, and Odessa southward to Millington constituted a sizeable Catholic enclave. Hugh Jones, the nearby rector of St. Stephen's Anglican Church on Sassafras Neck in Cecil County, was prompted to complain on July 30,1739, in a letter to the Society for the Propagation of the Gospel: "The Jesuits in my parish seem to combine our ruin by propagation of schism, popery, and apostasy in this neighborhood."[86]

King George's War (1744–1748)

Aggravated by the wars of religion and the revocation of the Edict of Nantes in the prior century, a common hatred of Catholicism remained extraordinarily virulent in England and its American colonies in the eighteenth century. With Catholic France and Spain joining in war on England in March 1744, rumors and panics again flourished, heightening the common suspicion of Catholics.

The decade of the 1740s began with a frenzy that seized England when Robert Jenkins brought back an ear that he claimed to be his own, cut off by the Spanish. In 1739 Britain declared war on Spain in "The War of Jenkins' Ear," which developed into open warfare with France in 1744, a struggle in the colonies known as King George's War.[87]

Each county in the colonies had to furnish its own quota of troops. A conscription was passed compelling men to join the militia. The threat to the almost unprotected coast of the middle colonies was very real, making the prospects frightening for colonists on the shores of the Delaware and Chesapeake bays. In 1741 Spanish privateers were infesting the Delaware coast, some even coming up the bay.[88]

Thomas Bladen, who became the first native governor of Maryland in 1742, alerted the Maryland authorities to be watchful for any pro-French sentiments on the part of the Roman Catholics in the province. Although the whole current of Maryland history should have silenced the cry that the Protestant religion was in danger, and although Catholics were only in the proportion of one to twelve or fifteen among the inhabitants, the words "papist" and "Jesuit" threw people into a delirium in which all reason and justice seem to have been cast aside.[89]

The Jesuit superior of the Maryland mission, Father Richard Molyneux, happened to be in Lancaster, Pennsylvania, on business for his order at the time that the commissioners of Maryland, Pennsylvania, and Virginia met there for a conference with the representatives of the Six Nations. Molyneux's presence was seen by the commissioners as an effort to aid the French in preventing the Indians from ceding their lands. Therefore, on March 21, 1745, Governor Bladen had Father Molyneux arrested for treason. The story gathered further embellishments as it traveled from place to place. Eventually, Father Molyneux was required to appear before the Maryland Assembly, where no specific charge was made, but Governor Bladen took the occasion to lecture the priest before he dismissed him.[90]

Governor Bladen's anxiety over Catholic loyalties was further excited when in August 1745, Charles Edward Stuart, "The Young Pretender," led an uprising in Scotland in quest of the English throne. The Stuarts, the rightful Kings of England, Scotland, and Ireland, had remained Catholic and were backed by the French, who attempted to cross the English Channel with "Bonnie Prince Charlie" in 1745 but were foiled by a violent storm. Undaunted, Charles Edward Stuart gathered some 2,000 adherents at Perth in Scotland in December 1745 and began to invade England. When news reached Maryland that London was in a state of panic, the Maryland Assembly declared unanimously for the Hanovarian King George II. On January 14, 1746, *The Maryland Gazette* published the royal call for able-bodied men to enlist themselves on his behalf against the French and the Stuarts. The king's proclamation, published in the Maryland paper, was a source of embarrassment to loyal Catholic colonists by its naming their religion as that of the king's enemies: "an unnatural Rebellion is begun and is now carrying on in the North Part of this our Realm, in favor of a Popish Pretender."[91]

The Stuart forces, and the Scottish clans that rose in their favor, were easily defeated at Culloden in Scotland on April 27,1746. For months afterwards, "Bonnie Prince Charlie" hid out with a price on his head but no one betrayed him. In October 1746, he escaped to France but was denied any aid by King Louis XV. Jacobism did not end with Culloden, but gradually faded away as Stuart sympathizers accepted the reality that the door was closed to them with the withdrawal of French support.[92] Charles Edward Stuart died without issue in 1788. His younger brother, Henry, who was a Catholic priest was made a cardinal in Rome. Although Henry should have been king, few, if any, ever gave it a thought that a Roman cardinal would ever become king of Great Britain. When Henry Cardinal Stuart died in 1807, the very last of Jacobite hopes died with him.[93] His brother Charles, and his Father James, lie in a tomb in St. Peter's at the Vatican.

During the Stuart uprising in 1745, strong anti-Catholic feelings were enkindled in Maryland. The Reverend Hugh Jones, rector of the North Sassafras Parish (St. Stephen's) in Cecil County, published repeatedly in 1745 a prominent advertisement for his work entitled "A Protest Against Popery, Showing the Errors of the Church of Rome."[94] In September 1746, after the defeat of the Stuart forces, Governor Bladen charged the Jesuits with "alienating the affections of some from the British crown in connection with the Stuart uprising."[95] *The Maryland Gazette* on September 21, 1746, published "A Thanksgiving Sermon on Occasion of the Suppression of the Unnatural Rebellion in Scotland," a discourse not kind to "papists."

When *The Maryland Gazette* repeated the advertisement for the Reverend Hugh Jones' "Protest Against Popery" on November 25, 1746, the Jesuits at Bohemia did not allow his charges to go unanswered. A scholarly reply was composed and circulated in manuscript form since no printer was available. It was well received by many whom it reached. The Reverend Hugh Jones tried to get his hands on a copy but, failing to do so, published the following notice in Benjamin Franklin's *Pennsylvania Gazette* on November 13, 1746:

> To the Jesuits established in Maryland and Pennsylvania—
> Learned Sirs: Imagining myself to be principally concerned in the applauded answer to my "Protest Against Popery," that has been handed about by some of you in these parts, I have used all means in my Power to procure one; in order for which I applied to the gentleman on whom it is fathered, but in a very handsome manner disowned it. I presume I may be excused for making this my public request that some one of you would vouchsafe to transmit me one of the books that I may rejoin to any sophistical fallacies or sarcastical falsehoods (those usual tropes of St. Omer) that I hear this smart performance (as your friends call it) abounds with; assuring you that any assertions of mine truly demonstrated to be erroneous shall readily be recanted. Your compliance with my request will confer a great favor on, Learned Gentlemen, Your humble servant, H. Jones.

This letter was reprinted in *The Maryland Gazette* on December 9, 1746. A week later, the same paper again carried the advertisement for Jones' "Protest Against Popery," with an attending article that in part told its readers:

> All the danger to which Great Britain has been exposed on account of the late barbarous, bloody, and unnatural Rebellion is now happily over. A sect of Popish enthusiasts have endeavored to the utmost of their power totally to overthrow King George (whom may God long preserve). Thanks to Providence they have miscarried in their Aim.

Anti-Catholic sentiments soared when, in July 1747, a shipload of political prisoners from the Culloden defeat, most of them Catholic, were unloaded at Oxford, on Maryland's Eastern Shore, to be sold as indentured workhands.[96]

The long coastline of Delaware on the ocean, bay, and river, as well as the ports around the Chesapeake Bay, remained exposed to attacks from French and

Spanish privateers. In July 1747, a band of privateers landed and plundered a few houses and farms near Lewes, and again in September of the same year a small band attacked two plantations on Bombay Hook, at the head of Delaware Bay.[97] In May 1748, a French privateer captured an American ship in Delaware Bay.[98] All through these years, those who lived along the coastlines were kept in a great state of excitement caused by these threats. And the enemy was regarded and feared as "papist."

King George's War ended in 1748. It was, however, just an early phase of the expanding struggle between England and France for dominance in North America. There was no abatement for Catholics, as the struggle known as the French and Indian War resumed in the colonies and erupted finally in the international conflict called the Seven Years' War.

The Jesuit Academy In Cecil County

In the mid-1740s, while England was at war with France, the Jesuits opened a small school for boys at the Bohemia Mission. The temper of the times was bitterly anti-Catholic. As a consequence, the school's origin was obscure and its existence precarious and brief. The tattered pages of a small account book, now preserved in the archives of Georgetown University, provide all we know directly concerning the school's operation. Still, those pages bear some of the most illustrious names in American Catholic history.

The only formal school that the Jesuits had sponsored in colonial Maryland prior to the eighteenth century was that conducted at Newtown in St. Mary's County on the Western Shore of the Chesapeake Bay. Ralph Crouch, a lay brother, had been schoolmaster there from its opening in 1640 for a period of 20 years. Crouch had been succeeded by Gregory Turberville, who directed the school until his death in 1684. The era of persecution aroused by the overthrow of James II caused the closing of the Newtown school in 1689.[99]

Only five years later, the Maryland Assembly passed a law "for the further prevention of the growth of Popery," making it illegal for Catholics to carry on any school work. The burden was thus thrown upon Catholic parents, who were by law liable to a fine of 40 shillings a day if they employed any but a Protestant tutor.[100]

From 1715 to 1751, however, Catholics were, for the most part, unmolested in the practice of their faith, provided that it was not public. The laws, nonetheless, were open to extreme interpretation by bigoted judges and were so framed that they empowered intolerant non-Catholics to rob the father of his child and the widow of her children. The Assembly in 1749 was attempting to pass a law to confiscate all Jesuit properties. After a dispute erupted publicly in 1751 between Charles Carroll of Annapolis and Dr. Charles Carroll over the estate of James Carroll, the Assembly sought to pass new anti-Catholic legislation.[101]

Wealthy Catholics could secure a private tutor from among the many capable schoolmasters fleeing persecution in Ireland. Maryland and Pennsylvania attracted an abundance of these, many of them coming as indentured servants. The annals of Maryland's court proceedings show several instances in which Catholic Irish schoolmasters were arrested for refusing to take the Test Oath, which denied their faith.[102] Still, in spite of the stringency of laws and the vigilance of some authorities, Catholic parents of means often provided Catholic tutors for their children without recrimination.

Catholic priests were forbidden by law to engage in education, although clergymen of all denominations were commonly employed as tutors. On their missionary journeys, the Jesuits privately instructed candidates for the sacraments and encouraged Catholic parents of means to send their sons and daughters to Europe for higher Catholic education. Poorer Catholic parents were left to instruct their children to the best of their ability.

After the Assembly in 1723 passed an act to erect schools and provide for local supervisors, or visitors, there were regular efforts to establish one good "free school," for boys only, in each Maryland county. The schoolmaster was required to be an Anglican. Some counties failed to provide a school, but Kent, Queen Anne's, and Somerset counties established notably successful schools. For instance, a 1740s Maryland Gazette advertisement states that at the Kent County Free School in Chestertown "Young gentlemen will be boarded and taught the Greek and Latin tongues, Writing, Arithmetic, Fencing, and Dancing."[103] A brief mention is made in the history of Mount Harmon, on the Sassafras River in Cecil County, of a young girls' school in the 1740s at the home of the Catholic Heath family.[104]

The Jesuits had wished to open a school in Cecil County in 1704. when they established the St. Xaverius Mission, so far away from the Annapolis government. Three decades and a half passed, however, before that plan became a reality. Father Thomas Poulton is credited with starting Bohemia Academy in the 1740s. Father Poulton was superior of the entire Maryland mission at that time, and Father Henry Neale, superior of the Old Bohemia mission. A paid schoolmaster by the name of Mr. Wayt was in charge of instruction at the academy.

Jesuits who were at the Bohemia mission during the years following establishment included the Reverend John Digges, 1742 (died in 1746 at the age of 34); the Reverend James Farrar, 1733–1745 (kept book of accounts for mission from 1735 and returned to England in 1747); and the Reverend Richard Molyneux, 1748 (returned to England in 1749 after 19 years in Maryland).[105]

Father Henry Neale, S.J., a native of Maryland and son of Anthony Neale and Elizabeth Digges, remained superior of Bohemia until his death in 1748 in Philadelphia, where he was assisting the ill Father Greaton, founder of St. Joseph's Church there.[106] Because of age, Father Greaton retired in 1750 to Bohemia, where he died and was buried in 1753.[107] Father John Lewis became superior of Bohemia in 1750.

There is tangible evidence that a separate building existed to house the academy.[108] Around that building, which served as both residence and classroom, swirled the frenzy of activity that was part of any mission plantation. Numerous workhands tended livestock and farmed the land. Among them were blacksmiths who shod the horses, mules, and oxen, and made tools, pots, rims for wheels, and runners for sleds. In the 1700s bricks for buildings were baked in a kiln at the mission. In 1747 the Jesuits opened a mill at Old Bohemia on the south branch of St. Augustine Creek, from which water was dammed for the wheel turning millstones to grind grain into flour. The Bohemia account book provides ample information regarding business transactions involved in the operation of a typical colonial plantation.[109]

Here and there in this record are bits of information that shed some light on the academy itself. Tuition for the elementary course (the rudiments of reading, writing, and arithmetic) was set at £30 currency per year. For those taking classes preparatory to higher education in Europe (in Latin, algebra, and perhaps Greek), the tuition was set at £40 a year, with room and board.

The Bohemia account book also gives information, sparse as it is, on those who were enrolled in the academy. The earliest students were Daniel Carroll II (born in 1730) and James Reynolds (born in 1731). Daniel Carroll II was a member of the Maryland Catholic gentry. His father had married Eleanor Darnall, daughter of Henry Darnall II. Daniel Carroll II prepared at Bohemia for an education abroad and left there in 1742 for six years of study on the Continent. He was only 18 when he returned to take over the burdens of his father's mercantile empire. His father died in 1751, and Daniel inherited his father's lands and money. He built a reputation for a solid, upright character and a sincere loyalty to his native Maryland. He became prominent in the political life of the new nation after the Revolution, was a framer of the American Constitution, and served as a commissioner for the new District of Columbia before his death in 1796.[110]

James Reynolds, on the other hand, was the son of a farmer in New Castle County, Delaware, just across the line in the Appoquinimink area. James Reynolds took only the basic course at Bohemia Academy and returned to the farm, where during and after his schooling he helped his father. He inherited Eleanor's Delight from his father and continued to farm it until his death in 1787.[111]

We might reasonably presume that other boys from the neighborhood of Bohemia received the rudiments of education at the academy. Mentioned in accounts were day students who rode their horses to school from the surrounding countryside. David Witherspoon, the son of Middletown's Captain Witherspoon attended the academy. In 1747 Philip Reading, the minister of St. Anne's Anglican Church near Middletown, reported to the Society for the Propagation of the Gospel that some 82 "papists" lived in his parish in Appoquinimink Hundred.[112] Michael and John Reynolds, sons of Daniel and Grace (Lowber) Reynolds, all Catholics, were about the same age as James Reynolds and probably also spent some time at the academy.[113]

Two cousins of the Reynolds boys, who definitely were enrolled as students at Bohemia, were Matthew and Peter Lowber, both from farms in Kent County, Delaware. Their grandfather, Peter Lowber, a Catholic from Amsterdam, Holland, had purchased land near Dover in 1684.[114] One son, Michael, inherited land from his father and in 1740 purchased an adjoining 270 acres at Petersburg in the Dover area.

Father Poulton purchased land farther north in Murderkill Hundred in 1745 from Matthew Lowber and John Cain, the first a tract of 135 acres called "Cavil Ridge." On November 3, 1747, he purchased a second tract, registered as the "Cavil Ridge Addition" (225 acres), contiguous to property owned by a second son, Peter Lowber II, who had attended Bohemia Academy around 1746 and had married Catherine Cain.[115] His home, known as the Peter Lowber House, in Frederica, was built around 1737.[116] He laid out the town on his property, and a Lober Street in Frederica remains today. Peter Lowber II died in 1770. A cousin, Manassey Cain, the same age, attended the academy with the Lowbers. He served in the colonial wars with them and the Reynoldses, as the Kent County muster rolls indicate.[117]

Two students at the Bohemia Academy were from nearby Worsell Manor: James and Daniel Charles Heath, sons of James Paul and Mary Heath. The Heath brothers were aristocrats destined to study in Europe. James Heath became a Jesuit in Europe before his father's death and remained there for the rest of his life. As a result, his younger brother, Daniel Charles Heath, inherited Worsell Manor and was the first of the Heaths to live there. After his continental studies, he lived a carefree life, marrying, first, Mary Key of St. Mary's County and, second, Hannah Clarke, the mother of his eight children.[118] He was the last Heath to own Worsell Manor. In 1788 it was deeded to his creditors.

From Queen Anne's County in Maryland came two other aristocratic students at the Bohemia Academy. These were Bennett and Edward (Neddy) Neale, sons of Edward and Mary (Lowe) Neale. Their record in the Bohemia account book begins in 1745.[119] By their grandfather (Anthony Neale), they were grandnephews of Madam Lloyd of Wye. By their mother, they were grandnephews of Richard Bennett III, the wealthiest person in America and the most prominent Catholic on the Eastern Shore during his time. In 1746, while they were students at the academy, their father married, secondly, Elizabeth Digges Hawkins, who owned the property called "Bolingly," adjacent to the village of Queenstown. Edward Neale became owner of Bolingly from 1746 until his death in 1760.[120]

Neither Benny (Bennett) nor Neddy (Edward) Neale survived their father. Bennett died while a student at Bohemia Academy in May 1746. A brief note appears in the account book of his illness and death: "To Doctor Matthews, 300 pds. tobacco, To a coffin for Ben. Neale 1 pound." Dr. Hugh Matthews was a Catholic

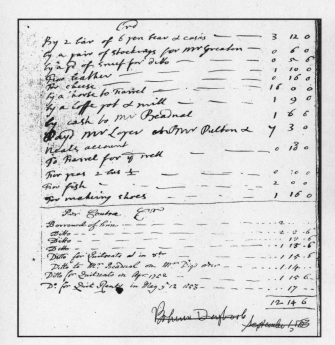

James Heath Chalice (c. 1695 Annapolis)

Page from Bohemia Daybook, Sept. 1, 1753

physician and parishioner of St. Xaverius. He died in 1756.[121] Neddy (Edward) Neale died in 1749 in Queen Anne's County. There is no information available regarding his death. The one daughter, Martha Neale (born 1737) married Francis Hall, a prominent Catholic. She inherited Bolingly in 1760. Her uncle, the brother of Edward Neale, the Reverend Bennett Neale (born 1709) became a Jesuit and served most of his life at Deer Creek in Harford County. He was stationed at Bohemia from 1749 to 1751.[122]

Two Neale cousins, Leonard and Charles, are alleged to have received early education at the Bohemia Academy but are not mentioned in the account book. These were sons of William and Ann (Brooke) Neale of Charles County. Through their father they were grandnephews of Madam Lloyd of Wye. Born in 1746, Leonard later studied in Europe and became a Jesuit priest. The Reverend Leonard Neale was president of Georgetown College, is credited with the establishment of the Visitation Monastery in Georgetown, was consecrated coadjutor-bishop of Baltimore in 1800, and succeeded to the archbishopric in 1815.[123] His brother Charles, born in 1751, also studied in Europe, joined the Jesuits, and returned to America with a group of Carmelite nuns to found the first Carmelite monastery in the United States, at Port Tobacco on the Western Shore of Maryland.[124]

Another cousin to the Neales who attended the academy in Cecil County was Robert Brent, oldest son of George and Mary (Wharton) Brent, of Woodstock, Virginia. Nephew of Giles and Margaret Brent, George Brent was a prominent Catholic lawyer. George's sister, Mary Brent, had married Oswald Neale, second son of Anthony Neale and brother of Edward Neale. Robert Brent studied at Bohemia at the same time as Daniel Carroll and accompanied him to Europe in 1748. After his formal education, Brent rapidly rose to prominence in business and politics. He married Ann, daughter of Daniel and Eleanor (Darnall) Carroll. Their sons were Robert Brent Jr., who became first mayor of Washington, D.C.; Daniel Brent, who was United States Consul to Paris; and George Brent, a member of the Virginia House of Delegates from 1787 to 1789. Robert Brent Sr., died in 1790.[125]

John Sayer Blake II and Philemon Charles Blake attended the Bohemia Academy. The Blakes were great-grandnephews of Peter Sayer. Their father, John Sayer Blake I, died in 1748.[126]

There is a persistent tradition, although no documentary evidence to prove, that Charles Carroll of Carrollton, only son of Charles Carroll of Annapolis, also attended Bohemia Academy before studying in Europe.[127] A steady supporter of George Washington, Charles Carroll of Carrollton was the only Catholic signer of the Declaration of Independence, and the last of all the signers to die.

The person who played the greatest

Portrait of young Jackie Carroll

role in the formation of the early American church, as founder of the American hierarchy, was John Carroll, younger son of Daniel and Eleanor (Darnall) Carroll, of Upper Marlboro Prince George's County, Maryland. At the age of 12, "Jacky" Carroll enrolled at the Bohemia Academy. He was a student at Bohemia Academy in 1745 and 1746.[128] In July 1748 he left for Europe with his cousin, Charles Carroll of Carrollton. Ordained a Jesuit priest in 1767, John Carroll remained in Europe until the eve of the American Revolution. With the support of Benjamin Franklin, he was consecrated the first bishop of the United States in 1790, and the first archbishop in 1808.

In 1751 the Maryland Assembly introduced various stringent acts to enforce the penal code for Catholics. Few of these passed in the upper house, but the climate was very threatening to any Catholic activity. With the beginning of the French and Indian War, the Reverend Hugh Jones, the Anglican rector of North Sassafras Parish in Cecil County, publicized the fact of a "popish seminary" in his parish and instigated efforts to enforce the "Act to Prevent the Growth of Popery."[129] Conditions were considered too dangerous to continue the academy, so its doors were closed in the early 1750s. No evidence exists that they were ever opened again.

The Bohemia academy was not, as sometimes stated, the predecessor of Georgetown University, since there was no connection between the two except that Bishop Carroll attended one and founded the other. The academy was, however, the first of many American Jesuit schools and colleges that have established a reputation for educational excellence.

The Seven Years War (1754–1763)

Events in the early 1750s set the stage for the final quarter-century before the American Revolution. For years the English and French had been fighting to gain mastery in North America. The final conflict erupted in the spring of 1754 in western Pennsylvania. It turned out to be one of the worst periods of trial for Roman Catholics in the colonies.

Maryland and Pennsylvania were panic-stricken during King George's War, and even more so during the French and Indian War. Fear of attack from water or land, suspicion of the Catholic minority, hostility toward Scot rebels in their midst, and dread of more arrivals direct from Ireland all contributed to an unreasoning fear of "popery."

In October 1750, the zealous and effective Father John Lewis, S.J., became superior of Old Bohemia mission in Cecil County. For the next 11 years, he recorded his coverage of the extensive mission stations under his care, noting some 210 excursions for those years.

Slaves at Bohemia Plantation

As a typical plantation of colonial times, Bohemia had its share of slaves on whom it depended to perform the household and farm work. Although the mission was founded in 1704, and in all likelihood there probably were slaves on the plantation almost from its founding, the earliest record that can be found is in the

Bohemia Daybook (1735-1761). It is contained in an entry dated February 7, 1756: "Mathias Nolend, to our negro, Ben, four shillings, to our negro, Tom, 8 shillings." From this date on there are occasional references to negro servants throughout the rest of the account book.

A knowledge of the names of these faithful blacks can be derived from the references to their respective deaths and burials as culled from the Jesuit records, and should be comprehensive of those who died while still under servitude to the Jesuit Fathers:

The Jesuits, like all typical colonial proprietors, owned negro slaves and depended on them to man the farms which provided the income to cover household, mission and educational expenses. From an economic point of view, the slaves were, therefore, essential to the advancement of the Jesuits missionary goals, and this ownership of them was in keeping with the accepted system of slavery in effect throughout the English Colonies of North America.

Father George Hunter's summary report for 1765 gives a total of 192 slaves for the seven Jesuit owned estates, and only 101 were working hands.

The Jesuit owned estates were managed by priests and the old Jesuit records indicate the considerate manner in which they avoided the term "slaves" and referred to them usually as "servant men, servant women, negroes and members of the family." Such consideration is an indication of the position these domestics held under the Jesuit management and the moral care taken of them. From an economic point of view, such considerations may explain in part the unprofitable conditions of the priests' farms, manned as they were with what were called by the Jesuits plantation neighbors "priests slaves," this latter term found in contemporary literature refers in a complimentary manner to the way in which Jesuit slave owners treated their Blacks.

The Jesuit literature on slaves holdings also shows examples of the priests-managers alienation or buying slaves under compulsion to prevent the separation of man and wife, and obligation of charity which did not appeal to other masters, and which necessarily imposed upon the missionary proprietor new arrangements without any regard to his convenience or his means.[130]

An influx of Irish, German, and French Catholics was increasing the attendance at the mission stations. Father Lewis was joined by Father James Beadnall by late 1750, and Father Richard Gailibrande arrived to work with them in 1753. Gailibrande went from Bohemia Mission to visit Catholics at Murderkill (Frederica) and Dover in Delaware. The town of Canterbury was first called "Irish Hill," a fact that indicates a number of Irish once lived there.

In several public documents, Father Beadnall is described as "of Queen Anne's County." There are good indications that after 1748 he resided at Kings Town on the Chester River opposite Chestertown, from which base he served the Catholics of Queen Anne's and Talbot counties. Kings Town was established as a town m 1735. Henry Cully, a Catholic of Chestertown, bought lot 12 there on March 1, 1741. He and his wife, Christian Beech Cully, sold their properties in Chestertown and moved to Kings Town by 1747. They had no children.

By his will, made in 1747 and probated after his death in 1748, Henry Cully left lot 12 (which included a house, chapel, and cemetery) to the Jesuit missionaries. Father James Ashby, the superior of the Maryland Mission, received the deed to it in March 1749. Christian Beech Cully died one-and-a-half years later, leaving in her will lots 1,13,24, and 25, other Kings Town properties that the Cullys had acquired, to the Jesuit Fathers. In 1785 Father Joseph Mosley, S.J., sold two of the lots to acquire money to build his plantation at Tuckahoe in Talbot County. The remaining properties were sold to John Quinby on November 2,1805, by Bishop John Carroll, at the time when he was making every effort to enlarge Georgetown Academy. The cemetery on lot 12 was reserved to the Roman Catholic clergy "forever." It was known for many years as the Primrose Cemetery, after a family that owned adjoining properties and buried their deceased there. The Jesuits at Georgetown are still in possession of the deed to lot 12.[131]

In 1750 four known Catholics were listed as living at Talbot Court House (Easton). Father Lewis began visiting the home of David Jones at Easton Landing in 1750.[132] Frances Pope Ungle, who died in 1750, had stated in her will her "desire to be buried by my father and mother in Oxford by the priest who attends the Romish Church." Hugh Linch specified in his will that his "son Hugh Linch is to be advised, tutored, and brought up in the Roman Catholic Religion."[133]

Father Robert Harding served from Bohemia from 1751 to 1756. He was pastor of St. Joseph's Church in Philadelphia after Father Joseph Greaton's retirement to Bohemia in 1751.[134] Until his death in 1753, Father Greaton continued to make trips to Mill Creek Hundred in New Castle County, Delaware, where he celebrated Mass in the home of Cornelius Hollahan. A son, David Hollahan, was born and baptized in 1753.[135]

Father James Beadnall made regular trips to Taylor's Bridge (near Dover), where "about five or six families" of Catholics were reported to the Anglican Society for the Propagation of the Gospel by the Reverend Hugh Neil of Dover.[136] Father Gailibrande cared for the mission at Murderkill (the Lowbers and Cains) between 1752 and 1755.[137]

In 1750 the Anglican minister at St. Anne's Parish near Middletown, Delaware, reported some 59 "papists" in his parish (the Appoquinimink area).[138] The mission chapel and school at Appoquinimink Forest were first mentioned in the records in 1750.[139] A son, Nicholas, was born to Nicholas and Eleanor Reynolds in that year, and a second son, John, was born and baptized in 1753.

In the spring of 1754, hostilities between the English and French erupted into an

Missal printed in 1645, used by Jesuit Priests from "Old Bohemia" when they said Mass at Ivy Mills Chapel during the early 1700's.

A Recusant Chalice. Recusant chalices were small enough to be hidden in the missionary's saddle bag. *Recusant* refers to a person who refused to take an oath of loyalty to the Monarch of England as the head of the English Church.

all-out war in western Pennsylvania.[140] Rumors multiplied that the Indians pushed on by the French were moving in to massacre the English colonists. Rising hysteria prompted fresh assaults against Catholics since French success was equated with Catholic success. To motivate men who were Puritan, Presbyterian, and Anglican to join the militia and to engender public support of funding for the war, public officials reached down to the common religious bias to galvanize war efforts.

On May 14, 1754, *The Maryland Gazette* printed an unsigned letter fiercely attacking Catholics. The writer urged the seizure of all Jesuit properties. The lower house of the Assembly was moved to propose such legislation, but the effort was defeated in the upper house.[141] A bill requiring the Test Oath before naturalizing immigrants was also rejected because the upper house refused to exclude Catholics from the advantages of citizenship.

However, schoolmasters were required to take the Test Oath in order to eliminate teachers who were suspected of being Catholic. In Dorchester County, Edward McSheky and 11 masters of the private schools abjured "popery." Another Catholic refused the oath, and two masters concerning whom there was doubt were ordered to appear before the court.[142] Several schoolmasters fled to Pennsylvania, where toleration was more liberally practiced.[143] Some courts were moved by the current panic to prosecute some who would not take the oath against their religion. On November 17, 1754, Charles Handley, a schoolmaster in Dorchester County, was summoned to court and "having the oath to the government tendered to him refused the same and declared himself to be Roman Catholic."[144]

On May 16, 1754, *The Maryland Gazette* published a long letter from Richard Brooke, again advocating the confiscation of all Jesuit properties. This was an obvious attempt to prejudice Jesuit ownership of an estate left by his mother in her will to Father Robert Brooke. Thomas Brooke, his brother, had tried unsuccessfully to prevent transfer of the title to the Jesuits. Brooke ended his letter with the offer to surrender to the government his claim "to the land which is detained from me by the Jesuits." The proposal was not acted upon, and the Jesuit properties remained intact.

Again, on October 17, 1754, *The Maryland Gazette* published a long, unsigned letter with the headline "Does Popery Increase In This Province?" The writer pointed out the number of "popish" chapels and the crowds that attended them. Next he focused attention on the number of young persons sent to foreign "popish seminaries." Then he brought up the large tracts of land and manors owned by the Jesuits, where they "live in a collegiate manner, hold public Masses, propagating their doctrine with the greatest industry and without control." Jesuit properties should be seized, he insisted, and those punished who send their children abroad for school. The writer concluded with an appeal to readers not to vote for any candidate in the next election unless that candidate agreed to revive in its most stringent form the Act to Prevent the Growth of Popery.

In November 1754, the citizens of Prince George's County instructed their delegates to urge a law:

> to dispossess the Jesuits of those landed estates which, under them, became formidable to his Majesty's good Protestant subjects of this

province; to exclude Papists from places of trust and profit, and to prevent them from sending their children to foreign Popish seminaries for education, whereby the minds of youth are corrupted and alienated from his Majesty's person and government.[145]

A commission was created to inquire into the affairs of the Jesuits in the colony, and also to ascertain by what tenure they held their land. One of the members of the commission was Nicholas Hyland, a resident of North Elk Parish near Bohemia. The commissioners were enjoined to tender the oaths of allegiance, abhorrence, and abjuration to Society of Jesus members.[146]

Governor Samuel Ogle had died in 1753 and was succeeded by Governor Horatio Sharpe, the next-to-last colonial governor of Maryland. Charles Calvert, fifth Lord Baltimore, had died in 1751 and was succeeded by his son Frederick, sixth and last Lord Baltimore. Even after 1753, when Frederick turned 21, he relied on his uncle, Cecilius Calvert, to manage his affairs in Maryland. The young baron wanted Cecilius to become governor in 1753, but Cecilius refused because of age and health. Both the baron and his uncle were influential in mitigating efforts to come down harshly on the Catholics and Jesuits. The new governor, Sharpe, appointed by the Calverts in 1753, was urged to block in the upper house of Assembly the intolerant measures proposed by the lower house. Governor Sharpe did not relish the outbursts of anti-Catholicism engendered by the war and exacerbated by politicians' local instructions to their delegates.[147]

In July 1755, the lower house urged Governor Sharpe to command all magistrates and other officers to execute the penal statutes against Catholics.[148] Protestants in Cecil County especially were frantic in their demands for proscriptive legislation. On July 9, 1755, Sharpe wrote Lord Baltimore:

> In the course of the session, they [the lower house] presented me with a furious Address against Roman Catholics which you will see enclosed. As I thought it contained some indecent Reflections I thought it improper to let it pass unanswered—For my part I have not heard but the Papists behave themselves peaceably as good Subjects.[149]

In 1756 the French and Indian War escalated into a worldwide struggle that became known as the Seven Years War that ended with the Treaty of Paris seven years later. By the war's end, Protestant Britain had emerged as mistress of the seas, and Protestant Prussia had gained dominance in Germany, while Catholic France, Spain, and Austria suffered decline. For Catholics in the English colonies, it was another bitter period, yet one that brought them to the edge of the American Revolution and its liberation from official religious persecution.

In the wake of Braddock's defeat in western Pennsylvania in 1756, the governors of Maryland and Pennsylvania called for troops and supplies for a new campaign. The militia law was revived to raise troops for frontier service, and the legislatures were pressed to make further appropriations for defense.[150] Anti-Catholic feeling was intensified by rumors that Irish and German Catholic immigrants were planning to cooperate with the French in overthrowing British rule. All kinds of false charges were hurled against Catholics, including the charge of a "papist plot," concocted on the basis of allegedly treasonable correspondence that purported to sell out English interests to the French. Father George Harding of Philadelphia came under suspicion, as we learn from a letter to Governor Robert Morris of Pennsylvania: "I am inclined to think the treasonable correspondence must have been carried on by some Roman Catholics. I have heard you have an ingenious Jesuit in Philadelphia.[151]

At the instigation of the Reverend Hugh Jones, the ever vigilant Anglican pastor in Cecil County, Maryland, the Protestants of Sassafras Neck, Middle Neck, and Bohemia Manor appealed to the lower house at the session of 1756 to take stringent measures against the Jesuits, whom they denounced as traitors.[152] The commander-in-chief of the British forces in America required that an exact count of Catholics be ascertained in each colony.[153] In Maryland, the Assembly passed an act in 1756 doubling the taxes paid by Catholic landholders, both to inhibit Catholicism and to raise funds for the war.[154] Charles Calvert, fifth Lord Baltimore, approved the measure, even though, as Charles Carroll of Annapolis remarked later, "he knew us innocent of the calumnies raised against us.[155] At the same time, a separate land tax was put on proprietary manors.[156]

In September 1756, Father James Beadnall journeyed from Kings Town, where he lived in upper Queen Anne's County, to visit the scattered Catholics of Queen Anne's and Talbot counties. He was arrested by the sheriff of Queen Anne's County on two counts: first, for celebrating Mass in July 1756 at the private homes of David Jones at Easton Landing and of Thomas Browning at Island Creek, and, second, for trying to win a Quakeress, Rachel McManus, away from her religion. He was obliged to give bail for his appearance at the provincial court, to be held at Annapolis on October 19, under the penalty of forfeiting 1,500 pounds of tobacco. The amount of bail demanded indicates the seriousness of the charges against him.[157]

After his arraignment, Father Beadnall petitioned Lord Baltimore for acquittal, with a reminder that Queen Anne had permitted Catholics to worship privately in their homes in order to prevent Catholics from leaving Maryland. The trial was delayed until April 16, 1757, when, at Talbot County court, Beadnall was acquitted of the first charge on the basis of the order issued by Queen Anne in 1705, and of the second charge because insufficient evidence was brought against him.[158]

After Beadnall's trial, he moved to the Western Shore of Maryland. Father John Lewis continued as superior of the Bohemia Mission until 1764. His visits to Catholics in Queen Anne's and Talbot counties in 1758 and 1759 are as follows: "Philemon Blake's at Blakeford, David Jones at Easton Landing, John Councill's at Tully's Neck [between Bridgeton and Roe's Crossroads in present-day Caroline County], John Blake's at Sportsman's Hall on the Wye, Still Pond in Kent County, Jaq. Seth's at Mount Mill in Queen Anne's County, and J. Burke's, also in Queen Anne's County."[159]

From 1756 to 1759, German Catholics increased greatly among the settlers in Pennsylvania and Maryland as a result of wars in their homeland. The lower house of the Maryland Assembly formulated a law forbidding the importation of both French and German "papists" seeking asylum from religious intolerance in Europe.[160] Although in the late 1750s Catholics in Maryland numbered 7,692, compared to 93,308 Protestants, the Committee on Grievances reported to the Assembly a dangerous growth of "popery" in the province and pointed out that

Catholic priests had access "in the back and removed parts" of the province to foreign immigrants who could be made ready to join the French and Indians in a war against the province.[161]

Charles Carroll of Annapolis strongly objected to this report of the Committee on Grievances and responded by posting a protest on the door of the State House in Annapolis. Carroll was arrested for this demonstration, but the Assembly refused to confine him in a public jail and adjourned, leaving no record of the outcome.[162]

In July 1757, Charles Carroll visited his son in Europe and looked further into the possibility of moving to Europe or Louisiana. Governor Horatio Sharpe of Maryland took note of this in his correspondence: "One Mr. Carroll, who is at the head of that sect [Roman Catholic]...it has been said that he has thought of leaving Maryland and of carrying his fortune to Europe."[163]

Many Protestants objected to the injustices done to Catholics and suffered with them, sacrificing honors and positions in defense of justice and decency.[164]

When the Mason-Dixon line was run down the peninsula in 1763, several Catholic families in Maryland found themselves on the Delaware side. Among these were Nicholas and Eleanor Reynolds, of the large estate and Catholic cemetery known as "Eleanor's Delight."[165] The Reynoldses attended Mass at Bohemia Mission and at the Appoquinimink Jesuit mission when Mass was offered there. Along with their neighbors, the Reynoldses were confronted with the eventual necessity of deciding for or against the mother country. They too felt the burden of increased taxes and were attracted by arguments for representative government. More and more they got caught up in the cause. In 1764 came the Sugar Act, which imposed a new tax on sugar and molasses. Colonists largely accepted this tax with little open protest. The Currency Act, which tightened the economy, soon followed, but still no great popular demonstrations protested the new taxes.

Strong ties of blood and language, and an inbred devotion to their king, caused those who did object to refrain from overt and radical action. The Stamp Act in 1765, however, did break down inhibitions and prompted loud and open protest. The colonists in 1764 had readily declared their "unshaken faith and true allegiance to his Majesty." By 1774 they were sufficiently roused to denounce the king as a traitor, as crowds did in New Castle, Delaware, on June 17 of that year.[166] In June 1776 a crowd burned the portrait of George III at a mass rally on The Green at Dover.[167] The Oath of Fidelity to that new state included the declaration, "I do not hold myself bound to yield any allegiance or obedience to the King of Great Britain."[168]

Almost to a person, Catholics in the Delmarva peninsula took the oaths of fidelity to the new state governments. The Reverend Matthias Manners, S.J., served as superior of Bohemia Mission from 1764 until his death at the age of 56 in 1775. Father John Lewis, S.J., succeeded him as superior and served there through the war until his death in 1788. Father Lewis, who was 55 years old when the war broke out in 1775, encouraged his people to take the fidelity oath. As a matter of fact, all the Jesuits approved of the oath, taking it themselves and counseling Catholics under their direction to take it also.[169] In contrast, the Anglican clergy generally remained loyal to the king, and most of them sailed for England or English colonies not in rebellion.[170]

When James Reynolds, the oldest son of Nicholas and Eleanor Reynolds, took the Oath of Fidelity, he was 47 years old. He enlisted in the service of "The United Colonies" on April 11, 1776.[171] James Reynolds' name appears frequently on the pages of the Bohemia sacramental registers as a sponsor.[172] He inherited Eleanor's Delight after his parents' death and continued to farm it after the Revolution, until his death in 1787. He married Rachel Seth, great-granddaughter of Jacobus Seth. She died on March 1, 1796, and was buried at Seth's Mill, her family's ancestral home. James and Rachel Seth Reynolds had one daughter, Frances, who inherited Eleanor's Delight. She married Raworth Weldon, of the numerous local Catholic Weldons.[173]

Raworth's brother, Jacob Weldon, son of Joseph Weldon (who lived on the further reaches of Duck Creek), served as a private in the Delaware militia under Captain George Evans from 1776 to 1780, when he joined the wagon brigades under Colonel Francis Wade of the Continental Service, where he served until the end of the war.[174]

The youngest son of Nicholas and Eleanor, John Reynolds, was 23 in 1776. John joined the Delaware militia and served as a private in the Christiana Company in White Clay Creek Hundred for the duration of the war.[175] Like the rest of his family, John was a regular Catholic. It is thought that he and his brothers received a superior education at the Catholic school in Appoquinimink Forest. The schoolmaster there, Samuel Watkins, lived until March 14, 1796, at which time he was buried at Bohemia cemetery, at the age of 70.[176]

John Reynolds' name, like that of his brother James, appears frequently in the sacramental register of Bohemia Mission. He was often called upon by family and neighbors to help settle estates, to appraise property, and to settle wills. The accounts of these transactions are written in such a beautiful hand that they have been preserved for generations and are now in the possession of the Clifford Pryor family.[177]

John Reynolds married Ann Taylor, the daughter of Richard Taylor, a Catholic who lived near Blackbird. Richard Taylor's son, also named Richard, was 21 in 1776. He served as a private in the company of Robert Kirkwood at the Wilmington Post in Delaware during the early part of the war, and later in the southern army of the United States, in the second battalion of Colonel William's Regiment of Infantry, to the end of the war.[178] He died in 1788 in his 33rd year. His mother, Rebecca Taylor, born in 1738, died December 24, 1798, and was buried at Bohemia Cemetery. Richard Taylor's wife, widowed, married John Weldon, a Catholic who died in 1821.[179]

Richard Taylor's daughter, Martha, married William Pryor (another local Catholic), who with his brother John served in Captain Isaac Alexander's Company of the New Castle County militia.[180] Joseph Pryor served in Colonel Henry Neale's Regiment of the Delaware militia.[181] William Pryor's son James, born in 1793, married Sarah Cole, of the numerous local Catholic family by that name. Her brother, Zebulon Cole, enlisted in the Delaware Regiment at the age of 20 and served throughout the war on the muster roll of Captain Peter Jacquet.[182] Jacob and Jeremiah Reynolds, sons of Edward Reynolds, who lived on King's Highway (Route 13 today) just south of Blackbird, were cousins of James and John Reynolds and also prominent laymen in the Bohemia congregation. Their names appear frequently in the sacramental records of Saint Francis Xavier Church. These brothers served through the war in the New Castle County militia.[183] Jacob and his wife had two daughters, Catherine and Elizabeth, born sometime within the seven years of revolutionary combat. Ann Reynolds died February 20, 1795.[184]

Another Reynolds of the revolutionary generation, Benjamin and his wife Rachel, lived in the Appoquinimink Forest and had one daughter, Sarah, who was baptized in 1791. Benjamin, who was too young to serve in the military during the war, died in 1800. Jeremiah Reynolds, who had served in the New Castle County militia, was buried at Bohemia in 1808 at the age of 75. Mary Reynolds, the wife of John Reynolds, was buried at Eleanor's Delight cemetery in 1795.

Others of the Reynolds family whose names appear in the sacramental records of the Bohemia Mission during the period of the Revolutionary War are Katy, Henrietta, Betsy, and Ann Reynolds.

William Heverin, member of the numerous New Castle County Catholic family by that name, joined the Delaware militia at the age of 36 in 1776[185] and signed the Oath of Fidelity to the state of Delaware in a notably bold and legible hand. William Heverin's land, Crispin's Ramble, was at the head of Black Stallion Branch, which flows into Cypress Creek, and 15 miles from Old Bohemia Mission. William's neighbor on the west was Nicholas Reynolds. His father-in-law, William Hill, bordered him on the northwest.

William Heverin (1714–1782) and his wife Ann (died 1780) were both buried at Bohemia cemetery. They reared numerous children: William, born 1740; Charles, 1746; Robert, 1748; James; Hannah, 1741; Ann; and Barbara, 1744. William and Charles remained in Delaware and in 1789 divided Crispin's Ramble between them. William received 127 acres, Charles the balance. William married Hannah McClerey and remained a devout Catholic until his death in 1804. Charles Heverin died on December 15, 1792. His wife, Sarah, was buried at his side in the Heverin family plot in 1796. Charles Heverin and his wife reared six children: John. born 1771; William, 1773; David, 1775; Temperance, 1777; Thomas, 1778; and Mary, 1793.[186]

Solomon Jones, of another New Castle County Catholic family, took the Oath of Fidelity and served in the militia of the state of Delaware.[187] He survived the Revolution and is listed as a witness to a wedding at Bohemia Church between Samuel Peter Watkinson and Mary Whittington, on September 15, 1790.

Benjamin Donoho, another local Catholic, enlisted as a private on April 17, 1777.[188] After the war he operated a family hotel on King's Highway at Blackbird. James Murphy, another Catholic neighbor, enrolled in Captain David Hall's Company of the Delaware Regiment on April 12, 1776. He marched as a part of the Flying Camp in the Delaware Battalion from the Dover barracks on August 24, 1776,[189] and continued throughout the war in the Delaware Regiment of the southern army.[190] Murphy was buried by Father Joseph Mosley on August 5, 1782. Catherine, James Murphy's widow, married Patrick Lyons, who was 32 years old in 1782. Patrick had received his education at the Jesuit Appoquinimink Mission school. His mother was a daughter of Sapien Harris. Patrick Lyons was prominent as the owner of a grist mill, influential in community affairs at large, and a strong patriot leader in the local Catholic group.[191] He married Catherine

Allfree Murphy, sister of William Allfree, justice of the peace for Appoquinimink Hundred and a soldier in the Delaware militia.[192] Patrick Lyons died in 1798.

Con Hollahan, with his wife and five children, lived at Cuba Rock in Mill Creek Hundred. He owned other lands in the vicinity of Coffee Run as early as 1747. John Hollahan, born on August 8, 1748, first son of Con and Margaret, was 28 years old in 1776. His name was "drawn for the colonial army," but his brother James, then 25 years old, went as a substitute, and his youngest brother, David, then 23 (born January 25, 1753), went with him. James and David were killed in action at the Battle of Camden as part of the immortal "Delaware Line." James was remarkable for his physical strength, being "able to lift a barrel of flour with ease."[193]

John Hollahan, the only one who survived his father, inherited Cuba Rock. He married Phoebe Way. Their house near Chadd's Ford became Washington's headquarters at the Battle of the Brandywine. They had a son Jacob. The southwest corner of Cuba Rock, usually called "The Old Homestead," touched the northeast corner of the 208-acre Jesuit property at Coffee Run. Con continued to live at Cuba Rock until about the time the church was built at Coffee Run. The clergy invited him to manage the property, so he moved to the priests' farm but retained Cuba Rock until his death in 1788. Cuba Rock passed out of the family by sheriff's sale on January 12, 1793, to Evans Phillips of Christiana Hundred.[194] In 1772 Father John Lewis purchased 208 acres at White Clay Creek for £565 from Samuel Lyle.[195] Father Lewis always referred to it as "Letitia Manor," after Penn's daughter Letitia, who had received the original grant of land, officially called Sterling Manor, containing more than 20,000 acres in northern New Castle and southern Chester counties. Sometimes the priests called it "Con Hollahan's." Father Lewis built a tenant house there in 1775, undoubtedly with a Mass room. A log chapel was built sometime after the Revolution, probably before Con Hollahan's death.[196] It was the first Catholic church built in upper New Castle County. After 1804 it was called Coffee Run after the stream that ran through it. Father Matthias Sittensperger (alias Manners) served the station at White Clay Creek from 1764 until his death on June 15, 1775.[197]

In Kent County, Delaware, on the Delaware-Maryland line, between Mud Mill Road and Willow Grove, the Jesuits owned 135 acres called "Cavil Ridge."[198]

The American Revolutionary War (1776-1783)

Father John Lewis, S.J., served the Catholics in the upper Eastern Shore of Maryland and New Castle County, Delaware, throughout the Revolution. He became superior of Bohemia Mission for the second time in 1775 and remained in that office until his death in 1788. Father Lewis and his congregation at Bohemia Mission played an important role in the long and bloody struggle for independence.

Father John Lewis was 46 when the war broke out. At the time, he was not only superior of Bohemia Mission, but also vicar-general of the Catholic missions in all the American colonies. Father Peter Morris, S.J., was his assistant throughout the war, from 1775 to 1782. Father Morris died at the age of 40 in 1783 at Newtown on the Western Shore. At Bohemia both priests took the Oath of Fidelity to the new State of Maryland with "cordial concurrence and consent."[199] In contrast, the

Reverend Philip Reading, Anglican Rector of the neighboring Appoquinimink Parish, discontinued services rather than take the Oath of Fidelity to the State of Delaware.[200]

Prior to the Revolution, on December 14, 1773, Father Matthias Manners, then superior of Bohemia Mission, had written to Father Lewis, then at Newtown in St. Mary's County, about Daniel Charles Heath, a grandson of James Heath, from whom a large share of the Bohemia lands had been purchased. Daniel Heath was attempting to eject the Jesuits from the farms they had purchased from James Heath (i.e., part of Worsell Manor, Woodbridge, and St. Ignatius) on the grounds that the land had been a gift from his grandfather for the support of the pastor. He maintained that such a transfer for Catholic purposes was illegal.[201] Father Manners died on June 15, 1775. The problem of Heath's attempts to dispossess the Jesuits was passed on to Father Lewis but was ultimately terminated by the Revolution.

Daniel Charles Heath had been born in 1744 and had married Mary Key, daughter of Richard Key of St. Mary's County. He had inherited Worsell Manor from his father, James Paul Heath.[202] With his older brother, James, Daniel Charles had been educated by the Jesuits at Bohemia Academy. James went to St. Omer's College in French Flanders to complete his education and never returned to America. He became a member of the Society of Jesus and died in England at an early age. Worsell Manor went to Daniel Charles Heath.

It was during his ownership that George Washington dined and lodged there, on the occasion of his passage through Cecil County on May 14, 1773. In Washington's party at the time were Governor Robert Eden of Maryland and John (Jackie) Parke Custis, Washington's stepson. Governor Eden was en route to Philadelphia to attend the spring horse races, and Washington was taking his stepson to New York City to enroll him at King's College (now Columbia University).[203] Daniel Charles Heath was a spendthrift and, as a consequence, frittered away his large property. In 1788 Worsell Manor passed out of the hands of the Heaths by deed of trust to James Hughes, trustee for Heath's creditors.[204]

The children of Daniel Charles Heath were Rebecca (who married Joseph Sims), Richard Key (who married Mary Hall), Hannah (born 1773), James Paul (born July 19,1775, and died in infancy), Daniel Charles (married Elizabeth McKim and was lost at sea), Susannah G. (married Matthias Bordley), Mary Key (married Thomas White), and Eliza Key (married Thomas H. Belt).[205]

There is a question as to Daniel Charles Heath's adherence to the American cause. In fact, in 1777, Daniel Heath was accused of inviting his neighbors to send their cattle to his pasture for "protection." He then allegedly sold the animals to the British fleet "for a very large bagg of Gold."[206]

Father Mosley described Daniel Charles Heath, a great-great nephew of Peter Sayer, as "a fallen Catholic" and added that he was very harsh in his treatment of indentured servants who were sold to him.[207] Daniel Charles Heath was listed as a pewholder at St. Anne's Episcopal Church, Middletown, Delaware, in 1795. After his death in 1799, very little is known historically about his descendants.

In 1796 Worsell Manor was purchased by Dr. William Matthews, of a local Catholic family. William Matthews was 41 years of age in 1776. He had joined the Bohemia Battalion and fought during the war.[208] He was the first son of Dr. Hugh

Matthews (1712–1774). Another son of Dr. Hugh Matthews, James Matthews (died 1792), also served in the Bohemia Battalion.[209] Two other sons were Arthur and Dr. Hugh Matthews III (died 1809). Hugh Matthews III married Margaret Morton and lived in New Castle County just over the Maryland line. Their daughters were Bridget, Rebecca, Susannah (died 1791), and Catherine (twin of William).

Dr. William Matthews resided at and is buried at Worsell Manor. He served several terms as judge of Cecil County (1778–1780, 1782–1786). He was a member of the Maryland General Assembly (1786–1789) and a member of the Fifth U.S. Congress (1797–1799).[210] Dr. William Matthews loaned the Jesuits enough money to purchase the plantation at White Clay Creek, New Castle County, Delaware, in 1772.[211]

Dr. Matthews' twin, Catherine Matthews, married John Leach Knight, who became a captain in the 18th Maryland Battalion under Colonel John D. Thompson on April 21, 1778.[212] He was one of the court justices who administered the Oath of Allegiance to the state of Maryland in March 1778.[213] John Leach Knight was among five persons appointed in May 1781 to superintend the issuing of bills of credit, or paper money, in Cecil County.[214] A daughter, Katherine (Kitty), the dauntless local heroine of the War of 1812 who saved at least some of Georgetown, Kent County, from being burned by the British, was born at Knights Island on the Sassafras River in 1775. Unmarried, Kitty Knight died in 1855 and is buried at Bohemia cemetery. William Knight, brother of John Leach Knight, died in 1815 at the age of 65. He also was buried at Bohemia.

Gilbert and John Nowland, of another Cecil County Catholic family, enrolled as privates in Captain Joshua George's Company in the 18th Battalion on August 18, 1776.[215] John, who took the Oath of Allegiance in 1778,[216] married Lydia Weldon on August 11, 1788. His son, Benoni, married Margaret Miller. Elias Nowland was commissioned an ensign in Captain Charles Heath's company in the 18th Battalion on June 22, 1778,[217] the same year he took the Oath of Allegiance.[218]

Gilbert, John, and Elias Nowland were great-grandsons of Desmond Nowland, who came to America from Ireland in 1680 and settled in Cecil County. He had one son, Darby, who bought Woodbridge, part of Worsell Manor. Darby sold Woodbridge to James Heath, who in turn sold it to the Jesuits. Jesse Nowland died in Sassafras Hundred in 1794; Bridget Nowland, at Bohemia Plantation in 1794; Stephen Nowland, son of Thomas and Mary, of Kent County, Maryland, in 1796; Thomas Nowland (age 25 in 1776), in 1824; and James Nowland, in 1826. Catherine Nowland married Nicholas Vosh at Elkton in 1790; witnesses were Michael Nowland, Hugh Grant, and Hannah McDermott. Sarah Nowland married Nathan Burk, widower, at Sassafras Neck on November 22, 1798; witnesses were Sylvester Nowland and James Council. Nathan Burk was godfather for Sylvester Carty, baptized on July 24, 1799. Joseph Burk and Mary Smith were married by Father John Lewis on April 15, 1776. Nancy Burk and Peggy Burk were baptized by Father John Lewis on August 4, 1779; Sally Casey was godparent. Sara Burk was buried at Bohemia on August 8, 1776.

In 1776 William Craddock, another Cecil County Catholic, who had come to the Warwick area around 1750, was 34. He and his wife, Mary, had three sons:

Thomas (born at Bohemia 1771, died 1833), John (baptized 1776, buried at Bohemia Mission), and Joseph (baptized 1779). William's brother, Charles Craddock, enrolled in the Cecil County Militia.[219] Daniel Craddock married Elizabeth O'Donald, of Sassafras Neck, at Old Bohemia Mission in 1792; witnesses were Alice, James, and John O'Donald. A son, Daniel Craddock, died in 1810 and was buried at Bohemia Mission. Daniel Craddock and Elizabeth Price were married at Old Bohemia Mission in 1794; witnesses were William Craddock and his wife, Mary, and Benedict Craddock. Captain Benedict Craddock, born in 1774, married Margaret Ryland, died and was buried at Bohemia Mission in 1845. Jeremiah and Bathsheba Craddock were sponsors for Joseph Craddock, baptized November 14, 1779. Margaret Craddock, who was born December 17, 1785, was buried at Old Bohemia Mission on March 20, 1851.

Other Cecil County Catholics during the Revolution were James and Barbara O'Donald, who were sponsors for Temperance Craddock, baptized in 1806. Barbara, wife of James O'Donald, died in 1810. Alice O'Donald died at Head of Little Bohemia in 1793. Catherine O'Donald died at Sassafras Neck in 1799.

The Erwins were also Cecil County Catholics during the Revolution. John Erwin married May Wadman on July 22, 1779; witnesses were Thomas, Edward, and Sally Burk Amy Erwin was godparent with Daniel Molkeye for the baptism of Margaret Ready on May 7, 1780. John Butler and Rachel Seth were godparents for Margaret Erwin, baptized November 28, 1780. Robert Erwin married Catherine Nugent, both of Cecil County, at Bohemia Mission, on February 27, 1791. Their son, James Caldwell Erwin, was born December 11, 1791, and died February 19, 1792. He was buried at the age of two months at Old Bohemia Mission. His godparents had been James H. Barnett and Eleanor Browning.

Lafayette wrote from Elkton on March 7, 1781, to Colonel Henry Hollingsworth, Commissary for the Eastern Shore:

> I do not think you will be able to collect the quantity of meat specified by tomorrow. You may, however, use your utmost endeavors with the civil power with which you are vested to collect as much as possible today, which we will take with us. The rest you will form into a magazine, and wait my orders for its following us. I do not suppose, on such an occasion as the present, a military guard necessary for enforcing the Governor's warrant, but should you find it is, you must have one.[220]

En route to Yorktown, General Washington arrived at Head of Elk in September 1781 with the main body of his army. Rochambeau's heavy artillery and baggage train camped on September 9, 1781, before fording the Susquehanna at Bald Friar. They, too, marched to Baltimore and on to Annapolis, where they boarded ships to Virginia.

When the war ended in 1783, Father Lewis continued as superior of Bohemia until his death five years later. The years that followed were a time of growth and development. Head of Elk became the county seat in 1786 and was renamed Elkton in 1787. Colonel John Rogers opened a ferry service and a tavern on Old Post Road (today Broad Street in Perryville), which had been an Indian trail when Europeans first arrived.[221] Over the years ahead, Washington and other prominent leaders frequented Rogers Tavern and ferry (Lower Ferry was incorporated as Perryville in 1882).

In 1782 an expanded Kent County Free School in Chestertown was incorporated as Washington College, a nondenominational institution where young men of the peninsula could continue their studies at the collegiate level.[222] In a letter from Newburgh, New York, where his army was encamped at the time, General Washington gave his consent for the college to bear his name and donated 50 guineas. In May 1784, Washington visited and took his seat as a member of the board of visitors and governors for the tenth-oldest college in the nation and the first established in the state of Maryland. During Washington's visit, an original play was performed in his honor, and in 1789 an honorary degree was conferred

Portrait of Charles Carroll of Carrollton

Sample page of *The Maryland Gazette*

Sample page of The Maryland Gazette (courtesy Hall of Records, Annapolis, Maryland)

upon him.

Responding to the energetic personal solicitations of the principal, the Reverend Dr. William Smith, for subscriptions to finance the new college on the upper Eastern Shore, Father John Lewis, superior of the Catholic clergy, became a contributor and an active patron.[223]

In 1783 the Maryland legislature passed an act entitled "An act for making the river Susquehanna navigable from the line of this state to tidewater."[224] Charles Carroll of Carrollton and 40 others obligated themselves to raise the sum for the purpose named in the title of the act.[225] This was the origin of the old Maryland Canal, which was one of the first works of its kind chartered in the United States. Irish Catholic workers began to gather on the shores of the Susquehanna to work on the canal, which extended from Conowingo nearly to Port Deposit. The influx of Catholic laborers resulted in the building of the old St. Patrick Chapel (built in 1819) at Pilottown, just above Conowingo. John Glackin, born in County Donegal in 1769. was the first to be buried in St. Patrick Cemetery there.[226]

At a September 23, 1783, meeting held at Newtown on the Western Shore, Father John Lewis was elected unanimously to remain superior of the missions.[227] Eventually, on June 9, 1784, in the first direct communique from the Holy See to the American Church, John Carroll was appointed "Superior of the Missions in the Thirteen United States of North America." In a letter to Carroll, Cardinal Antonelli stated the reasons for his appointment: he had given conspicuous proofs of his piety and zeal. He added, "And it is known that your appointment will please and gratify many members of that Republic and especially Mr. Franklin." From then on, France was no longer used as an intermediary, and the infant church in the United States was under the direct supervision of its own superior. John Carroll received the news of his appointment as prefect apostolic on August 20, 1784.[228]

Father John Carroll was an ardent patriot. He had returned from his education and ministry in Europe to his native Maryland in 1774, at the age of 37. In 1776 he had accompanied Benjamin Franklin and Charles Carroll of Carrollton, his cousin, on the mission to Canada. Father John Lewis, in his diary, records that John Carroll, returning from Canada, stopped at Old Bohemia Mission on June 5, 1776, and two days later set off again for Rock Creek, Montgomery County, where he lived with his mother.

During his term as prefect-apostolic, Father John Carroll lost to death two splendid co-workers. Father Joseph Mosley died on June 3, 1787, at the age of 56. For 31 years he had served the Church. Father John Lewis came from Bohemia Mission 50 miles away to attend Father Mosley in his last days. He buried Father Mosley under the floor in St. Joseph chapel.[229]

Less than a year later, on March 24, 1788, Father Lewis followed Father Mosley in death at the age of 68 at Bohemia Mission. In his will, proved April 7, 1788, Father Lewis bequeathed "wholly and solely" to Father Robert Molyneux of Philadelphia all his "real and personal estate, of what denomination soever."[230] This included the "plantation in New Castle County, State of Delaware, now in the tenure of Con Hollahan."

NOTES FOR CHAPTER ONE

1. Thomas Bacon, *Laws of Maryland: 1638-1763*, (Annapolis, Jonas Green, 1765), Art. 1715, Chapt. xxxix; reprinted by William H. Browne (ed), *The Archives of Maryland*, (Baltimore, 1887-1956), Maryland Historical Society, 67 Vols.) 36: 340-341. John Tracy Ellis, *Catholics in Colonial America*, (Baltimore: Helicon Press, 1965) 345; David William Jordan, "The Royal Period in Colonial Maryland, 1689-1715" (Ph. D. Dissertation, Princeton University, 1966) 284 Thomas Hughes, S.J., *A History of the Society of Jesus in North America* (New York: Longmans Green and Co., 1907-1917) Text 2:457-460 Edward I. Devitt, S.J., "A Dark Chapter in the Catholic History of Maryland," *United States Catholic Historical Magazine* 1 (April, 1857) 138-139; Henry S. Spalding, *Catholic Colonial Maryland* (Milwaukee: Bruce Publ. Co., 1931) 149. In this and subsequent chapters we refer to priests as "Father" or "Reverend," according to more recent custom. Before the Reformation, English priests were given the courtesy title "Sir" like a knight. Afterwards, things were different. William Schuyler, in *The Pioneer Catholic Church*, (Philadelphia, Pennsylvania: P. Reilly Co., 1944) 73, explains the title "Mr.": "The usual title by which all clergymen were addressed was Mr. This practice was common in Great Britain, Ireland and all the English colonies, including the U.S. It was a survival of the habit formed in penal times when religious were hunted down, when Catholic priests had to resort to the disguise of lay persons in order to perform their functions and even to save their lives." Cardinal Wiseman when the Catholic hierarchy was re-established in England in 1850, introduced the title "Father" for priests. It quickly spread to America.
2. William Hand Browne et al, eds., *Archives of Maryland*, 72 vols. (Baltimore: Maryland Historical Society, 1883 –) 26:44; J. Moss Ives, *The Ark and The Dove: The Beginning of Civil and Religious Liberties in America* (New York: Longmans, Green and Co., 1936) 265
3. *Archives of Maryland*, 26: 340; Hughes, Text 2: 440
4. *Archives of Maryland*, 25: 178 and 26: 44–46; Gerald P. Fogarty, S.J., "Property and Religious Liberty in Colonial Maryland Catholic Thought, *Catholic Historical Review* 72 (October, 1986): 585, note 54
5. *Archives of Maryland*, 26: 340–341; William Kilty, *Laws of Maryland* 1704 (Annapolis: Frederick Green, 1798-1800), LL, No.2: 435; Hughes, *History of the Society of Jesus in North America*, Text 2: 457; Jordan, *Royal Period*, 284; J. Thomas Scharf, *History of Maryland 1600-1765* (Baltimore: J. B. Piet, 1879) 1:370-371; Edwin Warfield Beitzell, *The Jesuit Missions of St. Mary's County, Maryland* (Abell, Maryland: the author, 1960, second ed. St. Mary's County Bicentennial Commission, 1976) 44; Ives, *Ark* and *Dove*, 268; William T. Russell, *Maryland, The Land of Sanctuary: A History of Religious Toleration in Maryland from the First Settlement Until the American Revolution*, 2nd ed. (Baltimore: J. H. Furst Co., 1908), 388
6. *Archives of Maryland*, 26: 340–341; Copy of a Memorial of Roman Catholics in Maryland to the Assembly, December 1704, Colonial Office Papers 5/715, VIII, No. 94, Public Record Office, London; Peter Guilday, *The Life and Times of John Carroll, Archbishop of Baltimore*, 1735–1815 (Westminster, Maryland: Newman Press, 1954), 44–46; Hughes, Text 2: 460
7. *Archives of Maryland*, 26: 451, 597; Devitt, "Dark Chapter," 140; Jordan, *Royal Period*, 285; Beitzell, *Jesuit Missions in St. Mary's*, 55; David Mathew, *Catholicism in England 1535-1935, Portrait of a Minority, Its Culture and Tradition* (London: Eyre and Spottswood, 1955) 130; Ellis, *Catholics in Colonial America*, 346; Russell, *Land of Sanctuary*, 392
8. John Kilty, *Land-Holder's Assistant and Land-Office Guide, Being an Exposition of Original Titles* (Baltimore: G. Dobbin and Murphy, 1808), 129; Jordan *Royal Period*, 285; Ives, *Ark and Dove*, 264; Ellis, *Catholics in Colonial America*, 347–348
9. George Johnston, *History of Cecil County, Maryland* (Elkton, Maryland, 1881, reprinted Baltimore: Regional Publishing Company, 1972) 137–138; Hughes, Text 2: 472–474; Jordan, *Royal Period*, 286; Ives, *Ark and Dove*, 268; Eugene Irving McCormac, *White Servitude in Maryland, 1634-1820* (Baltimore: Johns Hopkins University Press, 1904) 31; Edward I. Devitt, S.J., "Bohemia," *Records of the American Catholic Historical Society* (hereafter *RACHS*) 24 (June 1913): 101–102
10. William Stevens Perry, ed., *Historical Collections Relating to the American Colonial Church* 5 vols. (Hartford, Conn.: printed privately 1870-1878) 4:170-171; Scharf, *History of Maryland*, 1: 371; Hughes, Text 2: 483
11. Francis C. Nicholson, *Manors of Maryland* (Baltimore: The author, 1935), 11; Jordan, *Royal Period*, 286

12. Georgetown University Archives (hereafter GUA) Special Collections division, Box 571174, Washington, D.C. 20057. The searchable index to these Georgetown University Library Special Collections is found at this web address:: http://www.library.georgetown. edu/dept/spec-coll/index1st.htm. For the Jesuit Complex at Bohemia, this web address: http://www.library.georgetown.edu/dept/speccoll/mi/mi}176.htm. Bohemia Records are continued at: http://www.library.georgetown.edu/dept/speccoll/mi/mi}177.htm.
    BOHEMIA – ABSTRACT OF TITLE Archives, Maryland Province, Society of Jesus
    BOHEMIA – ACCOUNT OF FARMS AND VALUE Archives, Maryland Province, Society of Jesus
    BOHEMIA – LIST OF DEEDS to 1779's,
    BOHEMIA – LIST OF PRIESTS (1704-1855),
    BOHEMIA – LAND DOCUMENTS [103 W5-W18],
    BOHEMIA – LAND GRANTS [103 W1-W4],
    BOHEMIA – PROPERTY SUMMARY – (17TH C.)
    GUA – Society of Jesus, Maryland – New York Provincial Archives, Bohemia original parchment, warrant dated July 10, 1796, and surveyor's map, dated August 29, 1704; plat of Bohemia Manor. Edward I. Devitt, S. J., "Bohemia," 99-100, Joseph C. Cann, ed., *History of Saint Francis Xavier Church and Bohemia Plantation, 1704-1976* (Warwick, Md.: Old Bohemia Historical Society, 1976) 146; Hughes, *History of the Society of Jesus in North America*, Text 2: 471-473; John Gilmary Shea, *The Catholic Church in Colonial Days vol. 1 – A History of the Catholic Church Within The Limits of the United States* (New York: J. G. Shea, 1886) 368; Ellis, *Catholics in Colonial America*, 347; Beitzell, *Jesuit Missions of St. Mary's*, 56; Clifton E. Olmstead, *Religion in America, Past and Present* (Englewood Cliffs, NJ.: Prentice Hall, 1961), 29. For population of Cecil County in 1704, see Charles B. Clark, ed., *The Eastern Shore of Maryland and Virginia* (New York: Lewis Historical Pub. Co., 1950), 1:258. Cann 5: Superiors and Missionaries of St. Francis Xavier – ENGLISH JESUIT, THOMAS MANSELL Father Mansell (alias Harding) was founder and first superior of Bohemia from 1704 to 1712. In 1713 he became superior of the Maryland Jesuits. In 1722 he was appointed superior of St. Thomas Manor, Maryland, and in 1724 superior of St. Inigoe's, Maryland, where he died March 18, 1724. Jesuits who assisted Father Mansell were: Thomas Havers in 1706, who returned to Europe in 1707; Richard Latham (alias Kuknun) in 1706 and 1707, who died at sea at age 37; William Wood (alias Killick, born 1671, died at age 49 in August, 1720; George Thorold, in 1706, born 1670, died at St. Thomas Manor, Maryland, at age 72 on November 15, 1742. he was a missionary 42 years in Maryland.
13. Hughes, Documents 1: 220-221; Cann, 136, 161; Devitt, "Bohemia," 99
14. Land Office Records (Patent Records), Kent County, DD: 533, Maryland State Archives, S-11-4-6, MDHR 17371
15. Cann, 1; Devitt, "Bohemia," 102. Today the main complex includes three connected buildings. A kitchen dates to the 1700s. 'We feel it's on the foundation of where the original log house was when Father Mansell came here – " Marji Matyniak, current president of the Old Bohemia Historical Society.
16. Hughes, Documents 1: 234; GUA - Society of Jesus, Maryland-New York Provincial Archives, 103T-8; Cann, 156–162 Today Bohemia Covers 160 acres, a fraction of the 1200 acres on the Little Bohemia River that Father Mansell purchased in 1704.
17. Mary de Vine Dunn, "Heath's Warwick," *Bulletin of the Historical Society of Cecil County*, No. 32 (May 1968), 3–4; *Calvert Papers*, No. 1, Maryland Historical Society Fund Publication No. 28 (Baltimore: J. Murphy & Co., 1889–1899), 110, No. 884; Rent Rolls, Cecil County, 1658–1724, October 10, 1683—Mr. Charles Blake, 1,000 acres; Cann, 233–234, 244, 245. Mrs. Alfred N. Phillips, "A History of Worsell Manor," in Cann 264.
18. GUA – Maryland-New York Provincial Archives of the Society of Jesus, 103–78, original deed; Cecil County Land Records, TD: 279–282 (April 30, 1722)—originally granted to James Heath, February 6, 1711, Records of Land Office, PKE: 189, Maryland State Archives; Hughes, Documents 1:223; Cann, 156, 161, 245
19. Cann, 6; Ellis, *Catholics in Colonial America*, 347
20. Shea, *Catholic Church in Colonial Days*, 244; Thomas O'Gorman, *A History of the Roman Catholic Church in the United States* (New York: Christian Literature Co., 1895), 244
21. Hughes, Text 2: 469; Ellis, *Catholics in Colonial America*, 347; Donnell McClure Owings, *His Lordship's Patronage: Offices of Profit in Colonial Maryland* (Baltimore: Maryland Historical

22. Beitzell, *Jesuit Missions of St. Mary's*, 251; "Brooke Family," *Maryland Historical Magazine* (hereafter MHM) 1 (March 1906): 66–73, (June 1906): 184–188, (Sept. 1906): 284–289; James Hennessy, S.J., *American Catholics: A History of the Roman Catholic Community in the United States* (New York: Oxford University Press, 1981), 43
23. Dudley Lunt, *The Bounds of Delaware* (Wilmington: Star Pub. Co., 1947), 28; John H. B. Latrobe, *The History of the Mason and Dixon Line* (Philadelphia: Historical Society of Pennsylvania, 1855), 19-20
24. *Archives of Maryland*, 34: 4; Paul Walsh, *Maryland, A History 1632-1974* (Baltimore: Maryland Historical Society, 1974) 31
25. *Archives of Maryland*, 33: 480-481
26. Charles Petrie, *Jacobite Movement*, (London: Eyre and Spottiswood, 948) 308; Alistair Taylor and Henrietta Taylor, *The Old Chevalier, James Francis Stuart* (London: Cassell and Co., 1934), 132–134
27. GUA – No. 42, Maryland-New York Province Archives, Society of Jesus; Thomas Meagher Field, *Unpublished Letters of Charles Carroll* (New York: United States Catholic Historical Society, 1902), 17–19; Jordan, *Royal Period*, 62–63; Hughes, Text 2: 526
28. Esmeralda Boyle, *Biographical Sketches of Distinguished Marylanders* (Baltimore: Kelly, Piet and Company, 1877), 79
29. Perry, ed., *Papers Relating to the History of the Church in Delaware, 1706–1782*, 36; Devitt, "Bohemia," *RACHS* 23 (June 1913), 102
30. Cann, 6: ENGLISH JESUIT, THOMAS HODGSON (HUDSON) – Father Hodgson was superior of Bohemia from 1712 to 1726. He was born in 1682 an entered the Jesuits in 1703. He died at Bohemia at age 44 on December 18, 1726, and is buried there. Devitt, "Bohemia" *RACHS* 14 (1885) 345.
31. Cecil County Land Records, TD: 279–282 (recorded April 30, 1722), Maryland State Archives; Hughes, Documents 1: 285; Cairn, 161. Bohemia Plantation: Timber was felled and cut in the water powered sawmill. Later local paper was used to print money. (Framed samples of paper money are in the Bohemia Museum.) Tenant farmers, indentured servants, share croppers, and "negro servants" (who were treated with great dignity) grew and harvested tobacco, which filled hogsheads taken to market. Along with staples like corn, barley, oats, and wheat, Jesuit Diaries include references to potatoes, carrots, beets, beans, parsnips, cabbage, cucumbers, and peppers. They record the growing of onions, lettuce, artichokes, spinach, parsley, squash, cauliflower, peas, turnips, and pumpkins. (Letters from that period record that potatoes, apples, and turnips were shipped through Fredericktown, probably to Baltimore.) Trees included apple, pear, hickory, walnut, chestnut, cherry, plum, quince, persimmon, mulberry and fig. (After the War between the States Old Bohemia had over 8,000 peach trees!) Cattle, swine, sheep, turkeys, chickens, ducks and geese were raised, with an abundance of eggs, cheese, milk and butter, as well as cider, whiskey and wine mentioned in early records. Wine was needed for meals and for Mass, but the whiskey was probably for medicinal purposes only! Meat was salted, smoked, or pickled, although ice cut from two streams usually lasted long enough to keep meat until the summer. The plantation was not terribly successful, as was true of other Jesuit properties, since circuit-riding owners were seldom home to supervise the work.
32. Beitzell, 56, 252; Hughes, Documents 1: 233, Text 2: Appendix F, No. 55; Cann, 5; Devitt, "Bohemia," 102
33. Provincial Records, 1: 198, Maryland State Archives.
34. Hughes, Documents 1: 233; Cann, 182
35. Ellis, *Catholics in Colonial America*, 348
36. Beitzell, 31–33, 335, 337; Hughes, Text 2: Appendix F, No. 32
37. Cann, 6; Hughes, Text 2: Appendix F, No. 71; Carley, *Queenstown*, 19
38. Cann, 6: ENGLISH JESUIT, PETER ATTWOOD was superior of Bohemia from 1726 to 1733. He was born in 1682 and entered the Jesuits in 1703/4. He died at age 52 at Newtown, Maryland. Hughes, Text etc. Hughes, Text 2: Appendix F, No. 72, Documents 1: 237, No. 51; Will of Peter Attwood (1729), Wills, 21: 185, Maryland State Archives; Carley, *Queenstown*, 19. Devitt, "Bohemia" 14 (1885) 345
39. Hughes, Documents 1: 233, No. 48. Ellis, *Catholics in Colonial America*, 347; Cann, 162
40. GUA – BOHEMIA ACCOUNTS LEDGER/DAY BOOK – (1735-61) Archives, Maryland

Province, Society; of Jesus ADW – Xerox copies of Bohemia *Daybook* 1735-1761 and Bohemia *Ledger* 1735-1761

41. Martin I. J. Griffin, "The First Mass in Philadelphia," *American Catholic Researches* 12 (Jan. 1895): 39–43; Martin I. J. Griffin, *History of Old Saint Joseph's Church, Philadelphia* (Philadelphia: I.C.B.U. Journal Printing, 1882), 2; Joseph L. J. Kirlin, *Catholicity in Philadelphia* (Philadelphia: John Joseph McVey, 1909), 20; Quigley, "Catholic Beginnings in Delaware Valley," 12; Esling, "Catholicity in Lower Counties," 121; Hughes, Text 2: 495–496. St. Joseph's Church in Philadelphia, founded 1733, was the first public place of Catholic worship in the colonies, since Pennsylvania, unlike Maryland, had no prohibition against public Catholic worship. The churches in Maryland, including Old Bohemia, were all physically attached to the priest's residence, so that technically they were private house chapels. Philadelphia was not, strictly speaking, a daughter parish of Bohemia, although southeastern Pennsylvania had originally been within the area attended from Bohemia, and there was ongoing mutual assistance between the priests of the two churches after 1733. The Rev. Joseph Greaton, S.J., had been given responsibility for southern Pennsylvania soon after his arrival in the colonies in 1720, bit he visited that area, not from Bohemia, but from a base in Anne Arundel County across the bay until he took up residence in Philadelphia about 1729. (James F. Connelly, *The History of the Archdiocese of Philadelphia* [Philadelphia: 1976].) Bohemia, however, was probably a stop on his travels into Pennsylvania. In 1749 he was transferred from Philadelphia to become the superior at Bohemia, where he died in 1754.
42. Perry, *Papers Relating to the Church in Delaware*, 97; Quigley, "Catholic Beginnings in Delaware Valley." 29
43. Perry, *Papers Relating to the Church in Delaware*, 91–92; Carley, *Queenstown*, 18
44. Perry, *Papers Relating to the Church in Delaware*, 36
45. Hughes, Documents 1: 254; Cann, 6: ENGLISH JESUIT, JAMES JOHN QUIN was superior of Bohemia from 1734 to 1742. He was born in 1698 and entered the Jesuits in 1717. He died in Talbot County on November 27, 1845 and is buried at Bohemia cemetery. ENGLISH JESUIT, JAMES FARRAR was superior at Bohemia from 1742 to 1745. Born 1707, he entered the Jesuits in 1725. First sent to Maryland in 1733, he was bookkeeper (Account and Day Book) at Bohemia in 1735 and 1736. He was a teacher at the Bohemia school. He returned to England in 1747 and died at age 56 in 1763.
46. Joseph Willcox, "The Catholic Mission at Concord, Delaware County, Pennsylvania," *RACHS* 7 (Jan. 1896): 389–393; John Smith Futhey and Gilbert Cope, *History of Chester County, Pennsylvania, with Genealogical and Biographical Sketches* (Philadelphia: Louis H. Everts, 1881), 378; Quigley, "Catholic Beginnings in Delaware Valley," 15–16; Cann, 29. J. Thomas Scharf, *History of Delaware, 1609–1888* (Philadelphia: L. J. Richards & Co., 1888), 1: 631
47. Esling, "Catholicity in Lower Counties," *RACHS* 1:124-128; James L. McSweeney, "The Diocese of Wilmington," in Henry De Courcy, ed., *The Catholic Church in the United States of America* (New York: E. Dunigan and Bros., 1914), 3: 215; Henry Clay Conrad, *History of the State of Delaware, From the Earliest Settlement to the Year 1907* (Wilmington: The author, 1908), 2: 777; Anthony D. Michele, "A Few Square Miles and Two Centuries," in *Coffee Run, 1772–1960: The Story of the Beginnings of the Catholic Faith in Delaware* (Wilmington: William N. Cann, 1960), 28 Cann 174 – "Bohemia Day and Ledger Book 1735-1782" – September 1, 1753 – "Mr. Lewis going to White Clay Creek" – is the first documentary reference to Jesuit missionary presence in the Wilmington area.
48. Esling, 128; Cann, 184; John Munroe, "Catholicism's Start in Delaware," in *Coffee Run*, 11
49. Clifford Pryor, *The Forest of Appoquinimink* (Middletown, Del.: The author, 1975), 153; Eugene J. Kraemer, "The Catholic Church in Delaware," in Henry Clay Reed, ed., *Delaware: A History of the First State* (New York: Lewis Historical Pub. Co., 1947), 2: 681
50. New Castle County Deeds, D-3: 299, Delaware Hall of Records, Dover
51. Maryland Probate Records, 6: 469, Maryland State Archives.
52. Pryor, 2
53. Pryor, 4
54. Russell F. Heavrin and Charles A. Heavrin, *New Land: A Heverin-Heavrin-Hevrin Family History* (Bountiful, Utah: Family History Publishers, 1992), 27
55. Herbert L. Osgood, *The American Colonies in the Eighteenth Century* (New York: Columbia

University Press, 1930), 4: 55
56. William Lloyd Bevan, *History of Delaware, Past and Present* (New York: Lewis Historical Pub. Co., 1929), 1: 252; Clayton Colman Hall, *The Lords Baltimore and the Maryland Palatinate*, (Baltimore: John Murphy Co., 1902) 152; Clayton Colman Hall, ed., *Narratives of Early Maryland: 1633–1684* (New York: Charles Scribner's Sons, 1910), 412; Walsh 36–37
57. Hall, *The Lords Baltimore*, 157
58. Walter A. Powell, *History of Delaware* (Boston: Christopher Publishing Co., 1928), 116; Dudley Lunt, *The Bounds of Delaware* (Wilmington: Star Pub. Co., 1947), 64; Johnston, 299–300
59. Pryor, 99
60. Cann, 67, 135
61. Pryor, 88, 99
62. Pryor, 2
63. Pryor, 2, 5, 64; Maryland Probate Records, DC 3: 287–292; Charles A. Barker, *The Background of the Revolution in Maryland* (New Haven, Conn.: Yale University Press, 1940), 134; Walsh 37
64. Owings, *His Lordships Patronage*, 173; inventory of James Heath's will, April 17, 1730, Prerogative Court Wills, 16: 488–494, Maryland State Archives—"silver chalice and cover, and crucifix, and other things belonging to the chapel."
65. Cann, 233; will of James Paul Heath, Prerogative Court Wills, 25: 63–68; Geoffrey Holt, *St. Omer's and Bruges Colleges, 1593—1773: A Biographical Dictionary* (Thetford, England: Catholic Record Society, 1979), 130
66. Cann, 235; William Love, "Two Maryland Heroines," *MHM* 3 (June 1908): 134
67. Pryor, 2
68. Pryor, 2
69. Pryor, 5; John Gilmary Shea, *The Catholic Church in Colonial Days*, 244; Kraemer, "Catholic Church in Delaware," 681
70. Pryor 39
71. Will of James Heath, probated Jan. 31, 1732, Prerogative Court Wills, 20: 333–334; Cecil County Land Records, 2: 232–James Heath sold part of Sedgefield "except the present pathway being eight yards wide that leads from the plantation called St. Paul's to the plantation of Mr. Thomas Mansell"; Hughes, Documents 1: 233, Heath's Longlands; Cann, 182
72. Pryor, 82
73. Pryor, 154
74. Pryor, 153; New Castle County Wills, 0-1: 140, DH of R.
75. New Castle County Deeds, Y-3: 333, DH of R.
76. New Castle County Deeds, Y-l: 644, DH of R.
77. New Castle County Wills, T-l: 77; New Castle County Orphans Court Records, I-I: 628, DH of R.
78. "Willson v. Blackbird Creek Marsh Co. (1829)," in Francis N. Stites, *John Marshall, Defender of the Constitution* (Boston: Little Brown and Co., 1981), 150–151
79. Pryor, 24
80. New Castle County Book of Original Surveys, 289, DH of R; Heavrin and Heavrin, *New Land*, 37
81. J. M. Runk, *Biographical and Genealogical History of the State of Delaware* (Chambersburg, Pa.: J. M. Runk & Co., 1899), 2: 817; Heavrin and Heavrin, *New Land*, 27–28
82. Cann, 6
83. Pryor, 60
84. Beitzell, 31
85. Hughes, Documents 1: 219–220, "Mr. Londey's Will," dated May 13, 1693; Cann, ix; Carley, "Baptismal Register of Joseph Mosley, S.J.," 42
86. Perry, *Historical Collections*, 4 (Maryland): 322
87. Scharf, *History of Maryland*, 1: 432; Charles J. Stille, "The Attitude of the Quakers in the Provincial Wars," *Pennsylvania Magazine of History and Biography* 10 (Jan. 1886): 290; Leon De Valinger, Jr., *Colonial Military Organization in Delaware, 1638–1776* (Wilmington, Del.: Tercentenary Commission, 1938), 30–37
88. Scharf, *History of Maryland*, 1: 358; Munroe, *Colonial Delaware*, 216
89. Hughes, Text 2: 525; Walsh 46; Owings, *His Lordship's Patronage*, 172

90. *Archives of Maryland*, 28: 355; C, No. 63, articles 5 and 6, Province Archives; Hughes, Text 2: 528
91. Petrie, 363. *Maryland Gazette*, Annapolis, Maryland, Jan. 14, 1746.
92. Petrie, 385–388
93. Petrie, 451–456
94. Sister Mary Augustina Ray, *American Opinion of Roman Catholicism in the Eighteenth Century* (New York: Columbia University Press, 1936) 215
95. *Archives of Maryland*, 25: 341, 26: 597–598
96. Scharf, *History of Maryland*, 1: 435. Scharf lists the prisoners landed at Oxford in footnote 2 on the same page.
97. Powell, *History of Delaware*, 116; Munroe, *Colonial Delaware*, 216–217; Scharf, *History of Delaware*, 1: 138; Anthony Higgins, *New Castle on the Delaware* (New Castle, Del: New Castle Historical Society, 1973), 35
98. Leon De Valinger Jr., *Colonial Military Organization in Delaware 1638-1776* (Wilmington, Del: Tercentenary Commission, 1938) 42
99. William P. Treacy, "Some Early Catholic Grammar Schools," *United States Catholic Historical Magazine* 1 (Jan. 1887): 72–73; James A. Burns, *The Catholic School System in the United States: Its Principles, Origin, and Establishment* (1908; repr., New York: Arno Press, 1969), 109–111, 163; Bernard C. Steiner, *History of Education in Maryland* (Washington, D.C.: Government Printing Office, 1894), 16; Peter Guilday, *The Life and Times of John Carroll, Archbishop of Baltimore, 1735–1815* (Westminster, Md.: Newman Press, 1954), 9–10; Richard J. Purcell, "Education and Irish Teachers in Colonial Maryland," *Catholic Educational Review* 32 (March 1934): 143; Shea, *Catholic Church in Colonial Days*, 404. Harold A. Buetow, *The Story of Catholic Education in the United States*, (London, Collier-Macmillan, Ltd., 1970) 33,36_

Although the Protestant Committee on Grievances had obtained an enactment in 1654 resulting in the licensing of only those teachers who would take the Oath of Abhorrency Against Catholicism, the new legislation of 1704 provided that:

> If any Papist or person making profession of the Popish Religion shall keep school or take upon themselves the Education, Government, or Boarding of youth in any place within this Province, such persons being thereof lawfully convicted, (must) be transported out of this Province.

The only place left in the colonies where religious toleration was practiced was in the colony founded by the Quaker, William Penn. There, schools were started at Conewago by Father Wappeler, and at Goshenhoppen by Father Schneider, during the 1740's, and they seem to have prospered for many years. In addition to the school at Goshenhoppen, Father Schneider is said to have established schools at several other locations, meriting for him the title of "the founder of the parochial school system of the archdiocese of Philadelphia.

Although in the Province of Maryland the Church had to virtually go underground, and Catholics risked a fine of 100 pounds for attempting to educate their children according to their conscience, nevertheless, the wealthier families were willing to face whatever severe penalty, and sought ways to provide the forbidden education.

100. *Archives of Maryland*, 8: 431–432; Hughes, Text 2: 463; Edward J. Devitt, S.J., "A Dark Chapter in the Catholic History of Maryland," *United States Catholic Historical Magazine* 1 (April 1887): 145; Purcell, "Education and Irish Teachers," 145; John W. McGrain, Jr., "Priest Neale, His Mass House and His Successors," *Maryland Historical Magazine (hereafter MHM)* 62 (Sept. 1967): 255 John Gilmary Shea, *History of the Catholic Church in the United States*, (New York, J.G. Shea, 1890), 1:405 – The Protestant rector of St. Stephen's parish near the Jesuit Academy, was a Rev. Hugh Jones, who regarded his neighbors with no favorable eye. In 1739 he wrote to the Secretary of the Society for the Propagation, of the Gospel: Since the Jesuits in my parish favored and settled in Phila. seem to combine our problem by propagation of schism, popery and apostasy in the neighborhood, to prevent the danger of which impending tempert, "tis hoped you will be so good to contribute your extensive charitable benevolence to purchase a set of books of practical and polemical church history as you shall judge most profitable for the purpose."
101. Russell, *Land of Sanctuary*, 400–405
102. Purcell, "Education and Irish Teachers," 147; William Hand Browne, "First Free School in Queen Anne's County," MHM 6 (March 1911): 1–14
103. *Archives of Maryland*, 34: 680; Robert L. Swain, Jr., "Kent County," in Charles B. Clark, ed., The

Eastern Shore of Maryland and Virginia (New York: Lewis Historical Publishing Co., 1950) 2:935
104. Will of James Paul Heath, Prerogative Court Wills, 25: 63–68—inventory, the chapel at Mount Harmon; Johnston, 199–200; Hanson, *Old Kent*, 374; Marguerite du Pont de Villiers Boden, *Mount Harmon Plantation at World's End, Cecil County, Maryland* (Elkton, Md.: The author, 1976), 2–3; Hughes, Text 2: 519
105. Devitt, "Bohemia," 105; Henry S. Spalding, 138–139; Hughes, Text 2: 520, Documents 1: 238; Cann, 30–31; Burns, *Catholic School System*, 110; John Gilmary Shea, *A History of the Catholic Church Within the Limits of the United States*, 4 volt. (New York: J. G. Shea, 1886), 2: 27–28; ENGLISH JESUIT, RICHARD MOLYNEUX – Father Molyneux was born in 1696 and entered the Jesuits in 1715. He was at Bohemia from 1745 to 1750, and superior at St. Thomas Manor 1736 to 1747 before returning to Canterbury, England. He died there on May 18, 1766, at age 70. AMERICAN JESUIT, JOHN DIGGES – John Digges was born in Maryland in 1712 and entered the Jesuits in 1734. While stationed at Bohemia he was a teacher at the Academy. He died in Baltimore, Maryland, on December 14, 1746, at age 34. BELGIAN JESUIT BROTHER, HENRY DE GEE – was born in Liege, Belgium in 1696, and entered the Jesuits in 1740. He was at Bohemia in 1746. He returned to Belgium and was the last Brother sent from England. He died in 1772 at age 62 and was buried at Bruges, Belgium. ENGLISH JESUIT, RICHARD ARCHBOLD was born 1713 and entered the Jesuits in 1731. He was at Bohemia in 1746. He died in 1749 at age 36. Hughes 2:472 – Historians are not sure when the Jesuits first began taking in students at their plantation at the head of the Little Bohemia River. Some authors claim as early as 1735, others 1741, but we are certain that the academy was open in 1745 because of the written records which still exist. Hughes notes: "When Father Henry Neale had begun prospecting a landed foundation in Pennsylvania in 1741, we find soon afterwards a school was opened on the Maryland side of the border at Bohemia, under the direction of Father Thomas Poulton." GUA – Maryland Province, Society of Jesus, Mss. 174, A-6: Whether or not Father Poulton (or Pulton) was the founder of this academy is somewhat questionable. On the inside of the cover of the *Bohemia Day* (Account) *Book*, 1735-1761, there is a terse note that the students were admitted "in Mr. Neale's absence." Hughes 1:285 – Hughes observes: "…James Heath is seen as registered as the first scholar at the Jesuits' Latin school, which was opened under Father Henry Neale's superintendence on St. Xaverius plantation." Nevertheless, following an ancient tradition, most authors ascribe the foundation to Father Poulton. ENGLISH JESUIT, FATHER THOMAS POULTON was born on May 15, 1697, in England, of an illustrious family who were lords of Desborough, Northamptonshire. He was admitted to the Society of Jesus on December 7, 1716, became one of the professed fathers at Rome on February 2, 1734 and came to America in 1738. It is not known how soon after his arrival he came to Bohemia, but the records show he was there from 1742 until his death on January 23, 1749. Edward I. Devitt, "Bohemia," *Woodstock Letters, A Record of Current Events and historical Notes Connected With the College and Missions of the Society of Jesus* (Baltimore, Society of Jesus – Ma???? New York Province, 1872-1970) 63 (1934) 12.

Father Thomas Poulton, who founded and fostered the Bohemia Academy, had some measure of success in realizing the hope of Father Fedinando Pulton, as expressed to the General of the Society in the earliest days of the Colony. They were of the same family, Poulton or Pulton, of Desborough, County North Hampton (v. Foley, *Records of the English Province*), of whom three came to America, and ended their days on the Maryland mission. Father Ferdinando was accidentally shot whilst crossing St. Mary's River. On the ancient list which chronicles his death some ill-informed commentator makes a marginal note that "he was a Spaniard, as his name, and the names of his servants evidently show,…."

The Poultons were an old English family, staunch Catholics, who suffered severely for the Faith; the fines imposed on them for non-attendance at Protestant services would have beggared the richest landholders in England. In the Desborough Church, the church of the ancestors of Father Thomas Poulton of Bohemia, there stood a monument which bore the following inscription: "Sacred to the memory of the honorable family of the Poultons, who for fourteen generations were the lords of this town of Desburg or Desborough. Descended from princely, most noble, illustrious and holy progenitors of this kingdom." – "England's Letter From Brother Foley," *Woodstock Letters* 14 (1885) 347: Father Poulton came to Maryland in 1738, and was, perhaps, stationed at Bohemia. There are records to show that he was there from 1742 to

January, 1749. While Fr. Poulton was pastor a classical school was opened at Bohemia.... Fr. Poulton died January 23, 1749, at Bohemia says Fr. George Hunter and Fr. Bennet Neale makes the same statement. The old catalog puts his death at Newtown. Devitt, "Bohemia, Cecil County," *Woodstock Letters* 14 (1885) 353: Fr. Thomas Poulton, *alias* Underhill, Brook, Oswald, Thomas, son of Ferdinand Poulton, of Desborough, Esquire, and brother of Fathers Giles and Henry Poulton; a native of Northamptonshire, born May 8, 1697, made his humanity studies at St. Omer's College; entered the Society in December, 1716, and was professed of the four vows in Rome, February 2, 1734. In 1730 he was prefect of St. Omer's; in 1738, was sent to the Maryland mission and died Superior of it January 13-23, 1749 – Henry Foley, S. J. (Ed.) *Records of the English Province* (London: Burns, Oates and Co., 1883); 3:334 GUA – Archives of the Jesuit – Maryland Province 7-W-1-2 Poulton, Thomas, born May 15, 1697, admitted Dec. 7, 1716; numbered amongst professed fathera at Rome, Feb. 2, 1734; proceeded to Maryland, where he filled the office of Superior. Died Jan. 23, 1749

He was emminently equipped to prepare future students for the college at St. Omer's, having studied there himself and later returning to be the prefect of the college from 1730 until coming to Maryland. F. Edward Wright, *Vital Records of the Jesuit Missions of the Eastern Shore 1760-1800* (Silver Springs, Maryland: Family Line Publications, 1986) 49: Old Bohemia Mission, Warwick Dates of Death 1726 Rev. Thomas Hudson died; born 1682; 1746: Mar 20 buried Mary Betson; 1749 Rev. Thomas Pulton died Jan 23 1749; born 1697. "One records says he died at Newtowns but W. Neale and W. Hunter – say Bohemia."; 1753 Aug 19 Revd Joseph Graeton died; 1759 Feb 19 buried Old Mary.

106. Beitzell, 102; Hughes, Text 2: Appendix F, No. 103; Cann, 30–31; Quigley, "Catholic Beginnings in the Delaware Valley," 18–19; James Hennesey, S.J., 'Several Youth Sent from Here: Native Born Priests and Religious of English America, 1634–1776," in Nelson H. Minnich et al, *Studies in Catholic History in Honor of John Tracy Ellis*, (Wilmington, Del.: Michael Glazier, 1985), 11; AMERICAN JESUIT, HENRY NEALE was superior at Bohemia from 1742 to 1746. He was born in 1702 and entered the Jesuits in 1724. He assisted Father Poulton at Bohemia Academy. He died in Philadelphia, Pennsylvania, at age 46, on April 24, 1748.

107. Willcox, "Catholic Mission at Concord," 391
108. Cann, 31; Heavrin and Heavrin, *New Land*, 37
109. GUA – Ms ledger and day–book, Bohemia Manor, 1735–1761, Province Archives; "Bohemia Account Book" as transcribed in part in Cann, 34–36, 171–176; Hughes, Text 2: 520-521

Bohemia Accounts
1735-1761

The 1st part of the book is ledger, the 2nd part is the day book.
The accounts in that length of time were kept by different Fathers and consequently, in the ledger section are found diverse hands on the same page.
The order of the Bookkeepers.
James Farrar, began 1735 and 1736.
James Quin, 2 months, Feb. & March, 1736.
Vincent Philips, March, 1736 to Feb. 1740.
Richard Molyneux, Feb., 1740 to Oct., 1742.
Henry Neale, Oct. 1742 to June 1746.
Thomas Poulton, June, 1746 to Dec., 1748.
Richard Molyneux, Dec., 1748 to beginning of 1750.
Joseph Greaton, began 1750 until his death Aug., 1753.
John Lewis, Aug., 1753 to 1761.

1736 Stocked farm. Fr. Farrar repaired barn for tob. – accts. due to him.
Michael Cartwright, miller – contract
Rich Craddock – farmer – (The Craddocks lived on Kentucky for a long time after).
Darnly Dunsloy – another tenant – also Jackson – paid in tobacco p. 11.
Rev. Mr. Neale acc't.
Mr. H. Neale settled acc't. till March 1746.

1740 Jas. Noland plastered house 12 lb.
It appears F. F. had to store at house for supplying tenants and workman.

1740 Youg plasterer came to work and began the 25 Aug. at rate of 4 sh. per day; he was 4? days

	finish. and abroad about other business – in all he worked 29 days.
1740	Wilson, Dr., N.B. Runaway.
1746	A coffin for Ben Neale 1 lb. (may be for the boy Ben Neale at school).
1745	New design farm – Kentucky farm.
1745	To renting a house, 10 shill. a quarter.
	Bro. Henry Duchet acct.
	Fr. Wapelers, acct.
	Wayt. – the school teacher acct.
1747	They worked at chapel and house, vaulted cellar, raised the brick with partition walls and chimneys, put pillars in chapel under pinned mill.
1750	Fr. Greaton takes pay from Joshua George for the two horses he bought from Mr. Harding.
1745	School acct. with Edw. Neale for his two sons at school Bennet and Neddy (EDW. Neale comes from Queenstown) There was a Bro. Henry at Boh. at this time.
1745	School acct. with Dan Carroll for John (future archbishop of Baltimore) of Marlboro – he was there a year and six weeks it seems.
1745	Acct. with Mr. Wayt ye school teacher by schooling 2 Neale boys and John Carroll in all for 32 mos. at 40 sh. per year.
1746	The school master got a gall. of Whiskey in Dec. ? gall. in Jan. in April he took out horse for 4 days and damaged him and brought him back in back order – fine 10 shill.
1753	To Mathias Nolan for making Mr. Greatons coffin 16 sh. Bal. due Mathias Nolan for making Mr. Pultons coffin 21 sh.
1746	Peter Loper – for your sons board from 17 Feb. – 1746 till.
	Blacksmith at Boh.
1747	Clift Hammon made several door frames and window sashes.
	Mr. John Diggs was at Baltimore his acc. with Boh. Mr. Wappeler also visited Boh. & had his horse shod.
1748	John Toland and Ann Kelly our weaving and spinning.
	Bohemia's best beer 1? shilling per gall., also p. 20 malt bought. Plenty of whiskey drunk by workmen.
1748	Contract with miller, Thos. Murray 1/3 of grindings took away distills.
	Contract with Will Agges to make well from 14 to 40 ft. deep at the Quarter at 2 sh., 6 p. a foot.
1748	Jos. Lilly did the distilling of liquors.
	Rev. Henry Neale acct. with Phil – he traveled probably from Phil. to Balt. from Balt. to East Shore, from St. Jose. to Boh.
1748	Rev. Bennet Neale of Balt. acct.
	School, John Carroll came back Apr. 22, 1748 and stayed till Oct. 16.
	Rev. John Kingdon acct. Came to Boh. July 30, visited Molyneux perhaps 1744 or 45.
1748	School probably – Bob Brent came Aug. 5 left Oct. 25.
	Rich Molyneux acct. in Pulton's hand – I journed to Annapol. for you 13 sh. – to your journey to Appoquinimink. When Molyneux came back he marked down all he had to Poultons acct.
1749	Acct of Greaton & Beadnall. Fr. Greaton used to snuff.
1750	The cash left in house by Mr. Molyneux to Jos. Greaton 7 lb. 4 sh. Fr. Greaton seems to have borrowed money from Livers and Diggs.
1750	To pay for Beadnalls horse for my journey to Phil. 1 lb. 2 sh. Oct. 3, for my journey up & down to Phil 1 lb.
	For a crystal for Mr. Lewis watch 2 sh. 6 p. Took up cash for Mr. Lewis for traveling – stockings for Beadnall.
1751	Mill expenses, etc.
	April for Mr. Lewis travelling exp.
	April to Mending Mr. Greatons chair, travel to Phil.
	May for Mr. Lewis travell exp.
	June for Mr. Lewis travell exp.
	Oct. for Mr. Lewis travell exp., etc.
	Oct. Ralph and Thos. Ashton for their dinner, etc. at Fredericktown (Ralph was servant.)
1752	Fr. Greaton's acct with Robert Harding of Phil.
1752	Sep. to doctor for setting Mr. Greatons collar bone. 1 lb. 14 sh.

Jesuit Mission in Colonial Maryland 59

To travel up and down to Phil. 1 lb.
Oct. for portage of Mr. Gillibrands box from Annapolis lb. 1.
May Spent for Mr. Sneider 38 lb. 16 sh.
May Spent for winnowing engine 4 lb., 12 sh.
July to Mr. Harding for Mr. Sneider.
Oct. for newspapers.
To Bennet Neale pr. order of Mr. Diggs.

1752 Crop of wheat 843 bus.
1753 1st Barack   139 bus.   1st stack of Quarter   68.
     2 "   134   2 "   72
     3 "   118   3 "   82
     4 "   124   SOLD   222
There were 3 farms, Home, St. Inigoes, Quarter. Mr. Lewis made frequent little journeys.

1753 Cap for Mr. Greaton, 3 sh.
April Mr. Gillibrands horse goes astray – gave Ralph 7 sh. 6 p. to find him.

1753 Aug. ye 19, Mr. Jos. Greaton died. Left at his death cash in house 21 lb., 18 sh., ? p. Dr. Plunket for tending Mr. Greaton 1 lb. 7 sh. Sept. 1 Mr. Lewis going to White Clay Creek, 1 sh., 3 p. Ralph for going to W. C. Creek for cartwheels 4 sh., 8 p. Sept. 27 for Mr. Gillibrands travel exp. 1, 13, 6, Oct. 9 to Mr. Gillibrands cash 0, 8, 3.
Nov. 11 Borrowed of Mr. Gillibrands 4, 3, 8.
Oc. At Noxontown fair as Sock fairings, etc. (Noxon fair – a market fair for buying all kinds of goods.)
Two farms in operation – Quarter, St. Inigoes.
Cash in house for 1754 22, 1, 4.

1754 Jan. Mr. Lewis went to Talbot 0, 13, 6.
Ap. Mr. Lewis went to Newtown, 0, 2, 0 (Chestertown).
Rec'd. by Mr. Gillibrandt for rent for a tract of land lying in Kent on Delaware.
May to cash from Mr. Harding for "Essec's" passage.
Apr. 22 to Peter Lowber for a tract of land purchased by Mr. Pulton of J. Cain lying in Kent on Delaware in Motherkill hundred called Addition to Cavilridge layed out for 100 acres capital and int. thereof from the year 1745, 19th Nov. 42, 15, 4.
Watch string for Mr. Lewis, 0, 1, 0. A pair of garters 0, 0, 9 – 2 curling irons for Mr. Gillibrandt 0, 1, 4.
May To Mr. Harding interest money 9 lb.
June Mr. Lewis to White Clay 0, 2, 9.
Thea and coffee – Rum also.
July 14 Mr. Lewis to White Clay.

1754 Sept. Lewis to Talbot.
Sept. 16 Lewis to Balt. 9 sh.
Oct. Lewis to New Castle, 5 s, 9.
They bought cod & mackerel.
Nov. Suit of clothes for Mr. Gillibrandt 8, 14, 4. a vize 1 lb.
Mr. Gillibrandt to Phil. travel exp. 1 lb.

1755 Jan. 29 Ralph's journey with Mr. Gillibrandt to Phil. 0, 17, 6.
Pay to Davy Jones on Mr. Beadnalls order 16 lb.
Pay to Mr. Harding on Mr. Gillibrandt acc. 11, 15, 0.
To Mr. Harding int. 9 lb.
June to Travel to Newtown 0, 2, 6. This Newtown was place on eastern shore. (Chestertown, Md. Called Chester Newtown).
Mr. Harding on my acc. bought a Phil To White Clay Creek 2 sh.

1755 Crop of corn for 1755. Made at home 46 bills.
Hands at house Tom, Dick, Molly & 2 boys (Ben was jobber.)
Made at Askmore 56 blls. hands Peter & Moll.
Made at St. Inigoes 140 blls. hands Ralph, Tom, Nancy, Hanna & O. Mary + 2 plows & six horses. A very dry year.
Dec. 11. Distributed to people 1800 wt. of pork, 100 wt. to 18 hands young and old. To Mr.

	Lowbers (i.e., new farm) Kent To Beadnalls, by Mr. Hunters order 5, 9, 6. Travel to Dover 5 sh.
1756	Apr. 30 Travel to Kent
	Sep. to Mr. Farrar per order 8 lb., 2
	Dec. journey to Balt.
	Corn crop St. Inigoes 94 blls. Askmore 73?, Home 76? = 244 blls.
1757	To Mr. Harding int. 9 lb.
	To Mr. Beadnall packet money 4 sh., 1
	To Mr. Harding for purchase of sundries for house 12, 15.
	Travel to New Castle 0, 5, 3.
	June to New Castle.
	June 27 to Dover.
	To Mr. Harding for a horse.
	Sept. 12 to White Clay Creek.
1758	Apr. to White Clay Creek to Dover.
	June to Mr. Harding Int. 9 lb.
	Sept. to Mr. Manners returning to Conewage 6 lb. 15 s.
	Built a new house, milk house, corn crib 5, 9, 6.
	Oct. to Dover.
	Nov. to White Clay.
	Tobacco house – Mill race repairs.
	Dec. 7 to a French priest prisoner de guerre 1, 1, 0.
	Dec. 28 to ye French priest 0, 12, 6.
	Dec. 31 to Briant O'Daniel going after a stray horse 5 sh.
1758	Aug. To Mr. Farmer per order of Mr. Hunter 15 lb.
1759	March To White Clay to Queen Annes.
	Apr. 30. A hat for Mr. Manners, etc. 2 lb., 10 (he came here as he got one outfit).
	Travel expenses Mr. Manners 4 sh.
	Nov. 28 to cash of Mr. Hunter for purchasing a lot in Newport 40 lb.
1760	Mgrs. John returns to Frigal, 7 sh., 6.
	April 29 to Mr. Manners cash 14 lb.
	April 29 cakes and dinner for self & Mr. Manners 5 sh.
	May 1 Cash to Mr. Manners 22 lb.
	June sent cash to Mr. Harding for goods for house.
	July cash to Mr. Leonard by Mr. Hunters order 20 lb.
	Nov. 10 cash to Mr. Manners 15 sh.
1761	Jan. 1 cash from Mr. Manners 12, 11, 6.
	March cash to a French neutral 0, 1, 10.
	June Cash for Smollets history. 0, 1, 4.
	Cash for negro-man – Charles – 30 lb.
	July, Cash for Mr. Manners watch.

Cann 176 – Names From The Bohemia Day Book – 1735-1761; The following list of names, cover in many instances, the trades and professions of the various people who helped build and maintain this plantation in its first fifty-seven years.

Some helped to build, some were customers who purchased the various crops; tobacco, vegetables, meats, hides, wool, etc., and it was just as important for the vendors who hand many items to sell that were necessary for the maintenance of the plantation and the many people who lived on it.

Without this extensive business enterprise, it would have been impossible for the missionaries to the performed their many duties over their vast territory. Today, it could have been classed as big business.

Ailsbury, Christopher, 1745.; Anderson, Bartholemous, 1754, clothing.; Ailsbury, Henrietta (widow) 1742, dress maker.; Ashton, Thomas, 1739-1751, Factotum, this man would be classified as a manager today.; Brown, John, 1753.; Bayard, Peter, 1756, Nails.; Beard, Alexander, 1745 – Quit rent.; Bouchet, Dr., 1759 – Customer.; Brent, Robert, 1748.; Brown, Dan, 1758 – Linens.; Branham, Timothy, 1742 – Tailor.; Broderick, Thomas, 1755 – Laborer.; Best, Humprey, 1735.; Baine, John, 1750 – Shop keeper.; Bradford, Benjamin, 1744.; Base, William, 1759.; Betson, Mary,

1745, made Mr. Henry Neale, S. J. executor. Her will left quite and amount of money (paper currency, gold and sterling) to her daughter when she reached the age of 21.; Blake, Philemon.; Bartley, Mat, 1759 – Laborer.; Baldwin, John, Colonel, 1757-1751.; Branghan, Patrick, 1760.; Beatty, Peggy, 1756 – Farming.; Bradley, John, 1740-1746.; Brooks, William, 1754 – Weaver.; Bradly, Suzanna, 1747-1753 – Shoes.; Burke, John, 1759 – Merchant.; Bradford, William, 1742.; Bradford Charles, 1752.; Bannister, Thomas, 1750-1753.; Crosby, Susan, 1753-1755 – Spinner.; Cradick, Richard, 1735-1740 – Renter, 20 lb /yr.; Crosbey, James, 1753.; Crosbye, John, 1755-1756 – Factotum.; Colnil, Colonel, 1750.; Cazier, John, 1743-1748 – Shoemaker.; Cockran, Joseph, 1751 – Victualler.; Cane, John, 1744-1751 – Planter (Kent Co., Del.).; Crevet, J., 1755-1756 – Oxen.; Chreten, Francois, 1745-1746.; Carnan, John, 1751 – Merchant.; Cartwright, Michael, 1747.; Cully, 1751 – house in Newtown (Chestertown).; Carrol, Daniel, 1745-1748.; Cowgato, John, 1758 – Merchant.; Carnie, Nicholas, 1753 – Tanner and Shoemaker in Warwick.; Cretian, Ann, 1756 – Farming.; Carrol, Timothy, 1746.; Carnie, Jane, 1753 – Knitting.; Carty, Darby, 1753.; Costello, Edward, 1756.; Cassons, Thomas, 1759 – Smithy (Blacksmith).; Cotringer, 1756 – Tailor.; Cockeran, James, 1759 – Customer.; Campbell, Miller, 1759 – Millwright.; Couch, Thomas, 2-9-1751 – 30 lb. In part for ye mill.; Cullen, William, 1758 – Customer.; Cammel, Archibold, 1746.; Dunleavy, Darby, 1736-1745 – Renter.; Douglas, Marcellous, 1742 – Tailor.; Dixon, 1750.; Douglas, William, 1742.; Doherty, Patrick, 1758.; Douglas, Arch, 1742.; Doland, William, 1745-1751 – Butcher – Meat.; Doland, Catherine, 1754 – Spinner.; Dagnail, John, 1745.; Douglas, George, 1758.; Dun, Timothy, 1745.; Driscoll, J, 1758 – Tailor.; Driscoll, Steven, 1743 – Miller.; Dawson, Nathaniel, 1753 – Weaver.; Douglas, Valentine, 1745.; Dawson (Dorsy) Margaret, 1748.; Eyler, Robert 1745 – Carpenter.; Evans, Evan, 1750 – Lumber.; Eyler, Mary.; Evans, James, 1756 – Farming.; Farrell, Brian, 1745 – Well digger, tanner.; Foreigner, Edward, 1760.; Fitzsimmons, Thomas, 1756 – Merchant.; Farrell, William, 1748 – Well digger.; Farrell, Mrs. 1751, Tanning and currying leather.; Frisby, Peregrine, 1744 – Tanner.; Fayweather, 1751 – Merchant.; Frisby, James, 1744-1760 – Customer.; Fitzpatrick, Terence, 1751 – Wig maker.; Fowler, Archibold, 1753-1755 – Smithy.; Fowler, Jacob, 1755 – Smith.; Fitch, Patrick Lawrence, 1750 – Wig maker.; Foley, Denis 1759 – Merchant.; Graham, Bryon, 1744 – Smithy.; Gooding, Abraham, 1749-1750 – borrowed 10 lb.; Galaher, John, 1745.; Griffin, Hugh, 1756-1759 – Weaver.; Galaher, Neal G., 1747-1760 – Tailor.; Gallaher, Hugh, 1742.; George, Joshua, 1745 – Smith.; George, Sidney, 1760.; Galaher, Daniel, 1745-1755 – Laborer.; Gibbs, Joseph, 1753 – Harness.; Garrety, Briant, 1745 – Laborer.; Galaher, Peggy, 1756 – Shirt maker.; Grimes, Bryan, 1753 – Victualler and Smith.; Gordon, Charles, 1752.; Holland, John, 1751 – Druggist.; Heath, James Paul, 1744-1747 – Planter.; Hays, Darby, 1758 – Tallow – Hides.; Havring, William, 1744.; Harper, Even, Mrs. 1756 – Weaver.; Hall, William, 1743-1755 – Merchant and Customer.; Hemings, Cliff, 1755 – Renter.; Hagan, Owen, 1743.; Hanley, John, 1759 – Cobbler.; Hagan, James, 1745 – Butcher.; Hutchenson, Gavin, 1756 – Smith.; Hammon, Cliff, 1746 – (rented "New Design") – Carpenter.; Harper, Thomas, 1757.; Honis, John, 1752.; Himmings, Jr., 1759 – Picture frames.; Hollins, Jonathon.; Jackson, John, 1735-1740 (1 yrs. Rent 20 lb.) Doctor?; Jones, Jenny, 1750.; Johnson, James, 1750-1753 – Lumber.; Jones, Dave, 1755 – rec'd. on Mr. Beadnall order 16 lb.; Kaine, John, 1748.; Knarsborough, Mary, 1756 – Wax.; Kelly, Hugh, 1749-1750 – Merchant.; Kleinhoff, 1756 – Merchant.; Kelly, Anne, 1748.; Lloyd, Robt. 1755 – Servant.; Long, Christopher, 1750.; Loland, John, 1748.; Luna, 1751.; Lavin, Thomas, 1756.; Loy, Edward, M., 1754 – Laborer.; Lilly, Joseph, 1746-1752.; Lober, Peter, 1751 – Planter (Kent Co., Del.).; Lockwood, Richard, 1754 – Carpenter.; Lylly, 1750.; Mahoney, Cornelius, 1740-1754 – Customer.; More, 1751 – Millwright.; Murphy, William, 1745.; Meridith, Mrs., 1751 – Left money on deposit.; Murdock, William, 1758 – Shoemaker.; Murphy, Patrick, 1759 – Laborer.; Matthews, Dr. Hugh, J., Sr., 1744-1753 – Borrowed 40 lb.; Musgang, Dr., 1750 – Customer.; Mills, Thomas, 1755 – Axes.; Murray, Thomas, 1748 – Miller.; Meighan, Thomas, 1754 – Planter.; Marr, Thomas, 1752 – Smithy.; Maguire, Charles, 1756 – Merchant.; Mainer, Neddy, 1746.; McCabe, Francis, 1758 – Shoemaker.; McDermott, Edward, 1758.; McDermott, Dominic, 1760 – Tailor.; MacAdams, Mary, 1744 – Weaver.; McCombs, John, 1750 – Mason.; MacDermott, John, 1750-1753 – borrowed 10 lb. Good Customer.; McDerry, 1751 – Veterinarian.; McLaughlin, Thomas, 1748 – Customer.; McCarty, 1753 – Cobbler.; MacNeal, John, 1752.; McDuel, James, 1754 – Customer.; McDermot, widow, 1755 – Wool.; McLean, Thomas, 1758 – Customer.; Nugent, Peter, 1760.; Nicholas, Richard, 1751 – Millwright, 16 lb. for building Mill house.; Neale, Edward, 1745.; Nodine, Andrew, 1759 –

Tallow, hides.; Noland, Matthias, 1746-1751 – Carpenter, Wheelwright.; Noland, Esther, Mrs., 1755.; Noland, James, 1744 – Plasterer.; Noland, James, 1751 – Draper, suit of clothes for Mr. Lewis 3-10-0.; Noland, Dennis, 1742.; O'Daniel, Briant, 1755-1756 – Laborer.; O'Dell, John.; O'Castle, Denis, 1751 – Thresher.; Porter, James, 1753.; Patterson, James, 1753 – Smith.; Price, Nicholas, 1753 – Smith.; Plunket, Dr. John 1753 – cared for Mr. Greaton, S. J., Portlock, Mary, Mrs., 1750.; Quin, James, 1753 – Painter.; Ringgold, 1754 – Newspaper.; Ryon, William, 1754 – Laborer.; Roberts, Samuel, 1756 – Cartwright.; Richardson, Elizabeth, 1759 – Stocking maker.; Reyly, Brian, 1748.; Reyleigh, Briant, 1751 – Customer.; Reynolds, Nicholas, 1735 – Planter.; Rumsey, 1751 – Contractor.; Rutter, Thomas, 1744.; Reed, James, 1751 – Merchant.; Stampson, Sam, 1735-1740.; Swan, Daniel, 1751 – Horse trader.; Sergeant, Williams, 1737.; Scotty, Charles, 1752 – Cobbler.; Smith, Cornelius, 1735.; Savin, Williams, 1756 – Quit rents.; Sorrell, Dan, 1751-1754 – Culleys House, Newtowne (Chestertown) Paid Rent.; Spence, Captain, 1739.; Scots, Harry, 1750 – Negro.; Snow, Prince, 1744-1751.; Shaddock, Charles, 1753 – Laborer.; Stanley, James, 1744.; Sheppard, Mrs., 1758 – Knitting, Spinning.; Shoemaker, Anthony, 1747.; Shea, Martha, 1749-1755 – Customer.; Smith, Thomas, 1745 – Smithy.; Stell, Alexander, 1746 – Mowers.; Schloss, James, 1756 – Dry Goods.; Summers, Felix, 1745.; Tweedy, William, 1754 – Cobbler.; Taylor, Ann, 1744.; Toland, John, 1752 – Weaver.; Vicars, George, 1754.; Veasey, Edward, 1750 – Auctioneer.; Van Sant, Cornelius, 1753 – Smith.; Van Horn, B., 1755.; Wyatt, Andrew, 1745-1759 – School Master at the Bohemia Academy.; Williams, William, 1758 – Frederick, Nails and Planks.; Watherspoon, David, 1749-1753 – Planter.; Wallace, Joseph, 1751 – Ax Layer.; Watts, Thomas, 1738-1740.; Ward, Henrietta, Mrs., 1739-1756 – Midwife.; Woods, Nichols, 1743-1748.; Woods, Henry, 1751 – Stocking maker.; Waters, John, 1745 – Mason and Bricklayer.; White, James, 1753 – Merchant.; Wilson, Charles, 1753.

110. Sister Mary Virginia Geiger, *Daniel Carroll, A Framer of the Constitution* (Washington, D.C.: Catholic University of America, 1943), 21; Bernard C. Steiner, "Maryland's Adoption of the Federal Constitution," *American Historical Review* 5 (Oct. 1899): 22–24, (Jan. 1900): 207–224; Hannis Taylor, *The Origin and Growth of the American Constitution* (Boston: Houghton, Mifflin and Co., 1911), 226; *American State Papers, Documents Legislative and Executive* (Washington, D.C.: Gales and Seaton, 1832), 5: 5–8; Cann, 31–32; Guilday, *John Carroll*, 3; John Tracy Ellis, ed., *Documents of American Catholic History* (Wilmington, Del.: Michael Glazier Co., 1987), 1: 157–158, No. 51, "Daniel Carroll Argues for Marylanders to Ratify the Constitution, October 16, 1787."
111. Cann, 31, 181; Pryor, 101
112. Rev. Philip Reading to the Secretary, Appoquinimink, March 26, 1747, in William Stevens Perry, ed., *Papers Relating to the History of the Church in Pennsylvania*, also printed as vol. 2 of *Historical Collections Relating to the American Colonial Church* (Privately printed, 1871), 244–245; Carley, "Baptismal Register of Joseph Mosley, S.J.," 44; Quigley, "Catholic Beginnings in the Delaware Valley," 29; Elizabeth Waterson, *Churches in Delaware During the Revolution* (Wilmington, Del.: Historical Society of Delaware, 1925), 6–7; Kraemer, "Catholic Church in Delaware," 681–682
113. Cann, 31
114. Cann, 31, 179; Carley, "Baptismal Register of Joseph Mosley, S.J.," 1; Will of Matthew Lober, June 8, 1772, Register of Wills, L: 117, DH of R—heirs: wife Hannah; sons Matthew Jr., Peter, and Jonathan; daughters Susanna, Elizabeth, and Miriam; son-in-law William Virdin Durborrow; executor, son Peter.
115. Hughes, Documents 1: 260–261; Bohemia day-book, April 22, 1754, GUA, to Peter Lowber for a tract of land purchased by Mr. Poulton of John Cain lying in Kenton, Delaware called 'Addition"'; Cann, 182–184; Carley, "Baptismal Register of Joseph Mosley, S.J.," 44
116. Will of Michael Lowber, dated Jan. 2, 1744, probated April 7, 1746, Register of Wills, I: 122–123, DH of R—Heirs: daughters Unity (wife of John Emerson), Susannah Lewis; sons Michael, Peter, Matthew, Isaac; daughters Garty Muncy, Margaret Manlove, Agnes Walker; wife Rachel; grandchildren of daughter Grace Brown; grandsons Michael (son of Peter Lowber), John and Michael Reynolds, Michael Emerson (son of Unity and John Emerson); granddaughter Susannah Reynolds.
117. *Delaware Archives* (Wilmington: Mercantile Printing Company, 1911), 1 (Military): 13, "in the Company of which John Caton is captain—Manassey Cain, Matthew Lowber, John Reynolds"; Cann, 177; De Valinger, *Colonial Military Organization*, 37; Will of Owen Cain, dated Dec. 6, 1741, probated Dec. 9, 1741, Register of Wills, I: 126, DH of R—Heirs: sons Manassey, Owen. Wife

unnamed. Witnesses: Peter Lowber, John Cain, Thomas Thomas.
118. "The Heath Family of Worsall Manor, Maryland, "TMs, 1965, Cecil County Historical Society, Elkton, Md., 5; Cann, 31, 179
119. GUA – Bohemia Ledger, May 1745, Harry C. Rhodes, GUA *Queenstown: The Social History of a Small American Town* (Queenstown, Md.: Queen Anne Press, 1985), 31, 35
120. Rhodes, *Queenstown,* 30; Carley, "Baptismal Register of Joseph Mosley, S.J.," 42–43
121. Christopher Johnston, "Hall Family of Calvert County, *MHM 8* (Sept. 1913): 291–301; Rhodes, *Queenstown,* 30; Carley, "Baptismal Register of Joseph Mosley, S.J.," 37
122. McGrain, "Priest Neale," 265; Shea, *Catholic Church in Colonial Days,* 443; Cann, 7
123. Christopher Johnston, "The Neale Family of Charles County," *MHM 7* (June 1912): 208 ff.; Cann, 31
124. Cann, 31; Sister Clare Joseph Dickinson, *Diary of a Trip to America* (Brookline, Mass.: Carmelite Monastery, 1970), 1; Anonymous [a Carmelite nun], *A History of Port Tobacco Carmel* (Washington, D.C.: Nuns of Port Tobacco Carmel, 1985), 15
125. Sister M. Virginia Geiger, *Robert Brent II: One Man and His Descendants* (Baltimore: College of Notre Dame of Maryland, 1978), 300–302; Christopher Johnston, *Society of the Colonial Wars in the State of Maryland: Genealogies of the Members and Record of Services of Ancestors*
(Baltimore: Friedenwald Co., 1905), 7; Guilday, *John Carroll,* 3; Ray, *American Opinion of Roman Catholicism,* 249–251; W. B. Chilton, "Brent Genealogy," *Virginia Magazine of History and Biography* 12 (April 1905): 439–443; William P. Palmer, ed., *Virginia Calendar of State Papers, 1652–1781* (Richmond: Commonwealth of Virginia, 1875), 1: 46–47; Fairfax Harrison, "Brent Town, Ravensworth and the Huguenots in Stafford," *Tyler's Quarterly Magazine* 5 (Jan. 1924): 164–185
126. Hughes, Text 2: 523, note 14; Cann, 177; Carley, "Baptismal Register of Joseph Mosley, S. J.," 35, 39, 41
127. Thomas O'Brien Hanley, *Charles Carroll of Carrollton, The Making of a Revolutionary Gentleman* (Chicago: Loyola University press, 1982) 15 – "In 1747 Charles went to Bohemia to study for about seven months, and went again the following year for a similar period." Kate Rowland, *The Life of Charles Carroll of Carrollton, 1737-1832* (New York: G. P. Putnam, 1898) 1:15; (Rowland, *Life of Charles Carroll*), 1: 15; "Charles Carroll of Carrollton," in *Catholic World* [New York] 23 (July 1876): 541; Cann, 31, 34; Thomas Hughes, S.J., "Educational Convoys to Europe in the Olden Time," *The American Ecclesiastical Review* 29 (July 1903): 38
128. Guilday, *John Carroll,* 4; Cann, "Bohemia Academy" 30-32, "Bohemia Academy Accounts" 34-36
129. Perry, *Papers Relating to the Church in Pennsylvania,* 313; Hughes, Text 2: 532; Devitt, "Bohemia," 110–111
130. GUA – Ledger and Account Book, 1750–1761, Bohemia Mission.; Cann, 7–8, 36, 39; Beitzell, 246, 252; Hughes, Text 2: Appendix F, No. 123; Carley, *St. Peter's, Queenstown,* 24–25; Carley, "Baptismal Register of Joseph Mosley, S.J.," 43

SLAVES BAPTIZED AT BOHEMIA IN THE COLONIAL PERIOD: F. Edward Wright, compiler, *Vital Records of the Jesuit Missions of the Eastern Shore 1760-1800* (Silver springs, Maryland: Family Line Publications, 1986) 32 – Dick; Bohemia, bapt 1750; Betty; Slave; Nelly; Bohemia; bapt 1750; Ralph; slave; Ralph; Bohemia; bapt 1752; Nenney; slave; John; Bohemia; bapt 1755; Nenny; Spon Betty; slave; Sara; Bohemia; bapt 1760; Mary; slave.

SLAVES BURIED AT BOHEMIA IN THE COLONIAL PERIOD:
02/19/1759   Buried old Mary.
03/28/1776   Rose, Dian's child.
11/20/1779   Delia.
Indicative of the humane and tender care taken of the priests' slaves and of the efforts to fulfill their temporal needs are the following entries taken from the Bohemia Account Books:
11/05/1752   to a pair of breetches for Davi: 1 pound, 4 shillings.
10/29/1752   to ye negroes for a fairing (Noxentown Fair): 2 shillings and 7 pence.
12/18/1752   to Mr. Charles Scot for making ye negroes shoes: 7 shillings and 7 pence.
04/10/1753   to Peter for physick: 2 shillings and 6 pence.
04/23/1753   to Tho. Harper in full to his negro woman's teeth: 2 pounds and 10 shillings.

05/07/153 to Dr. Hugh Matthews, Jr. in full for his negroes foot service and all accounts, see his rec't. 19 pounds and 8 shillings.
10/31/1753 to 12 pounds upper leather for ye negroes shoes 1 pound and 1 shilling.
04/13/1754 to 2 physicks for negroe, Peter, 5 pounds.
05/22/1754 to 1 gallon of molasses to Ralph when sick, 2 shillings and 6 pence.
07/22/1754 to Ralph going to Phila. For his sick wife: 15 shillings.
11/09/1755 to negroe woman, Nanny, was brought to bed of a boy who was christened John on ye 11 of Nov. God-father Isaac; God-Mother Betty.
01/28/1756 to Mr. Charles Scott in part for negroes shoes: 15 shillings.
11/07/1756 by cash for shoes for negroes: 7 pounds.
11/21/1756 buttons for negroes clothes: 6 shillings and 4 pence.
12/05/1756 Negro woman, Molly, was brought to bed of a girl who was christened Bulah, on ye 7th Dec. God-father Davey, God-mother, Betty.
02/19/1759 Buried old Mary.
01/09/1759 to Jo Driscole for cutting negro clothes.
04/02/1760 to Franc (Bebe?) for 1 pr. negro shoes: 6 shillings and 6 pence.
07/31/1760 by cash for negro shoes: 4 shillings and 4 pence.

Cann 162-171: Slaves at Bohemia – In 1765 an official report from the Superior, Father George Hunter, to the Provincial, Father De Mutt, shows that there were 21 slaves buried in Bohemia cemetery.

131. Hughes, Text 2: 694, Appendix F, No. 120, Father Richard Gailibrande; John Lewis Missionary Account, Bohemia Day-book, 1750–1761, Georgetown University Archives; Hughes, Text 2: 693, Appendix F, No. 118, Father James Beadnall; Queen Anne's County Land Records, STW 7: 343–344; will of Henry Cully, probated 1749, Wills, Queen Anne's County 25: 571. The will of Christian Beech Cully was probated 1751.
132. Carley, "Baptismal Register of Joseph Mosley, S.J.," 43; Cann, 36
133. Will of Frances Pope Ungle (1754), Wills, Talbot County, 29: 263; will of Hugh Linch (dated April, 1748), Wills, DD4: 559, with instruction given to Terence Connolly, executor.
134. Beitzell, 252; Hughes, Text 2: 501; Cann, 7, 39. ENGLISH JESUIT, JOSEPH GREATON – was superior at Bohemia from 1750 to 1753. He was born in 1679 and entered the Jesuits in 1708. He died on August 19, 1753 at Bohemia at age 74 and is buried there. AMERICAN JESUIT, ARNOLD LIVERS – was at Bohemia from 1749 to 1750. He was born in Maryland in 1705 and entered the Jesuits in 1724. He died on August 16, 1767 at age 62 and is buried at St. Inigoes. AMERICAN JESUIT, BENEDICT NEALE – Father Benedict Neale was assistant to Father Greaton at Bohemia in 1751. He was born in Maryland in 1709 and entered the Jesuits in 1728. He died in 1787 at age 78. ENGLISH JESUIT, ROBERT HARDING – Father Harding was born in 1701 and entered the Jesuits in 1722. He died on September 1, 1772 at age 71 and is buried in Philadelphia. JESUIT, THEODORE SCHNEIDER – Father Schneider was at Bohemia in 1751. He was born in 1703 and entered the Jesuits in 1721. He died on July 10, 1764 at age 61 and is buried at Goshenhoppen, Pennsylvania.
135. Esling, 126–127; Carley, "Baptismal Register of Joseph Mosley, S.J.," 179; Hughes, Text 2: 508, Documents 1: 96, 102–104; Cann, 36
136. Reverend Hugh Neil to the Secretary, Dover, September 1, 1751, in Perry, *Papers Relating to the Church in Delaware*, 97; Cann, 39. JESUIT, James BEADNALL – Father Beadnall was at Bohemia from 1752 to 1757. He was born in 1718 and entered the Jesuits in 1739. He died on September 1, 1772 at age 54 and is buried at Newtown, Maryland.

Cann 162-171: Slaves at Bohemia – In 1765 an official report from the Superior, Father George Hunter, to the Provincial, Father De Mutt, shows that there were 21 slaves at Bohemia, of which 3 worked within doors, 12 in the fields, and the rest being children or old.

Like the Jesuits in general, as pointed out above, Bohemia depended on these black servants to man part of the plantation and help with the income to cover expenses. The Jesuit priests had no other source of income other than occasional contributions of the wealthier Catholics and an occasional bequest in their wills, and since, according to contemporary Jesuit letters, the larger part of their congregation was very poor, the Jesuits, of necessity, had to provide some means to support themselves to enable them to carry on the purpose of their Mission. Their faithful blacks then played no small part, even though indirectly, in bringing the consolations of religion to the Maryland and Pennsylvania Provinces. Thus, the slaves were essential to the advancement of the Mission's goals, and were in keeping with the way of life practiced throughout the English Colonies. In 1765, Father Hunter reported an annual income from the 12 slaves at Bohemia at 9 pounds sterling each, to be a total of 108 pounds.

137. Carley, "Baptismal Register of Joseph Mosley, S.J.," 44; Cann 39 FRENCH JESUIT, RICHARD GALLIBRANDE – Father Gallibrande was at Bohemia from 1752 to 1755.
138. Reverend Philip Reading to the Secretary, Appoquinimink, June 25, 1750, in Perry, *Papers Relating to the Church in Pennsylvania*, 261; Esling, 119–120
139. Pryor, 39; Esling, 119; Kraemer, "The Catholic Church in Delaware," 2: 681; John Gilmary Shea, *The Life and Times of the Most Rev. John Carroll, Bishop and First Archbishop of Baltimore* (New York: J. G. Shea, 1888), 454
140. Eugene Irving McCormac, *Colonial Opposition to Imperial Authority During the French and Indian War* (Berkeley, Cal.: University Press, 1911), 46; Arthur M. Schlesinger, "Maryland's Share in the Last Intercolonial War," *MHM* 7 (June 1912): 119–149; J. William Black, *Maryland's Attitude in the Struggle for Canada* (Baltimore: The Johns Hopkins University, 1892), 10: No. 7; Thomas P. Phelan, *Catholics in Colonial Days* (New York: P. J. Kennedy and Sons, 1935), 154
141. *Archives of Maryland*, 2: 86
142. Purcell, "Education and Irish Teachers," 149; "Proceedings of the [Anglican] Parochial Clergy," *MHM* 3 (Dec. 1908): 374
143. Scharf, *History of Maryland* 2: 511
144. Dorchester County Judgments, vol. 1, C-12: 148, no. 8913, 1-4-3-45, Maryland State Archives; John Cornelius Linehan and Thomas Hamilton Murray, *Irish Schoolmasters in the American Colonies* (Washington, D.C.: American-Irish Historical Society, 1898), 10
145. *Maryland Gazette*, Annapolis, March 6, 1755; Steiner, *Education in Maryland*, 36; Hughes, Text 2: 538; Hughes, "Educational Convoys to Europe," 24–39; Ray, 59
146. *Archives of Maryland*, 31: 525
147. *Archives of Maryland*, 1: 408; "Letters of Governor Sharpe," MHM 6I (Sept. 1966): 190; Barker, *Background of Revolution in Maryland*, 254–255; Black, *Maryland's Attitude in the Struggle for Canada*, 6l, 64; Hughes, Text 2: 540–541
148. Devitt, "A Dark Chapter in the Catholic History of Maryland," 146; Thomas O'Brien Hanley, "The Catholic and Anglican Gentry in Maryland Politics," *Historical Magazine of the Protestant Episcopal Church* 38 (June 1969): 143–151
149. Black, *Maryland's Attitude in the Struggle for Canada*, 25, 65
150. Mathew Page Andrews, *Tercentenary History of Maryland,* (Baltimore: S.J. Clark Publishers, 1925) 1: 467–468
151. George Hardy to Robert H. Morris, New York, July 9, 1756, *Pennsylvania Archives*, series 2, 1: 694
152. Devitt, "Dark Chapter," 146; Hughes, Text 2: 502
153. *Archives of Maryland*, 6: 497; Colonial Offices, 318, 2, part 1, 20, Public Record Office, London; Quigley, "Catholic Beginnings in Delaware Valley," 40
154. *Archives of Maryland*, 25: 609; *Compleat Collection of the Laws of Maryland* (Annapolis: William Parks, 1727), 59; Devitt, "Dark Chapter," 145; Michael J. Riordan, *Cathedral Records, From the Beginning of Catholicity in Baltimore to the Present Time* (Baltimore: Catholic Mirror, 1906), 6–12; McGrain, "Priest Neale, " 267
155. Charles Carroll to son, July 14, 1760, quoted in Rowland, *Life and Correspondence of Charles Carroll*, 1: 43
156. *Archives of Maryland*, 6: 539
157. *Archives of Maryland*, 2: 610
158. Hughes, Text 2: 545; Carley, "Baptismal Register of Joseph Mosley, S.J.," 33. Jones' inventory in 1757 included "a parcel of Romans Books," Maryland State Archives, Inventories, Prerogative Court 63: 450. Petition of Beadnall to Lord Baltimore, Ms 15, 489, folio 66, British Museum, London; Edward B. Carley, *The Origins and History of St. Peter's Church, Queenstown, Maryland 1637-1976* (Easton, Maryland: Tidewater Publishers, 1976) 23–24
159. *The Woodstock Letters, A Record of Current Events and Historical Notes Connected with the Colleges and Missions of the Society of Jesus* (Baltimore: Society of Jesus, Maryland-New York Province, 1872–1970), 10: 22–23; Devitt, "Dark Chapter," 141; Devitt, "Bohemia," 112. Ledger and Account Books, 1750–1761, Bohemia Mission, GUA; James Beadnall preached at the Seth's at

least twice in 1755. Georgetown University, Washington, D.C., Lauinger Library, Special Collections, *American Catholic Sermon Collection* Be-l,10
160. *Archives of Maryland*, 24: 89–91, 25: 626
161. *Archives of Maryland*, 24: 441–448, 25: 675
162. Andrews, *Tercentenary History of Maryland*, 485
163. *Archives of Maryland*, 2: 46; Hughes, Text 2:546; Rowland, 1: 31–32; Field, *Unpublished Letters of Charles Carroll*, 35; "Extracts from the Carroll Papers," *MHM* 10 (Sept. 1915): 255–256
164. Ives, 288; Hughes, Text 2: 545, note 11. GUA – Maryland Province, Society of Jesus – Bohemia 1764-1767
165. Clifford Pryor, 14
166. Walter A. Powell, *A History of Delaware* (Boston: Christopher Publishing Co., 1928), 122, 125; John A. Munroe, Colonial *Delaware: A History* (Millwood, N.Y.: KTO Press, 1978), 65; J. Thomas Scharf, *History of Maryland* (Baltimore: J. B. Piet, 1879), 1: 524-556; Charles A. Barker, *The Background of the Revolution in Maryland* (New Haven: Yale University Press, 1940), 293–302; Alfred F. Young, *The American Revolution: Explorations in the History of American Radicalism* (DeKalb, ill.: Northern Illinois University Ness, 1976), 241. The population of Delaware in 1775 was 37,219, according to United States Bureau of the Census, *US. Census of Population, 1950* (Washington, D.C.: U.S. Government Printing Office, 1952), 2: 4–8, table 1.
167. Harold B. Hancock, *A History of Kent County, Delaware* (Dover: Litho Printing Co., 1975–1976), 10
168. Pauline Maier, *From Resistance to Revolution: Colonial Radicals and the Development of American Opposition to Britain, 1765–1776* (New York: Alfred A. Knopf, 1972), 10
169. Beitzell, 70 – At the beginning of the American revolution there were some 25,000 professed and practicing Catholics in the colonies. Sixteen thousand were in Maryland and six thousand in Pennsylvania. The rest were scattered and isolated, cf. William L. Sperry, *Religion in America* (New York: Macmillan Co., 1947), 204. For Catholic population figures during the Revolution, see "The Catholic Church in the United States, 1776–1876," *Catholic World* 23 (July 1876): 434–452
170. Nelson Waite Rightmyer, *Maryland's Established Church* (Baltimore: Church Historical Society for Diocese of Maryland, 1956), 118
171. *Delaware Military Archives*, vol. 1 of *Delaware Archives* (Wilmington: Mercantile Printing Co., 1911), 43
172. Sacramental Registers of Saint Francis Xavier Church, Warwick, Maryland,1769, 1771, 1773, 1776, 1783, 1786, Archives of the Diocese of Wilmington, Wilmington, Del.
173. Pryor, 101
174. *Delaware Military Archives*, 701, 756, 768, 769, 997, 1179
175. *Delaware Military Archives*, 756, 793, 799, 800, 802, 810
176. "The Burial Register of Old Bohemia, 1726–1976," in Cann, 138
177. Pryor, 103; will of John Reynolds, probated Oct. 10, 1820, RG 2545, Register of Wills, New Castle County Probates, Reel 354 (microfilm), Delaware Hall of Records, Dover (hereafter cited as DH of R).
178. *Delaware Military Archives*, 247, 249–250,446–463
179. Pryor, 150; Administrative Papers of Estate of John Weldon, DH of R.
180. *Delaware Military Archives*, 782
181. *Delaware Military Archives*, 673
182. *Delaware Military Archives*, 468, 495–500
183. *Delaware Military Archives*, 996
184. Pryor, 117
185. *Delaware Military Archives*, 287, 290
186. Cann, 179
187. *Delaware Military Archives*, 996
188. *Delaware Military Archives*, 396, 1098
189. *Delaware Military Archives*, 313, 320, 321
190. *Delaware Military Archives*, 115
191. Pryor, 12, 18, 24, 82
192. *Delaware Military Archives*, 679–680, 904, 1262

193. Esling, *RACHS* 1 (March 1886): 126–127
194. New Castle County Deed Book, M2: 463, DH of R.
195. Esling, 134 AMERICAN JESUIT, JOHN LEWIS – Father Lewis was superior at Bohemia from 1753 to 1764 and again from 1775 to 1788. He was born in 1720 and entered the Jesuits in 1740. He served as superior of St. Mary's County in 1772, superior of St. Thomas Manor 1773-1774, and superior at St. Inigoes in 1775. He died at Bohemia on March 24, 1788 at age 68. He was Vicar general from 1773 to 1783. Cann 167 – An indication of care for the slaves under his charge, is the fact that in 1760 Father John Lewis salted down 100 pounds of pork for every negro man, woman and child. The same careful assumption of responsibility to feed the and clothe the servants is evident in the provision of a contract to lease them to a tenant of Bohemia in 1795: "The tenant is to provide them with the same victuals and clothing they had on our plantation, viz.: 2 pounds of bacon and 1 peck of Indian corn, for each one every week: and of the clothing for man, one woolen jacket, one pair of breeches, one pair of stockings, a new pair of shoes every winter. For women: 1 pair of shoes every year, on pair stockings every other year: for winter: one woolen petticoat and a jacket, for the summer, one linen petticoat and two shifts (shirts)."

And in accordance with the terms of the lease of a young black man, who was a blacksmith, the master was to provide him during the year with lodging, victuals and clothing as follows: "One pair of stockings, one pair of woolen trousers and shirts for the summer, and he has to have three days a week in harvest to work for himself." The blacksmith, unlike others, wore shoes in the summer to protect his feet from the red hot sparks he hammered out of the horseshoes and plowshares. The terms of his contract give us a good idea of what the servants wore in winter and summer and substantially the fact that provisions were made for a change of clothing with the change of seasons. Cann 213-227: Diary of Father John Lewis, S. J., Bohemia – 1775-76 – The Diary of Father John Lewis, S. J. for the years 1775-76, while not decipherable in places, is included here as it gives a day to day account of the weather, life on the plantation, the names of people to whom they sold produce, comments on affairs at the mill and the dam which impounded the water required for its operation, charity shown by Father Lewis to those in need, baptisms, marriages and deaths, attendance at church services and many other notations of life in the 1775-76 period of this section of the Maryland Colony.

AUGUST, 1775– (1). Cross'd ye Bay – Passage, dinner......etc. 15/ to Mr. Hall's at Queens-Town. 2nd Stay'd at do. (3). I got to Mr. Mosely's. (4). Stay'd at d'o. Spkoe?.... (5). Rain. (6). (7). (8). (9). (10). I wrote a letter to Mr..... sent Hamersly Bill of 29L and for Neale (?). (11). Stay'd (Still?) at Mr. Mosley's – (12). pay'd 5s for shoeing two horses – 2/6 to Jenny – 1/3d to Jef (or Jesse). (13). Left Mr. Mosely's – dinner – etc. 3/6 – got to Bohemia – (13). Read a Lesson: went to Ben Branham. (14). Mr. Molyneux & Mr. Wilcox came to Bohemia: by him I rec'd a Letter from An. Carol and Mr. de Ritter etc. an order for 2L 2s Stirl: (15). I went to assist Mrs. Gribbin – Mr. Molyneus kept Church – (16). Nothing remarkable. A great thunder & rain: (17). Mr. Mosley came up. I assisted? Branham & Gribbin. I marry'd Frank Lennon.... (18). I pay'd Mr. Moyneux for Mr. John Carrol's pipes?.... Boxes – 3L 10s. To d'o for Mr. Ashton's acc't for amt? for cash pledged 3L 10s. (19). (20). I confessed 3. Mr. Mosley preached – I buried Sara Webb's child. R'd cash 3/9 for 3 qts. of Rum. (21). Killed a lamb – R'd cash from mill ? B'l: 1/6 (22). For ? C of flower from ye mill 9/N.B. I rec'd of Mr. Mosley Bohemia talk? Page one at my taking charge..... 23 – 16? (23). (24). I buried Charles....child belong...George in? Middle neck.... (25). (26). Came to Fox....hole...Night the.... Rain. (27). Com. 2. I preach'd Without faith etc... etc... Martha, Mary Connolly?...

SEPTEMBER, 1775 – Rain Wind N.E. (2). N.E. with a prodigious storm of thunder, hail and rain. Dam of ye lake near eight foot. Millhouse damaged etc. Nobody at church. (4). Nothing remarkable. I & Mr. Molyneux set off for Philadelphia. Left Mr. Mosley to manage – Expended at ye Red Lion 6/2 – at Wilmington 12/3d – at Brandywine ferry 6d. – At Marcus Hook – 2/8d – at Schulkill (4). 6th arrived at Philadelphia – Expended there 4d to Dougherty – 2d for beer. R'd 100 L of Ritchie – Riddle's order – Letters from Messrs. Walton, Boarman, & Dunlop, etc. 7th Dined at Cottringer. Bespoke a suit of cloathes (8). Dined at Bourn's – (9.) Pay'd for a hat 2L 7/6 to ye Barber 2/6 (10). Mr. Farmer kept Church – I gave to ye poor 1/8 – (11). Pay'd O'Hara for a wig 1L9 to Boots 2L 7/6. Shoes 10/. Stockings 4 pair 1L grave stone 4L 17 – Mr. Mosley killed 3 sheep – (12). to Mr. Cottringer for a whole suit of cloathes of 9L 17/3 dined at

Fitzsimons. I wrote to Messrs. Reisler & Ratter (or Rutter). (13). I ans'd Messrs. Walton & Boarman's letters – postages for letters – 4/5 to Mr. Farmer. Bought 4 pieces of Jersey (?) 13L16/. To Mr. Molyneux 12/ for Mr. Mosley's watch. Shoeing my horse 2/6. 14th. (15). To Beng. Hemings stabling and feeding of my horse 1L2/6 left with Mr. Molyneux 15L for leather, lime, etc. (16). I left Philadelphia. To Nanny I gave 2/6. Boys 3/. (16). I left Philadelphia. To Nanny I gave 2/6. Boys 3/. Schulkill 2d. Marcus Hook 2/ brandywine ferry 3/.? Wilmington 1/6 Arrived Con Hollahan. (17). Rain – no Church kept. (18). At Bunkers 2/7. Returned home to Bohemia – (19). Heavy rains…ye dam stood, but much damaged. (20). Mustered a large Gang. Killed two sheep. 3 dyed. (21). Continued to work on ye dam. Fine weather. Amy? Had 1 prvk og Rye meal – on cr. (22). Rain – I wrote to Mr. Mosley afternoon was fair. R'd 1L from ye mill – ye mill work. (23). Kept to ye dam. Rd 17/ for molass and corn from mill. (24). Fine weather. Com. 4. Buried Deb. Brannan. Preached on ye raising of Lazarus I part.? R'd 2/6 for molasses. Killed 2 sheep. (25). R'd 8/ for ?C of Midlings. 1/10? for 1/2 of Mutton. Pay'd Dan Linch 15/7 for weaving. Began to sow wheat at home. R'd of Mat's Bartley 3/8 for Corn. Of Bell 8/ for 1/2C Midlings. Sowed 12 B. seed wheat. (26). 3? sowed below ye thorn hedge (in all 15?). N.B. to Mad'm Douglas 1/2C. Middlings 2/ for Middlings. Began ye square next to ye thorn hedge, sowed 2B. (27). R'd 2? B. Corn 7/6 for mutton of Brian O'Daniel. 4/5d from Mill 1 B. Corn 3/. Sowed 15 B. wheat. (28). Sowed all above in ye house. 6/? Bush. N.B. 34? Cash for one B. of Corn 3/. ? C. flower 5/. Killed a sheep…from ye Granary. 4 for ? B. Corn 1/6. (29). Sowed 7 B. (30). Pay'd to Mr. Ethrington for public dues 21 taxables 14L16s 7?d for 2 years Quit Rents 4L6s 2d Ster. Sowed 12B. of wheat 4 from ye mill of ye h. six. N.B. sowed in all ye first week 50?B.

OCTOBER, 1775 – (1). Sold to James Brady one Christ. Director. 7/6. 5 Com. Preached on ye Raising Lazarus, 2'd point. (2). Killed 2 sheep. Sowed 8 B. wheat. Assisted Jo. Teague. Christened Rachel Anderson. R'd a letter from Mr. Molyneux. Ally O'Daniel had…3/4 Mutton, 1/3, from mill 4/. (3). Ans'd Mr. Molyneux letter. 2/ from ye mill. Sowed 8B. from Mill. Red 5/. Letters from Mr. Matthews by Mr. Wheeler. Isaac brought home ye goods, Kuseys, leather, lime, etc. (4). Ans'd Mr. Matthews Letter. R'd from Mill 8/. Sugan 1/4. P'd postage 10d. Rained all day, N.E. (5). Rain all ye day, N.E. 6th. Drizzling Rain. r'd 7/ from mill. N.E. 7th. Hard rain all ye day. N.E. Mr. Wheeler returned to Harford City with my letter and pamphlet to Mr. Matthews. Pd Ralph 1/. (8). Preach'd on final Impenitence. No Com's. N.W. (9). N.W. Fine weather. Killed one wether and sold 1 to Dan Noland. Rec'd 8/, 6 from Mill. N.B. Mr. Boyce owes 2/ for corn, 1 B., p'd 1/. Sowed 7B. (10). Fine weather. Sold to R'd Thompson Plank etc.? 1L7/4d from mill 1 ? B. Corn 4/6d. Sowed 2-1/3 in all 86A. (12). Wm. Casey died. (13). from mill 1/4C. flour 5/ Wm. Casey was buried. Notable fine weather. Grey mare strangled by coupling with another horse. (14). I went to Laetitia Mannor. (15). Preached on final Impenitence, 1a p. Com. 2. Christened Ja. Connelly. (16). I pay'd Mr. Richardson 209L Capital and Interest in full for Sam Lyle's mortgage, 200 of which I borrowed of Dr. Matthews. I pay'd 3L to Con for Dr. Latimer. 11L10/ to ditto towards his house. 6/7 my journey to and from ye Mission. R'd 15/from mill. (17). From mill 8/, 1/2C Middlings. Sow'd ye oat patch 2? B. finished for ye season. N.B. 78? of which from ye Granary, 7 ? from Mill. (18). R'd from mill 1/4C flour 5/. Pay'd Jo Astivens? 1L10/ for Smith's work. N.B. 1/ above acc't. (19). Visited Deb. Brankam, found in no danger. R'd 10/for flour. Rain very heavy all night long. (20). Rain all ye day. Mr. Nowland brought home ye ten? Which his charges p'd 2L6. For a wether he p'd 12/6. (21). Cold and raw. Messers. Diggs & Blake came here and lodg'd. I rec'd a letter from Rob't Molyneux and one from Mr. de Ritter. d'o from Mr. Mosley & Reynolds. (22). Com. 2 Preach'd on Final Impenitence, 2'd p't. Messers. Diggs & Blake went off to Mr. Heath. Smokey weather. (23). Killed a wether. Gave Ralph 7/6. Lent to Jo. Crosbye 20/ to Wm. Cradock 10/. Ans'd Messers. Mosley & Molyneux ye 1st? James Reynolds 2d? Mrs. Spangler, by whom I sent 8L15/ advanced on my acc't by Mr. Molyneux. (24). R'd 2/ for 2B. Corn. 1/6 for 1/2 B. d'c. Assisted Joseph Smith. R'd 6/ for 2 BC. 1/. Ship stuff. Jos. Smith dy'd ye 27. (25). Messers Diggs, Hagan & Matthews dined here. I gave my Bond to Dr. Matthews. Dated ye 11th Inst. for 200L Rd 7/8 from Mill. (26). Messers Diggs, etc. went off. R'd 1L3 / from Mill. (27). Rain – all day. R'd 8/6 from Mill. 4/6 from granary – Rye Pay'd Ralph junior for bottoming 2 chairs 2/6. (28). Cold Raw and like for snow? Wm. Craddock had 11/2B. from Mill – of wheat. (29). More moderate by cloudy. Com. 5. Buried Joseph Smith. Preach'd on Final

Imptenitence 3d p't. Christened Sara Wittington. God-f. Holland Webb, God-M. Sara Webb. R'd a letter from Mr. Mosley dated 7ber 30, ans'd d'o. (30). Assisted John Teague. Gave in charity 5/8. Charles Reed came to work. Isaac carry'd 25 B.W. to landing 23 ? of it came from mill, 1 ? granery. Killed an old wether. I bought and killed a cow of John Crosby. P'd freight for ye gravestone 2/6. 2 lbs. Rosin 8d. Beef weigh'd 222 lbs. (31). Charles Reed had 17 lbs. flour from mill on Cr. 3/3d.

NOVEMBER, 1775 – (1). Com. 5. Read a lesson. Christened John Rankin, God-f. Matt. Bartley, God-m. Sara Casey – 1/. To J. Crosbey 1/4 beef of Mr. Rawlins 92 lbs. – 1L10/8d. (2d). I assisted Dick belonging to Doctor Matthews. Buried John Teague. Dick dyed eod. die. Cloudy? R'd 4/ ? midlings from mill. Rain at night. (3). Rain. Afternoon N.W. I buried Dick. Jo Crosby had ? B.C. from mill. (4). N.W. Spey'd 9 sows and cut 3 Boars. Sold a wether to Dan Nowland 12/6. Lofted 77? Barrels of Corn. My letter to Mr. went by ye days post. (5). Com. 7. Preach'd "Every Free etc." on ye Pain of Sense. (6). Cash R'd from mill for 2 B. Corn 6/. N.E. wind – Rain. (7). N.W. R'd from Mill for 1 B.C. 3/. 5B Rye 15/. (8). R'd of Ralph Jun. 1/3 for quart of Rum. John Castevens bought 2 B.C. from mill on Cr. Wm. Cradock 1? d'o on d'o. (9). Rain. Jo. Crosbye had 14 lbs. middlings and some – before 14 lbs. flour. Ye whole 4/ on Cr. To ye house 94 lbs. flour. (10). R'd 1/3 2t. Rum from mill 1/10. Sold to Reed on Cr. 1 B. W. To Jo. Crosbye on d'o half B. of Corn. Lofted 15 B. Corn. Windy & cold. (11). N.W. cold & raw. Rachel had half gal. Molas. 1/3. Finished lofting ye home field 20 B. Assisted Molly Coleman. R'd a letter from Mr. Molyneux and Mr. Geizler. Sold 1 B. corn from mill 3/. I gave to a poor man 1/6. Molly Coleman dyed eod. die. (12). I preached on ye Pain of Sense. Com. I. I buried Mary Bell, Alias Coleman and child. R'd 2/6 for half gal. Rum. N.W. cold & raw. (13). N.W. Sold from mill 1=1/2 B. W. 7/3. 1 B.C. 2/6. 1/2 gal. Mollass to Ralph sen. 1/3. 12t Rum to Johny 1/3. 1? B. Corn from mill 3/8. Mr. Mosley came up. R'd a letter from Bob. (14). Raw and Rainy. W'd East, Rain'd all night Dr. Matthews dined with us. Killed ye calf. (15). Rain. Then N.W. We dined at Doctor Matthews. (16). N.W. & very cold. Sold 1/2 gal. Molass 1/3. Calf skin 6/4d. Pay'd to J. Shanon 7/6. (17). N.W. Mr. Mosley returned home. R'd 2/6 for sugar of Peter J. Crosbye jun'r began to work. (18). John Crosbye jun'r had a wether 12/6 on Cr. Pay'd Forkner & Chaple 3L15/ for repairs ye Mill stonework. I went to Laetitia Manor. (19). COM. 6. R(?)c. 3. Preached on final Impenitence 2d. Pt. Marry'd corn. Buckley – Bridget Nivell. Item Rich'd Begley (Reyly)? – Joanna Taylor. N.W. Raw. (20). Expended 3/6. Returned home. R'd 6/ for corn from mill. N.W. Raw. (21). R'd for 1 Qt. Rum of J. Crosbye 1/3. Let d'o have one d'o on Cr. Foreigner finished walling in cellar. (22). Hard black frost. N.W. 5 B. W. from mill 23/9. (23). Mild weather. Sold 1? B. Corn from mill & buckwt. Jon. Holland 4/8. Timothy began to cut out ye negroes cloathing. (24). Mild & moderate. Mr. Reed had B.W. from mill. (25). I went to Jo Cole. Called to assist Skooley. J. Crosbye finished boarding ye East of ye mill House. (26). Com. 2. Small flock. Returned home. (27). Sold on Cr. To John Crosbye Jun' or 4 B. Corn 10/. To J. Crosbye sen'or 1/2 B. Rye on d'o. (28). From mill 1 ? B. Corn 3/9. To Castevens 2 B.d'l on Cr. Overseer 1 gall. molas. 2/6. 2 lbs. sugar 1/6. 1 Qt. Rum Rachel 1/8. N.E. Rain and very cold. (29). Moderate but cloudy. (30). From Mill 2B. wh. McCullough 9/6. One pint Rum to Jo. Crosbye, Jun'or on Cr. Wind w. cold & raw.

DECEMBER, 1775 – (1). Moderate and warm. R'd 1/3 for 1/2 B.C. Bartley. Pay'd J. Crosbye, jun'r 1L10/. (2d). Moderate weather. Finished gathering corn. I went to Middle-Town to assist Neal O'Donnelly. R'd 5/ for 2 B. Corn from mill. Brannan, Tim. (3d). Dca Adventus Wind S. Rain, moderate and warm. Com. 2 Reach a Lesson. Sold 12L Rum to Sam 1/3. (4). N.W. Black frost. Timothy Brannan came to cut out Negroes clothes. Ye day finished lofting our corn. N.B. 112? BB from Quarter 137 at Home. Overseers' share took there from 31 BB ye 8th. (5). Hard frost. J. Crosbye jun'or had 12t Rum by Daniel. (6). Rec'd 19/ 4B, wheat from mill McCullough. Tim Branham finished cutting out Negro cloathing. (7). White frost. Rain in ye afternoon. J. Crosbye sen'or. 1 B.C. from mill on cr. (8). Rain all ye day. Few at Mass. R'd ? from mill for 1? B.C. O'Donahoe. ? B. d'o to ye Scotch woman. (9). Fine weather. R'd from mill 2? B. Corn 6/3. To J. Crosby June. 12t Rum on Cr. Cato (cats?) came up. (10). Cloudy weather. Com. 7. Preach'd on ye, Pain of Loss. Pay'd 1L1/ to Dan Lynch for weaving. Sold to Betty 1/2 Qt. Rum 1/3. Rain all night. (11). N.W. and very cold. R'd 5/ for 2 B Corn – Young. Gave to a poor man 1/10. Cato return'd home. (12). Very hard frost. N.W. R'd 10/ for 4 B. Corn from Mill. (13). White frost. Cloudy and like for snow. Killed hogs – 32. R'd 5% for 2 B. Corn – McCullough.

(14). Salted ye Pork: Weighed 2550 exclusive of ye Overseers share. Moderate by cloudy – wind at South. (15). Moderate, cloudy and hazy. I christen'd Wm. Disprat. At Warwick; Patrina, Mary Hissey. P'd J. Crosby jun'or 10/. Lent Wm. Matthews a large side of sole leather. (16). To. J. Crosbye Jun'or double channel shoes 15/. Wind N.E. Rain. 1 Pint Rum J. Crosbye jun'or 7d?. To d'o 2 B. wheat from mill 9/6. (17). Rain and very warm. Few at church. Read a Lesson. (18). N.W. but moderate. Sold six B.W. to McCullo' & 2B. 1L13/6. One B. to Haff, 4/9. 2B d'o to Wm. Craddock on cr. (19). To Wm. Craddock for his mother 2B.W. on Cr. N.W. (20). N.W. and very cold. Some snow. Huff 1? B. Corn 3/9. Sol. Styles brought a letter from Mr. Morris. I pay'd to do's 5/ hire of horse. J. Crosbye Sen. ? B.C. 2? B. Rye d'o. Branham 1B. Corn on Cr. (21). N.W. moderate wether. 3 B.W. to ye House. (22). N.W. and hard frost. (23). Bitter cold, hail and snow. My truck was brought from Elk-ferry. Jo. Crosbye had 14 wt. of Middlings on Cr. Mat Noland 1 B.W. to pay for Ralph's Box. Jack foot 1 B. d'o. p'd 1/9, ye rest I owed for harvest last. (24). Snow all day and all night. Con Hollahan lodg'd here. a laborer from Pencader. Com. I. Read a lesson; few at Church. (25). Snow pretty deep. Com. 3. Preached "and Suddenly, etc." Sold Dina 1? lbs. sugar 1/. 2 sheep dyed. (26). West wind and very cold. Thin flock. 4 Com. Preach'd "Who of us shall dwell, etc." R'd 1/6 for a Prayer Book 6d from Davi ball' ce due." (27). West Very cold. Few at Church. I bought J. Mac Taggart's Indenture and pay'd 18L to d'o he serves 15? Years? I am to find him in Victuals and House. (28). More moderate. No Body at Church but our own family. (29). I gave out to J.M. Taggart 85L Pork and 1? Bush. of Potatoes. Cloudy. East wind. Thaw. (30). From mill 2/ for midd's 10/s. Rain – East. Mr. Neilson came after John for stealing (?). Thaw. (31) South wind. Thaw. Preached "Bring Forth therefore." Few at church. Com. 3.

JANUARY, 1776 – (1). Com. 11. Preach'd "Delay not to be Converted, etc." Moderate and mild weather. Thawing all day. Ye snow partly gone. (2). Matthew Cottringer dined here. R'd a letter from Mr. de Ritter. Sold 2 B. Corn from mill. 6/. Warm weather, but very sloppy. (3). Fine moderate weather. Johny was whipped. Pay'd Johnny Savin 2 B. W. for 3 days attendance on ye survey. To J. McTaggart 1 B. C., 1 gall. Molass. (4). Fine weather. Cleaned Oats 43 B. (5). Rain. Sold ye Oats to Thomas Skully and carry'd 'em. Wrote letters to Messrs. Molyneux, Ritter and Morris. (6). Fine weather. N.W. Few at Church. 3 Com. Preach'd "Without faith etc." Married Peter Nugent and Mary Hughes. Deliv'd ye above letters to Cottringer. (7). D'ca infra Epip. Christn'd Rich'd Ben. Nowland's godf. Davi, godm. Betty. Com. 5. Preach'd on ye 1st article of ye Creed. Mild, soft weather. Cloudy. S. (8). Mild weather. Rec'd for 4 B. 19/, McCullough. 3/9 for a B? of Corn, O'Donahoe. J. Crosby Sen's 1 B.C. Cr. Jos. Mr. Tribye cancl. S. wind. Rain. (9). Jos. and our people began to mawl. W. and towards evening N.W., very freezing weather. (10). N.W. and very cold. Mawl'd rails. (11). Evening rain. 2 B.C. to M. Cull's. Cr. (12). Nothing singular. Mowled. (13). Lent J. Crosby 5/. R'd ? B.C. 1/3. for oats 3L Cottringer dined here. Cut wood all hands. (14). D'ca 2'd da post Epip. Preach'd on ye 1st Art of ye Creed. Com. 5. Soft and thawing. (15). Drizzley and wet. Mawled. (16). Fog and and drizzly all ye day. Messrs. Matthews and Cottringer set off for Philadelphia. (17). Small drift of snow and thin N.W. and very cold. (18). R'd 1/3 for 1/2 B.C. from mill, Robinet. Very cold. N.W. (19). N.W. P'd Anderson for Smith's work 2/18/5. Sold 1/2 B. Oats to McCullough. Pay'd. (20). Hard frost. N.W. P'd Mr. Reed 5/. Rec'd 1/16/9d for oats. P'd Mr. Cradock his share 12/5. To J. Crosby Sen. 1 B.C., Cr. (21). Com. 3 Preach'd on ye 2d article of ye Creed. Very cold. (22). Snow, then N.W. Cut wood all hands. J. Crosbye Jun'r enlisted. (23). Andrew Briant was here for wheat. Pay'd to Dan Lynch 7/ for 12 yds. Linnin. Rec'd 14/3 for wheat. Mr. Josias Wheeler from Harford, Deer Creek, lodged here. Brought a letter from Mr. Matthews dated 20 Jan. (24). I answ'd ye s'd letter. P'd d'o. Cloudy, dull, and snow. (25). Cloudy and very cold and snow all night. Mr. Wheeler returned from Dr. Matthew's. (26). Mr. Wheeler returned to Harford. R'd a letter from Mr. Molyneux by Dr. Matthews. Wind N.W. and cold. (27). Very sharp weather, N.W. Mr. Reed finished ye People's shoes – 29 pr. I p'd ye whole as pr. acc't. (28). Preached on ye 2'd article, 2'd Discourse. No C. (29). Sharp and cold. Snow, N.E. Visited Patr. Nugent daughter; did not assist her. R'd 7/ from Betty for Wm. Shoes. 3/9 Huff for 1? B. Corn in ye Even. Rain and a thaw. A great Fogg. McTagg't 1 B.C. (31). South wind. Thaw. Preached "Bring Forth therefore." Com. 3. Publish'd Peter Nugent and Mary Hughes. Few at Church.

FEBRUARY, 1776 – (1). Wind N.W. and snow again. McTaggart ? B. Salt. (2d). Very cold. Preach'd on ye 3'd Art. Com. 2. (3d). Very cold. Tim Brannan came to work. (4). Com. 2.

Preach'd on ye 4th Article. Marry'd James and Prudens (?). Very cold. Wind N.W. Bought of Shelly 2 Qtrs. Beef 3L16/. (5). N.W. and very Raw. 6 N.W. I sent to assist James Humings in Thoroughfare Neck. Clean. 62 B.W. (7). Jo Crosbye 9B. Rye from mill. Took up our fax. Housed a stack of wh. Freezing weather. (8). Sent 40 B.C. to Landing. W. at S. Moderate and thaw. (9). Wind South and very warm. Thaws apace. Hung-up our Bacon. Gammon 54. Shoulders 50. Middlings 45. 10th. N.W. Sold 2 lb. Sugar to Molly Scot. (11). N.W. Com. 2. Preach'd on ye 4th Article. (12). West wind and moderate weather. (13). N.W. R'd 7L10/ of McCullough for 72 B. Oats. Pay'd Mr. Cradock for his share of 102 B. 25/ of whom I received in return for cash lent 10/. Mr. Molyneux came down unexpectedly from Philadelphia. (14). Killed ye English Sow. Weigh'd 294 lbs. Bought a Turkey hen 2/6. South wind and warm. (15). Fine weather, W.S. Sold 2 B.C. to Brockson from mill 5/. 3B wheat for house use. (16). Southerly and warm. At night Rain. Thrash'd ye O. (17). N.W. and freezing weather. Sold 1 B. Corn to ye Taylor. (18). D'ca. Com. 7. Mr. Molyneux Preach'd. N.W. and hard weather. (19). N.W. Sent to ye Landing 44 of wheat. Mr. Molyneux returned to Phila. Sent by him 63L 13/9 Stir. A Bill on Dunlop and Wilson. Item, Letters of novice to Mr. Rupel and Messrs. Fearron etc. (20). W. Frost. South wind. Sent 22 B. wh to ye Landing per Jos. 1 B.C. from mill 2/6. (21). White frost. Johny helpt to thrash. In afternoon Rain. Visited Peter Braughan. (22). Rain all ye Day and Drizzle. (23). Mr. Matthews return'd ye side of Sole Leather. Sold 4 B.C. to Young 5/. Fine day. (24). Small white frost. Fair, wind N.E. Sold ? B.W. to Annabelle McTaggart, 2/4? Pay'd. (25). D'ca Quad. La. Com. 5. Cloudy and like for Rain. N.E. Lent Johny 2/2d to pay Mr. Cradock for cobbling. (26). Cloudy all day. S.W. Made fences towards ye rack (?) (27). Rain all day. Matthias Barkly had 1 B. Corn. Cleaned 46 B. Wheat. (28). N.W. Housed a stack of wheat. Sold ? B.W. and 1 B.C. to Matthew Noland from mill 4/10. Freezing hard. (29). N.W. Bitter Cold. 1 gall. molas. To J. McTaggart. 12t to Lucy.

MARCH, 1776 – (1) N.W. Hard, freezing weather. Rec'd 26L10 from Andrew Briant for 106 B.W. at 5/ pr. Bushel. (2). Moderate and warm South wind. Pay'd Mr. Credon his shoes of 106 B.W. or 3L6/3d. McTaggart 1 B.C. from mill cr. To ? C. to Robinet 1/3. (30). N.E. Raw and cloudy and smoky. Com. 3. Preach'd on ye 5th Art of ye Creed, 2nd Discourse. (4). Fine warm Day – S.W. I visited Wm. Casey, did not assist him as he appeared not dangerous. Matt Barklay had ? B.C. Jo Crosby 7/6. (5). South. Housed a stack of wheat. ? B.C. from C. H. for Ralph's sow. A shower of Rain, then ceased. Prodigious storming with Lightning. (6). S.W. and bustring weather; then N.W. Bought a hackle of Matthias Bukley 5/. (7). S.W. and good weather. Sold 2 B. Com from corn house to young, 5/. (8). Smokey and warm, S.W. and by S. Sold 1 B.C. from Mill. 2/6. (9). Pay'd Shirkey per J. Crosby for a cheese 14 lb. wt. 14/. R'd 1/3 for ? B.C. Matt Nowland. N.W. and Cold. (10). Preach'd on ye 6th Article, 1st Discourse. Com. 3. R'd 7/8 for a "Daily Exercize," Geo. Wright. 1 Cold and raw. Wind and East. In ye night Rain. (11). South. Warm a d pleasant. Evening, East and like for Rain. R'd 4/6 for flour mill London. (12). South and moist weather. Sent 73 lbs. wt of wooden Yarn to Patrick Nugent. In ye afternoon, N.W. (13). S.E. and small frost. R'd by Mr. Dougherty 2 Letters from Mr. Molyneux and one per Post from d'o. Item 289 dollars. Ans'd d'o's Letters. Sent letters to Dunlop and Wilson per d'o. inclosed. Clean'd 104 B. Wheat. (14). Rain. S.E., then Fair. P'd for 1 Bottle Snuff 7/6. Fish 15/. Truss 15. Letter 10d to ye Post. (15). Foggy and moist and drizzly. S.E. R'd ye fish and Truss. Rain all night. Lightning and Thunder. (16). Remarkable warm and sultry. S.W. (17). Few at church. Read a Lesson. No Com's. After church Rain all day – East. (18). Drizzly weather – S.E. Patt came down from Whiteclay Creek. (19).W – but fine day. Mr. Blake came hither. Timothy Brannan cut out Patt's cloaths. Sett ye ware. (20). White frost. 2 B. corn from ye corn H. Young 5. d'o. Kitchen 2 B. from d'o. Ralph's Qtrs. 2 from d'o. Jos. 2 from d'o. S.W. 2 shower in ye night. (21). N.W. housed a stack of wheat. Sold 1 B. Corn from mill, Robinet, 2/6. Matthias Bartley 1/d'o. 2/6 Cr. Annabella 1 1/2 B. What. Cr. (22). S.E. Rain all ye day. No working out. Rainy eve. (23). Sent per Jos. 20/ for 2 plows to Isaac Logue. Pay'd John ye Flaxbreaker 20/ for 240 wght. Wind S.W. Showers off and on and squally, then N.W. (24). N.W. Hard Frost. Few at Church. No Com's. Preach'd on ye necessity and obligation of Con'f'n. Ia pcs. (25). Patrick return'd to Con's. N.W. and hard frost gave Patt 15d. Few at Church. In ye afternoon Wind S.E. R'd from mill 5/. 2 B.C. Tompson. (26). S.W. – fine day. Sold 1 B.W. to Mrs. Douglass from ye mill 4/. 1 B.C. to Jo Crosbye, Cr. (27). Cold, Raw day. N.E. and Northerly, etc. Rosa dyed – Dina's child. Braint O'Daniel had 2 B. wh. from mill on Cr. (28). Hard black frost. P'd

Matt's Barkley 12/6 a yearling dead. Cleaned 83B. Wk. Buried Rosa. (29). White frost. Brought in 7 B.W. Housed ye last stack of wh. S.E. and Raw weather. (30). East, Raw and drizzly Rain all ye day. No working out. ? B.C. Robinet, 1/3. (31). Com. 10. D'ca Palmarum. Many at church. Preached on ye Obstacles to a good Confession. A Prayer Book to Sara Casey, 2/. Rainy and drizzly weather in afternoon and all night without clearing – N.E.

APRIL, 1776 – (1). Rain all ye day – N.E. Sold 2 B. Corn from ye mill to Young, 5/. Pay'd Logue 10/, a 3d Plow. (2). S.E. & Raw & Cloudy. Sold 2 B.C. Corn Houe 5/. Brian O'Daniel. Mr. Cradock 1? B.W. Mill. (3). S.W. & Rain almost all ye day. No working out. Killed ye old cow. Sent 1 Quarter to Mr. Mullikens. (4). N.W. but fine mild weather. R'd 3 dollars from Benj. Bodice at 2/6 per B. He takes it as he wants it from ye mill. Sold ye cow hide 16/8d. Annabella had ? B. Wh. Cr. Work'd ye dam? (5). Finish'd thrashing. Worked on ye dam. Fine moderate day. S. wind. ? wh. from Mill 1/3, Phil. (6).Work'd ye dam. P'd 3L to Hanking. Rain toward Even. R'd Letters from Messrs. Farmer & Molyneux. Gentle calved. (7). Rainy. Soft growing season. Com. 25. Preach'd on ye Resurrection, la pars. (8). N.E. Rain. A good many at Church. Preach'd "We all shall rise again, etc." 2 a p'ct. Com. 31. Still rain all ye day & night. I answer'd Messrs. Molyneux & Farmer's Letters. (9). Rainy & drizzly. Com. 11. Read a lesson. Sold 2 B.C. from C.H. 5/. N.E. (10). More drizzly weather – then thunder & rain. 2? B.C. from Corn H. Patr. Nugent, Cr. N.E. Sold ? B.C. to Robinet 1/3. (11). N.W. & very Cold. For 2 B.C. from C.H. Anderson, 5/. Matt's Bartley ? . d'o from d'o, Cr. Annabella 2 B. from d'o. Cr. For 2 B. from d'o Dan Noland, 5/, from Mill 2B. 5/ In ye evening set in to Rain again – all ye night with drifts of snow. (12). N.W. – very cold & squawly. ? B.C. from mill, J. Crosbye. (13). Squawly & Raw. Went to Jo. Coles. (14). Raw weather Com's 13. Christened 4 children. Preach'd "Cum queasier is Dom." Pay'd Mrs. Cole 4s for wax. Returned home. (15). S.E. Sold 2 B. from C.H. 5/, Young. Rain ye even. & all night. Married Jo. Burk & Mary Smith. (16). Rain & drizzly. No working out. Sold 1? B.C. from C.H. to Charles Wolton 3/9. 7? B. to family use. 2 B. from mill, Rumsey 3/. 52? B.W. Clean'd. Sprayed 3 pigs cut Boars. (17). Sold to Brian O'Daniel 2? B.C. from C.H., Cr. From Mill 2 B.C. Rumsey 5/. Dry day – S.W. (18). Sold 1 B.C. from C.H. Matthias Berkley, Cr. Fair all day – S.E. Sowed our Flaxseed. Sent 72 yds. Woolens to ye fulling? Mill by J. Crosbye. (10). Fair – N.W. Christened John Rickets Spurious. Assisted Neale Shirkey. (20). Fair, but cold and raw. I went to Laetitia Mannor. (21). Com. 11. Preach'd on Hell, "Hast thou seen, etc." Christened 2 children. Rain all ye afternoon & night. (22). Settled and pay'd all charges for ye Building & finishing ye dwelling House of ye Tenant 58L 14/4d. Item pay'd David Hahan 9/ for 4 days & half's assistance. Return'd home. Spent 2/3 journey. R'd 15/ for corn. Began to furrow out for Corn. (23). N.W. Received 20L for Corn & 9/6 for 2 B. wheat. (24). White frost. R'd 2L5/ of Mr. Rumsey for Corn. P'd to Briant O'Daniel 2L5/ to Mauling logs. R'd from Tompson 5/ for 2 B.C., C.H. Closed ye meadows. (25). Finish'd ye mill dam. Bought 1 gall. vinigar 2/. (26). Bought a wheelbarrow of Dan. Noland 15/. (27). Fine growing weather. Finished listing ye home field. Briant O'Daniel had 2 B.C. Rumsey 2 B. d'o. from C.H. McCullough 3 d'o C.H. 7/6. Dan Noland 2 d'o Cr. (28). Com. 13. Christened 2 negro children. Preached, "Suffer both to grow, etc." Went to assist Nancy Craig. (29). R'd for corn 2/ B? James Hussey 5/. Broxon 1 d'o 2/6. M'Clan 2? from C.H. 6/3. Rain. A Prayer Book ? - Reynolds. (30). Rain & Thunder & a great fresh. Lent Wm. Cradock 2L5/. Pay'd Nell for Turkeys, 5/. Ralph for a Canoe 15/. Phil on Hankins acc't 5/. Ralph Jun'or on Matthias Bartley acc't 2/6. Lucy 2? B. Beans 10/. Rebecca Crosby knitting 8 pr. stocking 16/. 1 milk Bucket 1/6.

MAY, 1776 – (1). Sold 1 B.W. & 1? B.C. to C.H. Young 8/6. ? B.C. from mill Robinet. 2 B. C. to C. H. Reed 5/. Hankin 1 B. C. H. 2/6. (2). Black frost. Began to plant Corn at both places. 2 B.C. from C.H. for family use at ye Quarter. 2 d'o trom d'o Thompson. 1 ? d'o from mill Broxon. 1 B. Rye Crosbye, Cr. (3). White frost – S.E. Sold 2 B.C. C.H. Anderson 5/. (4). Wm. Rumsey had 4 B.C. C.H. Rain part of ye day. (5). Com. 6. Christen'd David Mr. Matthew's negro child. Preached "Accedamus, etc." la P'rs. S.E. Wind. Raw. (6). Finished planting corn at home. Sold 2 B.C. C.H. Aug. Savin, 5/. D'o 1 B.C. Young 2/6. 1 B.W. mill d'o 4/6. Very warm all day: stormy at night & Thunder. (7). Bought 3000 herrings 15/. Sold 3 B.W. from mill to McCullo' 14/9. 1 B.C. d'o Broxon 2/6. Cold, drizzly weather – N.E. (8). Raw & drizzly Rain. (9). Fine, warm day. Sold 2 B.C. C.H. to Rumsey, 2? to Nugent, 3 to Fitzgerald, 7/6, all from ye C.H. (10). S. Wind & high, very warm. Sold from Mill 2 B.C. Young 5/. 2 B. d'o from d'o Anderson Cr., at 2 o'clock Heavy thunder & Rain. (11). S.W. & very sultry. Sold 2 B.C. to Mr. Rumsey. 2 B. d'o to O'Daniel. Rec'd ye same from Wm. Cradock. Pay'd Briant O'Daniel in full for 2000 Logs 24/5d. Finish'd planting at ye Quarter. (12). Com. 6. Preached 'Accedamus and Deum, etc.' 2d kt. Thunder & a shower, sultry hot. Mr. Mosley & Mr. Hall came up. (13). Sold 5 B.C. C.H. to strangers 12/6. Cutt 5 Colts; sheep & calves cut & marked. Rumsey had 2 B.C. C.H. Small showers off & on. (14). R'd a letter per Th's Price from Mr. Morris & one from Mr. Walton. P'd Matt's Bartley 5/. Lee 7/6. 2 B.C. to Hankins. R'd 6/ & 3d for 4? B.C. C.H. Ans'd Mr. Morris Letter per Price. (15). Killed a veale. Pay'd Dr. Matthews for 1 lb. tea 1 bottle snuff 7/6. Pay'd Mr. Mosely 10L C'cy. (16). Ans'd Mr. Walton's Letter & sent per Ralph. 1 box of China to Mr. Morris per Thos. Price. R'd for 2 B.C. C.H. 5/ Gantre. 3 B.W. mill McCullo' 14/3d. Gave to Ralph 2/6. Com. 2. Mr. Mosley officiated. (17). Dined at Dr. Matthews. Sold 10 B.C. 1L5/. (18). Rec'd for 2? B.C. from mill 6/3 – McClan. ? B.W. from d'o 1/3. 2 B.C. C.H. Robinson 5/. (die pracced.) 2 B.C. C.H. Anderson 5/. 1 B.W. Mill, Young 4/9. Rain all ye day. Roan horse dyed with ye Hooks. (19). Com. 4 Mr. Mosley officiated. Item 2 Sheep & a Yearling. (20). Rain good part of ye day. P'd Rumsey ye whole & half a B. over from ye C.H. from 2L5/ before rec'd. Item 2 B from d'o. Bodice. 3B sold to Reynolds 7/6 from d'o. Lent Dr. Matthews 31 lbs. nails. 2000 per Peter. Rain all ye night & part of ye (day). (21). Sold 10 B.C. C.H. 1L5/. Began to plow ye orchard. (22). Sold 3 B.C. C.H. 7/6. Mr. Mosely returned home. (23). Sent for ye cloth to ye fulling mill, 53 yds. P'd 17/6. Lent Briant O'Daniel 15/. 1 B.C. Mill 2/6. (24). Lent Dr. Matthews 36 wt. nails. Lent ... wife 15/6. Another colt got ye Hooks. (25). The colt dyed. Sold 1 B.C. 2/6. Christn'd Dan O'Daniel. (26). Com. # Easter 11. Preach'd "accedamus" 3'a p's. Rain. (27). Easter Com's 3. Read a Lesson. Rainy & drizzly. 2 sheep died: remain 57 alive & 14 lambs. (28). Com. 1 Washed sheep. Sold 2 B.W. mill McCullough. 2 B.C. C.H. Anderson Cr., 3 B. d'o O'Daniel Cr. To Peggy Neal 2? B. d'o Cr. 1? B.C. mill Young 3/9. Cold – N.E. (29). Shear'd ye sheep, 57 fleeces. Sold 2 B.C. C.H. Bodice. Jos. 2 B.C. C.H. Phil 1? B. d'o. Very cold – N.E. (30). White frost & cold 1 sheep dyed. Put up 9 Skates for harvest. N.W. Robinet had 1 B.C. p'd 21d. (31). Raw & cold & dry. Sold 4 B.C. C.H. Wm. Reynolds 10/. Another Colt has ye hooks. Ben. Sapinton cut 'em out. Dyed on ye 3'd Sequentis.

JUNE, 1776 – (1). Dry weather & windy. Finished double furrowing ye Quarter field. Put up a Shoter for harvest. Pay'd Lee & Hankins in full for grubbing ye Quarter Meadows 7L7/6d. (2). No Communicants. Preach'd "Hast thou Seen, etc." on Hell. (3). Rain all ye day, wind at East. No working out. (4). Began to harrow at both places. Sold 3 B.C. C.H. 7/6. ? B. to Crosbye, Cr. ? d'o Bartley Cr. – Mill. 2 more sheep dead. Cool for ye season. (5). Sold 2 B.W. Mill McCullo' 9/. 2 B.C C.H.J. Anderson Cr. Messers. Molyneux & Carrol came down from Philad. (6). Sold 10 B.C. to John Cockran 2L4/ ... Mrs. Ecert for paying Dina 15/. Few at church. Read a Lesson. Com. 6. (7). Mr. John Carrol set off for Rock Creek. Sold ? B.W. C.H. to Mr. M'W. Noland. 2 B.C. to Hankin C.H. 5/... 5/ Gantz. 1? D'o from d'o 3/9d. Id'o Mil. Id'o.

MARRIAGES AT BOHEMIA – 1775 (Extracted from Registers of Bohemia) – F. Edward Wright, *Vital Records of The Jesuit Missions of the Eastern Shore 1760-1800* (Silver Springs, Maryland: Family Line Publications, 1986) 46: Francis Lanon and Hellen McDermot Aug 15 1775; by Rev Mr. Lewis with license; Priest: Rev. Mr. Lewis performing following marriage ceremonies. Cornel. Buckley and Bridgett Nivell; Nov 19 1775; Richard Reyly; Johanna Taylor ___ eod."; Peter Nugent and Mary Hughes Jan 6 1776; James and Prudence Feb 4 1776; Jo. Burk and Mary Smith Apr 15 1776; John and Lucy Dec 9 1776; James Bournes and Nancy O'Donald Jul 12 1779; William Boyls and Susanna Bushull (?) Oct 28 1779; Jack and Mary Write Nov 7 1779; Mr. Beard's/Sylv. Nowlands. Devitt, "Bohemia," *Woodstock Letters* 15 RECORDS OF BURIALS AT BOHEMIA (1886) 228: The oldest I met with were: Mary Belson, 1746, and Aug. 19, 1753, Rev. Joseph Greaton. These had been copied apparently from an older record which is no longer extant. In the old burial register now at Bohemia, I notice that mention is made of the person deceased, the residence, the occupation, the malady, and finally the funeral sermon; with a note sometimes about the people present. Dr. William Matthews in Sassafras (*frax* in the old writings) had a burying-ground which was used also by his Catholic neighbors.

For Jan. 21, 1796 the following record is made by Rev. Ambrose Maréchal: "Mr. Walter Fullam departed this life.

The Genealogists Post (February, 1966) vol. 3, No. 2. 3-14: The Burial Register Of Old Bohemia 1726 – All persons listed are buried in the church yard unless otherwise noted. 1726-12-18+Hodgson, Rev. Thomas (S.J.), Age 44, born in England; 1731 Reynolds, John, Age 65 at

"Sarah's Joynture" in Cecil Co., Md.; 1731-11-10 Heath, James, Age 73; 1745-11-27+Quinn Rev. James (John) (S.J.), Age 47; 1749-1-23+Pulton, Rev. Thomas (S.J.), Age 52, born in England; 1750-9-2 Knaresbrough, William, Age 65; 1753-8-19+Greaton, Rev. Joseph (S.J.), Age 74, born in England; 1775-6-15+Manners, Rev. Matthias (S.J.), Age 56-born in Germany; 1773-6-26 Wood, Ann, Age 64; 1775-2-2 Wood, Nicholas, Age 57; 1778-3-22 Wood, Nicholas, Age 51; 1780-10-6 Wood, Nicholas, Age 13; 1788-3-24+Lewis, Rev. John (S.J.), Age 67, born in England.

BURIALS AT BOHEMIA – WRIGHT, *Vital Records* 49: 1775 – Aug 19 Sara Webb's child; Aug 23 Charles, Sidney George's; Sep 24 Deborah Branham; Oct 12 William Casey; Oct 29 Joseph Smith; Nov 2 John Teague; Nov 3 Dick. D. Matthews's; Nov 12 Mary Bell, alias Coleman with her child; 1776 – Mar 28 Rase, Dina's child; Aug 8 Sara Burk; Aug 13 Charles; Aug 29 John White; Sep 20 James Neale; Oct 15 John Taggard; 1779 – Feb 24 Elisa Doughlass; eod. (same day) Wm Skooley and child; Mar 2 Dan. Nowland; Aug 12 Nancy Casey; Sep 23 William B…b..n; Nov 19 Molly Neale; Nov 20 Delia; Nov 25 Matthew Berkley.

196. Esling, 129
197. Cann, 7, 184 GERMAN JESUIT, MATTHIAS MANNERS (*alias* SITTENSPERGER) – Father Manners was superior at Bohemia from 1764 to 1775. He was born in 1719 and entered the Jesuits in 1737. He died at Bohemia on June 15, 1775 at age 56 and is buried there. WRIGHT, *Vital Records* 32-33: BAPTISMS BY FATHER MANNERS – Martin, Stephen; bapt 1775; Cogen, Mary; bapt 1775; Anderson, Rachel; bapt 1775; Connelly, ____n; bapt 1775; spon: Holland Webb, Sarah Webb; Millington, Sarah; bapt 1775; Hawkins, John; bapt 1775; spon: Matthew Bartley, Sarah Casey; Deprat, William; bapt 1775; spon: Mary Hissey; Richard; bapt Jan 7 1776, "Ben Nowlands' negro"; spon: Davi, Betty; Priest: BAPTISMS BY FATHER LEWIS – Ricketts, John; bapt 1776; Mar 19; "Spurius"" David; bapt 1776 ____ 5; "Mr. Matthews' negro"; O'Donald, Daniel; 1776; Smith, Mary; bapt 1776; spon: Denys Haggerty; Kelly, Mary; bapt 1776; spon: John Casey, Mary Casey; Hooby, Mary; bapt 1776 ____ 25; "Twins"; Hooby, Catharine; bapt 1776 ____ 25; "Twins"; Delia; bapt 1776; "Sylvester Nowlands negro girl"; Sara; bapt 1776; "Mr. Scotts' negro girl"; Benedict; Bohemia; bapt 1776; spon: Charles Havering, Miss Havering; slave; Reynolds, Jacob; bapt 1776; Parker, Samuel; Bapt 1776; Mull, Sarah; bapt 1776; Tolend, Edward; bapt 1776, Sep 18; Duhall, Nancy; bapt 1776 Sep 21; Craddock, John; bapt 1776 Oct 5; son of William Craddock; spon: John Craddock, Beths. Craddock; Robinet, Ann; bapt 1776 Oct 13; Reynolds, Katy; bapt 1776, Oct 13; Garrah, Margaret; bapt 1776 Oct 19; McCawley, John; bapt 1776 Oct 19; Barnet, Adam; bapt 1776 Nov 17; Vicars, John 1779 Jan; "spurius"; Esther, Ev; 1779 Jan 13; spon: Mary Reynolds; slave; Sally; Bohemia; bapt 1779 Jan 14; "Lucy's child"; slave; Dick; Bohemia; 1779 Feb 7; mother: Rachel; spons: Isaac, Betty; Crouch, Ann; bapt 1779 Feb 14; spon: Jac. Reynolds, Katy Nowland; Cole, John; 1779 Feb 28; son of Perry Cole; sponsors: Mr. O'Denahoe, Suz. Wright; Carnee, William; 1779 Mar 25; spon: Mr. Bromighan, Nancy Neale; Clinus; bapt 1779 Apr 4 "Mr. Blake's"; spon: Ignatius, Cate; Rose; bapt 1779 Apr 4; "Mr. Hall's"; spon: Tom, Duck, Henny; Knight, William; bapt 1779; spon: Arthur Matthews, Sally Mathews; Reynolds, Jerem.; bapt 1779 Apr 11; spon: Richard Craddock, Bethsabee Craddock; Craig, Walter; 1779 Apr 18; spon: Davis Vaughn, Monica Hollahan; Reed, Jenny; 1779 Apr 25; spon: Miss Branhan, Sally Daly; "twins"; Wood, Catherine; bapt 1779 May 16; spon: ____ Dougherty, Johanna Dempsy; Boys, Obediah; bapt 1779 May 22; spon: William Craddock, Margaret Neale; Antony; bapt 1779 May 24; "Mr. Hall's"; spon: "Our Betty," slave; Lucy; bapt 1779 May 24; "Mr. Hall's"; spon: "Our Betty," slave; Weldon, Eliz.; bapt 1779 May 30; spon: Miss Havering, Miss Reynolds; twins; Weldon, Amelia; bapt 1779 May 30; spon: Miss Havering, Miss Reynolds; twins; Ralph; Bohemia; bapt 1779 Jun 13; mother: Nell; spon: Old Ralph, Cate; slave; Elizabeth; Bohemia; bapt 1779 Jul 4; spon: Ralph, Jr, Nancy Su's girl; slave; Burk, Nancy; bapt 1779 Aug 4; spon: Sally Casey; Burke, Peggy; bapt 1779 Aug 4; spon: Sally Casey; Hellen; bapt 1779 Aug 29; Sylvester Nowland's; spon: Jack, Susan; slave; McCawley, Nancy; bapt 1779 Sep 19; White, Eliasa; bapt 1779 Sep 19; James; Bohemia; bapt 1779 Oct 3; mother: Jenny; spon: Matthew, Phillis; slave; Jones, Matthew; bapt 1779 Oct 18; spon: Bernard McCormac, Nelly McCormac; Craddock, Joseph; bapt 1779 Nov 14; spon: Jerem. Reynolds, Bethseba Craddock; Counsell, Edward C.; bapt 1760 Jan 15; Nowland, Brigitt; bapt 1760 Sep 24; Councell, John L.: bapt 1787 Nov 21.

On August 6, 1776, Dr. Thomas Bennett Willson married Mary Theresa Hall, daughter of Francis Hall and Martha Neale.

THE "DOUBLE LL" WILLSONS OF KENT COUNTY, MD. – Compiled by Joseph A. Dickerson, Rock Hall, Maryland FIRST THREE GENERATIONS – John Willson was born about 1680 in Edinburg, Scotland c. 1632 and died after 1749. He was a shipbuilder. See Peterman, *Catholics in Colonial Delmarva* 62, 229, 287. Children of John Willson and Mary his wife were Dr. Thomas Bennett Willson, born 1727 in Edinburgh, Scotland, came to America, lived at Greenwood on the Wye, Queen Anne County, died 1762. He married Margaret Smith, daughter of Roger Smith and Elizabeth Hutchins. She died 1780. Dr. Thomas Bennett Willson was educated between 1737 and 1745 at the University of St. Omer's Flanders. Children of Dr. Thomas Willson and Margaret Smith were Dr. Thomas Bennett Willson, born c. 1752, resided at Greenwood on Wye, died between 1790-1819; Richard Willson, died June 27, 1818, was a captain in the Revolutionary War. Dr. Thomas Bennett Willson married Mary Theresa hall, August 6, 1776, daughter of Francis Hall and Martha Neale. She was born between 1757-1760 and died August 20, 1810. Dr. T. B. Willson was educated at the University of Edinburg, Scotland. Mary Theresa Hall was buried on August 22, 1810 at the Dr. Willson Burying Ground "Overton "in Queen Anne County. The children of Dr. T. B. Willson and Mary Theresa Hall were: Francis Hall Willson, born 1777; Dr. Thomas Bennett Willson II, born September 28, 1778, died October 28, 1859; Martha Theresa Willson, born August 10, 1780, died October 27, 1863; Edward Willson, born c. 1782, married Henrietta Brooke; Richard Aloysius Willson, born May 6, 1783, Queen Anne County, died February 19, 1854.

198. Edward B. Carley, *The History of St. Joseph's Mission, Cordova, Maryland 1765-1965* (Euston, Maryland: Tidewater Publishers, 1965) 41: "The Baptismal Register of Joseph Mosley, S.J.," 41; GUA, Land Records, N-l-182—Peter Lowber to Thomas Poulton (1747); Hughes, Documents 1: 260–261. William Lowber inherited Cavil Ridge. According to local tradition, there was a building used as a school and chapel on Cavil Ridge property. A now deceased native of the area testified to Father Edward Carley some 30 years ago that he used to go hunting around the ruins. Father John Lewis sold the property to Daniel Lowber, Dec. 9, 1785; Land Records, 1785, DH of R. At a later date, all of the other Lowber property went to Catherine Cooper. The cemetery was thenceforth known as Cooper Cemetery. Cavil Ridge – 120 Acres – Addition to Cavil Ridge – 106 Acres These property acquisitions were in Kent County, Delaware, Murderkill Hundred.

 The first was made November 18, 1745 when Thomas Pulton, S.J., ten superior of Old Bohemia, purchased 120 acres of land and buildings from "John Cain, Planter."

 The second purchase was made just two years later on November 13, 1747 when Thomas Pulton, S.J. bought 106 acres (contiguous to the first purchase) from Peter Lowber, yeoman. The first tract is called "Cavil Ridge" and the second "Addition to Cavil Ridge." The first was "cleared" and with buildings and the second was uncleared." The Jesuits from Bohemia had been coming down to the area for a generation or more, and evidently wanted to establish a permanent mission. It is interesting to note that a son of Pete Lowber (Loper) was a student at the Bohemia Academy in 1745. This land was in the area now known as Frederica, Delaware and a street in this town is named Lober.

199. WL, 42: 145
200. Rightmyer, 170
201. Hughes, Documents 1:286, no. 3, "Bohemia Disputed, 1773"
202. Johnston, 302; Henry C. Peden, Jr., *Revolutionary Patriots of Cecil County, Maryland* (Westminster, Md.: Family Line Publications, 1991), 47; Anonymous, *The Heath Family of Worsall Manor, Maryland* (Elkton, Md.: Cecil County Historical Society, 1965), 1-4; Hughes, Documents 1:285-286, No. 83, "Bohemia Disputed, December 14, 1773"—Copy of letters from Mrs. James McMillan of Conesus, Livingston County, New York, a descendant of James Heath, February 10, 1898; Mathias Manners, S.J., Bohemia, December 14, 1773 to the Rev. John Lewis at New Town [Chestertown], 2 pp., fol. 1 and 2 of appendix, Box C, Maryland-New York Province Archives, Society of Jesus, Hughes suggests a possible connection between these claims now put forward and the Suppression of the Society of Jesus, an event that occurred in Europe four months previously.
203. John R. Michel, "The Heaths of Warwick," *Bulletin of the Historical Society of Cecil County*, No. 30 (Oct. 1966): 2; Geoffrey Holt, *St. Omer's and Bruges Colleges, 1593–1773: A Biographical Dictionary* (Thetford, England: Catholic Record Society, 1979), 130
204. Cann, 246

205. *Heath Family of Worsall Manor*, 5
206. Margaret Hodges, *Unpublished Records of Revolutionary Maryland* (Baltimore: Maryland Historical Society, 1941), 1: 56—"Charles Heath, Oath of Allegiance in 1778, Captain of Militia in 18th Battalion under Colonel John B. Thompson 1777–1778."
207. *WL*, 35: 53
208. *Maryland Militia Muster Roll*, 104, 121, 186, 193, 197, 202, 209, 230
209. Peden, 70; *Maryland Militia Muster Roll*, 38, 187, 205; *Cann*, 238–240
210. Papenfuse, *Biographical Dictionary*, 2: 583; Papers of Hugh Matthews of Cecil County, Maryland, and New Castle County, Delaware, 1770–1825, Maryland State Archives; William Love, "Two Maryland Heroines," *MHM* 3 (June 1908): 133–141; Usilton, *History of Kent County*, 64–71
211. Diary of John Lewis, S.J., 6-3B, carton 12, folder 4l2A, Province Archives:—"I borrowed 200 pds. from Dr. William Matthews and paid for house chapel at Letitia Manor."; Hughes, Documents 1: 296, No. 87, No. 178N
212. *Maryland Militia Muster Roll*, 29
213. Ms 1146, Maryland Historical Society, Baltimore.
214. Johnston, 347
215. *Maryland Militia Muster Roll*, 103; Peden, 84; Anonymous, *Cecil County in the Revolutionary War, 1776–1783* (Elkton, Md.: Cecil County Bicentennial Committee, 1976), 84, C-84, G-61
216. Ms 1146, A-6, Maryland Historical Society; Cann 180, 241
217. Hodges, *Unpublished Revolutionary Records of Maryland*, 1: 56; Ms 1146, A-17, Maryland Historical Society; Original manuscript 6636-9-93, Maryland State Archives.
218. Ms 1146, Maryland Historical Society;
219. Peden, 84. *Maryland Militia Muster Roll*, 142
220. *Archives of Maryland*, 47:131
221. Margaret Campbell, "History of the Perryville Area," *Cecil Whig*, Elkton, Md., 125th Anniversary Issue, August 31, 1966; Morton F. Taylor, *A Historical Sketch of Perryville* (Perryville, Md.: Perryville Chamber of Commerce, 1969), n. p.
222. Fred W. Dumschott, *Washington College* (Chestertown, Md.: Washington College, 1980), 6-9. *Honorary Degrees Conferred by Washington College, 1785–1790* (Chestertown, Md.: Washington College, 1971), 11
223. Dumschott, 25; John Bach McMaster, *A History of the People of the United States* (New York: D. Appleton Co., 1883), 2: 501. L. Wethered Barroll, "Washington College, 1783," *MHM* 6 (June 1911): 164-179
224. Mollie Howard Ash, "The Susquehanna River," TMs, Cecil County Historical Society, Elkton, Md., n. d., 3; R. G. Ringliffe, *Conowingo: The History of a Great Development on the Susquehanna* (New York: Newcomen Society in North America, 1953), 11–12
225. Gerald Smeltzer, *Canals Along the Lower Susquehanna* (York, Pa: Historical Society of York, 1963), 10; Ash, "The Susquehanna River," 3
226. Thomas J. Peterman, "Old St. Patrick's at Pilot," *The Upper Shoreman* 12 (Dec. 1973): 7, 21, 31, 37; Leone R. Terrell, *Tombstone Records of Cecil County* (Elkton, Md.: Head of Elk Chapter, Daughters of the American Revolution, 1973), 4: 173–177—"St. Patrick's Catholic Chapel, Pilot, Maryland."
227. *WL*, 10: 90
228. B. U. Campbell, "Memoirs and Times of the Most Rev. John Carroll," *United States Catholic Magazine* 3 (June 1844): 377–378
229. *WL*, 35: 240–242 ENGLISH JESUIT, JOSEPH MOSLEY – Father Mosley founded St. Joseph's in Talbot County in 1765. He was at Bohemia from 1764 to 1765. Born in 1731 he entered the Jesuits in 1748. He died on June 3, 1787.
230. Register of Wills, Cecil County, EE5 (C-646-4): 178-179, Maryland State Archives. "Copy of the Last Will of Reverend John Lewis," *RACHS* 1(1884-1886): 158–160; *Private Acts*, New Castle County Recorder of Deeds, Wilmington, Delaware, 1: 137. GUA – BOHEMIA CORRESP. RE (1788) Archives, Maryland Province, Society of Jesus

CHAPTER TWO

The Episcopate Of John Carroll
1789-1815

New Nation, New Bishop

*I*n the papal bull Ex Hac Apostolicae, issued on November 6, 1789, Pope Pius VI established the See of Baltimore and named John Carroll as its first bishop. He was consecrated in The Weld family chapel at Lulworth Castle in Dorsetshire, England. John Carroll headed the American church for the next twenty-five years.

English Former Jesuit, Robert Molyneux

Portrait of Archbishop John Carroll

Father Robert Molyneux (1738-1808) was pastor of St. Francis Xavier Church in Cecil County on the Eastern Shore of Maryland at the time when George Washington was sworn in as first president and when his former student, John Carroll, was designated as first Catholic bishop of the United States.[1] Arriving in Maryland from England in 1771, Father Molyneux had served as pastor of St. Mary's Church in Philadelphia during the whole Revolutionary War.[2]

Philadelphia was temporarily America's national capital, while Washington-on-the-Potomac was being built. Prominent persons of the Continental Congress and in the military forces, both French and American, were familiar with Father Molyneux. On four occasions members of the Continental Congress had attended services at Molyneux's church. The first occasion had been the anniversary celebration of the Declaration of Independence on July 4, 1779. On another occasion Molyneux celebrated the Solemn Mass of Thanksgiving at the arrival of the French forces on August 25, 1781, prior to the surrender of Cornwallis at Yorktown on October 17, 1781. The Mass was attended by Chevalier Caesar de la Luzerne, minister of the King of France, members of the Continental Congress, and, tradition has it, by General George Washington himself.[3] Molyneux had preached again in the presence of the French minister on the occasion of King Louis XVI's birthday. During Luzerne's stay in Philadelphia, his tutor in the English language was Father Molyneux.[4]

As pastor of St. Joseph's in Philadelphia, Molyneux had established the first parochial school in that city, and had personally prepared the first class of students to be confirmed in this country by John Carroll, then Superior of the Mission with faculties to confirm.[5] Molyneux published textbooks for his school and was among the first promoters of an American Catholic press.[6]

Molyneux's assistant pastor in Philadelphia during the entire Revolution was another very visible missionary priest, Ferdinand Farmer (alias Steinmeyer), a German and former Jesuit. Farmer had come to Pennsylvania twenty years earlier than Molyneux. He had covered thousands of miles on horseback serving Catholics scattered over Pennsylvania, New Jersey, and New Castle County in Delaware. When Farmer died in August, 1786, Molyneux's sermon preached at his funeral was printed in all the newspapers of Pennsylvania and was translated into German for the German immigrants that Father Farmer had so faithfully served.[7] Beginning with 1787 the sacramental registers at St. Joseph's Church in Philadelphia reflect his activities.[8]

At the end of February, 1788, Molyneux traveled to St. Francis Xavier Church in Cecil County, Maryland, to attend the seriously ill Father John Lewis. When Lewis died on March 24, 1788, Molyneux, then aged 49, succeeded as pastor.[9] For two years, Father Molyneux enjoyed the comparative peace of the Eastern Shore countryside, and experienced the contrast between the refined society of the new nation's capital and association with simple farmers. There is evidence of his active ministry as a country pastor in the baptismal and marriage registers for 1788-1789.[10] The Bohemia registers begin with 1790 but there are some notes from earlier records apparently collected by Father John Lewis and by Father Robert Molyneux, some of them going back to the time of Father Joseph Greaton and probably copied from his notebook. Father Molyneux made the first entries in the Bohemia *Marriage Register* and *Baptismal Register*. The only marriage he recorded took place on July 4, 1790, between, Flora and Sampson, slaves of Dr. William Matthews. Witnesses were Rev. Francis Beeston and Alice O'Donnell.[11]

On July 1, 1790, after more than two years as pastor of Bohemia, Father Molyneux was transferred to Port Tobacco on the Western Shore of the Chesapeake Bay. He was listed as Vicar General for the Northern District at the First Diocesan Synod convoked by Bishop Carroll in Baltimore, November 7-8, 1791.[12] In 1793, Carroll persuaded him to accept an appointment as second president of Georgetown College. Georgetown Academy had opened its doors in 1791.[13]

In October, 1806, Father Molyneux joined with other ex-Jesuit priests in petitioning Pope Pius VII for permission to reestablish the Society of Jesus in the United States.[14] He became the first provincial of the American Jesuits when the order was restored.[15]

Some months after the reestablishment of the Society, Molyneux accepted a second term as president of Georgetown College. On October 10, 1806, he established a Jesuit novitiate opposite Trinity Church at Georgetown.[16]

Father Molyneux died on December 8, 1808. The funeral was held at Georgetown College, and his remains were the first to be interred in the cemetery there.[17] Molyneux had been a mutual friend to Father Charles Plowden and Bishop John Carroll. From the Carroll - Plowden correspondence we can piece together a heart-warming portrait of Father Molyneux's character. His friendship and good sense were a great support to Bishop Carroll who esteemed his counsel and spoke of him in high praise. Carroll considered him his "oldest friend" after Charles Carroll of Carrollton, his relative and companion at St. Omer's in France. Robert Molyneux emerges from Carroll's descriptions as good-natured, popular, effective, useful, and reliable.[18] Father Ambrose Maréchal who studied English from Father Molyneux in Philadelphia, also gave testimony to Molyneux's good character.[19]

English Former Jesuit, Francis Beeston

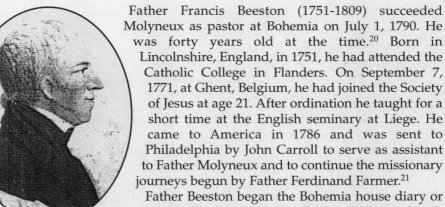

Portrait of Rev. Francis Beeston

Father Francis Beeston (1751-1809) succeeded Molyneux as pastor at Bohemia on July 1, 1790. He was forty years old at the time.[20] Born in Lincolnshire, England, in 1751, he had attended the Catholic College in Flanders. On September 7, 1771, at Ghent, Belgium, he had joined the Society of Jesus at age 21. After ordination he taught for a short time at the English seminary at Liege. He came to America in 1786 and was sent to Philadelphia by John Carroll to serve as assistant to Father Molyneux and to continue the missionary journeys begun by Father Ferdinand Farmer.[21]

Father Beeston began the Bohemia house diary or Memoranda Book, as it is inscribed in Beeston's handwriting, with the first entry: "1790, July 1 - I, Francis Beeston, began to take care of Bohemia Plantation."[22]

On the next day he wrote in the diary: "July 2 - last night the dogs killed a sheep and wounded three more, so my overseer and myself shot six of the dogs, allowing for the future no more than one dog for each quarter."[23] Besides his parochial duties, Beeston was charged with the management of a large plantation. The first United States Census (1790) has for Cecil County under "Heads of Families," Francis Beeston - Whites 1, Slaves 49.[24] Beeston's diary records farm activities, data on the sawmill, lists clothing given to slaves, and shows that he knew a great deal about crops, cattle, and workmen.[25]

Father Francis Beeston served his three and more years at Bohemia unassisted by any other clergy except for one French priest who lived for some months with him there. Beeston noted in his diary on December 10, 1791: "Rev. M. Louis de Barth, a native of Alsace, came to live with me at Bohemia." Born at Munster in 1764, he arrived in Baltimore in 1791, and was sent by Carroll to Bohemia.[26] In the spring of 1792 Father de Barth ministered to the Catholic families in

Page from Father Beeston's Financial Records

Appoquinimink Forest, New Castle County, Delaware.[27] He left for Port Tobacco, Maryland, on June 12, 1792, and went from there to Lancaster, Pennsylvania in 1795. He was manager of the church farm owned by the Jesuits' Clergy Corporation at Conewago, Pennsylvania, in 1814. For six years he was administrator of the Diocese of Philadelphia after the death of Bishop Francis Egan.[28] He retired to Georgetown College in 1838, and died there in 1844.[29]

While Father Beeston was pastor at Bohemia, Mathew Carey published the first American edition of the Douay - Rheims version of the Bible. Among those subscribers listed at the front of the book is "Francis Beeston, Bohemia, two copies."[30] The opening session of the first national synod of Catholic clergymen was held on November 7, 1791. It brought to Baltimore twenty-one priests, of whom twelve had been Jesuits. Beeston wrote in the Bohemia diary: "November 3, 1791. Went to Baltimore to the first Diocesan Synod assembled by the Rt. Rev. Father in God, John Carroll, D.D., Bishop of Baltimore, and first Bishop in the United States of America." Francis Beeston was delegated by Carroll to act as secretary for the synod. The twenty-four decrees enacted concerned themselves with the uniform administration of the sacraments. Hymns or prayers in English were allowed during Mass and the performance of the sacraments. Priests were obliged to dress in black ordinarily and to wear the cassock at Mass. Carroll encouraged parochial congregations to form vestries or bodies of trustees, and to seek incorporation as legal bodies under the laws of the state. No other synod was held in Carroll's lifetime.[31]

The sacramental records of Bohemia reveal that Father Beeston not only ministered at Bohemia but made regular trips from St. Francis Xavier Church to near-

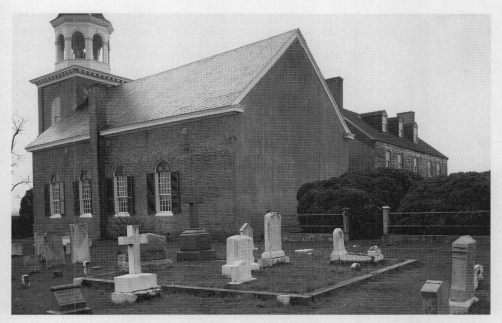

St. Francis Xavier Church. After the Bill of Rights and its guarantee of religious freedom was ratified, work began on St. Francis Xavier Church. It was completed in 1797.

by Warwick and to Appoquinimink Forest in New Castle County, Delaware.[32] In 1790 alone there were twenty-three baptisms; in 1791 forty-four baptisms.[33] Names of those who fought in the Revolutionary War appear as witnesses of the sacraments, such as Reynolds, Weldon, Heverin, Burke, and Cole.[34] Beeston is credited with at least five trips to Chestertown and other places in Kent County, Maryland.[35] He made trips to Elkton and Sassafras Neck in Cecil County, Maryland.[36] Other trips were made by Father Beeston to Queenstown, Tully's Neck and Kingstown in Queen Anne County, Maryland.[37] Less frequently Father Beeston ministered to Caroline County, Maryland.[38] He showed a special solicitude for Blacks under his care.[39]

On January 16, 1792, a duel took place near Bohemia between Richard Key Heath, for his father, Daniel Charles Heath, and James V. Matthews, for his brother Dr. William Matthews. A quarrel had taken place between Dr. William Matthews and Daniel Charles Heath at the Buck Tavern, near Summit, Delaware on November 7, 1791, when Dr. Matthews resented remarks made by Mr. Heath about his professional character. The doctor asserted that the calumny was that of an infamous liar. A challenge to a duel was then accepted by Dr. Matthews. James Matthews, the younger brother of Dr. William Matthews and a Roman Catholic, eventually stepped in for his brother, although the Church forbade duels. Richard Key Heath stepped in for his father, Daniel Charles Heath. James Matthews was mortally wounded in the duel which took place at the home of Mr. Hodgson at 10 o'clock on January 16, 1792. Matthews was wrapped in a blanket and driven in a sleigh to the home of his brother Dr. William Matthews at Worsall Manor. Summoned from nearby Bohemia, Father Beeston arrived in time to receive the

Original Wrought Iron Thumb Latch, Dated 1792. This picture shows one of the original wrought iron thumb latches that had been on some of the doors at Old Bohemia. It had been removed during the period when the buildings were uncared for and was, many years later, found in an antique shop by Mr. Titus Geesey of Wilmington, Delaware, who kindly presented it to The Old Bohemia Historical Society. This particular latch, dated 1792, was found to fit perfectly the nail holes in the door from which it had been removed.

wounded man's repentance and to administer the last rites of the church. Two days later Father Beeston preached at the graveside and offered prayers over the mortal remains of James V. Matthews at the burial site near Worsall Manor.[40]

Besides his pastoral responsibilities Father Beeston was charged with the management of the farm and its several buildings. He did all in his power to pay off the debts which at his coming exceeded 925 pounds (about $100,000 in 2004 dollars). He felt that he could go forward now with plans to build a new church. In his diary he wrote on April 21, 1792, that he threw down the old chapel - pulled down the parlour chimney and part of both the gable ends of the house... began to rebuild... to dig the foundations of the new church...[41] On October 11, 1792, he began a road leading straight from the new church to Warwick.[42] On November 2, 1792, he began to frame the roof of the new church. By May 1, 1793, "the roof for the church was raised"[43] Father Beeston was pushing the project forward when suddenly he was taken away from Bohemia.[44]

On May 19, 1793, Francis Beeston was appointed rector of St. Peter's pro-Cathedral in Baltimore.[45] Although sixteen years younger than Bishop Carrol, Beeston was a close friend and confidante to the prelate for the next twenty years. After the death of Lawrence Graessel, coadjutor-elect, in July, 1793, Beeston was generally considered the most likely candidate to take his place.[46] Beeston was regularly of a cheerful disposition, esteemed as excellent company and was himself fond of good companionship. He became the most intimate friend that Carroll allowed himself in later life.[47] Like Carroll an ex-Jesuit and alumnus of Liege, Belgium, Beeston chose not to reenter the Society of Jesus when it was restored in Maryland on June 21, 1805.[48]

Through his ministry to the sick, he twice contracted yellow fever but recovered. After years of devoted service, he died on December 20, 1809, at the age of 59. Bishop Carroll himself wrote a tribute commemorating his priestly zeal, his charity towards the poor, and his heroism in attending victims of the yellow fever.[49]

French Sulpician, Ambrose Maréchal

When he was consecrated first Bishop of Baltimore, Carroll faced the task of forming a native American clergy. He had no seminary and no seminarians. While he was still in Europe, Carroll considered himself fortunate to enlist the help of the Society of St. Sulpice, a body of secular priests committed to the training of diocesan clergy in France since 1641. A group of this Society arrived in

Baltimore on July 10, 1791.⁵⁰ Father Charles Sewall, Baltimore's first resident priest and first rector of St. Peter's pro-Cathedral gave them a cordial welcome.⁵¹ The Sulpician Fathers opened St. Mary's Seminary in Baltimore on October 16, 1791.⁵² Father Louis Caesar Delavan, S.S., former canon of Tours, France, was in their company.⁵³ After the first year and a half, the Sulpicians found their resources exhausted. Bishop Carroll sent them to Bohemia with the plan of reviving the old academy as a means of income along with the farm. At a chapter meeting of the Corporation of the Clergy at White Marsh on November 7, 1792, Carroll made the case on behalf of the Sulpicians.⁵⁴ It was resolved at the same meeting that profits arising from the Bohemia estate should be granted to the Seminary of St. Sulpice at Baltimore.⁵⁵ The possession of the property was revocable, however, at the will of the Jesuits.⁵⁶

On May 18, 1793, Father Beeston left Bohemia, entrusting the care of it to Father Delavan. At first another Sulpician, Louis Regiol Deluol, joined Father Delavan at Bohemia. Both were replaced by Father Ambrose Maréchal, S.S., the first Sulpician to be named pastor of St. Francis Xavier mission and temporal administrator of the farm. Maréchal, newly-ordained and energetic, had arrived in Baltimore from France on June 24, 1792.⁵⁷ Immediately upon assuming the administration of Bohemia, Maréchal made a minute inventory of every possession at Bohemia.⁵⁸

From 1793 to 1798, Father Maréchal devoted himself to pastoral ministry at Bohemia and its several mission stations. A copy of one of Father Maréchal's sermons given at Bohemia, now in the archives of the Archdiocese of Baltimore, shows a logical and well composed homily with a good choice of words.⁵⁹ He made as many as twenty-two trips to Appoquinimink Forest in New Castle County, Delaware.⁶⁰ In addition, he made trips to Head of Elk (now Elkton) and Sassafras Hill in Cecil County, Maryland,⁶¹ to Georgetown and Sassafras Neck,⁶² to Warwick in the same county,⁶³ to Kingstown in Queen Anne County, Maryland⁶⁴ and to Taylor's Bridge (north of Dover) in Kent County, Delaware.⁶⁵

In 1793, Father Maréchal completed the new church begun by Father Beeston, personally joining in the building of the church and turning the wooden stiles of the altar railing (destroyed in the fire of 1912).⁶⁶ Stephen Theodore Badin, one of the seminarians at St. Mary's Seminary in Baltimore, had finished most of his studies in the Sulpician Seminary, Orleans, France, before he came to the United States. He made his retreat before ordination at Bohemia with Father Maréchal before he was ordained in Baltimore on May 25, 1793.⁶⁷ Father Badin, the first priest ordained in the United States, became a missionary to Kentucky.⁶⁸

Another Sulpician priest, Jean Baptiste Chicoisneau, had come to the United States on March 29, 1792. From time to time he traveled to Bohemia to assist Father Maréchal and other pastors over the years 1793 to 1799. Father Chicoisneau spent July, 1793, at the Bohemia plantation making an even more detailed survey than that of Maréchal. He served as économe of St. Mary's Seminary, was assigned to the Grande Seminaire in Montreal on May 2, 1796. He died on March 2, 1818.⁶⁹ Father Antione Garnier was at Bohemia on occasion. On May 19, 1797, while Garnier was serving as pastor there, Bishop John Carroll arrived from Baltimore. On May 21, 1797, Carroll preached and confirmed some fifty persons. Carroll left for Baltimore on May 23, 1797.⁷⁰

Worsall Manor, Home of William Matthews from 1790-1806

While Ambrose Maréchal was pastor at Bohemia, a Miss Kitty (Catherine) Knight attended Mass there from Essex Lodge on the Sassafras, where she lived. She was the only daughter born of John Leach Knight and Catherine Matthews at Knights' Point on the Sassafras River. Her uncle Hugh Matthews served both in the Maryland legislature and the United States Congress. Another uncle, Dr. William Matthews, owned Worsall Manor from 1796 to 1806.[71] In her twenties (she turned twenty in 1795) she was a devoted parishioner of Father Maréchal and declared when he was transferred that she wouldn't attend church unless he were brought back.[72] According to local legend, Kitty came to Mass with a big hat and fashionable dress and brought a boy slave to fan her in church and to shield her with a parasol while out in the sun. Kitty spent some winters in Philadelphia, then the national capital. According to her own account, Kitty Knight spoke with President Washington at a theater event in Philadelphia. He said to her: "You are well guarded, Miss," and "then I said to him, 'I surely am, sir, in your presence, and courtsied."[73]

On July 14, 1794, Father Maréchal baptized seven of Kitty Knight's slaves' children. She was their sponsor. The children were Ephrem 14, George 12, Henry 12, Ned 14, Mary 14, Jane 5, and Elizabeth 12 years of age.

When Kitty Knight was in her late thirties, she displayed a courage that has made her a famous heroine of the War of 1812. When the British sailed up the Sassafras River to burn Georgetown and Fredericktown, she intervened and saved two homes that have since been joined together and are known today as The Kitty Knight House. Her own account of the incident is recorded:

> The British, after landing, commenced to burn all the lower part of the town, she said, and this was largely frame. There were; however, two brick dwellings on top of the hill, in the town, which had not as yet been fired. In one of them was an old lady, sick and almost destitute, and toward that building the Admiral and his sailors and marines proceeded at a rapid gait. I followed them, but before I got to the top of the hill, they had set fire to the house in which the old lady lay. I immediately called the attention of the

Picture of Kitty Knight's and William Knight's Graves

Admiral to the fact that they were about to burn up a human being, and that a woman, and I pleaded with him to make his men put the fire out. This I finally succeeded in doing, when they immediately went next door, not over forty feet distant, and fired the second of the brick houses. I told the commanding officer that, as the wind was blowing toward the other house, this old lady would be burned up anyway, when apparently affected by my appeal, he called his men off, but left the fire burning, saying, 'Come on boys,' As they went through the door one of them struck his boarding axe through the panel of the door.[74]

Kitty Knight lived to the age of 84. She died on November 22, 1855, at her home Essex Lodge, the Knight home on the Sassafras. She is buried beside her uncle William Knight, brother of John Leach Knight, at Saint Francis Xavier Cemetery, Bohemia, Cecil County.

In 1795 Father Maréchal was transferred from Bohemia.[75] For a period he occupied the chair of mathematics at Georgetown Academy. He then became a professor of theology at St. Mary's Seminary in Baltimore. In July, 1803, he was recalled to France by his Sulpician superiors, but would return to America later and become the third Archbishop of Baltimore. He was consecrated on December 14, 1817, and died on January 29, 1828.[76]

French Sulpician, Jean Marie Tessier

Another Sulpician priest, Jean Marie Tessier, served as pastor of Bohemia after Ambrose Maréchal. At the age of 33, he had come to Baltimore with the first group of Sulpicians in 1791. For almost two years, Tessier capably managed the large farm at Bohemia and attended its many missions in Delaware and the Eastern Shore of Maryland.[77] In those two years Tessier made several trips to Appoquinimink Forest,[78] to Kent County, Delaware[79] to Elkton,[80] to Lynch,

Maryland[81] to Little Bohemia,[82] to Queen Anne County,[83] and to, Chestertown.[84] He kept a record of burials.[85]

Father Tessier also kept a *Journal*, now preserved in the Sulpician Archives, Baltimore.[86] He remained at Bohemia until April 1796, when he returned to the seminary in Baltimore. He served as superior of St. Mary's Seminary from 1810 to 1829.[87]

Succeeding Father Tessier as pastor of Bohemia was the Sulpician priest, Reverend Antoine Garnier. He was 29 when he came to Baltimore in 1791, and was sent to Bohemia in 1796.[88] In Garnier's time it became evident that what was intended to be a benefaction to the Sulpicians was not becoming a reality. The attempt to revive the Bohemia Academy had come to nothing. The location was remote and there were too few students available. The record of 1798 gives only 54 whites and 36 blacks as the Bohemia congregation.[89] The whole number scattered over the rest of the missions was not more than that. The Sulpicians decided that their full efforts would be directed to the success of their Baltimore seminary. A report of the financial condition of Bohemia was sent to Bishop Carroll on March 26, 1798, in answer to the "false opinion, which some in the diocese have conceived that we are being enriched at the expense of Bohemia, whereas we are still in a straightened condition."[90] The agreement had been from the beginning that the possession of the property was revocable at the will of the former Jesuits.[91]

On April 30, 1799, three trustees of the Corporation of the Roman Catholic Clergy wrote a letter to Father Nagot, the Sulpician superior in Baltimore, demanding the return of Bohemia in order to aid in the payment of debts incurred by Georgetown College.[92]

Father Francis Beeston was designated by the three trustees as administrator of the estate. All the financial accounts of the Sulpicians at Bohemia, letters pertaining to the estate, a map of the plantation and contemporary accounts of the Sulpicians' stay on the Eastern Shore comprise a rich trove of documents preserved in the Sulpician archives in Baltimore.

French Capuchin, Sebastian DeRosey

In the register of Bohemia Mission in Cecil County, Maryland, it is evident that Abbé Sebastian de Rosey (Durvoisier) was ministering to Catholics of Maryland as early as 1797. A Capuchin, he had been chaplain on the French man-of-war *La Reflechie* during the American Revolutionary War. After Yorktown he went to Saint-Domingue. At the time of the slave insurrection he fled to the United States. He became missionary pastor of St. Mary Church, Meekins Neck, in Dorchester County, and other congregations in the counties of Talbot and Queen Anne on the Eastern Shore. One contemporary says "he was highly esteemed for his worth and great ability." By 1806 he was at St. Nicholas Church on the Patuxent River on the Western Shore of Maryland, where he died December 27, 1812.[93]

Irish Augustinian, George Staunton, Irish Capuchin, Lawrence S. Phelan,

The name of Rev. Ambrose Maréchal appears for the last time on the Bohemia Mission sacramental records in the Spring of 1799. The Sulpicians were methodical and exact in their keeping of the sacramental records at Bohemia, but the registers were neglected for nearly seven years after their departure. From 1799 to 1805 there is a break in the records except for a few unsigned entries seemingly by French priests, though in 1801 Fathers Staunton and Phelan were there. Rev. George Staunton, an Augustinian friar, came to the United States in 1799 and was appointed manager of that part of the Bohemia estate allotted for the clergyman's support. During the summer of 1800, Staunton, was sent to St. Mary's Church, Philadelphia, where he served until 1804. After five more years of service in New Jersey, he left for Spain in 1809. He died in 1815.[94] Reverend Laurence Silvester Phelan, from Cork, Ireland, was his immediate successor at Bohemia, remaining until 1801, and probably till a later date. It is difficult to determine who were the pastors from 1800 to 1806. Phelan was sent by Bishop Carroll in 1805 to Buffalo Creek, Westmoreland County, Pennsylvania. He was later transferred to Chambersburg, Pennsylvania, and then to Holy Trinity Church, Philadelphia.[95]

French Secular Priest, William Pasquet

The successor to Father Laurence Phelan was William Pasquet de Leyde, who had been a French Jesuit but now was a secular or diocesan priest assigned by Bishop Carroll as superior to Bohemia and manager of the farm. There is evidence that he was at Bohemia and entrusted with the management of the plantation as early as 1802.[96]

At this time a project was begun just north of Bohemia which would result in the development of the Chesapeake and Delaware Canal, and would involve the ministry of priests from Bohemia. The idea of connecting the Delaware Bay with the Chesapeake Bay by digging a canal dates back as far as Augustine Herman, but any plan to dig such a canal was not put into effect until the new nation came into existence and President Jefferson had made the 1803 Louisiana Purchase. Preliminary surveys for the canal began in July, 1803.[97] Benjamin Latrobe was employed as the chief engineer, and was authorized to hire one or more groups of laborers to begin digging immediately.[98] By May of 1804, a crew of fifty Irish laborers were at work.[99] Wages were extremely low, living conditions were indescribably poor. Makeshift houses were constructed for the laborers which were torrid and mosquito-ridden in the summer and freezing in the winter. With those conditions, at times wagon loads of laborers sick with pneumonia and tuberculosis were unloaded at the poor house in Elkton.[100] Liquor and gambling provided their only diversion and led to many troubles. In October, 1804, for instance, at the Elkton race track (horse races) nearby, a riot was triggered when the proprietor disputed the win of an Irish canal worker. A fight followed, the Elkton men were routed by the Irish workers. One Irishman was killed and thirty other persons injured.[101]

From the beginning Latrobe experienced a deficiency of funds. He was eventually forced to discontinue the work. In November, 1805, he announced that all employees would be fired. The release date of all workers was December 1, 1805.[102] The project was suspended and not resumed until 1824.[103] Hardly a year between passed without the need for the canal being brought before the federal government. Many of the workmen and their families continued to live in poor conditions on the canal in hopes that they would be reemployed.[104]

On July 29, 1807, Father Ambrose Maréchal returned to the Eastern Shore to baptize Sara Maria Mitchell, born December 22, 1806, daughter of Joseph T. and Sophia Mitchell. Sponsors were James and Ann Mitchell, uncle and aunt of her child. Sponsor was Reverend William Pasquet. During the first half of the nineteenth century a chapel was located at the Mitchell farm, just north of Tolchester Point, in Kent County, Maryland. Joseph T. Mitchell had bought 1000 acres there on December 6, 1811, from William Ringgold and his wife, Martha. He possibly owned other property there as early as 1807. He built a large wide – porched dwelling which came to be known through the years as the *Mitchell House*. [105]

In the spring of 1813 the British blocked the Chesapeake Bay and ravaged several unprotected communities on Maryland's Eastern Shore. British Navy Captain Peter Parker and his ship, HMS Menelaus, was thirty days in the Bay in 1814 as part of the buildup of forces to attack Washington, D.C. Parker moved up the Chesapeake to prevent the Maryland militia from marching to defend Washington. Parker's force landed on the property of John Waltham and marched through the woods to meet the Marylanders in what is known as the Battle of Caulk's Field. In the encounter Captain Parker was wounded on the battlefield on August 30, 1814. He was carried to the Mitchell House where he died in a bedroom on the second floor. His body was taken to Georgetown on the Sassafras River, where a surgeon embalmed his body in a barrel of rum and shipped it back to England. The British, on the next day, September 3, 1814, invaded Mitchell's farm again, removed some livestock and kidnapped Mitchell's son, Joseph Jr. The son was taken aboard *HMS Surprise*. On September 6 the British returned to take away some of Mitchell's slaves. The slaves were sent on to Tangier Island. Their fate is not known, nor is there any record of Joseph Jr.'s release. He found his way back home, however, because he was present at his father's death in 1830, and inherited the farm upon his mother's death.[106]

On June 21, 1812, *at Bohemia*, Father Pasquet baptized Charles O'Neal, born February 9, 1812, son of Bernard and Jane O'Neal. Sponsors were Benedict Craddock and Elizabeth O'Donald. On the same day *at Bohemia* he baptized Janette Eleanora Reynolds, born January 1, 1812, daughter of James and Rachel Reynolds. Sponsors were James O'Donahoe and Sarah Reynolds. On the same day, *at Bohemia*, he baptized Sarah Anne Lee, daughter of David and Martha Lee. Sponsors were Bernard O'Neal and Sarah Reynolds.

On April 3, 1814, *at Bohemia*, Father Pasquet baptized William O'Neal, born on December 20, 1813, son of Bernard and Jane O'Neal. Sponsors were James Councell and Sarah Nowland. On April 26, 1815, *at Bohemia*, Father Pasquet baptized Amelia Read, born March 31, 1815, daughter of Benjamin Read and Anne, his wife. Sponsors were Jacob and Sarah Reynolds. On April 30, 1815, *at Bohemia* he baptized George Craig, born February 26, 1815, son of Levi and Elizabeth Craig. Sponsors were Jacob Reynolds and Mary Nowland. On September 14, 1815, *at Bohemia* he baptized Joseph, born September 6, 1815, son of Abigail, a slave belonging to Mrs. Elizabeth O'Donald. Sponsor was Lucy.

Father William Pasquet officiated at the following weddings at Bohemia: November 21, 1824, between Henry Helm and Rachael Lee. Witnesses were James O'Donald and Ignatia B. Brooke. On February 15, 1825, between John V. Price and

Ann Nowland. Witnesses were John Corbaley and Sarah Crouch. On February 20, 1825, between John Burke and Martha, negro slave of John Hanson. Witnesses were Moses and James, slaves.

Maurice Delaney died May 3, 1807, and was buried at Bohemia. J.G.E. Durand died July 20, 1814, age 33, and was buried at Bohemia. Theresa Durand died October 15, 1814, age 50, and was buried at Bohemia.

Although Father Pasquet did not keep careful sacramental records, and did not record that he visited the many Catholic workers and their families at work on the Chesapeake and Delaware Canal, they must have attracted his attention as he traveled in or through the vicinity.

In a short time after work on the C & D Canal was curtailed, many Irish immigrants were employed to work on a transpeninsular turnpike from 1809 to 1814. It had been an important thoroughfare since early colonial days. The roads that did exist across the isthmus between Chesapeake Bay and Delaware Bay were little more than dirt paths over which horse-drawn stages and wagons crept about thirty miles a day. When the federal government was moved to Washington in 1800, travel over the route became even more important.[107] Demands were made to legislators for the thoroughfare from New Castle to Frenchtown to be improved. Residents of Cecil County, Maryland, petitioned the court to improve the road, which they noted was "very crooked and in extreme bad repair."[108] A group of New Castle men took the initiative and promoted a plan to build a highly-improved road, which passed by the General Assembly of Delaware on January 24, 1809. The plan approved was subject to a similar charter from the legislature of Maryland. The road was to be completed from New Castle to the Delaware State line enroute to Frenchtown on the Elk River in Cecil County, Maryland.[109] That portion of the road from New Castle to Hare's Corner on State Road (Route 13) was commenced on August 1, 1811, and was completed and opened on March 13, 1813.[110]

The advent of steam-powered ships provided an added stimulant to building a better road across the isthmus. The first steamboat, the "Chesapeake," arrived from Baltimore at Frenchtown on June 21, 1813.[111] Two more miles of the turnpike had been completed by February, 1814, and the entire project finished to Frenchtown by 1814.[112]

Irish immigrants unloaded at New Castle supplied the labor to build the road.[113] The turnpike was hailed as a major transportation improvement, but it was no more than a poor gravel road. The work on it didn't end, as labor crews struggled to keep the highway in good repair. Nevertheless, it provided the main route across the Delmarva peninsula for fifteen years until the Chesapeake and Delaware Canal broke the land barrier between the bays in 1829.[114]

At the request of Bishop Carroll, on February 15, 1805, Father Pasquet accompanied a new Irish immigrant priest Father Patrick Kenny, on a tour of the Jesuit mission at White Clay Creek and of Wilmington in New Castle County, Delaware.[115] These mission stations were founded from Bohemia and were under the care of the priests there. From Wilmington Pasquet consigned a letter to Bishop Carroll which outlined to Carroll the dissatisfaction many parishioners in Wilmington felt with Father Charles Whelan, whose illness had increased to the point that he would retire to Bohemia that year and die at Bohemia in 1806:

As to charges forwarded by the congregation, it was mortifying, even humiliating, to Clergyman to inquire into imputations so unbecoming the nicety of clerical character and unfortunately too strongly and too uniformly well-supported. Whatever members of the congregation residents of Wilmington that could be convened, were requested to meet at Mr. Paul Maginns', where they attended to the number of nine, amongst whom there was a single dissentient voice, a Mr. Patrick Trainor who deposed that Rev. Mr. Whelan always behaved well to him and his family and that all who contributed to the demands were equally well attended to – and that his name was put to the list of subscribers without his knowledge or consent — - the names of the nine are Mr. Wm. McBride, Francis Cunningham, Paul Maginn, Francis Kane, Jas. Fitzgerald, Thos. Maguire, Dennis McCready, Patk. Higgins, and Patk. Trainor – Since writing this report three persons appeared to say they had nothing to accuse Rev. Mr. Whelan of, to wit – Bernard McEnemy, Thos. Arjoin, Stephen Murphy. We remain, Rt. Rev. Sir, with every respect yr. most humble and obedt. servts.

          Patrick Kenny
          William Pasquet[116]

When Carroll had wrote to Francis Neale, fiscal agent of the Congregation of the Clergy regarding Pasquet and the management of Bohemia, in June, 1805, he said that his planned trip to Bohemia might have to be deferred because Pasquet was to be at White Marsh the next day or so, and added that Pasquet had sent 500 bushels of corn to him (Carroll) that had been expected at Baird's Point, South River the previous Monday.[117] The following spring Carroll wrote to Robert Molyneux that "Pasquet has been expected for some time on his way to Georgetown —— it is fitting if not necessary for me to go to the E. Shore which will be when Pasquet returns."[118]

In 1806 Bishop Carroll agreed to accept the Bohemia property in Cecil County awarded to him by the Corporation of the Clergy in lieu of the $800 that had been paid him annually from the general fund.[119] From that year on till his death in 1815, Bohemia constituted Carroll's benefice, his "table," his "manse," the property for his episcopal maintenance, his principal source of income. An interesting memorandum appears in Carroll's letterbook which describes the deplorable state of the Bohemia plantation at the time:

Observations on the temporal state of Bohemia.

House in a most decayed state, and no sign of the least reparation for many years—The front doors perfectly unsafe and rotten—Kitchen, outhouses, stables and particularly the last as bad as can be, so as to afford neither shelter nor safety to the horses. No places provided for the black people, who cultivate the farm—they inhabit the brick building near the mill pond, belonging to the Abps manse.[120]

Carroll had assigned the management of Bohemia to Rev. William Pasquet, who was also assigned to minister to its congregation.[121] Pasquet's sacrament records at Bohemia appear to be poorly kept.[122]

As proprietor of Bohemia, Carroll was master of approximately twenty four slaves.[123] Technically the slaves belonged to the Corporation of the Clergy. Still Carroll could not avoid involvement in decisions concerning the slaves at Bohemia. Always a bit defensive on the question of slavery, in the last year of his life, Carroll insisted that he had not owned a single slave.[124]

In 1808, Carroll wrote Pasquet concerning a slave at Bohemia named Barney, that Pasquet should have the mill with Barney [a slave] at £100 for the year 1809, paying all expenses for the mill during that term and restoring it the same as before. Mr. Corbaley has replaced the lost or damaged articles. Carroll is thus freed from expenses for Barney. Pasquet should see that Corbaley makes good the deficiencies as promised. Carroll will send a line to Mr. Craddock to pay the taxes. If Dr. Scanlan and others who owe for the hire of Negroes do not pay a reasonable amount at the end of the year, Pasquet should look for other masters. If they pay, the money will remain with Pasquet as part of the $200 due him.[125] In response to a letter from Pasquet, July 23, 1811, Carroll wrote. "If Fillingham is unacceptable, [Carroll] would prefer the mill continue under Barney's management. Listen to Barney [a slave] and don't compel him into service if he has good reasons for wanting otherwise. If no one else will give $70 for him, Carroll will try to find him employment. Pasquet intended to make an inquiry into the character of Mr. George Fillingham. If Pasquet found him acceptable, Pasquet is permitted to bargain with him on his terms for the mill. [126]

Again in December of the same year, Carroll wrote Pasquet regarding business at Bohemia and the question of the mill and Barney:

> Bohemia, postmarked Wilmington 18th is just rec'd. I depend on your acting in behalf of the mill, as for yourself, and hereby authorize you to bargain with George Eton, owner of a farm in the area of Bohemia and user of the Bohemia Manor Mill, according to the terms specified in yours; tho' I have never been able to understand the reason of the great reduction made in the rent of the mill for a few years past, it having been est[imated] before the £100. As to loading of the grind stones with plaster of Paris, I am totally ignorant of the cost of the operation, which for cost and materials will not probably exceed 8 or ten dollars: there must be wheat and corn enough in the mill to cover the expense, for whoever contracts to do the work, you will be pleased to require of him receipts for my examination. I have been calculating the profits of the mill since January, 1811 to this day, & have only received in corn and every other article $35..50c. This is the whole for work of the mill & Barney bindes [a term of local usage for the process of storing or preparing grain for shipment]. It is impossible to believe that justice has been done me, and rather than suffer imposition longer, I am not only willing but glad to rent out the property at $200 (Carroll was supported by this property, which belonged to the Corporation of the Clergy.) If you can discover whence the fraud proceeds, you will render me an essential service. You said, I think, that there remained in the mill about five bushels of wheat (the entire produce of one year, not a grain besides being accounted for)... I am sorry to give you this trouble of searching into the matter; but it is necessary to my existence. You do not say that Eton wants to employ Barney next year. He therefore must be hired out; perhaps he knows how to load

the grind-stones with plaster, which will save me some money. How can the race (Millrace, or duct leading water to mill wheel) be cleaned immediately: no one should be compelled to work in water at this season. As soon as possible, it shall be done by Barney or some hirelings. Barney has never hired for less than $80 p an: But being so far off; I shall abide by your agreement. You have been fav[ore]d. with Servts. hire [them]; if not paid, my credit will be lost. In that Statement, some blanks were left instead of charges with respect for instance to Barney, whilst serving you. Must I write to Mr. Coleman for the balance due to Corbally,? or will you collect it; none of Mr. Reynold's wood yet come (These persons are identified only by what is shown in this and similar letters to Pasquet. They were farmers or estate owners who negotiated with produce, the work of servants, and loans. Barney is more likely a slave than an indentured servant.) Did Barney raise no pork?[127]

Carroll again wrote Pasquet on January 18, 1814, penning a notation on the letter regarding slaves at Bohemia: Carroll says to note the contents about Rachel but particularly Phyllis, whom Pasquet had hired out, Joe, and Jacob.[128] On May 5/6, 1814, Carroll complained to Pasquet of a letter just received from him that dealt for the most part with the disposition of slaves at Bohemia. Carroll could not decide about James's family. At times Pasquet proposed selling them to make good [the Corporation's] claim on him. At other times he would have nothing to do with such a settlement. Carroll is of the opinion that Pasquet and Mr. [Francis] Neale [the agent] should work it out between them. He is surprised that nothing has yet been done about old Jack, after Pasquet's telling him that the bargain had been concluded for $130 or $120 and that Jack was gone to the neighborhood of Notthingham. Carroll would be much dissatisfied if the old man was turned out without any security for a home or his last year's wages. How was he to reconcile Pasquet's two reports?[129]

Pasquet had written that a buyer was interested in a daughter of a slave named James, but James' wife wanted her daughters to be sold for a term of years and wanted to go with them. Pasquet informed her he would have to get Carroll's consent: "She has so many children, and she has not done breeding," Pasquet explained. James also wanted his wife and children sold for a term of years but he himself wanted to stay with Pasquet. The affairs of another "Old Jack" were still not settled. Although Pasquet had wanted from $120 to $130 for him, he asked Carroll if $100 would be acceptable. Jack's son wanted to buy his father's freedom.[130]

Carroll was annoyed at Pasquet's indecision on James's family. He would leave the decision to Pasquet in consultation with Rev. Francis Neale, fiscal agent of the Corporation. "I shall be most dissatisfied," he added, "if the old man [Jack] has been turned out of doors, without having any security for a home or your obtaining the money for him."[131]

Carroll again expressed his concern for the slaves at Bohemia in a notation made on an unrelated letter dated May 29, 1814. "Fanny" and her family wish to be sold. Carroll offers his opinion [not given] and lists the members of the family.[132] In the ledger Carroll kept on the Bohemia plantation, he listed the names of

Fanny, age 48, and her nine children, two of whom had infants, and of Phyllis, 36, and her six children. Molly also had a son; her husband Harry was willing to buy them both in the spring of 1816 for $150. And there was Barney, 53, Joe, 45 and Dick, 32, but no mention of James (Fanny's husband) or Old Jack. Fanny's three oldest boys were estimated to be worth $350 each if sold for a term of twelve years. The next two if they served until 24, were valued at $120 and $60 respectively. The two oldest girls with infants, if they served for ten and twelve years respectively and their infants till age 24, were worth $200 each; the next girl, if she served eleven years, $150. No value was placed on an 18-month-old daughter. Only Fanny's children were so evaluated. Barney was to be manumitted after four years if it could be done legally. Later (19 September 1815) Carroll made provisions for the manumission of Joe after six years and Dick after eight.[133]

In the spring of 1815, the last year of his life, Carroll went to Bohemia to investigate affairs there for himself, including the status of the slaves, whose future disposition he wished to determine.[134] Concerned as he was with the care of the slaves at Bohemia, Carroll was just as concerned for the rest of the congregation there and Pasquet's failure to minister to them. On 15 July 1815 Carroll sent Pasquet a rather harsh letter dismissing him for having failed to serve properly the needs of his congregation. He wrote:

> Rev. Sir You must be sensible, that for some time past I have been made uneasy by the state, in which the congregation of Bohemia, if congregation it can be called, is now found. My general duty over all parts of the Diocess demands my vigilance; but more especially, the station, in which you now are. At my visitation before the last, in 1810, or 1811, I observed to you, that having received the profits of that estate, as my Episcopal maintenance, I took upon myself the obligation of allowing out of the estate a competent subsistence for a Clergyman to live there, & have spiritual charge of the Congregations dependant on it. You were continued in that place: but, as was intimated to you at the period of my former visitation, I was not satisfied of yr. having paid due attention to the Xtians; and constancy of divine service & Xtian instruction. I expostulated with you; you gave assurances of more diligence. On revisiting you this last spring, so far from observing any improvement, every thing connected with religion was in a more deplorable state; few Catholic families, even amongst the Laity, were more remiss in the sacred practices of Xtian piety; the black children were neglected; Mass was celebrated on Sunday to about half a dozen people; which had the appearance of its being done, merely thro human respects, because a chapel existed there. I abstain for the present from repeating the universal language of your parishioners, who have lost all confidence in you. Whilst you held out the idea of your immediate departure for France, it was my earnest wish to let you depart without censure or canonical investigation of the truth of charges preferred against you by your most respectable parishioners; [now] that you have declined going, I must provide, as much as in me lies, for the benefit of the faithful under my care, and protect the honour of religion, and credit of its sacred ministry. You will therefore choose elsewhere your habitation; for I cannot leave you any longer in the care of souls, who have been so much neglected. For their and your own sake, depart qui-

etly whenever you go; I expect that your Successor will be ready to go about the last of August or beginning of Sepr. Give all comfort in yr. power to James's wife &c. I am respectfully, Rev. Sir, Yr. most obedt. st. J. Abp of Baltre Carroll. The following passage, it will be more for your credit & tranquility, than to provoke an investigation; which would not altar my final determination; to employ you no longer, as my vicar in discharging me of the duty I owe to the altar faithful, who are or were formerly attached to the congregations at & in the neighborhood near Bohemia."[135]

Carroll had made a visit to Bohemia in May 1815 and another in September 1815, accompanied by Father Francis Neal. Regrettably Carroll did not keep a diary. Knowledge of his visitations to Catholics on the Eastern Shore must be gleaned from correspondence. Carroll mentions he visited Bohemia from June 26-30, 1812, in a letter to Pasquet and speaks of "my visitation before the last one (i.e. the one in 1812) in 1810 or 1811. There are no Confirmation records by Carroll in the archives of the Archdiocese of Baltimore nor in any of the early parish records. The only notation of his name to be found in the records of Bohemia is the following: "Margaret Craddock, buried at Bohemia in 1834, nee Ryland, first married John Thomas and after his death Benedict Craddock, converted by Abp. John Carroll."

On 3 October 1815 Carroll wrote Francis Neale: "You have been informed already, that all has been done there [Bohemia], which depended on me: but Jem's [James's] family are not disposed of; the purchasers for a term of years could be had; and in my own estimation I had settled that term, and its correspondent price." It was necessary, Carroll added, to have Francis Neale's concurrence on the terms.[136] Archbishop John Carroll died on December 3, 1815. Coadjutor – Archbishop Leonard Neale was his successor.

Neale was looking for a replacement for Pasquet in early 1816. He was eager to repair the damage of Pasquet's tenure at Bohemia.[137] Pasquet announced in the beginning of May, 1816, his intention of returning to France, but he lost his passage by falling sick at Georgetown and could not go before the Fall.[138] Neale agreed he should remain until September. Pasquet left America before August, 1816.[139]

NOTES FOR CHAPTER TWO

1. Joseph C. Cann, compiler and editor., *History of Saint Francis Xavier Church and Bohemia Plantation, Now Known As Bohemia* (Warwick, Maryland: Bohemia Historical Society, 1976) 8. Father Molyneux succeeded Father John Lewis at Bohemia at the end of February, 1788. Edward I. Devitt, S.J. "Bohemia," *Woodstock letters* 63 (June, 1913) 20
2. Philip S. Hurley, S.J., "Father Robert Molyneux, 1738-1808," *Woodstock letters* 67 (1938) 282. Thomas Hughes, S.J., *History of the Society of Jesus in North America, Colonial and Federal* (London: Longmans, Green, and Co., 1917) Text 2:698, Documents 1: No. 178. Born in Lancashire, England, on June 24, 1738, Molyneux was admitted to the Society of Jesus on September 7, 1757. He was an instructor in philosophy at Bruges, came to Maryland March 21, 1771, and was soon thereafter stationed by Carroll in Philadelphia. Thomas W. Spalding, *John Carroll Recovered, Abstracts of Letters and Other Documents Not Found in the John Carroll Papers, with the Assistance of Paul K. Thomas* (Baltimore, Maryland: Cathedral Foundation Press, 2000) 55n.1
3. John Tracy Ellis, *Catholics in Colonial America* (Baltimore, Maryland: Helicon Press, 1965) 409; William P. Tracey, "A Biographical Sketch of Father Robert Molyneux, S.J." *American Catholic Quarterly Review* 11 (1886) 140-153

4. James J. Walsh, "The Chevalier de la Luzerne," *Records of the American Catholic Historical Society* (hereafter *RACHS*) 16 (1905) 182; Hurley 278. Other occasions were Requiem Masses, one for a French officer who was drowned in the Schuylkill River and the other for the Spanish ambassador who succumbed in 1780. Until 1800 the government was by the Residence Act decreed to remain in Philadelphia temporarily while Washington-on-the-Potomac was being built.
5. Patrick Aloysius Jordon, S.J., "St. Joseph's Church, Philadelphia," *Woodstock letters* 2 (1875) 97-102
6. Wilfred Parsons, S.J., "Early Catholic Publishers of Philadelphia," *Catholic Historical Review* 24 (July, 1938) 143
7. John M. Daley, S.J., "Pioneer Missionary, Ferdinand Farmer, S.J., 1720-1786," *Woodstock Letters* 75 (1946), 211, Delaware Missions of Father Farmer. Molyneux's funeral sermon is published in *Woodstock letters* 13 (1884) 297-302
8. Father Molyneux started entries in the surviving sacramental registers at St. Joseph's Church, Philadelphia in 1787. Few Catholic churches in this country have registers that go back before 1790. Except in Pennsylvania, a policy of silence was necessitated by the fact that recorded administration of sacraments might be used as documentary evidence against the priest or the persons involved.
9. Devitt, "Bohemia" *Woodstock letters* 63 (1934) 20; Georgetown University Archives, (hereafter GUA) Maryland Province, Society of Jesus, Series 57, Correspondence 202-228, Molyneux at Bohemia writes May 26, 1788, on continuing progress on plans for Georgetown Academy. GUA. Special Collections Division, Box 571174, Washington, D.C. 20057. The searchable index to these Georgetown University Library Special Collections is found at this web address: http://www.library.georgetown.edu/dept/speccoll/indexlst.htm.
For the Jesuit Complex at Bohemia, this web address:
http://www.library.georgetown.edu/dept/speccoll/mi/mi}176.htm – Archives, Maryland Province, Society of Jesus BOHEMIA-DAY-BOOK-(1790-1871).
10. Cann 42; Charles H. A. Esling, "Catholicity in The Three Lower Counties, or, The Planting of the Church in Delaware," *RACHS* 1 (1884-1886) 145 - When Margaret Holahan, wife of Con Holahan, died, Father Molyneux preached at her funeral August 18, 1788. Her granddaughter who was present on the occasion reflected: "And I mind to have heard him say that she never let the poor go empty-handed from her door." Con Holahan died ten weeks later, on November 1, 1788. Both were buried beneath the trees at Coffee Run.
11. According to the 1790 Federal Census, Bohemia had 49 slaves, i.e., men, women and children. In 1800 there were 26 blacks and 46 whites on the plantation. The location of the July 4, 1790 marriage was the farm of William Matthews, *Worsall Manor*. From time to time there will be given a detailed genealogical account on names that appear in the sacramental records. The reader is urged to consult the index to gain a more cumulative record about individuals or families. THE MATTHEWS FAMILY was among Cecil County's first families and possessed significant properties, such as *Vulcan's Rest*, owned by Dr. Hugh Matthews, Jr., *Worsall Manor*, owned by Dr. William Matthews from 1790 to 1806, and *Bohemia* or *Milligan Hall*, owned by William Matthews Knight. The American progenitor of the family was *Dr. Hugh Matthews*, who was born in Ireland in the late 1600s. He died in Maryland in 1756. His will was probated in Cecil County on October 1, 1757, in which he freed two slaves and left the rest of his estate to the four daughters of his son Hugh, Jr., naming him executor. He gave his other son Patrick five shillings sterling. Cecil County Land Records, Elkton, Maryland, Liber 8, folio 456 (MD 4-5130) Vulcan's Rest, Deed James Douglas to Hugh Matthews, January 18, 1757. Historical Society of Delaware, Wilmington, Delaware, Notes on Vulcan's Rest, April 14, 1790, Hugh Matthews advertised his property for sale as follows: Three miles of Appoquinimink Hundred Landing, Cecil County, Maryland. His son, *Dr. Hugh Matthews, Jr.* was born in Philadelphia in 1712, died in June 1774, and is buried at Vulcan's Rest, a farm he owned which adjoins the Bohemia churchyard and plantation. The Historical Society of Cecil County (135 E. Main Street, Elkton) is in possession of some 100 pieces of correspondence of Dr. Hugh Matthews, Jr. His will was probated in 1774. The tomb board or pattern for the marble stone for his tomb was given to The Old Bohemia Historical Society by Mrs. Rachel Ullman of Bethlehem, Pennsylvania, a direct descendant, in 1967. The name of his first wife is not known. They had four daughters and four sons: (1) Bridget, unmarried, (2) Rebecca, unmarried, born 1755, died January 5, 1825, buried at Bohemia. Her will was written on October 30, 1824 and probated

January 26, 1825, (3) Susannah, who married Dr. James Scanlon. She died of consumption of March 30, 1791, and is buried at Worsall Manor, Sassafras Neck, the home of her brother Dr. William Matthews, (4) Catherine, who was born April 26, 1735 and was twin sister to Dr. William Matthews. She married John Leach Knight as his second wife in 1770, and was mother of Kitty Knight. She died on November 22, 1855, (5) *Doctor and Judge William Matthews* was born April 26, 1735. At the age of 41 in 1776, he joined the Bohemia Battalion and fought during the Revolutionary War – *Maryland Militia Muster Roll* 104, 121, 186, 193, 197, 202, 209, 230. From 1778 to 1780 he was a judge of the Cecil County Court, and a member of the General Assembly from 1786 to 1789. He was one of the six electors from Maryland when George Washington was unanimously chosen to be the first president on April 6, 1789. In the presidential election in October, 1796, Dr. Matthews was again the Federalist candidate for elector from the Sixth Congressional District of Maryland, which was composed of Cecil, Harford, and Kent counties. He defeated his opponent on the Republican ticket, Gabriel Christie, and cast his vote for John Adams as the second president. Edward C. Papenfuse *et al, A Biographical Dictionary of the Maryland Legislature 1635-1789* (Baltimore: The Johns Hopkins University Press, 1979-1985) 2:583. In the 1790 U.S. Census, William Matthews is reported as a doctor in North Sassafras Hundred. In 1796 he purchased Worsall Manor. In 1806 he deeded Worsall Manor to his step-brother Richard Davis, who owned Worsall Manor until 1819. Dr. William Matthews' will was probated on February 25, 1808. It mentions his deceased brothers James and Arthur, and makes bequeathals to his sisters Catherine and Rebecca, and to his brother Hugh, to nephews James Knight, William Knight, to his niece Kitty Knight, to Dr. James Scanlon and his sister Catherine, to the three children of his nephew John Knight (Edward, Caroline, and John) and to Patrick Edwards, a schoolmaster in Georgetown, Maryland. Executors of his will were William Knight and Doctor Scanlon. Dr. William Matthews loaned the Jesuits enough money to purchase the plantation at White Clay Creek, New Castle County, Delaware in 1772. Georgetown University Archives, 6-3B, carton 12, folder 12A, Maryland Province – "I borrowed 200 pds. from Dr. William Matthews and paid for house chapel at Letitia Manor." Thomas Hughes, *History of the Society of Jesus in North America* (New York: Longmans Green and Co., 1907-1917 Documents 1:296, No. 87, No. 178 N, (6) Arthur Matthews, unmarried, served in the Maryland Legislature, died before 1807, (7) James Matthews, unmarried, served in the Bohemia Battalion in the Revolutionary War – Henry C. Peden, Jr., *Revolutionary Patriots of Cecil County, Maryland* (Westminister, Md.: Family Line Publications, 1991) 70, *Maryland Militia Muster Roll* 38, 187, 203, Cann, *Saint Francis Xavier and Bohemia Plantation* 238-240: James Matthews was shot by Richard Key Heath in a duel, and was buried with a sermon by Rev. Francis Beeston, S.J. on January 18, 1792, at Worsall Manor, (8) Hugh Matthews III, unmarried, died 1809, will proved 1809, leaves property to Mrs. Margaret Morton, for her two sons, appointing her trustee of the estate (Vulcan's Rest). Dr. Hugh Matthews, Jr. married as his second wife the widow of Joseph Davis, who had two daughters and one son, Richard Davis. There were two other daughters, Sarah and Elizabeth, who were probably the children of this marriage to Mrs. Davis.

12. Thomas O'Brien Hanley, *The John Carroll Papers* (Notre Dame, Indiana: University of Notre Dame Press, 1976) (hereafter *JCP*) "Synod Report"1:526
13. John Gilmary Shea, *Memorial of the First Centenary of Georgetown College, D.C., Comprising a History of Georgetown University* (New York: P.F. Collier, 1891) 12-13. William Gaston of North Carolina, a boy of thirteen and future associate justice of the state's supreme court, was the first student. John M. Daley, *Georgetown University: Origin and Early Years* (Washington: Georgetown University Press, 1957) 68 - The second student was Philemon Charles Wederstrandt from the Eastern Shore of Maryland. Through 1791 and early 1792 Gaston and Wederstrandt were joined by more and more classmates. Philemon Wederstrandt at the age of 18 received his warrant as a midshipman in the United States Navy. In 1808 he received command of the *Argus*. He served in Tripolitan wars and assisted in the apprehension of Aaron Burr - Isaac Edward Morse, "Notes for a Life of P.C. Wederstrandt" Catholic University of America Manuscript 311.5. Ellis, *Documents* 1:169 - No. 54 – "Beginnings of the First Catholic College in the United States, 1789" - Subscribers from the Eastern Shore of Maryland: John Blake, Charles Blake, Francis Hall, William Matthews, and John Tuite.
14. Hurley 67:286

15. Hanley 1:55; Thomas Hughes, S.J., *History of the Society of Jesus in North America*. Documents 2:820; AAB 2-C-Z, Thaddeus Brzozowski to Bishop Carroll, February 22, 1806. The former Jesuits of Maryland, on December 23, 1792, won from the Maryland legislature an act that created a Corporation for the Roman Catholic Clergy of the state. The corporation was to be a board elected by representatives of the clergy. In the corporation was vested title to all former Jesuit estates as well as to Georgetown College. Those elected first to the board of the Corporation included Robert Molyneux.
16. Father Molyneux was rector of Georgetown College from October 1, 1806, to December 8, 1808. Daley, *Georgetown* 141; Hurley 67:283; Georgetown University Archives, Maryland Province, Society of Jesus, Series 57, Correspondence 202-228, folder 203, R1-10, John Carroll to Robert Molyneux, Baltimore, February, 1807, Carroll expresses his desire to keep Georgetown Academy open; John Carroll to Robert Molyneux, Baltimore, July 1, 1808 - regarding sparse attendance at Georgetown; Carroll to Molyneux, Baltimore, September 19, 1808, on the unfitness of Georgetown for the Jesuit novitiate.
17. Daley, *Georgetown* 141
18. Hurley 67:290; The Will of Robert Molyneux, S.J., *Woodstock letters* 15 (1886) 186
19. Hurley 67:290-291: Maréchal's estimate of Molyneux in Latin: "Erat enim vir humilitate ac mira morum suavitate conspicuus." – "He was a man conspicuous for his humility and wonderful grace of manner."
20. Cann 8; Hughes, Text 2:700. In his diary, under the date of July 15, 790, Beeston wrote: "Mr. Molyneux left Bohemia for Portobacco. I accompanied him as far as Mr. Bolton's [St. Joseph's, Talbot County]." GUA, Maryland Province, Society of Jesus, Series 21 folder 103-W5-W8, Bohemia Manor Land Documents, concerns number of acres at Bohemia, power of attorney from Robert Molyneux, S.J., to Francis Beeston, S.J.
21. Devitt, "Bohemia" *Woodstock letters* 63 (1934) 23; Annabelle Melville, *John Carroll of Baltimore, Founder of the American Hierarchy* (New York: Charles-Scribner's Sons, 1955) 101. In February 1786, William Strickland at Liege wrote to Carroll: "Mr. Beeston has been a very perceivable man at the academy and, I doubt not, will prove a valuable recruit to your mission," Catholic University Transcripts, Strickland to Carroll, February 25, 1786.
22. GUA, Maryland Province, Society of Jesus, Series One, Bohemia, Cecil County, Maryland: a significant diary, ledger or record book, kept first and best by Father Beeston, July 1, 1790 (hereafter *Beeston Diary*). Beeston kept the diary till the day of his departure from Bohemia. Others continued the ledger, sometimes in French. AAB, *Bohemia Plantation Book 1790-1796*: Father Beeston's carefully kept records of Plantation Expenses (page one) July 1, 1790 to (page 21) May 16, 1793. Cann 167 – In a leather bound book at Georgetown University, marked "Record of Bohemia" 1790, made by the Rev. Francis Beeston, resident priest of Bohemia from July 1, 1790 to May 1793, were found the following entries: February 12, 1791 – Hands cutting wood for brick kiln; February 22, 1791 – 20 of my negroes innoculated. I sent part of these who were innoculated to the quarter near Warwick, and the rest to the quarter at St. Inigos. Here we have definite evidence of the measures taken to protect their health in the days when such precautions were very rarely administered anywhere and today's new medicines were undreamed of.; July 27, 1792 – paid for making a grey coat for Dick: 4 shillings; May 11, 1792 – paid cash for making negroes clothes: 8 shillings and 4 pence. Archives of the Diocese of Wilmington (hereafter ADW), *Burial Register of St. Francis Xavier, Warwick, Maryland, 17546-1963, A Register of the Deceased Catholics of the Congregation of Bohemia, Cecil County, Maryland, and Other Congregations Depending Thereon*: The volume begins September 10, 1790 – Rachel Ward, wife of William Ward, in the burial ground at Bohemia, died near Warwick, Maryland; 1790-10-17 Boils, Eleanor, Wife of Robert Boils of Kent Co., Md.; 1790-11-12 Connor, Charles, Died at Warwick, Md., 1791-1-20 Lee, Sarah, Died at Sassafras Neck, Md.; 1791-3-8 Reynolds, Mary, Died at New Castle, Del.; 1791-3-14 Knott, Edward, Died in New Castle, Del.; 1791-3-30 Scanlon, Ann, Died at the home of Dr. Matthews. Buried near his house, Worsell Mannor.; 1791-5-24 Prudence, Slave of Rev. F. Beeston of the Plantation.; 1791-5-31 Wright, George, Died in New Castle Co., Del. Buried in the family _?_; 1791-6-26 Maguire, Wife of George Maguire of Sassafras Neck, Md.; 1791-6-26 Gibbin, Rachel, Widow, near Bohemia; 1791-6-26 Knott, Catherine, Died in New Castle, Del; 1791-11-28 Cain Roger, Died at New Castle, Del. Native of Ireland; 1792-1-16 Matthews, James, Shot and killed by Richard Heath, his remains were interred on the 18th near

the Worsell Mannor mansion of his brother, Dr. William Matthews in Sassafras Neck, Md. A sermon was preached by Rev. Francis B. Beeston. He was killed in New Castle, Del.; 1792-1-21 Brady, James, Died in Kent Co., Md.; 1792-2-2 Lee, Barbara, Died at Georgetown, Md.; 1792-2-19 Irvin, James Caldwell, Head of Little Bohemia; 1792-5-13 Manseur, Christiana, Died in Queen Anne Co., Md. Buried in the burial ground of his late residence.; 1792-9-3 Robinson, Edward, Died at Duck Neck, Crossroads, New Castle Co., Del. Buried at Bohemia; 1792-12-15 Erwin, Charles, Son of William and Hannah. Died in New Castle Co., Del. Buried in Family Burial Ground of his late residence.; 1792-12-15 Heverin, Charles, Son of William and Hannah of New Castle Co., Del. Buried in family lot.; 1793 A.O.D. Field Stone. 1793-7-17 O'Donald, Alice, Head of Little Bohemia; 1793-9-30 Pennington, John Rigs, Son of John and Eleanor Rigs, died in Warwick, Md.; 1793-10-10 Gribben, Henry; Son of James and Sarah of Warwick, Md.; 1794-1-1 Craddock, Francis, Son of Daniel Craddock and Elizabeth O'Donald of Sassafras Neck, Md.; 1794-2-10 Kelegum, Morris, Died in Cecil Co., Md.; 1794-2-17 MacFall, Anna, Wife of Stephen, died in Warwick, Md.; 1794-3-15 O'Conar, Wm. Henry, Death "contessed by signs" at Warwick, Md.; 1794-5-16 Clerk, Sarah, Daughter of Bergaman & Theresa Clerk at the head of the Sassafras River; 1794-6-11 Nugent, Mola, Wife of Peter Nugent, Cecil Co., Md.; 1794-8-10 Wise, Frederick, Shot in the forest of his uncle at Duck Creek, Smyrna, Del.; 1794-12-9 Nowland, Jesse, Died in Sassafras Hundred, Md.; 1794-12-21 Nowland, Bridget, Died at Bohemia Plantation; 1794-3-20 Bayards, Elizabeth, Daughter of Jacob and Ann New Castle Co., Del.; 1794-12-9 Boraling, Mary Ann, of the Plantation.; 1794-12-21 Burns, Thomas, Irishman of Warwick, Md.; 1795-11-2 Biggers, Daniel, Son of David and Athea, of Warwick, Md.; 1795-12-27 Burk, William, of Sassafras Neck, Md.; 1795-2-3 Carey, Jermiah, of New Castle, Del; 1795-5-1 Reynolds, Mary, Wife of John, buried in family burial ground in New Castle Co., Del.; 1795-8-10 Gaffard, Rachael, Died in March, Queen Anne Co., Md. Prayers said at grave in Queen Anne Co.; 1795-10-10 Cabby, Mary, Dau. Of Richard & Mary Cabby; 1795-10-12 Severs, Peter, Died and was buried in Queen Anne Co., Md. Mr. Rev. J. Tessier said prayers at grave.; 1795-11-5 Gribbin, Matthew, Son of Henry & Sarah of Warwick, Md.; 1796-1-8 Craddock, Elizabeth, Wife of Daniel Craddock of Sassafras Neck, Md.; 1796-1-13 Cassy, Mary, Near Warwick, Md.; 1796-1-21 Fullam, Walter, Died in Dragans Neck about 64 years old. Buried at Bohemia. (Note: After this entry the following notation was written). On the 21st of January in the year of our Lord one thousand seven hundred and ninety six, Mr. Walter Fullam departed this life. He left to the church of Bohemia a legacy of 100 pounds and by way of grateful remembrance, it has been determined by the Rt. Rev. Dr. Carroll that, on the day above mentioned, a Mass will be said for the benefactor's soul by the priest living on the State of Bohemia, every year forever.; 1796-1-21 Dermott, Anne, Wife of Charles, Fredericktown, Md.; 1797-3-14 Davey, John, The Forest, New Castle Co., Del.; 1796-3-14 Watkins, Samuel, School Master in the "Forest" in New Castle Co., Del.; 1796-3-21 Crout Burnice, of Kent Co., Md.; 1796-8-17 Mullen, Thomas, Died in Middletown, Del.; 1796-8-22 Causell, E.C., near Warwick, Md.; 1796-9-1 Ryan, Mary, Died near Warwick, Md.; 1796-9-18 Nowland, Stephen, Son of Thomas & Mary, Kent Co., Md.; 1796-9-20 Heverin, Sarah, Wife of Charles, died in New Castle Co., Del Buried in family lot.; 1796-11-2 Martin, James, Died in Warwick, Md.; 1796-11-11 Riggs, Daniel, Died at Warwick, Md.; 1796-11-30 Robinson, Peggy, Died at Warwick, Md.; 1797-1-20 Sala Lee, Sassafras Neck; 1798-1-13 Nicks NED, Slave of Mr. Nowland; 1798-2-28 Wright, John, Died in New Castle Co., Del.; 1798-8-2 Craddock, Daniel, of Sassafras Neck, Md.; 1798-8-21+Faure, Rev. Etienne, Buried close to north end of church. Grave head begin at east side of border of the Epistle window. France; 1798-11-10 Johns, Molly, Died at Knoxtown, Del.; 1798-12-24 Tatler, Robena, Died at Bohemia Neck; 1799-1-18 O'Donald, Catherine, Died at Sassafras Neck; 1799-7-14 Hogan, Jermiah, Native of Ireland; 1806-3-21+Whelan, Rev. Charles (O.S.F.C.), Age 65, born in Ireland, Buried close to the grave of Rev. Faure, at the north end of the church at Bohemia.; 1807-5-3 Delaney, Maurice, 1807-10-22 Delapoolee, L. Clandmore, died at Bohemia; 1807-10-23 Ciety, Sylvester, Died in the forest of his uncle Sylvester Nowland.; 1808- Reynolds, Jermiah, Age 75; 1810-1 O'Donald, Barbara, Wife of James; 1810-5-24 Craddock, Daniel son of Daniel Craddock; 1810-5-24 Reynolds, William, Accidentally killed self; 1811-2-5 Vincum, Joseph Stephen; 1810-11-24 Reynolds, Jermiah, 1811-3-10 Heverin, Charles, of New Castle Co., Del.; 1811-3-29 McCredy, Bridget, 1812-1-25 Harling, Mary, 1812-4-27 Craddock, Mary, wife of William; 1814-7-20 Durand, J.G.E., Age 33; 1814-10-15 Durand, Theresa, Age 50; 1815-3-26 Knight, William, Age 65;

CHRISTIAN BURIAL OF SLAVES AT BOHEMIA – March 24, 1791 – At the priest's plantation at the head of Little Bohemia, died Prudence (a negro slave). She was buried in the church yard on said plantation; December 26, 1791 – On the priest's plantation, at the head of Little Bohemia, died Frances, a negro child, aged 2 years, daughter of Robert and Henny, negro slaves of Rev. Francis Beeston. He was buried the next day in the church yard; 1791-11-26 Frances, child of Robert & Hetty. Died at the Plantation.; 1792-3-5 Jonathan, "Free Mulotto" son of Perry and Henethea "Dr. Matthews" died at the home of the doctor.; 17-4-23 Hannah, At the head of Little Bohemia, died of a consumption, Hannah, negro slave of Rev. Francis Beeston. She was buried the next day in the Catholic church yard at the head of Little Bohemia.; 1793-1-7 Robert, Slave of Daniel Craddock, died Sassafras Neck.; 1793-12-17 Isaac, Slave of the Seminary in Baltimore, died at the Plantation.; 1793-11- A. Brown, Widow, slave, died at the Plantation.; 1794-3-30 Beak, Son of Patrick & Molly, slaves of Rev. Amb. Marechal, died at the Plantation.; 1794-11-28 Venus, Slave of Dr. William Matthews, buried in the burial ground of Dr. W. Matthews at Sassafras Neck.; 1795-3-15 Betsy, Dau. Of Dilly, slave, married to Slate. Died on the Plantation.; 1795-10-4 William, Son of William & Ester, salves of Mr. Milligan. Died on the farm.; 1794-11-8 Slak, Prayers were said at the grave. He died a month ago in Queens Anne's County, buried in Queen Anne County, Md.; 1795-11-27 Ned, Son of Ned and Rachael, slaves of Dr. Matthews. Rev. Tesseur said the prayers. He died on his farm. Buried in Bohemia.; 1796-1-17 Susie, Dau. Of Sale of Doris. Slaves of Dr. Wm. Matthews of Worsell Manor. Buried there.; 1796-3-4 John, Slave of Nowland, died at Sassafras Neck.; 1796-3-14 Kate, "Negro" woman, Sassfras Neck.; 1796-6-9 Joseph, Free Negro, has belonged to Plantation.; 1796-8-4 Stephen, Slav, died on Plantation.; 1796-8-17 Chims, Slave of Boehmia Plantation. Died at the Plantation, Thorough Fair Neck. Buried at his mother" place.; 1796-1-23 Samuel, Son of Delahan, died in Warwick, Md.; 1796-5-27 Anna, Dau. Of Dilly & Hamy. Died at Bohemia.; 1796-2-8 Margaret, Slave of Mr. Biddle, died at Sassafras Neck.; 1798-2-28 Ned, Slave of Mr. Millighan the head of Bohemia; 1807-10-18 Ralph, Slave of the Corporation, died at Bohemia.; 1808-10-12 Betty, Slave of the Plantation, died at Bohemia.; 1809- Hannah, Wife of John, Died at Bohemia.; 1810-7-17 Edward, Slave of Shop John Carroll buried at Bohemia.; 1811-3-15 Mary, Old Miller Ralph's wife buried at Bohemia.; 1815-12-28 Rachel & Joseph, Slaves, Age 76 and 26

23. Devitt "Bohemia" 63 *Woodstock letters* (1934) 21
24. *Heads of Families at the First Census of the United States taken in the year 1790: Maryland* (Washington, D.C., 1907)
25. Devitt "Bohemia" *Woodstock letters* 63 (1934) 24; Devitt, "Bohemia," *RACHS* 24 (1913) 119
26. Joseph George Rosengarten, *French Colonists and Exiles in the United States* (Philadelphia: J.B. Lippincott Co., 1907) 89
27. Devitt, "Bohemia" 63:22; Cann 40; Archives of Diocese of Wilmington (hereafter ADW), 8 Old Church Road (at Route 100); enter from St. Joseph on the Brandywine Church parking lot), Greenville, DE 19807, mailing address: PO Box 2030, Wilmington, DE 19899): Sacramental Records St. Francis Xavier, Warwick, Maryland: Record Group 49. *May 27, 1792* - New Castle County, Delaware: Father deBarth baptized Elizabeth Culley, born August 2, 1791, of William Culley and his wife Rebecca, both Catholics. Sponsors were Samuel Watkinson and his wife Mary, both Catholics. *May 28, 1792* - New Castle County, Delaware, baptized Hannah Reynolds born March 29, 1792, of Benjamin Reynold's, Catholic, and his wife, Rachel, Protestant. Godmother Sarah Cole, Catholic. *May 28, 1792* - New Castle County, Delaware - baptized Amelia Beck, born April 7, 1791, of Samuel Beck and Amelia, his wife. Godfather Jacob Reynolds. For background on these families, see Thomas J. Peterman, *Catholics in Colonial Delmarva*: (Devon, Pennsylvania: Cooke Publishing Company, 1996): Culley 233, Watkinson 265, Reynolds 264, Cole 263, Beck 216. Clifford Pryor, *The Forest of Appoquinimink* (Milford, Delaware: Shawnee Printing Co., 1975) 55. Amelia, daughter of Samuel and Amelia Beck, died in childhood.
28. Devitt, "Bohemia" *Woodstock letters* 63 (1934): 23; Hughes, Documents 1:346; Francis Edward Tourscher, *The Hogan Schism and Trustee Problems in St. Mary's Church, Philadelphia 1820 - 1829* (Philadelphia: Peter Reilly Co., 1930) 78
29. Jules Foin, "Rev. Louis Barth, A Pioneer Missionary and an Administrator of the Diocese of Philadelphia," *RACHS* 2 (1889) 36; Hughes, Documents 1:882.
30. First American Catholic Bible, published 1790 by Mathew Carey, Philadelphia. List of

31. Subscribers. Copy is available in the Archives of the Diocese of Wilmington.
31. Peter Guilday, *The Life and Times of John Carroll, Archbishop of Baltimore, 1735-1815* (New York: The Encyclopedia Press, 1922) 1:7; Hanley 1:526. In this session the synod adopted the beautiful prayer which John Carroll had composed for the civil authorities. John Tracy Ellis, *Documents of American Catholic History* (Washington, Delaware: Michael Glazier, 1987) 1:174 No. 57 – "John Carroll's Prayer for Civil Authorities, November 10, 1791."
32. Cann 39; ADW, Bohemia Sacramental Registers, Baptisms at Bohemia: *October 3, 1790* - Andrew Looby, age 6 years, son of Patrick Looby, Catholic, and his wife, Elizabeth, Protestant. Godfather was Peter Watkinson. *Catholic marriages at St. Francis Xavier Church performed by Father Beeston: August 15, 1790* - between Holland Webb, widower, and Catherine Fieter, widow. Witnesses were Edward Councill, Daniel Carney, and Sarah Carney; *September 15, 1790* - between Samuel Peter Watkinson and Mary Whittington from New Castle County, Delaware. Witnesses were Solomon Jones, Benjamin Webb, and Nehemiah Webb; *October 17, 1790* - between John Carty and Elizabeth Nowland. Witnesses were Daniel Craddock, Hannah McDonald, and Edward C. Councill; *February 2, 1791*- between Hugh Grant and Mary Marshall. Witnesses were Mary Nugent, Daniel Craddock, and James O'Donato; *February 27, 1791* - between Robert Irwin and Catherine Nugent. Witnesses were Hugh Grant, Mary Grant, and Hannah McDermott; *April 8, 1792* - between James Dailey, Protestant, and Mary Gafford Catholic. Witnesses were Samuel Gafford and Jacob Gafford; *June 27, 1792* - between Charles McDermott and Hannah Nugent. Witnesses were Thomas Dixon and Mary Grant; *November 11, 1792* - between Pierce Neal and Mary Neide. Witnesses were John Neide, Michael Neide, Thomas McLaughlin and William Ellis; *December 30, 1792* - between Daniel Craddock and Elizabeth O'Donald, Witnesses were Alice O'Donald, James O'Donald and John O'Donald.
33. Devitt, "Bohemia" *Woodstock Letters* 63 (1934): 21
34. F. Edward Wright, compiler, Vital Records of the Jesuit Missions of the Eastern Shore 1760-1800 (Silver Springs, Maryland: Family Line Publications, 1986) 33 – Councell, James; bapt 1789 Jan 30; Priest: Francis Beeston; Councell, Mary; bapt 1790 Dec 26; Patterson, Alexander; about 4 yrs of age when bapt on Jul 4 1790; father: James Patterson (prot.), mother: Catherine Patterson; spon: James O'Donald, Alice O'Donald; Priest: Robert Molyneux; "Bohemia"; Samson and Flora; negroes from Guinea; bapt Jul 4 1790; slaves of Wm. Matthews, Esq."; spon: Isaac, Rachael; "sponsors, slaves of Rev. Francis Beeston" "Bohemia"; Agnes; b Apr 30th; bapt Jul 11 1790; father: "John a negro slave of Mr. Lloyd," mother: Dina, a negro slave of Wm Nielson"; spon: "Joseph – a free negro," Jenny – a negro slave of Mr. Lloyd"; Priest: Francis Beeston; "Bohemia"; Fife, Elizabeth; Elkton," b Sep 12; bapt Aug 13 1790; father: James Fife, Mother: Grace Fife; spon: Nicholas Veal, Cath. Veal; "Elkton" Parents and sponsors all Catholic. ADW, Bohemia Sacramental Records, Father Francis Beeston baptized, "in the forest" of Appoquinimink, New Castle County, Delaware: *July, 1790* - William Reynolds, born 1787, of Benjamin Reynolds, Catholic, and his wife Rachel Sponsors were William and Mary Reynolds, Catholics. *August 22, 1790* - Catherine Reynolds, born June 1790, of William Reynolds and Mary, both Catholics. Sponsors were James Reynolds and Mary Reynolds, Catholics. *October 24, 1790* - Jane Weldon, an adult. Godfather was Samuel Peter Watkinson, Catholic. *October 24, 1790* - Elizabeth Heverin, born April 13, 1790, of Charles Heverin, Catholic and wife, Alize, Catholic. The child had already received private baptism. Supplied ceremonies. Sponsors were Thomas Nowland, Catholic, and Teresia Crouch, Catholic. *September 5, 1791* - Abraham and Samuel Watts, twins, born August 5, 1791, of James Watts and Anne, his wife, both Protestants. *September 22, 1791* - Anne Webb, born August 18, 1791, of Holland Webb and Cornelia, his wife, both Catholics. Sponsors were Jacob Reynolds and Catherine Reynolds, daughter of Jacob, both Catholic. *October 23, 1791* - Sarah Heverin, born October 22, 1791, of Charles and Sarah Heverin, Catholic. Sponsors were Benjamin Reynolds and Sarah Bowman, Catholics. *December 29, 1791* - Saloman Cole, born November 21, 1791, of Peregrine Cole and Sarah his wife, both Catholic. Sponsors were Jacob Reynolds and Sarah, his wife, both Catholic. *March 13, 1791* - James Reynolds, born January 11, 1791, of Nicholas Reynolds, Catholic, and Elizabeth Farmer, Protestant. Sponsors were Jacob Reynolds and Catherine Knott, both Catholics. *May 20, 1791* - Jacob and William Bourke, twins, born of Thomas Bourke, Catholic, and Elizabeth, his wife. Sponsors were Edward Fitzgerald and Elizabeth Heverin, both Catholics. *May 22, 1791* - Samson Heverin, born November 6, 1790, of Abraham and Elizabeth

Heverin, both Catholic Sponsors were Benjamin Crouch, Catholic, and Elizabeth Bourke, Protestant. *August 28, 1791* - Sarah Reynolds, born May 17, 1790, of Benjamin Reynolds, Catholic, and Rachel, his wife, Protestant. Sponsors were Peter Nugent and Mary Reynolds, both Catholic. *April 22, 1792* - Stephen Heverin, born March 9, 1792, of Isaac Heverin and Elizabeth, his wife. Sponsors were Charles and Alice Heverin. *April 22, 1792* - John Reynolds, born December 29, 1791, of Nicholas Reynolds, Catholic, and Elizabeth, his wife, Protestant. Sponsors were John Reynolds and Barbara Heverin. *November 22, 1792* - Nathan Wright, born October 5, 1792, of John and Mary Wright, Catholics. Sponsors were Holland Webb and Mary Watkinson, Catholics. *December 15, 1792* - James Simpson, age 9 years, born of Isaac and Margaret Simpson. Godmother was Alice Heverin. *December 15, 1792* - Hannah Bowman, born June 25, 1792, of Charles Bowman and Sarah, his wife. Godmother was Rachel Wright. *June 4, 1793* - Temperance Cook, born December 12, 1792, of John and Mary Cook. Sponsors were William Reynolds Sr. and Sarah Reynolds, wife of Jacob Reynolds. *June 4, 1793* - Sarah Wheeler, born January 2, 1793, of John and Ruth Wheeler. Sponsors were Mary and Samuel Watkinson. *June 4, 1793* - Isaac Beck, born October 17, 1792, of Samuel Beck and his wife, Amelia Beck, Catholics Sponsors were Holland Webb and Catherine Reynolds, daughter of Jacob, Catholics. *June 4, 1793* - Ann Reynolds, born November 15, 1792, of William and Mary Reynolds. Sponsors were Holland Webb and Elizabeth Reynolds, daughter of Jacob, Catholics. For background of these families, consult Peterman, *Catholics in Colonial Delmarva*: Reynolds 210, 211, 223, 264; Heverin 210, 212, 214, 216, 264, 265; Cole 214, 216; Weldon 214, 215, 263; Burke 294. One Marriage by Father Beeston at Appoquinimink Forest: January 23, 1793 - between Thomas Scott and Ruth Edwards. Witnesses were Jacob Reynolds, Solomon Jones, and Peregrine Cole.

35. ADW, Bohemia, Records - Baptisms by Rev. Francis Beeston at Kent County, Maryland: *April 12, 1791* - Robert Holmes, born October 13, 1790, of Robert Holmes (Calvinist) and Celia, his wife, Catholic. Sponsors were Daniel Conroy, Catholic, and Sarah Perkins, Protestant. *November 25, 1791* - Francis Vechel Severs born December 13, 1790, of Peter Severs, and Margaret, his wife, both Catholic. Godmother was Ann Neill, Catholic.

36. ADW, Bohemia Records: Marriage by Father Beeston at Elkton: *August 13, 1790* - between Nicholas Vosh and Catherine Nowland. Witnesses were Michael Nowland, Hugh Grant, and Hannah McDermott. THE NOWLAND FAMILY: The first of this branch of the family to come to America from Ireland was Desmond Nowland, who in 1680 settled in Cecil County near where the Jesuit Bohemia Mission was established in 1704. He had a son Darby, who bought Woodbridge, part of Worsall Manor, and sold Woodbridge to James Heath who sold it to the Jesuits in 1721. Richard, James, Mary, and Henry Nowland are the earliest known descendants of Darby Nowland. Henry Nowland died in 1746. Cecil County, Maryland Wills, Elkton, Maryland, Will of Henry Nowland. Liber B.B. Folio 20: "I Henry Nowland of Cecil County Province of Maryland. Planter. To brother Richard Nowland etc, To brother James Nowland etc, To sister Mary, wife of Matthew Hodgson of Cecil County, Sadler, etc., Appoints said sister Mary and Matthew Hodgson Executors. Dated 29th, May 1739. In presence of John Herbert, Mich, Wallace, William Crage, Henry Nowland. Probated 13th, day of June 1746." Dennis Nowland, who died in 1756, married Elizabeth. Cecil County Courthouse, Elkton, Maryland. Will of Dennis Nowland. Liber B.B. Folio 152: I Dennis Nowland of Cecil County, Province of Maryland, Planter. To son Silvester Nowland etc, To my daughter Rachel Craddock, etc, To my daughter Ann Lilly, Etc, To my granddaughter Christiana Lilly etc, To my son-in-law John Lilly, etc, To my son James Nowland Plantation I now live on it being a part of Woodbridge, Bandenbridge, Weselmanor, Coxes Forest and part of Vulcans Rest. To grandson Dennis Nowland son of my son James Nowland etc, Son James Nowland to take good care of his brother Stephen. Appoints son James Nowland and Joseph Lilly Executors. Dated September 12th, 1751. In presence of John Jackson. Barnet Vanhorn. Edward Rumsey, Jr, Denis Nowland. Probated 15th, January 1756. Daniel Nowland was born 1715, Stephen Nowland was born 1719, Rachel Nowland was born 1719 and married a Craddock. James Nowland was born 1721. Ann Nowland was born 1725 and married Joseph Lilly. Thomas Nowland was born in 1724 and died 1760. Cecil County, Maryland. Wills. Will of Thomas Nowland. Liber B.B. Folio 191: "I Thomas Nowland of Cecil County, Province of Maryland. To wife Elizabeth Nowland etc, To Alexander Beard etc, Appoints wife Elizabeth Nowland Executrix. Dated 29th, May 1760. In presence of Mary Lowe. Wm, Bordley. WM, Pearce. Thomas Nowland. Probated August 23rd, 1760. Will

of Daniel Nowland. Liber B.B. Folio 297: "I Daniel Nowland of Cecil County, Province of Maryland. To my grandson Benjamin Nowland the son & Augustine Nowland, and John Nowland his brother etc, To daughter Hannah Nowland etc, To son Benjamin Nowland Green Spring, lying in Cecil County at Head of Sassfras River. To sons Benjamin Nowland and Ephriam Nowland personal estste. Appoints son Benjamin Nowland Executor. Dated 5th, December 1766. In presence of Hugh Matthews. Wm, Savin. Thomas McDonough. Daniel Nowland. Probated 30th, day of March 1768." Michael Nowland died at age 40 on March 12, 1826. James Nowland's children were Daniel who died in 1807 and Dennis (1771-1807). Sylvester Nowland died on May 6, 1790. Will of Silvester Nowland. Liber E.E. Folio 239: "I Silvester Nowland of Cecil County, Maryland. To son Jessee Nowland etc, To son Thomas Nowland etc, To son Silvester Nowland Land in Kent Co., Md, To daughter Bridget Council etc, To daughter Sarah Nowland etc, To daughter Elizabeth Nowland etc, Appoints wife Sarah Nowland Executor. Dated 6th, May 1790. In presence of John Mercer, Joseph Pennington, and James Fulton. Silvester Noland. Probated 22nd, June 1790." Dennis Nowland married Mary Mansfield Foard (1770-1844). Dennis James Nowland died July 26, 1807. Mary Nowland was godmother to George Heverin at Baptism at Bohemia May 11, 1817. Sponsor was Sarah Nowland. John Lusby and Sarah Nowland were married August 12, 1817. Witness was Thomas Nowland. Cecil County, Maryland Wills. Will of Dennis James Nowland. Liber F.F. Folio 479: "I Dennis James Nowland of Cecil County, Maryland. To wife Mary one third of real and personal estate. The rest of my property shall be under the direction of my wife for the support and education of all my children, but, should she marry, a guardian or guardians are to be appointed for my children. My land is not to be sold until my youngest child comes of age. Appoints wife Mary Executrix. Dated 25th, July 1807. In presence of William Matthews, James Scanlon, William Dowdall, Dennis James Nowland. Probated October 2nd, 1807." Dennis Nowland's children were Agustus Nowland who married Mary J. Sluyter (1817-1885), and John Nowland who died in 1815. Cecil County, Maryland, Wills, Will of John Nowland. Liber G.G. Folio 506: I John Nowland of Cecil County, Maryland. To wife Lydia Nowland etc, The remainder of estate to be equally divided between among my children, excepting Richard Simpsons wife and Francis Gillespies wife, I allow seventy-five dollars less to them than the other children. Appoints Richard Simpson and William Nowland Executors. Dated 175h, February 1815. In presence of Jno, Williams, Richard Lamborn, James Fulton, John Nowland. Probated June 15th, 1815. Mary his wife died 1844. Cecil County, Maryland. Wills. Will of Mary Nowland. Liber B. Folio 235: "I Mary Nowland of Bohemia Manor, Cecil County, Maryland. To my granddaughter Mary Matthews Nowland, daughter of my deceased son Henry Nowland, etc, To my grandson Edward Foard Nowland son of my son Lambert, whom he is twenty-one years of age. To my children Viz, Augustus James Nowland. Alfred C. Nowland. Frisby M. Nowland. (if he shall be living at time of my death and come forward in two years thereafter) Lambert D. Nowland. Mary R. Mansfield wife of James C. Mansfield. Sarah Sluyter wife of Benjamin Sluyter, and Louise H. Staples wife of Samuel H. Staples. Appoints son Augusts James Nowland Trustee for children of Louise H. Staples Appoints son Alfred C. Nowland Executor. Dated 1st, November 1841. In presence of B.W. Harris, John W. Wirt, Richard J. Foard, Mary Nowland. Probated May 31st, 1844." Sylvester Nowland died in 1819. He married Elizabeth, who died on October 28, 1824. Thomas Nowland (1757-1824) married Mary Brady (1750-1824). Their children were Stephen who died 1796, Ann (1793-1866) who married John Veazey Price (1781-1849) and Sarah who married Lemuel Wooters. The first son of Ann Nowland and John Veazey Price was Thomas T. Price (1826-1885) who married Mary Ann Corbaley (1826-1908). Children of Thomas T. Price and Mary Ann Corbaley were Henrietta Price, Nolan Price, Aloysius Price (born 1855), Theresa Price (born 1860) and Elizabeth Price (1857-1947). Other children of John Veazey Price were Mary Price (1828-1831), John N. Price (1829-1870), Susannah (1832-1924) who married Dr. Charles Perkins, and Margaret Ellen (1835-1915) who married Henry Van Bibber Crawford. The children of Margaret Ellen Price and Henry Van Bibber Crawford were Edward Crawford who died in infancy, Charles Henry Crawford (1876-1925) who married Alice Irvin Woodall. The children of Charles Henry Crawford and Alice Irvin Woodall were Henry Van Bibber Crawford who was born in 1916 and married Edith Jean Keith, Alice who was born in 1917 and who married Joseph Dale McGuire, Margaret (1918-1964) who married first Bob Sheldon and second Harvey Atkinson and Andrew (1920-1944). The children of Henry Van

Bibber Crawford and Edith Jean Keith were Henry Van Bibber Crawford, Edith Jean Crawford, Margaret Alice Crawford, Cynthia Crawford and Keith Crawford. Alice S. Crawford, daughter of Henry Van Bibber Crawford and Alice Irvin Woodall was born 1917 and married Joseph McGuire. Their son was William Preston McGuire Margaret Crawford (1918-1964) married (1) Eli Sheldon (2) Henry Atkinson. Their children were Margaret Price Atkinson, Charles Crawford Atkinson, and Elizabeth Elyson Atkinson. A third child of Thomas Nowland (d. 1824) and Mary Brady (d. 1824) was Sarah Nowland who married Lemuel Wooters. Their children were Laura Wooters who married Anthony Johnson. Their children were Bradford, Clayton, Alan, and Fannie Johnson. Clayton married Maricen Reynolds. Their children were Maxine, Gwendolyn, and Andy Johnson. Fannie Johnson married Frank Huey whose son Frank Jr. married Carolyn Lynch. Lelia Wooters, daughter of Sarah Nowland and Lamuel Wooters, married Stonewall Johnson. Their daughters were Blanche and Marie. Marie Johnson married first a Rosen and second a Poore. Their daughters Mary Jane Rosen married George Sherwood and Frances Poore married John Quinn. Ann Nowland Price lived at "Daley's Desire" now known as the Price Farm. It belongs to the children of Charles Henry Crawford. The Crawford Farm is next door, called "Coloton," with a windmill, and belongs to the widow of Charles H. Crawford. James Nowland born 1721, in 1740 plastered interior of Bohemia, had two sons Daniel who died in 1807, and Dennis (1777-1807). Dennis Nowland married Mary Mansfield Foard (1770-1844). Their son Agustus James Nowland (1800-1879) married Mary J. Sluyter (1817-1885). Their son Henry Agustus Nowland married Lizzie Blackeston. Their two children were Maria Hepburn Nowland and Henry Augustus Nowland.

37. ADW, Bohemia Records, Baptisms by Francis Beeston in Queen Anne's County: *October 30, 1790* - at Tully's Neck, Margaret Tully, born January 20, 1788, of Michael Tully, Catholic, and his wife Ann Catholic. Sponsors were John Keith and Elizabeth Cruze. *June 6, 1791* - Elizabeth Leary, born February 24, 1791, of Laurence and Mary Leary, Catholics. Sponsors were Charles Seth and Elizabeth Cruze. *December 19, 1791* at Queenstown, William Tate, born November 11, 1791, of Richard Tate and Hannah, his wife, both Catholics. Sponsors were Reverend Beeston and Margaret Bailey. *April 12, 1792* - Benjamin Gafford, born January 28, 1792, of Jacob Gafford and Sarah, his wife, Catholics. Sponsors were Samuel Gafford and Mary Dailey, Catholics. *May 13, 1792* - Sylvester Nowland, born July 14, 1791, of Thomas Nowland and Mary, his wife, both Catholics. Sponsors were James Sweeny and Elizabeth Cruze, both Catholics. *May 13, 1792* - Rachel Cain, born February 29, 1792, of John Cain, Catholic, and Ann, his wife, Protestant. Sponsors were John Carey and Rachel Seth, both Catholics. *June 12, 1792* - Charolette McKinsey, born February 24, 1792, of Kennard McKinsey and Eleanor Lamb. Sponsors were Charles Seth and Mary Danskin, both Catholics. *November 11, 1792* - Elizabeth Evans, born May 12, 1792, of Jonathan and Mary Evans. Sponsors were James Sweeny and Margaret Kean, Catholics. *November 11, 1792* - Frederic Osborn, born July 2, 1792, of John and Ann Osborn, Protestants. Sponsors were Samuel Gafford and Mary Daily, Catholics. *December 9, 1792* - Mary Hadder, an adult Godfather was Reverend Francis Beeston. *April 14, 1793* - Thomas Gafford, born December 10, 1792, of Leir and Sarah Gafford, Catholics. Sponsors were Samuel Gafford and Sarah Gafford, wife of Jacob Gafford, Catholics. For earlier background of these families in Queen Anne's County, consult Peterman, *Catholics in Colonial Delmarva*: - Cain 235, 294; Carey 283, 285; Gafford 291; Nowland 312; Cruze (Cruse) 294; Seth 281, 285, 290; Tate 298; Tully 184, 243, 281. Marriage performed by Father Beeston in Queen Anne County: *July 17, 1790* - between Joseph Callahan of Talbot County and Ann Armstrong of Queen Anne's County. Witnesses were Daniel Conroy and Robert Tuite; *January 25, 1791* - between John Cain, Catholic of Queen Anne's County, widower, and Ann Smith Hamilton, Protestant of same county, widow. Witnesses were Daniel Cain, John Tippens, and Charles Seth; *December 12, 1791* - between Edward Goodwin, Calvinist, and Elizabeth Seth, Catholic. Witnesses were Charles Seth, George Washington Seth, Maurice Oliver and John Cain; *December 9, 1792* - between Isaac Jackson and Mary Hadder. Witnesses were James Ewen, Joseph Jackson, Anastasia Ewen, Sarah Boggs (at Tully's Neck); Burial by Father Beeston in Queen Anne County: *May 13, 1792* - Christina Monsieur, died at age 12, buried in family burying ground of Jacob Gafford (near Sudlersville).

38. ADW, Bohemia Records - November 15, 1792, Father Beeston baptized James Meredith, son of James and Anastasia Meredith. Child was born October 26, 1792. Witnesses were James and Anastasia Ewing (Catholics). Baptismal Register of Bohemia Church, September 9, 1792, Father

Beeston baptized Francis Councell, born 1792. THE COUNCELL FAMILY (from genealogical notes of Rodney V. Councell published privately, Greensboro, Maryland, 1997): Henry Councell, son of Dennis Councell, was born in England about 1691: He migrated to Maryland and settled on "The Relief," a tract of land along the western side of the Tuckahoe Creek in 1729. Queen Anne County, *Land Commission Book 3*, folio 38: Henry Councell was 68 years old in 1759. He purchased land in Queen Anne County on September 11, 1729, 52 acres for 2500 pounds of tobacco. Queen Anne County Levy Court Records 31, 59- "Bounty paid for squirrel heads to Henry Councill." 1734, Index 58, drawer 17: "Debt Rolls for Queen Anne's due on Lady Day in the Land Office" 1734 – Henry Councell married Hawkins Pharsalia, of French parentage. Property. first purchased land in Queen Anne's County, Maryland on 11 Sep 1729; 52 acres for 2500 pounds of tobacco. Later acquisitions occurred until the death of two of Henry's sons, Joseph and John. Queen Anne County Land Records: 19 May 1729 – 25 June 1729 William Turbutt, Gent., to Henry Councill, Carpenter – consideration 15,000 pounds of tobacco – 271 acres, part of "Hawkins Pharsalia" and "Reliefe," in Tully's Neck, on Millson's Branch. Adjoining the lands possessed by Michael Hussey; the land possessed by Thomas Baynard, part of "Reliefe." Wits: J. Earle, John Beck. Acknowledged before Arthur Emory and Thomas H. Wright. (William Turbutt was the surveyor in charge of dividing the county from Talbot in 1706) Lib 1KC fol 213. 11 Sep 1729 – 13 Sep 1729 Henry Councill, carpenter, and Elizabeth his wife, to Michael Hussey, planter – consideration 2,500 pounds of tobacco – 55 acres, part of the "Reliefe," on the west side of Tuckahoe Creek in Tully's Neck – adjoining "Hawkins Pharsalia" and a part sold to Michael Hussey by Major William Turbutt. Henry and Elizabeth (she being first privately examined out of the hearing) acknowledge before Augustine Thompson and Solomon Clayton. Lib iKC, fol 231. William COUNCELL was born about 1766 and died on 15 Oct 1812. William married Mary Polly EWING, daughter of James EWING and Anastasia COUNCELL, on 19 Jul 1802 in Caroline County, Maryland. Mary Polly EWING was christened on 2 Jun 1776. General Notes: Married William Councell (son of John & Sarah Councell) in 1802. William died 15 Oct 1776. Children of this marriage were: I. Clotilda COUNCELL was born on 14 Jun 1803 in Caroline County, Maryland and; II. Anastasia COUNCELL was born about 1745 and died in 1801. Anastasia married James EWING on 17 May 1767 in Councell Home, Queen Anne County, Maryland. James EWING died in Oct 1796 and was buried on 23 Oct 1796. Witnesses were Thomas Carey & Elizabeth Seth. Children from this marriage were: i. John EWING was buried on 22 Dec 1800.; ii. Susannah EWING General Notes: Married John Richardson 29 Jan 1799.; iii. Anastasia EWING, died on 19 Apr 1801. Noted events in her life were: Baptism: 18 Dec 1768, St. Joseph's Mission Godparents: John Counsil & Mary Wright.; iv. James EWING Jr., died on 25 Mar 1798.; v. Mary Polly EWING was christened on 2 Jun 1776. Mary married William COUNCELL, son of John COUNCELL and Sarah CAREY, on 19 Jul 1802 in Caroline County, Maryland. William was born about 1766 and died on 15 Oct 1812.; vi. Henry EWING, died about 1803. Baptism: 29 Mar 1780, St. Joseph's Mission.; vii. Joseph EWING was born in 1781 and died on 14 Aug 1842.; III. Joseph COUNCELL was born about 1747. Will: 14 Oct 1766. COUNCEL, Joseph, Queen Anne's County MD WB 35, p. 131 14 Oct 1766 13 Dec 1766 To wife Rebeccah, 1/3 pt of estate, or a mare if wife shall be fully satisfied. To son John Councel, tract called "Hog Pen Ridge," with all right of land to me belonging or pertaining to him, lying and being in Queen Anne's Co. to son John Councel, Gun and Surveying Instruments. To dau. Mary Councel, personals. Balance to children: Mary, John and Ann Council. If servant man Peter Corban, shall get any person to discharge my bond to Thomas Smith and Emory Badclar for 17 lbs money, then he shall have liberty of chosing his master. Wife Rebecca, who is known to be a lunatic or crazed person and quite incapable of managing her affairs and education of my children, I appoint, as Ex. Bro, John Councel, may educate and place children in such a manner as I have enjoyed him. Appoint this as my last will. Ex: Affectionate bro. John Councel Wit: Henry Councell, Thomas Baggs Jr., John Huebank. Occupation. He was a school master. Joseph married Rebecca GRAY on 6 May 1784 in St. Peter's Church. Children from this marriage were: i. John COUNCELL was born about 1770.; ii. Mary COUNCELL. Another name for Mary was Name From Father's WILL.; iii. Ann COUNCELL. Another name for Ann was Name From Father's WILL.; iv. Catherine COUNCELL was born about 1749. Catherine married Benedict JACKSON.; v. Martha COUNCELL was born about 1750. Martha married Henry BAGGS, son of Thomas

BAGGS and Sarah HARRINGTON. Henry was born in 1738. Children from this marriage were i. Henry BAGGS, died in 1810.; vi. Mary COUNCELL was born about 1751. Mary married Henry WRIGHT. Died on 27 Nov 1850. Attended St. Joseph's College, Emmitsburg, became a Nun in 1823. Dau. Of Charity, 1823, Emmitsburg, MD. Baptism: 19 Jun 1803, St. Joseph's Church, Near Cordova, Maryland. Baltimore *The Catholic Mirror*, April 5, 1856: A meeting of the corporators of St. Joseph's Hospital, President Ex Officio Right Reverend Bishop John N. Neumann, Vice President Reverend F. J. Barbelin, S.J. The Treasurer is Edward Ewing. One of the managers of the hospital is Robert Ewing and he is from Denton, Maryland. The reason I want to write that in is that he apparently kept his faith." Listed with Robert Ewing is Mark Wilcox and Dr. William V. Keating and also John Devereux all important Catholics of Philadelphia.

39. ADW, Bohemia Records, negroes baptized by Father Beeston at Appoquinimink Forest: *May 20, 1791* - Teresia, four years old, of Samuel, Catholic, and his wife, not baptized, both slaves of George Wright, Sr. Sponsors were Jeremiah Reynolds and Sarah Broxon, both Catholic. *June 24, 1792* - at Appoquinimink Forest, Charles, age 9 years, negro slave of William Heverin. Godfather was William Heverin. *June 24, 1792* - Appoquinimink Forest, Thamar, age 12 years, negro slave of Charles Heverin. Godmother was Alice Heverin, Catholic. *April 23, 1792* - at Appoquinimink Forest, Rachel, negro, an adult, slave of Charles Heverin. Sponsors were Richard, negro slave of Reverend Beeston, and Patience, negro slave of Jacob Reynolds. *April 13, 1792* - at Kent County, Maryland - William, negro, born March 6, 1792, of James (free negro) and Ann Leich, his wife, negro slave of Elizabeth Brady, widow. Godmother was Frances (Fan) negro slave of widow Brady. *October 13, 1792* - at Kent County, Maryland - Joseph (negro) born September 25, 1792, of Edward (free negro) and Frances (negro slave of Elizabeth Brady, widow). Godmother was Elizabeth Brady. Marriages of negroes by Father Beeston: *December 12, 1790* - at Tully's Neck, Queen Anne County - between William, Catholic, negro slave of George Williams and Susanna, widow, Catholic, negro slave of John Bewly. Witnesses were John Councill, Sr., Sarah Councill, Sr., and Sarah Councill, Jr. For background of the Councill family, consult Peterman, *Catholics in Colonial Delmarva* 274, 281, 282, 294, 299, 327. *December 12, 1790* - between William, negro slave of George Williams, and Susanna, widow, slave of John Buly at Tully's Neck, Queen Anne County. Witnesses were John Councill, Sr., Sarah Councill, Sr., and Sarah Councill, Jr.; *February 10, 1791* - between Henry Stephen Biddles, negro slave, Protestant, and Mary, Reverend Beeston's mulatto slave, Catholic, daughter of Reverend Beeston's slave Rachael, at Bohemia. Witnesses were Edward Carey Councill, Samuel Councill, Bridget Councill, and Hannah McDermott; *February 25, 1791* - between Bernard, Charles Blake's negro slave and Rebecca, Arthur Matthew's negro slave, at Bohemia. Witnesses were Bridget Councill and Hannah McDermott; *May 8, 1791* - between Joseph, Protestant slave of Ruth Faulkner, and Frances, Catholic slave of James Brady, at Bohemia. Witnesses were Edward Councill and Alice O'Donato; *April 23, 1792* - between Samuel and Rachael, both negro slaves of Charles Heverin, in New Castle County, Delaware. Witnesses were, Jacob Reynolds, Elizabeth Reynolds, and Sarah Reynolds;

40. Cann 251-3; Richard Key Heath was son of Charles Daniel Heath, the last Heath to own Worsall Manor, and grandson of James Paul Heath. James V. Matthews was son of Dr. Hugh Matthews II.

41. In 1792 Father Beeston laid Cornerstone of the Church, N. W. Corner. Devitt 63:24; GUA, Maryland Province Society of Jesus, Series One, File one: *Beeston Diary*, April 21, 1792, Beeston records farm activities, frequently describes weather conditions, and lists clothing given to slaves.

December 21, 1791	Began to uncover the north side of my dwelling house which was extremely leaky not do it sooner, the whole summer and fall having been so dry, that I had not a sufficient head of water to saw the laths and scantlings.
Jan. 5, 1792	This evening finished covering the house.
April 21, 1792	Robert Erwin, carpenter, finished working for me. threw down the old chapel.
May 7, 1792	Pulled down the parlor chimney and part of both gable ends of house.
May 8, 1792	Began to rebuild the parlor chimney, etc.
May 10, 1792	Began to dig the foundations of the New Church.
May 15, 1792	(Tuesday) Rev. Francis Beeston laid the first stone of the New Church at the NW corner.

Aug. 25, 1792	Sent load of wheat to Appoquinimink; brought back a load of shingles (1200) for the New Church.
Aug. 29, 1792	Sent to Appoquinimink, brought back 1200 shingles.
Aug. 30, 1792	1200 more shingles
Aug. 31, 1792	1200 more shingles.
Oct. 11, 1792	Began the road leading straight from the new church to Warwick.
Oct. 19, 1792	Clearing the new road to Warwick.
Oct. 22, 1792	Getting in timber to the saw mill for the roof of the new church. Working at the new road to Warwick.
Oct. 23, 1792	Hauled stocks to the saw mill for the roof of the new church.
Oct. 24, 1792	Worked at the new Warwick road. Cut stocks for the new church.
Oct. 25, 1792	Work as yesterday.
Oct. 26, 1792	Work as yesterday.
Oct. 29, 1792	Worked at the new road; brought stocks to the saw mill for the new church.
Oct. 30, 1792	Work as yesterday.
Oct. 31, 1792	Worked at the new road.
Nov. 2, 1792	Began to frame the roof of the new church.
Jan. 12, 1793	Began to raise the scaffold for the roof of the church.
Jan. 25, 1793	Helpt (sic) to raise the scaffold for putting the roof on the church.
April 9, 1793	Hauling more stocks for the new church.
May 1, 1793	Raised the roof of the new church without difficulty or hurt.
May 19, 1793	Bohemia in charge of Father Delavan."

Father Beeston's records indicate that the church was essentially completed, except for the interior, when he was transferred in 1793.

42. *Beeston Diary*, October 11, 1792. In 1789, the new U.S. Constitution guaranteed freedom of religion. Fr. Francis Beeston laid the foundation and cornerstone for this church three years later. He also laid the road to Warwick, which received supplies transported by land from Cantwell's Bridge, through Middletown, to Bohemia Landing. (This was the shortest route from the Atlantic Ocean to the Chesapeake Bay until the canal was dug.)
43. *Beeston Diary*, January 25, 1793 – "scaffold for roof;"
    March 7, 1793 – "made the graveyard;"
    April 9, 1793 – "more stocks for the church;"
    May 1, 1793 – "roof for church raised."
44. *Beeston Diary*, May 19, 1793
45. J. Alphonse Frederick, "Old Saint Peter's, or Beginnings of Catholicity in Baltimore," *Historical Records and Studies* 5 (1909) 383. Spalding 50n.1
46. Melville 215
47. Melville 101
48. Devitt 63:23
49. Communicated by John Carroll to John Kingston, *The American Biographic Dictionary* (Baltimore: Warner and Hanna, 1810) 40-41, the Beeston obituary was published in Thomas O'Brien Hanley, *The John Carroll Papers* 3:108-110. Spalding 141n.1.
50. Joseph W. Ruane, *The Beginnings of the Society of St. Sulpice in the United States* 1791-1829 (Washington, D.C.: The Catholic University of America Press, 1935) 24; Hughes, Documents 2:745
51. Melville 143; Ellis, *Documents of American Catholic History* (Wilmington, Delaware: Michael Glazier 1987) 1:175, No. 58- "The French Sulpicians and St. Mary's Seminary, Baltimore, April 23, 1792
52. Charles G. Herbermann, *The Sulpicians in the United States* (New York: The Encyclopedia Press, 1916)
53. Ruane 72; Devitt, "Bohemia," 39 *RACHS* 24 (1913):123
54. Ruane 73; Hughes, Documents 2:744, No. 170
55. Hughes, Documents 1:766
56. Ruane 36.
57. Ruane 36; Ronin John Murtha, "The Life of the Most Reverend Ambrose Maréchal: Third

Archbishop of Baltimore, 1768-1829" (doctoral dissertation, Catholic University of America, Washington, D. C., 1965) 1-16- Ambrose Maréchal, born December 4, 1768, at Ingre in the diocese of Orleans, had been destined for the study of law but chose instead the priesthood. Surrounded by the fury of the French Revolution, he was ordained March 25, 1792, in the library of the Irish College in Paris and the following day fled to America. His first Mass was said in Baltimore, July 8, 1792. Father Maréchal suffered severe attacks of fever during his stay at Bohemia. Long rides on horseback caused him frequently to be ill. Associated Archives, 5400 Roland Avenue, Baltimore, MD 21210 (hereafter AAB): ZZ-A-S, Maréchal Diary - August, 1792 Father Maréchal was assigned first to St. Mary's Church, Philadelphia, where he learned English, and was impressed by the virtues and learning of Fathers Francis Fleming and Lawrence Graessel. Maréchal Diary, December 9, 1794 – In December of 1792 Maréchal took the stagecoach for Bohemia in Cecil County where he had been appointed to assist the Reverend Francis Beeston, whose personality he summarized in a single word: "honnetête." From February until early June of the next year he attended the mission at Newtown, Maryland, after which he went again to Bohemia. Father Charles Bowling joined him there at the end of November and took care of Maréchal's needs during an attack of fever in the following July and August, but he himself succumbed to the sickness during Maréchal's convalescence and died on December 9, 1794.

58. Dated May 19, 1793, it is in AAB together with all financial accounts pertaining to the Bohemia plantation while in the hands of the Sulpicians. Hughes, Documents 2:748 – note of Father Peter Kenney, Jesuit Visitor, on the debt of Bohemia 1790 and changes of personnel 1790 - 1793. GUA, Bohemia Manor Varia, 103, N1-6.5, Series 21 – Lease (1795) between Ambrose Maréchal, S.S. and James O'Donald; Lease (1796) of Negro slave by Ambrose Maréchal to James O'Donald. A. Maréchal order to Mr. Hynan for Mrs. Morton. Contract (1797) by Patrick Barnes and Ambrose Maréchal; Bond (1797) between A. Maréchal and his Negro slave Patrick Barnes, for purchase of freedom. Petition for Freedom, Patrick Barnes, slave, Ambrose Maréchal, S.S.; Certificate of Contract (1798) for hire of negro slave by Ambrose Maréchal to John Morton; Account of Ambrose Maréchal with George Reece (1797-1798).; Maréchal settlement with S. Forge before leaving Bohemia (1797). GUA – Archives, Maryland Province, Society of Jesus – BOHEMIA PLANTATION MAP (1795) – BOHEMIA PLANTS/SURVEYS [103 S1-T9]
59. AAB Z1A-V-Z, June 19, 1794
60. ADW, Bohemia, Sacramental Records: Appoquinimink Forest, New Castle County, Delaware, Baptisms performed by Father Maréchal: *June 12, 1796* - Daniel Sweetman and Martha, his wife. Sponsors were John Reynolds and Sarah Heverin; *June 12, 1796* - Catherine Pennington about two months old, daughter of Otho Pennington and Katie, his wife. Sponsors were John Gorman and Mary Heverin; June 12, 1796 - James Reynolds, eighteen months old, son of William and Mary Reynolds; *June 12, 1796* - Abraham Heverin, three months old, son of Isaac Heverin and Betsy, his wife. Sponsors were Abraham Heverin and Polly Heverin. *June 12, 1796* - Mary Heverin, about six months old, daughter of Abraham Heverin and Elizabeth, his wife. Godfather was Isaac Heverin; *June 12, 1796* - Martha Hardin, about 4 months old, daughter of Edmond Hardin and Mary. Sponsors were John and Mary Heverin; *June 12, 1796* - Robert Reynolds, about 3 months old, son of Nicholas Reynolds and Betsy. Sponsors were John Reynolds and Mary Heverin; *June 25, 1796* - William Alexander Scott, son of Thomas and Ruth Scott. Sponsors were Jack Reynolds and Sarah his wife; *October 9, 1796* - Sarah Cole, daughter of Peregrine and Mary Cole. Sponsors were Holland Webb and Mary Heverin; *November, 1796* - Stephen, about four months old, son of Sam and Mindy. Sponsors were Sam and Robert. *January 16, 1797* - Sarah Reynolds, born January 14, 1797, daughter of Billy and Mary Reynolds. Sponsors were Jack and Sarah Reynolds; *January 16, 1797* - Nancy Reynolds, born November 7, 1796, daughter of John and Sarah Reynolds. Sponsors were Francis Barnard and Mary Heverin; *January 16, 1797* - Becky Cole, born in February 1796, daughter of William and Rebecca Cole. Sponsors were Jack Reynolds and Kate Pennington; *June 25, 1797* - William Alexander Scott, son of Thomas Scott and Ruth, his wife. Sponsors were Jack Reynolds and Sarah, his wife; *September 17, 1797* - Jeremiah Reynolds, two months old, son of James Reynolds and Mary Reed. Sponsors were Jeremiah Reynolds and Katy Reynolds; *February 25, 1798* - George Crouch, about three years old, son of Benjamin Crouch and Theresia, his wife. Sponsors were Elisha Crouch and Katy Pennington; *February 25, 1798* - Sarah Harding, about one month old,

daughter of Edward Harding and Mary, his wife. Sponsors were John Gammon and Barbara Heverin; *April 22, 1798* - Prudence Little, daughter of John and Temperance Little. Sponsors were John Gorman and Polly Heverin. Marriages performed by Father Maréchal at Appoquinimink Forest: *May 24, 1796* - between James Reynolds and Mary Bunker, widow. Witnesses were William Reynolds and Barnie Reed; *September 24, 1797* - between Benedict Crouch and Catherine Donoho. Witnesses were John Gammon and ?Crouch.

61   ADW, Bohemia Records, At Sassafras Hill, Father Maréchal baptized: *March 19, 1794* - Notley Young, 19 days old, son of Benjamin and Martha Young. Sponsors were Rev. Maréchal and Susanna Hall; *March 19, 1794* - Peter, son of Dick and Mary, both slaves of Benjamin Young. Sponsors were Tony and Jenny; *March 19, 1794* - Isaac, born of Rachel, slave of Benjamin Young. Sponsors were Molly and Jake; *March 19, 1794* - Luke, born of Nellie, slave of Benjamin Young. Sponsors were Ned and Dolly; *March 19, 1794* - Cecil, born of Jake and Luke, slaves of Benjamin Young. Sponsors were Dick and Suzanne. ADW, Bohemia Sacramental Records: Father Maréchal baptized at *Head of Sassafras* - *August 27, 1797* - Richard Henry and Daniel Coleman, sons of Charles Coleman and Hannah Heath. No sponsors. *August 27, 1797* - John McCoit, son of John McCoit and Polly Heverin. Sponsors were Jack Reynolds and Nancy Reynolds; At Sassafras Hill - *September 4, 1796* - Richard, 11 months old, son of Richard and Poll, slaves of Benjamin Young. Sponsors were Ralph and Molly. *September 4, 1796* - Michael, about 2 years old, son of Jack, slave of Mr. Chew, and Suzannah, slave of Mr. Young. Sponsors were Jack and Mollie.

62.   ADW, Bohemia Records, Baptisms by Father Maréchal at Sassafras Neck, Cecil County: *December 8, 1795* - Rachel, born November 7, 1795 - daughter of Phillip, Mr. Heath's slave and Jimmie, his wife, slave to Mr. Nowland. At Georgetown, Maryland: *January 7, 1796* - Anna Nicholson, about 7 months old, daughter of William Nicholson and Mary his wife. Sponsor was Rev. Maréchal. Marriage at Sassafras Neck: *June 3, 1794* between Samuel Councill and Margaret Craddock. Witnesses were James Councill and Jepe Nowland. Marriage by Father Maréchal at Sassafras Neck: *November 22, 1798* - between Nathan Burk, widower, and Sarah Nowland. Witnesses were Sylvester Nowland and James Councill.

63.   ADW, Bohemia Records, at Bohemia - Father Maréchal baptized: *April 8, 1798* - Charles Nicholson, about six months old, son of William Nicholson and his wife, Mary. Sponsors were Peter Haggard and Barbara Heverin; *August 3, 1799* - Richard Nicholson, born August 1, 1799, son of William Nicholson and Mary Lee. Sponsors were William and Mary Craddock; Father Maréchal performed marriages at Bohemia, *January 2, 1794* - between Isaac Holden and Anne Cole, of New Castle County, Delaware. Witnesses were Solomon Jones and Isaac Clayton; *1794* - between Daniel Craddock and Elizabeth Price. Witnesses were William Craddock and Benedict Craddock. *January 29, 1797* - between Bartholomew Lyons, widower, and Sarah Riggs, widow, at Bohemia. Witnesses were Mr. Mahoney and James Lyons; *January 29, 1797* - Samuel, slave of Mrs. Ryland, and Atee, slave of Mr. Barnett, at Bohemia. Witnesses were Teal and Tom; *April 24, 1797* between James, free negro, and Theresia, slave of Mr. Blake, at Bohemia. Witness was Daniel Conningin; *May 25, 1797* - between James Clancy and Biddy O'Donald, at Bohemia. Witnesses were Daniel Craddock and James O'Donald; *February 1, 1798* - Tilghman Jackson and Elizabeth Jackson, at Bohemia. Witnesses were William Lee and Rachael Lee; *December 26, 1795* - between Moses, slave of Mr. Bakey Matthews, and Mary, slave of Pierce Sappington, at Head of Bohemia. Witnesses were Father Marechal, Harry, a free man; *January 3, 1796* - between Harry, slave of Henry Pierce and Nelly, slave of Sarah Biddle, at Head of Bohemia. Witnesses were Stephen and Barney; *February 6, 1796* - between Charles, free negro man, and Phyllis, slave of George Reise, at Head of Bohemia. Witnesses were Ned Brown and James Brown; *May 4, 1796* - between John Davis and Anna Lynch, at Head of Bohemia. Witnesses were Martin O'Connor and his wife; *May 26, 1796* - between Jacob, slave of Benjamin Flintham, and Mary, slave of Reverend Maréchal, at Bohemia. Witnesses were Samuel Francis and Thomas Black; *February 1, 1798* - between James O'Donald and Catherine Reynolds, at Bohemia. Witnesses were Jeremiah Reynolds and Marie Faullanier; *February 13, 1798* - between Henry Gibben and Catherine McCardle, at Bohemia. Witness was Sylvester Nowland; *February 20, 1798* - between Charles Herring and Mary Linkhorn, widow, at Bohemia. Witnesses were James O'Donald and William Craddock; *June 21, 1798* - between Charles and Betsy, free negroes, at Bohemia. Witnesses were Suky and Phyllis; *December 31, 1798* - between Adam Kennell, slave of S.

George, and Susanna, slave of Reverend Marechal, at Bohemia; *February 12, 1799* - between Hugh Harkins and Barbara Lee, at Bohemia. Witness was William Nicholson; *February 17, 1799* - between Peter, slave of Mr. Carman, and Minty, slave of Mr. Reynolds, at Bohemia. Witnesses were Suky and James.

THE CRADDOCK FAMILY: William Craddock and Charles Craddock of Cecil County, Maryland were brothers. Born in 1742 *William Craddock* came to the Warwick area around 1750. He was a tenant of the farm known as "The Quarter," which was part of the Askmore Tract of the Bohemia Mission. Father John Lewis wrote in his diary that William Craddock purchased wheat flour from the mill in October, 1775, also on December 8, 1775: "two bushels of wheat due William Craddock on crop," and "lent Johnny money to pay Mr. Craddock for cobbling." *William* died on March 26, 1816, at age 74. His wife *Mary* died on April 27, 1814, and is buried at Bohemia. They had three sons: (1) *Thomas*, born at Bohemia in 1771 and died on January 24, 1833 at age 63 (20) *John*, baptized on October 5, 1776 and was buried at age 62 at Bohemia, and (3) *Joseph*, was baptized November 14, 1779 and was buried at Bohemia. Sponsors at a baptism on November 14, 1779 were *Jeremiah Craddock* and *Bathsheba Craddock* (buried at Bohemia). William's brother *Charles Craddock* enrolled in the Cecil County militia in the Revolutionary War. *Maryland Militia Master Roll* 142. *Daniel Craddock* married *Elizabeth O'Donald* of Sassafras Neck at Bohemia in 1772. The first son *James Francis Craddock* was born on October 24, 1773 and died at age 21 on January 1, 1794. Another son, *Daniel* died in 1810 and was buried at Bohemia. A daughter *Sarah* was baptized on March 16, 1796 and is buried at Bohemia. Another daughter *Temperance* was born on December 21, 1806, and died December 6, 1807. *Benedict Craddock* (b. 1774) married *Margaret Ryland* (b. 1785). She died on February 20, 1834. He died April 30, 1845 at age 71 (buried at Bohemia). Their son *Thomas Theodore Craddock* was born in 1809. Sponsor at his baptism was William Craddock, Jr., uncle of the child. Five children were born to Richard Craddock and his wife Ann Springer: (1) William Alfred Craddock born 1816, (2) Joseph Taylor Craddock born in 1818, (3) Richard Craddock born in 1820, and (4) twins Elizabeth and (5) Henry Craddock born in 1822. Wilson, *Rose Hill* 319: October 5, 1832 "Mrs. Richard Craddock departed this life who has been ill." October 6, 1832 –" went to Mrs. Craddock's funeral. She left three orphan children," 367 – March 10, 1836 – "Mr. Craddock here." 367 – June 19, 1836 – "we all went to Mr. Craddock's funeral." James Craddock was born in October, 1816, to William Craddock and his wife Elizabeth Hill. Captain Benedict Craddock was sponsor at the baptisms of all the children born to Richard Craddock and Ann Springer. Benedict Craddock (born 1774) married after 1834 a second wife Susan Hessy. Their children were John Benedict Craddock was born in 1837, and Mary Ann (Molly) Craddock born July 20, 1843 (died September 17, 1920 at age 77. Molly Craddock married Hugh McAleer in 1873. Their children were Ned and Elsie. Eugenia May Craddock was born on May 23, 1840 to Joseph Craddock and Helen Green. Sponsors were Elizabeth Craddock nee wheeler and John Craddock. Theodore Craddock was born in 1841 to Joseph Craddock and his wife Helen Amelia Green. Another son Joseph Clement Craddock was born on March 7, 1844. He was baptized on May 5, 1844. Sponsor was Thomas Theodore Price. A third child, Corinne Helen Craddock was born April 21, 1846. Mary Janet Craddock was born in 1842 to Thomas and Margaret Craddock. Margaret Craddock was born in 1841. Susan Craddock was born in 1842 to Joseph Craddock and Catherine Antoine Sharon. Sponsor was Ann Price nee Nowland. William Craddock was born in 1843 and died 1916. Elma Gertrude Craddock was born July 17, 1842 to Joseph Craddock and his wife Helen Green. Sponsors were Benjamin Green and Temperance Craddock. Jane Elizabeth Craddock was born August 28, 1844 to Thomas Craddock and Margaret Frances. Sponsor was Mary Ann Hessy. Wilson, *Rose Hill* 368 – July 7, 1836 "Mr. Benedict Craddock here to tea." 378 – February 6, 1837 "The general left for Philadelphia and stayed all night at Benedict Craddock's" *Rose Hill* 332 – February 13, 1834 "Elizabeth Craddock here – she is 12 years of age," 361 – March 23, 1836 – "Elizabeth Craddock here to dine," 360 – March 6, 1836 "Mr. Joseph Craddock here to dinner," March 10, 1836 – "Mr. Craddock here," 258 – October 16, 1828 "My husband went up to Richard Craddock's to see his horse Sassafras run," 367 – June 18, 1836 "Mr. Craddock found dead at the blacksmith shop gate. His gig turned bottom upwards and he under it, supposed to have been in a state of intoxification." "Rose Hill" is located on the Grove Point road on the Sassafras River. It was the home of General Thomas Marsh Foreman (1758-1845), aide to General William Alexander, known as Lord Sterling, and a representative in The General Assembly, 1790 and 1800. He served with Major George Armistead, Fort McHenry, 1814. A later owner, William Ward, represented Cecil County in the General Assembly, 1875 and married Charlotte Ringgold Knight of "Essex Lodge."

64. ADW, Bohemia Records, Queen Anne County, near Sudlersville, *February 12, 1794* - Jacob Waters, born January 31, 1794, son of Jacob Waters and Sally Gafford. Sponsors were James Sweeny and Elizabeth Cruze; *September 4, 1796* - Richard, eleven months old, son of Poll and Richard, slaves of Benjamin Young. Sponsors were Ralph and Mely; *September 4, 1796* - Michael, about two years old, son of Jack, slave of Mr. Chew, and Susannah, slave of Mr. Young. Sponsors were Jack and Meble; *May, 1797* - Anna, daughter of Jacob and Sala Gafford. Sponsors were Levy and Sala Gafford; *September 10, 1797* - Mary Gafford, 9 2 months old, daughters of Samuel and Mary Gafford. Sponsors were Levy and Anna Gafford; *September 10, 1797* - Edward Gafford, six months old, son of Leonard Leary and his wife, Mary. Sponsor was James Jevers; *June, 1798* - Anna, eight months old, daughter of James and Anna, slaves of Perry Blake. Godmother was Elizabeth, slave of Perry Blake; *June, 1798* - Elisha, three months old, son of George, slave of Thomas Ringgold and Elizabeth, his wife, slave of Perry Blake. Sponsors were James and Anna; *June, 1798* - Adam, eight weeks old, son of James a free mulatto, and Susanna, slave of Perry Blake, Sponsors were James and Lucy.

65. ADW, Bohemia Records, At Taylor's Bridge, Delaware, Father Maréchal baptized: *May 9, 1796* - Thomas and Elizabeth Heron, children of John Heron and Susanna, his wife, Protestants. No sponsors; *May 9, 1796* - Catherine Bassett, daughter of Thomas Bassett and Becky, his wife. No sponsors; *May 9, 1796* - Nely Bassett, daughter of Ned Bassett and Judith, a mulatto woman; *May 9, 1796* - Henny Green, daughter of Perry Green and Henny, both black people. No sponsors.

66. Devitt, "Bohemia," *RACHS* 24 (1913) 126. The two niches on either side of the main altar which now hold statues of the Sacred Heart and St. Francis Xavier, were originally windows. This can be plainly seen by the outlines in the stucco on the rear wall of the church and confirmed by the following from Rev. Ambrose Maréchal's entry in the Burial Register: "1799. Aug. 21. Died at the Head of Bohemia, the Rev. Stephen Faure, a French Priest, residing at Wilmington, Del. He was about 37 years old. His eminent piety, extreme erudition, and active charity made him an object of respect and veneration to those who knew him. His remains were buried close to the North end of the Church of Bohemia: grave head being at the East side or border of the Gospel window." This entry is definite proof that there were two windows in the rear wall of the church. When they were bricked-up remains unknown.

67. Devitt, "Bohemia," *RACHS* 24 (1913): 117; Ellis, *Documents* 1:179; Sister Mary Doris Mulvey, O.P., *French Catholic Missionaries in the Present United_States, 1604 - 1791* (Washington, D.C.: Catholic University of America Press, 1936) 117; no author given, "The Church in Kentucky," *RACHS* 23 (1912) 141

68. Maurice C. Moreau, *Les Pretres Francais Emigrés Aux Etats-Unis* (Paris: Charles Duoniol, 1856) 85, 133; Devitt, "Bohemia," *RACHS* 24 (1913): 123-125

69. Ruane 36

70. Hanley, *JCP* 3:343-344, Carroll to Pasquet, Baltimore, July 15, 1815.

71. Mary de Vine Dunn, "The Family Background of Kitty Knight," *Bulletin of the Historical Society of Cecil County*, No. 39, (May 17, 1971) 6-8: THE KNIGHT FAMILY – John Leach Knight was born 1741, son of William Knight of Kent County, Maryland, who married Rachael Dulaney, daughter of Honorable Daniel Dulaney of Annapolis. William Knight died in 1787, leaving two sons, William Knight and John Leach Knight. William was born in 1750, died in 1815 and was buried at Bohemia Cemetery. John Leach Knight married first Mary Ward and had three daughters, Mary, Cordelia, and Elizabeth. Mary Ward was buried at Ward's Knowledge. John Leach Knight married second Catherine Matthews, twin sister of Dr. William Matthews, a neighbor of the Jesuits at Bohemia. Their children were James, who died unmarried John, Catherine, and William. John Knight married Sarah and had three children: John Carroll Knight and Edward Henry Knight (baptized July 6, 1807) and William Knight (baptized June 6, 1809). Sponsors at the baptism on July 6, 1807, and of John Carroll Knight of Edward Henry Knight were Dr. James Scanlan and Catherine Matthews Knight. Catherine (Kitty) Knight was born in 1776 and died November 22, 1855 and was buried at Bohemia. John Leach Knight, who married Catherine Matthews, became a captain in the 18th Battalion under Colonel John D. Thompson on April 21,

1778. *Maryland Militia Muster Roll* 29 He was one of the court justices who administered the Oath of Allegiance to the State of Maryland in March 1778 – Maryland Historical Society, Baltimore, Ms. 1146. John Leach Knight was among five persons appointed in May 1781 to superintend the issuing of bills of credit, or paper money, in Cecil County – Johnson, *History of Cecil County* 347. William Knight, son of John Leach and Catherine Knight married Rebecca Ringgold of Chestertown, Maryland. They had one son William, who married Arabella Veazey and had six children: Catherine, Charlotte, Nellie, Annie, Julia and William Matthews Knight. William Matthews Knight was born in 1837, baptized May 14, 1837, at age three months. He married Marie Groome, daughter of Colonel C. Groome. They had five children: Elizabeth, Ethel, Rebecca, Mrs. Lyndon Tracey and James Groome. Mary Carter Roberts, "Kitty Knight" article in Maryland State Library, Annapolis, Maryland, printed by the Maryland Department of Economic Development, 1964, n.p. Wilson, *Mount Harmon* 66: April 12, 1839 – "Sent Dick to William Knight's to get some spruce pines," 67 – April 13, 1839 – "Dick to get from Knight's about 20 spruce pines," 188 – May 26, 1846 – "went to Rose Hill. Mr. and Mrs. William Knight were there. Had some talk with Knight about farming." 197 – June 24, 1846 – "sent note to Mr. Knight inviting him to dine here tomorrow," 215 – December 6, 1846 – "Knights Island, opposite me which by the way is no island but is always called one." Wilson, *Rose Hill* 316: May 6, 1832 – "Mr. Knight here to tea," 361 – March 13, 1836 – "William Knight and his bride made their first appearance at church today," 367 – June 16, 1836 – "spent this afternoon with Mrs. William Knight," 367 – June 19, 1836 – "We all went to Mr. Craddock's funeral. Mr. Knight returned with us to dinner," 367 – June 3, 1836 – "Mr. Knight here to dinner."

72. The Matthews educated their children at Catholic schools both at home and abroad. A school for young girls called Shinai Woods was held at Mount Harmon, owned by James Heath. Kitty's grandmother, Rachael Dulaney, daughter of Honorable Daniel Dulaney, was a sister of Rebecca Dulaney, the wife of James Paul Heath, founder of the town of Warwick. Cann 235 – Story told by Mrs. George Lockwood, eldest daughter. Hamilton Morton related to her daughter Miss Marie Lockwood of Middletown, Delaware was that her mother told how Miss Kitty would arrive at church very much dressed — wearing her diamonds — and that a young colored boy would accompany her. She got out of her carriage, and the boy would enter church with her, walking backwards all the way up the aisle fanning her with a large palm leaf fan, up to the front pew, and then stand all through the Mass fanning her continually. Mrs. Lockwood's youngest son, James Booth Lockwood, a veteran of World War I, said that Miss Kitty came into church "with all sails set." Dunn 8 Cann 237; GUA, Bohemia Manor Varia 103 – N1 – P65, Maryland Province, Society of Jesus Series 20, folder 54 R1-26 Hugh Matthews to Ambrose Maréchal, August 29, 1798: Apparently Maréchal's successor did not socialize as much as Maréchal. Kitty Knight's uncle, Hugh Matthews told Father Maréchal in a letter that his aunt said she would not return to church unless Father Maréchal came back to Bohemia. Cann 236 – In a letter to Hugh Matthews dated May 2, 1800, Maréchal indicates that he and Miss Knight were good friends and that she was good natured and enjoyed a good laugh.

During the pastorate of Father Maréchal, Catherine Knight, as a parishioner of Bohemia, had seven little negro children baptized there, ranging in age from fourteen down to one and a half years. They were baptized by Father Maréchal and she was the Godmother. All the children were her slaves. This shows that she had their spiritual as well as material interest at heart. She was also Godmother for the post humous child of Walter and Marie Fullum, nee O'Donald. This is the Walter Fullum, who left a legacy to Bohemia.

Doctor William Matthews was very solicitous of the deportment of his twin sister's darling daughter as is indicated in the following excerpt from a letter written to his brother, Hugh, dated 10-4-1798: "I have cautioned Kitty as to having any communication with E. Hall, who is frequently at Mrs. Fullerton's, where Miss Ward is. This coxcomb makes himself agreeable to the giddy girls." He concludes the letter by saying "I have been very unwell, sore throat and disordered bowels etc. etc. Wm. Matthews."

W. Emerson Wilson, ed., *Plantation Life at Rose Hill: The Diaries of Martha Ogle Forman, 1814-1845* (Wilmington, Delaware: The Historical Society of Delaware, 1976) 261- "November 18, 1828 – Mr. William Knight here for dinner and all night" 339- "August 29, 1834 – Mr. Knight here with Mr. Biddle to dine with Mr. Bryan Lewis brought back young William Knight" 361- "William Knight and his bride made their first appearance at church today." 367- "June 16, 1836 – The general and I spent this afternoon with Mrs. William Knight and was much pleased with Mrs. Knight and our visit." 439- "May 21, 1843, Mr. Knight buried today." 359- "Feb. 2, 1836 – Lewis took 24 lbs. of butter to Miss Knight for Judge Chambers."

73. Cann 235; Cann 237. Kitty Knight never married and there is no report of romance in the surviving records of her life. Her escort at the Philadelphia event with President Washington was Benjamin Harrison, former Governor of Virginia. Joseph Horgan, *History of St. Dennis Church, Galena, Maryland, 1855-1970* (Philadelphia: William T. Cooke Publishers, 1971)19. Colonel John Veazey, Jr., who commanded the Bohemia Battalion, called upon Kitty Knight often. William Joynes, "He Swore By Kitty," *Baltimore American* November 24, 1963. The following is an excerpt from a letter written by Rev. Ambrose Maréchal, Pastor at Bohemia from 1793-1799 and later Third Archbishop of Baltimore, dated: Baltimore 5-2-1800 to Hugh Matthews, Barrister:

"Besides many reasons I have of going once more to Bohemia, there is a most weighty one with me. it is the promise Miss Katie Knight made me per Doctor Scanlan to become a practical Christian, if I be willing to come back again to my former station: and surely I have too much charity for that young and amiable lady not to be second, as much as it weighs in my power, her pious resolutions. Although she is so very cunning that when there —?—, she will perhaps laugh, and she is so good natured as to believe the Doctor proved me -?— —?—never made such an agreement. However, present her my respects and to the other ladies, I remain with the same sentiments, Your most obedient servant, Ambrose Marechal"

Larry O'Hare, "Kitty Knight: The Revolutionary Era's Grand Lady," *Cecil Whig*, Elkton, Maryland, July 8, 1970: At the time of her death she had read all the English classics and "could quote page after page of favorite authors." She is also remembered as "having had rare conversational powers."

74. George Johnston, *History of Cecil County, Maryland* (Elkton, Maryland: the writer, 1881, Historical Society of Cecil County, 1956) 408. Devastation was caused by the British invasion from 1812 to 1815. The Maryland militia defeated the British at the Battle of Caulk's Field on August 30, 1814. This preceded only by twelve days The British attack and defeat at the Battle of Baltimore and Fort McHenry and the end of their occupation of Tangier Island that had acted as their major headquarters for the navy operations in the Chesapeake Bay for more than two years. Our War of 1812 was due briefly to results brought about by Napoleonic European Wars. In 1793 Washington had issued a proclamation of neutrality. Peace with England was declared in 1814. Larry O'Hara, "Kitty Knight: The Revolutionary Era's Grand Lady" *Cecil Whig*, Elkton, Maryland, July 8, 1970: The British were burning each house in Georgetown. Unwilling to yield to the command of the British officer Admiral Cockburn, Kitty remained inside her house. When they tossed a flaming brand into her house she twice "beat out the flames with her broom." The admiral declared: "so brave a bird was worthy of its nest" and he ordered the house to be spared. A novel has been written about this incident and Kitty Knight: Gertrude Crownfield, *Conquering Kitty* (Philadelphia: Lippincott Co., 1935). The Kitty Knight chapter of the War of 1812 is the only chapter on the Eastern Shore with active members from Kent, Caroline, Talbot, Dorchester, and Queen Anne counties as well as some from Delaware. Cann 236: Two houses in Georgetown were connected and enlarged to make the present Kitty Knight House, a restaurant and inn.

A bronze plaque attached to the river side of the Kitty Knight House reads as follows:

In honor of Mistress Kitty Knight
Revolutionary Belle and Beauty
A friend of General George Washington
When the British burned Georgetown in 1813
Her heroic efforts saved this house which
later became her home.
Placed by London Bridge Chapter DAR.

Kitty Knight's will is dated December 7, 1852 and probated on March 18, 1856. Recorded Liber IF No. 1, folio 60. Executor was William Knight, son of her brother William, Knight to whom she left her earthly belongings.

75. Devitt, "Bohemia," *RACHS* 24:128 – Maréchal's name appears for the last time in the baptismal register. Cann 236; Hughes, Documents 2:749 - sale of negroes at Bohemia, objected to by a resolution of the Corporation of the Clergy, Maréchal's notes of purchase and sales of slaves 1794,

1795, 1796; Cann 235; AAB, ZZ-A-S, Maréchal Diary; Georgetown University Archives 174-C-Bohemia Day Book - Maréchal closed his account on August 13, 1799. Georgetown University Archives, *Bohemia Manor Varia* 103 N1 - P6.5, Series 21, Maryland Province, Society of Jesus, Series 20, folder 54R1-26: Letter August 29, 1798 - Hugh Matthews to Ambrose Maréchal and James O'Donald; letters - September 15, October 17, 1799, February 20, May 2, 1800, Ambrose Maréchal to Hugh Matthews; Lease (1795) between Ambrose Maréchal, S.S. and James O'Donald; Lease (1796) of negro slave by Ambrose Maréchal to James O'Donald; Maréchal settlement w. S. George before leaving Bohemia 1797; Account of Ambrose Maréchal with George Reece 1797 - 98; Bond 1797 between Ambrose Maréchal and his negro slave Patrick Barnes for purchase of freedom; petition for freedom, Patrick Barnes (slave) v. Ambrose Maréchal, S.S.; certificate of contract (1798) for hire of negro slave by A. Maréchal to John Morton. In 1795 Marie Jacques Dominique D'Orlic from San Domingo was business manager at the Bohemia plantation. Memorandum by Maréchal, January, 1795, from Georgetown University Archives, J.A. Frederick, "Notes taken from the Papers at the Baltimore Cathedral, April 17, 1898" Series One, folder four: Adjustment of outstanding debts, January, 1795. Jane Campbell, "San Domingo Refugees in Philadelphia, Compiled from the Original D'Orlic - Rodrique Papers," *RACHS* 28 (1917) 97-144, 30 (1919) 309-330. CHRISTIAN BURIAL OF SLAVES AT BOHEMIA – March 15, 1795 – On the priest's plantation area Betsy, negro girl, daughter of Dilly, slave on the same plantation; the girl infant was born and baptized on the 7th of January in the same year. She was buried in the Catholic church yard of the aforesaid place. December 27, 1795 – Died in the Sassafras's Neck, Ned, son of Ned, slave of the Rev. Mr. Tessier, and of Rachel, slave of Mr. Matthews. He was buried in this church yard. March 14, 1796 – Died in Delaware State, Joseph, free negro about 60 years old. He belonged to the priests. August 4, 1796 – Died on the priest's plantation a negro man named Stephen, of a cancer. His remains were buried in the Catholic church yard of Little Bohemia. August 17, 1796 – Died in thorough fair (sic) Neck a negro man belonging to the priests named Clinus, about 24 years old. He was buried at his mother's place. May 27, 1797 – Died on the priest's plantation, Anna, daughter of Dilly and Barney.

76. Ronin John Murtha, "The Life of the Most Reverend Ambrose, Maréchal, Third Archbishop of Baltimore, 1768-1829" (Doctoral dissertation, Catholic University of America, 1965) 4; Hughes, Documents 2:766
77. Devitt, "Bohemia," *RACHS* 24 (1913) 126
78. ADW, Bohemia Records, Father Tessier baptized, at Appoquinimink Forest, New Castle County, Delaware, *December 28, 1794* - Steven, son of Catherine, slave of Mrs. Reynolds, about one month old. Sponsors were Dick, Tessier's slave, and Patience, Mrs. Reynolds' slave; *May 3, 1795* - William, son of Michael Brian and Ann Morris, his wife, born January 12, 1795. Sponsors were Samuel Peter Watkinson and Mary, his wife; *June 28, 1795* - Rachael, negro girl, about five months old, daughter of Charles and Grace, slave of Sarah Cole. Sponsor was Peregrine Cole.
79. ADW, Bohemia Records - May 9, 1796, Thomas and Elizabeth Hirons, children of John and Susanna Hirons. No witnesses.
80. ADW, Bohemia Records - August 30, 1795, Father Tessier baptized Margaret Burgoin, six years old, daughter of James Burgoin and Sarah Wheelan, his lawful wife. Sponsors were Collins and Laura Nowland.
81. ADW, Bohemia Register, Father Tessier baptized at Lynch - town - *April 16, 1795* - William Connor, three weeks old, son of John Martin Connor and Suzannah, his wife. Sponsor was Becky Hankey.
82. Father Tessier performed marriages: *April 18, 1795* - at Bohemia - marriage between Samuel and Esther, slaves of Dr. William Matthews. Witness was Rev. Francis Beeston; *September 11, 1795* - at Bohemia, marriage between Sam, slave of Reverend Tessier, and Monto, slave of Abigail Ryland. Witnesses were Reverend John Ray and John O'Donald; *December 21, 1795* - at Head of Bohemia marriage between Joseph, slave of Reverend Tessier, and Elizabeth, slave of 82. Father Tessier performed marriages: *April 18, 1795* - at Bohemia - marriage between Samuel and Esther, slaves of Dr. William Matthews. Witness was Rev. Francis Beeston; *September 11, 1795* - at Bohemia, marriage between Sam, slave of Reverend Tessier, and Monto, slave of Abigail Ryland. Witnesses were Reverend John Ray and John O'Donald; *December 21, 1795* - at

Head of Bohemia marriage between Joseph, slave of Reverend Tessier, and Elizabeth, slave of Richard Flintham. Witnesses were Daniel and Stephen, free men.

83. ADW, Bohemia Records - Queen Anne County: Father Tessier baptized Sudlersville mission station - *June 14, 1795* - Thomas Larey, born October 26, 1793, son of Laurence Larey and Mary his wife. Sponsors were John Cain and Nancy Seth; *August 10, 1795* - Juliana, two years old, daughter of John and Nelly Gafford. Sponsors were James Sweeny and Sophia Gafford.

84. ADW, Bohemia Registers, Father Tessier baptized at Chestertown (Head of Chester), *November 9, 1794* - Elizabeth about four years old, and Biddy, about one year old, daughters of John Williams and his wife. There were no sponsors.

85. ADW, *Burial Records of Bohemia*: Jesse Nowland, died in Sassafras Hundred, Md. December 9, 1794; Bridget Nowland, died at Bohemia Plantation, December 21, 1794; Stephen Nowland, son of Thomas and Mary, Kent Co., Md., September 18, 1796; Jeremiah Carey of New Castle, Del buried at Bohemia, February 3, 1795; Elizabeth Bayards, daughter of Jacob and Ann Bayards of New Castle County, Del. Buried March 20, 1794; Jeremiah Carey, of New Castle, Del. Buried February 3, 1795; Francis Craddock, son of Daniel Craddock and Elizabeth O'Donald of Sassafras Neck, buried January 1, 1794; Elizabeth Craddock, wife of Daniel Craddock of Sassafras Neck, January 8, 1796; Daniel Craddock, son of Daniel Craddock, buried August 2, 1798.

Father Tessier said funeral prayers over grave in Queen Anne County: *August 10, 1795* - Rachael Gafford, about 70 years old, died in March, 1795; *October 12, 1795* - Peter Severe, died in September, 1795, about forty-six years old; *November 8, 1795* - Sarah Gafford, about thirty-five years old, died November 3, 1795.

86. Hughes, Documents 2:763 - Tessier on the grant made of Bohemia to the Sulpicians; Hughes, Documents 2:764 – Tessier's Memoirs 1792-1805, transactions regarding Bohemia, extracts from Jean Marie Tessier, *Epoques du Seminaire de Baltimore Redigées par M. Tessier le 28 Juillet 1804 et Continuees Successivement*

87. Ruane 36; AAB *Bohemia Plantation Book 1790-1796* Financial Records, (page 22) September, 1795 to (page 29) December, 1796. Hughes, Documents 2:750 – specimen of Bohemia debts discharged June 28, 1796.

88. Devitt, "Bohemia," *RACHS* (June, 1913) 125; *Woodstock Letters* 15:227 - Charles Sewall, S.J., and financial troubles at Bohemia.

89. GUA, Maryland Province, Society of Jesus (hereafter GUA), Series One, Folder One:

Bohemia, 1798
White People:

Men

Don Craddock	Thomas Nowland	Peter Haggart
Charles Heverin	William Nicholson	Joseph Cain
William Reynolds	Livy Gafford	Thomas Craddock
Tally Reynolds	William Craddock	Uriah Crout
John Reynolds	E. C. Counsell	William Heverin
Jeremiah Reynolds	John Wright	Mick McKervan
Jeremiah Reynolds	William Craddock	Liger Cometele
P. Taggart	James Cometele	Charles Seth
Thomas Campbell		

Women

M. Fullam	Margaret Nowland	M. Reynolds, John's wife
Barbara Heverin	Nancy Reynolds	Sara Reynolds
Sarah Flintham	Polly Reynolds	Mary Wright
Mary Nowland	M. Severe	Margaret Craddock
Mary Carty	Sara Gafford	Alice O'Donald
Sally Gafford	Biddy O'Donald	Alma Gafford
Margaret Reynolds	Catherine Pennington	Sally Nowland
Helena Bernard	Sally Counsell	Margaret Nugent
Margaret Watkins	Mary Carty	Margaret Heverin
Polly Horning	Margaret Reynolds	

Black People

Men

Old Ralph	Jacob Anderson	Old Ned of Mr. Millegan
Will, of Dr. Matthews	Jake of Hugh Matthews	Dick
Jack	Barny	Jacky
Dary	Charles	Barny
Moses, of Mr. Pennington		

Women

Jenny, of Mr. Lloyd	Sarah	Phyllis
Jake's wife	Suky	Rachel
Mary, of Mr. Onde	Becky, of Dr. Matthews	Isabelle, of Mr. O'Donald
Jenny	Sarah, of Dr. Matthews	Teresia, of Mr. Blau
Margaret, of Mr. Beetle	Jenny, of Llyod's	Betsy, of free mullatto girl
Sarah	Dithy, of Mr. Campbell	Sally, of T. Reynolds
Susanna	Diana	Poll
Betty	Nelly, of Mr. Nowland	

90. Hughes, Documents 1:766; Ruane 74
91. Kauffman 45-47; Ruane 36-39; Hughes, Documents 2:754 - Restoration of Bohemia to the Corporation, August 22, 1799.
92. Ruane 81; Georgetown University Archives, Maryland Province, Society of Jesus 103-S1-T9, series 21-map in French of Bohemia Manor (sic) Plantation (1795), Varia 103-R1-R7, Series 20, folder 54 R1-Z6, Receipt January 1800 of Robert Molyneaux, S.J., Series 21: (1800) notice of a Cecil County commission to mark and bound land tracts at Little Bohemia. Letter, Francis Beeston, S.J. to Hugh Matthews, February 24, 1801; Petition, March 1, 1801, to the justices of Cecil County to mark and bound lanes at Bohemia; letter, Archbishop John Carroll to Father Beeston or Hugh Matthews, March 3, 1801; Order of Cecil County Court (1801) appointing commissioners to mark and bound Bohemia tracts; official survey of Bohemia tracts (1801); Survey by commissioners Box 4, 103R4.5 map; letter; Father Beeston to Hugh Matthews, June 16, 1801; map (copy) of Bohemia farm (1801). Hughes, Documents 2:756 - Corporation proceedings winding up the Bohemia accounts October 9, 1799.
93. Also known as Deroset and Derosier, Devitt, "Bohemia" *RACHS* 24 (1913): 125, 128, 139; Leo F. Ruskowski, *French Emigré Priests in the United States, 1791-1815* (Washington, D.C.: Catholic University of America, 1940), 37-38; Norbert Miller, "Pioneer Capuchin Missionaries in the United States, 1784-1816," *Historical Records and Studies of New York* 21 (1932): 175-176; *RACHS* 1 (1887): 142, 373; *RACHS* 7 (1896): 51-53; Thomas Hughes, *History of the Society of Jesus in North America, Colonial and Federal* (New York: Longmans, Green and Co., 1907), Documents 1:296-297. John Gilmary Shea, *History of the Catholic Church in the United States* (New York: P.J. Kennedy, 1879) 2:451; Devitt, "History of The Maryland - New York Province," *Woodstock Letters* 63 (1934) 30. GUA – Archives, Maryland Province, Society of Jesus BOHEMIA FARM-MAP [COPY]-(1801)
94. Devitt, "Bohemia" *RACHS* 24:129; Staunton was a native of Mayo County, Ireland, and was ordained in Galway about 1792. McGowan 22, Francis E. Tourscher O.S.A., *Old St. Augustine's* (Philadelphia: 1937) 19; *RACHS* 7 (1896) 4 – "Extracts from the Minute Book of the Proceedings of the Association of Roman Catholic Clergymen" – meeting at St. Thomas Manor, Charles Co., Md. – August 28, 1799 – "Rev. Mr. Staunton appointed Manager of that part of Bohemia estate allotted for the clergyman's support." Tourscher 33 – records of baptism at St. Augustine's, Philadelphia, December 19, 1803, Fr. Staunton baptized Arthur Lafferty, born in New Castle, Del., October 16, 1803; McGowan 22 – Staunton left this country shortly after 1807, and was stationed at Seville and Cadiz in Spain, as vicar of the Catholic Church at Gibralter, at Lisbon in Portugal, and at Dublin, Ireland, where it is supposed he died in 1815.
95. Devitt, "Bohemia," *RACHS* 24:128 - Laurence Phelan, immediate successor to Maréchal; Francis X. Reuss, "Sacramental Registers of St. Joseph's Church, Philadelphia," *RACHS* 16 (1905) 202; Hanley 1:368 - John Carroll to Laurence Phelan, Baltimore, December 27, 1801:

Phelan will have to pay board if he remains at Bohemia. Rev. Mr. Fitzpatrick has been appointed in his place. 1801 - Phelan to St. Mary's, Philadelphia. Hanley 1:386 - Carroll withdraws Phelan's faculties citing sobriety." - AAB-6-6-12; Cann 8; J. Thomas Scharf, and Thompson Westcott, *History of Philadelphia* (Philadelphia: L.H. Everts and Co., 1884) 2:1373; "Letters from the Baltimore Archives" *RACHS* 19 (1908) 462: Steven Badin to Bishop Carroll, at Ralph Lancaster's, Kentucky, March 4, 1798. "Mr. Phelan is endowed with a talent for speaking." "Extracts from the Minute Book of the Proceedings of the Association of Roman Catholic Clergymen - August 28, 1799," *RACHS* - ? (1896) 4; Spalding 27, No 28 - October 9, 1795 - Notation for Rev. Laurence Silvester Phelan: Bishop Carroll wrote a formula for Phelan to use concerning title to land left by Rev. Theodore Brouwer. Spalding 63 No. 64 - December 21, 1801 - Carroll wrote Phelan, a former priest of Philadelphia then at Bohemia about a transfer back to Philadelphia. The priest signed all his letters to Carroll as "Laur. Silv. Phelan." Hanley, *JCP* 2:372 Carroll to Laurence Phelan: Carroll expresses surprise at Phelan's remaining at Bohemia; AAB, *Carroll Letterbook* 3:49; Spalding 64, No. 66 – Carroll to Rev. Laurence Silvester Phelan, Jan 11, 1802 – Carroll is surprised that Phelan has not gone to Philadelphia. He had not insisted, but Phelan had written he would return to live there, this before he had sown any wheat for the next crop. Carroll never told anyone that Phelan might remain at Bohemia if he liked, and he is determined not to retract the promises he made in Philadelphia. The rest of Phelan's letter is a matter for the Corporation of the Clergy, to whom it will be referred. The opinion of Phelan's lawyer's may have some effect upon the Corporation but not upon Carroll. AAB, *Carroll Letterbook* 3:54; Spalding 70, No. 73 - Hanley, *JCP* 2:386 - Carroll to Rev. Laurence Silvester Phelan, March 15, 1802: In consequence of Phelan's failure to abide by Carroll's arrangements and earlier directives he is to consider himself as no longer having a pastoral charge and his faculties "for the present" are withdrawn. n.1 – Phelan would later be named pastor at Chambersburg, Pennsylvania. AAB, *Carroll Letterbook* 3:48; Hanley, *JCP* 2:368; Spalding 63, No. 64—Carroll To Reverend Laurence Silvester Phelan, December 27, 1801— Mr. Beeston has informed Carroll of Phelan's refusal to leave Bohemia to go to Philadelphia before he received full value for the crop on the ground. This is not Carroll's concern. Mr. Fitzpatrick alone has the right to the house. If Phelan stays, he must pay rent. n.2 – Rev. R. FitzPatrick, Phelan's replacement, may not have gone to Bohemia since he is still found at St. Mary's in Philadelphia in 1802. AAB, Bohemia Plantation Book 30-34: "Inventory of the Effects, Goods, Utensils etc. found at Bohemia at my taking possession of the place on the 1st of April, 1802. House Furnitures, Kitchen Furnitures, Farming Utensils, Poultry and Bees." (Document is unsigned).

96. Devitt, "Bohemia," *RACHS* 24 (1913) 129. Pasquet had previously (1797) been at Newtown, St. Mary's County and (1800) at Deer Creek, Harford County. "Newtown Manor," *Woodstock Letters* 15 (1886) 28. Hughes, *Documents* 1:770 - Members of the Select Body of the Clergy, June 5, 1795, Reverend William Pasquet is among those listed. Hughes, *Documents* 2:785 - says William Pasquet, elected to the Corporation of the Clergy, had no previous connection to the Jesuits. Cann 8, 40, 46. GUA – Archives, Maryland Province, Society of Jesus – COMMISSION TO BOUND & MARK-(1800) BOHEMIA-RENTS (1808) F. Edward Wright, *Vital Records of the Jesuit Missions of the Eastern Shore 1760-1800* 49 – BURIALS AT BOHEMIA: 1790 Sep 10 Died near Warwick Rachael Ward, wife of William Ward, buried on 12th Catholic burying ground at Bohemia; Oct 17 died Kent Co, Eleanor Boiles wife of Robert Boiles, buried 19th in Catholic burying ground at Bohemia; November 12 Died at Warwick, Charles Connor, buried next day in Catholic burying ground at Bohemia; 1791 – Mar 8 in New Castle Co, Del, Mary Reynolds died of a putrid sore throat, buried next day in Catholic Church yard at the head of Little Bohemia; Mar 14 at his house in New Castle Co, Del, Edward Knott died of an appoplexy, buried 16th in Catholic Church yard at head of Little Bohemia. Mar 30 – Died at the house of Doctor William Matthews in Sassefrass Neck, Ann Scanlan, widow died of a consumption, buried next day in family burying ground near the dwelling of Doctor William Matthews. May 24 – on the priest's plantation at the Head of Little Bohemia, died Prudence a negro slave, buried in Church yard on the plantation. May 31 – in New Castle Co, Del, died of the small pox, George Wright, Senr, in an advanced age, buried next day in family burying ground. Jun 26 – in New Castle Co, Del, died of the smallpox, Catharine Knott, aged 6 yrs, dau of Edward Knott, lately decd, and Catharine Knott, buried next day in Catholic church yard at the Head

of Little Bohemia. In Sassafras Neck died of a putrid sore throat, (blank) Maguire, wife of George Maguire, buried Catholic Church yard at head of Little Bohemia. Near the head of Little Bohemia died of a dropsy in an advanced age Rachael Gribbin, widow, she was buried next day in Catholic Church Yard at the Head of Little Bohemia. Dec 26 on the Priest's plantation at the Head of Little Bohemia died Frances, a negro child, aged 2 yrs, dau of Robert and Henny, negro slave of Revd Fran: Beeston, buried next day in Church yard. Dec 28 in New Castle Co, Del, died Roger Cain, a native of Ireland, buried next day in Catholic Churchyard at the head of Little Bohemia. Died this year White males 3, females 5, negroes females 2. 1792 – Jan 16 – in New Castle Co, Del, James Matthews, was shot by Richard Heath. His body was interred 18th near mansion of his brother Doctor William Matthews in Sassafras Neck. Jan 21 – Kent Co, Md, James Brady died of a gathering in his throat, in an advanced age, buried on 23d in Catholic Churchyard at the head of Little Bohemia. Feb 2 – at George Town, Kent Co, Md, Barbara Lee died of a consumption in an advanced age, buried next day in Catholic Church yard at the Head of Little Bohemia. Feb 19 – At the Head of Little Bohemia died James Calowell Erwin, aged 2 mos., son of Robert and Catharine Erwin, buried next day in Catholic Church yard at the Head of Little Bohemia. Mar 5 – Near the Head of Little Bohemia, died Jonathan aged 2 yrs, son of Perry Greenwood and Henrietta his wife, both free mulattoes, buried next day in Catholic Church yard Head of Little Bohemia. Apr 23 – At the Head of Little Bohemia, died of a consumption, Hannah, negro slave of Revd, Fran: Beeston, buried next day in Catholic Church yard at Head of Little Bohemia. May 13 – in QA Co, Christina Monsieur died aged 12 yrs, of a fever, buried next day by in family burying ground of Jacob Gafford. Sep 3 – at Duck Creek Cross Roads, New Castle Co, Del, of a fever, Edward Robinson, native of Ireland, blacksmith, by trade, buried Catholic Church yard at Head of Little Bohemia, Cecil Co. Dec 15 in New Castle Co, Del, Charles Heverin, Junr. Son of Wm and Hannah Heverin, died of a fever, interred 17th in family burying ground near his late dwelling. 1793 – Jan 7 in Sassafras Neck Cecil Co, Robert, negro slave of Daniel Craddock, died of the cholera, in and advanced age; interred next day in Catholic church yard head of Little Bohemia. Jul 17 - at the head of little Bohemia, Alice O'Donald, widow, about 56 yrs, buried Church yard of little Bohemia. Aug 12 – At Warwick died Maria wife of John Sappington, converted to the Catholic faith in her last sickness, buried in fam burying ground. Aug 13 – At Warwick died Eleanor Rigs wife of John Pennington Rigs, 29 yrs old, buried church yard of little Bohemia. Aug 28 – Kent Co died Anne Lusby (?), about 50 yrs old, buried in Church yard of little Bohemia, widow. Aug 30 – at the Head of little Bohemia died Clement son of Elizabeth slave of Rev A. Maréchal, buried in Church yard of little Bohemia, widow. Sep 25 – in New Castle Co, died John, about 11 mos old, son of John and Maria Wright, buried in Church yard of little Bohemia. Sep 30 – at Warwick died John, son of John Penington and Eleanor Rigs, buried in Church yard of little Bohemia. Oct 10 – in Cecil Co died Henry son of James and Sala Gribbing, buried Church yard, head of Bohemia. Nov – buried at head of little Bohemia A. Brown, widow. Dec 17 on Priests plantation died Isaac, slave of the Seminary of Balt, buried in Church yard of Bohemia. 1794 – Jan 1 In Sassafras neck died Francis son of David Craddock and Elizabeth O'Donald, 8 days old buried Church yard of Bohemia. Feb 10 – in Cecil Co, died Morris Kelegan (Calahan?), 74 widower, buried Church yard of little Bohemia. Feb 27 – at Warwick Anna, wife of Stephen Makefall(?), about 28, buried in Church yard of little Bohemia. Mar 16 – at Warwick died William Henry O'Conor about 38 yrs old, extraordinary deaf, buried Church yard of Bohemia. Apr 30 – At Warwick died Isak 3 ? yrs old, son of Patrick, slave of Rev Abm. Maréchal and of Molly, buried in church yard of Bohemia. May 16 – at head of Sassafras's river, died Sara dau of Benjamin Clerk and Theresia, his wife, about 9 yrs old; buried Church yard of little Bohemia, Jun 11 – in Cecil Co, died Mole Hugh wife of Peter Nugent, about 50 yrs old, buried Church yard of Bohemia. Aug 9 – at Bohemia died Nely Kolegan, about 30 yrs old, buried Church yard of Bohemia. Aug 10 – at Duck Creek cross roads died Frederic Wise about 45 yrs old, buried Church yard of little Bohemia. Nov 28 – Died in Sassafras Neck, Venus about 90 yrs old, slave of Dr. Wm. Mathews, buried in burying ground f the doctor. Dec 9 – at the Priest's Plantation at the head of little Bohemia died Mary Anna Bowling, about 52 yrs old, buried next day at Church yard of little Bohemia. Dec 9 – at Sassafras Hundred, died Jesse Nowland bout 45 yrs old, buried Catholic Church yard of little Bohemia. Dec 8 – at Priest's plantation died Jonathan, infant negro, son of Ralph and Jenny, slave of the same plantation, he was 5 yrs old buried

Catholic Church yard. Dec 21 at Warwick died Thomas Burns, an Irishman, about 22 buried Catholic Church yard of little Bohemia. Dec 21 – on Priest's Plantation died Briditt Nowland, wife of Mr. Carey Counsell, about 35 yrs old, buried Catholic Church yard of little Bohemia. 1795 – Feb 3 New Castle hundred, Del, died Jeremiah Carty, about 46 yrs old, 2 days after, he was buried in Catholic church yard Head of Little Bohemia. Feb 20 – in New Castle Co, died Elizabeth, dau of Jacob Reynolds and his late wife Ann, about 19 yrs old, buried Catholic Church yard Head of Little Bohemia. Mar 15 – on the Priest's plantation died Betsy, negro girl dau of Dilly, slave on the plantation, infant born and bapt of 7 Jan same year, buried Catholic Church yard. May 1 – in New Castle Co, died Mary Reynolds, wife of late John Reynolds, about 61 to 62 yrs old, buried sun net in fam burying ground. Aug 10 – in QA Co., prayers were said on grave of Rachel Gafford, about 70 yrs old when she died in Mar 1795. Oct 4 – buried in Catholic Church yard of little Bohemia, William, son of William slave of Mr. Meleghan and Ester his wife. Oct 10 – buried in Catholic Church yard of little Bohemia, Mary dau of Richard Corbely and Mary his wife, about 3 yrs old. Oct 12 – in QA Co, Revd John Tessier, said the funeral prayers on the grave of Peter Severe, who died a month ago, about 46 yrs old. Nov 2 – Died at Warwick Daniel a boy almost 3 yrs old, son of Daniel Riggs and Alithea his wife, buried in Catholic Churchyard at head of little Bohemia. Nov 5 – Died nr Warwick, Mathew about 6 weeks old, son of Henry Gribbin and Sarah his wife, buried in Catholic church yard head of little Bohemia. Nov 8 – in QA Co funeral prayers said at grave of Salah about 45 yrs old, died 3 of inst. Dec 27 – died in Sassafras's Neck, William Burke, about 60 yrs old buried in Church yard of little Bohemia. Dec 27 – died in Sassafras's Neck Ned son of Ned, slave of Rev Tessier and Rachel slave of Mr. Mathews, buried in this churchyard. 1796 – Jan 8 – died in Sassafras neck Elizabeth wife of Daniel Craddock, buried in Catholic Church yard of little Bohemia. Jan 13 – died nr Warwick, Mary Cassy(?) buried Catholic Church yard of Little Bohemia. Jan 17 – died in Sassafras's Neck Luisa dau of Tate and Daris, both Doctor Mathew's slaves, buried Church yard of little Bohemia. Jan 21 Walter Fullam died. Jan 21 – died in Dragon's Neck, Walter Fullam about 64 yrs old, buried Church yard of little Bohemia. Died at Frederick town, Anna wife of Charles Dermott about 25 yrs old, buried Church yard of little Bohemia. Mar 4 – died in Sassafras Neck, John about 66 old, slave of Mistress Noland. Mar 14 – died in New Castle Co, Samuel Watkins, about 70 yrs old, buried Church yard of little Bohemia, school master in the forest. Died in Sassafras Neck a negro woman named Kate about 70 yrs old, buried Catholic Church yard of little Bohemia. June (?) died in Delaware state, Joseph, free negro, about 60 yrs old, he belonged once to the priest. Aug 4 – died on the Priest's plantation a negro man named Stephen, of a cancer, buried in Catholic Church yard of little Bohemia. Aug 17 – died near Middletown, Thomas Mullen, about 40 yrs old, buried Church yard of Bohemia. died in Thorough-fair neck, negro man belonging to the priest named Clinus, about 24 yrs old, buried at his mother's place. Sep 1 – Died near Warwick, Mary Lyon about 46 yrs old, buried in church yard of Bohemia. Sep 18 – Died in Kent Co, Sylvester about 5 yrs old son of Thomas Nowland and Mary his wife, buried Church yard of Bohemia. Died in New Castle Co, Sarah about 42, yrs old, wife of Charles Hevering, buried Church yard of Bohemia. Oct 23 – died at Warwick, Samuel, son of Thomas Delahand and Casey his wife, about 22 months old, buried Church yard of Bohemia. Nov 2 died at Warwick, James Martin about 40 yrs old, buried Church yard of Bohemia. Nov 3 – Died at Warwick, Peggy Roberson, about 40 yrs old, buried Church yard of Bohemia. Nov 11 – died at Warwick, Daniel Riggs, about 44 yrs old buried church yard of Bohemia. New Castle Co – Nov 26 died in the Forest, Holland Webb about 57 yrs old; buried Church yard of Bohemia. 1797 – Jan 20 – Died in Sassafras Neck Sala Lee , buried Catholic church yard of Bohemia. New Castle Co, Mar 14 died in the Forest, John Davy about 34 hrs old buried Church yard of Bohemia. Kent Co, Mar 21 – died in Kent Co, Benjamin Crout, about 50 yrs old, buried Church yard of Bohemia. May 5 – died on Bohemia Mannor, Mary Carty about 82 yrs old, buried Church yard of Bohemia. May 21 – died in Kent Theresia Crout about 16 yrs old, buried cemetery of Bohemia. May 27 – Died on the Priest's Plantation, Anna dau of Dilly and Barney. Aug 22 – died near Warwick, E. C. Counsell, about 36 yrs old, his remains buried in Church yard of Bohemia. 1798 – Jan 13 – died in Sassafras Neck, negro man named Ned, slave of Mistress Nowland, buried in Church yard at Bohemia. Feb 8 – Died in Sassafras Neck, Marguerit slave of Mistriss Bidle; buried Church yard of Bohemia. Feb 28 – died in New Castle Co, John Wright about 36 yrs old, buried Church yard of Bohemia. Died at head of Bohemia, Ned about 65 yrs old, slave of Mr. Milligan, buried Church yard of the same place. Aug 2 – died in Sassafras Neck, Daniel Craddock about 48 yrs old, buried Church yard of Bohemia. Aug 21 – died at the Head of Bohemia, Rev Stephen Faure A French Priest residing at Wilmington Del. About 37 yrs old, buried north end of the church of Bohemia, grave head burying at the east side of border of the gospel window. Nov 10 – died in Knox-town, Molly Johns, about 80 yrs old, buried Church yard of Bohemia. Dec 24 – died in Bohemia Neck, Rebecca Tailor, about 60 yrs old, buried Bohemia grave yard. 1799, Died in Bohemia Neck, Catharine O'Donald, about 20 yrs old, buried in Church yard of Bohemia. July 14 – died at Bohemia, Jeremiah Hogan, native of Ireland, about (blank) yrs old; buried in Church yard of the chapel Bohemia. GUA – Bohemia Daybook, September 16, 1796 – "bought half gallon of honey from Rachel: 3 shillings and 9 pence." Cann 167 – CHRISTIAN BURIAL OF SLAVES AT BOHEMIA 1793-8-30 At the head of Little Bohemia, died Clement, son of Elizabeth, widow, slave of the Rev. A. Maréchal. He was buried in the church yard of Little Bohemia. 1793-12-17 On the priest's plantation, died Isaac, slave of the Seminary of Baltimore. His remains were buried in the church yard of Bohemia. 1794-3-30 At Warwick died, Isaak, three years and one half old, son of Patrick and Molly, slaves of the Rev. Amb. Maréchal. His remains were buried in the church yard at Bohemia. 1794-12-8 At the priest's plantation died Jonathan. He was five years old, and was buried in the Catholic Church yard.

97. Ralph D. Gray, "Delaware and Its Canal, The Early History of the Chesapeake and Delaware Canal, 1796-1829" (Master's Thesis, University of Delaware 1958) 49, published in *Delaware History* 8 (March, 1959) 383 – 97; Post-Revolutionary agitation for the canal, Gray 16; Alice E. Miller, *Cecil County, Maryland, A Study in Local History* (Port Deposit, Maryland: the author, 1949) 45

98. AAB 6-0-1, Latrobe to Carroll, New Castle, Delaware, April 10, 1804; AAB 6-0-2, Latrobe to Carroll, New Castle, Delaware, May 16, 1804. Scharf, *History of Delaware* 2:650 - Latrobe lived in New Castle, Delaware in 1804, and in Wilmington 1805-1806 at a home on the east side of Market Street a few doors below Second Street. He settled in Washington, D.C. in 1807. Talbot Hamlin, *Benjamin Henry Latrobe* (New York: Oxford University Press, 1955) 203: Latrobe was born in May, 1764. His father was an Irish Protestant, his mother a devout Moravian who now lived in Pennsylvania. In the summer of 1784 Latrobe came to America to claim land left him by his mother. He lived in Virginia until 1798 when he moved to Philadelphia. When commissioned to survey for the Chesapeake and Delaware canal, he moved to New Castle, Delaware. While engaged in the work of the canal he lived later at Iron Hill and in Wilmington. From the spring of 1804 throughout Latrobe's years in the eastern United States Latrobe worked spasmodically on the Roman Catholic Cathedral of Baltimore – Fiske Kimball, "Latrobe's Designs for the Cathedral of Baltimore" *Architectural Record* 42 (December, 1917) no. 6 and 43 (January, 1918) no. 1. Also J. M. Riordan, *Cathedral Records From the Beginning of Catholicity in Baltimore to the Present Time* (Baltimore: Catholic Mirror Publishing Co., 1906) 42; On July 7, 1806, the cornerstone for the Baltimore cathedral was laid. Archbishop Carroll would not live to see the completion of the cathedral some fifteen years later. John Gilmary Shea, *Life and Times of John Carroll* 598 – "The plans of the Cathedral were the work of an eminent architect, B. Henry Latrobe, who at first submitted plans for a Gothic cathedral, but as Roman or Greek architecture was preferred, he prepared the plan for the present Cathedral." John W. Bowen, S.S., "A History of the Baltimore Cathedral to 1876" (Catholic University of America, Master's Thesis, 1962) 10. AAB, Benjamin Latrobe to Rt. Rev. John Carroll from Wilmington, Delaware, May 16, 1804, from New Castle, Delaware, May 16, 1804; from Wilmington, Delaware, April 16, 1805; from Wilmington, Delaware, April 27, 1805; from Wilmington, Delaware, April 28, 1805; from Wilmington, Delaware, July 9, 1805. *Centenary of St. Mary's Seminary, Baltimore, 1791-1891* (Baltimore: John Murphy Company, 1891): Benjamin H. Latrobe, 1821-1823, oldest son of the architect, and Osmun Latrobe, 1848-1849, another son, were students at St. Mary's College, Baltimore. *RACHS* 1:370. Herberman, *Sulpicians* 120 – Latrobe was the scion of a French Huguenot family which left France after the revocation of the Edict of Nantes. Hamlin 463 – In religion, Benjamin Latrobe was a humanist. His thorough Moravian education led him to consider the ministry. In America he joined the Episcopal Church. Hamlin 512 – He developed a close friendship with Father William Dubourg, head of St. Mary's College in Baltimore, later Administrator Apostolic of the Roman Catholic district of

Louisiana in 1812, and first Bishop of New Orleans. Hamlin 515 – Benjamin Latrobe, architect for central tower of Cathedral of St. Louis, New Orleans. Historical Society of Delaware: Latrobe's survey and plan for New Castle, Delaware.

99. Gray 106
100. Hamlin 387
101. Gray 50
102. Hamlin 211
103. Gray 57
104. Gray 58
105. Kent County, Maryland, Land Records, Deed BCT-39-44. Joseph T. Mitchell, Sr., bought property which included Gresham College Hall, 208 acres, Arcadia and Swamps 478 ? acres plus ten acres adjoining. The main tract called Tolchester was 375 acres. Cecelius Calvert in 1659 awarded a parcel of land on the Chester River and the Chesapeake Bay to a man named Toulson. The name of the plot was later abbreviated to Tolchester, "beginning at a bounded stone at the N.E. corner of tract called Tolchester and running with the division fence between said land and the land of John Waltham deceased to the Chesapeake Bay thence with the Bay the said Joseph Thomas Mitchell's land, thence with his land to the main road and from thence to the beginning for $6000. He has paid this in full."
106. Office of Public Records, London, England, A-D-M, 37-5361 lists Joseph Mitchell on *The Menelaus* muster. Joseph T. Mitchell Sr. deed without a will. His property has to be itemized in Orphan's Court, December 7, 1830. In 1830 Joseph T. Mitchell's mother Ann Marie Mitchell, was alive. Until she died, she owned the property and 29 slaves. Courthouse Kent County, Maryland, 1832 – Administration Account of Ann Maria Mitchell, administrator of Joseph T. Mitchell late of Kent County. Kent County Courthouse, JNE 6-431, January 13, 1840: Mortgage between Joseph T. Mitchell, Jr., Baltimore, and George B. Westcott and Thomas R. Browne. "Tolchester 375 acres, Gresham College 208 acres, Arcadia and Swamps 478 ? acres plus 10 acres adjoining – being lands and premises which descended from Joseph T. Mitchell, late of Kent Co., deceased, to his son the said Joseph T. Mitchell." Kent County JFG 2/146 – December 6, 1853 – Agreement of Sale From Joseph T. Mitchell, Kent Co., To George Handy and James Gordon. 1852 Total Assessment, Inventory 20/114 of Joseph T. Mitchell, submitted by Ann Marie Mitchell, Administrator Acct. 15/272 Kent County Mention is made of a Bennett Mitchell, Laura Mitchell born May 22, 1819 baptized June 2, 1819. After the Civil War it was impossible to keep up the plantation. In mid – 1876 the Mitchell estate was under litigation for property settlements. Involved were Catherine J. Mitchell and Robert Brent Mitchell grandchildren of Joseph T. Mitchell. John Ambruster of Camden NJ bought 1050 acres for $23,500. He constructed a pier where a steamboat link to and from Baltimore unloaded thousands to Tolchester Amusement Park.
107. Ralph D. Gray, "Transportation and Brandywine Industries, 1800-1840," *Delaware History* (Wilmington, Delaware: The Historical Society of Delaware) 9 (October, 1961) 303. William F. Holmes, "Turnpikes Across The Peninsula," *Delaware History* 10:71; Johnson 406
108. Holmes 83
109. George Rogers Taylor, *The Transportation Revolution* 1815-1860 (New York: Rinehart, 1951) 5
110. Holmes 84
111. New Castle Historical Society, Delaware Federal Writers Project, *New Castle on the Delaware, 1651-1936* (Wilmington, Delaware: William Cann, Inc., 1937) 50; Seymour Dunbar, *History of Travel in America* (Indianapolis: Bobbs Merrill Co., 1915) 3:1028; Johnson, *History of Cecil County, Maryland* 424. The introduction of steamboats on Chesapeake Bay in June, 1813, led to an increase of travel across the peninsula, and to the organization of the Frenchtown and New Castle Railroad Company. About seventeen miles long, it was among the first railroads built in this country and the very first upon which steampower was applied to the transportation of passengers. Anthony Higgins, *New Castle, Delaware 1651-1939* (Boston: Houghton, Mifflin Co., 1939) 8: as a port of entry for half a century, New Castle received thousands of immigrants, mostly Scotch-Irish.
112. Holmes 88; *Delaware Gazette*, May 7, 1817 – Another turnpike between Elkton and Christiana was completed by 1817.
113. Holmes 75

114. Holmes 89
115. *RACHS* 7 (1896) 18 - Patrick Kenny to Bishop John Carroll, Wilmington, February 16, 1805: "According to your directions, Rev. Mr. Pasquet and I attended at White Clay Creek and Wilmington on the 15th inst. As to the plantation business the surmises contained in your letter to Rev. Mr. Whelan as to the new tenant he was about to engage with, appears to us to be well-founded...."
116. *RACHS* 7 (1896) 18-19
117. Spalding 92, No. 101 - Carroll to Rev. Francis Ignatius Neale, Baltimore, June 6, 1805. Francis Ignatius Neale (1754-1836), a younger brother of Bishop Leonard Neale and Charles Neale, would enter the restored Jesuits in 1806. Francis Neale was formerly a student at Bohemia Academy with James Heath and Robert Brent. Francis Neale was added to the first faculty of Georgetown College. - Daley, *Georgetown*, 68. AAB 6-D-4, Hanley *JCP* 2:486: William Pasquet to John Carroll, September 9, 1805 - Pasquet asks Carroll for settlement of his account with Deer Creek in Harford County where he had served in 1800. Pasquet was opposed to Jesuit tenure of property of which Deer Park was a part. Spalding 93 n. 2: Hughes, Documents 1:378 - Carroll's manager of Bohemia, William Pasquet. On October 13, 1802, The Corporation of the Clergy at their annual meeting authorized William Pasquet, then rector of St. Francis Xavier mission at Warwick, Cecil County, "to obtain from Rev. Mr. Sougé the plot and deed for certain lots lying in Kingstown, Queen Anne's County, and sell the same at the best terms he can obtain." It was not until September 7, 1805, that William Richmond, agent for the Corporation of the Clergy, sold 20 acres of Poplar Hill, Kingstown, to John Quimby of Maryland for 35 dollars current money of Maryland. John Quimby owned and operated an ordinary (tavern) and ferry house at Kingstown, and had bought part of this property earlier in 1785. There are still six acres of land and two town lots unaccounted for. This property was the location of the Queen Anne's County Jesuit Mission Center from 1735 to 1757.
118. Hanley, *JCP* 3:19 - Carroll to Molyneux, Baltimore, May 10, 1807.
119. Hughes, Documents 1:870 - Carroll agrees to have the estate Bohemia subject to conditions. GUA – Archives, Maryland Province, Society of Jesus, BOHEMIA BEQUEST OF (ABP) CARROLL, BOHEMIA-INCOME (1807). By a vote of the Corporation, Sept. 9, 1806, the revenues of Bohemia are given to Right Rev. John Carroll. This took the place of the eight hundred dollars that had been allotted him by our Fathers for his support. As early as May 26, 1790, the Bishop had written a paper in which he asserted that he considered that no words in the Bull of Pius VI., appointing him Bishop of Baltimore, gave him any claim to the property of the old Society.
120. AAB 11-S-5; Hanley, *JCP* 3:168-169, Carroll's Memorandum on Bohemia Manor: AD Maj. D. G. Bohemia-C[oun]ty-Spiritual affairs-No.1-Chapel-newly & solidly built-of fine proportions, in length, breadth & height-Length—52 ? feet Breadth-32 ? Height-. Inside in a most deplorable condition-no plaistering-windows broken; swallows building & roosting in it; even over the altar; most dreadful irreverences to be apprehended, even in time of Mass. Every thing else appertaining to divine service in the same deplorable state. Vestments neglected & Altar linnen scanty and ragged, especially purificatories -One of, the two chalices & the best of them without gilding at present. Not the least amendment in the state of the chapel since the last visitation, notwithstanding repeated promises to have it plastered, the broken panes replaced, and the birds with their filth excluded-Wherefore I intimated to the Cong[regatio]n. my resolution; and must enforce it before my departure of interdicting the Chapel-No. 2. Mass scarce celebrated but on Sundays; little, or rather no preparation and instruction for Conf[essio]n made previously to the Abps' coming tho so long announced. Black boys and girls, from 16 years of age downwards, had never been called to and instructed even for the Scmt of penance; so that when they wished for Confirmation, the Abp was either obliged to reject them from it entirely or take upon himself to give them such instruction, as the time will allow, admitting them only half-prepared. No. 3. The Congn. has dwindled to nothing-the whole number, which has been & will be confirmed during the visitation will not exceed ten or twelve, and that of Easter Communicants has not been more than between 21, and 30, if so many. No. 4. Only Congn., that of the home place, is attached to or served from Bohemia. That formerly of the forest is in Delaware, out of the Bre. Diocess. It is said to consist of no more than five or six families, who have no places provided for divine service. But I was pleased to understand, that

the sick of those families are attended from Bohemia, when the Clergyman is sent for, & that most of them come to church there. Hanley, *JCP* 3:148 - Bohemia estate, administered by Pasquet, was used to subsidize the students (named at Georgetown College - Davis, Corbaley, and Graham. Hanley, *JCP* 1:403-408. "Account of the Conditions of the Catholic Church c. 1790," quoted by John Gilmary Shea, *History of the Catholic Church in the United States*. (II) *Life and Times of the Most Rev. John Carroll 1763-1815*, (New York: published by the author, 1890) 49. Carroll attributed the problem of meager financial support by the laity to the previous penal colonial status of Catholics. The Jesuits had kept a low profile and supported themselves from their farms. Carroll pointed out that the practice continued and asserted "Catholics contribute nothing to the support of religion or its ministers; the whole charge of their maintenance, of furnishing the altars, of all traveling expenses, fell on the priests themselves, and no compensation was ever offered for any service performed by them.." To this failure of the laity to recognize their financial obligations, Bishop Carroll addressed his Pastoral Letter of May 28, 1792, wherein he stated that this "back-wardness of the faithful" to contribute to the support of the Church was the greatest amongst all the obstructions to the due celebration of divine service. Shea 399-400; Hanley *JCP* 2:43-52 Citing the Statutes of the First Synod of Baltimore, 1791, which inaugurated the custom of offertory collections, Bishop Carroll impressed upon his flock their binding force and prescribed that: ... two should be appointed in every church to take up the offertory collection of the faithful after the Gospel had been read. Where no provision was made for the support of the priest or the poor, one third of the collection was to go to each purpose, the third was to be applied to the purchase of plate or investments, the repair of the church, and all was to be devoted to this purpose in other cases. Hanley; *JCP* 1:533

121. Hughes, Documents 1:870; Griffin, ed., "Extracts," *RACHS* 7 (1896) 99: In 1806 Father Patrick Kenny recorded for the first time in his diary a journey to Bohemia in Cecil County, Maryland, where Reverend William Pasquet de Leyde was the superior and manager of the farm. Hanley, *JCP* 3:42-43 Carroll to Ambrose Maréchal, Baltimore, February 7, 1808: "[William] Pasquet has under him your congregation of Bohemia which still misses you." GUA – Archives, Maryland Province, Society of Jesus – BOHEMIA-JURISDICTION OVER (1814)

122. Cann 46 – entries made in Old Bohemia sacramental registers from 1807 to 1812. There are two entries by Pasquet, on December 28, 1805, and another April, 1814. Another mentions Pasquet July 29, 1807: Father Maréchal returned to Bohemia to baptize Sarah Maria Mitchell, born December 22, 1806, daughter of Joseph T. and Sophia Mitchell. Sponsors were *Reverend William Pasquet* for James and Ann Mitchell, uncle and aunt of the child. AAB-6-0-9, Hanley, *JCP* 3:148. In a letter of complaint to Archbishop Carroll Pasquet stated that he sometimes was called from Bohemia to minister in Queen Anne and Talbot counties when the proper pastors were away or sick. ADW, Bohemia Records, Marriages by Father William Pasquet, at Bohemia, Alexander Patterson and Priscilla Stevens, July 19, 1807, witnesses James O'Donald and John B. Brooke; at Appoquinimink Forest, New Castle County, Delaware, John Crouch and Mary Tygard, January 12, 1808, witnesses Sarah Crouch and John Corbaley; at Bohemia, Thomas, slave of Mr. Green, and Mary, slave of John Hanson, n.d., witnesses Moses and Benjamin, Negroes; in 1810, trip to Kenton, Kent County, Delaware; two trips to Camden, Kent County, Delaware.

123. Spalding 215-219, Appendix: "John Carroll's Slaves"

124. Hanley, *JCP* 3:313 - Spalding 218-219; In the late spring of 1815, Carroll told Archbishop Troy that the members of the Corporation, "anxious to suppress censure," had begun some years ago and were still in the process of gradually emancipating the older slaves on their estates. "To proceed at once to make it a general measure, would not be either humanity towards the Individuals, nor doing justice to the trust, under which the estates have been transmitted and received. This and Carroll's insistence to Plowden that he owned no slaves was occasioned by statements that a Dominican named John Ryan, who had served in Philadelphia, had lately circulated in London and in Ireland, to Bishop Francis Moylan of Cork. Carroll wrote that Ryan's statements had "caused me more displeasure than I can express." Ryan had said that the Jesuit planters had trafficked in slaves and "that the Archbp. himself was a great slaveholder." The "retailers" of that "most wicked calumny" should have mentioned, Carroll insisted, as he had to Archbishop Troy, that the clergy were now gradually freeing their slaves. Carroll repeated that, since he had renounced his paternal inheritance at age twenty-six, he had not owned a single slave. In 1838 the Maryland Jesuits still had 272 slaves. These they sold that year to a

planter in Louisiana. Blacks in southern Maryland told an agent of the Maryland Colonization Society that they now put no more trust in priests than in kidnappers. See Robert Emmett Curran, "Splendid Poverty, Jesuit Slaveholding in Maryland, 1805-1838," in Randall M. Miller and Jon I. Wakelyn, eds., *Catholics in the Old South: Essays on Church and Culture* (Macon, GA.: Mercer University Press, 1983), pp. 125-46.

125. AAB *Carroll Letterbook* 3:91 Spalding p. 129, No. 129 – To Rev. William Pasquet, Baltimore, December 14, 1808
126. AAB 6-D-10 Spalding p. 129, No. 129 - Carroll to Rev. William Pasquet, Baltimore, July 23, 1811;
127. AAB 6-D-10, Spalding No. 150 - Carroll to Pasquet, Baltimore August 2, 1812 Hanley, *JCP* 3:202, Carroll to Enoch Fenwick, Seneca, September 25, 1812: "I am anxious to hear of the wood being come from Bohemia: if Pasquet has again deceived me, let me request you to see Bonner (not the coppersmith) who will immediately send boats for it, provided you can obtain certain advice of the wood being at the landing, Coxe's landing, Bohemia River. The boatman must always bring a certificate of the quantity delivered to him: freight $2.50 pr cord. The certificates must be given for Wm. Craddock, or Jacob Reynolds. Is Mr. Ryan with you? My most affectionate compliments to good Mr. Mertz & him, & all friends. Poor Eliza Jones! Nothing good for her with Bp. Neale's family."
128. AAB 6-E-5, Spalding No. 173 - Notation for Rev. William Pasquet, January 18, 1814: Carroll says to note the contents about Rachel but particularly Phyllis (whom Pasquet had hired out), Joe, and Jacob. Hanley, *JCP* 3:165 - Carroll to William Pasquet, Baltimore, December 20, 1811
129. AAB 6-E-13, *Carroll Letterbook* 3:107; Spalding No. 176, Carroll to Pasquet, Baltimore, May 5/6, 1814 - Pasquet appears to have resided in Baltimore for some time in 1812, as we learn from a letter from John Carroll to John Vaughan, member of the American Philosophical Society of Philadelphia, Baltimore, July 16, 1812: "If the Rev. Mr. Pasquet, who is the Professor of natural philosophy in St. Mary's College here, can take time to deliver this into your hand, allow me to recommend him to your polite attention...." Hanley, *JCP* 3:200, Carroll to Enoch Fenwick, September 23, 1812: "I was yesterday at the College – (St. Mary's, DuBourg's College)... The Trustees are to sit again for a short time this morning, when they will probably take up the subject of Mr. Pasquet's refusal, mentioned on the back of your letter." Pasquet often visited Baltimore from Bohemia, as for instance, as mentioned in Carroll to John Grassi, Baltimore, October 15, 1813, *JCP* 3:233: "Mr. Pasquet... returned some days ago by the Marsh;" Hanley, *JCP* 3:358: Carroll to Enoch Fenwick, Bohemia, September 10, 1815, "Mr. Pasquet goes for Baltimore, as he says, today or tomorrow."
130. Spalding 174 no. 176 Carroll to Pasquet, May 16, 1814
131. AAB 6-E-9 Pasquet to Carroll, Bohemia, May 2, 1814
132. Spalding No. 177, Appendix 3; AAB 11-N-2;
133. AAB 6-E-12: AAB, Bohemia Plantation Book; AAB 6-E-11, November 28, 1814 Carroll's Comment on William Pasquet's Letter. William Pasquet to John Carroll, Bohemia, November 23, 1814; Cann 255-256; AAB Bohemia Plantation Book 6-E-11, November 28, 1814, Carroll's Comment on William Pasquet's letter.

In the midst of this, Pasquet wrote Carroll on November 28, 1814, of the deterioration of the waterpowered mill at Bohemia:

Most Rt. Rev. Sir:

Last week I wrote you in answer to your favor of the 10th inst. In speaking of your mill I mentioned to you that it was doubtful to me whether she would stand this winter, that the flood gates had given away many inches, that the safe gates were shaking, and that the fore bay was all but gone. The great rain we had yesterday completed the business and finished what was threatening since long while, what I was aware of and afraid. Barney was working all day long, giving vent tot he waters as much as he could, and in spite of his endeavors, at 10 p.m. when he was at the mill, the water undermined the piling of the safe gates, and of the warfage next to it. Vast quantities of dirt has been carried away by the strength of the current, and the proper fall of water is now done away. How must it be mended, and whether must it be mended? That is the object of the present. To do it well will cost at least $100. But, pray is it worth mending in the present condition of the mill? All her works and frames are in so bad condition, unless you intend just to patch her up, it must be the subject of your consideration. Therefore, be pleased, R. Rev. Sir, to acquaint me as soon as possible with your intention about it. The hands are very scarce indeed in this neighborhood, and the wages are very high, for such work they are higher..besides the..liquor and accommodation which will make the expense great, considering the price of everything...the pilings being carried away, and likewise the wings, the wharfage rotten, it will require a workman to-?- things-substantially Secundum artim. A mill-wright will cost at least $2. per day and found like a gentleman, and will he do but little work. If you could get old Isaac and James from White Marsh, they would do what is required, and a great deal chaper. Besides doing what is wanting in the interior of the mill, a millhouse in the present urgency, I see no other way, unless you have more money to spend than I presume. After all, will the mill pay for all these expenses? But during that time, where must your people get their meals? I expect there is grain enough in the mill to fatten your hogs in the pen, though tight work if not I will let Barney have some for that purpose, and if you give the order to. Some of your tenants are the same. But no matter how the breach will be repaired, it will take many hundred feet of planks. A floor will have to be laid more than 25 feet long, and nine or ten feet wide as far as the frames of the old gates, and some side work. The fact is that I see a great deal of work to be done and more expenses than it will really afford for the income. Considering the scantiness of the stream, if it was my property, I would have a saw mill and fulling mill instead of a grist mill, they would cost less than the repairs now wanting and be more profitable. But why do I give you my opinion when you are better judge what to do in the present circumstances. Neverless if you have mind to have the havoc done, made up, write to me immediately, for it must be done before the frost set in, if it is done at all this fall, for the dirt could not and would not join solidly together, if it is frozen or it is very apt to go to nothing in the spring. In expectation of your answer, I remain, Most Rt. Rev. Sir,

Your most humble and obt. ser. W. Pasquet

134. AAB, 6-E-13: From Pasquet's letter to Carroll, December 22, 1814, it was evident that the administration of a large estate such as Bohemia was too great for him. Hughes, Documents 2:858—Carroll to Grassi, Baltimore, May 7, 1815— "Mr. Pasquet's tergiversations and evasions"—Pasquet is away from Bohemia to New York. GUA, Bohemia Correspondence, 204—G1-10, Series 57—John Carroll to Francis Neale, July 26, 1815, requesting Neale to go to Bohemia to settle with Rev. Wm. Pasquet on question of land. Hughes, Documents 2:863—Carroll to Enoch Fenwick, Bohemia, September 10, 1815—"the whole duty [at Bohemia] must be performed by me"—Pasquet was off to Baltimore. Hughes, Documents 2:947—"The Business of Pasquet." GUA, 90-T1-5, Series 35—Receipt 1815 by Rev. Wm. Pasquet to Francis Neale, S.J. Hanley, JCP 3:324, Carroll to John Grassi, Baltimore, February 21, 1815: "You saw Mr. Pasquet lately: he had declared by letter, that he would remonstrate publicly against certain proceedings, and I know that he has no delicate feelings to prevent him from appearing as a public accuser, and representing facts, not in their truth, but according to his own jaundiced view of them: there are in our legislative bodies such men as Fr. John Hippesley ready to embrace the erroneous statements of misinformed men. But there is one security for us, he knows that he is in my power."

134. Cann 255-256; AAB, Bohemia Plantation Book 6-E-11, November 28, 1814, Carroll's Comment on William Pasquet's letter. Hanley, JCP 3:36—Carroll to Enoch Fenwick, Washington, June 1, 1815: "I am uneasy for Mr. Pasquet. He was ill at Ge. Town and appears to have been no better, when he left Baltimore on Saturday, of course, the morning after his going from this place." Hanley, JCP 3:343-344, Carroll to Pasquet, Baltimore, July 15, 1815. Hughes, Documents 2:879—"The Pasquet Trouble." Hanley JCP 3:353, Carroll to Enoch Fenwick, Bohemia, September 10, 1815: "Today (Sunday) the whole duty must be performed by me. Mr. Pasquet does nothing, not even mass." AAB, Bohemia Plantation Book. Hanley, JCP 3:183—Carroll to Enoch Fenwick, O.P., Easton, June 23, 1812: "I returned thus far yesterday from Dorset and mosquitoes, shall go this morning to St. Joseph's and hope to be at Bohemia before Sunday." Hanley, JCP 3:185—Carroll to John Grassi, Baltimore, July 9, 1812: "At my return from the Eastern Shore last week….." It is interesting to note that when John Carroll died on December 3, 1815, his successor as Archbishop of Baltimore, Leonard Neale (consecrated December 7, 1800), declined to accept the Bohemia estate as his principal source of income and returned the estate to the trustees of the Corporation of the Clergy, who reassumed its management—Hughes, Documents 1:885, No. 180. AAB *Bohemia Plantation Book 1790-1796* 35: "Molly and her

son David, Harry, her husband, would be glad to buy them in the spring of 1816 for $150. September, 19, 1815 – Dick, if he serves faithfully the Clergymen of St. Francis Xavier, Bohemia, for eight years from the date hereof, is to be free. In the meantime he is to be carefully maintained. September 19, 1815 – Joe, if he faithfully serves the Revd. Gentlemen at the head of Little Bohemia for six years from the date hereof will be entitled to his freedom."

135. Hanley, *JCP* 3:343-344, Carroll to Pasquet, Baltimore, July 15, 1815 – Carroll mentions that he visited Bohemia from June 26-30, 1812, and speaks of "my visitation before the last (i.e. the only in 1812) in 1810 or 1811." GUA – Archives, Maryland Province, Society of BOHEMIA-ABP CARROLL'S VISIT TO (1812); GUA – Archives, Maryland Province, Society of Jesus – BOHEMIA-PROPERTY (1815).

136. Hanley, *JCP* 3:360—Carroll to Francis Neale, Baltimore, October 3, 1815

137. Hughes, Documents 2:890—February 16, 1816, "The Pasquet Investigation is Suspended."

138. Devitt, "Bohemia," *Woodstock Letters* 63 (1934) 32. Since Pasquet met Patrick Kenny in 1805 and introduced him to St. Mary's Church at Coffee Run in New Castle County, Delaware, he continued to be a friend and visited Coffee Run occasionally, perhaps enroute to Philadelphia and back. Kenny noted these visits in his diary, as for instance, on July 29, 1812: "Rev. Mr. Pasquet leaving Coffee Run went off for Bohemia"— *RACHS* 24 (1913) 129.

139. Griffin, ed., "Extracts," *RACHS* 7 (1896) 120: When Pasquet retired from Bohemia, Patrick Kenny noted in his diary, May 8, 1816: "letter from Mr. Pasquet, sailed for France for Bordeaux," Griffin, ed., "Extracts," *RACHS* 9 (1898) 65. ADW, Bohemia Burial Records, Rev. Francis Neale buried Elizabeth Allen, wife of James Allen, at Bohemia on July 16, 1816. Father Francis Neale covered Bohemia for Carroll until Pasquet would be replaced with Father James Moynihan.

CHAPTER THREE

Bohemia Under The Next Four Archbishops Of Baltimore
1815-1852

When Baltimore became an archdiocese in 1808, Delaware became part of the new Diocese of Philadelphia. The nine counties of Maryland on the Eastern Shore of the Chesapeake Bay remained under the immediate jurisdiction of the archbishops of Baltimore until 1868..

THE EPISCOPATE OF LEONARD NEALE

Portrait of Archbishop Neale

Archbishop John Carroll died on December 3, 1815, and was succeeded by Most Reverend Leonard Neale, who had been consecrated as Carroll's coadjutor on December 7, 1800.[1] Neale had served as president of Georgetown College from 1799 to 1806. He was 68 years old when he succeeded Carroll as archbishop. By then he lived in virtual retirement at the Georgetown Visitation.[2]

Though he had attended the Jesuit Academy at Bohemia in his youth and had spent some time there as a priest, he left no record of any visit there as coadjutor or archbishop. Only from correspondence between himself and the priests whom he assigned there can we learn about his dealings with Catholics on the Eastern Shore.

In 1815 there were two parishes on the Eastern Shore of Maryland: *Bohemia*, with one church and *Tuckahoe*, later Cordova, on the Wye River in Talbot County. The Jesuits at St. Francis Xavier, Bohemia Mission, in Cecil County, in addition to ministry to Catholics in Cecil and Kent counties in Maryland, had agreed to continue their care of the Catholic Irish farmers in the Forest of Appoquinimink, now Blackbird Hundred, in southwestern New Castle County in Delaware. The Jesuit priests at St. Joseph's in Talbot attended mission churches at Meekins Neck

(Golden Hill) and at Queenstown, and a burial ground at Kingstown across the Chester River from Chestertown. They also agreed to visit scattered Catholics in Kent and Sussex counties in Delaware. There was a Catholic burial ground at Laurel and possibly one at Lowber's, near Petersburg, south of Dover in Delaware.[3]

Irish Secular Priest, James Moynihan

As successor to Father Pasquet, Reverend James Moynihan was assigned as superior at Bohemia in 1815.[4] He had been born in Ireland, had come to Baltimore at an early age, and had attended, Georgetown College and St. Mary's Seminary before his ordination by Archbishop Carroll on August 7, 1813. He was first assigned to Saint Francis Xavier Church at Newtown in St. Mary's County.[5]

Concerned about the management of the large farm at Bohemia, Archbishop Carroll had written to his coadjutor Leonard Neale on August 3, 1815:

> I conferred with you at Georgetown about appointing Mr. Moynihan to go to Bohemia, and altho' I would gladly designate another more fit person, if there were one at my disposal, yet there is not one whom I can now remove...at all hazards; it is impossible to leave Bohemia vacant.[6]

Ordained in 1813, and now in 1815, less than thirty years old, Father Moynihan's youth and inexperience caused the archbishop to question his capability to manage the Corporation's largest holding of 12000 acres and 29 slaves. The profits from the Bohemia plantation were the archbishop's principal source of income. Nevertheless, Father Moynihan soon proved himself to be an excellent priest and administrator. He was soon out visiting his extensive charge and bringing the sacraments to his people.

On October 15, 1815, Father Moynihan baptized Sarah Reynolds, a three months old daughter of Jeremiah and Sarah Reynolds, of Appoquinimink Forest, New Castle County, Delaware. Sponsors were Jacob Reynolds and Sarah Pennington.[7]

Early in the new year, on January 24, 1816, Father Moynihan visited Father Patrick Kenny at Coffee Run in northern Delaware and took breakfast with him.[8]

On February 2, 1816, Father Moynihan baptized Betsey, two months old, daughter of Hoys and Phillis. Sponsors were Sarah, a free woman, and Dick, a slave. On May 12, 1816, he baptized Maria (22 months), Nanny (14 years), Elizabeth (18 years), Catherine (8 years), Mary E. (6 years), Harriet (3 years), Becky (4 years), Joseph (one year), Hannah (14 years) and Hester (2 years) all slaves belonging to James Blake farm near Chestertown. Sponsors were James and Jane Blake.[9] He returned to Chestertown to baptize on August 20, 1816, three more children of slaves: Harriet (18 months), Catherine (16 months) and Juliet (12 months), all slaves belonging to James Brooke near Chestertown. Sponsors were Lucy and David.[10]

On August 22, 1816, Father Moynihan baptized James (2 years old), Joan (2 years old) and Sarah (2 years old), all slaves belonging to Mr. Joseph Mitchell in Kent County Maryland. On August 24, 1816, Father Moynihan baptized Millie (2 years old) and Hannah (13 months old), daughters of Catherine, a slave belonging to Jacob Reynolds. Sponsors were Barney and Phyllis.[11] On September 15, 1816, he baptized at Bohemia an infant named Dick (13 months old), child of Dick and Diana, slaves. Sponsors were Richard, a slave, and Molly, a free woman. In all, in 1816, Father Moynihan baptized 22 Blacks.

On May 2, 1816, at Appoquinimink Forest, Father Moynihan baptized Samuel Corbaley (14 months old), son of Richard and Hannah Corbaley. Sponsors were Francis and Elizabeth McCreedy. All Catholics.[12]

On March 26, 1816, at Bohemia, Father Moynihan buried William Craddock, aged 74. On July 16, 1816, at Bohemia, Father Francis Neale buried Elizabeth Allen, wife of James Allen.

In August of 1816, Archbishop Neale received a letter from Father Moynihan informing him that Moynihan had visited a mission about forty miles from Bohemia where he found many Blacks twenty years old and above who had not yet been baptized. "Such is the state of religion in those parts and I am sorry that it is very little better in these parts." He added that much of the religious indifference in these sections was due to the scarcity of priests and to the bad example of some of the few priests who did minister to them.[13]

In the same letter, Moynihan made a report to Archbishop Neale concerning his congregations: "I now proceed to inform your grace that I have lately returned from a mission distant about 40 miles, where I attend three families, namely Messrs. Brooke, Blake, and Mitchell, who have many black people, many of whom

Script of emancipation of slaves at Bohemia – 1816

I have christened, some twenty years old and upwards, who were not even baptized. Such is the state of religion in those parts."[14]

I attend another small congregation about twelve miles distance from here where there are few Catholics.... There are about eight families only in the congregation of Bohemia, some of whom come regularly to their duty."[15]

On October 24, 1816, Father Moynihan again wrote to Archbishop Neale: "I shall do all in my power to justify the confidence your Grace is pleased to repose in my zeal and diligence... I am in hopes we shall be able to finish our church here next spring, as it has never been plastered."[16]

As we learn from this letter, Father Moynihan had hoped to see the church at Bohemia completed by the next spring, but three months later, Archbishop Neale transferred him as pastor from Bohemia to St. Joseph's Church in Talbot County.

While still at Bohemia, on January 2, 1817, Father Moynihan baptized John, an eighteen month old son of Nancy, a slave belonging to Dr. James Scanlon. Sponsors were Phillis and Barry, slaves belonging to the Corporation of the Clergy. On the same day, he baptized Milly, daughter to Milly, slave belonging to Dr. James Scanlon. Sponsors were Barry and Phillis. On January 13, 1817, he baptized Rosetta Ann, daughter of Dr. James Scanlon and Rosetta, his wife. Sponsors were Rev. James Moynihan and Catherine Scanlon, aunt of the child.[17]

Archbishop Neale appointed Father Moynihan to St. Joseph's in Talbot County on January 24, 1817. When Father Moynihan learned of his transfer, he wrote Archbishop Neale, on February 24, 1817, hoping to reverse the unwelcome transfer. He said, "I fear the air and especially the water of St. Joseph, which is very bad, will incapacitate me to perform the duties of that mission. However, if it be y'r will, I shall attempt it, if the following consideration does not avail." Moynihan had improved the plantation considerably, constructing several new buildings, planting a crop of wheat, and preparing to complete the church at Bohemia built in 1797, but never finished. He hoped the church when finished "would inspire some with devotion and others with awe and respect for our religion."[18]

Belgian Jesuit, John Henry

On the occasion of Father Moynihan's transfer from Bohemia, Archbishop Neale chose to return the charge of the plantation and church there to the Jesuit superiors, the Corporation of the Catholic Clergy, who appointed to it one of their own priests, for the first time since 1793. The name of Father John Henry, S. J., appears in the Bohemia registers from May 11, 1817, until June of the following year.[19] Born September 15, 1765, at Opont in the Duchy of Bouillon, Belgium, John Henry was ordained in Belgium and entered the Society of Jesus in Russia on June 18, 1804. He came to America from White Russia in 1806. He served on other missions in Maryland until his assignment to Bohemia at age 52.[20]

On May 11, 1817, Father Henry baptized *at Bohemia* George Heverin, son of George and Rebecca Heverin, his wife. George Heverin was born March 25, 1817. The godmother was Mary Noland. On May 15, 1817, Father Henry baptized Mary O'Neale, born on March 25, 1817, daughter of Bernard and Jane O'Neale. Sponsors were James Councell and Sarah Noland. On May 25, 1817, Father Henry baptized Levy Brier, born March 1, 1816, son of Isaac Brier and Patricia his wife. Free negroes. Sponsor was Betsy. On May 26, 1817, Father Henry baptized Mary Ann Gilze, born April 26, 1817, daughter of John Gilze and Fanny his wife, slaves. Sponsor was Phillis. On June 15, 1817, Father Henry baptized *at Bohemia* Catherine Ann, child of Jeremiah and Sarah Reynolds. Catherine Ann was born April 19, 1817. Sponsor was Ann Read. On the same day *at Bohemia* he baptized Rebecca, a fifteen-year old slave of Benjamin Read.

On July 6, 1817, *at Bohemia*, Father Henry baptized Susannah, born the day before, daughter of Abigail, slave of Mrs. Elizabeth O'Donald. Sponsor was Anna. On July 8, 1817, *at Bohemia*, Father Henry baptized John Corbaley, one day old, son of Richard and Hanna Corbaley. On July 19, 1817, *at Bohemia*, Father Henry baptized Elizabeth Lee, born December 4, 1816, daughter of David and Patty Lee. Sponsor was Katy Pennington. In July, 1817, Father Henry buried John Corbaley, son of Richard and Hanna Corbaley. He died on July 20, 1817. On July 29, 1817, Father Henry baptized James Craddock, born October, 1816, a son of William Craddock and Elizabeth Hill. Witness was N. Pennington. On August 10, 1817, *at Bohemia*, Father Henry baptized Charles Coalman, born January 1, 1817, son of Henry and Henrietta Coalman. Sponsor was Charles Coalman. On August 10, 1817, *at Bohemia*, Father Henry baptized Sarah Coalman, born March 25, 1802, near Chestertown, daughter of Henry and Henrietta Coalman. Sponsor was Charles Coalman. August 12, 1817 – Father Henry officiated at the wedding *at Bohemia* between John Lusby and Sarah Nowland. Witnesses were Thomas Nowland and James Councill. On August 16, 1817, at Bohemia, Father Henry baptized Levy Bowing, born on October 8, 1757, son of Lewis and Rebecca Bowing. Sponsor was Charles Coalman. On August 25, 1817, Father Henry baptized William, born July 20, 1817, son of Edward and Henny, slaves of Dr. James Scanlan. Sponsor was Mary.

On September 1, 1817, Father Henry baptized Henri Ferret, born on May 17, 1817, son of James and Jane Ferrit. Sponsor was Sarah Reynolds. On October 16, 1817, Father Henry baptized at the farm of Mr. William Lee *at Grove Point*, Cecil County, Sallie and Suzie, twin daughters of Jack and Polly. Sponsors were Robert and Mary. All were slaves of William Lee, of Grove Point. [21]

Father John Henry officiated at the following weddings *at Bohemia*: On April 6, 1825, between James and Rebecca. Witnesses were Thomas Nowland and James Councell. On May 20, 1825, between Maurice O'Flinn, slave of William Craddock, and Elizabeth Farrell, slave of the Roman Catholic Clergy of Maryland. Witnesses were Joe and Barney. On May 28, 1825, between Abraham Pennington and Elizabeth Reed. Sponsors were James and Mary Wering.

Archbishop Neale died on June 18, 1817. Father Henry continued to serve *at Bohemia* under vicar-general Ambrose Maréchal until the spring of the next year. He would have continued to serve at Bohemia for a longer time, but a troublesome incident developed with the slaves there that brought about his transfer. We learn of it from the diary of Brother Joseph Mobberly, S. J., who served as farm supervisor at Bohemia at that time. Brother Joseph wrote:

> After years of loose supervision the negroes had become ungovernable and very loose in their morals. Father Henry deemed it better to send some of

the worst of them away from the estate and he sold five of them to a neighbor who was in the habit of purchasing Blacks for planters in Louisiana. A little before this, a severe law had been enacted by the Legislature of Maryland against "kidnappers" who, it seems, had become pretty common on the Eastern Shore. The negroes were sent off in the mail stage to some place on the Chesapeake Bay, where they were to be put on board of a vessel bound for New Orleans. The stage was stopped at Centreville, and the negroes were lodged in jail by a magistrate who was also a Methodist preacher. Father Henry was also to have been arrested as a "kidnapper," although he had full authority for the transaction. Still, a malicious interpretation of the late law might have caused him trouble, and his friends advised him to retire, in order to avoid the disagreeable necessity of attending court.[22]

Brother Mobberly met Father Henry in Baltimore and started for Bohemia with two thousand dollars commissioned to release the prisoners and refund the money to the purchasers. This he accomplished, not without extortionate demands of the jailer and trader."[23]

At the beginning of the year 1818, Father Henry visited Father Patrick Kenny at White Clay Creek in northern Delaware.[24] He was at White Clay at the time of a major explosion at the du Pont Mills.[25]

Before moving to his new assignment in the Spring of 1818, Father Henry again visited Father Kenny in northern Delaware.[26] Father Henry was assigned to Frederick 1819-1820, to St. Inigoes 1821-1822, and to Newtown 1823. He died there on March 12, 1823.[27]

Portrait of Archbishop Maréchal

THE EPISCOPATE OF AMBROSE MARÉCHAL

Belgian Jesuit, Michael J. Cousinne

Born in Belgium on November 8, 1767, Michael Cousinne was already a priest when he entered the Society of Jesus in 1817.[28] He was assigned to Bohemia Mission in Cecil County in 1817 at age 50.[29] At Bohemia he buried John Corbaly, son of Richard and Hannah Corbaly, who died on July 20, 1817. In August he buried at Bohemia Henrietta M. Corbaly, who died on August 11, 1818.

In a letter to Archbishop Maréchal on June 8, 1819, Father Cousinne reported on the various congregations under his charge as pastor of Bohemia. He added: "I had the honor to receive a visit from Mr. Moynihan, who has engaged me to take care of some Catholics near Chestertown and its neighborhood. I accompanied him to these places and it seems there are at least 20 Catholics..."[30]

Moynihan had cared for these Catholics when he was at Bohemia, and apparently had continued to do so after he went to St. Joseph's, in Talbot County, but now it was too much for him, so he called upon the pastor of Bohemia.

On January 20, 1819, Father Cousinne was at Coffee Run in New Castle, Delaware to visit Father Patrick Kenny: "Cousinne from Bohemia came most providentially, for about 12 o'clock in the night I was taken so ill with the humors of both legs that flew up to my head. Rev. M. Cousinne administered unto me the rites of the church *hora mortis*"[31]

On February 17, 1819, *at Bohemia*, Father Cousinne baptized Rebecca Gil, six weeks old, daughter of John and Magdalen Gil. On April 11, 1819, he baptized Maria Helene Mortland, born August 10, 1818, daughter of John and Cecelia Mortland. On May 2, 1819, *at Bohemia*, he baptized Richard Corbaly, born July 26, 1818, son of Richard Corbaly and Hannah Johnson. Sponsor was Catherine Reynolds. On May 11, 1819, he baptized *at Elkton*, Eleanor Grady born January 26, 1817, and Anne Grady born October 6, 1818, daughters of Philip and Elizabeth Grady. Sponsors were Hughey Dugan and his wife Eleanor.

On June 4, 1819, he was at the Blake farm *near Chestertown*, where he baptized Samuel, five months old, and Martha, four months old, slaves belonging to Alphonsa Blake. Alphonsa Blake was the sponsor. On June 5, 1819, he was *near Chestertown* at the farm of Mr. Tilghman, where he baptized Augustine, ten months old, slave belonging to Mr. Tilghman. Harriet was the sponsor. On June 20, 1819, *at Grove Point* in Cecil County, he baptized David Lee, four months old, son of David Lee, Sr. There were no sponsors. On June 24, 1819, he baptized Laura Anna Mitchell, born May 22, 1819 *at the Mitchell House*, 12 miles from Chestertown. She was the daughter of Joseph and Maria Anna Mitchell. At the same time he baptized *at the Mitchell House* in Kent County Perry, six months old, William, nine months old, Grace, ten months old, Martha, fourteen months old, and Elizabeth, twenty years old, slaves belonging to Joseph Mitchell. Cousinne – made two trips to Elkton in 1819, and two trips to New Castle Co. in 1819.[32]

A lay brother, John S. Heard, S.J., resided with Father Cousinne at Bohemia as a helper in domestic concerns and general supervision of the farm.[33] On

November 17, 1819, Father Peter Kenny, S.J., administered conditional baptism to Aquila Charles Coleman. Witness was Brother Joseph Heard, S.J. Father Michael Cousinne died at Bohemia at the age of 52 on July 31, 1819. He was buried there behind the church on August 1, 1819.[34]

American Jesuit, John Francis Hickey

Father John Hickey spent only one year at Bohemia.[35] He was there when Father Cousinne died on July 31, 1819. On August 1, 1819, he baptized Harriet Derrow, daughter of James Derrow, free man, and Abigail, slave of Elizabeth Stanley. The baptism was at the home of Elizabeth Stanley. Sponsor was Anne. Father Hickey buried Sylvester Nowland on April 28, 1819. He left Bohemia sometime in 1820.[36]

French Jesuit, Peter Epinette

The successor to Father Cousinne as pastor at Bohemia was Peter Epinette, S.J., born in France on September 24, 1760. He entered the Society of Jesus at Duneburg, Russia, on June 2, 1805. He spoke English, French, Hebrew, and Italian. He was sent by the Russian superior general to America and arrived in Baltimore in 1806. He served as a professor of theology at Georgetown College until 1813. There he was appointed superior of St. Thomas Manor, Charles County, Maryland, until 1817 when he returned to Georgetown to teach philosophy. He was appointed pastor of Bohemia and its mission in 1819.[37]

Father Epinette's first baptism *at Bohemia* was on October 17, 1819, when he christened Elizabeth Hopkins, five week old daughter of Edward Hopkins and Hannah Fatin. On October 26, 1819, he baptized *at Bohemia* Ginet Eliza Reed, seven weeks old, daughter of Benjamin Reed and Ann Reynolds. Sponsor was Amelia Reynolds.

Photo of residence of Jesuit Fathers at Bohemia, built in 1825, using bricks from the 1700's that were part of the original rectory-chapel building.

On January 19, 1820, he baptized Amelia Leahy, daughter of John Lusby and Sara Nowland. Sponsor was Ann Nowland. On January 16, 1820, he baptized Mary Jane Cora Pennington, daughter of John Pennington and Mary Carty. Sponsors were Sylvester Nowland and Ann Nowland. On March 19, 1820, he baptized Sara Jane O'Neil, 8 weeks old, daughter of Bernard O'Neil and Jane McCleland. Sponsors were Benedict Craddock and Margaret, his wife. On March 26, 1820, he baptized Catherine, five weeks old, daughter of George and Anna. Sponsors were Richard and Rachel. On the same day he baptized Suzan, four weeks old, daughter of Ann. Sponsors were Richard and Mary. On April 20, 1820, he baptized James Brady, two months old, son of Robert Brady and Mary Brady. Sponsors were Bernard and Felissy. On May 14, 1820, he baptized Thomas Craddock, son of Daniel and Elizabeth Craddock. Sponsors were Benedict and Margaret Craddock. On May 28, 1820, he baptized William Gustavus Farrell, seven months old, daughter of James Farrell and Jane Scofield. Sponsor was Elizabeth Stanley.

In 1820 he buried *at Bohemia* John Reynolds of Appoquinimink Forest, born in 1791 of Nicholas Reynolds I and his wife Eleanor on a farm known as Eleanor's Delight. John Reynolds probably attended the Catholic school called Appoquinimink Mission.[38] Janet Boyce Reynolds, wife of Jeremiah Reynolds, died in 1821 and was buried *at Bohemia* next to her husband who died in 1808 at age 75.[39] Their son Jeremiah died in 1823 at age 45. Other children of Jeremiah were James, Sarah (who married William Weldon III) Amelia (unmarried, buried at Bohemia) Ann (married William Price) and Mary (married Benjamin Green).[40]

In 1821, Nicholas Reynolds II, born in 1750 and son of Nicholas I and Eleanor Reynolds, of Appoquinimink Forest, died at age 71. His farm of forty acres was located west of Kings Road, between Blackbird and Smyrna, Delaware, adjoining the lands of his kinsman James Reynolds of Kings Road. His wife Betsy was Protestant, but their children were all baptized at Bohemia church.[41]

In October 1821 Archbishop Maréchal went to Europe and presented his second report on his archdiocese to Roman authorities.[42]

On June 24, 1821, Father Epinette buried *at Bohemia* Daniel Craddock. On November 21, 1821, he buried *at Bohemia* Richard Craddock.

On January 28, 1821, *at Bohemia* he baptized Joseph, son of Hays and Philis. Sponsor was Maria. On March 4, 1821, he baptized Ann, daughter of Edward and Henrietta. Sponsor was Maria. On March 4, 1821, he baptized *at Bohemia* Edward Scanlan, born the previous day, son of James Scanlan and Rose Walker. Sponsor was Catherine Scanlan. On May 15, 1821, *at Bohemia*, he baptized John Corbely, son of Richard Corbely and Hannah Johnson. Sponsor was Rebecca Dickson. On June 7, 1821, *at Bohemia*, he baptized William Alfred Craddock, (about five years old) Joseph Taylor Craddock (3 years old) and Richard Craddock (one year old) children of Richard Craddock and Anne Springer. Sponsor was Benedict Craddock.

On August 19, 1821 *at Bohemia* he baptized Esther Haverin, four months old, daughter of George Haverin and Rebecca Dickson. On August 31, 1821, *at Bohemia* he baptized Rebecca Ann Heverin, seven months old, daughter of Stephen Heverin and Ann Fenlon. Sponsor was James Scanlon.

In Appoquinimink Forest, William Pryor died in 1822 and was buried by Father

Epinette at the old Catholic cemetery at Eleanor's Delight."[43] William Pryor, a Catholic, died in 1822 and was buried in the old Catholic burial ground located in "Eleanor's Delight" estate. His wife Martha then married Elisha Crouch, member of Bohemia church. Crouch's first wife was Millie Weldon, daughter of Abraham Weldon. Elisha Crouch was active in local politics. He was probably also buried in the old Catholic cemetery at "Eleanor's Delight."[44] Janet Boyce Reynolds, wife of Jeremiah Reynolds, died in 1821 and was buried *at Bohemia*, next to her husband who had died in 1808, at age 75. Their son, Jeremiah, died in 1823 at age 45. Parmelia Reynolds, child of James Reynolds and Sarah Cole, born October 21, 1823, died on August 29, 1831.[45] William Reynolds, child of James Reynolds and Sarah Cole, was born on December 24, 1825 and died on June 3, 1833. Peregrine Cole a devout Catholic, died in 1826. When his first wife died, he married Elizabeth Weldon, daughter of Abraham Weldon. They had seven children: John, Benjamin, James, Andrew, Martha, Elizabeth and Sarah.[46]

On June 24, 1821, *at Bohemia* Father Epinette buried Daniel Craddock. On November 21, 1821 *at Bohemia* he buried Richard Craddock. On November 13, 1823, *at Bohemia* he buried William Alfonso Craddock. On November 25, 1824, *at Bohemia* he buried Isabella Brady. On November 21, 1825, *at Bohemia* he buried Jeremiah Michael Boland. On August 13, 1826, *at Bohemia* he buried Bernard Burns. On January 15, 1827, *at Bohemia* he buried Michael Butler, age 27. On October 15, 1828, *at Bohemia* he buried Mary Brickley, age four years. On March 12, 1829, *at Bohemia* he buried Mary Brazil, age five months.

On January 6, 1822, *at Bohemia* Father Epinette baptized Sylvester Pennington, four month old daughter of John Pennington and Mary Carty. Sponsor was Ann Nowland. On January 29, 1822, Father Epinette officiated at the wedding between Baker Truitt and Mary Stephen. No location nor witness given. On January 11, 1822, *at Bohemia,* he baptized Amelia Reynolds, one year old, daughter of Jeremiah Reynolds and Sara Booth. Sponsor was Mary Green. On March 3, 1822, *at Bohemia* he baptized Richard, two months old, son of Sara. Sponsor was Rebecca. On June 2, 1822, he baptized Mary Elizabeth, two months old, daughter of Abigail. Sponsor was Maria. On June 16, 1822, *at Bohemia*, he baptized Robert, three months old, son of Robert and Mary. Sponsor was Rebecca.

On July 18, 1822 *at Bohemia* Father Epinette baptized Benjamin Amos Read, four month old son of Benjamin Read and Ann his wife. Sponsors were Richard Corbely and Sara Reynolds. On September 5, 1822, he baptized Mary, four days old, son of Ezechias and Phillis. Sponsor was Maria. On October 16, 1822, *at Bohemia* he baptized James Lusby, six months old, son of John Lusby and Sara Nowland. Sponsors were Thomas and Mary Nowland. On December 1, 1822, he baptized John Bernard O'Neale, five months old, son of Bernard O'Neale and Jane McCleland. Sponsor was Elizabeth O'Neale.

On January 29, 1822, *at Bohemia,* Father Epinette officiated at the wedding between Baker Truitt and Mary Stephen. On April 9, 1823, Father Epinette baptized *at Bohemia* Isaac Heverin, three months old, son of Stephen Heverin and Ann Fowler. Sponsor was Catherine Scanlon. On April 11, 1823, he baptized *at Grove Point,* Cecil County, Apollonia Rohn, four month old daughter of Simon and Apollonia Rohn. Sponsors were William and Mary Lee. On May 25, 1823, *at Bohemia* he baptized Edward George Hopkins, son of Edward Hopkins and

Anne Foulting.

On June 16, 1823, *at Bohemia*, he baptized Elizabeth Ann Pennington, five month old son of John Pennington and Mary Carty. Sponsor was Mary Nowland. On July 13, 1823, *at Bohemia*, he baptized John, born the previous day, son of Maria. Sponsor was Rebecca. On November 1, 1823, *at Bohemia*, he baptized Anna Mayard, twelve years old, daughter of Samuel and Margaret Mayard. Sponsor was Molly, wife of Henry Mayard. On November 16, 1823, *at Bohemia*, he baptized Araminta Maria Reynolds, nineteen months old, daughter of the late Jeremiah Reynolds and Sara Booth. Sponsor was Ann Nowland.

On November 13, 1823, *at Bohemia* Father Epinette buried William Alfonso Craddock. On March 13, 1825, *at Grove Point*, Father Epinette baptized Charles and Lydia, slaves of William and Helen Lee. Sponsor was Father Epinette himself. On October 25, 1827, Father Epinette officiated at the wedding between Peter Conley and Maria Millegan. On January 9, 1828, he officiated at the wedding between Henry Martin and Ann Brown. On January 22, 1828, he officiated at the wedding between John McIntire and Honored Money.

On May 23, 1823, Miss Alphonsa Blake of the Blake farm *near Chestertown* wrote to Archbishop Maréchal, making a strong plea for a priest of their own in Chestertown. She spoke of a mission near Chestertown that was attended only ten times a year. She went on to assert: that it "would be a likely place for converts if the archbishop could have a priest visit there more often." She further requested permission to attend Protestant services "in order to induce some of those adherents to reciprocate by attending the Catholic Mass." Without more frequent pastoral attention, she maintained: "the poor, often the most faithful servants of God, would be left to themselves, and perhaps, as several have done, become members of the same dissenting church. The loss of souls would indeed be great, for we are almost certain had there been a church here ten years ago, it would now probably be filled."[47]

On July 4, 1824 he baptized *at Bohemia* Henrietta, seven years old, son of Mary. Sponsor was Rebecca. On the same day, *at Bohemia*, he baptized Elizabeth, five months old, daughter of Richard and Mary. Sponsor was Molly. On August 1, 1824, *at Bohemia*, he baptized John Ennis, two weeks old, son of Patrick and Catherine Ennis. Sponsor was Thomas Nowland. On September 5, 1824, *at Bohemia*, he baptized Henrica Emerentia Corbely, ten months old, daughter of Richard Corbely and Anna Johnson. Sponsor was Amelia Reynolds. On November 25, 1824, he baptized Mary Buchlin, three weeks old, daughter of Jeremiah Buchlin and Mary Barry. Sponsor was Phillis.

Father Epinette officiated at weddings (no location, no witnesses given): on January 29, 1822 – between Baker Truitt and Mary Stephen; on February 15, 1825 – between John V. Price and Ann K. Nowland; on May 22, 1825 – between Maurice Flinn and Elizabeth Farrell; on May 28, 1825 – between Abraham Pennington and Elizabeth Reed; on May 29, 1825 – between James Warter and Suzanne Shiffey; on July 24, 1825 – between Patrick Murphy and Catherine Cavender; on July 31, 1825 – between John McEnestry and Ann Foley; on April 23, 1826 – between Nicholas Smith and Ann Dougherty.

Work on the Chesapeake and Delaware Canal had begin as early as 1805, but the company had been forced to close down. Many Irish laborers had remained in the area. Father Moynihan had notified Archbishop Carroll in 1815 that he needed to care for the many Irish still living along the Canal.

The project was revived in 1821, and work was resumed on April 15, 1824.[48] Matthew Carey, a prominent Catholic publicist and economist in Philadelphia, was the one most responsible for an awakened interest in the completion of the canal. Fearful of the decline of Philadelphia's commercial life, Carey actively supported the Chesapeake and Delaware Canal as a means of capturing the ever-increasing trade of the Susquehanna River for Philadelphia.[49]

By June of 1824 a work force of 85 men and 150 horses was actively employed. Carts and wagons drawn by horses were used to transport the earth from the excavation.[50] The work was grueling in the heat of summer and the cold of winter. Wages were again extremely low and living conditions bad. Most of the workers were Irish immigrants.[51] The workmen were employed by the contractor rather than by the canal company. They averaged ten to twelve dollars per month, although in the winter months wages often fell to five dollars or less per month. In a plea for improvement of their wages, Matthew Carey pointed out that most canal laborers could not support a wife and two children at even a subsistence level, even if the wife earned separately fifty cents a week.[52]

In 1827 there were as many as two thousand engaged in digging the canal. By June 1828, the company reported that the canal was in use from the Delaware River to the Summit Bridge, a span across the deep cut of the canal completed in 1826.[53] In 1829, excursion steamboats were used to transport touring groups through the canal to Summit Bridge.[54] The company directors announced the completion of the canal to stockholders in June, 1830.[55] At the time it was considered one of the outstanding works of human skill and ingenuity in the world.[56] Father Peter Epinette was the first priest to record baptisms *at Canal*. On May 22, 1825, he baptized *at Canal* James Doyle, two months old; son of Thomas Doyle. On the same day *at Canal* he baptized John Larkin son of Michael Larkin and Margaret Nowland. Sponsors were James Nowland and Catherine Kavanaugh. On May 26, 1825, *at Canal* he baptized Benjamin, two months old, son of Abigail. Sponsor was Suzanne. On June 23, 1825, *at Canal* he baptized Charles John Ganly, son of John Ganly and Mary Haydn. Sponsor was Nicholas Smith. On July 3, 1825, *at Canal*, he baptized Esther Ann Hopkins, born of Edward Hopkins and Ann Fountain. On April 25, 1827, *at Canal*, he baptized George Patrick and Jeremiah Warren. Sponsors were Patrick and Mary McCormick. On May 27, 1827, *at Canal* he baptized Margaret Cecily McNolty, born of John and Elizabeth McNolty. Sponsors were Patrick Furly and Rose Ann Mulligan. On June 13, 1827 *at Canal* he baptized Anne Rebecca Proctor, five months old, daughter of James and Rebecca Proctor. On June 13, 1827 *at Canal* he baptized William McGee. On July 2, 1827, *at Canal*, he baptized Bridgit Ganley, born June 29, 1827, daughter of Thomas Ganley and Catherine, his wife. Sponsors were John Dunn and Mary Lynch. On July 17, 1827, he baptized *at Canal* Thomas Gaffney, son of James and Jane Gaffney. Sponsors were Michael Hagan and Elizabeth Sylvan. On November 4, 1827, he baptized *at Canal* John Francis Ryan, son of John Baptist Ryan and Mary Gleason. Sponsors were Daniel Hogan and Maria Conley. On December 7, 1827, he baptized *at Canal* Mary McGlanogen, daughter of James McGlanogen and Elizabeth his wife. Sponsors were John

McNamee and Catherine Smith. On November 21, 1827, he baptized *at Bohemia* Sara Jane Heverin, four years old, daughter of Mary Heverin. Sponsor was Elizabeth Stanley. On December 23, 1827, *at Canal* he baptized Robert Alexander McGuire, son of James and Margaret McGuire. Sponsors were John McNamee and Catherine Smith. On the same day, *at Canal* he baptized Margaret, daughter of Timothy. On January 12, 1828, *at Canal* he baptized Catherine Ganley, born of James and Brigid Ganley. Sponsors were Thomas and Mary Ganley. On March 7, 1828, *at Canal* he baptized Lawrence Farragar, three days old, son of David Farragar and Winifred Daly. Sponsors were Lawrence Dowling and his wife. On March 7, 1828, he baptized *at Canal* Lawrence Daly, son of David and Gertrude Daly. Sponsor was Thomas Downing: On March 7, 1828 *at Canal* he baptized John Strane, four weeks old, son of Robert Strane and Helen Carey. Sponsors were James Meghan and Amelia Flanary. On May 11, 1828, *at Canal*, he baptized Suzanne Sheridan, five weeks old, daughter of John Sheridan and Catherine, his wife. Sponsors were Arthur Magee and Catherine Sheldon. On the same day, *at Canal* he baptized Michael Brashler, three weeks old, son of Timothy Brashler and Helen Flin. Sponsors were Bartholomew and Mary Scanlan.

On May 11, 1828, *at Canal* he baptized Ann Elizabeth King, two years old, daughter of George and Rachel King. On the same day, *at Canal*, he baptized Edward Burke, two weeks old, daughter of Jacob and Suzanne Burke. Sponsor was Suzanna Hall.

Father Epinette continued to visit Canal until 1831.

On October 7, 1829, *at Bohemia* he baptized George Moffitt, six months old, son of George Moffitt and Mary Heverin. Sponsor was Elizabeth Stanley.

On January 6, 1824, *at Bohemia*, Father Epinette baptized Sara, six months old, daughter of Mary. Sponsor was Rebecca.

On February 1, 1824, Father Epinette baptized *at Bohemia* Edward Morris, one month old, son of James Morris and Mary Hopkins. Sponsor was Rebecca.

On February 29, 1824, *at Bohemia* he baptized Charles, three months old, son of Ann. Sponsor was Phillis. On July 1, 1824, *at Bohemia* he baptized Eliza, nine years old, daughter of Mary. Sponsor was Rebecca.

On January 16, 1825, *at Bohemia*, Father Epinette baptized Henry, six weeks old, son of Jane. Sponsor was Phillis. On March 11, 1825, *at Bohemia*, he baptized Susan August O'Neale, five months old, daughter of Beenard O'Neale and Jane McCleland. Sponsor was Charles O'Neale.

On March 13, 1825, he baptized *at Grove Point*, Cecil County, Charles and Lydia, slaves of Mr. Kee, witness was Mr. Kee.

June 19, 1825, *at Bohemia*, he baptized Robert Lusby, 12 months old, son of John Lusby and Sara Nowland. Sponsor was John Pennington.

On June 19, 1825 he baptized *at Bohemia* the two months old son of John Pennington. On September 11, 1825, he baptized *at Bohemia*, Araminta Johnson, daughter of Stephen and Suzanna Johnson. Sponsor was Phillis. On the same day *at Bohemia* he baptized Stephen, parents unknown. On November 1, 1825, at Bohemia he baptized Ambrose, two months old, son of Sara. Sponsor was Rebecca. On May 4, 1826, he baptized at Bohemia Mary, daughter of Nancy. Sponsor was Suzanne. On the same day he baptized *at Bohemia* Margaret Anne, four weeks old, daughter of Jane. Sponsor was Prudence.

On May 25, 1826, Father Epinette baptized *at Bohemia* William Henri Craddock, two years old, son of Richard Craddock and Anne Springer. Sponsor was Benedict Craddock. At the same time he baptized Anne Elizabeth Craddock four years old, of same parents and with same sponsor.

On September 15, 1826, he baptized *at Bohemia* John Roderick Hevelow, son of Roderick and Anne Sabina. Sponsor was Ann Read.

On September 17, 1826, he baptized at Bohemia Eliza Harris, two months old, daughter of James and Mary Harris. Sponsor was Phillis. On September 26, 1826, he baptized at Bohemia Mary Emely Corbaley, four months old, daughter of Richard and Ann Corbely. Sponsor was Sara Reynolds. On October 17, 1826, he baptized *at Bohemia* Thomas Theodore Price, two months old, daughter of John Price and Ann Nowland. Sponsor was Suzanne. On the same day he baptized *at Bohemia* Charles Hopkins, two months old, son of Edward and Ann Hopkins. Sponsor was Prudence.

On December 14, 1826, he baptized *at Bohemia* Ann O'Neale, ten days old, daughter of Bernard O'Neale and Jane McCleland. Sponsor was Edward O'Neale.

On June 29, 1827, he baptized *at Bohemia* Margaret Row, born that day, daughter of Patrick Row and Mary Lynch. Sponsors were Patrick Ganly and Sarah Crossgrove.

On July 29, 1827, *at Bohemia* he baptized John Hinson, one month old, son of Henry and Jane Hinson. Sponsor was Phillis.

On August 15, 1827, *at Bohemia* he baptized Jane Anderson, fifty-four years old, daughter of Rebecca Anderson. Sponsor was Rebecca.

On August 21, 1827, *at Bohemia* he baptized Rachel Brady, daughter of Robert and Mary Brady. Sponsor was Rebecca.

On November 10, 1827, *at Bohemia* he baptized Joseph, son of Gemana. Sponsor was Rebecca Sprig.

On November 21, 1827, *at Bohemia* he baptized Sara Jane Heavrin, four years old, daughter of Mary Heavrin. Sponsor was Elizabeth Stanley.

On December 31, 1827, *at Bohemia* he baptized Ann, daughter of Louisa. Sponsor was Sara. On January 4, 1828, he baptized Andrew Hares, seven years old, Eliza Hares and James Hares, three years old, children of James and Elizabeth Hares. On January 8, 1828, *at Bohemia*, he baptized Thomas Saving, thirteen years old, "dying" son of John Saving.

Father Peter Epinette officiated at the following weddings at Bohemia: On May 29, 1825, between James Wortey and Suzanna Shiffley. No witnesses given. On July 24, 1825, between Patrick Murphy slave of General Forman, and Catherine Cavender, slave of Mrs. Horsey. On July 31, 1825, between John McEnestry, slave, and Ann Foley, slave. On April 23, 1826, between Nicholas Smith, free, and Anne Dougherty, slave of this place. On December 24, 1826, between John McCormick, free, and Bridget Kerrigan, slave of Mrs. Horsey. On October 26, 1827, between Patrick Conley and Maria Millegan. On January 4, 1828, between Henry Martin, slave to General Forman, and Ann Brown, slave to Mr. William Lee. On January 22, 1828, between George Grady and Judith Purcell. On January 22, 1828, between John McIntire and Honored Money. On February 4, 1828, between James Milon and Ann Baxter. On February 14, 1828, between Jack McIntire and Honored Money. On February 21, 1828, between Henry Mallon and Juliana O'Donnell.

Archbishop Maréchal had died on January 29, 1828. He had conducted regular visits throughout his archdiocese from 1818 until mid-July, 1827. His greatness depended largely on the fact that he was a man of his times, forming his people in a spirit not alien to America, furthering order and discipline in an infant church struggling with lay trusteeism. He stressed the need for American priests and felt that the next most acceptable, given the prejudices of the times, were Englishmen. He was extremely optimistic about Catholic prospects in the United States, but stressed that steps must be taken to overcome internal dissensions related to the trustee system and the notion that Catholics could choose and dismiss pastors as they pleased. He was not afraid to speak his mind. Maréchal's victories over trustees and the Jesuits marked an important milestone in the ever-widening rise of episcopal power in the United States.

Archbishop Maréchal is remembered for his learning, eloquence, piety, and firm disposition. He suffered protracted battles over local control in other places, but not on the Eastern Shore of Maryland.[57]

Archbishop Maréchal was personally unassuming. A short bespeckled prelate, unpretentious and unprepossessing, he enjoyed a good rapport with Protestants and was at home with most Americans. Admittedly he was authoritarian and held the reins tightly. He knew his diocese intimately through extensive visitations.

In December of 1826 Maréchal contracted a chest infection from which he never fully recovered. After spending much of the summer of 1827 resting in a attempt to recover his health, he returned to Baltimore to resume his obligations, but requesting of Rome a much needed coadjutor.[58]

THE EPISCOPATE OF JAMES WHITFIELD

The metropolitan who presided over the American Church in its single ecclesiastical province from 1828 to 1834 was James Whitfield, born on November 3, 1770, at Liverpool, England. He was the only native of England to serve as Archbishop of Baltimore. He spent fifteen years in Leghorn, Italy, learning to be a merchant. Then as a result of meeting Ambrose Maréchal, who was then teaching in France, he spent eight years in the Sulpician Seminary in Lyons, studying to be a priest. He was ordained there in 1809. In 1817 Maréchal persuaded him to come to Baltimore, where he remained a secular priest, serving as assistant rector at the Cathedral from 1818 to 1820, and then as rector until May 25, 1828, when he was consecrated fourth Archbishop of Baltimore.[59]

Portrait of Archbishop Whitfield

French Jesuit, Peter Epinette

When Archbishop Maréchal died on January 29, 1828, Father Epinette was already serving at St. Francis Xavier in Cecil County. He continued to serve there under Archbishop Whitfield.

On March 8, 1828, *at Bohemia*, Father Epinette baptized Mary Rebecca Roberta Price, two months old, daughter of John Price and Anne Nowland. The sponsor was Sarah Hessy.

On March 7, 1828, *at Canal*, Father Epinette baptized Lawrence Daly, 3 days old, son of David and Gertrude Daly. Sponsors were Thomas Dowing and his wife. On the same day, *at Canal* he baptized John Shane, four weeks old, son of Robert Shane and Helen Carey. Sponsors were James Meighan and Amelia Flanary. On May (no date given) *at Canal*, he baptized Suzanne Sheridan, five weeks old, daughter of John and Catherine Sheridan. Sponsors were Arthur Mahan and Catherine Killen.

On May (no date given) *at Canal* he baptized Michael Braskeld, three weeks old, son of Timothy and Helen Braskled. Sponsors were Bartholomew Scanlon and Mary Scanlon. On May (no date given) *at Canal* he baptized Ann Elizabeth King, two years old, daughter of George and Rachel King. There were no sponsors. On May 18, 1828, *at Canal* he baptized Edward Burke, two weeks old, son of Jacob and Suzanne Burke. Sponsor was Suzann Hall. On June 8, 1828, he baptized Thomas Burns, six days old, son of John Burns and Catherine Murphy. Sponsors were Daniel Burns and Mary McHale.

On August 21, 1828, *at Canal* Father Epinette baptized Lucinda Atwell, two weeks old, daughter of John Atwell and Mary Farrell. Sponsors were Edward Scanlon and Margaret O'Connor. On August 31, 1828, *at Canal* he baptized John Cain, three years old, son of John and Johanna Cain. Sponsors were Jeremiah Sullivan and Elizabeth Burns. On the same day, *at Canal* he baptized Margaret Kenney, daughter of Hugh Kenney and Susan McHugh. Sponsors were David Morris and Frances Brannon.

On September 12, *1828*, *at Canal* he baptized Elizabeth Johnson, seven years old, and Catherine Jane Johnson, five years old, and John Johnson, sixteen months old, children of William and Ann Johnson. On September 13, 1828, *at Canal* he baptized William Henry Story, three years old, son of Elizabeth Story. Sponsor was Jane Farrell. On October 28, 1828, *at Canal* he baptized Thomas Ganley five days old, son of Tom and Catherine Ganley. Sponsors were James Gaffney and Brigid Ganley. On November 11, 1828, *at Canal* he baptized Daniel Dugan, born that day, son of Matthew Dugan and Ann Deran. Sponsors were Henry Flanery and Hannah Molony.

At Bohemia on June 8, 1828, Father Epinette officiated at a marriage between Hugh Kelly and Sarah White. On June 13, 1828, between Philip McCaffry and Nancy Turner. On August 16, 1828, between James Barney and Grace Youth. On October 18, 1828, between George Vizey and Germana Blake. On January 4, 1829, between Jacob Brey and Henrietta Jefferson. On January 21, 1829, between David Bayard and Jane Harris. On June 16, 1829, between Alfred B. Thomas and Alice O'Donnell.

On February 8, 1829, *at Canal* Father Epinette baptized Ann Finy, two weeks old, daughter of John Finy and Helen Greias. Sponsors were John McHugh and Catherine Martin. On the same day, *at Canal* he baptized Mary Brasil, three days old, daughter of John Brasil and Bridgit Shy. Sponsors were Matthew Ryan and Margaret O'Connor.

On May 24, 1829, *at Canal* he baptized Ann Fury, three weeks old, daughter of John Fury and Honora Glisson. Sponsors were William Robertson and Mary Carson. On July 12, 1829, *at Canal* he baptized Margaret Boyle, eight years old, daughter of Sarah Ann Boyle. Sponsor was Margaret Nicholas. On August 9, 1829, *at Canal* he baptized Philip Neale, seven months old, son of Richard and Eliza Neale. No sponsors.

On August 13, 1829, *at Canal* he baptized John Coklan, born the day previous, son of Jeremiah Coklan and Mary McNelty. Sponsors were John Toman and Mary Coklan. On September 13, 1829, *at Canal* he baptized John Bradley and Suzan Meyers. Sponsors were John Marshall and Agnes Kidd.

On September 20, 1829, *at Canal* he baptized Letitia Rudden, one year old, daughter of William Rudden and Mary Hannon. Sponsor was Margaret Sastre. On October 6, 1829, *at Canal* he baptized Michael Burke, four days old, son of Patrick Burke and Catherine Mogurn. Sponsors were Edward Whistler and Mary Lyons. On November 2, 1829, *at Canal* he baptized David Tom, born that day, son of James Tom and Margaret McKan. Sponsors were Michael Mooney and Helen Dougherty. On the same day (Nov. 2, 1829) *at Canal* he baptized Elizabeth Merrycroft, two months old, daughter of William Merrycroft and Jane Boyle. Sponsors were Thomas and Margaret Smith.

On January 4, 1829, he officiated at the wedding between Jacob Nery and Henrietta Jefferson. On January 21, 1829, he officiated at the wedding between David Bayard and Jane Harris. On June 16, 1829 he officiated at the wedding between Alfred B. Thomas and Alice O'Donnell.

On September 6, 1829, *at Bohemia* Father Epinette buried Lucinda Otwell, age 2.

On February 21, 1830, *at Canal* Father Epinette baptized James Burke, born the same day, son of Patrick Burke and Mary Dougherty. Sponsors were Matthew Ryan and Catherine McCormick. On March 22, 1830, *at Canal* he baptized Elizabeth Leek, born March 5, daughter of John Leek and Hannah Savage. Sponsor was Anna Leek. On April 11, 1830, *at Canal* he baptized Martha Bayard, eleven months old, daughter of James and Mary Bayard. Sponsor was Rebecca Sprig. On July 12, 1830, *at Canal* he baptized William Caughlen, four days old, son of Jeremiah Caughlen and Mary McNary. Sponsors were John Fine and Margaret Tom. On October 5, 1830, *at Canal* he baptized Michael Dougherty, two weeks old, son of Charles Dougherty and Helen Sleven. Sponsors were John and Helen Finey. On October 30, 1830, *at Canal* he baptized Rebecca Govin, twenty months old, daughter of Henry Govin and Ann Johnson. Sponsor was Rebecca Sprig. On November 16, 1831, *at Canal* he baptized Albert Harrison, son of James Harrison and Mary Hopkins. Sponsor was Rebecca Sprig.

This was the last baptism by Father Epinette. At age 72, he died at Bohemia on January 8, 1832, and was buried there.[60]

American Jesuit, Richard B. Hardey

Father Richard B. Hardey was transferred from St. Joseph's, Talbot County, to succeed Father Epinette at Bohemia Mission in April, 1831. The construction of the first railroad in the eastern United States from New Castle, Delaware, to Frenchtown, Maryland, was at that time in progress. Many legislators realized the practical value of railroads by 1826 after steam locomotives had been successfully demonstrated in England.[61] The authority to build a railroad along or near the New Castle Frenchtown turnpike was granted by the general Assembly of Maryland in December, 1827, and by the Delaware Assembly in February, 1829. The project was begun to construct a road of rails nearly parallel with the turnpike. Cedar rails and blocks of gray stone from the quarry in Port Deposit, Maryland, arrived in New Castle in July, 1830. By April of 1831, eleven hundred men were working on the road, strung across the entire roadbed from New Castle to Frenchtown. The track was laid on large stone cross ties on a base of sand and gravel. Most of the laborers were Irishmen.[62]

Seventeen miles of railroad from New Castle terminating at the wharf landing of Elk River below Frenchtown were completed by the end of 1830. Crowds of curious people attended the grand opening on Monday, July 4, 1831. Exhausted but exuberant workers had to work on Sunday, July 3, to complete the track in time.[63]

The road was equipped with two passenger cars resembling stage coaches and having the capacity of ten or twelve passengers and each drawn by one horse. The horses were changed at Glasgow and Bear, the two stations along the road. This mode of travel over the rails continued one year. Then in 1832 a steam locomotive was imported from England. The railroaders went to work assembling the new engine in New Castle. It was named "Delaware" and was introduced on the road February 28, 1832.[64] Farmers along the route were startled to see the strange device chugging along the countryside belching sparks and clouds of smoke. Passengers had to beat out large sparks landing on them and threatening to set their clothing on fire. One local observer called the engine "harnessed hell," and didn't wonder that horses on the countryside bolted away in terror of the fiery monster. The first trips took longer since the train had to stop for wood and water along the way, but soon the trip was reduced to one hour. There were two trips each day.[65]

From the outset the railroad was successful. During March, 1832, some 4, 413 passengers traveled over the line. When warm spring weather arrived, hundreds of curious people took Sunday excursions over the novel railroad.[66]

The development of the railroad was an important source of employment for Irish immigrants. The wage and grocery bills submitted by the contractor to the financiers of the New Castle and Frenchtown Railroad show none but Irish names. For instance., the work force employed on the New Castle - Frenchtown Rail Road January - February, 1832 contains the following names:

Patrick Managan	John McCake	John Hennessy
James Longon	Daniel McManus	Arthur McClone
Charles Haskins	James Molen	David Gibson
Patrick McGovern	Michael Butter	Philip Sheridan

Joseph Rodgers	Patrick Donovan	John Horgan
Denis Slattery	James Walsh	James McGovern
Michael Horgan	Florence Flinn	Edward Gogan
Hugh McGee	David Gilkison	John Harrigan
Michael Harrigan	Patrick Dunivan	Owen Gorman
Thomas Tracy	Michael Kenny	John Slaltery
John Ryan	James Fliming	Thomas Riley
John Kelley	James Whelahan	John Thornton
Hugh McGee	Patrick Welsh	Lawrence Kane
Michael Haley	Daniel McManus	Edward Keath
Charles Haskins	James Dortty	Isaac Mitton[67]

The Jesuit priests at Bohemia were the closest to the workplace of these men and their families. Father Hardey's baptisms were as follows: *January 29, 1832 – at Railroad*, Bridget Cashman, born of Maurice and Bridget Cashman Sponsor: Simon McCleese and Catherine Flynn; *February 14, 1832 – at Railroad*, Mary Finney, born of John and Ellen Finney. Sponsors were Philip Carland and Margaret Connors; *February 14, 1832 – at Railroad*, Bridget Dougherty, born of Daniel and Bridget Dougherty. Sponsors: James Magee and Bridget Cashman; *February 24, 1832 – at Railroad*, Anthony Brady, born of Robert and Mary Brady;[68]

On March 1, 1831, *at St. Elizabeth Church, Denton* Father Hardey baptized Joseph Philip Walter Richardson, son of Joseph Richardson and Lucy Potter, his wife. Sponsors were Catherine and Zebediah Potter. It was the first baptism performed in the new church there.[69] On March 3, 1831, *at St. Elizabeth's Church, Denton,* he baptized William Jerome, son of Sylvia Coinish. On March 6, 1831, *at St. Elizabeth's Church, Denton,* he baptized Constantine Augustine Richardson, son of Joseph Richardson and Elva Martin, his wife. In 1832 Father Hardey was assigned to White Marsh, and again in 1834 to Trinity Church, near Georgetown College. In 1836 he was transferred to St. Joseph's Church, Philadelphia.[70]

American Jesuit, William McSherry

Father William McSherry was born on July 19, 1799, the third son of Richard McSherry, an Irishman, and his wife Anastasia Lilly, of Harper's Ferry, Virginia. William entered Georgetown College in 1813, and the Society of Jesus in 1815. After studies in Rome, he was ordained and taught at Georgetown until he became provincial and later president of the college. He died at age 41, on December 18, 1839.[71] On June 21, 1832, Father William McSherry baptized *at Railroad* Harriett Gemina, daughter of Tom and Ann Jones. Sponsors were Mary Harris and Anthony Thomas (all colored persons). This child was about two years old and belonged to Benedict Craddock.

Irish Jesuit, Peter Kenny

On October 21, 1832, Father Peter Kenny baptized *at Bohemia* Clara Elizabeth, daughter of Thomas and Ann Jones. Godmother was Mary Harris. All were Black persons. The child was someweeks old and had received private baptism from

Photo of Rev. Peter Kenny, S.J.

Mr. Benedict Craddock to whom all belonged.

In 1830 Father Peter Kenny, S. J. had come back to America to finish the Audit or Visitation, broken off in 1821 by the death of the Father General. He made out a report for all the "residences, houses and farms including the residence of St. Francis Xavier, Bohemia, Cecil Co., Md., June, 1831," not in his own words, but in those of Brother Heard, upon whose statement Father Kenny's observations were based. Brother Heard's statement:

"Slaves, males 5, females 2: males under 18, 2; females under 16, 1. Males married, 3; none of their wives belong to us, and one of those men married a free woman of the worst character; she has lived in wickedness for many years; another of these men has married a slave woman, who since has turned methodist; the third has lived three years with a married woman whose husband has left her some years before; but now he has left her and tells me he is married to another, without asking leave of anyone. The greatest number that lives together is four: one old woman, her little daughter of 10 year, and two boys of 14 year. Illegitimate male children on the farm for twelve years, one. We have two that gets drunk 10 or 12 times a year and some Times Fights at home and abroad. As for their honesty I have not heard any complaints against them abroad, and for what they take at home is not of meterial consequence, though I have to take all possible care to prevent it."

"The people sold at common price would bring $1,050. Jacob $250, Jim $250, Tom $250, Jerry $150, Bill $150, the little girl would have to be given to support the old."[72]

While Father Kenny was there he instructed Brother Heard how to keep the Account Book, which had not been used since August 13, 1799, when the Abbé Maréchal left Bohemia for Baltimore. The Brother began well by placing the date 1831 on two pages, under the caption of Charge and Discharge, the Irish way of saying Debtor and Creditor, but after a few entries he used his own way as more intelligible. On the last pages of the book he recorded his sales of negroes:

Jan. 23, 1832. Sould Jacob To Jacob Caulk for 9 years and 6 months for . . . . . . $250 after that Term of years he is to be free.

Feb. 5th. Sould James To David Mackey for 10 years for . . . . . . $150 after that Term of years he is to be free.

Jan. 23rd. Sould the little Boy Jerry to Alfred B. Thomas for $150

Feb. 2nd. Sould Phillis and Mary To Wm. & Joseph Craddock. mary 9 years old and Phillis 54 for the sum of $80.50

Sent Lucy & Betsey to St. Joseph's."

The men to whom the servants were sold were our neighbors, Thomas and Craddock our tenants. There is no mention of Tom in the Brother's account, but he was sold too, because Father Kenny in October, 1832, wrote from Bohemia.: "Brother Heard has disposed of all his slaves except a boy." This boy was called Bill, and Bill remained a servant at Bohemia till 1852; and with Bill there was another boy, called Sam, who came from St. Joseph's to help Bill; Sam appears in the expense columns till 1859. Bill and Sam were very faithful servants, and the Fathers always gave them a bonus at harvest time and fifty cents extra for Christmas.[73]

Even after Brother Heard had sold his slaves at Bohemia, he employed some of the negroes who had gained their freedom before. Thus he engaged old Joe, who got the surname of Wells, for many years at $40 a year and his working clothes; and Jane his wife used to cook for him at $2 a month. Every year he made a new contract: "I promise to give to our old Joe $40," – then it is $50, and finally $55 a year and working clothes. He made the same kind of contracts with David, surnamed Bayard, after the Knight without fear and reproach, and Dick Johnson; and there was also a Dick Lilly who helped Sam and Bill long after the headings of "Charge and Discharge" were changed into "Reserved and Plate," and when the war prices were put on such ordinary things like a pair of "drors, shirtbatins, sosbentoes, sopp, mosterd, dost-pans and aggbeeters."[74]

Father Kenny in his Visitation of 1831 was kept pretty busy going around on all the plantations. H examined the Account Books, added up columns and struck balances; when there were no books because the Superior kept everything in his head and the rest in his pocket book, the examination was not quite so satisfactory perhaps but very easy. Then he examined the farms, the houses, barns and quarters and everything else, and put an evaluation on them, as if they were going to sell out. "The fact is we were going to sell out, but Father General, before the reports reached him, sent over word 'You had better hold on to your lands and improve them;' right on improving them every year, and the taxes are going right on improving also at the same rate. According to the Concordat signed by Father Charles Neale, the Superior of the Jesuits in America, and Bishop Dubourg, on March 19th, 1823, the Superior promised to send with the Fathers and Brothers, who should go to Missouri, at least four or five or six negroes, to be employed in preparing and providing the additional buildings, or in cultivating the farm.

When the slaves saw Father Kenny going around from plantation to plantation and making all kinds of inquiries they got somewhat suspicious; in fact, Father Havermans wrote from Newtown to Father George Fenwick in 1832: "The slaves have heard they have been sold or are going to be sold: they are in suspense and I hope they will continue to work." And their suspicions were not altogether without foundation, since Father Kenny wrote to Father Neale at St. Thomas'. "Let me know how many blacks you have and what kind. Mr. John Lee and Horsey wish to purchase for plantations in Louisiana" but some time after in his letter to Father McElroy at Frederick, Father Kenny put off the sale saying, "When you see Mr. Horsey or Lee, tell him his letter came too late. My letter to them gave my final answer as to proposed purchase of slaves."[75]

In 1833, the Maryland Jesuit Mission was erected into a Province, and Father William McSherry was made its first Provincial, and at the suggestion of Father Kenny, he made St. Thomas' his official residence. Here then the final sale of slaves began.

The Provincial Congregation was held in July, 1835, and the Fathers deliberated on the postulatum to sell the servants. After having considered the matter and formulated the reasons, they sent it to Father General. The reasons given, may be summed up under three heads: the Fathers who have charge of the farms and negroes, neglect their spiritual duties–the servants are unprofitable– the farms if hired out to tenants would be more productive. The reasons under the first head had the greatest weight, for here the cunning of Satan, or of the "farming devil," as Father Debarth called him, came into play: his trick was to give them a passion for farming, "and in order to hinder the children of St. Ignatius to become good missionaries, he would try to make them bad farmers, and thus the spiritual is neglected and the temporals ruined." The answer to the postulatum was: This matter needs further deliberation and cannot be decided on the spot. So they went on deliberating for a whole year, and finally on December 27, 1836, Father General approved of the sale of our servants, but only on the following conditions, namely:

"1. That they have the free exercise of the Catholic religion and the opportunity of practising it.

Therefore a) they are not to be sold except to proprietors of plantations so that the purchasers may not separate them indiscriminately and sell them;

b) it must be stipulated in the sale, that the negroes have the advantage of practicing their religion, and the assistance of a priest:

c) that husbands and wives be not at all separated, and children not from their parents, quantum fieri potest.

d) if a servant, male or female, have wife and husband on another plantation they are to be brought together, otherwise, they are by no means to be sold into a distant place:

e) that those who cannot be sold or transported on account of old age or incurable diseases be provided for as justice and charity demands.

2. That the money received from the sale be in no way spent in making purchases, nor in paying of debts, but it must be invested as Capital which fructifies. The best way would perhaps be *ground rents* in the cities especially of Pennsylvania and New York–but in this you shall have to ask counsel both from ours and externs.

Of everything that is done in this matter your Rev. will inform me as on it depends the subsistence of the Province, namely for the Novitiate and scholasticate. Therefore act with consideration and consultation and prayer, in order that the business may proceed for the good of the Province and all others.

The only ones of these who had been on the St. Joseph's, Talbot County, farm in 1803, were old Nan and young Ned; Lucy and Beller or Bettey came from Bohemia in 1831, and the boy Sam was sent to Bohemia in 1833 to help Bill. This is Father Hardy's report about his negroes to Father Kenney in 1831: "With regard to our servants I have but little to say favorably. Very few regard the frequentation of the sacraments, and most of them I fear are immoral. Old Nancy is a good woman, the boy Sam does very well, Ned is a good man as a servant, and as a Christian careless and indifferent. The rest sometimes go to confession and communion, but they are unworthy of the least praise. Admonition is of little avail with most of our servants, and surrounded as they are by methodist, free blacks and careless colored Catholics, their reformation will be difficult. The Brother is unpopular and will never rule the servants, who are determined to oppose him in their sly way, right or wrong." In 1839, after the slaves had been sold on the other plantations, there still remained at St. Joseph's Old Nancy, Michael and his wife, Ned and his wife, Sam and one or two others; Ned was hired out at $40 a year until 1863. As I cannot find the Charge and Discharge book before 1855, I do not know what became of the others.[76]

German Secular, Francis Varin

Succeeding Father Hardey as pastor of St. Francis Xavier Church in Cecil County was Father Francis Varin, who was born of a noble family at Shonewalt in Saxony, Germany, on September 14, 1777. After his ordination as a secular priest, he left Dresden and arrived in the United States in June, 1813. He became a priest of the Diocese of Philadelphia and gave instructions in the teachings of the Church there in different languages. In 1833 he arrived at Bohemia to serve as pastor.[77]

On January 24, 1833, *at Bohemia* Father Varin buried Thomas Craddock, aged 62. In 1834, *at Bohemia* he buried Margaret Ryland Craddock, the wife of Benedict Craddock. She was a convert of Archbishop John Carroll.

In 1833, Father Varin officiated at the wedding between Thomas Philips and Elizabeth Pryor, daughter of William Pryor and Martha Reynolds. Susan Heverin, born in 1834, daughter of David Heverin and Jane Gribbins, was baptized. David Heverin was a devout Catholic who regularly attended Mass at the Bohemia Mission. William Peregrine Reynolds, son of James Reynolds and Sarah Cole, was born on September 12, 1835, and was baptized at Bohemia. Father Francis Varin officiated at the following other weddings at Bohemia: On May 4, 1834, between James Boilt, convert, and Mary Milton, Catholic. Witnesses were Molly and Bayard. All free colored people. On June 6, 1835, between John Martin, free, working at the Railroad and Roseanna Silk, free born. Witness was Patrick. On March 2, 1836, between Henry Gibbs, slave to Mr. Lockwood, and Laetitia Brady, slave to Mr. Benedict Craddock. Witness was Patrick Makin. All colored persons. Father Varin would serve at Bohemia for three years beyond the date of Archbishop Whitfield's death.

Archbishop Whitfield died on October 19, 1834.[78] His years as archbishop were a leveling off period during which the young American Church would stabilize itself with carefully drawn up legislation. He presided over the First and Second Provincial Councils of Baltimore.[79] Religious congregations of both men and women took quantum leaps in the Whitfield years.

Irish and German immigrants were drawn in considerable numbers to canal and railroad projects on the upper Eastern Shore although no new parishes were established. While the massive waves of immigration were coming, the increase of Catholic numbers resulted in a revival of anti-popery. *The Protestant* was launched in January 1830 with the avowed purpose to warn the nation of the growth of papacy. The nativist assault began two months before Whitfield's death, when a mob burned the Ursuline convent and school in Charlestown, Massachusetts.[80]

THE EPISCOPATE OF SAMUEL ECCLESTON

Portrait of Archbishop Eccleston

Samuel Eccleston was the only child of the second marriage of Samuel, Sr., and the first marriage of Martha Hynson, both Episcopalians, who lived near Chestertown, Maryland. The father died shortly after Samuel Jr.'s birth on June 27, 1801, and the mother moved to Baltimore. There she married an Irish Catholic named William Stenson, adopted his faith, and had by him four children.[81]

At age twelve Samuel was enrolled at St. Mary's College, from which he graduated at age eighteen. Two years after graduation Samuel entered the seminary. He was ordained a priest on April 24, 1825, and not long after that he became the second American to enter the Sulpician novitiate at Issy near Paris in France. At St. Mary's College after his ordination, Eccleston soon proved himself as vice-president from 1827 to 1829, and as president from 1829 to 1834.[82] He was an eloquent speaker and congenial companion, frequently accompanying Archbishop Whitfield on visitations of the archdiocese. He remained a Sulpician till his death. Consecrated on September 14, 1834, at 33, he was the youngest by far of those chosen to govern the premier see. He was the first convert in the American hierarchy. It fell to his lot to preside over the transition of the American Catholic Church from a small integrated minority into a burgeoning immigrant church with many educational and charitable institutions.

German Secular, Francis Varin

Father Francis Varin was already a year at Bohemia when Samuel Eccleston became Archbishop of Baltimore. In his first year he had made two trips to Kent County, Maryland, and for the remainder of his years at Bohemia, till 1837 he concentrated on Cecil County. He was a secular priest a great linguist, and had been professor of German at Georgetown College.[83]

On March 31, 1835, Father Varin baptized conditionally Catharina Sexthon, four months old, daughter of Laurence and Johanna Sexthon. She had received private baptism from Mr. Key, a Catholic teacher in Smyrna. On the same day he baptized Mariana Boilt, four months old, daughter of James and Mary Boilt, free colored persons. Sponsor was Beth Harland. On August 22, 1835, Father Varin baptized Jeremia Camillus, five weeks old, son of George and Jeannette Reynolds. Sponsors were Father Varin and Emilia Reynolds. On September 23, 1835, *at Bohemia* he baptized James Morgan, 8 months old, son of James and Jan Heveran. Sponsors were Father Varin and Elizabeth Stanley.

On April 16, 1836, Father Varin baptized *at Smyrna* Elizabeth and Johanna Sexton, seven months old twins. Sponsors were Thomas Craddock and Alice Thomas.

On October 15, 1835, Father Varin officiated at the wedding between John Martin and the widow Rosanna Silte, both of Ireland, and working *at the Railroad*. Witness was Patrick Makin. On June 17, 1835, he officiated at the wedding between William January, a slave belonging to the Misses Reynolds of Delaware (Appoquinimink Forest) and Betsy Williams, a slave belonging to Mrs. Johns of Bohemia Manor. Witnesses were Dave Bayard and Anna Anderson, both free colored persons.

On March 21, 1836, Father Varin officiated at the wedding between Henry Gibbs, slave to Mr. Lockwood and Letitia Brown, slave of Benedict Craddock. Witness was Patrick Makin, all colored people.

On June 13, 1835, he recorded the wedding between Benedict Craddock and Susan Hessy by Reverend Patrick Reilly, pastor of Wilmington, and he recorded that it was with his pastoral consent that Father Reilly officiated at the wedding.

On October 11, 1837, Father Varin officiated at the wedding between Isaac Hilsen, a Protestant slave belonging to John Francis and Mary Brady, a Catholic slave belonging to Mr. John Price. Witness was Mattilda Anderson, all colored people.

In May, 1836, a large number of Irish laborers employed in grading the roadbed near Charlestown in Cecil County attended the fair at Kent Place, and "having imbibed freely of whiskey, engaged in an old-fashioned Irish riot," The rioters were driven out of town and the sheriff was summoned. On the next day the Cecil Guards, a military company composed of citizens of Elkton, arrested some 25 to 30 rioters. Seven of them were indicted for riot and tried at the October term of court. Two were convicted and sentenced to pay a fine of one dollar and be imprisoned for two years. The county commissioners paid their fine since they had no money, and because they were costing too much to keep, discharged them.[84]

In 1837 Father Varin was transferred to Goshenhoppen, Pennsylvania, where he died at age 62 on May 21, 1840.[85]

American Jesuit, George King

Father George King was born on February 8, 1796, in Laurel, Sussex County, Delaware. His mother was a Waples, a native of Laurel, Delaware. While home to visit her folks in Laurel, she gave birth to a son, George. After graduation from Georgetown College. George married and raised a family. One son Charles entered the Jesuits.[86] After the death of his wife, George himself entered the Society of Jesus on June 13, 1830.[87]

After five years of ministry in Wheeling, West Virginia, in November, 1837, at the age of forty-two, Father George King was sent as pastor to Bohemia, where he would spend the next eighteen years.[88] He was alone at Bohemia until 1844. The first recorded baptism by Father King as pastor of Bohemia was on August 16, 1838, when he baptized Margaret Ann Keating, about two years old, daughter of Michael and Elizabeth J. (Palmer) Keating. The child was born at Church Hill, Queen Anne County, and was baptized there.

In September 1839, Father Monnelly who was in charge of St. Peter's Church, Queenstown, fell from a roof and died as a result at the age of 84.[89] Father John B. Carey, who was approaching age 70, was pastor at St. Joseph's Church, Talbot County. In 1841, he retired to Bohemia for his health.[90] With the death of Father Monnelly and the aging of Father Carey, Archbishop Eccleston was forced to turn to Father George King to reorganize the entire Eastern Shore mission. King would serve as superior of the whole missions, with one and sometimes two assistant priests living with him at Bohemia. Father King kept for himself the charge of St. Peter's, Queenstown, and all of Queen Anne County, and St. Mary Star of the Sea, Meekins Neck in Dorchester County. His assistants were assigned to serve Talbot and Caroline counties, as well as the Delaware missions at Laurel and Smyrna.[91]

On October 28, 1841, Father King baptized Ann Maria Roe, born September 17, 1823, daughter of Thomas Roe and Rebecca Pearson. Sponsor was Elizabeth (Ford) Bryan.

On November 12, 1841, *in Kent County, Maryland*, Father King baptized Rosalia, two years old, Frances, about four years old, Brooke and Dianna, servants of Joseph T. Mitchell. Sponsor was Mrs. Mary (Horsey) Mitchell. On the same day he baptized Victoria, Mary, and Susan, children of Nicholas and Araminta, servants of Joseph T. Mitchell. Sponsor was Mrs. Mary (Horsey) Mitchell. On the same day he baptized Stephen, Moses, James Henry, belonging

Mitchell House

to Richard Haly and Michelle, belonging to Joseph Mitchell. Sponsor was Mrs. Caroline Mitchell. Also, Frances, child of Ann, belonging to Joseph Mitchell. Sponsor was Mrs. Caroline Mitchell.

On November 13, 1841, *in Kent County, Maryland*, Father King baptized Minnie, Emeline, Caroline, Rachel, and Elizabeth, children of John Hall, a free negro, and Maria, belonging to Richard Thomas. Sponsor was Jane Blake.

On April 3, 1842, Father King baptized *at Bohemia* Gervase Briscoe, nine weeks old son of Susan and Moses, "free people of color." Sponsor was Richard Johnson.

On May 27, 1846, *in Kent County, Maryland*, Father King baptized Mary Ann, daughter of David Murray belonging to James Weeks and his wife, Catherine, belonging to George H. Willson. Sponsor was Ann, belonging to George H. Willson.

On December 16, 1846, *in Kent County, Maryland*, Father King baptized John Charles Willson, born September 29, 1846, son of John Charles Willson and his wife Ann Elizabeth Brooke Willson. Sponsors were Thomas Willson and Mary Ann Held Willson.

On December 16, 1846, *in Kent County, Maryland*, he baptized Henry Hayward Willson, born July 25, 1846, son of George H. and Henrietta Eleanore Brooke Willson. Sponsors were Alexander H. Willson and Mary Ann Woolisby Ozenon.

On December 9, 1846, *at Chesapeake City*, Father King baptized Ann Morenan, born March 17, 1844, daughter of Peter Morenan and his wife Ann McGirr. Sponsor was Edward Scanlon. On the same day, *at Chesapeake City*, Father King baptized William Thomas Scanlon, born June 20, 1846, son of Edward Scanlon and his wife, Margaret Vance. Sponsors were John Conlan and Mary Conlan.

On February 22, 1847, Father King baptized Richard, two months old, and Caroline, two years old, children of Charlotte. Sponsor was Araminta. All belonging to Captain V. Bryan. On February 22, 1847, Father King baptized Jeremiah, born February 20, son of Jeremiah Haselton, a free colored man, and his wife Susanna, belonging to Henrietta Blake. Sponsor was Margaret, belonging to Eleanore Blake.

On March 14, 1847, *at Smyrna in Kent County, Delaware*, Father King baptized William Reilly Smyth, born in Smyrna, Delaware, on December 23, 1846, son of James Smyth and his wife Bridget McGillis. Sponsor was Patrick Mackin.

On March 19, 1847, Father King baptized Esther Goldsborough Jones, born in Kent County, Maryland on July 31, 1846, daughter of Richard J.C. Jones and his wife, Mary G. Pascault. Sponsor was Esther A. Pascault Goldsborough.

On June 25, 1847, Father King baptized Thomas Smyth Willson, born May 30, 1847, son of Thomas Smyth Willson and his wife, Ellen Emily (Brown) Willson. Sponsors were Charles J.B. Mitchell and Martha Louisa Mitchell.

On December 22, 1847, *in Kent County, Maryland*, Father King baptized Wilfred Manning, born September 17, 1847, son of Richard E. and Anna Young Willson. Sponsors were Daniel C. Willson and Julia Compton.

On December 22, 1847, *in Kent County, Maryland*, he baptized John Henry, belonging to P. Weaks and Elizabeth, his wife, belonging to J.C. Willson and Eleanore Willson.

On December 22, 1847, *in Kent County, Maryland*, he baptized Maria, daughter of Thomas and Ann Margaret, all belonging to Dr. Thomas Willson.

On July 7, 1848, *at Elkton*, Father King baptized Catherine Toomey, born May 14, 1846, daughter of William Toomey and his wife Mary McEveney. Sponsor was Constantine McEveney.

On November 11, 1848, *at Chesapeake City*, Father King baptized Mary Amanda Scanlon, born September 27, 1848, daughter of Edward Scanlon and his wife, Mary Vance. Sponsors were Luke Conlan and Mary Conlan.

On the same day, *at Elkton*, Father King baptized Benjamin, son of William Toomey and his wife, Mary Anne McEveney. Sponsor was Constantine McEveney.

On May 7, 1849, *at Appoquinimink Forest*, Father King baptized Margaret Heverin, about six years old, daughter of Stephen Heverin and his wife Harriet McCoy. Sponsor was Elizabeth Slye Stanley.

On May 12, 1849, *at Appoquinimink Forest*, Father King baptized Benjamin Read, born January 13, 1849, son of Benjamin Read and his wife Elizabeth Walsh. Sponsor was Ann Reynolds Cann.

On March 26, 1849, *in Kent County, Maryland*, Father King baptized Horace James Kindle, son of Stephen Kindle and his wife Sarah Downy. Sponsor was H.E. Brooke Willson.

On May 29, 1849, he baptized Henrietta Marie Willson, born November 20, 1848, daughter of John C. Willson and his wife Ann Elizabeth Brooke Willson. Sponsors were Ignatius O. Farrell and Henrietta J. Hill Kennedy.

On June 24, 1849, Father King baptized Charles Stephen Smith, born January 17, 1849, son of William W. Smith and his wife Eliza Ann Stephens Smith. Sponsor was Laura Jane Hobbs.

On July 14, 1849, Father King baptized Alexander Joseph born May 14, 1849, son of Sally, belonging to the estate of Bennett Mitchell. Sponsor was Mary E. Browne. Also, Charity Ann, born May 14, 1849, daughter of Sally, belonging to the estate of Bennett Mitchell. Sponsor was Mary E. Browne.

Father George King Officiated at the Following Weddings at Bohemia:

On December 28, 1838, between Thomas Lusby of Cecil County, Protestant, and Mary Ellen Lusby, of Kent County. Witnesses were Benjamin Donoho and Elizabeth Craddock. On January 17, 1834, between Joseph Craddock and Helena Green. Witnesses were Patrick Mackin and Joseph Flant. On January 20, 1839, between David Hagan and Milcah Lowe. Witnesses were James Bears, George Bears, Patrick Mackin, and Owen Downey.

On September 21, 1839, between Vincent J. Taylor, of Georgetown, D.C., and Anne Massey, of New Castle County, Delaware. Witnesses were Andrew Naudain, Mary Naudain, John Driver, Joanne Driver. On September 26, 1839, between William P. Green and Elizabeth H. Craddock. Witnesses were Benedict and Susan Craddock, Thomas N. Price, and John M. Price. On October 15, 1839, between Alfred Thomas of Cecil County and Jane A. Shields, of Cecil County. Witnesses were Jacob Jones, Ruth Jones, James Shields and Margaret Shields.

On January 7, 1840, between John C. Wilson and Ann Elizabeth Brooke. Witnesses were Robert Brown, Henry Wilson, Thomas S. Wilson and Ann Young.

On May 10, 1840, between Perry Conegys, slave to E. A. Longfellows and Mary Boyer, slave to Joseph L. Craddock. Witnesses were Clara Bacchus, a free woman, Richard Johnson, a free man, John Johnson.

On January 20, 1840, between Perry Brady slave of Benedict Craddock, and Tabitha Davis, slave to George T. Price. Witnesses were William, slave to R. C. Corporation, Clara Bacchus, free, and Patrick Mackin. On August 16, 1840, between John McCaffery and Mary Hughes. Witnesses were James Hunt and Ellen Hunt. On September 1, 1840, between John E. Applegarth, of Dorchester County, and Ann Keene, of Dorchester County. Witnesses were John Augustus Tubman, Mary Tubman, Rachael Keene.

On December 26, 1840, between William, slave of Bohemia, and (no name given) free woman. Witnesses were Richard Liddy, free negro, and Clara Bacchus, free negro. On December 27, 1840, between Barnabas Hutching, free colored man, and Sarah Johnson, slave to Dr. Thomas S. Willson, Queenstown. Witnesses were Samuel Blake, Miss M. Brown, Hannah Johnson, slave to Mrs. Nichols, Peter Hinson, free. On April 29, 1841, between John K. Griffin, Queen Anne Co., and Elizabeth Clements (nee Bryan). Witnesses were William K. Griffin, Debora Larrimore, Arthur Bryan, John Holfer.

On September 9, 1841, between Thomas P. Davis and Catherine Willoughley, both of Kent County. Witnesses were Henry Edgar and Ann Edgar. On October 8, 1840, between Elijah Chance and Martha Blount of Queen Anne County. Witnesses were Arthur Bryan, James Blount, and Elizabeth Clements. On October 7, 1841, between Thomas Craddock and Margaret Shields. Witnesses were John Craddock, Temperance Craddock, and Alfred B. Thomas.

On December 13, 1841, between Isaac Dunnock of Dorchester county and Margaret Dunnock of Dorchester County. Witnesses were Thomas Willson, Susan King, and John Dunnock. On December 25, 1841, Nace (no other name given) belonging to Henry S. Mitchell and wife, belonging to J. Boyle of Annapolis. Witnesses were John of Mrs. M. Brown and Mary of Henry S. Mitchell. On December 26, 1841, between Ezechiel a freeman, and Margaret, belonging to H. S. Mitchell. Witnesses were John, of Mrs. Brown, and Fanny and Ann of Mrs. M. Brown.

On May 24, 1842, between Edward Bryan and Anna M. Tilghman, of Queen Anne County. Witnesses were Richard Grason Samuel O. Tilghman, and John Bryan. On August 28, 1842, between Samuel Johnson, belonging to Gerard Coursey, and Martha, belonging to Henry F. Blake. Witnesses were Ann, Alex, and John, belonging to Mrs. Brown. On January 17, 1843, between Timothy Sullivan and Jane Cannon. Witnesses were James Mulhulrane, Patrick Mackin, and Frances Brady.

On June 24, 1843, between John Palmer, of color, and Martha Harwood, of Mrs. Ann Louisa Gibson. Witnesses were John Thomas, Dorrington Gibson, and Ann Gibson. On February 18, 1843, between Martin Meagher and Catherine Beers. Witnesses were Thomas Beers, James Beers, and Mary G. Beers. On March 13, 1843, between James Dunnock, slave to Miss Susan King, and Susan Chancy, slave of Robert F. Tubman. Witnesses were John Dunnock, Dorothy Creighton, and Mary G. Tubman.

On April 24, 1843, between William, of the estate of Bennett Mitchell, Queen

Anne County, and Mary, of Charles C. Brown, Maria E. Tilghman, Ogle Tilghman, and Elizabeth Fairburn. On June 22, 1843, between John Pinkind and Mary Larrimore, of Queen Anne County. Witnesses were Arthur Bryan, Debra Larrimore, and Henrietta Pinkind. On November 21, 1843, between Isaac, of Joseph Callahan, and Ann, of Mrs. Martha Brown. Witnesses were John Williams and Sarah, of Mrs. M. Brown.

On March 14, 1844, between Henry Anderson, of Edward Ringgold, and Sarah Robertson, a free colored woman. Witnesses were William A. Blake, James Blake, and John Miller. On March 22, 1845, between Henry, of Gov. Grason, and Henny, of Captain Valentine Bryan. No witnesses given. On April 24, 1845, between William Smith and Mary Ellen Lilly, free persons of color. Witnesses were Paul J. Durney, Ignatius Lancaster, and Patrick Mackin.

On June 25, 1845, between Ignatius Lancaster, of Maryland, and Elizabeth Spearman, of Delaware. Witnesses were John F. Maitland, Thomas Betton, and Alfred Spearman.

On October 2, 1845, between Thomas Ford and Helen M. Wheeler. Witnesses were Hanilton Morton, Mary Morton, and Benjamin Green. On December 2, 1845, between Henry May and Henrietta M. deCourcey, of Queen Anne County. Witnesses were Edward Paca, Thomas S. Willson, and William deCourcey.

On September 23, 1846, between John R. Brown, of Dorset, and Mary Creighton, of Dorset. Witnesses were John Shenton, John Tubman, and Robert Creighton. On November 10, 1846, between Lewis Pascault, of Queen Anne County and Emily M. Rhodes, of Talbot County. Witnesses were Francis Pascault, William L. Goldsborough, and Howes Goldsborough. On December 23, 1846, between William Dadds and Sarah E. Plumer. Witnesses were Robert Callahan, John Council, and Ann Golt.

On January 27, 1847, between John, of Bennett Mitchell, and Frances, of Mrs. Martha L. Browne. Witnesses were Samuel and John. On February 25, 1847, between Charles Moody, of Charles I. Bryan, and Eliz Cooper, of Captain Valentine Bryan. Witnesses were Charles I. Bryan, Edward Bryan, and Rachel Tate. On May 10, 1847, between William Goldsborough and Rebecca R. Pasco, both of Queen Anne County. No witnesses given.

On May 24, 1847, in Denton, Caroline County, between Edward D. Martin and Sallie L. Richardson. Witnesses were Z. W. Potter, John Franklin, and Thomas Martin. On December 11, 187, between Prosper Libre and Marguerite La Paire. Witnesses were Rainé La Paire and D. Katley.

On December 27, 1847, between William Smith and Eliza A. Stephens. Witnesses were Charles Carbery, Edward Smith, and Richard Wilson.

On March 19, 1848, between Richard J. Lilly and Sarah Jane Lewis. Witnesses were Patrick Mackin and Michael Burns. On August 27, 1848, between Henry Stewart and Araminta. Witnesses were Robert Callahan, John Council, and Ann Golt. On April 5, 1848, between William H. Taylor, of Charles I. Bryan, and Harriett M. Taylor, of Captain Valentine Bryan. Witnesses were Charles I. Bryan, Edward Bryan, and Robert Tate.

On May 2, 1848, between William Partridge and Priscilla Keene. Witnesses were Matthew Meekins, John Tubman, and Sara J. Meekins. On August 27, 1848, between Henry Stewart, of William Paca, and Araminta, estate of Captain

Valentine Bryan. Witnesses were John Moody, Charles Bryan, and Henrietta Pinkind. On September 5, 1848, between William H. Taylor and Harriett M. Taylor. Witnesses were David Taylor, William Taylor, Patrick Mackin.

On December 17, 1848, Father King officiated at a wedding between John R. Keene and Priscilla J. Meekins. Witnesses were Matthew Meekins, John Tubman, and Thomas H. Keene. On December 25, 1848, between Thomas A. Bryan and Henrietta Pinkind. Witnesses were Henry Blake, Rachel Tate, and Mary E. Browne. On April 22, 1849, between Benjamin Wilmer, of W. G. Hobbs, and Henny, of Mary E. Browne. Witnesses were Richard Hall, William Hobbs, and George McCubbin.

On May 29, 1849, between Thomas Smith, of Richard Jones and Ann Hammersly of Dr. Thomas Willson, both of Kent County. Witnesses were John, of Hiram Jones, and Louise and Margaret, of Dr. Thomas Willson. On November 4, 1849, between George Brady, estate of John V. Price, and Harriett Jones, estate of Benedict Craddock. Witnesses were Patrick Mackin and Mary Sullivan.

On December 13, 1849, between Jacob Cooper, of R. C. Tilghman, and Alice Plater, of R. J. Browne. Witnesses were Charles B. Mitchell, Mary E. Browne, and Maria L. Mitchell. On December 29, 1849, between John Rafferty and Ellen Ennis. Witnesses were Patrick Mackin, Bernard McCaffery, and Mrs. B. McCaffery. On March 31, 1850, between John Deshane and Mrs. Ann Bahan. Witnesses were Bartholomew Brady and Patrick.

On April 7, 1850, between James Fleming and Mary Beers. Witnesses were James B. Lupill, Ellen B. Lupill, and Thomas Murry. On May 7, 1850, between James Price and Ellen H. Hessy. Witnesses were Thomas A. Price, William Flintham, and John W. Flintham. On June 9, 1850, between John Coresky, of Smyrna, Delaware, and Johanna Flemming. Witnesses were John R. Rafferty, Ellen Rafferty, and Patrick Mackin.

On December 1, 1850, between Jacob Boulden and Ann Wells, free people of color. Witnesses were James Brady and Henny, free. On December 28, 1850, between Edward Dougherty and Ellen Bray. Witnesses were Joseph Flant and Patrick Mackin. On January 8, 1851, between Christopher Burns and Mary Dougherty. Witnesses were James Shea, Maria Cosgrave, and Patrick Mackin.

There were many Irish digging the Susquehanna Canal and the Chesapeake and Delaware Canal as well as many working in the iron furnaces located around Cecil County. Mass was already celebrated in the Elkton area at two places: Mount Pleasant and Wilna Place. Wilna Place was owned by Henry B. Mackall, an attorney at law. Wilna Place is north-northwest of Elkton on Blue Ball Road along the Little Elk Creek. In the 1840's a wealthy widow from New York, Margaret Butler Lyons, rented the property from Mr. Mackall and invited area Catholics to make her home there a place for the regular celebration of Mass. In time Mrs. Lyons purchased an acre of land on the western outskirts of Elkton on what is now Bridge Street.[92]

In 1847 she transferred the deed to Samuel Eccleston, the Archbishop of Baltimore. In July, 1849, Archbishop Eccleston purchased an additional one and a quarter acres of ground for $500 to add to the parish property. There were seven Catholic families in Elkton when the land for the church was deeded.[93]

Mrs. Lyons proposed to Father King of Bohemia and the people that enough stones were on her farm near Child's Maryland to build a church. The members of the community both Catholic and non-Catholic hauled stones over several winters to build the church. Father King oversaw the building of the church. George Rambo of Newark, Delaware, served as head stonemason and Jacob Rambo was the chief carpenter. The church built of limestone was plastered on the outside to give the building a smooth appearance. The walls were two feet thick. The finished church did not have a bell tower but did have a few plain windows and pews that were discarded from a church in Baltimore.

Father King had written his Jesuit superior regarding ownership of the new church:

"I wrote a letter to the Most Rev. Archbishop of Baltimore at the request of those who subscribed the money for the purpose of building a church at Elkton. Asking the Most Rev. Archbishop to consent to have the church deeded to the Society. I thought that as the congregation wishes the Society to have the church his Most Reverence would have no difficulty about it, particularly as Father Comby has said that the Most Reverend Archbishop told him all the churches our Fathers built might belong to the Society. This I stated in my letter to the Archbishop. In my letter to his Grace's I enclosed yours the archbishop's reply and place the matter where it should be – in your Very Reverend's hands.

The missions are going on well. Since Christmas I have had the happiness of receiving five persons in the church."[94]

Later that month he wrote again:

"I hope his grace the Archbishop will give a favor in response to the wish of the Elkton congregation which is to permit them to have the church about to be built to be deeded to the Society."[95]

As King planned the ceremony he wrote:

"The Most Rev. Archbishop has agreed to go over to Elkton and lay the cornerstone of the new church now about being built there which is to be called the Church of the Immaculate Conception of the Blessed Virgin. The stone will be laid at 10 o'clock on Sunday next. I would be very much pleased if your Very Reverend could come over for the occasion and bring some of ours with you. If you cannot conveniently come yourself be pleased to send some of ours over if any can be spared. The Archbishop with Mr. Donelan who is to be here on the occasion will leave Baltimore by the nine o'clock car and arrive at Elkton a little after twelve where they will remain during the night. Your Very Reverend and ours could do so too, or if you or they prefer they could leave Baltimore at one o'clock by the Union Line boat bound for French Town, which arrives there about six o'clock from whence your Very Rev. and they could go over to Elkton or Bohemia. We will have Confirmation at Bohemia on the Monday following. Begging a remembrance in your prayers, I am your most humble and obedient servant."[96]

The cornerstone was laid on September 15, 1849.[97] King wrote his Jesuit Superior: "I had hoped it would have been convenient for your Very Reverend to have come over at the laying of the cornerstone of the new church at Elkton which was laid last Sunday under the most holy patronage of the ever blessed Virgin's Immaculate Conception.

I had written your Very Reverence begging you to favor us with your presence or attempt to send some of ours for that occasion. I regret that your or their occupations did not permit you Very Reverence or any of them to come. We had Confirmation last Monday at Bohemia. Nineteen were confirmed by the Archbishop who returned to Baltimore the following day."[98]

Archbishop Eccleston wrote Father King regarding debts on the Elkton church.[99] Father George King continued to serve at Bohemia until after Archbishop Eccleston's death in 1851.

On September 24, 1849, Father King baptized Anna Ridout Tilghman, born August 9, 1849, daughter of Samuel O. Tilghman and his wife Mary Fairbairn Heuston Tilghman. Sponsor was Elizabeth Ann Fairbairn. On the same day he baptized Robert, born May 8, 1849, son of John Goldsborough, belonging to the estate of William G. Tilghman, and his wife Henny, belonging to Samuel Ogle Tilghman. Sponsor was Mary E. Tilghman.

On September 24, 1849, Father King baptized conditionally and with the ceremonies of the church, Joseph Elias McLean, born May 23, 1849, son of William McLean and his wife Mary Ann Marsh McLean. Sponsors were Mary E. Brown and Charles J.B. Mitchell.

On October 28, 1849, Father King baptized Abraham, three months old, son of Margaret, belonging to Henry S. Mitchell. Sponsor was Ann, belonging to Mrs.

Church of the Immaculate Conception, Elkton (1850)

Handwritten letter of Father George King, 1850

Martha T. Browne.

On November 26, 1849 *in Kent County, Maryland*, Father King baptized Richard Bennett Willson, born July 16, 1849, son of Richard Bennett Willson and his wife Ann Martha Young Willson. Sponsors were Alexander H. Willson and Martha A. Willson.

On November 26, 1849, *in Kent County, Maryland*, he baptized Abraham, born October 28, 1849, son of Daniel Murray, belonging to James Weeks, and Catherine, his wife, belonging to George H. Willson. Sponsor was Elizabeth Hill Willson.

On November 26, 1849, *in Kent County, Maryland*, Father King baptized Charlotte Ann, daughter of Andrew Murray, belonging to Antoinette Weeks, and his wife Eliza, belonging to John M. Willson. Sponsor was Elizabeth H. Willson.

On April 24, 1850, *in Kent County, Maryland*, Father King baptized Mary Margaret, born March 21, 1850, daughter of James Smith, belonging to Hiram Jones and his wife, Ann Elizabeth, belonging to Richard Bennett Willson. Sponsor was Ann S. Willson.

On February 7, 1851, *in Kent County, Maryland*, Father King baptized Ann Maria Smythe Willson, born October 20, 1850, daughter of John . Willson, and his wife, Ann E. Brooke Willson. Sponsors were Alexander H. Willson and Anna Maria Willson.

In April, 1851, Father George King was transferred to St. Joseph's Church Talbot County. In 1855, because of failing health he was sent to Newtown in St. Mary's County. He died at Loyola College in Baltimore on June 20, 1856.[100] He had labored on the Eastern Shore of Maryland for nearly twenty years. His obituary notice praises him as follows: "He was remarkable for his simplicity of manner, his kindness to all, and his admirable humility. He lived contented and unmurmering in every privation. His patience and meekness were all that could be desired whilst his zeal for the welfare of others led him to brave the scorching heat of summer, and the storms of many a severe winter, to visit the sick, sometimes at the distance of a hundred miles."[101]

French Jesuit, James F. M. Lucas

In 1840 Father James Lucas was born at Rienes, France on February 7, 1788, he came to America in 1815, and entered the Society of Jesus in Norfolk, Virginia. He served as professor of French at Georgetown College and pastor of Holy Trinity Church there until 1838. He came to St. Joseph's in Talbot County from Norfolk in 1840.[102]

In 1844, St. Joseph's was consolidated with Bohemia mission with Father George King as the superior. Bohemia became the central house and fixed residence for all the fathers. This enabled them to live a community life, but caused enduring long distances of travel. Father King was first assisted by Father James Lucas who had been at St. Joseph's since 1840. He would continue to serve St. Joseph's and its missions while being based at Bohemia until 1846.[103]

Swiss Jesuit, George Villiger

Father George Villiger joined the missionary team at Bohemia with Fathers King and Lucas in 1844. Born in Canton Aargau, Switzerland, on September 14, 1808, he became a Jesuit in 1838. After serving a year at Georgetown College, he was assigned as assistant to Father George King *at Bohemia* in 1844. Though he would return to serve as pastor of Bohemia for many years, he was transferred in 1845.[104] On January 26, 1845, *at Bohemia* Father Villiger baptized Mary Jane Mulherin, daughter of James Mulherin and Mary Murphy. Sponsors were Luke Konelin and Elizabeth Henry. On April 18, 1845, *at Bohemia*, Father Villiger baptized Mary Ellen Price, daughter of Edward and Elizabeth Price. Sponsor was Jane Harris. On May 5, 1845, *at Bohemia* he baptized Margaret Anne Perkins, born April 20, 1844, daughter of Edward Perkins, belonging to W. Caulk, and Susan, free colored. No sponsor given. On May 25, 1845, *at Bohemia*, Father Villiger baptized Benedict O'Neal, born in Cecilton January 29, 1845, son of Charles O'Neal and Emily Robertson. Sponsor was Elizabeth O'Neal.

French Jesuit, John Baptiste Carey

Father Carey had served at St. Joseph's under the previous archbishop and continued to serve there many more years under Archbishop Eccleston. *At Bohemia*, Father John Carey officiated at the following wedding:

On April 29, 1841, between Charles O'Neal and Emily Robinson. Witnesses were Michael Carroll and Patrick McKim.

In 1841, Father Carey was transferred to Bohemia from St. Joseph's, Talbot. On April 24, 1842, he baptized *in Queen Anne County* John Fisher, son of John and Mary Fisher. Sponsors were David Ewings and his wife Jane. Broken in health, he came at last to live permanently at Bohemia.

During his last years he was mentally unbalanced. His chief aberration manifested itself when he would be seized with the persuasion that it was time for him to set out on any Saturday for his mission. He would endeavor to get a wagon ready, as in the days of his active ministry and that failing he would wander off afoot. One Sunday morning he had disappeared and the whole congregation turned out to search for him. He was found unconscious down near the stream in a damp place where he had spent the night, having fallen exhausted from this wanderings. He died at Bohemia May 20, 1843.[105]

German Jesuit, Michael Tuffer

During the late summer of 1845, Father Michael Tuffer, a native of Germany, replaced Father Villiger as Father King's assistant at Bohemia. He remained in that assignment until 1851.[106]

On April 29, 1849, Father Tuffer baptized *at Bohemia* Mary Johama Huchardson, born February 24, 1849, daughter of Andrew Huchardson and Mary Joanna (colored). Sponsor was Isabella Robinson.

On May 20, 1849, *at Bohemia* he baptized John Sharter, born *in Smyrna* on April 27, 1849, son of Michael Sharter and Margaret Hobey. Sponsors were Dennis O'Brien and Eleanore Ennis.

On February 21, 1846, Father Michael Tuffer officiated at a wedding between Anthony Huchesan, free colored, non-Catholic, and Rachel Harris, Catholic servant. Witnesses were Jeanson Huchesan, William Roberts, and Jean Brown.

German Jesuit, Nicholas Steinbacher

When Father Michael Tuffer was away temporarily in the late spring of 1846, Father Nicholas Steinbacher was assigned to assist Father George King from Bohemia. Born in Germany on December 27, 1796, he entered the Society of Jesus on December 3, 1832. In 1840, Father Steinbacher had served at Georgetown College, then at Newtown until 1847. He remained with Father King only one year, at which time he attended Queen Anne, Dorchester and Talbot counties.[107]

On May 30, 1846, Father Steinbacher officiated at a wedding between William Harrington and Rebecca Cooper, widow. No witnesses given. He was baptized after making a profession of faith.

American Jesuit, William F. Clarke

Rev. William F. Clarke served at Bohemia from 1847 to 1849. He made one trip to Dorchester County and one trip to Queen Anne County.[108]

On August 15, 1844, Father Clarke baptized Thomas Henry Maitland, born *at Bohemia* on July 9, 1844, son of Thomas Maitland and Catherine Kipp. Sponsors were William P. and Elizabeth Green. On December 20, 1846, he baptized Mary Agnes Carty, born *at Bohemia* on September 1, 1846, daughter of Elizabeth Carty, belonging to John Craddock.

On January 4, 1848, Father Clarke baptized Joseph Cephas Henson, two months old, born *at Bohemia*, child of Mary Henson. Sponsor was Patrick McKim. On January 6, 1848, he baptized Isaac Harris, twenty-four years of age, born *at Bohemia*, servant of Thomas Craddock. Sponsor was Thomas Craddock. On January 23, 1848, he baptized Isaiah Carty, born *at Bohemia* on December 22, 1847, son of Elizabeth Carty, slave of Joseph Craddock. Sponsor was Margaret Durney.

On January 30, 1848, he baptized Felix Brady, born *at Bohemia* on December 2, 1847, son of James Brady and Lydia Ann Harris, servants of George Reynolds. Sponsor was Harriett Jones, slave of Susan Craddock. On February 1, 1848, he baptized Charles Augustine Craddock, born *at Bohemia* on January 24, 1848, son of Joseph Craddock and Helena A. Green. Sponsor was Margaret Durney. On February 25, 1848, he baptized Hannah M. Corbely, born *in Kent County, Maryland*, on March 22, 1794. Sponsor was Agnes R. Johnston (born Malaberger).

On March 6, 1848, Father Clarke baptized Sarah Jane Lilly (born Lewis), a convert, twenty years old, born *at Bohemia*, daughter of Deborah Lewis. Sponsor was Ellen Greenwell.

On April 30, 1848, Father Clarke baptized John Waugh, born *at Bohemia* on February 8, 1847, son of Benjamin Reed and Elizabeth Waugh. Sponsors were Benjamin and Elizabeth (Craddock) Green. On June 12, 1848, Father Clarke baptized Mary Elinore Lusby, born *at Bohemia* February 26, 1848, daughter of Thomas and Mary Ellen Lusby. Sponsor was Sarah Wootis.

On July 17, 1848, he baptized Mary Catherine Darcy, born *at Bohemia* on July 13, 1848, daughter of John Darcy and his wife (Dynan). Sponsor was Ann Dynan. On July 20, 1848, he baptized Wilson Morton, born *at Bohemia* on July 6, 1848, son of Hamilton Morton and Mary Theresa Durkee. Sponsors were John B. and Elizabeth E. Durkee. On August 6, 1848, he baptized John Frisby Cooper a convert, born *at Bohemia* in 1845, son of Henry Cooper and his wife. Sponsor was Susan Ann Craddock.

On August 13, 1848, he baptized Laura Virginia Gibbs, born *at Bohemia* on

July 10, 1848, daughter of Henry Gibbs and Letitia Brady. Sponsor was Mary Henson, slave of J. V. Price. On August 27, 1848, he baptized William Callahan, born *at Bohemia* on September 22, 1845, son of Thomas Callahan and Ann Register. Sponsor was Patrick McKim.

On December 24, 1848, Father Clarke baptized Ann Theresa Ford, born *at Bohemia* on November 28, 1848, daughter of Thomas Ford and Helen Wheeler. Sponsors were Benjamin and Mary Green.

On October 31, 1847, *at Bohemia*, Father William Clarke officiated at a wedding between Abraham Riley, free colored, and Caroline Price, servant of J. V. Price. Witnesses were J. V. Price and his wife and Elizabeth Bardis. On March 19, 1848, between Richard J. Lilly and Sara Jane Lewis. Witnesses were J. B. Gillespie, Charles Lancaster, Ellen Greenwell. On June 5, 1849, between John Flintham and Susan A. Craddock. No witnesses given.

American Jesuit, James Power

In 1851 Father James Power was in charge of Bohemia for a few months.[109] On May 11, 1851, Father Power baptized Charles Andrew Gibbs, two months old, colored child, born at Bohemia, son of Henry and Letitia Gibbs. Sponsor was Lisa Ann. On August 15, 1851, he baptized Edwine Slater Hanson, seven months old colored child seven months old, son of Thomas P. and Mary Hanson. Sponsor was Adele Dulin. On September 7, 1851, he baptized Thomas Rourke, seven weeks old colored child, born *at Elkton*, son of Timothy and Mary Rourke. Sponsor was Mary Riley. On September 27, 1851, Father Power baptized Thomas Holliday, five months old colored child, born *at Elkton*, son of Richard and Mary Holliday. Sponsors were Thomas Sullivan and Mrs. Devine.

On February 23, 1851, *at Bohemia*, Father James Power officiated at a wedding between William Henry Chiffens and Temperance Craddock. Witnesses were John Craddock and Mary Craddock. On October 18, 1851, in Elkton, between Cornelius Hanlon and Catherine O'Connell, both of Delaware. Witnesses were Mr. McGrath and M. McKim.

Jesuit Brothers, John and James O'Sullivan

Brother John O'Sullivan, S.J., born March 17, 1804, County Kerry, Ireland, entered the S.J. April 7, 1840, died February 15, 1884 and is buried at Frederick, Maryland, age 80. He was procurator of "The Home Farm" at Bohemia from 1849 to 1861. During this time he tutored his nephew James O'Sullivan, who became the first and only vocation of the Bohemia mission. John later tutored his nephew, Thomas deVine at Bohemia when James went to Georgetown, Brother John was in charge of the boys there. Thomas O'Sullivan, born 1803, County Kerry, Ireland, was the father of James whose mother died at his birth. Thomas came to Cecil County, Maryland with his son James in 1845. James O'Sullivan was born December 26, 1841, and was three years old when his father, Thomas, brought him to Cecil County, Maryland. Thomas O'Sullivan was a tenant of Bohemia plantation and ran the farm known as "The New Design," where James grew up. Brother James O'Sullivan, S.J., died in the year 1902 and was buried at

Dorsey's House on one of the five farms of St. Xavier Church

Woodstock, Maryland. He entered the Society of Jesus June 23, 1856.[110]

Having become Archbishop of Baltimore at age 33, Samuel Eccleston governed his province with prudence and kindness for sixteen and a half years. He was notable for his dignity of person and suavity of manner, thrust as he was into a demanding role at a bewildering time in the development of the Catholic Church in the United States.

He held one diocesan synod from October 29 through November 1, 1835, to put the decrees of the Second Provincial Council into effect. As metropolitan he held five provincial councils over which he presided over with singular ability and wisdom. These councils reflected the overriding problems and concerns of the American church as the mid-century approached: the status and conduct of the clergy, trusteeism, and the manner of securing church property, the perils of secret societies, the dangers of public schools, the value of Catholic schools, the need for Catholic publications, the necessity of creating new dioceses.[111]

As metropolitan he presided over the transition of the American church from a small minority into an exploding immigrant church. The greatest influx of foreigners in proportion to the population in the history of the nation took place between 1845 and 1855, three million in a country of twenty million.[112] The Catholic population doubled through immigration.

Anti-Catholic bigotry expressed itself in many violent ways. Anti-Catholic animus surfaced political nativism in Maryland. The American Republican Party was organized in Baltimore in 1844.[113]

The tasks of his pastoral office took their toll on Archbishop Eccleston. In the spring of 1845 he suffered a serious head injury when he lept from a runaway carriage hurtling down a hill. After that his mental and physical faculties declined. In the spring of 1851 he went to Georgetown and died there on April 22, 1852. His obituary declared him to be "good and virtuous, gentle in manner and graceful in speech."[114]

NOTES FOR CHAPTER THREE

1. M. Bernetta Brislen, O.S.F., "The Episcopacy of Leonard Neale, Second Archbishop of Baltimore," *Historical Records and Studies* 34 (1925) 20-111. Leonard Neale (1746-1817), an ex-Jesuit, was Carroll's second choice. The first choice was Lawrence Graessl, who died in the yellow fever epidemic of 1793. Thomas W. Spalding, *John Carroll Recovered* (Baltimore: Cathedral Foundation Press, 2000) xxii, 31- Neale was a native of Charles County, Maryland, 92n. – Francis Neale, Leonard's youngest brother entered the restored Jesuits in 1806. The Neale family of Charles County – Breslin 21. Leonard Neale was a grandnephew of Madam Henrietta Maria Neale Beanett Lloyd of Wye – Thomas J. Peterman, *Catholics in Colonial Delmarva* (Devon, Pennsylvania: Cooke Publishing Company 1996) 94: Leonard Neale is alleged to have received his early ealucution at Bohemia Academy in Cecil County. He returned from his European studies in 1783. At the death of Archbishop Carroll the Corporation could resume the Bohemia property by paying a thousand dollars annually to his successor. Afterwards the income of White Marsh was allotted for the same purpose instead of the revenues of Bohemia. The Corporation did this act of kindness as to ex-Jesuits, and even allotted five hundred and sixty dollars to Archbishop Maréchal for three years. Of what followed after this generosity, of the claim of the Archbishop to the White Marsh property, and the decree of the Propaganda, the protest of Fr. Charles Neale, the Superior at the time, and the final compromise in the time of Archbishop Eccleston will be dealt with elsewhere.

2. Thomas W. Spalding, *The Premier See, A History of The Archdiocese of Baltimore 1789-1989* (Baltimore: The Johns Hopkins University Press, 1989) 66; *Records of the American Catholic Historical Society* (hereafter *RACHS*) 1 (1884-1886) 150: As a priest in Philadelphia, Leonard Neale had received into the church Phoebe Way, wife of John Holohan. Leonard Neale was a close friend to Father John Rosseter, when Rosseter was at White Clay Creek in Delaware and in Philadelphia.

3. Edward B. Carley, et al., *This History of St. Joseph's Mission, Cordova, Maryland 1765-1965* (n.p.n.d.) 15; Thomas Hughes, S. J., *A History of The Society of Jesus in North America* (New York: Longmans and Green, Co., 1907-1917) Documents 1:927– List of Jesuit Stations, 1816 – "Bohemia" and "St. Joseph's and three others on the Eastern Shore." When word came in December, 1814, of the complete restoration of the Jesuit Order, Carroll was pressed to fix the congregations that would be exclusively committed to the Order. Carroll replied that a conference would be required with Bishop Neale and others, but such a conference was not held in the six months of life left to Carroll. Thomas Hanley, S. J., *The John Carroll Papers* (Notre Dame, Indiana: University of Notre Dame Press, 1976) 3:335 – Carroll to Grassi, Baltimore, May 19, 1815.

4. Georgetown University Archives (hereafter GUA) Special Collections Division, Box 571174, Washington, D.C. 20057. The searchable index to these Georgetown University Library Special Collections is found at this web address: http://www.library.georgetown.edu/dept/speccoll/indexlst.htm. For the Jesuit Complex at Bohemia, this web address: http://www.library.georgetown.edu/dept/speccoll/mi/mi}176.htm. – The Bohemia Records are continued at: http://www.library.georgetown.edu/dept/speccoll/mi/mi} 177.htm - Maryland Province of the Society of Jesus, *Varia Bohemia*, Series 20, Folder 54R1 – Z – 6, "List of the Priests Who Lived at Bohemia, 1704-1855," E. I. Devitt, "Bohemia," *RACHS* 24 (1913) 131; Devitt, "Clergy List of 1819," *RACHS* 22:261; Devitt, "Bohemia," *Woodstock Letters* 63 (1934) 32. GUA, *Varia Bohemia*, 103N1-K5, Series 21 – Decisions of arbitrators (1816) in dispute between James Moynihan, and William Pasquet, S. J.; Observations on the arbitration of James Scanlon and Benedict Craddock concerning the Settlement of Dispute (1816) between Moynihan and Pasquet.

5. Joseph C. Cann, *History of Saint Francis Xavier Church and Bohemia Plantation* (Warwick, Maryland: Bohemia Historical Society, 1976) 8; Edward B. Carley, *The Origins and History of St. Peter's Church, Queenstown, Maryland, 1637-1976* (hereafter *Queenstown*) 53

6. Associated Archives, 5400 Roland Avenue, Baltimore, MD 21212 (hereafter AAB) 9-R-2, John Carroll to Leonard Neale, Baltimore, August 3, 1815.

7. ADW, Bohemia Registers. Clifford Pryor, *The Forest of Appoquinimink* (Middletown, Delaware: the author, 1975). In 1701 William Penn made a grant of land to Joseph Weldon who had emigrated from Ireland. In 1710 Edward Mitchell began the development of Mitchell's Park. Other

Catholic Irish farmers who settled there in colonial times were John and Nicholas Reynolds, Thomas Heverin, Richard McWilliams, and the Coles. Thomas J. Peterman, *Catholics in Colonial Delmarva* 264, 266, 214

8. Martin I. J. Griffin "Extracts from the Diary of Patrick Kenny, From 1816-19" *RACHS* 7 (1896) 64: "January 24, 1816 – Rev. Mr. Moynihan, successor to Rev. Mr. Pasquet at Bohemia, called this morning – took breakfast, had his horse fed and set out."

9. THE BLAKE FAMILY (THE IRISH BLAKES) –
The Blake farm of five hundred acres (Rousbey's Recovery) was located on the northeast branch of Langford Bay near Chestertown in Kent County – Maryland State Archives, Annapolis, Maryland, LAND OFFICE (Patent Records) 12, 149-150, Christopher Rousby's Patent of Rousby's Recovery 1668. MSA SM2-SR-7354-2pp. James Blake was married to Alfonsa Carmichael. His sister Jane Blake lived with them on the farm. These were the Irish Blakes in contrast to the English Blakes of Corsica and Wye. James Blake died on August 30, 1816, and was buried at the family burial ground on the farm near Chestertown. Alphonsa Carmichael Blake died on February 26, 1844, at age 58, and was buried in the family plot near Chestertown. Jane Blake died on April 6, 1844, at age 65 and was buried in the family plot near Chestertown. Register of Wills, Kent County, Maryland Will Book, 10, folio 14, August 12, 1816: *Will of James Blake*:

I James Blake of Kent County – do make the following disposition of my estate – to my beloved wife, Alphonsa Blake a farm called Rousby's Recovery in Kent County, which contains about five hundred acres of land and a small tract adjoining it called Thomas' Purchase resurveyed containing about ninety – three acres and also a farm in Queen Anne's County called Park resurveyed and containing about four hundred acres. I hereby bequeath these three farms to my dear wife and the heirs of her body but the farm in Queen Anne County is now advertised for sale previous to my death for the payment of her Father's debts. Then after the paid debts are discharged, I bequest the annual interest arising, from the remainder of the purchase money to go to her during her life. I also bequeath to my beloved wife the annual dividend arising from nine shares standing in my name in the Farmers and Merchants Bank of Baltimore and the said nine shares after her death to go to the heirs of her body. I bequeath to my wife the present crops of wheat on the said farms, also the furniture, including the plate, books, and the two – wheel carriage. I also bequeath to my beloved wife all the negroes or I call them Black People which I own, to be disposed of as she may think proper. I have the most implicit confidence in her humanity and most devoutly wish that the said Black People will conduct themselves in such manner as to give her entire satisfaction for they have much to expect from their obedience and orderly behavior towards her and little or nothing from insubordination. I recommend to my dear wife's tender care Charley and Ted. I also bequeath to my wife all the farming utensils which I own or shall own at my death and all the stock.

As my beloved wife and myself have invited my dear sister Jane to this country promising her our kind protection and affectionate regard and whereas we are highly pleased with her conduct for five years during which time she resided with us and also in consideration of the great services she has rendered us during that period which I feel for her in a strange courting to make a reasonable provision for her. Therefore I bequeath to her during her life two hundred dollars to be paid her annually out of the produce of my personal estate. I also bequeath to my dear sister Jane the annual dividend arising from nine shares of stock standing in my name in the Farmers and Merchants Bank of Baltimore. I bequeath to my beloved brother Dominick T. Blake, counsellor at law in New York my gold watch as small token of my affection for him.

I also bequeath to my worthy friend Richard Bennett Carmichael, Esq. A travelling case of handsome razors, little used.

I hereby nominate and appoint to this my last Will and Testament as executrix my beloved wife and William Carmichael, Esq. Attorney at law. August 12, 1816, James Blake. Witnesses: James Moynihan, Samuel Hodges, Isaac Spencer. To find his wife Jane Blake's Will consult Register of Wills, Kent County, Maryland, Will Book JFB-1-folio 260.

10. THE BROOKE FAMILY –
The Brooke farm was at Eastern Neck, near Trumpington estate in Kent County. The Will of James Brooke can be found in *Will Book* 10 – folio 260, Register of Wills, Kent County, Maryland. The wife of James Brooke, Mary Ann Hill, survived him to marry Dr. Thomas Bennett Willson

of Trumpington in 1825. James Brooke died in 1822, three years previous to her second marriage leaving with her three small daughters, Mary Hester, Ann Elizabeth, and Henrietta Eleanor Brooke. These Brookes were descendants of Robert Brooke, who was the first to establish a manor on the Patuxent River and descendants of James Neale, whose wife was one of the ladies – in – waiting to Queen Henrietta Maria, and of Richard Bennett I., a colonial governor of Virginia. A pedigree of this family can be found in "The Brooke Family," *Maryland Historical Magazine* 1 (1906) 66-73, 184-188, 284-289, 376-378. James Brooke was third son of Basil Brooke and Henrietta Neale.

11. THE REYNOLDS FAMILY OF KINGS ROAD –
Clifford Pryor, *The Forest of Appoquinimink* (Milford, Delaware: Shawnee Printing, 1975) 117: Farm of 246 acres, south of the village of Blackbird. Jacob Reynolds, brother of Jeremiah, was active in community affairs and a prominent layman in Bohemia Catholic Church. Both Jacob and Jeremiah served in the militia during the Revolutionary War. Jacob's sister married Edward Knotts. Edward Knotts, his wife, and Catherine their daughter, all died in 1791; 14: "Eleanor's Delight" was willed in 1776 to Sarah Wooderson who married, second Jacob Reynolds. Jacob and Sarah Reynolds transferred ownership in 1811 to John Garman. The Garman family became Methodists. The Catholic cemetery marked with its wooden crosses was abandoned. If there were stones they were moved and the exact site now unknown became part of a tilled field called now "The Graveyard Field;" 15: By 1816 there were 103 black taxables in Appoquinimink Hundred, about twenty black families living in the Forest.

12. THE CORBALEY FAMILY –
Richard and Hannah (B. Johnson) Corbaley were parents of *Samuel Corbaley* who was baptized on May 2, 1816 at fourteen months of age, died on July 6, 1876, at age 61. Elizabeth Craddock, daughter of Richard Craddock and Ann Springer of Cecil County, married first William P. Green. After his death she married second Samuel J. Corbaley who lived on his farm between Millington and Massey's Crossroads in Kent County. After the death of Samuel Corbaley, she resided with her son William Green on a farm at Bohemia in Cecil County, then to a farm near Sudlersville in Queen Anne County, then to Bloomingdale farm near St. Peter's Church, Queenstown. She died in 1890 and is buried at St. Peter's Church, Queenstown. Helen Springer Green born on November 30, 1884 in Galena, Maryland, was baptized on April 9, 1885 at St. Francis Xavier Church, Bohemia. After her mother's decease, she was in the care of Mrs. Samuel Corbaley, her grandmother, until her decease and then cared for by her aunt, Varine J. Corbaley, until her marriage to John Jacob Raskob on June 18, 1906, at St. Peter's Cathedral, Wilmington, Delaware. Cann 232-233. n.a., Raskob – *Green Record Book* (Claymont, Delaware: Franklin Printing Co., 1921) 54 John Corbaley, a son of Richard and Hannah Corbaley was baptized July 8, 1817. He died and was buried July 20, 1817. Hannah Corbaley born 1794, died January 6, 1861, at age 67 and was buried at Bohemia. Henrietta M. Corbaley died August 11, 1818 and was buried at Bohemia. William J. Corbaley was born in 1831, died January 10, 1856, and is buried at Bohemia. John B. Corbaley died September 21, 1832 and was buried at Bohemia. Hanna T. Corbaley was born 1820 and died May 8, 1881. Richard Corbaley was born on July 20, 1818, and baptized May 2, 1819. Mary Ann Corbaley (1826-1908) married Thomas T. Price, first son of John Veazey Price and Ann Nowland. Wilson, *Rose Hill* 9 – February 3, 1815 – "Capt. Corbaley came here with Mr. Ford," note 5: "John N. Corbaley had served as a captain in the militia."

13. AAB 12A-K-2, Moynihan to Neale, Bohemia, August 24, 1816
14. AAB 12A-K-2, Moynihan to Neale, Bohemia, August 24, 1816
15. AAB 12A-K-3, Moynihan to Neale, Bohemia, October 24, 1816
16. AAB 12A-K-4, Moynihan to Neale, Bohemia, October 24, 1816; GUA – Archives, Maryland Province, Society of Jesus BOHEMIA-CORRESP. RE (1815), BOHEMIA-CORRESP. RE (1816)
17. THE SCANLAN FAMILY –
Eugene Fauntleroy Cordell, *The Medical Annals of Maryland* (Baltimore: Williams and Wilkins, 1903) 560: James Scanlan, 1801, of Georgetown, Maryland. Census 1819-1822 Wilson, *Rose Hill* 71: November 16, 1818 – "Doct. Scandling (Dr. James Scanlan had been practising medicine in Georgetown since 1801) was here to see Samuel.," 192: January 5, 1825 – "The General (the husband of Martha Ogle Foreman) and I went to Doctor Scanlin's funeral." 247: February 20, 1828 – "Mr. Biddle here. My husband gave him a check for ten dollars which he subscribed to

James W. Scanlan to enable him to attend the lectures at Philadelphia." Cann 238: Dr. James Scanlan married first Susannah Matthews, daughter of Dr. Hugh Matthews, Jr. She died on March 30, 1791, and is buried at Worsall Manor, home of her brother Dr. William Matthews. Dr. James Scanlan married second Rosetta (Rose) Walker. They had a daughter Rosetta Ann Scarlan, baptized January 2, 1817. Catherine Scanlan, aunt of the child, was the sponsor. On March 4, 1821, Edward Scanlan, the son of James Scanlan and Rose Walker, was baptized. Again Catherine Scanlan was the sponsor. William Thomas Scanlan, son of Edward Scanlan and Margaret Vance, was baptized December 9, 1846. A daughter of Edward and Mary Scanlan, Mary Amanda Scanlan was baptized on November 11, 1848. "List of Subscribers to Washington College, 1783," Cecil County Maryland Historical Magazine 6 (1911) 172: Edward Scanlan.

WILLSON FAMILY – FOURTH GENERATION:

On February 1, 1825, Father Moynihan officiated at the wedding between Dr. Thomas Bennett Willson and Mary Ann Hoskins Hill Brooke. Dr. Thomas Bennett Willson II was born in Warrington Farm, Queen Anne County, inherited through his *wife Trumpington* and died October 28, 1859. He married Anna Maria Smythe on June 3, 1806 in Rock Hall, Kent County. She died April 28, 1823. He then married Mary Ann Hoskins Hill Brook on February 1, 1825, daughter of Captain Henry Darnall Hill. She was born on August 25, 1795 in Price George County and died June 4, 1847. Children of Dr. Thomas Bennett Willson II and Anna Smythe were Dr. Thomas Smythe Willson, born March 18, 1807, died March 28, 1878; James Henry Willson, born September 17, 808, inherited Trumpington; George Hayward Willson, born May 25, 1810, died April 2, 1873; Anna Maria Smythe Willson, born August 10, 1811, died February 16, 1835; Mary Elizabeth Willson, born April 5, 1813, died May 22, 1894; John Charles Willson, born April 5, 1816, died January 25, 1858; Richard Bennett Willson, born December 10, 1817, inherited Trumpington 1859, died December 30, 1901; Alexander Willson, born November 15, 1819, died July 21, 1820; Robert Willson, born May 16, 1821, died May 19, 1821. Children of Dr. Thomas Bennett Willson II and Mary Ann Hoskins Hill Brooke were: Charles Joseph Willson, born May 21, 1826, died July 31, 1830; Daniel Carroll Willson, born October 21, 1828, died March 5, 1876; Martha Neale "Patty" Willson, born July 22, 1831, died December 9, 1919, buried December 11, 1919 at St. John's Cemetery, Rock Hall; Alexander Hoskins Willson, born May 11, 1834, died September, 1877. Richard Aloysius Willson, child of Dr. Thomas Bennett Willson II and Mary Theresa Hall, was born on May 6, 1783 in Queen Anne County and died there on February 19, 1854. He married Anne Matilda Coale May 7, 1811. Their children were Charles Bennett Willson, born 1821 in Libertytown, Maryland, and died April 24, 1891; Mary Theresa Willson, born c. 1816, died August 9, 1820.

18. AAB 12A-K4, Moynihan to Neale, Bohemia, February 24, 1817
19. Edward I. Devitt, "Bohemia Mission: Its Registers," *RACHS* 21 (1910) 247; Devitt, "Bohemia," *RACHS* 24 (1913) 132. In 1808 Father Henry was at St. Thomas, in charge of Newport and Bryantown in Charles County – Charles W. Currier, "An Historic Corner of Old Maryland," *RACHS* 20 (1909) 348. From 1816 to 1817, he was at St. Inigoes.
20. Devitt, "Clergy List of 1819, Archdiocese of Baltimore," *RACHS* 22 (1911) 253
21. THE LEE FAMILY – W. Emerson Wilson, ed., *Plantation Life at Rose Hill, The Diaries of Martha Ogle Foreman 1814-1845* (Wilmington, Delaware: Historical Society of Delaware, 1976) 35: January, 1817 "Mr. William Lee purchased Grove Point from its former Baltimore owners, Mr. Smith and Dr. Warring, 64: July 18, 1818 – "Mrs. Pearce, the general, and I spent the afternoon with Mrs. Lee. Mrs. Lee's sister, Mrs. Chambers there from Baltimore" 64: August 9, 1818 – "We have just heard that our neighbor, Mrs. Lee, now in Wilmington, has a fine son. She calls him Thomas Sim Lee. 102: April 28, 1820 – "Mr. Lee and his three little daughters Molly, Eliza, and Ellen spent the day with us. We have 7 dozen bottled cider left from last year." 215: "February 20, 1826 – Miss Sophia Lee spent the day here." 249: "March 27, 1828 – Miss Molly Lee sent us a fine rock fish." 211: "Mr. John Lee spent the day with us." Edmund Jennings Lee, *Lee of Virginia, 1642–1892, Biographical and Genealogical Sketches of The Descendants of Colonel Richard Lee* (Baltimore: Genealogical Publishing Co., 1974) 388 – Thomas Sim Lee (1745-1819) was elected the second governor of the State of Maryland in 1779. He married Mary Digges in 1771. They lived in Frederick County and were progenitors of many prominent Marylanders. *Their third son, William* was born June 23, 1775. He married on October 2, 1809, Mary, the fifth daughter of Robert Hollyday. She died August 23, 1818, leaving five daughters and an infant son. William

Lee died on July 8, 1845. His will, dated December 8, 1842, was probated in Frederick County, Maryland on July 15, 1845. Item 3 – my son Thomas, my daughter Ellen Lynch, my daughter Mary Diggs. William and Mary Hollyday Lee had the following children: (1) Mary Digges Lee, born June 20, 1810, married Samuel L. Governeur of New York, (2) Sarah Brooke Lee, born September 29, 1811, died in infancy, (3) Eliza Horsey Lee, born January 25, 1813, died 1838, unmarried, (4) Eleanor, born May 5, 1814, married Eugene Lynch, died July 7, 1873, without issue, (5) Anna Gaston Lee, born August 25, 1816, died quite young, and (6) Thomas Sim Lee born August 8, 1818 and died 1891. He married April 7, 1840 Josephine, a daughter of General Columbus O'Donnell. The daughter Mary, married again Charles Carroll. (Mary Digges Lee Carroll). They visited Grove Point in 1832, perhaps other times. Charles Carroll of Carrollton the Signer owned a very extensive estate in the present Howard County of Maryland. His other estate "Carrollton Manor" was situated in Frederick County, Maryland, near the Lee home. Wilson, *Rose Hill* 316 – May 28, 1832 – "Mrs. Charles Carroll called," note: Mrs. Charles Carroll was the former Harriet Chew of Philadelphia. Her husband was the son of Charles Carroll of Carrollton, the signer of the Declaration of Independence. Cann 97; Wilson, *Rose Hill* 35: January 20, 1817 – "Mr. William Lee, our new neighbor, dined here for the first time." 64 – August 9, 1818 – "We have just heard that our neighbor Mr. Lee, now in Wilmington, has a fine son. She calls him Thomas Sim Lee. 71 – November 20, 1818 "Mr. Lee called this morning." 102 – April 28, 1820 – "Mr. Lee and his three little daughters Molly, Eliza, and Ellen spent the day with us. 249 – March 27, 1828 64 – July 18, 1818 – "Mr. Pearce, the General and I spent the afternoon with Mrs. Lee. Mrs. Lee's sister, Mrs. Chambers, there from Baltimore. 215 – February 20, 1826 – "Miss Sophia Lee spent the day here. 249 – March 27, 1828, "Miss Molly Lee sent us a fine rock fish."   Maryland State Archives, Annapolis, Maryland, CECIL COUNTY COURT (Land Records, Index) MSA CM344 from 1810-1850 and CECIL COUNTY CIRCUIT COURT (Land Records, Index) MSA CM342 form 1851-1887 for Grantor William Lee, contains the following references: William Lee to Richard T. Earle, deed, JS 23, folio 100-101, MSA CM 343, WK 962-1, 1825-6, William Lee to Maviche & Susan (negroes), manumission, JS 24, folio 442, MSA CM 343, WK 962-2, 1826-7, William Lee (et al) to William M. Beall, deed of trust, JS 25, folio 106, MSA CM 343, WK 962-963-1, 1827-8, William Lee & Outerbridge Horsey to William M. Beall, deed, JS 25, folio 417, MSA CM 343, WK 962-963-1, 1827-28, William Lee & Other to John Heckart, mortg., GMC 16, folio 54, MSA CM 343, WK 977-2, 1848-9, William T. Lee to James Denny, HHM 8, folio 609, MSA CM 341, CR 5536-1, 1856-7, William Lee to African M.E. Church (port deposit), deed, DS 2, folio 470, MSA CM 341, CR 5543-1, 1869-70, William Lee to James Merrey, assigning lease, DS 2, folio 306, MSA CM 341, CR 5543-1, 1869-70, William Lee to Bridget McNitty, lease, IWM, folio 533, MSA CM 341, CR 5545-2, 1874-5.

Father Epinette made several trips to *Grove Point*, the farm of William Lee in Cecil County. On April 11, 1823, Father Epinette baptized at *Grove Point* Apolonia, a slave born of Simon and Apolonia. Sponsors were William and Mary Lee. On March 13, 1825, at *Grove Point*, Father Epinette baptized Charles and Lydia, slaves of William and Helen Lee. Sponsor was Father Epinette himself. William Lee's wife died August 23, 1818. Thomas Sims Lee, her last child, was born August 8, 1818. William continued to rear the children at Grove Point until 1825-6, when he sold his property and moved from Grove Point to Frederick County where he had grown up. There was a strong relationship with Outerbridge Horsey, a prominent politician in Delaware. Outerbridge Horsey (1777-1842) was an attorney with an office at 9th Street and West St. in Wilmington, Delaware. He was admitted to the Bar in 1807 – Thomas J. Scharf, *History of Delaware* (Philadelphia: L. J. Richards and Co., 1888) 573. On November 14, 1809, Samuel White, U.S. Senator from Delaware, died and on January 12, 1810, Outerbridge Horsey was appointed his successor. He was elected and began a new term of service March 4, 1815, and continued until March 3, 1821 – John A. Munroe, *History of Delaware* (Newark, Delaware: University of Delaware Press, 1984) 266. On April 16, 1812, Outerbridge Horsey married Eliza Lee, daughter of Thomas Sims Lee, at Georgetown, District of Columbia. Several attempts were made in Congress during the spring of 1814 to effect a repeal of the Embargo Act. In the Senate on March 23rd, Senator Outerbridge Horsey of Delaware presented a petition signed by citizens of Delaware demanding the repeal of the measure. Mr. Horsey secured the appointment of a select committee to consider the bill, but further efforts to repeal the embargo proved futile. Scharf 296:   Outerbridge Horsey was born in Somerset County, Maryland, in 1777. Having studied law under James A. Bayard, he became prominent in his profession, and represented Delaware in the U.S. Senate from 1810 to 1821. He was chosen attorney general of Delaware and filled the office for many years. He died at Needwood, Maryland on June 9, 1843 – Scharf 281 n. 2. He was a member of the Board of Safety for Delaware in the War of 1812. Scharf 288: At a large meeting in Wilmington on January 19, 1820, Caesar A. Rodney addressed the people in favor of Congress prohibiting the further extension of slavery, and resolutions to that effect were adopted. Those emphatic manifestations of public opinion called forth a letter from Senators Outerbridge Horsey and Louis McLane. He was a member of the original board for the academy to be known as the "College of Wilmington" – Scharf 686. John A. Munroe, *Federalist Delaware 1775-1815* (New Brunswick, New Jersey, Rutgees University Press, 1954), 250: The charter of the Bank of Delaware in which prominent Federalists as James Bayard, Outerbridge Horsey, and Louis McLane held stock was extended for ten years in 1812.

22. "The Diary of Brother Joseph Mobberly, S. J.," *Woodstock Letters, A Record of Current Events and Historical Notes Connected With The Colleges and Missions of the Society of Jesus (Woodstock College)* 32 (1903): 14-16. GUA – Archives, Maryland Province, Society of Jesus, BOHEMIA-NEGRO SLAVES-ACCOUNTING, BOHEMIA-NEGROES-MANUMISSION: SLAVES-(C.1817); Cann 168-169: Between the late spring of 1793, when the Jesuits gave the management of Bohemia to the Sulpicians and 1799, when they took back the management, it is evident in the old records that the English were able to handle the slaves but the French were unable to do so.

Father John Henry, who was assigned to Bohemia shortly after the take over found that conditions were unstable, so he deemed it better to send the slaves off to some distant state, probably supposing that a change of climate and a new location could produce a more stable change for the blacks. He, therefore, sold five of them to a neighbor who, it seems, was in the habit of purchasing blacks for planters in New Orleans. A little time before this, a severe law had been enacted by the Maryland Legislature against kidnappers who, it seems, had become pretty common on the Eastern Shore of Maryland. These blacks were sent off in the mailstage, down the Chesapeake Bay to some place where they were to be put on board a vessel for Louisiana. The state, however, was stopped at Centreville, Maryland, by a magistrate and the blacks were lodged in jail. Father Henry was also to have been arrested as their kidnapper, according to the interpretation of the late law.

Although Father Henry had obtained permission from his superiors for what he had done, and was supposed to be in the clear, his superior deemed it advisable to transfer him in order to avoid the disagreeable necessity of his attending court. This was done and the Superior of the Mission sent a Jesuit lay brother to the Eastern Shore to negotiate the settlement of the difficulty, which was to retain the blacks and restore the money to the purchaser. The was done. GUA – Ashton Papers – Emancipation of Slaves at Bohemia – Reverend Francis Neale, S.J. – Estimate on the price of Fanny and Family, i.e. Fanny, about 40 years of age, Regis $350. Jacob #350, Bill $350, Dick $170, John $60, Nancy $200, Polly $200, Misty $150, Lucy about 5. 1815, Sept. 19 – Dick, if he serves faithfully the clergymen of St. Francis Xavier, Bohemia, for 8 years, from the date hereof is to be free. In the meantime he is to be carefully maintained as other servants. 1815, Sept. 19 – Joe, if he faithfully serves the Rev. Gentlemen at the Head of the Little Bohemia for 5 years from the date hereof will be entitled to his freedom.
Dear Rw. Father,

When last I had the pleasure of seeing you here, I remember you asked me whether the late Archbishop (Carroll) left any record of promised emancipation of the negroes of Bohemia farm. The above is literally copied from a book in his own handwriting which lately fell into our hands. I take the liberty likewise to send you my account against you as it stands in our books for the purpose of receiving a pecuniary remittance from you, assuring you at the same time that I am very much pushed for money, having some time ago advanced unto Tom gross $420 to enable my Brother to leave New York. I must observe that some arrangement ought to be made about Ordo's and holy oils. You will perceive that you owe me for the oils purchased last year. Il faut de l'arbeit; Il faut beaucoup d'anguish. Affeitionalety yours. Enoch Fenwick, S.J.
GUA – BOHEMIA-PILLAGE AND DEVASTATION-(1817)

23. Devitt, "Bohemia," *RACHS* 24 (1913) 132; no author given, "The Jesuit Farms in Maryland, The Negro Slaves," *The Woodstock Letters* 41 (1912) 275. As Father Henry's Account Book has not been preserved it is impossible to say how many slaves were sold, on what terms, and what

became of the money. Two years afterwards Father Peter Kenny was sent over from Ireland as Visitator of the Mission, to bring about a unanimity or conciliation between the Trustees of the Corporation and the Superior of the Mission in regard to the administration of the farms.

24. "Extracts," *RACHS* 9 (1898) 70 – "January 5 – Rev. Mr. Henry, Priest of Bohemia, Maryland, came on a visit. January 6 – Epiphany – Rev. Mr. Henry celebrated. January 7 – Rev. Mr. Henry started home."
25. "Extracts," *RACHS* 9 (1898) 70 – "Rev. Mr. Henry and I went over to Dupont's."
26. "Extracts," *RACHS* 9 (1898) 72 – June 11, 1818 – Rev. Mr. Henry of Bohemia, Cecil County, Md. visited here this afternoon. June 12, 1818 – Rev. Mr. Henry set out for his home this morning after breakfast. June 25, 1818 – Rev. Mr. Henry came from Bohemia – went in afternoon to Newark"
27. Devitt, "Clergy List of 1819" *RACHS* 22 (1911): 253. Father Leonard Edelen, the Superior, wrote an account of his last illness and death.
28. Devitt, "Clergy List of 1819," *RACHS* 22 (1911) 246
29. Cann 8; Devitt, "Bohemia," *RACHS* 63:132
30. AAB 15-E-3, Michael Cousinne to Archbishop Maréchal, Bohemia, June 8, 1819. This is Cousinne's only letter to Maréchal in AAB. There are no letters from Cousinne to Archbishops Carroll or Neale in AAB.
31. "Extracts," *RACHS* 9:75
32. Cann 40
33. Devitt, "Bohemia," *Woodstock Letters* 63:35. Sometime after this date two brothers were stationed at Bohemia to fulfill this task. Brother Joseph Heard, S. J., resided at Bohemia for nearly twenty years.
34. GUA 54T3: *The Diary of Father John McElroy*, under date of August 4, 1819, Georgetown College, says: "Received information this evening of the death of Father Cousinne, at Bohemia, on the Feast of our Holy Father, 31st ult.: at 8 o'clock P.M. He had been up the same day and assisted at part of Rev. Mr. Hickey's Mass. He had been nearly two years in the noviceship, and was just expected at the College, to make his retreat with his fellow-novices, in order to take his Vows on the Feast of the Assumption. He was a most strict observer of the Rules, and of Religious discipline." The Burial Register of Bohemia has this entry: "1819. August 1. Was buried behind the Church, at the altar, and near two other Priests, close to the wall, Michael J. Cousinne, S. J. He died yesterday about 8 P.M. Buried by J. Hickey."; Devitt, "Bohemia" *Woodstock Letters* 63:133

BURIAL RECORDS AT BOHEMIA –
1816-7-16 Allen, Elizabeth, Wife of James, Buried by Rev. Francis Neale; 1816-8-30 Blake, James, Buried 3 weeks after his death in the family burying ground (Blake, Sayer, Heath). Residence near Chestertown, Kent Co., Md. A funeral sermon was preached.; 1817-10-11 Beard, Rebecca; 1824-4-30 Brady, Bernard; 1824-11-25 Brady, Isabella; 1825-11-21 Boland, Jermiah Michael, Age 33; 1826-8-13 Burns, Bernard, Age 14 mos.; 1826-9-2 Buttler, Michael, Age 27; 1826-9-28 Baxter, Mary, Age 18 mos.; 1827-1-15 Buttler, Edward; 1828-10-15 Buckley, Mary, Age 4; 1829-9-6 Atwell, Lucenda, Age 2; 1829-3-12 Brazel, Mary, Age 5 mos.; 1832-4 Black, Rebecca Barns, Age 65; 1836-5-25 Baggus, Mary Adaline, Age 3 mos.; 1836 Boils, Mary Jermina, Colored – Free; 1838-10-17 Bond, William G., Age 29; 1839-10-4 Brady, Thomas Johns, Son of Robert & Jane Brady; 1841-9-11 Brady, Martin, Plantation of Bohemia; 1844-1-2 Bears, George, Elkton, Md. (From Cork Ireland); 1844-2-26 Blake, Alfonsa, Age 58 widow of James Blake, near Chestertown, Kent Co., Md. Buried in family plot.; 1844-4-6 Blake, Jane, Age 65, near Chestertown, Kent Co., Md. Buried in family plot.; 1846-1-19 Blake, Susan, Age 2, daughter of Susan Blake who belonged to Ellen Blake. Buried at Queen Anne, Md.; 1850-4-1 Brady, Mary, Slave of advance age on this plantation.; 1851-2-20 Brady, Sara, Dau. of Martin and Jane; 1816-3-36 Craddock, William, Age 74; 1817-7-20 Corbaley, John, Son of Richard & Hannah.; 1818-8-11 Corbaley, Henrietta M.; 1818-11-1 Craddock, T. T., Age 9; 1819-9-2 Corbaley, Richard, 1819-7-13 Cousinne (S.J.) Rev. Michael J., Age 52 born in Belgium; 1821-6-4 Craddock, Daniel; 1821-11-21 Craddock, Richard; 1823-11-13 Craddock, Wm. Alfonso; 1825-1-23 Ciller, Charles, Age 30; 1826-3-19 Campbell, Thomas, Age 30; 1826-7-11 Cavanaugh, Anthony, Age 40; 1827-2-17 Clark, Michael, Age 22; 1828-10-19 Cleffaro, Timothy, Age 20; 1829-5-8 Craddock, Age 1 mo.; 1829-9-5 Coglan, John, Age 6 weeks; 1829-10-7 Coglan, Helen; 1833-1-24 Craddock, Thomas, Age 62 –

District; 1834- Craddock, Margaret, Wife of Benedict. Married John Thomas and after his death married Benedict Craddock. Converted by the Most Rev. Archbishop Carroll (nee Ryland); 1835-1-1 Callahan, Mary, Widow "Ireland" from the Bridge.; 1837-12-31 Craddock, J. Benedict, Son of Benedict and Susan.; 1838-9-19 Callahan, Ann, Age 87; 1839-10-14 Craddock, Arthur, Died at Warwick, Md.; 1841- Craddock, Margaret, Age 1 day; 1843-5-20+Carey (S.J.) Rev. John B., Age 71 born in France.; 1844-5-1 Craddock, Capt. Benedict, Age 71; 1846-11-20 Creeghtan, Sara, Nee Tuleman, Dorchester Co., Md. Buried there.; 1846-11-22 Conlin, Elizabeth, (Mrs.) Died at Poorhouse, Cecil County, Md.; 1849-7-16 Corby, Henrietta, Dau. of Richard of Kent Co., Md.; 1851-3-20 Craddock, Margaret, Age 66; 1852-9-21 Corbaley, John B., 1819-9-10 Drugger, 1824-7-31 Daguin, Daniel, Age 22; 1825-11-29 Dunn, Patrick, Age not known; 1827-3-9 Dazeman, John, Age 35; 1827-4-27 Donahan, Peter, Age 26; 1827-5-3 Doyle, James, Age 36; 1828-12-20 Dunn, Francis, Age 27; 1844-6-18 Dunmeck, Isaac, Buried in Dorchester Co., Md.; 1844-7-11 Donavan, Richard B., Age 27, son of James & Ellen.; 1844-7-20 Duraind, James, Age 67, son of Francis, died at Millington, Kent Co., Md.; 1844-7-26 Duraind, F. J., Age 19; 1847-11-4 Durney, John, Died in Montgomery Co., Md.; 1849-8-15 Daughterty, John, Native of Ireland; 1851-1-25 Durney, Ann Marie, Widow of John, 1832-1-8+Epinette, Rev. Peter S.J., Age 72, died & buried at Bohemia. Born in France. 1849-8-6 Ennis, Charles, Age 37 of Ireland; 1849-10-5 Ennis, Anna, Dau. of Charles & Elizabeth.; 1821-2-13 Foot, Abegail, Age 37, wife of Jack France.; 1826-4-28 Farrell, Matthew, 1826-5-5 Farrell, Edward, Age 27; 1826-10-1 Falls, Dennis, 1826-10-13 Fitzsimmons, Matthew, 1827-2-28 Farrell, John, Age 37; 1827-4-17 Fannie, Nickolas, Age 46; 1828-10-7 Feneman, Lawrence, Age 40; 1829-1-21 Farrell, Michael, Age 59; 1829-3-28 Farrell, Edward, Age 20; 1829-4-7 Ford Walter, Age 30; 1841-9-30 Flintham, Wife of John; 1843-9-18 Flintham, John M., Age 17; 1849-8-13 Ferris, John, Age 30 of Ireland.; 1829-9-29 Ganly, Bridget, Age 2; 1839-9-18 Green, Ellen, Daughter of widow Green near Back Creek, Cecil Co., Md.; 1841-7-28 Goodham, Harriet, Age 1 mo. Buried in Queen Anne Co., Md.; 1826-9-18 Hagerty, Catherine, 1827-1-17 Hagerty, Alfred, Age 40; 1828-1-4 Hagerty, Mary, Age 39; 1828-1-13 Hayes, James, Age 3; 1834-3-24 Hessey, Elizabeth, Age 48, widow; 1839-10-5 Hill, Mary, Died near Frenchtown, Cecil Co., Md. Native of Ireland; 1841-7-14 Heverin, Susan, Age 5; 1844-9-7 Heverin, David, Died in New Castle Co., Del.; 1846-5-31 Hede, James Al, Age 3 mos.; 1846-12-7 Heverin, David, died in New Castle Co.; 1849-1-7 Harris, Isaac, Servant of Thomas Craddock; 1826-7-26 Kelley, James, Age 29, native of Ireland; 1826-9-28 Kell, James, Age 29; 1828-9-28 Kerney, Margaret, Daughter of Hugh Kerney; 1836-6-18 Karkite, James August, Age 9 mos.; 1847-9-16 Kingan, Stephen, Orphan living with Ham Morton, Died at Strawberry Hill.; 1850-5-6 Kenarly, Ann, Dau. of John & Margaret; 1824-7-11 Larkin, Catherine; 1824-8-16 Lynch, Alexander, Age 85; 1825-4-10 Larkin, Catherine; 1826-4-8 Lynch, Edward; 1826-5-15 Larkin, Michael; 1826-8-20 Lafferty, Dorothy, Age 14; 1826-10-5 Lestrange, Michael, Age 28, Parrish of Gillain, Ire.; 1826-12-6 Leonard, Edward, Age 24; 1836-3-2 Linch, Peregenus, Age 59; 1847-3-5 Larkin, Leana, Died at Dr. M. S. Larkins.; Buried at Centerville, Md.; 1822-6-15 Miller, Edward, Age 55; 1824-8-15 Mulnigrie, Sara, Age 5; 1825-1-15 Matthews, Rebecca, Age 70; 1825-8-23 Mair, Michael, 1826-1-27 McKann, John, Age 39; 1826-9-11 Mulligan, Peter, 1826-10-7 McGuire, Patrick, Age 50; 1826-11-9 McLaughlin, John, Age 30; 1827-3-1 Mallaix, Bridget, Age 7; 1827-11-2 McCan, Andrew, Age 40; 1828-8-10 McGreff, John, Age 24; 1828-10-10 McGaw, John, Age 50; 1829-10-4 Manry, James, Age 35; 1831-8-7 McPhelan, Catherine, Age 7; 1831-11-11 Mullen, James, Age 50; 1835-4-7 Manly, John James, Age 38; 1844-7-26 McLane, John, of Ireland. Died at Cautwely Bridge, Del. (Cantwells); 1844-4-27 McCafferty, Bernard, Son of Francis and Catherine; 1845- McKing, Matthew, Died & buried in Dorchester Co., Md.; 1847-9-21 Meekins, Margaret, Died & buried in Dorchester Co., Md.; 1847-11-7 McCaffry, Thomas, Died at Bohemia, of Ireland.; 1849-10-16 Murray, Arthur, of County Donegal, Ireland; 1850-9-20 Malsberger, Joseph, Age 61, Massey, Kent Co., Md.; 1851-7-2 Morton, Frank, Age 1; 1816-10-17 Nugent, Mary, Died at William Craddocks; 1819-4-28 Nowland, Sylvester; 1824-2-3 Nowland, Mary Brady, Wife of Thomas Nowland; 1824-9-21 Nowland, Thomas, Age 73; 1824-10-28 Nowland, Elizabeth, "Relict" of Sylvester, age 50.; 1826-3-12 Nowland, Michael, Age 40; 1826-9-10 Nowland, James; 1831-8-21 Naughten, Mary, Age 3; 1850-4-28 Nowland, Wm. (Mrs.), Died near Smyrna, Del.; 1819-6-2 O'Donald, Daniel; 1821-9-12 O'Donald, John; 1824-9-31 Owres, Phillip, Age 30; 1825-10-7 O'Neal, John Bernard, Age 4; 1826-8-17 O'Neill, Thomas, Age 33; 1826-9-13 O'Relly, James, Age 68; 1827-5-23 O'Flin, Thomas, Age 13 mos. 1829-11-27 O'Neill,

Susan, 1831-8-20 O'Neal, Sarah Jane; 1831-8-22 O'Neal, Bernard; 1831-8-22 O'Neill, Margaret Rosalin, Age 5 mos.; 1841-10-20 O'Neil, Daughter of Charles O'Neil; 1847-12-20 O'Neil, Susan Adela, Daughter of Charles O'Neil, Age 4 mos.; 1819-11-3 Pennington, Joseph; 1829-4-27 Pennington, Ann Rebecca, Age 17 mos.; 1831-1-1 Price, Mary Rebecca R., Age 3 mos.; 1849-10-19 Price, John Veazy, Age 68; 1821-7-24 Quinn, Joseph; 1827-4-24 Queen, John, Age 50.; 1819-1-15 Reynolds, Cecilia Carmela, Wife of Jacob; 1819-6-3 Reynolds, Jacob, Husband of C. C. Reynolds; 1821-3-23 Reynolds, Janet, Widow of Jermiah (nee Boyce); 1823-4-18 Reynolds, Jermiah, Age 45; 1824-10-26 Riley, Dennis, Age 40; 1825-1-4 Reynolds, Armenta, Age 2; 1825-5-20 Reynolds, Amelia; 1827-5-18 Rosny, Barthanew, Age 35; 1829-9-5 Ralty, Hugh, Age 50; 1829-10-7 Ragen, Hugh, Age 40; 1834-10-14 Reynolds, Jannette T., Age 4 mos. 15 days infant of Elizabeth McCredy.; 1841-9-20 Reynolds, Jarud, Age 70; 1819-7-7 Scanlon, Arthur; 1821-10-3 Scanlan, Thomas; 1824- Selooquin, James, Age 28; 1825-1-5 Scanlan, James, Age 51; 1826-2-27 Scanlan, Rose, Age 9; 1826-6-27 Sweeney, Edward, Age 50; 1826-10-7 Strange, Michael L.; 1827-11-27 Scanlon, Rebecca, Age 20 mos.; 1828-1-10 Savin, Thomas, Age 13; 1828-6-30 Skellen, Sara Ann, Age 10 mos.; 1828-10-16 Spriggs, James, Age 28; 1830-1-29 Smith, Margaret, Age 30; 1833-2-20 Savin, Susan Fullum, Age 2 days; 1839-5-12 Savin, William Morris, Son of John and Betsy, died near Buck, New Castle Co., Del.; 1846-8-11 Smith, Caroline, Dau. of John and Elizabeth; 1847-7-18 Scanlan, Wm. Thomas, Age 18 mos.; 1849-8-12 Scanlan, Mary Amanda, Age 70; 1826-2-6 Terry, John, Age 26; 1828-12-9 Tweed, Mary, Age 27; 1829-11-4 Tom, David, Age 10 days; 1830-8-17 Tom, Margaret, Age 35, Dau. of James and Elizabeth O'Donald near Back Creek; 1838-8-4 Thomas, Alice, Wife of Alfred B. Thomas Died in Baltimore, Md. Buried at St. Peter's in Queen Anne Co., Md.; 1851-1-9 Tassell, Catherine Butler; 1850-9-3 Usher, John, Age 27 of Smyrna, Del.; 1826-10-6 Wrery, Ann, Age 2 weeks; 1827-4-2 Welsh, John, Age 66; 1827-12-9 Wood, Patrick, Age 35; 1827-11-31 Wright, Marie; 1828-2-23 Welch, Martin, Age 30; 1835-8-10 Wells, Jane, Free Colored Person; 1840-10-31 Walt, Ricco, Sr., Died in Queenstown, Md.; 1844-5-1 Wooters, Samuel; 1847-4-10 Wilson, Mary Ann Harkins, Wife of Dr. Thomas Wilson, Kent Co., Md.; 1847-9-8 Wells, Joseph, Servant died at the Plantation.; 1816-10-20 Betsy, A tree woman, wife of Moses, slave of William Craddock.; 1817-7-10 James, Black child, at Mrs. O'Donald's farm.; 1817-7-28 Nan, Slave of Sylvester Nowland; 1818- Amelia, Slave of Dr. James Scanlan; 1823-10-7 Frances, Wife of Moses; 1823-10-20 Joseph, Age 3 months; 1825-1-20 Molly, Age 8; 1825-3-17 Henry, Age 3 months; 1825-4-16 Charles, 19 years old; 1826-10-8 Dolly; 1827-11-21 Ann Rebecca, Age 20 mos.; 1828-1-27 Dick, Slave, Age 50; 1828-10-1 George, Slave, Age 18; 1829-2-11 Prudence, Age 28; 1829-3-20 Patrick, Slave; 1830-7-26 Mary, Slave, Age 69; 1830-12-20 George, Age 3 mo.; 1832-4-1 Bryne, From the Railroad "Old".; 1834-4-10 Elizabeth Bayard, 20 weeks old – colored.; 1835-3-15 Thomas John, Son of Thomas John, slave of Mr. Alfred Thomas and Ann Jane slave of Benedict Craddock. Baby and parents are colored people.; 1836-8-5 Molly Mitilda, Dau. of James & Molly Harris, colored.; 1841-7-28 Maria Louisa, Dau. of "Jones," 5 years old.; 1844-1-22 Amanda, Dau. of Steven, Free Colored.; 1844-10-29 Isaac, Slave of Mrs. Matthew Bean, died in Queen Anne Co., buried St. Peters Church, Queen Anne Co., Md.; 1844-11-8 Richard, Johnson, slave, died at the Plantation in Bohemia.; 1844-10-2 Nancy, Salve of the Plantation at Bohemia; 1846-3-21 Richard, Slave of Capt. John Griffan.; 1846-9-20 Rachel, Slave of Matthew Meekin who disowned her. Died in Dorchester County, Md. Buried there.; 1850-4-1 Mary Brady, Slave of Advanced age. Died on the Plantation at Bohemia.

CHRISTIAN BURIAL OF SLAVES AT BOHEMIA –

1823-10-7 Frances, Moses wife, 56 years old., 1823-10-20 Joseph, 32 months old., 1825-4-16 Charles, 19 years old., 1827-11-21 Anne Rebecca, 10 months old., 1828-1-27 Dick, 50 years old., 1828-10-1 Georges, about 18 years old., 1829-2-11 Prudence, 28 years old., 1830-7-26 Mary, 9 years old., 1830-12-20 Georges, 3 months old. GUA – Archives, Maryland Province, Society of Jesus – BOHEMIA-BURIAL REGISTER-(1798-1843)

35. Cann 9; Devitt, "Clergy List of 1819" *RACHS* 22 (1911): 253; GUA, Maryland Provincial Archives 54T3. Father John Hickey was born at Georgetown, D.C., on September 4, 1789. After studies at Mount Saint Mary's Seminary, Emmitsburg, he was ordained by Archbishop Carroll in Baltimore on September 24, 1814. He was a teacher at St. Mary's College, Baltimore from 1812 to 1818. After years of parish ministry, he taught at Mt. St. Mary's College, Emmitsburg, from 1826 to 1844.

36. Devitt, "Bohemia" 22 (1911) 258 – Father John Hickey died February 15, 1869, at age 80, at St.

37. Cann 9; Devitt, "Clergy List of 1819" *RACHS* 22 (1911): 250; Epinette at Newport, Maryland 1818 – *RACHS* 20:348-349, at Bohemia *RACHS* 21:247; 24:137;139, at Georgetown College 1819 – *RACHS* 22:240;250; Hughes, Documents 1:362 – Epinette, pastor of Bohemia, 110 acres home farm, revenue expected from Bohemia $2000 *per annum*. Hughes, Documents 1:875 – certificate of citizenship of Peter Epinette, declared to be a member of the Select Body of the Clergy. AAB 3-N-8 Peter Epinette to Archbishop Carroll, St. Thomas Manor, January 9, 1813. This is the only letter from Epinette to Carroll in AAB. There are no letters from Epinette to Archbishops Neale or Maréchal in AAB. Thomas W. Spalding, *John Carroll Recovered* 109: John Carroll to Rev. Robert Molyneux, S. J., Baltimore, November 24, 1806: "it seems that Mr. Epinette will have no theology students this year, only a lesson on Holy Scripture to the novices and preparation of candidates for the novitiate, an employment unheard of before." Molyneux was provincial of the restored Society of Jesus in Maryland. Spalding, 162: John Carroll to Rev. John Anthony Grassi, S. J. Baltimore, November 11, 1812: Carroll says that he has just received Grassi's letter concerning Mr. Peter Epinette, S. J.. His only reason for forbidding him to preach at the college is his imperfect command of English. Carroll knows French and Italian better than Epinette knows English, but he would never attempt to preach in either, in or out of the time of the sitting of Congress. If Epinette insists on leaving the college, Grassi may do as he pleases. Epinette is needed more at St. Thomas Manor. GUA – Archives, Maryland Province, Society of Jesus, BOHEMIA-INSPECTION OF (1825). Cann 169: In 1820, Father Kenny was sent over from Ireland as official Delegate of the Missions, among other things, to bring about a unimity between the trustees of the Corporation of Catholic Clergy and the Superior of the Missions, in regard to the administration of the farms. On April 28, 1820, Father Kenny wrote to Father Louis de Barth, the manager of the Jesuit Mission of Conewago (in Pennsylvania): "All the trustees are quite content with the arrangements I have made on the Temporalities (i.e., Physical aspects) and are desirous to have them carried into effect. They seem inclined even to part with the slaves and let the lands out, or to manage them without blacks. This, of course, is no order of mine; I leave this to themselves, but such a change cannot suddenly take place, or even without sure prospect of its being better." This conciliation between the trustees of the Catholic Clergy and the Jesuit Superior was brought about by making him (Father Kenny) President of the Corporation and his consultors the trustees. In the meantime, only a few servants were sold and the Jesuit plantation managers were allowed, with the consent of the Superior, to exchange their women blacks in order to give them an opportunity to marry.

At Bohemia, as reported in the note of Father Peter Kenny in the Bohemia Day Book 1790-1870, we find in 1821 there were 28 whites and 15 blacks.

In an additional list, Father Kenny listed for the same year 10 whites and 6 blacks. that year had 500 African men bounded to them in slavery, at an average value of about $200 each. Thomas Morrissey, S.J., *As One Sent: Peter Kenney, S.J., 1779-1841, His Mission in Ireland and North America* (Dublin, Ireland: Four Courts Press, 1855) 20.

38. Pryor, 104-105, the will of John Reynolds. Wilson, *Rose Hill*, 107: August 9, 1820 – "Mr. Epinette, the Catholic Priest, here to attend poor Manuel who is very low. He dined with us."
39. Pryor 118
40. Pryor 103
41. Pryor 88. His wife Martha then married Elisha Crouch, member of Bohemia Church, whose first wife was Millie Weldon, daughter of Abraham Weldon.
42. Archives of Propaganda Fide, Rome (hereafter APF) Congressi 7: 167R to 170V, 1821, "General Description of the Metropolitan Province of Baltimore in the United States of America"
43. Pryor – "Eleanor's Delight" 101
44. Pryor 88, 156
45. Pryor 110
46. Pryor 60-61: Inventory of the Goods of Peregrine Cole, 1826. The Cole farm remained in the possession of the Reynolds family until 1912 – James Lattomus, "Log Cabin Near Townsend, An Interesting Reminder of Other Days (Built by Peregrine Cole in 1798)," Wilmington, Delaware: *The Delmarva Star*, January 28, 1934
47. AAB 13-L-3, Miss Alphonsa Blake to Archbishop Maréchal, Chestertown, May 23, 1823, quoted in Murtha, *Maréchal* 120.

48. Ralph D. Gray 62, "Delaware And Its Canal, The Early History of the Chesapeake and Delaware Canal, 1769-1829," (M. A. Thesis, University of Delaware, Newark, Delaware, 1958) 62.
49. Kenneth Wyer Rowe, *Mathew Carey: A Study in American Economic Development* (Baltimore: John Hopkins Press, 1933) 107-108: Selections from the Correspondence of the Deceased Mathew Carey, Writer, Printer, Publisher," *RACHS* 13 (1902) 237-247; *Delaware Gazette*, February 22, 1822 – C & D Canal, Board of Directors, Mathew Carey, Chairman; Hagley, *The Winterthur Manuscripts*, Series A, Letters of Victor du Pont to Mathew Carey, 1819-1827; Gray 83 – Mathew Carey in Philadelphia is raising funds to complete the canal. On April 16, 1823, Carey gave a long address and distributed 2000 copies of the pamphlet promoting the canal; Gray 83 – In 1823, subscriptions from the three state legislatures and a great subscription in Philadelphia led by Mathew Carey were received. Mathew Carey, *Address to the Citizens of Philadelphia* (Philadelphia: Mathew Carey, 1823); Mathew Carey, *Autobiography of Mathew Carey* (New York: Mathew Carey, 1942) 118; Eugene F. J. Maier, "Mathew Carey, Publicist and Politician," *RACHS* 39 (1928) 82-86; Gray 93 – At the annual meeting in 1824, the stockholders adopted the following resolution: "Resolved unanimously, that the thanks for the stockholders be presented to Mathew Carey, Esquire, for the zeal and ability with which he promoted a new subscription to the work in the year 1823;" Gray 101 – Mathew Carey published an *Address To The Stockholders of the Chesapeake and Delaware Canal, On The Subject of the Route* (Philadelphia, 1824) to allay the fears and suspicions about the adoption of John Randel's plan to relocate the canal and to prove that the directors had taken the proper action in choice of the route. Historical Society of Pennsylvania, Gardiner Collection, Mathew Carey Papers. Rowe 20 – Carey's children were baptized at St. Joseph's and St. Augustine's Churches in Philadelphia, Francis Anna, daughter of Mathew Carey, married Isaac Lea, born in Wilmington, Delaware, December 3, 1792. He was admitted into the Carey business in 1821 and remained until his death in 1851. After Mathew Carey retired in 1824, the firm became "Carey and Lea." Joseph Wilcox, *RACHS* 15 (1904) 420-421. "Notes and Queries," Rowe 31 – Born in Dublin, Ireland, in 1760, Carey died in 1837 and was buried in St. Mary's Churchyard, Philadelphia, Rowe 22 – "The Carey Bible," the first American Catholic publication of the Douay – Rheims version of the Bible, was published by Carey in Philadelphia 1790. Arthur J. Ennis, O.S.A., "The New Diocese of Philadelphia" in Connelly 95: Mathew Carey was a well-known and rather bellicose but generally fair-minded publisher.
50. *Fifth General Report* 13, Gray 105
51. Wilmington, Delaware *American Watchman and Delaware Republican* May 17, 1823: "The men are summoned to meals and work by a bell, which must be punctually obeyed or a forfeiture incurred. The workmen live in companies of fifteen or twenty in shanties, frame buildings, along the canal, provided with a cook, or board in more private houses erected for the purpose." Wilmington *Delaware Gazette*, October 21, 1825 – "If not death from exposure, destitute sick laborers, incapacitated by fevers, become wards of the county, brought in by the cartload to the poorhouse."
52. Mathew Carey, *Address To The Wealthy of the Land* (Philadelphia: Mathew Carey, 1831) 9; *A Plea For The Poor* (Philadelphia, Mathew Carey, 1837), Carey shamed civil leaders by his exposure of the terrible living conditions of the poor workers and moved them to some reforms. Carey died in 1837, a militant crusader for justice and freedom to the end. Newspaper editorials told of drunken Irishmen and the misery of their families, of canal riots, murders, brawls, and the gamut of crime involving the Irish, representing an effort on the part of the editors to satisfy their readers' desire for unfavorable news about the Irish.
53. Gray 106
54. Gray 115; *Niles Weekly Register* 31 (October 7, 1826) 96
55. Philadelphia *Gazette and Daily Advertiser*, August 8, 1829
56. Gray 118; Alvin F. Harlow, *Old Towpaths* (New York: D. Appleton & Co., 1926) 225, From 1922 to 1927 the locks were removed and the canal enlarged to sea level. From 1935 to 1938 the canal was again enlarged. Throughout the years it has been enlarged many times.
57. In 1728 the English Jesuit Provincial asked that the custom be kept of not asking for financial support from the laity. The Jesuits and other clergy relied mainly on the farms they owned for their livelihood through the nineteenth century. Hughes, Documents 1:238, 241.

58. Spalding, *The Premier See* 100; Shea, *Defenders of Our Faith* (New York: Callahan and Clifford, 1894) 68; *RACHS* 28 (1917) 322; At the time of his death he was also administrator of the Diocese of Richmond which included the counties of Accomac and Northhampton on the Eastern Shore of Virginia.

59. Bosco David Cestello, "James Whitfield, Fourth Archbishop of Baltimore, The Early Years: 1770-1828," *Historical Records and Studies* 4 (1957) 32-78. Devitt, "Clergy List of 1819," *RACHS* 22 (1911): 266. Hughes, Documents 1:1104 – Father Jean Tessier, announced the death of Archbishop Maréchal on February 4, 1828, and Maréchal's recommendation of Whitfield as his successor; 1105 – James Whitfield's policy if appointed to succeed Maréchal, 1109 – Whitfield becomes archbishop-elect, and anti-Jesuit animus of the new archbishop. Matthew Leo Panczyk, "James Whitfield, Fourth Archbishop of Baltimore, the Episcopal Years, 1818-1834," *RACHS* 75 (1964) 222-251; 76 (1965) 21-53

60. Devitt, "Bohemia," *RACHS* 24: 227; *Woodstock Letters* 15 (1886) 22; GUA – Archives, Maryland Province, Society of Jesus – BOHEMIA-REPAIRS (1828), BOHEMIA-LIST OF BOOKS-1831; BOHEMIA-CORRESP. RE (1828). Cann 163: In time, the slaves became a burden to the Maryland-Pennsylvania Missions. In 1835 the record shows that hardly a fourth part of the large farms were cultivated for want of capital. The produce and therefore the profits were in great part consumed by the ever increasing number of slaves who, by reason of conscientious obligations to them, could not be sold, and could not be set at liberty, because of the great dangers to soul and body which they would incur if set free. Since the only morally justifiable grounds upon which the Jesuit fathers could pretend to possess slaves was that they were able to give them the true faith of Christianity, which they would not have been able to enjoy on the Dark Continent, necessarily then the Fathers could not sell them into a situation where they could not practice their Christian religion, or where its practice would be in jeopardy.

61. William F. Homes, "Canal versus Railroad," *Delaware History* 10 (1962): 153
62. Holmes 10:173
63. Holmes 10:177
64. Richard E. Hall, "The New Castle and Frenchtown's First Locomotive," *Transfer Table*(Wilmington, Delaware: National Railway Historical Society, 1997) 11; Betty Harrington, New Castle and Frenchtown Railroad" typewritten paper, October, 1949, Historical Society of Delaware, Box 90A, 3; George Johnston, *History of Cecil County, Maryland* (Elkton, Md., 1881; repr. Baltimore Regional Publ. Co., 1972) 426
65. *Niles Weekly Register*, March 3, 1832
66. Holmes 10:245
67. Historical Society of Delaware, Box 88, Folder 3, *New Castle and Frenchtown Railroad Manuscripts*, Payrolls and Way Bills, Account Book of the New Castle Turnpike Company. The workmen were paid 80 cents a day. It was difficult to keep laborers because other railroads and canals were being constructed in nearby states and the men would go wherever the wages were the highest.
68. The New Castle and Frenchtown Railroad was outmoded only a decade after its inception. By May of 1837, the New Castle company had constructed a second track parallel to the original one. However, in December of 1837, the railroad was completed from Philadelphia to Wilmington, and in the following year the independent lines merged to form a single corporation–the Philadelphia, Wilmington and Baltimore Railroad Company. The New Castle and Frenchtown Railroad attempted to compete with this powerful foe until 1843, when it was finally absorbed by its rival.
69. Carley, *St. Joseph's* 18: Father James Moynihan started the church in 1823.
70. *Woodstock Letters* 15 (1886) 22. Cann 170-171: In 1833, the Maryland Mission was made a Province, and Father William McSherry was made its first Provincial at the suggestion of Father Kenny, he made St. Thomas Manor, Charles County, Maryland, his official residence. Here he began the final sale of the slaves.
71. Devitt, "Bohemia," *RACHS* 24 (1905); 227 *Woodstock Letters* 33 (1904) 14-16
72. Joseph Zwinge, S. J., "The Jesuit Farms in Maryland," *The Woodstock Letters* 41 (1912) 278-279. Father Peter Kenny was sent over from Ireland as Visitor of the Mission amongst other things to bring about a unanimity or reconciliation between the Trustees of the Corporation and the Superior of the Mission in regard to the administration of the farms. Hughes, Documents

1:1150-1153: Peter Kenny, Irish Jesuit, superior of the reconstituted Irish Mission. In 1830, Father Kenny came back to America to finish the Cannonical Visitation broken off in 1821 by the death of the Father General of the order. He subsequently made out a report for all the residences, houses and farms. GUA – Archives, Maryland Province, Society of Jesus, BOHEMIA-FARM, BOHEMIA-FARM (1832).

73. Zwinge 279
74. Zwinge 280
75. Zwinge 281
76. Zwinge 282-283. Cann 165: CHRISTIAN BURIAL OF SLAVES AT BOHEMIA – August 16, 1835, Jane Wells, lawful consort of Joseph Wells, both free coloured persons. she was educated a Methodist, but by the grace of God, and the exertions of the deceased Rev. P. Epinette, she became a Catholic and was the mother of many children, and a faithful servant at this farm house. She died in her 70th year of age, after having been repeatedly provided with the Holy Sacraments. Rev. F. Varin.
77. Devitt, "Bohemia," *The Woodstock Letters* 63:35, "Bohemia Registers" *RACHS* 24:134; Cann 9
78. Devitt, "Clergy List of 1819," *RACHS* 22:266; Obituary Notice, Catholic Almanac, 1837; *The United States Catholic Almanac or Laity's Directory, For The Year 1835* (Baltimore, published by James Myres, at the Cathedral, 1835) 144, under *Obituary, 1834*: "October 19, Most Rev. James Whitfield, 4th Archbishop of Baltimore, aged 64."
79. Spalding, *The Premier See* 105; Peter Guilday, *A History of the Councils of Baltimore 1791-1884* (New York: Arno Press and The New York Times, 1969) 81-111.
80. Ray Allen Billington, *The Protestant Crusade, 1800-1860, A Study of the Origins of American Nativism* (New York: Rinehart and Company, Inc., 1952) 53
81. Columba Halsey, "The Life of Samuel Eccleston, Fifth Archbishop of Baltimore, 1801-1851," *RACHS* 76 (1905) 70; Hughes, Documents 1:118
82. Halsey 90-104; Judge Eccleston of Kent County is mentioned in Fred Usilton, *History of Kent County, Maryland 1630-1916* (Chestertown, Maryland: Perry Publications, 1980) 239
83. Devitt, "History of the Province" *Woodstock Letters* 63:55; Devitt, "Bohemia," *RACHS* 24:134; Cann 9; Francis X. Reuss, "Catholic Chronicles of Lancaster County, Pa.," *RACHS* 9 (1898) 211-212, Varin was the second priest to assist Father B. Keenan in Lancaster; Martin I. J. Griffin, *History of the Right Reverend Michael Egan, D.D.* (Philadelphia: printed privately, 1893) 20,: "Varin a Dutch clergyman from Gutenberg arrived here in May or June 1813." "Diary of Rev. Patrick Kenny," *RACHS* 7 (1896) 131 – July 18 – "A Dutch priest was introduced yesterday evening by Rev. Mr. Roloff – just arrived from Gottenbourg via New York – by name Varin," 133 – August 14 – "Rev. Mr. Varin Rev. Mr. Marshall – Rev. Mr. O'Brien to West Chester," 135 – October 16 – "Rev. Mr. Varin"
84. Johnston, *History of Cecil County, Maryland* 431
85. Martin I. J. Griffin, *American Catholic Historical Researches* 8 (July, 1897) 134; Devitt, "Bohemia" 139: an account is given of his last illness and death. In old age he was sent to Goshenhoppen by the Jesuit provincial. He died there of old age and infirmities May 21, 1840, aged 62 years and nine months. Father Varin is referred to in "letter from Rev. Fideluis DeGrivel, S.J. to Rev. Joseph Tristam, S.J., Worcester, England, Relating to The History of St. Inigoes, Maryland," *RACHS* 16 (1905) 48. William B. Schuyler, "Memoirs of the Rev. Augustin Bally, S.J.," *RACHS* 20 (1909) 213. The book *Life of Father Varin* refers to a contemporary, Rev. Joseph Varin, a Jesuit superior general in France.
86. John Jr. Ryan, "St. John's College, Frederick, A. Half Century Ago," *Woodstock Letters* 30 (1901) 212-213. Charles King was one of the lights of St. John's College, Frederick, Maryland, for over fifty years. He was a professor of rhetoric and prefect. In his early years he was sent to Loyola College, Baltimore, in its early years. He is described as a man of fine classical taste and a master of choice English. In the catalogue of 1835 he is listed as professor of poetry. He was a good preacher and a cultivated musician. After his mother's death his father entered the Society of Jesus four years before his son. Charles King died in March, 1870, at the age of 52. GUA, Correspondence 217-P-1-9, Series 57, Maryland Province Society of Jesus, two letters from Charles King, S.J., May 3 and 24, 1849
87. Devitt, "Bohemia," *RACHS* 24: 134-136; *Woodstock Letters* 63: 37 Carley, *Queenstown* 67 The first listing of George King in the Catholic Directory is in "A List of Catholic Clergymen in the

United States," *United States Catholic Almanac or Laity's Directory For The Year 1836* (Baltimore: James Myres at the Cathedral, 1836) 87; *The Metropolitan Catholic Almanac and Laity's Director For The Year 1839*, 70 – "Bohemia, Cecil County – Rev. George King," "Newtown Manor – Appendix," *Woodstock Letters* 15 (1886) 23-24; GUA, Bohemia Manor Varia 103 N1765, Series 21, Bohemia Material, Statement of Account from Father King up to January, 1855. The only letter from Father George King in AAB is dated July 14, 1832, and was written to Archbishop Whitfield. The content of the letter has to do with his arrival in Wheeling, West Virginia, and his work there. "Letter from Father George King S.J. to His Son, Charles King, S.J., Bohemia, Cecil County, 1838, *Woodstock Letters* 15 (1856) 230-231

"Dear Charles,

It gives me pleasure to find that you have at least so far overcome yourself as to write to me, and I hope you will continue to write, at least occasionally. I do not wish by any means to trespass upon your time, which I make no doubt is much better employed than in writing to me, but I might now and then fill up some of your moments of recreation. – I had heard before you wrote that Messrs. Donavan, Brogard, Frs. Smith and Grace had left the Society, or had been dismissed from it, which is enough to make us all tremble, and guard ourselves against anything that might be a most distant cause of such a most dreadful misfortune happening to us. Nothing is better calculated to preserve us from sad occurrences than humility and a hidden life in religion, desiring earnestly to be unknown in the midst of others; to do for God what men do to please the world. – The other pieces of news you gave are highly interesting. The three missionaries for Brazil should meditate frequently on the advice given by my good old Superior: to be careful lest whilst we preach to others we ourselves may become reprobates; this care, according to the Apostle, must be the chastising and mortifying ourselves for that end. I hope God will grant the necessary grace in their arduous undertaking. – I was equally pleased to hear of the arrival of the reinforcement of eight persons for the Missouri Mission; it will become a very important one in time. I hear that there is one likely to go to the Noviceship, a priest from Canada; though I hope and expect that next year there will be some from the College, where you say there is much edification among the boys.

I do not want you to give up German, as it is becoming very useful in this country, and is now taught in all the high schools, and many from that nation are coming to this country.

Senator Benton will succeed in doing all that he wishes for the Society in the West for the benefit of the Red Men. – I am pleased to hear that Fr. McSherry has recovered, and I hope his health will continue to improve, but sorry that Br. Heard does not improve. Tell him we have been looking for him all the fall. – Br. Flaut and Mr. Mackin return respects to Mr. Maguire, and desire to be remembered to him and by his prayers.

There is scarcely any news here; the only thing of importance is that the Episcopalians have quarreled with their parson, and are publishing pamphlets against each other, which I hope will open the eyes of his flock. However, four of the most respectable ladies of his congregation are reading Catholic books; one of whom has declared that she will become a Catholic; the others will come in time.

88. Carley, *Queenstown* 67-68;
89. Cann 9. Sometime in the year 1835, probably in June, Thomas D. Monnelly was transferred to the charge of St. Peter's Church, Queenstown. Whether this was the church or rectory roof; or a barn is not known for certain. One account relates that the roof of his house at "Clover Hill" fell in on him. Mrs. Richard Bennett Willson, of Trumpington in Kent County, refers to the "tragic end of Fr. Monnelly." He was close to eighty years old and was over fifty years a priest. He had spent eighteen years earlier as pastor of St. Peter's, Queenstown. His former parishioners referred to him in 1834 as "The most accommodating and laborious of pastors." He is probably buried in St. Peter's churchyard, Queenstown.

WILLSON FAMILY – FIFTH GENERATION:
On November 17, 1835, Father Thomas D. Monnelly of Queenstown officiated at the wedding between Dr. Thomas Smyth Willson and Ellen Elizabeth Browne. Dr. Thomas Smyth Willson, child of Dr. Thomas Bennett Willson II and Anna Maria Smythe, was born on March 18, 1807 and died March 28, 1878. He married Ellen Elizabeth Browne on November 17, 1835 (by Rev. Thomas D. Monnelly). She was born October 15, 1815 and died July 31, 1891. Their children were Anna M. S. Willson, born October 8, 1842 and died August 18, 1914; Ellen E. Willson, born

December 28, 1844, and died December 7, 1922. Mary Elizabeth Willson, child of Dr. Thomas Bennett Willson II and Anna Maria Smythe, was born April 5, 1813, and died May 22, 1894. She married Bernard Browne on August 13, 1835. He was born in Queen Anne County, inherited Trumpington. The son of Mary Elizabeth Willson and Bernard Browne was Charles Clarence Browne, born June 11, 1836 and died January 5, 1877. Martha Theresa Willson, child of Dr. Thomas Bennett Willson II and Mary Theresa Hall was born on August 10, 1780, and died October 27, 1863. She married Charles Cochrane Browne in 1802. He was born in 1777 and died 1825. Their daughter was Mary E. Browne, born November 2, 1805, and died April 22, 1867. George Howard Willson, child of Dr. Thomas Bennett Willson II and Anna Maria Smythe, was born May 25, 1810 and died April 2, 1873. He married Henrietta Eleanor Brooke on June 13, 1837 (Rev. John B. Cary). She was daughter of James Brooke and Mary Brook. She was born on June 5, 1820, and died April 17, 1877. Their children were Elizabeth Hill Willson, born September 29, 1839, died November 25, 1920; Mary Georgiana Willson, died May 11, 1906; William Eugene Willson, born February 25, 1849, died May 10, 1928.

90. Cann 9 At age 71, Father Carey died on May 20, 1843, at Bohemia and was buried there.
91. Carley, *Queenstown* 67. Father King was alone at Bohemia until 1844. In 1840, *at Appoquinimink Forest* he baptized Sarah C. Reynolds, born December 8, 1839, daughter of James Reynolds and Sarah Cole, his wife (Pryor 110). In 1841 he baptized David Heverin, son of David Heverin and Jane Gribbins. The child born 1841 died in 1844. His father was a devout Catholic (Pryor 75). Martha (Reynolds) Pryor, wife of William Pryor, died in 1844. (Pryor 89). In 1841 Elisha Crouch, a Catholic, was elected on the Whig ticket as Assessor for Appoquinimink Hundred (Pryor 156). David Heverin, *of Appoquinimink Forest* died on December 7, 1845, aged 65, and was buried in Bohemia churchyard. "Uncle Dave" Haverin was opposed to slavery. His farm hands were free Blacks and he paid them wages. David, third son of Charles Heverin, bought from his brothers and sisters all the Heverin land except portions that went to Martha Sweetman and John Heverin, New Castle County, Delaware, Deeds Book I-2, p.360,. P-4, p.156 and 491, P-4 p.158. *The Burial Register of Bohemia*: Mary Adaline Baggus, May 25, 1836, age 3 months. Mary Jermina Bolls, 1836, free Black. William G. Bond, October 17, 1838, age 29. Thomas Johns Brady, October 4, 1839, son of Robert and Jane Brady. Martin Brady, September 11, 1841, plantation of Bohemia. George Bears, January 2, 1844, from Cork, Ireland, Elkton, Maryland. Alfonsa Blake, February 26, 1844, age 58, widow of James Blake near Chesterown, Kent County. Buried in family plot. Jane Blake, April 6, 1844, age 65, near Chesterown, Kent County, buried in family plot. Susan Blake, January 19, 1846, age 2, daughter of Susan Blake, who belonged to Ellen Blake, buried at Queen Anne, Maryland. Mary Brady, April 1, 1850, slave of an advanced age on Bohemia plantation. Sara Brady, February 20, 1851, daughter of Martin and Jane Brady. Jane Wells, August 10, 1835, free colored person. Walt Ricio, Sr., October 31, 1840, died in Queenstown. Samuel Wooters, May 1, 1844. Mary Ann Hoskins Willson, wife of Dr. Thomas Hoskins Willson, Kent County, Maryland, April 10, 1847. Joseph Wells, September 8, 1847, servant, died at Bohemia plantation. Thomas John, March 15, 1835, son of Thomas John, slave of Mr. Alfred Thomas and Ann Jane, slave of Benedict Craddock Molly Matilda, August 5, 1836, daughter of James and Molly Harris. Maria Louisa, July 28, 1841, daughter of "Jones," five years old. Amanda, January 22, 1844, daughter of Steven, free Black. Isaac, October 29, 1844, slave of Mr. Matthew Bean, died in Queen Anne Co. buried at St. Peter's Church. Richard Johnson, November 8, 1844, slave, died at Bohemia plantation. Nancy, October 2, 1844, slave at Bohemia plantation. Richard, March 21, 1846, slave of Captain John Griffin. Rachall, September 20, 1846, slave of Matthew Meekin, died in Dorchester County and buried there. Mary Brady, April 1, 1850, slave of advanced age. Died at Bohemia.
92. Immaculate Conception Parish, Elkton, Maryland, *Celebrating Our Faith Past, Present, Future 1849-1999*. (Devon, Pennsylvania: Cooke Publishers Company, 1999) 7 Annapolis, Maryland, Maryland State Archives, Land Records, Cecil County. AAB – no documentation on transfer of land from Mrs. Lyons purchased land – Elkton Margaret Butler to Archbishop Eccleston GUA Maryland Province, Society of Jesus, Box 72, Folder 3, Correspondence 218 W 10-19) George King on progress at Elkton church, exodus from Smyrna, March 12, 1850. GUA Maryland Province, Society of Jesus Box 69, Folder 12, Correspondence 216 H 1-11 Series 57 from Clarke to Brocard on neglect at Bohemia, delay in building of church at Elkton September 5, 1848 George King to Brocard on construction of Elkton church September 10, 1848 GUA Maryland

Province, Society of Jesus, Box 70, Folder 14, Correspondence Series 57 217-K-1- 4 – April 2 and April 27, 1849 Archbishop Eccleston's refusal to allow S.J. control of Elkton church. Full index terms: King, S.J., George Correspondence of (1849). Two letters from George King on the beginning of construction of Elkton church, September 12 and September 21, 1849. GUA Maryland Province, Society of Jesus, Box 70, Folder 18, Correspondence 217-P1-9 – one letter from George King to Barbelin on misc. May 7, 1849 Lien Elkton church March 26, 1850; GUA Maryland Province, Society of Jesus, Box 70, Folder 18, Correspondence 217-P-1-9 – two letters from George King on disposition of the Elkton church.

93. Cecil County Land Record, Courthouse, Elkton, Maryland RCH No. 1, July 24, 1844: Archbishop Eccleston purchased 1? acres on east side of road leading to Fair Hill. GUA Maryland Province, Society of Jesus, Box 71, Folder 11, Correspondence (218-P1-10) George King on consecration of Elkton Church August 5, 1850.

94. GUA Maryland Province, Society of Jesus, Box 70, Folder 18– George King to Ignatius Brocard, S. J., Bohemia, April 2, 1849   GUA Maryland Province, Society of Jesus, Box 72, Folder 3, Correspondence 218 W10-19, two letters from Archbishop Eccleston on debts on Elkton church March 16, 1850, March 18, 1850

95. GUA Maryland Province, Society of Jesus, Box 70, Folder 18– George King to Ignatius Brocard, S. J., Bohemia, April 27, 1849 Miller, 15 St. Elizabeth's Church, Denton, remained a mission of St. Joseph's after construction, but existing St. Elizabeth's records do not give any specifics as to early use of St. Elizabeth's. Receipted bills for carpentry, an altar, benches, etc., indicate that Father Lucas, who became pastor of St. Joseph's in 1840, went about completing the furnishing of St. Elizabeth's nine or more years after the date the church presumably opened.

96. GUA Maryland Province, Society of Jesus, Box 70, Folder 18– George King to Ignatius Brocard, S. J., Baltimore, September 12, 1849 Devitt *Woodstock Letters* 63:36 Cann 9 – Lucas is considered the pastor of St. Joseph's for seven years 1840-1846, though he served under Father King from Bohemia 1844-1846. The fathers living at Bohemia visited Elkton, Queenstown, Chestertown, Denton and some stations in Delaware GUA 103.5 – W7-W16, Series 44, Maryland Province Booklet contains parish records for St. Joseph's, Talbot.

97. Alice E. Miller, *Cecil County, Maryland: A Study In Local History* (Port Deposit Heritage, 1949) 72; Elkton, *Cecil Democrat*, November 22, 1947. Devitt, "Bohemia" RACHS 24 (June, 1913) 97-139

98. GUA, Maryland Province, Society of Jesus, Box 70, Folder 14– George King, S. J. to Francis Dzierosinski, S. J., Bohemia, September 21, 1849.

99. GUA Correspondence 218 W 10-19, Series 57, Maryland Province, Society of Jesus: two letters from Eccleston to King regarding debts on the Elkton church, March 16, and 18, 1850; GUA Correspondence 219-6-1-15, Series 57, Maryland Province, Society of Jesus, George King on brief stay of mission at Smyrna January 25, 1851; *on Elkton debt payment*, January 27, 1851; on discord at St. Joseph's, Talbot, May 2, 1851; on miscellaneous, June 6, 1851.   Nicholas (Steinbacher) place of birth, ate of birth, when became Jesuit, where assigned *Woodstock Letters* 15:30 In May of 1847 Father Tuffer returned to St. Joseph's and its missions. Father King retained charge of Bohemia with Queen Anne, Kent and Dorchester missions. GUA, Maryland Province, Society of Jesus 219 G1-15, Series 37: BOHEMIA-NEGLECT (1848); George King on discord at St. Joseph's, Talbot, May 2, 1851; George King on miscellaneous, June 6, 1851; GUA Maryland Province, Society of Jesus, Correspondence 218 W10-19, Series 57: two letters from Archbishop Eccleston on debts of the Elkton church, March 16 and 18, 1850; George King on debt payment at Elkton April 27, 1851.

100. Devitt, "Bohemia," *Woodstock Letters* 63:37. Baltimore *The Catholic Mirror*
June 28, 1856: The death of Reverend George King, S.J. on the 20th instant at Loyola College in this city whither he had come to avail himself of the best medical attendants, the Reverend George King, S.J. in the 61st year of his age R.I.P.

The Reverend Father whose death we notice above has been for several years Treasurer of Georgetown College, D.C. until the increasing wants of the missions entrusted to the care of the society of which he was a member determined his superiors to send him to the Eastern Shore of Maryland and the various missions of that portion of the state as well as in the neighboring towns and towns of Delaware, the performed for nearly twenty years all the duties of an active and zealous missionary to the spiritual profit of the scattered Catholics. The labors he had to undergo and the contradictions he frequently encountered sufficient to frighten one of more healthy and vigorous constitution were only incentives to animate his zeal with a greater fervor and generosity. From that first scene of his apostolic labors he was removed at the close of the last year in order to take charge of the house and missions attached to Newtown in St. Mary's County. But God was satisfied with his labors. The change of place though more pleasing to nature could not removed the seeds of disease planted in his constitution by his former exposure and he gradually sank under its effects. He died fortified with all the rites of religion and helped in the awful moment on which eternity depends by the presence and prayers of his religious brethren whom he had edified by a life of simplicity and labor.

Baltimore *The Catholic Mirror*, August 2, 1856: The following article slightly remodeled in parts as to facts and dates we copy from *The Catholic Herald* of July 19 Alderman Leonard Town, Deacon. *The late Reverend George King whose recent death in Baltimore June 20, 1856 has been noticed was born at Laurel, Delaware* during a temporary sojourn of his parents, his brother being of the Waples family of that state. His father, Charles King, Esq., a native of St. Mary's, but raised from an early age in Charles County, Maryland, shortly after his marriage settled in Georgetown, District of Columbia where he prosecuted an extensive mercantile business until his death in November, 1847 leaving behind him the priceless memory of a long life well spent, characterized by a daring uprightness and unsullied business integrity and adorned by the Christian graces of piety and benevolence. His truly excellent wife, a convert to his faith died several years previously having vied with her husband in the possession of these beautiful virtues which elevate and ennoble human nature. His active almoner among the suffering and needy, his ready and sympathizing assistance in the performance of all pious and good works. Thus blessed with pious parents in the enjoyment of ample means and the subject of this sketch entered at an early age the Catholic College of Georgetown so long celebrated for the perfection of its classical arrangements and for the high character and unassuming piety of its learned professors of the Society of Jesus. This institution, the alma mater of some of the most eminent and distinguished Americans, is beautifully situated on a height commanding a view grand and imposing. Its effect on the mind of the young student is calculated to inspire bright inspiration but in the heart of the subject of this sketch these aspirations were not after earthly honors. What though three cities lay beneath the eyes glance and the magnificent structure of our country's capital crowned the eastern view, yet there was in this silvered stream of the Potomac and its richly wooded banks something of milder calmer being and when moonlight swept on its waters or the stars were reflected from its bosom, the effect left the gazers soul heavenwards, thus it was with him that the providence of God had destined him to enter the world's busy scene so little suited to his retiring habits, yet the strict probity and truthfulness with which he fulfilled the trust of business gained the respect of all who knew him.

He married in November 1816 Miss Susanna M the daughter of the late John Gerard Ford of Georgetown originally of St. Mary's County, Maryland; who reared under the pious example of her parents brought to his domestic hearth the peculiar charm.

101. *Catholic Almanac 1857*
102. Devitt, "Clergy List of 1819," *RACHS* 22:257; Carley, *Queenstown* 69
103. Devitt, "Bohemia," *RACHS* 24:135; Carley, *Queenstown* 72; Cann 241
104. Devitt, "Bohemia," *RACHS* 24:135, 20:213. GUA 103.5, W7-W16, Series 44– Booklet (1840-1846) contains parish records for St. Joseph's, Talbot. "St. Joseph's, Talbot." *Woodstock Letters* 20 (1891) 33; *Catalogus Provinciae Marylandiae Societatis Jesu 1858* (Baltimore, Lucas Brothers Printers, 1858) 71. George Villiger entered the Jesuit Novitiate in Brieg, Canton of Wallis, Switzerland on October 4, 1838. He arrived at Georgetown College on July 19, 1844. After a year at Bohemia in 1845, he was transferred to Frederick, Maryland. In 1847 he was assigned to Goshenhoppen, Pennsylvania. For two years (1848-1849) he served at Conewago, Pennsylvania. In 1850 he served in Baltimore, and in 1851 he was assigned to Philadelphia. In 1853-1854 he served in Alexandria, Virginia, and from 1855-1856 he was again at Conewago, Pennsylvania. He returned to Bohemia in 1856.
105. Devitt, "Bohemia," *RACHS* 24:134
106. Devitt, "Bohemia," *RACHS* 24:135, 20:213; GUA 103.5, W7-W16, Series 44, Maryland Province, Society of Jesus: St. Joseph's, Talbot Subscription List (1848) for the enlargement and repairs of St. Joseph's Church, Talbot; GUA Maryland Province, Society of Jesus, Box 70, Correspondence 217, P1-9, two letters from Tuffer on building a residence at St. Joseph's; painting at Bohemia,

March 12 and September 3, 1850 GUA, Correspondence 219 G-H-13, Series 57, Maryland Province, Society of Jesus (Full Index Term: King, S.J., Correspondence of 1851) from Brother Thomas Hickey, March 4, 1851, complaining to Tuffer; February 26, 1851 from Tuffer on replacement of Power and Hickey; March 10, 1851, Power responding to complaints; March 12, 1851, Power complaining of Tuffer; October 18, 1851 Tuffer on efforts to pay Bohemia's debts; April 1, 1851, petition of some of the congregation of St. Joseph's, Talbot, asking for Tuffer's removal and Power's return.

107. Spalding, *Premier See* 153 Cann 10; *Woodstock Letters* 15 (1856) 30 Father Steinbacher died at St. Mary's, Boston, on February 14, 1861. "Memoir of the Rev. August in Bally, S. J.," *Woodstock Letters* 15:213. In addition to Father Steinbacher, other co-workers over the years with Father Bally were Fathers Villiger, Varin, and Tuffer.

108. Devitt, "Bohemia," *RACHS* 24:135; *Woodstock Letters* 63 (1934) 36, 15 (1856) 228; Cann 42 *Woodstock Letters* 32 (1903) 126-130: Father William Francis Clarke, S. J. was born in the city of Washington, D.C. on March 19, 1816. He attended Gonzaga College and Georgetown College, graduating in 1833. He joined the Jesuits on August 14, 1833. He was ordained by Archbishop Eccleston in July 4, 1842. In 1843 he taught at Georgetown College, and then at Frederick, Maryland. To recover his health he was assigned to Bohemia in 1846. After Bohemia he served at St. Joseph's Church in Baltimore. In the ninth year of his pastorate in Baltimore, he became president of Loyola College. In August of 1888 he returned to Gonzaga College. On October 17, 1890 he died in the seventy-fourth year of his age, and fifty-seventh year of his religious life. GUA – Archives, Maryland Province, Society of Jesus, BOHEMIA-DIFFICULTIES (1848), BOHEMIA-EXPANSION (1848)
BURIALS BY FATHER CLARKE AT BOHEMIA:
November 8, 1844 – Richard Johnson, belonging to the Society. Died yesterday in the 65th year of his age, and was buried in the St. Francis Xavier burial ground; September 8, 1847 – Joseph Wells, (a servant formerly belonging to this place). Aged about 75 years, was this day buried at Bohemia. W. F. Clarke.; April 1, 1850 – Mary Brady, slave of advanced age, died on the plantation. Buried at Bohemia.

109. Cann 241-242; Devitt, "Bohemia" 24:135

110. Devitt, "Bohemia," *RACHS* 24:135, *Woodstock Letters* 15 (1856) 228. GUA – Archives, Maryland Province, Society of Jesus, BOHEMIA-DEBT (1851)

111. Spalding, *The Premier See* 118-120

112. Maldwyn Allen Jones, *American Immigration* (Chicago: University of Chicago Press, 1960) 94

113. Billington 388-390

114. Halsey, "Eccleston," *RACHS* 76:85-86

CHAPTER FOUR

The American Civil War and Reconstruction
1853-1868

THE EPISCOPATE OF FRANCIS P. KENRICK

Francis Patrick Kenrick, Third Bishop of Philadelphia, was chosen as the Sixth Archbishop of Baltimore on August 3, 1851. He received notice of his appointment to Baltimore on October 9, 1851, and received the pallium on November 9, 1851.[1] The new archbishop brought to Maryland a range of talents and depth of experience. He was at once appointed apostolic delegate and convener of the First Plenary Council of Baltimore, which was held in 1852.[2] As early as 1850 Catholics had become the largest single body of churchgoers in the nation. At that time American Catholics numbered over one and a half million members with fifteen hundred priests. Evangelical antipathy to Catholics was alive and well. Largely a church of immigrants the church projected an image of foreignism and was again the object of insults and mob violence. This reappearance of anti-popery was the most violent outbreak of nativism in American history.[3] The First Plenary Council of Baltimore did not recommend any direct response to this hostility, but simply consolidated previous church legislation and confirmed the American Church in its mission.[4]

Portrait of Archbishop
Francis Patrick Kenrick

American Jesuit, James Power

In 1851, less than a month after Archbishop Eccleston's death on April 22, 1851, Jesuit Father James Power was appointed superior at Bohemia, with its missions at Elkton, Chestertown, and parts of Delaware. Father Power had entered the Jesuits on February 15, 1846, at age 48. In 1847 he had been assigned to Alexandria, Virginia, and in 1848 he had become superior of the Jesuit establishment of St. Thomas Manor on the western shore of Maryland. He came to Cecil County to serve at Bohemia and performed his first baptism there on May 11, 1851. In 1854 he was transferred to White Marsh. From 1855 to 1858 he served at St. Joseph's in Talbot County where he died at age 65.[5]

Belgian Jesuit, Matthew F. Sanders

The successor to Father Power at Bohemia in March, 1852, was Father Matthew Sanders, born in Holland on November 30, 1807. He was already ordained a priest when he joined the Jesuits in 1832.[6] He spent four and a half years at Bohemia during a time when the onslaught of Know-Nothingism was most violent. The controversy over Bible reading in public schools was raging. Anti-Catholicism was everywhere in the air. In 1852 a block of marble arrived in Washington, D.C., as a gift from the pope to become part of the Washington monument then being constructed. In 1854 a mob forced its way into the shed where the slab was stored, and threw the block into the Potomac.[7] Another anti-Catholic interlude began with the arrival at New York on June 30, 1853, of a papal diplomat, Archbishop Gaetano Bedini. His cover story was that he was enroute to take an appointment as papal nuncio at the court of Dom Pedro II, Emperor of Brazil, but his real assignment was to visit the United States, and report to Rome on the state of affairs in the country. He was also to investigate the possibility of reciprocal diplomatic relations between the United States and the Holy See. There was an American minister in Rome but no nuncio had been accredited to Washington. It turned out to be a disastrous visit. Bedini visited east coast cities Baltimore and Philadelphia first, and headed for the Midwest, where trouble started. Protesting mobs converged on the Cincinnati and Wheeling cathedrals. A second visit of Bedini to Baltimore was cancelled when on January 16, 1854, mobs burned an effigy of Bedini a few blocks away from the cathedral. The nuncio finally had to be secretly taken aboard a ship in New York harbor and smuggled out of the country. He never reached Brazil. There was no more talk of a nunciature in Washington for many years thereafter.[8]

The passage of the Kansas-Nebraska Act in 1854 plunged the nation into a controversy that ended in Civil War. The disintegration of the Know-Nothing Party occurred over the issue of slavery. A wholesale exodus began of former Know-Nothings into the Republican Party, but the first Republican Party platform didn't even mention the subject of anti-Catholicism.[9] Under Lincoln's leadership, the emphasis continued to be anti-slavery, not anti-popery. Father Sanders spent four and a half of these critical years (1852-1856) at Bohemia. His sacramental records were well kept.[10]

In April of 1853, Archbishop Kenrick conducted a Confirmation tour on the Eastern Shore. On April 22 he confirmed at Cambridge and on April 28 at St. Peter's Church, Queenstown. He then went on to Bohemia. After a visit with Father Sanders, he went on to Elkton where he boarded the train to Baltimore.[11]

As pastor at Bohemia, Father Sanders was responsible for the spiritual care of

First Church of St. Dennis, Galena, 1855   Dennis McCauley

Catholics in all of Cecil and Kent counties, Maryland, in addition to stations at Middletown, Odessa, and Dover in Delaware. There were only a handful of Catholic families in Kent County, Maryland in 1854. There were perhaps more, but they were not willing publicly to express their allegiance to the faith in such an anti-Catholic atmosphere. One person courageous enough to announce his Catholicism openly was Dennis J. McCauley. He had come from Ireland as a young man and had moved his family from Philadelphia in 1854 to a farm he bought at Lambson's Station in Kent County, two miles from the town of Galena, which was then known as Georgetown Crossroads.[12] He was attracted to the Galena area after making trips to buy hay for his horses. He soon became a successful Kent County farmer.

A short time after he had settled at Lambson's Station (the new railroad tracks crossed the fields near his farm), Dennis McCauley obtained permission from Archbishop Kenrick to build a brick church on his farm. Deeding an acre of his best land for this purpose to the archbishop on September 17, 1853, he personally contributed a large part of the three thousand dollars total cost of constructing the 50 by 30 feet church, collected some from others, and made himself responsible for seeing that the church was paid for. The blessing and laying of the cornerstone for the new church (named for his baptismal patron saint, the first Bishop of Paris, France, a martyr) took place on August 29, 1855. The Reverend Thomas Foley, Baltimore's first chancellor, appointed soon after Kenrick's arrival, performed the ceremony, assisted by Father Sanders of Bohemia and by Father Bernard J. McManus, pastor of St. John's Church in Baltimore. At the appointed hour "a large and respectable concourse of persons" of different denominations gathered to witness the ceremony. After the blessing, Father Foley ascended a temporary platform and explained to those present the nature and meaning of the ceremonies they had witnessed. He pointed out the blessings that would come from the house of God which would be constructed, where sacraments would be administered and the gospel would be preached. His discourse was received with marked attention.[13] On February 3, 1856, Father Foley returned to dedicate the completed church. Assisting him was the Reverend Bernard J. McManus, pastor of St. John's Church in Baltimore, who celebrated the first Mass in it.[14]

The church was dedicated to the service of Almighty God under the invocation of the Blessed Virgin Mary, Conceived Without Stain of Original Sin and of St.

Dennis, Patron of France.[15]

The witness reporting to the Baltimore *Catholic Mirror* related that, notwithstanding the intense cold, the new brick structure (50 feet long and 30 feet wide) was filled to utmost capacity with persons of different denominations. After the blessing, Father Foley eloquently preached on the high sense of reverence with which all should regard this new house of prayer. After Mass, Father Foley gave an additional discourse on the divine authority and mission of the church. A collection was taken up towards the expenses of the church which amounted to $150.[16]

Five months later, in July 1856, Archbishop Kenrick visited Bohemia again. Having confirmed twenty persons at Elkton on July 5, he confirmed seventeen at Bohemia on Sunday morning, July 6.[17] He was then met by Dennis McCauley and taken by carriage that afternoon to Dennis' home at Lambson Station. Though there were none to be confirmed on this occasion, Archbishop Kenrick preached a sermon in the new church that Sunday afternoon at five o'clock on the Primacy of St. Peter.[18]

Reverend Bernard McManus became the first pastor of St. Dennis, the first Catholic parish in Kent County, Maryland.[19] He could take the train to Havre de Grace and crossing the Susquehanna, ride the train to Lambson's Station, say Mass, meet with parishioners, and catch the train back to Baltimore. After almost three years of ministry to St. Dennis, Father McManus sent his newly ordained assistant, Father Dwight E. Lyman on the third Sunday of each month to St. Dennis, from 1857 to 1859. For two years Lyman served as second pastor of St. Dennis Church at Lambson's Station.[20]

In November 1856, Father Sanders was transferred from Bohemia to White Marsh.[21]

Swiss Jesuit, George Villiger

Father George Villiger, at age 48, came from the Jesuit Mission in Conewago, in south central Pennsylvania, to serve as pastor of Bohemia from October 1856 to 1878.[22] He had already served as a Jesuit missionary for eighteen years, serving earlier as assistant to Father George King in 1844 and 1845. He preferred to remain alone at Bohemia, choosing to do all the work himself without assistance. His many years at Bohemia were marked by relentless toil and a burning zeal for souls. He was "sturdy in build and rugged in constitution."[23]

In an effort to defend the faith and to spread it, Father Villiger wrote two pamphlets during his time at Bohemia. These pamphlets dealing with points of controversy were entitled: "Letters to a Protestant Friend" and "The Catholic Church and the Roman Catholic Church."[24]

During Father Villiger's pastorate, the church bell tower and vestibule were added to St. Francis Xavier Church, with a marble slab over the entrance which reads:

INDEED THE LORD IS IN THIS PLACE AND I KNEW IT NOT. "THIS IS NO OTHER BUT THE HOUSE OF GOD AND THE GATE OF HEAVEN."
(from Genesis 28:16, 17)[25]

Though written histories have made no note of it, Father Villiger may have benefited from the development of the railroad in his mission territory. The main track of the Pennsylvania and Delaware railroad ran through the Appoquinimink Forest in 1856. Two stations were located on this line: the Sassafras Station, later called "Greenspring," and the Forest Station usually referred to as "Blackbird Station." The Smyrna Railroad ran through the extreme southwestern corner of the Appoquinimink Forest.[26]

Father Villiger became pastor of Bohemia just before the onset of the American Civil War and served there throughout the duration of the war. Just before the Civil War, Roger Brooke Taney, a Catholic descended from several old Maryland Catholic families, was Chief Justice of the United States. On behalf of the majority of the Supreme Court, he wrote the Dred Scott Decision which, though now repealed, declared that negro slaves, as opposed to free blacks, were property and not entitled to the rights enjoyed by U.S. citizens.[27]

Although the decision was on the wrong side of history, the view of slaves as property was widely held at the time. Few Catholics argued for abolition. Economic conditions, particularly the need of work for Irish immigrants, was a factor. No Catholic bishop spoke out for abolition in the pre-war years.[28]

Archbishop Kenrick, the American church's theological light, in his moral theology textbook, regretted: "that there were so many slaves whose liberty and education were restricted." His emphasis was that the American civil law must be obeyed to avoid chaos.[29]

Reflecting Kenrick's own opinion, the American bishops declared in the pastoral following the Ninth Provincial Council that while the church had striven always to mitigate the condition of slavery, "She has never disturbed established order or endangered the peace of society, by following theories of philanthropy."[30] Soon after the election of Abraham Lincoln, the Baltimore *Catholic Mirror* editorialized that it would rather have the Union broken up than see the new president and his party "destroy what we believe to be Southern States Rights."[31] The *Mirror* became increasingly sympathetic to the newly-formed Confederacy.[32] A week after the firing on Fort Sumter, the passage of Union troops through

Portrait of Father George Villiger, S.J.

At. Bohemia Museum – Desk made by Father Villiger while he was pastor at Bohemia 1856-1878.

Baltimore occasioned a riot that claimed several lives. In September, Archbishop Kenrick ordered Carroll's prayer for civil authorities read in all churches. Later he informed Propaganda Fide that he had ordered the prayer discontinued so as "to avoid suspicion of our loyalty to the present government."[33] He urged all priests and religious of his diocese to be cautious not to take sides in the politics dividing the country, to pray for peace, and to respect the constituted authorities.[34]

By now there were less than a handful of slaves on the Jesuit plantations on the Eastern Shore. There is no evidence of any by now at Bohemia. From the 1830s the Jesuits had begun to replace slaves with hired hands. Slaves owned by Jesuits on their farms in Maryland had been well treated, housed, and fed. They attended regular religious services in a chapel on the farm. The slaves were taught the catechism as well as reading and writing. The Jesuits baptized and officiated at slave funerals. The baptisms were recorded with all others. The deceased were buried in family burial grounds.[35]

Father Villiger has left no testimony of his northern or southern sympathies during the Civil War. Like Father Mosley during the Revolutionary War, he may have minded his own work and avoided embroilment in the issues that brought on the war. Sacramental records show that during these years he was not distracted from his work and that he was about "His Father's business."[36]

On September 2, 1860, the year Abraham Lincoln was elected to the presidency, Archbishop Kenrick administered the Sacrament of Confirmation at Bohemia to the following persons: Thomas (Stanislaus Dowell (convert), James Francis Bond (convert), Charles Jeremiah Bowls, Cornelius Bowls, John Thomas Bowls, Charles Edward Burns, Benjamin Michael Reynolds, Thomas Lucas Roberson, Mary Elizabeth Cayot (Convert), Mary Smith (Convert), Marie Helena Ford, Elizabeth Bowls, Francisca Bowls, Mary Elizabeth Roberson.

Neapolitan Jesuit, Leonard Nota

On the eve of the War between the States, from April, 1859, to September, 1859, Father Leonard Nota filled in for Father Villiger at Bohemia. Father Nota was born on November 23, 1807, in Naples, Italy. In 1850 he was at the Jesuit Novitiate in Frederick, Maryland, making his third year of probation. He was at the same time professor of rhetoric for the Juniors there. In 1851 he was at Georgetown College teaching dogmatic theology. In 1855 he resided at Newtown and attended the missions at Medley's Neck and St. John's. In 1855 he was professor of dogmatic theology at Georgetown. In 1858 he was at St. Thomas Manor on the western shore. He left there to serve at Bohemia.[37]

American Diocesan Priest, Lawrence S. Malloy

In August, 1857, Archbishop Kenrick purchased a large building and residence and chapel for a resident priest at Port Deposit, Maryland. At first the priest from Havre de Grace was given responsibility for Catholics there and at Elkton. In June, 1859, Kenrick ordained and assigned Reverend Lawrence S. Malloy to residence at Port Deposit. From there he attended Havre de Grace, Elkton, and Conowingo. Father Malloy was pastor of St. Patrick's, Havre de Grace, 1859 to

1861. He died in Baltimore July 25, 1885.³⁸

George Steinheiser

Father George Steinheiser, who succeeded Malloy at Havre de Grace, wrote Archbishop Kenrick on February 24, 1863, that "There are about 40 families of good practising Catholics and about 40 lapsed Catholic families here (in the Port Deposit, Elkton area)."³⁹

This arrangement ended at the end of the Civil War and with the establishment of the new Diocese of Wilmington. Four days after the battle of Gettysburg, on July 8, 1863, Archbishop Kenrick died, the apparent victim of a heart attack at age 61. Deploring conflict, he had suffered stress at the development of the war, and is said to have died of a broken heart after the Battle of Gettysburg. He was an outstanding example of gentle reaction to persecution and wished Catholics to extend the hand of friendship to non-Catholics. He was the most cerebral of the archbishops of Baltimore to that time, perhaps the most systematic bringing order to the administration of the archdiocese. He was undeviating in the application of the disciplines promoted by the Holy See.⁴⁰

THE EPISCOPATE OF MARTIN JOHN SPALDING

The archdiocese had to wait ten months to learn the name of Archbishop Kenrick's successor. On May 6, 1864, the Bishop of Louisville, Martin John Spalding, was promoted to Baltimore as its seventh archbishop. He was installed on July 31, 1864, the feast of St. Ignatius Loyola, patron of the Maryland missions.⁴¹ A man of enormous size and descended from an old Maryland Catholic family, Spalding was welcomed by Maryland Catholics as one of their own.⁴²

The new archbishop was naturally bewildered by the problems of the ongoing war. He made clear his conviction that churchmen should remain aloof from politics, and convinced Rome of the necessity of nonintervention in the war. He personally concerned himself with the welfare of soldiers held in the Union prisons and hospitals, and urged everyone to do all in their power to bring an end to the internecine war.⁴³

Swiss Jesuit, George Villiger

Throughout the American Civil War Father Villiger continued to serve his people at Bohemia and its missions without interruption and with remarkable earnestness and zeal.⁴⁴ Ominous events stirred the heart of the priest. He was keenly aware of inflammatory statements made on all sides around him, but following the instructions of Archbishop Spalding the priest kept his counsel, fully aware that greater forces reached into his parish and divided the allegiance of his people who lived along the Mason Dixon Line. During the war, munitions and supplies were often sent through the nearby Chesapeake and Delaware Canal by boat. In one incident every bridge on the Philadelphia, Wilmington, and Delaware Railroad between Baltimore and the Susquehanna River was burned or damaged. There was a concentration of federal troops at Perryville. The Union

Portrait of Archbishop
Martin J. Spalding

Michael Sullivan, Baptized at
Bohemia, August 30, 1863

officers used the Mansion House at Perry Point for quarters.[45]

On April 3, 1865, Maryland buzzed with excitement at the news of the fall of Richmond, and on April 9, the surrender of Lee and the Confederacy at Appomattox Court House. On April 15, less than two weeks after Appomattox the people were stunned and apprehensive as church bells began to toll at the announcement of Lincoln's death. Archbishop Spalding penned a circular urging Catholics to "join together in humble and earnest supplication to God for the prosperity of our beloved but afflicted country... We enjoin that the bells of all our churches be solemnly tolled on the occasion of the President's funeral."[46]

With the end of the Civil War, slavery was no more. The Church had survived the scourge of Know-Nothingism. Economic and social differences between the North and South had been modified drastically. Immigration was beginning to make the United States almost a new country. After five long years of deadening civil strife, the entire country turned to reconstruction.

In the early winter after the close of the war, Archbishop Spalding announced through the Baltimore *Catholic Mirror* that he was embarking on a pastoral visitation of the Eastern Shore of Maryland.[47]

At St. Patrick's in Havre de Grace, On Friday, November 24, 1865, Archbishop Spalding appealed to the congregation, reminding them to contribute to the decent maintenance of their pastor, Mr. Steinhouser, who also served Port Deposit and Elkton in Cecil County.[48] The archbishop took the train for Elkton on Saturday morning, November 25, and he confirmed 41 persons at Immaculate Conception Church in Elkton.[49]

At Elkton, the archbishop was met by Father Villiger. "After a pleasant drive of thirteen miles over a level road in rich country," he arrived at St. Francis Xavier's, Bohemia, where on Sunday morning November 26, he confirmed 45 persons

Richard Bennett Willson

including nine converts: Thomas Divine, Joseph McCallister, John Craddock, Michael Dignan, James Divine, Luis Druka, Clarence Walmsly, William Morton, Harrington Morton, R. L. Walmsly, Charles Perkins, Theodore Craddock, William Hill, Daniel Pascault, Francis Pascault, George Morris, Charles Queen, Jane Craddock, Anna Craddock, Rachael Newsome, S. A. Newsome, Emma Price, Araminta Price, Mary Walmsly, Eva Druka, Elsie Price, Margaret McCallister, Caroline Lotringer, Mary Dynan, Catherine Dolan, Maggie Bowls, Margaret Dorsey, Fanny W. Walmsly, Mrs. Mary Lockwood, Rose Money, Bridget McNeal, Maria Morris, Felice Queen, Emilia Morris, Maggie Queen, Melvina Queen.[50]

On Sunday evening the archbishop was met at Bohemia by Dennis McCauley who conducted him and his companion to his farm two miles from Galena at Lambson's Station. At St. Dennis Church there, on Monday November 27, at 10 a.m., Archbishop Spalding confirmed 12 persons, nearly all adult converts. After High Mass he preached to a respectable congregation, many of whom were non-Catholics.[51]

In the evening of Tuesday, November 28, he proceeded to Chestertown, fourteen miles away, where at seven o'clock in the Courthouse he delivered a powerful lecture on the divine institution of the Church. At Chestertown there was at that time no church building and only a few Catholics.

The next morning, Mr. Bennett Willson met Archbishop Spalding in Chestertown and conveyed him in his private carriage to Reese's Corner, a distance of ten miles, where the archbishop was again to lecture. However, inclemency of the weather, because of rain and snow, prevented any sizeable turnout, and the lecture was postponed.[52]

From Reese's Corner, Archbishop Spalding continued to Trumpington, near East Neck Island, the home of Richard Bennett Willson. Cold rain was soon forgotten in the warm reception given to the archbishop by the Willson family at Trumpington. The next morning, in the private chapel there Archbishop Spalding confirmed eleven persons.[53]

On the next day, Friday, December 1, 1865, the archbishop proceeded to Gray's Inn Landing, only three miles from Trumpington towards Rock Hall, to take the boat for Queenstown.[54] There he administered the Sacrament of Confirmation to the following: Billy Blunt, Joe Blunt, James O'Toul, Daniel Friel, Bernard Friel, John Griffin, Stanley Bryan, James Hampton, James Tracey, Robert Wilson, Frank Goldsborough, William Goldsborough, Theodore Slaughter, Elijah Chance, Samuel Ogle Tilghman, Billy (colored), John Friel, Catharine Calinan, Mary Ward, Catherine Friel, Mary Friel, Anne Hampton, Susan Hampton, A. Amelia Slaughter, Mary Slaughter, Mary Jones, Anne Maria Councell, Lizzy Wever, and

Lizzy Matthews.[55]

After dinner the archbishop was accompanied from Queenstown by Doctor Thomas S. Willson to Centreville, a distance of ten miles. There at the courthouse he was introduced by Mr. John Palmer to an audience who listened with interest to his lecture which lasted one hour and fifteen minutes.[56] From Centreville, Archbishop Spalding returned to Warrington, the home of Doctor Thomas S. Willson, where early on Sunday morning, December 3, 1865, he celebrated Mass in the family's private chapel, and immediately after left for St. Joseph's Church in Talbot County. After further visits to Denton and Easton, he took the boat for Annapolis.[57] On his Episcopal Visitation of the Eastern Shore, Archbishop Spalding confirmed a total of 195 persons, 48 of whom were adult converts. He had taken an inventory himself of the state of Catholicism there and was personally made cognizant of the need for priests and churches.

The archbishop wrote Father Villiger in early January of the new year, thanking him for his gracious hospitality, and Father Villiger in turn acknowledged Archbishop Spalding's correspondence, discussing some of the plans for new churches which different communities were hoping to build.[58] A chief motivation for the whole community to support the building of new churches was to lure and keep the immigrants who continued to pour in from Ireland, and now in greater numbers, Germans.[59] By 1865 the German had equaled the Irish influx.[60]

Father Villiger's fluency in German gave him a decided advantage in ministering o these new immigrants. We have seen German names appearing in the sacramental records of Bohemia in increasing numbers since 1850, following the failure of the liberal revolutions in Europe in 1848.[61] Following the close of the Civil War, German immigration was given new impetus. In the first year that peace had been declared 50,000 German immigrants entered New York harbor alone, and by 1871 the number had risen to over 17,500 more arrivals.[62] German farmers and craftsmen found employment on the farms of the Eastern Shore. Many worked on the building of railroads and the expansion of the Chesapeake and Delaware Canal.

Father Villiger regularly visited a growing German congregation at Chesapeake City, where he was accustomed to leaving his horses with the Stapp family and staying with the Schafers until Sunday morning when he would celebrate Mass.[63] Increasing numbers of Germans and German-speaking Polish were settling in Kent County near Rock Hall as farmers and watermen. In January of 1866, Father Villiger wrote the archbishop telling him: "Monday after the 3rd Sunday of February will be the regular day for me to go down to give service at Chestertown and at the Willson's. After my return I will inform your Grace of what has been done by this time towards St. John's Church."[64] This was the church proposed to be built at Reese's Corner between Chestertown and Rock Hall, discussed with the archbishop during his most recent visit there. The church proposed to be built there never materialized. Instead a Church of St. John's was built in Rock Hall in 1890.[65] In the last week of November that year, Archbishop Spalding wrote Father Villiger asking for a progress report on the proposed church in Chestertown. Father Villiger responded:

Your Grace's favor of the 25th inst. has come to hand yesterday. Accordingly I immediately commenced to write to Thomas Dixon, the only

Catholic who has a little money in Chestertown that we have to go to work, and what is to be done first, second, etc. but I soon came to an obstacle which, if it not be removed by some charitable and generous person or persons, will force us to drop the question of buying that house and lot for the present. It is this: if we borrow money on a mortgage on the lot, who will pay the yearly interest? Mr. Dixon is by far not able to do it and there are no Catholics able to help him. If therefore, no generous and charitable person or persons come to our assistance lending the balance to be borrowed for some years without interest, the question of buying that lot has to be dropped, which would be a pity indeed! But if the thing be undertaken, it ought to be done without interest in the proportion of two to one, and advancing one dollar as often as your Grace advances two of them. If then after the lapse of five years the congregation will not be able to pay our advanced money, if your Grace makes a donation of your part to that church, I will follow your example.

This, Most Rev. Archbishop, is the only plan I see that can be adopted. I cannot, however, enter into this engagement, without Father Provincial's permission, but he will make no objection to it. It will tax my little energy and means to the utmost extent, but seeing the importance of the object I shall cheerfully strain every nerve in helping to accomplish it."[66]

The most significant event in Archbishop Spalding's career was the Second Plenary Council of Baltimore held October 7-22, 1866. One of the main items of business the council undertook was to suggest new dioceses to be established by the Holy See and to propose candidates to fill the new sees. One of the proposed dioceses would encompass the Delmarva Peninsula and thus include the entire State of Delaware, the nine counties of the Eastern Shore of Maryland, and two

Canal Workers 1867

Picture of Father Thomas Becker and Archbishop Spalding at the Second Plenary Council of Baltimore

counties on Virginia's Eastern Shore.⁶⁷

From his recent tour of the Eastern Shore churches, Spalding brought to the Council a fresh and direct knowledge of the proposed diocese. He saw the area as a fertile field, and though the visitation involved considerable hardship and discomfort, he found this last and longest pastoral circuit most satisfying.⁶⁸ In a session held on October 13 there arose the subject of choosing candidates to be nominated to the Holy See for filling the new diocese.⁶⁹ In the original *terna*, a priest from the Diocese of Richmond, Thomas A. Becker, was third proposed for the Diocese of Wilmington.⁷⁰ A Presbyterian convert to Catholicism, Becker, whose last name was originally Baker before he changed the spelling, was an accomplished linguist and theologian.

After the Council, Archbishop Spalding wrote Propaganda Fide pleading convincingly on behalf of Thomas Becker's appointment.⁷¹ The archbishop arrived in Rome in the spring of 1867, and reinforced his preference for Becker as first Bishop of Wilmington. Spalding returned from Europe in October, 1867, and waited until the documents arrived from Rome in mid-February and took up pen to notify Father Becker in Richmond that his nomination had been confirmed.⁷² The news soon became public.⁷³ Becker was consecrated bishop on August 16, 1868, and was installed as the first Bishop of Wilmington on August 23, 1868.⁷⁴

NOTES FOR CHAPTER FOUR

1. John P. Marshall, "Francis Patrick Kenrick, 1851-1863: The Baltimore Years" (doctoral dissertation, The Catholic University of America, Washington, D.C.) 10; Thomas W. Spalding, *The Premier See, A History of the Archdiocese of Baltimore 1789-1989* (Baltimore The Johns Hopkins University Press, 1989) 153
2. Peter Guilday, *A History of the Councils of Baltimore, 1791-1884* (New York: The Macmillan Company, 1932) 173; James Hennessy, S.J., "Councils of Baltimore," *The New Catholic Encyclopedia* (Palatine, Illinois: Jack Healy and Associates, 1981) 2:38-43; Hugh J. Nolan, *Pastoral Letters of the American Hierarchy, 1792-1970* (Washington, D.C.: U.S. Catholic Conference, 1984) 173-184. Annual financial reports required of parishes by this synod provided Kenrick with a grasp of archdiocesan finances. Michael Moran, "The Writings of Francis Patrick Kenrick, Archbishop of Baltimore 1791-1863," *Records of the American Catholic Historical Society* (hereafter *RACHS*) 41 (1930) 230-262
3. Ray Billington, *The Protestant Crusade 1800-1860* (Chicago: Rinehart and Company, 1938) 322; Carlton Beals, *Brass-Knuckle Crusade: The Great Known-Nothing Conspiracy 1820-1860* (New York: Hastings House Publishers, 1960) 171; Mary St. Patrick McConville, *Political Nativism in the State of Maryland, 1830-1860*. (Washington, D.C.: The Catholic University of America, 1928) 64
4. Guilday 184-185
5. On May 11, 1851, Father Power *at Bohemia* baptized Charles Andrew Gibbs, two months old, son of Henry and Letitia Gibbs. All colored persons. Sponsor was Lidia Ann. On August 15, 1851, *at Bohemia*, he baptized Edwina Slater Hansen, seven months old, child of Thomas and Mary Hanson. Sponsor was Adebe Dulin. On September 7, 1851, *at Elkton* he baptized Thomas Rourke, seven weeks old, child of Timothy and Mary Rourke. Sponsor was Mary Riley. On September 27, 1851, *at Elkton* he baptized Thomas Holliday, five months old, child of Richard and Mary Holliday. Sponsors were Thomas Sullivan and Mrs. Devine. Georgetown University Archives (hereafter GUA) Special Collections Division, Box 571174, Washington, DC 20057. The searchable index to these Georgetown University Library Special Collections is found at this web address: http://www.library.georgetown.edu/dept/speccoll/indexlst.htm For the Jesuit Complex at Bohemia, this web address: http://www.library.georgetown.edu/dept/speccoll/mi/mi}176.htm - Archives, Maryland Province, Society of Jesus BOHEMIA-ROAD CASE-(1854)
6. Edward I. Devitt, "History of the Province" *Woodstock Letters, a record of Current Events and Historical Notes connected with the Colleges and Missions of the Soc. of Jesus in North and South America.* (hereafter WL) 63 (1934) 38 – Father Sanders was at Bohemia until November, 1856:

"He was simple and abstemious in his habits, and at one of the Missions at which he lived, he had solved the question of the high price of living by reducing his annual personal expenses to $26 – living on corn and bacon which he raised himself, his only indulgence being smoking tobacco which he also raised." 1853-1857 Rev. Matthew F. Sanders, S.J. Born in Holland, November 5, 1807, joined S.J. November 4, 1832, already a priest before joining order. Novitiate at White Marsh 1833, 1834 at St. Thomas Manor, 1837 at Newtown (Chestertown), 1840 Superior at White Marsh, 1853 sent as Superior to Bohemia and had Elkton, Chestertown and the State of Delaware, 1857 in Catholic Directory, Assistant to Rev. George Villiger and is said to attend Kent a station, 1858 at White Marsh, 1859 Superior at St. Josephs, Talbot County and attended Queenstown, Denton and Dorset, 1868 at Frederick, Md. Died there February 2, 1868, aged 61.

7. Boston *The Pilot* March 25, 1854; July 1, 1854; May 12, 1855
8. James F. Connelly, *The Visit of Archbishop Galtano Bedini To The United States of America, June 1853, - February, 1854* (Rome: Gregorian University 1960) 211-212
9. Billington 423 –427. Millard Fillmore, the Know-Nothing candidate for president in 1856, won the electoral vote in only one state – Maryland, and the party showed great strength in another state – Delaware. The Know-Nothing phase of Nativism died with the American Civil War. Slavery was the issue, not Catholicism. On August 21, 1855, Abraham Lincoln said: "As a nation we began by declaring that all men are created equal. We now practically read it: all men are created equal except Negroes. When the Know-Nothings obtain control, it will read: All men are created equal except Negroes, foreigners and Catholics." – Roy P. Basker, ed., *The Collected Works of Abraham Lincoln* (9 vols: New Brunswick 1952-55) 2:323
10. On March 13, 1852, *at Smyrna, Kent County, Delaware*, Father Sanders baptized Robert Pearson, 5 months old, son of Mr. and Mrs. Robert Pearson. Sponsor was Mrs. Woodward of Kent County. On March 14, 1852, he baptized Mary Magra, born January 24, 1852, daughter of Martin and Mary Magra. Sponsors were Ellen and William O'Brien of Smyrna, Delaware. On March 20, 1852, he baptized Sara Elma Riley, three months old, child of Caroline Riley, servant of Mrs. Price. Sponsor was Patrick Mackin. On March 20, 1852, he baptized *near Cecilton* Sarah Jane Lilly, five weeks old, daughter of Sarah Lilly. Sponsor was Patrick Mackin. On April 11, 1852, Father Sanders baptized William Donlon, two months old, child of Peter and Bridget Donlon. Sponsors were John Congrey and Anne Welsh. On April 11, 1852, he baptized Emily Elizabeth Robert, born October 4, 1851, child of Mr. and Mrs. Charles Robert. Sponsor was Louisa Lusbie. On April 11, 1852, he baptized George, town years old daughter of Caroline, servant of Thomas Lusbie. Sponsor was Laura Lusbie. On April 18, 1852, *at Elkton* he baptized Francis Rourick, born March 8, 1852, child of James and Mary Rourick. Sponsors were John Wall and Bridget Rosewick of Newark. On May 2, 1852, *at Elkton* Father Sanders baptized John Ward, three weeks old, child of John and Mary Ward. Sponsors were Michael Holdin and Margaret Dorethy. On May 2, 1852, he baptized Anne Burns, born October 1,, 1851, child of Christopher and Mary Burns. Sponsor was Ellen Dorethy. On May 2, 1852, he baptized Mary Ellen, born May 21, 1852, daughter of Lindy, servant of George Reynold. Sponsor was Margaret. On May 2, 1852, Father Sanders baptized Emely Jane, two months old, child of Samuel and Isabelle. Sponsor was Lindy Ann. On May 2, 1852, *at Elkton,* he baptized Mary McCormick, child of John and Anne McCormack. Sponsors were James McGuire and Eliza Connelly. On May 3, 1852, Father Sanders baptized Augusta Horace Smith, fourteen months old, daughter of Richard Bennett Willson and Martha Ann young. Sponsor was Elizabeth Willson. On May 3, 1852, he baptized *at Kent County*, Francis Thomas Willson, thirteen months old, child of Captain George Willson and Henrietta. Sponsor was Agnes. On May 3, 1852, he baptized, *at Kent County*, he baptized Charles William, child of Thomas and Ann Smith. Sponsors were Thomas and Elizabeth Smith. On May 3, 1852, *at Kent County* he baptized Martha Ellen, child of Daniel and Catherine. Sponsor was Ann Martha Willson. On May 3, 1852, Father Sanders baptized *at Kent County* Joseph Henry, child of Henry and Julia. Sponsor was Henrietta Willson. On May 3, 1852, he baptized *at Kent County* Maria, daughter of Isaac and Nancy. Sponsor was Margaret. On May 3, 1852, he baptized *at Kent County* Susan Ann, daughter of Louisa. Sponsor was Margaret. On August 15, 1852, *at Kent County*, he baptized Notley Oswald Willson, born July 8, 1852, son of Richard B. Willson and Ann Martha Young. Sponsors were Thomas Willson and Ann Hill. On September 7, 1852, at Kent County, Delaware, Father Sanders baptized Mary Anne Sullivan,

born September 30, 1849, daughter of Jeremiah Sullivan and his wife Hannah Ragan. Sponsor was John Lucey. On May 5, 1853, *at Dr. Willson's Kent County* he baptized Leonard Willson born February 20, 1853, son of Mr. and Mrs. George Willson. Sponsor was Ann Willson. On May 30, 1852, Father Sanders baptized John Hamilton Morton, born March 25, 1852, son of Mr. and Mrs. Morton. Sponsors were John Durkey and Mary Curnan. On May 30, 1852, he baptized *at Elkton* Francis Victor Prosper Libre, born May 2, 1852, child of Mr. and Mrs. Libre. Sponsor was Victor Lapiri. On June 2, 1852, *at Elkton* he baptized Anne Corbit, born March 4, 1852, child of Robert and Mrs. Corbit. Sponsors were Patrick Corbit and Ellen O'Donnell. On June 13, 1852, he baptized Stephen William Andrew fifteen months old, child of Rachel, servant of William Boldin. Sponsor was Mary History. On June 13, 1852, Father Sanders baptized Dennise Fitz Gerald, five weeks old, daughter of Dennis Fitzgerald. Sponsor was Patrick Magee. On June 20, 1852, he baptized John Rourick, two weeks old, child of Timothy Rourick and Alice Rourick. Sponsors were James Rourick and Bridget King. On August 1, 1852, he baptized William MacArtney, born July 7, 1852, child of James MacArtney. Sponsor was Eliza McKerob. On August 2, 1852, Father Sanders baptized Jane Rourick, born July 1, 1852, child of Bartholomew Rourick. Sponsors were Martin Cavanaugh and Catherine Lowney. On August 8, 1852, he baptized Mary Laura Price, born May 17, 1852, child of James and Ellen Price. Sponsor was Mary Price and Corbaley. On August 8, 1852, he baptized Dennis Moloney, four weeks old, son of Francis and Mary Moloney. Sponsor was Catherine Shahan. On August 15, 1852, *at Kent County, Maryland*, Father Sanders baptized Mary Maguinney, born June 3, 1852, daughter of Edward Maguinney. Sponsor was Mary Hassett. On August 15, 1852, Father Sanders baptized Notley Otwell Willson, born July 8, 1852, son of Richard Bennett Willson and Martha Anne Young. Sponsors were Thomas Willson and Anne Hill. On September 6, 1852, he baptized Mary Smith, five months old, child of James and Margaret Smith. Sponsor was Margaret Griffin. On September 6, 1852, *at Elkton*, he baptized Mary Ellen Heddevelt, three months old, child of Thomas and Mrs. Heddevelt. Sponsors were Edward Carty and Mrs. Rodriguez. On October 26, 1852, Father Sanders baptized Lucey, twelve years old. No parents given. Sponsor was Mrs. Green. On November 14, 1852, he baptized Susan Burns, born October , 1852, child of Mr. and Mrs. Burns. Sponsors were Daniel Dorethy and Rosey Carol. On December 10, 1852, *at Elkton* he baptized Edward Dorethy, born November 6, 1852, son of Patrick and Mary Dorethy. Sponsor was Bridget McCorklin. December 26, 1852. On March 13, 1853, he baptized James Mullan, thirty years old. No parents given. Sponsors were John MacKee and Anne Shahan. On December 26, 1852, Father Sanders baptized Francis Wheeler Ford, born November 4, 1852, child of Thomas and Ellen Ford. Sponsor was Mrs. Norton. On January 2, 1853, *at Elkton* Father Sanders baptized Catherine Ellen Carol, born Easter Sunday, 1852, child of John and Mrs. Carol (from New York). Sponsors were John and Mary Freebery. March 13. On March 29, 1853, he baptized *at Mrs. Leslie's,* Mary, four weeks old. No parents given. Sponsors were Mrs. Dorsey. On April 3, 1853, he baptized John Thomas Light, born *at Old Town*, five years old, son of John and Anne Light. Sponsors were James Norres and Jane McKully. On April 3, 1853, he baptized Nicholas Light born *at Old Town*, two years old, child of John and Anne Light. Sponsors were James Norres and Jane McKully. On March 13, 1853, Father Sanders baptized Jane Cosgrove, one month old, child of Patrick Cosgrove. Sponsors were Thomas Cosgrove and Mary Kirk. On May 1, 1853, he baptized *at Elkton* John O'Rourick (twin), six weeks old, son of James and Mary O'Rourick. Sponsors were Thomas Norres and James O'Rourick. On May 1, 1853, he baptized *at Elkton* Thomas O'Rourick (twin), six weeks old, child of James and Mary O'Rourick. Sponsors were Thomas Norres and James O'Rourick. On May 1, 1853, he baptized *at Elkton*, Thomas O'Rourick (twin), six weeks old, child of James and Mary O'Rourick. Sponsors were Thomas Norres and James O'Rourick. On May 5, 1853, Father Sanders baptized *at Dr. Willson's* Leonard Willson, born February 23, 1853, child of George and Mrs. Willson. Sponsor was Anne Willson. On May 15, 1853, he baptized *at Elkton* Anne Sabina Heanelow, four months old, child of John and Mrs. Heanelow (grandson of Mrs. Kern). Sponsor was Mrs. Rodgers. On May 29, 853, he baptized Mary Fitch Gerald, born in Chester County, Pennsylvania three months old, child of James Fitch Gerald. Sponsors were Dennis and Margaret Magunniger. On June 12, 1853, Father Sanders baptized Mary Mullan, seven months old, child of Patrick and Jane Mullan. Sponsors were John Dean and Catherine Manning. On June 19, 1853, he baptized Joseph Divine, *at Elkton*, four weeks old, son of James Devine and Emily O'Donald. Sponsors were Thomas Dougherty and

Bridget Key. On June 19, 1853, he baptized *at Elkton* Margaret Reidy, two years old, child of Robert Reidy and Mary Conner. Sponsors were Mary Reidy and John Connor. On June 19, 1853, Father Sanders baptized *at Elkton* Mary Sullyvan born May 1, 1853, child of Patrick Sullyvan and Mary Burres. Sponsor was Michael Holden. On June 26, 1853, he baptized John Hartnett, born May 18, 1853, child of Edward Hartnett and Mary Lions. Sponsors were Lawrence Hartnett and Joanne Lions. On July 3, 1853, *at Elkton* he baptized Thomas Foran, seven months old, child of Robert Foran and Bridget Power. Sponsor was Mrs. Rodgers. On July 3, 1853, Father Sanders baptized at Elkton Philip Green, born May 11, 1853, child of Francis Green and Sarah Connelly. Sponsors were Matthew and Margaret Smith. On July 10, 1853, he baptized Timothy Devine, six weeks old, child of Morris Devine and Mary Sullyvan. Sponsors was Rosa Carol. On July 10, 1853, he baptized *at Mrs. Price* Henrietta, eleven years old, child of servant of Louis McClain. Sponsor was Mrs. Mac Kim. On July 10, 8153, he baptized William Henry Ruley, seven months old, child of Caroline and Henry Ruley. Sponsor was Isabella. On July 10, 1853, Father Sanders baptized Catharine Brady, four months old, child of George and Henrietta Brady. Sponsor was Isabella, wife of Sam. On August 2, 1853, Father Sanders baptized, *at Dr. Willson's, Kent County*, Martha Elizabeth Willson, born July 29, 1853, daughter of John Willson and Ann Elizabeth (Brooke) Willson. Sponsors *were Jim and Martha Willson*. On November 8, 1853, *at Dr. Willson's, Kent County* Father Sanders baptized Ellen Theresa, three months old, daughter of Ann Smith, property of Robert Bogle. Sponsor was Elizabeth Smith. On June 6, 1854, at Dr. Willson's, Kent County, he baptized Frances, born October 5, 1853, daughter of Kitty. Sponsor was Mary. Belonging to George Willson. On August 14, 1853, Father Sanders baptized *at John Corbaley's* Charles Hamilton, six months old. No parents given. Sponsor was John Corbaley. On August 15, 1853, he baptized William H. Gibbs, five weeks old, child of Henry and Letitia Gibbs. Sponsor was Isabella. On August 20, 1853, he baptized *at Elkton* Peter Deur, born April 6, 1853, child of Thomas Craddock and Margaret Shield. On September 20, 1853, he baptized Peter Philip Martin, *at Elkton*, born September 4, 1853, son of John Martin and Mary Brady. Sponsors were Joseph Camel and Isabella Duffy. On September 20, 1853, Father Sanders *at Elkton* baptized Joseph Sleigh, born September 1, 1853, child of Joseph Sleigh and Ellen O'Brien. Sponsor was Bridget Rosewick. On October 2, 1853, *at Elkton*, he baptized William Maginnis, three weeks old, child of Peter Maginnis and Hanna McFadden. Sponsors were James Holden and Ellen Maginnis. On October 2, 1853, he baptized *at Elkton* John Screws, four weeks old, child of Thomas Screws and Catharine Maloney. Sponsors were Patrick Corbit and Catherine Foley. On October 10, 1853, Father Sanders baptized James Henry Clarck, five weeks old, child of James Clarck. Sponsor was Mary McCaffrey. On October 30, 1853, he baptized *at Elkton* John Rourick, three weeks old, child of Timothy Rourick and Mary Wall. Sponsors were James Rourick and Bridget Rourick. On November 1, 1853, he baptized Mary Ellen Hutchinson, three months old, child of Andrew and Rachel Hutchinson. Sponsor was Isabella, wife of Samuel. On November 8, 1853, *at Dr. Willson's* Father Sanders baptized Ellen Theresa Smith, child of Anna Smith, servant of Robert Boyle. Sponsor was Elizabeth Smith. On November 25, 1853, he baptized Robert, six months old, servant of Robert Lusbie. Sponsor was Virginia Lusbey. On December 11, 1853, he baptized Margarita Laura Martin, six weeks old, child of Alexander and Clara Martin. Sponsors were Gracian Bond and Anne Marie Loughlan. On December 11, 1853, he baptized Ellen Moloney, born December 9, 1853, child of Francis Molony and Mary White. Sponsors were Patrick Shahan and Mrs. John White. On December 18, 1853, Father Sanders *at Smyrna* baptized Andrew Rofferty, five weeks old, child of John Rafferty and Ellen Ennies. Sponsors were William Niorden and Mary Byrne. *Bohemia Burial Records*: Patrick Brennan died by accident working on the Delaware railroad at Middletown, Delaware in 1854. He is buried in the cemetery at Bohemia. On January 10, 1854, Father Sanders baptized Rose Anne Mooney, born January 9, 1854, child of Daniel and Mrs. Moloney. Sponsors were Patrick Dorsey and Mary Fay. On January 15, 1854, he baptized Mary Jane Plunket, two weeks old, child of Patrick and Mrs. Plunket. Sponsors were John Plunket and Catherine Bateman. On January 15, 1854, Father Sanders *at Dover, Delaware*, baptized Mary Jane Plunket, two weeks old, daughter of Patrick and Mrs. Plunket. Sponsors were James Plunket and Catherine Batesman. On January 15, 1854, Father Sanders baptized Martin Magra, two weeks old, son of Martin Magra and Mary Magra. Sponsors were John and Mrs. Finn of Smyrna and Dover. On August 30, 1854, *at Smyrna, Delaware* he baptized Elizabeth Reily, three weeks old, daughter of Mr. and Mrs. Reily. Sponsors were William Mollen and Mrs. Plunket. On February 5, 1854, *at Elkton* Father Sanders baptized Catherine Elizabeth McCormick, born January 15, 1854, child of John McCormick and Hanna Shearin. Sponsors were James Dungan and Elizabeth Maguire. On February 12, 1854, he baptized John Donnelan, three months old, child of Peter Donnelan and Bridget Cosgrave. Sponsor was John Mackin. On March 20, 1854, he baptized Mary Cavanaugh eight weeks old, child of Martin Cavanaugh and Maria Guilford. Sponsors were James Rigney and Mary Cavanaugh. On April 2, 1854, Father Sanders baptized Alice Marie McCaffrey, two months old, child of Patrick and Margaret McCaffrey. Sponsors were Thomas Norris and Margaret Flannegan. On April 9, 1854, he baptized Sarah Conwell Cromdigging, thirty years old, child of Michael Keenan Cromdigging. Sponsors were John Simmons and Bridget McClocklin. On April 9, 1854, he baptized Elizabeth Jane Murphey, four months old, child of William Murphey. Sponsors were James Donohoe and Margaret Meginnis. On April 9, 1854, Father Sanders baptized Francis Kearney, ten weeks old, child of Thomas Kearney. Sponsors were Martin Conlan and Ellen Conlan. On April 30, 1854, he baptized Elizabeth Ruley, *at Smyrna*, three weeks old, child of Mr. and Mrs. Ruley. Sponsors were William Mocken and Mrs. Plunket. On May 7, 1854, he baptized *at Elkton* Joannah Kennedy, born April 10, 1854, child of Daniel Kennedy and Ellen O'Donnell. Sponsors were Patrick O'Donnell and Margaret Tierney of Newark. On May 30, 1854, Father Sanders baptized *at Kent County, Maryland*, Jane Lavinia Dixon, born April 4, 1854, daughter of Thomas Dixon and Jane Thomas. Sponsors were William and Mary Thomas. On May 30, 1854, he baptized *at Kent County* Harriette, eighteen months old, and Caroline, three years old, daughter so Elizabeth. Belonging to John Willson. Sponsors were Mrs. Elizabeth and Mary Willson. July 6, 1854. On May 14, 1854, Father Sanders baptized Catherine Maulsburgher Johnson, born February 11, 1854, child of Mr. and Mrs. Johnson. Sponsors were Thomas Price and Mrs. Mary Price. On May 21, 1854, he baptized *at Elkton* William Brinnan, four weeks old, child of Patrick Brinnan and Ellen Ferral. Sponsors were Michael Holden and Eliza Herold. On May 21, 1854, *at Elkton* he baptized Sarah Anne Green, born February 26, 1854, child of Francis Green and Sarah Connelly. Sponsors were Joseph Carlin and Margaret Smith. On May 28, 1854, Father Sanders baptized Amelia Lilly, born February 12, 1854, child of Dick and Sarah Lilly. Sponsor was Isabella (of Bohemia). On June 3, 1854, at Elkton he baptized Margarate Corbit, three months old, child of Rodger and Bridget Corbit. Sponsors were John McCartney and Margaret Scanlan. On June 6, 1854, he baptized *at Dr. Willson's* Francis born October 5, 1853, child of Kitty (of Mrs. George Willson). Sponsor was Mary (of George Willson). On June 6, 1854, he baptized *at Dr. Willson's* Jane, six months old, child of Nancy. Sponsor was Mary (of Dr. Willson). On June 7, 1854, *at Joseph Craddock's* Father Sanders baptized James Andrew Fanny, child of two belonging to Joseph Craddock. Sponsors were Joseph and Gertrude Craddock. On June 16, 1854, he baptized Charles Abraham Reiley, born June 8, 1854. No parents given. Sponsor was Susan Perkins (of Mrs. Price). On July 2, 1854, at Elkton, he baptized *at Elkton* Edward McGunniger three weeks old, child of Edward McGunniger. Sponsors were Michael Keiley and Eliza Dun. On June 10, 1854, Father Sanders baptized *at Smyrna* Martin Magraw, two weeks old, child of Martin and Mrs. Magraw. Sponsors were John and Mrs. Finn. On July 6, 1854, *at Kent County* Father Sanders baptized Jane, six months old, daughter of Nancy. Sponsor was Mary. Belonging to Dr. Thomas Willson. On July 6, 1854, *at Kent County*, he baptized Catherine, two weeks old, daughter of Julia. Sponsor was Nora. Belonging to Dr. Thomas Willson. On August 1, 1854, *at Elkton* Father Sanders baptized Catharine Ahern, born May 12, 1854, child of John and Mary Ahern (of Newark). Sponsors were Michael Ahern and Bridget Flin. On August 1, 1854, he baptized *in Chester County* John O'Day, six weeks old, child of Neal O'Day. Sponsor was Amy Katen. On August 1, 1854, he baptized Matilda Mary Keenan, two weeks old, child of Michael Keenan. Sponsor was Laurence Connolly. On August 1, 1854, he baptized John Fox, nine weeks old, child of Mark Fox. Sponsor was Mike Brown. On August 1, 1854, Father Sanders baptized Margaret Henny Heddevel, nine days old, child of Thomas Heddevel. Sponsors were Peter Tighe and Mrs. Connor. On October 1, 1854, *at Elkton* he baptized Peter John Brady, born September 23, 1854, child of James Brady and Isabella Duffy. Sponsors were John Martin and Bridget Holden. On October 1, 1854, he baptized Francis Thibaud Sibre, born August 20, 1854, child of Prosper Sibre and Josephine Caijo. Sponsors were Francis Thibaud and Josephine Cajo. On October 2, 1854, Father Sanders baptized Joseph Henry Woodle, born August 31, 1854, child of Edward Woodle and Elizabeth

Marlsburger. Sponsors were Augustine Marlsburger and Catherine Marlsburger. On October 8, 1854, he baptized Maria Van de Griff, born February 13, 1853, child of Percy Van de Griff and Mary Congray. Sponsors were Patrick Congray and Margaret Congray. On October 15, 1854, he baptized Charles Dorr, born October 2, 1854, child of Peter Dorr and Anne Froment. Sponsors were Joseph Luber and Clementine Froment. On October 15, 1854, Father Sanders baptized Catharine Fitzgerald, born September 19, 1854, child of James Fitzgerald and Mary Dougherty. Sponsor was Dennis Magunniger. On October 15, 1854, he baptized Mary Anne Dougherty, born September 26, 1854, child of Daniel Dougherty and Rose Carlin. Sponsors were James Dougherty and Anne Kelly. On October 22, 1854, he baptized Anne Neil, born October 1, 1854, child of James Neal and Ellen Maginnis. Sponsors were John Newton and Margaret Maginnis. On October 28, 1854, Father Sanders baptized James O'Rourke, born August 24, 1854, child of James O'Rourke and Mary Anglin. Sponsors were John Corbit and Mrs. Sullivan. On November 4, 1854, he baptized Anne Rafferty, born October 20, 1854, child of Patrick Rafferty and Margaret Gartleney. Sponsors were John Bradley and Jane Brothers. On December 9, 1854, he baptized John Sullivan, five months old, child of Simon and Ellen Sullivan. Sponsors were John Kirivan and Anne Kelley. On December 17, 1854, Father Sanders baptized Margarate Ward, born December 2, 1854, child of John Ward and Mary Ryan. Sponsors were Patrick Ryan and Margret Ryan. On December 25, 1854, he baptized Margarate Rourke, born December 2, 1854, child of Timothy Rourke and Alice Flin. Sponsors were John McCarthy and Amy Roach. On December 25, 1854, he baptized Rebecca Madden, twenty three years old. No parents given. Sponsors were John and Bridget Holden. On January 1, 1855, Father Sanders baptized John Othoson, born September 12, 1821. Sponsor was Michael Holden. On January 21, 1855, he baptized Ellen Agnes McDonnal, six weeks old, child of Edward McDonnal and Margarate O'Calnon. Sporsors were Michael and Ellen Reiley. On January 21, 1855, he baptized Denis O'Connor, five months old, child of Cornelius O'Connor and Mary Scanlan. Sponsors were John and Anne Prendegrast. On February 4, 1855, Father Sanders baptized Robert Harold, born January 8,1855, child of William B. Harold and Eliza Lavery. Sponsors were James Cusack and Mrs. Cusack of Wilmington. On February 18, 1855, *at Dover, Delaware*, Father Sanders baptized Dennis Connor, born January 27, 1855, son of Patrick Connor and Julia Murphy. Sponsors were Timothy Murphy and Mary Connor. On February 18, 1855, *at Dover, Delaware*, he baptized Michael Connor, turn of Dennis, born January 27, 1855, son of Patrick Connor and Julia Murphy. Sponsors were Michael Connor and Mary Margaret Welch. On march 4, 1855, Father Sanders baptized Ellen Devine, born February 9, 1855, child of James Devine and Emily O'Donnal. Sponsors were Joseph Carlin and Anne Carlin. On March 18, 1855, at Kent County he baptized Francis Crommy, two months old, son of James Crommy and Frances Malloy. Sponsors were Neil Crommy and Belindey Boskin. On March 18, 1855, Father Sanders baptized *at Kent County, Maryland* Thomas Dixon, about 30 years old. On March 18, 1855, he baptized *at Kent County* Julia Rena Compton Willson, born November 28, 1854, daughter of Alexander Willson and Martha Ann Young. Sponsors were Julia Compton and Thomas Willson. Also sponsor was Mary Esther Willson. On March 18, 1855, he baptized *at Kent County* Leonard Ambrose Willson, born March 19, 1855, son of George Willson and Elizabeth Brooke. Sponsors were Georgina and Henry Willson. On March 31, 1855, *at Cherry Hill* Father Sanders baptized Martha Smith, two months old, child of Matthew Smith and Margaret Carley. Sponsors were Cornelius Cotter and Mary Cotter. On March 31, 1855, he baptized William Denver, born march 12, 1855, child of William Denver and Mary Ginley. Sponsors were James Givey and Bridget McKay. On April 8, 1855, at Newark he baptized James Reddy, born March 8, 1855, child of Charles Reddy and Kate Reiley. Sponsors were Patrick O'Donnal and Kate Duffy. On April 22, 1855, he baptized Sally Anne, seven week old, child of George and Henrietta (of Mrs. Flintum). Sponsor was Mrs. Price. On April 22, 1855, Father Sanders baptized Arthur Troy, born April 2, 1855, child of Michael Troy and Joanne Murphy. Sponsors were Patrick Dorsey and Anne Murphy. On April 29, 1855, Father Sanders baptized Peter Gray, born April 6, 1855, child of Michael Gray and Anne Gray. Sponsor was David Hays. On April 29, 1855, he baptized Mary Savin Ford, born January 30, 1855, child of Thomas Ford and Ellen Whalen. Sponsor was John D. Whalen. On May 12, 1855, he baptized Thomas Van de Griff, born January 17, 1855, child of Percy Van de Griff and Maria Cosgray. Sponsors were William Berry and Bridget Doyle. On May 12, 1855, he baptized Rose Ellen Cosgray, six weeks old, child of Patrick Cosgray and Margarate Donnelan. Sponsors were

Hugh McEntire and Marie Cosgray. On May 20, 1855, *at Federal Hill*, Father Sanders baptized David Harnet, born April 29, 1855, child of Michael Harnet and Julia Murphy. Sponsors were George Beards and Ellen Murphy. On May 27, 1855, Father Sanders baptized Mary Katen, two weeks old, child of James Katen and Bridgett Holland. Sponsors were Edward O'Day and Anne Hughston. On May 30, 1855, he baptized Margaret Jane Lavinia Dixon, born April 4, 1855, child of Thomas Dixon and Jane Thomas. Sponsors were William and Mary Thomas. On May 30, 1855, he baptized Harriette, eighteen months old. No further information given. On May 30, 1855, he baptized Caroline, three years old, child of Eliza (of John Willson). Sponsor was Mrs. Elizabeth and Mary Willson. On June 10, 1855, Father Sanders baptized Emma price, born December 25, 1855, child of James Price. Sponsor was Mary Anne Radick. On June 13, 1855, *in Delaware* Father Sanders baptized Sarah Simpkins, born March 1, 1855, daughter of Jerry Simpkins and Ann Williams. Sponsors were Edmond Dougherty and Jane McGoverin. On June 13, 1855, *in Delaware*, he baptized Francis Eisele, born March 31, 1855, son of Mathias Eisele and Manelille Kanz. Sponsor was Sylvester Kanz. On July 1, 1855, Father Sanders baptized Samuel Scot Graham David, born March 9, 1855, child of Jacob David and Anne Lyons. Sponsors were Patrick Corbit and Bridget Fling. On July 1, 1855, he baptized Mary Ellen O'Connor, born June 6, 1855, child of Richard O'Connor and Liddy Garcy. Sponsors were John O'Connor and Mary Roderick. On July 1, 1855, he baptized Mary Anne Flannagan, born May 19, 185, child of James Flannagan and Anne Kelly. Sponsors were Michael Ahern and Mary O'Donnel. On July 1, 1855, he baptized John O'Rourke born May 13, 1855, child of Bartholomew O'Rourke and Bridget Convery. Sponsors were James O'Rourke and Bridget O'Rourke. On July 8, 1855, Father Sanders baptized John Clarck, born May 6, 1855, child of James Clarck and Cusies Knoell. Sponsors were Patrick Dorsey and Ellen Brown. On July 8, 1855, he baptized Mary Morton, born May 24, 1855, child of Hamilton Morton and Mary Morton. Sponsors were Ben Green and Louisa P. Middifield. On July 8, 1855, he baptized John, six months old, property of Mrs. Thomas Lusbie. Sponsor was Augusta. On July 8, 1855, he baptized John James Martin, born July 19, 1855, child of John Martin and Mary Brady. Sponsors were James Hogen and Mrs. Anne Mullen. On August 10, 1855, Father Sanders baptized Edward Byrne, born June 25, 1855, child of Christopher Byrne. Sponsors were John Lockman and Catherine Devine. On August 10, 1855, *at Mrs. Flinthams'*, he baptized John Anthony Gibb, two months old, child of Henry and Sissee Gibb. Sponsor was Mary. On August 11, 1855, he baptized Alice Mary Thomas, born July 31, 1855, child of John Thomas and Sarah Goram. Sponsor was Mary Thomas. On August 20, 1855, he baptized William Charles Perkins, born May 24, 1826, son of John D. Perkins and Elizabeth Bradshaw. Sponsor was Ellen Grunwell. On August 22, 1855, Father Sanders baptized Ben and Anna Becks, twins born April 15, 1855, children of John Becks and Elizabeth Prindall. Sponsors were Bennett Willson and Elizabeth Willson. On September 4, 1855, Father Sanders baptized Anne, twenty years old, property of John Green. Sponsor was Isabella. On October 14, 1855, he baptized Thomas James Plunkett, born October 8, 1855, child of Patrick Plunkett and Anne Conley. Sponsors were Thomas Plunkett and Elizabeth Conley. On October 8, 1855, he baptized Martin Rafferty, born August 20, 1855, child of Thomas Rafferty and Anne Brophey. Sponsors were John and Mary Barry. On October 21, 1855, he baptized James Coile, born October 8, 1855, child of Edward Coile and Anne Gray. Sponsors were John Murphy and Roseann Callan. On October 24, 1855, Father Sanders baptized Ellen Ryan, born September 7, 1855, child of Peter Ryan and Anne Welch. Sponsor was Mrs. Mary Greenwell. On November 4, 1855, he baptized William O'Rourke, born September 30, 1855, child of Timothy O'Rourke and Mary Wall. Sponsors were Bill Carthy and Margaret O'Rourke. On November 7, 1855 *at Kent County*, Father Sanders baptized William Henry James, born October 1, 1855, son of Charles James and Eliza, belonging to Dr. Thomas Willson. Sponsor was Maria. On November 16, 1855, Father Sanders baptized Frances Anne Woodle, born October 29, 1855, child of Edward B. Woodle and Elizabeth Marlburger. Sponsors were Anthony Hookey and Catherine Tucker. On November 20, 1855, he baptized Mary O'Day born October 1, 1855, child of Edward O'Day and Bridget Coghlan. Sponsors were John Simmons and Mary O'Day. On November 20, 1855, he baptized Bridget Learner, born October 20, 1855, child of Thomas Learner and Winny Holland. Sponsors were Lawrence Connelly and Mary Laiden. On November 20, 1855, Father Sanders baptized Mary Hud, three months old, child of Sam Hud and Julia Murphy. Sponsors were Thomas Learner and Biddy O'Day. On November 20, 1855, he baptized Francis Dougherty, born April

30, 1855, child of Francis Dougherty and Bridget Martin. Sponsors were James Power and Selly McCloghlin. On December 2, 1855, he baptized Mary Kennedy, born November 2, 1855, child of David Kennedy and Ellen O'Donnal. Sponsors were John McCarthy and Mary O'Donnal. On December 23, 1855, Father Sanders baptized Aloysius Bisco Price, born November 18, 1855, child of Thomas Price and Mary Corbelley. Sponsors were John Corbelley and Margaret Price. On December 25, 1855, he baptized Frances Benedicta Reiley, born December 11, 1855, child of Abraham and Caroline Reiley, property of Dr. Perkins. Sponsor was Rachael. On December 25, 1855, he baptized Mary Christian, born October 10, 1855, child of Adam Christian and Mary Younger. Sponsor was Rachael Christian. On December 25, 1855, Father Sanders baptized Mary Smith, born October 13, 1854, child of William Smith and Mary Simmons Kanthing. Sponsor was Rachael Christian. On March 12, 1856, *at Kent County* Father Sanders baptized Cecelia Willson, born December 18, 1855, daughter of John Willson and Betsy Hill. Sponsors were Thomas and Mary Willson. On March 12, 1856, Father Sanders *at Kent County* baptized Thomas Frisbey, born in October, 1855, son of Thomas and Ann Frisbey. Belonging to Mr. Bogle. Sponsor was George Willson. On March 12,1856, *at Kent County* he baptized Michael Cahill, born March 8, 1856, son of Michael Cahill and Catherine Kennedy. Sponsors were Mary Kennedy and Michael Adhearne On March 16, 1856, Father Sanders baptized Bedelia Coglan, born February 5, 1856, child of James Coglan and Catharine Brackin. Sponsors were John and Mary Rigney. On March 16, 1856, he baptized John White, born February 1, 1856, child of Patrick White and Isabella Brackin. Sponsor was Catherine Devine. On March 16, 1856, he baptized Catherine O'Rourke, born January 31, 1856, child of Timothy O'Rourke and Alice Fling. Sponsors were Michael Corbit and Mary Angeline. On March 25, 1856, he baptized John Daniel Craddock, born March 24, 1856, child of Thomas Craddock and Margarate Shield. Sponsor was Netty Craddock. On April 16, 1856, Father Sanders baptized Michael Riley, born March 24, 1856, child of Michael Riley and Ellen Magrak. Sponsors were Michael Devine and Bridget Hammon. On April 16, 1856, he baptized Joseph Thomas Malsburgher, child of Augustus Malsburgher and Emily Woodall. Sponsor was Anthony Hoecken. On April 20, 1856, he baptized Catherine Cavanaugh, born February 4, 1856, child of Martin Cavanaugh and Marie Guilford. Sponsors were Patrick Corbit and Julia Doyle. On April 16, Father Sanders baptized Catherine Kantz, born December 7, 1855, child of Sylvester Kantz and Frances Grisley. Sponsors were Fred and Mrs. Kantz. On April 20, 1856, he baptized Catherine O'Neil, born April 14, 1856, child of Joseph O'Neil and Catherine McGinnis. Sponsors were Thomas Murray and Catherine Burns. On April 20, 1856, he baptized Mary Elizabeth Catener, born January 19, 1856, child of Joseph Catener and Mary Churley. Sponsors were John and Mary Smith. On April 27, 1856, Father Sanders baptized Charles Collins, four weeks old, child of Patrick Collins and Ella Dorsey. Sponsors were J. M. Conlon and Anny Cooney. On April 27, 1856, he baptized Thomas Finnegan, born December 22, 1855, child of Dennis Finnegan and Sarah Lyons. Sponsors were Daniel Collins and Catherine Hedley. On April 27, 1856, he baptized Mary Anne Doodey, born January 2, 1855, child of Daniel Doodey and Anne Gainley. Sponsors were Eugene Doodey and Mary Reardon. On April 29, 1856, Father Sanders baptized Daniel Healey, born April 16, 1855, child of Daniel Healey and Catherine Stacks. Sponsors were Edward Hussey and Ellen Leary. On April 29, 1856, he baptized Daniel Lyons, born December 11, 1854, child of Patrick Lyon and Joannah Hartnett. Sponsors were Patrick Lyons and Mrs. Lyons. On April 29, 1856, he baptized Mary O'Connor, born October 12, 1855, child of Martin O'Connor and Ellen Huston. Sponsors were Michael O'Connor and Ellen Kane. On April 29, 1856, he baptized Mary Horn, born December 16, 1855, child of Richard Horn and Catherine Lyons. Sponsors were John Horn and Joanna Collins. On April 29, 1856, Father Sanders baptized Margarate Horn, born December 6, 1854, child of Richard Horn and Catherine Lyons. Sponsors were Michael O'Connor and Elizabeth Lyons. On May 10, 1856, he baptized James Simmons, born February 21, 1856, child of John Simmons and Mary Murphy. Sponsors were John Hennisley and Nancy Harrogan. On May 10, 1856, he baptized William Simmons, born February 1, 1856, child of John Simmons and Mary McMahon. Sponsors were Martin Conlin an Sarah Cavanaugh. On May 10, 1856, he baptized Ellen Joice, born February 1, 1856, child of Martin Joice and Winny Gutley. On May 10, 1854, Father Sanders baptized Patrick Fox, born February 1, 1856, child of Mark Fox and Mary Brown. Sponsors were John Brown and Mary Maguinnegan. On May 10, 1856, he baptized Mary Anne McShane, born April 20, 1856, child of John McShane and Anne Manes. Sponsors were Patrick Morgan and Anne Houghton. On May 10, 1856, he baptized Edward Wells, born May 4, 1856, child of Patrick Wells and Margaret Fahey. Sponsors were John Brown and Margaret Brown. On May 14, 1856, *at Kent County* he baptized Emmaline, born September 15, 1855, daughter of Andrew and Eliza, belonging to John Willson. Sponsor was Mrs. Beck. On May 14, 1856, Father Sanders *at Kent County* baptized Mary Charlotte Willson, born May 7, 1856, daughter of Richard Bennett Willson and Martha Ann Young. Sponsors was Mary Willson. On May 14, 1856, he baptized *at Kent County* Agnes, three months old, daughter of Kitty, belonging to George Willson. Sponsor was Georgia Willson. On May 18, 1856, Father Sanders baptized James Maney, born April 27, 1856, child of Patrick Maney and Bridget Guinere. Sponsors were Thomas Ney and Marge Prendergast. On May 18, 1856, he baptized Francis Maloney, born May 4, 1856, child of Francis Maloney and Mary White. Sponsors were Patrick Dorsey and Anne Shahan. On May 22, 1856, he baptized Thomas Hutchinson, born April 9, 1856, child of Andrew and Rachel Hutchinson. Sponsor was Isabella. On May 25, 1856, Father Sanders baptized Charles Glen Mullen, twenty three years old, child of Daniel and Mary Mullen. No sponsors given. On May 25, 1856, he baptized Mary Bradley, born May 8, 1856, child of John Bradley and Mary O'Neil. Sponsors were Patrick Shahan and Ellen Connor. On May 25, 1856, he baptized Catherine Bradley born May 8, 1856, child of John Bradley and Mary O'Neil. Sponsors were Hugh O'Neil and Rose O'Neil. On June 2, 1856, he baptized Patrick O'Rourke, born April 16, 1856, child of James O'Rourke and Mary Angeline. Sponsors were James Sullivan and Ellen Bryan. On June 2, 1856, Father Sanders baptized Charles David Rosine, born March 22, 1856, child of Charles D. Rosine and Clementine Fremont. Sponsors were Charles Fremont and Generosa Lepiere. On June 2, 1856, he baptized William Feeheley, four weeks old, child of John Feeheley and Mary Ann Murphy. Sponsors were Patrick and Margaret Murphy. On June 2, 1856, he baptized Mary Corbit, born May 8, 1856, child of Patrick Corbit and Bridgett Fling. Sponsors were John McCarthy and Jane McBride. On June 8, 1856, Father Sanders baptized Eliza Donnel, born February 20, 1856, child of Peter Donnel and Bridget Cosgrave. Sponsors were Thomas and Margaret Cosgrave. On June 8, 18156, he baptized Joannah O'Connor, born February 20, 1856, child of Peter Donnel and Bridget Cosgrave. Sponsors were Thomas and Margaret Cosgrave. On June 8, 1856, he baptized Joannah O'Connor, born May 7, 1856, child of Bat O'Connor and Ellen Day. Sponsor was Timothy Hartnett. On June 8, 1856, he baptized Henry Larkin, born September 7, 1855, child of Patrick Larkin and Mary Murther. Sponsors were James McCallister and Mrs. McCallister. On June 8, 1856, Father Sanders baptized Mary Cavanaugh, born April 18, 1856, child of Philip Cavanaugh and Bridget Lauftis. Sponsor was Catherine Kennedy. On June 29, 1856, he baptized Marie O'Toul, born June 21, 1856, child of Lawrence O'Toul and Mary Connolley. Sponsors were Rodger Feeheley and Mrs. Brophy. On July 10, 1856, he baptized Mary Catherine Wilmer, two months old, child of Caroline Wilmer (of Mrs. Thomas Lusbie). Sponsor was Miss Augusta Lusbie. On July 28, 1856, Father Sanders baptized John Keeley, born July 22, 1856, son of Thomas Keeley and Anne Keeley. Sponsors were Thomas Conlon and Bridget Keeley. On July 31, 1856, he baptized Michael Dignan, born July 12, 1856, son of Patrick Dignan and Catherine Dorsey. Sponsors were Thomas Sullivan and Anne Murphy. On August 3, 1856, he baptized Jane Schone, born May 13, 1856, child of Thomas Schone and Catharine Maloney. Sponsors were John Corbit and Elizabeth Dorn. On August 17, 1856, he baptized Mary Elizabeth Martin, born August 5, 1856, child of John Martin and Mary Bradly. Sponsors were Joseph Gunner and Mrs. Gunner. On August 24, 1856, Father Sanders baptized Louise Brady, born July 24, 1856, child of George Brady and Henrietta Brady. Sponsor was Isabella, wife of Sam. On August 29, 1856, *at Dover, Delaware*, Father Sanders baptized John Kennedy, born August 5, 1856, son of Michael Kennedy and Mary Connor. Sponsor was Patrick Hickey. On September 7, 1856, he baptized Michael O'Leary, born July 19, 1856, son of Timothy O'Leary and Abbey Lions. Sponsors were John Leary and Mary Connor. On September 7, 1856, Father Sanders baptized Agnes Murray, born August 18, 1856, child of Andrew Murray and Catharine Carthy. Sponsors were John Connor and Bridgett Connor. On September 7, 1856, he baptized Rose Anne Fitzgerald, born August 21, 1856, child of James Fitzgerald and Mary Dougherty. Sponsors were Hugh Queen and Mary Dougherty. On September 14, 1856, he baptized Joseph Henry McCallister, born August 30, 1856, son of Robert McCallister and Mary Dillan. Sponsor was John Glenn and Mary O'Neil. On September 14, 1856, Father Sanders baptized Margaret

Mullan, born September 13, 1856, child of Patrick Mullan and Jane Thomas. Sponsors were Daniel and Margaret Mullan. On September 20, 1856, he baptized Mary Jane Green, born July 20, 1856, child of Francis Green and Sarah Conley. Sponsors were James Devine and Catherine Frail. On September 20, 1856, he baptized Joannah Connor, two months old, child of John Connor and Joannah Bennett. Sponsors were Neil Crimney and Mary Ready. On October 5, 1856, Father Sanders baptized John Holtz, born September 16, 1856, son of George Holtz and Mary Isley. Sponsors were Joseph Genn and Manilla Kertz. On October 26, 1856, he baptized Mary Susannah Sibre, born September 18, 1856, child of Prosper Sibre and Margaret Lapiere. Sponsors were George and Jenny Sibre. On October 26, 1856, he baptized Lizzy White, born October 10, 1856, child of Michael White and Mary Casey. Sponsors were Leroy Burns and Mary Queen. On October 26, 1856, Father Sanders baptized Jeremiah Michael Norris, born October 12, 1856, son of Thomas Norris and Sarah Brysan. Sponsors were Jeffrey Norris and Catherine Burns. On October 26, 1856, he baptized John Ysley (Eisele), born September 20, 1856, child of Huber Ysley and Manilla Kinz. Sponsor was George Holtz. On November 9, 1856, he baptized James Ahearne, born December 31, 1855, child of John Ahearne and Mary Brady. Sponsor was Michael Ahearne. On November 9, 1856, Father Sanders baptized Mary Kanz, born October 30, 1856, child of Fredoline Kanz and Frances Berger. Sponsors were Matthew Eisele and Barbara Hausleman. On November 9, 1856, he baptized Catherine Britt, born November 4, 1856, child of John Britt and Jane Bailey. Sponsors were John Lockman and Mrs. Sullivan. On June 14, 1860, Father Sanders *at Bohemia* baptized Mary Morton, born May 24, 1855, child of Hamilton Morton, and Mary Durkan. Sponsors were John L. Durkan and Mary Kernan. On June 23, 1861, Father Sanders baptized Elizabeth Campbell, born November 3, 1860, child of Levi and Catherine Campbell. Sponsors were Denis and Aherne Aherne. On June 23, 1861, Father Sanders *at Bohemia* baptized Bernard (colored), seven weeks old, property of Mrs. Flintham. Sponsor was Martha Burke. On June 23, 1861, *at Bohemia* Father Sanders baptized John Molony, four months old, child of Frank and Mary Molony. Sponsors were Thomas and Catherine Sullivan.

Joseph A. Dickerson, THE DOUBLE LL WILLSONS OF KENT COUNTY, MD. (joebeaches@firendly.net) - *Notley Oswald Willson*, born on July 8, 1852, *purchased Trumpington with his wife Julia R. Ringgold*. He died December 21, 1922, at Trumpington Farm, Eastern Neck Road, 5 miles south of Rock Hall in Kent County, Maryland. He married Mary R. Camp in 1918. She was born September 6, 1873. *She was willed Trumpington by her husband.* She died June 11, 1944. Julia Rena Ringgold Compton Willson was born November 28, 1854 and died June 30, 1935. Mary Charlotte Willson was born May 7, 1856. Peter Coninone Willson was born December 24, 1857. He died in 1920. Paul Alexander Willson was born June 2, 1859. Clement Joseph Beauregard Willson was born May 5, 1861. Alexander Hoskins Willson was born May 11, 1834 and died September 1877. He married Mary Tilden Browne on December 22, 1859, daughter of James Browne and Ann Tilden. She was born March 24, 1834, and died December 11, 1903. Children of Alexander Willson and Mary Browne were: Alexander Carroll Willson, born October 9, 1860 and died March 6, 1947, Frisby Browne Willson born July 2, 1864 and died September 28, 1865; Anne Tilden Willson born October 15, 1865 and died June 28, 1866; William Dalton Willson; Bennett Neal Willson born October 23, 1872, died February 21, 1941; Mary Tilden Hill Willson, born 1863, died 1941. Henrietta Maria Willson was born November 10, 1848 and died July 25, 1837. She married Dr. Thomas Bennett Willson on January 3, 1872, son of Richard Willson and Anna Young. He was born September 13, 1843, practised at Reese's Corner, and died March 23, 1923. He graduated from University of Maryland Medical School in March, 1866.

WEDDINGS BY FATHER SANDERS AT BOHEMIA:

On August 9, 1852, between James Powers and Sarah McLauchclain, both of Port Deposit, Cecil County. Witnesses were Molly Greenwell and Patrick Mackin. On November 14, 1852, between Thomas Schools and Catherine Molony, both of Elkton, Maryland. Witness was Patrick Mackin. On November 16, 1852, between Thomas O'Donnell and Catherine Shahan. Witness was Thomas Molony. On February 7, 1853, between J. Ben Thomas and Benitia A. Booker. Witnesses were Patrick Mackin and Mr. Stephens, Storekeeper.

On April 3, 1853, between Martin Cavanaugh and Maria Gilfoyle, both of Cecil County. Witnesses were Patrick Corbit and Catharine Gilfoyle. On July 17, 1853, at Elkton, between Joseph Gumer and Mary Martin. Witnesses were Prosper Libre and Margaret Connor. On

September 20, 1853, between James Brady and Isabella Duffy. Witnesses were Joseph Gumer and Mary Martin. On July 28, 1853, between Thomas P. Dixon and Mrs. Jane A. Thomas. Witnesses were Thomas P. Craddock and Patrick Mackin.

On September 25, 1853, between Daniel Dougherty and Rosanna Carlin Witnesses were Bernard Council and Mary Conroy. On November 1, 1853, between Daniel Dugan and Catherine Manning, both of Cecil County. Witnesses were Bartholomew Brady and Anne Chaira. On December 6, 1853, between Michael Brian and Susan Kilt, both of Queen Anne County. Witnesses were John Sweeny and his son.

On January 8, 1854, between William Morken and Mary Byrne, both of Kent County, Delaware. Witnesses were Daniel Morken, Patrick Byrne and his sister. On April 8, 1854, between Michael Keenan and Sarah Conwell. Witnesses were John Simmons and Bridgit McClocklin. On April 23, 1854, between James Flanagan and Anne Kelly, both of Chesapeake City. Witnesses were Thomas Lafferty and Mary Kelley.

On April 23, 1854, between James Coghlan and Catharine Brackon. Witnesses were James Dungan and Elizabeth Murphy. On May 7, 1854, between James O'Neil and Ellen McGinness, both of Cecil County. Witnesses were James Holdin and Michael Holdin. On May 13, 1854, between John T. Thomas and Sarah L. Goram, both of Cecil County, near Warwick. Witnesses were L. V. de Ward and John Sullyvan.

On June 4, 1854, at Elkton, between John Feehely and Mary Ann Murphy. Witnesses were Rodger Feeheley and Margaret Scantlan. On July 16, 1854, at Elkton, between Michael Norris and Bridget Norris. Witnesses were Thomas and James Norris. On August 7, 1854, at Chester County, between Patrick Connelly and Winny Katen.

On August 7, 1854, between James Dougherty and Catherine Keheler. Witness was Christopher Byrne. On October 25, 1854, between Michael E. Harnett and Julia Murphy. Witnesses were Matthew Smith and Ellen Harnett. On November 19, 1854, between Andrew Campbell and Catherine Byrnes. Witnesses not recorded.

On January 4, 1855, between John Atkinson and Mary Ann Pierson. Witnesses were Ben Green and Gracey Bond. On January 16, 1855, between Robert Welch and Mary Murphy, both of Kent County, Delaware. No witnesses given. On April 15, 1855, between Thomas Beers and Mary Hurley. Witnesses were John Hurley and Margarate Hurley. On April 12, 1855, between Augustine Malsberger and Emily Woodall. Witnesses were John Corbaley and Catherine Hoeckey.

On June 3, 1855, between John Casey and Margaret Ryan both of Port Deposit. Witnesses were Peter Ryan and Mrs. White. On August 18, 1855, between John Brown and Mary Fohey, both of Harford County. Witnesses were William Devine and James Beirs. On September 4, 1855, between Emory and Anne, property of Ben Green. Witnesses were Samuel and Isabella. On December 25, 1855, between Eliza and (name not given), servant of Dr. Perkins. Witnesses were Dr. Perkins and Mrs. Price.

On December 25, 1855, between Michael White and Mary Casey. Witnesses were Thomas Norris and Mrs. Byrne. On May 17, 1856, between Charles Hickey and Amy McBride, both of Cecil County. Witness was Mrs. Biddy Gaffney. On July 2, 1856, between Patrick Collins and Sarah Brason, both of Cecil County. Witnesses were Denis Collins and Margaret Queen. On July 20, 1856, between Thomas Norris and Sarah Bryson, of Chesapeake City. No witnesses given.

On July 20, 1856, between Thomas Nea and Catherine Maney, of Newark, Delaware. Witnesses were Mrs. Maney and James Coglan. On August 8, 1856, between Maurice Burns and Mary Norris, both of Cecil County. Witnesses were Thomas Norris and Mrs. B. Norris. On August 14, 1856, between Patrick Dorsey and Anne Sheehan, both of Cecil County. Witnesses were Patrick Sheehan and Mrs. Thomas O'Donnell.

11. Associated Archives, 5400 Roland Avenue, Baltimore, MD 21212 (hereafter AAB), Kenrick, *Acta Episcopalia* (written in Latin) gives a detailed account of his Confirmation tour: "1853 Aprilis 22, nave vectus sum ad oppidum Cambridge" – (By ship I came to Cambridge). "On the 28th I confirmed 13, in the Church of St. Peter near Queenstown. Hospitality was provided by a pious widow of 72 years named Browne (formerly Willson) whom nearly all my predecessors knew." On April 28, 1853 – Abp. Kenrick confirmed at St. Peter's, Queenstown: Martha A. Skinner, Mary Whiting, Charles Whiting, Lydia Griffin, Ann Jones, A. Francis Greaves, Richard L. Jones, Charles Jones, Mary Gleaves, Anthony, Samuel, Mary and Frances. Carley, *Queenstown*

79: Kenrick left Queenstown and next visited Saint Francis Xavier's near Warwick in Cecil County, then Elkton – St. Mary's of the Immaculate Conception. From there he returned to Baltimore by the railroad.

12. Joseph Horgan, *History of St. Dennis' Church, Galena, Maryland, 1855-1970* (Philadelphia: Cooke Publishers, 1970) 20-21: Dennis J. McCauley was born in County Donegal, Ireland, on May 14, 1814. At a young age he came to Philadelphia and was successful in business. On January 31, 1837, Dennis married Mary Gallagher in St. John's Church, 13th Street in Philadelphia. She was born at Letterkenny, County Donegal, Ireland, on May 12, 1812. They had five children, one of whom died at age three.

13. Baltimore *The Catholic Mirror*, August 31, 1855; Spalding, *Premier See* 179 – Thomas Foley was Vicar General of the Archdiocese of Baltimore from 1863 to 1869. He was a possible successor as archbishop. In 1870 he was consecrated Coadjutor – bishop of Chicago.

14. Baltimore *The Catholic Mirror*, February 5, 1856; Spalding, *Premier See* 166 – Bernard J. McManus was pastor of St. John the Evangelist parish in Baltimore for 35 years. It was the largest and most active parish in the Archdiocese of Baltimore.

15. "Kent County, State of Maryland, erected mostly by the zeal of Dennis McCauley, Esq. of Kent Co. Maryland." The dogma of the Immaculate Conception was promulgated for the entire Catholic Church in 1854.

16. Horgan 24

17. Kenrick, *Acta Episcopalia, Confirmed at Elkton, July 5, 1856*: Cornelius Cotter, James Burns, Catherine Burns, Robert Reedy, Anne Rigney, Catherine Brady, Monica Brinan, Joanna White, Catherine White, John White, John and Michael Keiley, Nancy Wheeler, Thomas Ney, James Sullivan, John Divine. *Confirmed at Bohemia, July 6, 1856*: Eliza Elizabeth Fin, Helena and James McGrath, Margaret Cosgray, Maria Cosgray, James Sullivan, Mary Ann Burns, Henry Clement Morton, Adela Maria Morton, Emily Theresa Thomas, Rose Anne, Ellen Connor, John Congray, Ellen, May of Mrs. Flintham, Susan of Tom Price, Charity May of Thomas Price.

18. Horgan 24

19. Horgan 29 – "It is a reasonable assumption that Father McManus and Dennis McCauley were already well acquainted when Dennis was inspired to build a church on his farm. It is not even difficult to imagine Father McManus implanting the idea in Dennis' receptive and spiritually fertile soul. Saddened by the unhappy plight of their fellow countrymen back home in Ireland, it is easy to further imagine both of them envisioning Kent County as a sanctuary of freedom and opportunity where their friends and relatives in Ireland might come to raise their families in peace and where they might have their own parish church in which to worship. The fact is that many Irish did come to settle in St. Dennis' Parish, as is evidenced by parish records of the past and of the present, listing such names as Duggan – the first recorded parish Baptism, Connor, Donahoe, Dougherty, Dunn, Fitzpatrick, Flanagan, Haley, Laverty, McGugan, McInerny, McKee, Mullen and Quinn. Regarded in his day as the lay theologian of Kent County, Dennis McCauley was ever conscious of the importance of regular religious instruction. Accordingly, he sent his two daughters, Elizabeth and Mary, to study at St. Joseph's Academy, run by the Sisters of Charity, in Emmitsburg, Maryland.

20. Horgan 30; Spalding, *Premier See* 162. Born at Mount Pleasant, New York, December 3, 1818, Dwight Edward Lyman was baptized in the Episcopalian Church. While he was receiving his advanced education at Columbia College in New York, he also served as organist in a Protestant Episcopal church. After completion of his course of studies at Columbia, he was ordained to the Episcopalian ministry and became a member of the faculty of St. James College in Hagerstown, Maryland. After teaching there for the six years from 1842 to 1848, he was made rector of St. Paul's Episcopal Church in Columbia, Pennsylvania. He was rector of St. Paul's Episcopal Church in Columbia, Pennsylvania, from 1848 until 1853, when he was received into the Catholic Church. Sydney E. Ahlstrom, *A Religious History of the American People* (New Haven; Connecticut: Yale University Press, 1972) 555 – The Oxford Movement in America: Dwight E. Lyman, an Episcopal clergyman made his profession in the Catholic faith on August 27, 1853, at St. Joseph's Church in Baltimore. He became pastor of St. Mary's, Govans, and died at St. Joseph's Church in Baltimore. December 29, 1893.

21. In the *Catholic Directory 1857* (Baltimore: Lucas Brothers, 1857); Father Sanders is marked as an assistant to Father Villiger at Bohemia and is said "to attend in Kent a station" (Trumpington

or Chestertown?). He was at White Marsh in 1857. In 1859 he was appointed pastor o St. Joseph's Church in Talbot County. In 1866 he returned to Frederick, Maryland, in a bad state of health. He died there on February 2, 1868 – "Newtown Manor," *Woodstock Letters* 15 (1886) 29. The only letter from Father Sanders to any of the archbishops of Baltimore was written in 1857: Associated Archives at St. Mary's Seminary, 5400 Roland Avenue, Baltimore, MD 21210. E-mail address: archives@St.Mary's.EDU (hereafter AAB) 31-I3, M. T. Sanders to Archbishop Kenrick, White Marsh, July 15, 1857, regarding Christian burial of slaves. GUA Archives of the Maryland Province of the Society of Jesus, Bohemia Varia, Folder 103-N1-P6.5, Vault Series 21 – Bohemia Material – "Statement of Account From Father King Up to January, 1855."

22. GUA *Catalogus Provinciae Marylandiae Societatis Jesu* (Baltimore: Lucas Brothers Printers, 1858) 69; Devitt, "Bohemia," *RACHS* 20:213, 24: 135-139

23. He is said – to have often walked the distance of thirteen miles to the church at Lambson Station – Horgan 32. *Woodstock Letters* 15 (1886) 228: "By his zeal and long days of toil in visiting the outlying districts did a great deal for religion." 229: "There have been some conversions in the church, especially during Father Villiger's pastorship."

24. *Woodstock Letters* 15 (1886) 229

25. Horgan 33

26. Clifford Pryor, *The Forest of Appoquinimink* (Milford, Delaware: Shawnee Printing, 1975) 6

27. Over thirty years before he wrote the Dred Scott Decision, Roger Brooke Taney had freed his own slaves except two who he felt were too old to be put on their own. Taney was a member of the American Colonization Society, which had as its purpose the liberation of slaves and their resettlement in Liberia, Africa. His fellow Maryland Catholic and last surviving signer of the Declaration of Independence, Charles Carroll of Carrollton, was another member of that Society. A slave owner himself, Charles Carrollton, in 1791, introduced in the Maryland State Senate an unsuccessful bill for gradual abolition.

28. Madeline Hooke Rice, *American Catholic Opinion on the Slavery Controversy* (New York: Columbia University Press, 1944) 89

29. Joseph D. Brokhage, *Francis Patrick Kenrick's Opinion on Slavery* (Washington, D.C.: The Catholic University of America, 1955) 170; John Joseph Larder, "Kenrick's Moral Theology: Its Adaptation to American Conditions," (Washington, D.C.: Catholic University of America, n.d.) Kenrick's *Theologia Dogmatica and Theologia Moralis* were published in his Philadelphia years and revised and republished when he was in Baltimore.

30. Benjamin J. Blied, *Catholics And The Civil War* (Milwaukee: Bruce Publishers, 1945) 70-82; Judith Conrad Wimmer, "American Catholic Interpretation of the Civil War," doctoral dissertation, Drew University 1980) 107-109

31. Baltimore *The Catholic Mirror* May 22, 1850

32. Baltimore *The Catholic Mirror* December 1, 1860

33. *Archives of Propaganda Fide, Rome* (hereafter *APF*) Congressi 20: 213r-214v, Kenrick to Barnabo, Baltimore, May 11, 1863

34. Spalding, *The Premier See*, 176

35. Robert K. Judge, S.J., "Foundation and First Administration of the Maryland Province vs. The Slave Question," *Woodstock Letters* 88 (1959) 392-401. Pope Gregory XVI had condemned the slave trade in 1838, but not slavery itself. Jesuits were not the only clergy who owned slaves. The practice was common in religious institutions in southern and border states until after the Civil War. Cann 168: In 1860, which was just prior to the War Between the States in 1861, and Abraham Lincoln's Emancipation Proclamation, in 1863, the record showed only one male slave by the name of Sam, age 31, and valued at $400.00. This is the last record found of slaves at Bohemia. Slavery was not officially abolished in Maryland and Delaware until 1865.

36. On October 3, 1856, Father Villiger baptized John Backes, born March 28, 1856, child of John Backes and Catherine Philips. Sponsor was Heber Eirele. On October 8, 1856, he baptized Michael McGrath, born October 5, 1856, child of Martin McGrath and Mary Rien. Sponsors were Patrick Mulchanoch and Anna Fin. On October 8, 1856, he baptized Margaret Connor, born June 20, 1856, child of Cornelius Connor and Mary Scannal. Sponsors were Martin and Ellen McGrath. On October 26, 1856, Father Villiger baptized Sarah Joanne Holiday, born August 24, 1855, child of Richard Holiday and Mary Burns. Sponsors were Christopher Buns and Rose Dougherty. On October 30, 1856, he baptized Thomas Brady, born October 6, 1856,

child of Christopher Brady and Catherine Reilly. Sponsor was Mary O'Donnell. On October 30, 1856, he baptized Margaret Anne Phalan, born October 7, 1856, child of James Phalan and Ann Hays. Sponsors were John Gifford and Joanne Lane. On November 11, 1856, Father Villiger baptized Robert Edward Welsh, born November 5, 1856, child of Robert Welsh and Mary Murphy. Sponsors were Edward Halloran and Ellen Healy. On November 23, 1856, he baptized Alexis Victor Cahill, born October 7, 1856, child of Dominic Cahill and Elizabeth Mouthrie. Sponsors were Charles Gerardin and Mary Victor Cujay. On November 23, 1856, he baptized John Murry, born October 31, 1856, child of Henry Murry and Julia Bentley. Sponsor was Catherine Murry. On November 23, 1856, Father Villiger baptized John Edward Sweeney, born November 2, 1856, child of John Sweeney and Mary McLain. Sponsors were Edward Collins and Mary Collins. On November 26, 1856, he baptized Elizabeth McDonnel, born September 15, 1856, child of Edward McDonnel and Margaret Calliner. Sponsors were John and Joanna Behan. On December 5, 1856, he baptized Vincent Hamilton Flintham. Price, born November 23, 1856, child of James Price and Ellen Hessey. Sponsor was Susanna Flintham. On December 19, 1856, he baptized Thomas Gerber, born November 29, 1855, child of Christopher Gerber and Genevieve Molitor. Sponsors were Daniel and Mary Collins. On December 20, 1856, Father Villiger baptized Dennis Robert Ahern, born November 19, 1856, son of Dennis Ahern and Anna Alworth. Sponsors were Patrick Hickey and Margaret Luber. On December 20, 1856, he baptized Elizabeth Collins born October 23, 1856, child of John Collins and Joanna Lions. Sponsors were Dennis Finnigan and Ellen Hartnett. On December 21, 1856, he baptized James Bear, born November 2, 1856, child of Henry Bear and Mary Nichol. Sponsors were Robert and Catherine School. On December 26, 1856, Father Villiger baptized William Emile Crawford, born December 7, 1856, child of Samuel I. Crawford and Ann Marie Langler. Sponsors were Jeremiah Reynolds and Julia Good. On December 27, 1856, he baptized Christopher Newman, born September 19, 1855, child of John Newman and Ellen Shirden. Sponsors were Patrick and Bridget O'Donnal. On December 28, 1856, he baptized Joanne Daly, born October 12, 1856, child of James Daly and Mary Brothers. Sponsors were Patrick and Catherine Brothers. On January 1, 1857, Father Villiger baptized Joanna Higler, born December 26, 1856, child of Francis Xavier Higler and Barbara Pfitzer. Sponsors were Francis Xavier Eisele and Petronella Renz. On January 4, 1857, he baptized James Keely, born December 29, 1856, child of Michael Keely and Margaret Keely. Sponsors were Daniel McBride and Frederica Henly. On January 7, 1857, he baptized Lucy Elizabeth Horst, born January 3, 1857, child of Catharine Horst. Sponsor was Adelaide Morton. On January 14, 1857, he baptized George Peter (colored), born January 9, 1857. Sponsor was Alma Craddock. On January 17, 1857, Father Villiger baptized Catherine Christian Miller, born October 24, 1856, child of Christian Miller and Louise Philomena Pensil. Sponsors were John Schmidt and Mary Martin. On January 19, 1857, he baptized John Henry Hartnett, child of Michael Hartnett and Julia Murphy. Sponsors were James Beers and Mary Murphy. On February 10, 1857, he baptized Michael Jordan, born January 7, 1857, child of Patrick Jordan and Mary McAfee. Sponsors were John and Elizabeth Finn. On February 10, 1857, Father Villiger baptized Anna Joanna McCloskey, born January 16, 1857, child of James McCloskey and Mary Bradley. Sponsors were Michael Collins and Mary Innes. On February 10, 1857, he baptized Margaret Sheridan, born January 4, 1857, child of Lawrence Sheridan and Mary Innes. Sponsors were John and Elizabeth Finn. On February 22, 1857, he baptized William Henry Walters (colored), born December 5, 1856, child of Henry Walters and Ann Elizabeth Hughes. Sponsor was Mary Huston. On February 28, 1857, Father Villiger baptized Margaret Smith, born January 3, 1857, child of Matthew Smith and Margaret Curley. Sponsors were James Hearly and Catherine Bird. On February 28, 1857, he baptized Dennis McGunnigan, born December 11, 1856, child of Edward McGunnigan and Bridget Keely. Sponsors were Michael and Margaret Keely. On March 16, 1857, he baptized Martin Conley, born November 10, 1856 child of Patrick Conley and Veronica McKatin. Sponsors were William Hennessy and Ellen Roach. On March 16, 1857, Father Villiger baptized Catherine Keenan, born November 14, 1856, child of Michael Keenan and Sarah Caldwell. Sponsors were Thomas Devine and Mary O'Day. On March 15, 1857, he baptized Charles Hicky, born March 7, 1857, child of Charles Hicky and Anna McBride. Sponsors were Francis Suter and Joanne White. On March 19, 1857, he baptized Anna McCarty, born December 7, 1856, child of James McCarty and Anne Hughes. Sponsors were Thomas Brophy and Catherine

Frail. On April 4, 1857, Father Villiger baptized Mary Emma Malsberger, born March 13, 1857, child of Augustine Malsberger and Emily Woodall. Sponsor was John Corbaley. On April 9, 1857, he baptized George Edward Roberson, born March 31, 1857, child of Samuel Roberson and Isabel Gasaway. Sponsor was Mary Huston. On April 14, 1857, he baptized Dennis Finnigan, born March 17, 1857, child of Dennis Finnigan and Sarah Lions. Sponsors were John and Joanna Collins. On April 15, 1857, Father Villiger baptized Timothy Phelz, born March 7, 1857, child of Timothy Phelz and Mary Scanlan. Sponsors were Daniel and Ellen Scanlan. On April 19, 1857, he baptized Mary Rourke, born March 24, 1857, child of Timothy Rourke and Alexis Fling. Sponsors were T. Rourke and Catherine Kelly. On May 1, 1857, he baptized Eugene Owen Sweeny, born April 11, 1857, child of Edward Sweeny and Julia Donigan. Sponsor was Thomas Peters. On May 6, 1857, he baptized Lane, born January 5, 1857, child of Timothy Lane and Margaret Connor. Sponsors were Ines Lane and Susan Hunter. On May 6, 1857, Father Villiger baptized Athanasius Gregory Hagan, born March 12, 1857, child of Bernard Hagan and Alice Prior. Sponsors were Patrick Drew and Catherine Conley. On May 6, 1857, he baptized Hanna M. Cooper (colored) born November 15, 1856, child of Cooper and Caroline Bready. Sponsor was Anna Theresa Ford. On May 12, 1857, he baptized Ann Catherine McDermott, born April 19, 1857, child of Patrick McDermott and Bridget Dugan. Sponsors were Hugh Durney and Catherine McDermott. On May 12, 1857, Father Villiger baptized Joseph Berriman (colored), born February 10, 1857, child of Mary Berriman. Sponsor was Anna Willson. On May 15, 1857, he baptized Leonard George Ford, born May 11, 1857, child of Thomas Ford and Helen Wheeler. Sponsor was Mary Teresa Martin. On May 16, 1857, he baptized Agnes Elizabeth Connor, born February 4, 1857, child of Richard Connor and Lydya Gerry. Sponsors were John Weldon and Winifred Roche. On May 18, 1857, Father Villiger baptized Richard McCavick, born Mary 9, 1857, child of William McCavick and Helen O'Neil. Sponsors were Mark Fox and Mary Brown. On May 25, 1857, he baptized George Simpkins, born January 22, 1857, child of Darius Simpkins and Anna McWilliams. Sponsors were Robert Davis and Mary Gillespie. On May 31, 1857, he baptized Joseph Schmid, born February 10, 1857, child of William Schmid and Mary Kinlin. Sponsors were Joseph and Maria Kirchman. On June 3, 1857, Father Villiger baptized Dorothy Kenny, born April 10, 1857, child of Patrick Kenny and Catherine Breen. Sponsor was Rose Dougherty. On June 7, 1857, he baptized Mary Dorsey, born May 17, 1857, child of Patrick Dorsey and Honora Shehan. Sponsor was Mary Jeannette Craddock. On June 14, 1857, he baptized Mary Ann Troy, born May 28, 1857, child of Michael Troy and Joanna Murphy. Sponsors were Patrick Digney and Catherine Lusby. On June 28, 1857, Father Villiger baptized James Franklin Bradley, born June 27, 1855, child of Edward Bradley and Elise Scurry. Sponsor was Alice Scurry. On June 28, 1857, conditionally Father Villiger baptized George Robert Price, born February 18, 1841, son of Robert Price and Araminta Coffin. No sponsors given. On July 12, 1857, he baptized George Vandegrift, born April 2, 1857, son of Perry George Vandegrift and Mary Cosgriff. Sponsors were Thomas Cosgriff and Margaret Cosgriff. On July 26, 1857, Father Villiger baptized Jeremiah Callaghan, born July 14, 1857, son of Richard Callaghan and Joanna Foley. Sponsors were Richard and Anna Haley. On August 10, 1857, he baptized Thomas Edward Cahill, born July 23,1857, child of Thomas Cahill and Eleanore Ahern. Sponsors were Thomas Herrigan and Catherine Ahern. On August 23, 1857, he baptized Margaret Crescentia Mratz, born March 31, 1857, child of John Mratz and Elizabeth Eisly. Sponsors were Emmanuel Holz and Anna Maria Eisly. On August 25, 1857, Father Villiger baptized William Helpern, born March 11, 1856, child of Francis Helpern and Mary M. Reynolds. Sponsor was Anne Honora Connor. On September 14, 1857, he baptized Thomas Dixon, born September 11, 1857, child of Thomas P. Dixon and Joanna A. Shields. Sponsors were William and Mary Thomas. On September 15, 1857, he baptized Henry Flower, born July 22, 1857, child of Joseph L. Flower and Catherine Kriss. Sponsor was Henry Kriss. On September 24, 1857, Father Villiger baptized John Christian, born May 17, 1857, child of Adam Christian and Anne Marie Youngker. Sponsor was John Christian. On September 27, 1857, he baptized John Finley, born September 22, 1857, child of William Finley and Bridget Lawler. Sponsors were Charles and Joanne Moss. On October 30, 1857, he baptized conditionally Benjamin Rocher, born November 11, 1828, son of Samuel Rocher and Mary Ann Oldham. On October 30, 1857, Father Villiger conditionally baptized Reuben Rocher, born. January 18, 1837, child of Samuel Rocher and Mary Anne Oldham. Sponsor was Helena

Greenwell. On November 4, 1857, he baptized Thomas Cosgriff, born October 10, 1857, child Patrick Cosgriff and Margaret Donlan. Sponsors were John and Rose Cosgriff. On November 4, 1857, he baptized Mary Ahern, born May 11, 1857, child of John Ahern and Mary Brady. Sponsor was Michael Ahern. On November 4, 1857, Father Villiger baptized Thomas Haden, born September 19, 1857, child of Thomas Haden and Margaret O'Brien. Sponsors were Darby O'Brien and Ellen O'Brien. On December 18, 1857, he baptized Honora Hicky, born November 15, 1857, child of Michael Hicky and Margaret Con. Sponsor was Maria Moore. On December 18, 1857, he baptized Mary Elizabeth Philomena Price, born November 11, 1857, child of Thomas T. Price and Mary A. Corbaley. Sponsor was John Corbaley and Margaret E. C. Price. On January 1, 1858, Father Villiger baptized Margaret Murphy, born December 13, 1857, child of Patrick Murphy and Mary Horan. Sponsor was Patrick Phalan. On January 1, 1858, he baptized Henry Madden, born December 22, 1857, child of George Madden and Ann Turner. Sponsor was Walter Carr. On January 11, 1858, he baptized John George Augustus Dreka, born November 18, 1857, child of August Dreka and Teresa Schneffy. Sponsor was John Sebastian Eberhard. On January 13, 1858, Father Villiger baptized Mary Eisele, born December 31, 1857, child of Matthew Eisele and Barbara Heinzleman. Sponsors were Francis Xavier Hiigler and Petronella Kantz. On January 23, 1858, *at Kent County, Maryland*, Father Villiger baptized Alice Josephine Willson, born October 21, 1857, daughter of John Willson and Anna Elizabeth Brooke Willson. Sponsors were Thomas and Martha Willson. On March 14, 1858, father Villiger baptized Josephine Messer, born January 31, 1858, child of Michael Messer and Bridget Doyle. Sponsor was John Hiigler. On March 4, 1858, he baptized Mary Ann Victoria Bates, born September 2, 1857, child of Henry Bates and Mary Strassner. Sponsors were Patrick A. McDermott and Mary Ann Farrell. On March 14, 1858, he baptized Gafney, born February 19, 1858, child of Thomas Gafney and Mary McAvoy. Sponsors were William Berry and Mary Ann Cleary. On March 15, 1858, Father Villiger baptized Catherine Driskel, born February 17, 1858, child of John Driskel and Catherine Sullivan. Sponsors were John Sullivan and Mary Ann Martin. On March 15, 1858, he baptized James Denniston, born February 13, 1858, child of Patrick Denniston and Rachael Farrell. Sponsors were Michael Joyce and Margaret Lions. On March 28, 1858, he baptized Thomas Dowell, born December 1, 1833, child of Henry Dowell and Febe Taylor. Sponsor was Rose Dougherty. On March 29, 1858, Father Villiger baptized Lydia Mary Man, born in February, 1805, child of Thomas Man and Lydia Davis. Sponsor was Mary Riley. On March 29, 1858, he baptized Arthur Morton, born January 20, 1858, child of Hamilton Morton and Mary Theresa Durkee. Sponsors were Henry Morton and Anna Maria Crawford. On April 4, 1858, he baptized William As, born in November, 1857, child of Peter As and Elizabeth Carty. Sponsor was Mary Houston. On April 11, 1858, Father Villiger baptized Catherine Skelly, born February 15, 1858, child of William Skelly and Mary Caral. Sponsors were Richard and Ellen Fin. On April 11, 1858, he baptized Michael Malony, born March 14, 1858, child of John Malony and Mary Hurney. Sponsors were Matthew and Honora Donohoe. On April 3, 1858, he baptized John Bradly, born March 31, 1858, child of John Bradly and Mary McGainly. Sponsors were George McGainly and Adeline Metzinger. On April 13, 1858, Father Villiger baptized Mary Murphy, born April 4, 1858, child of John Murphy and Bridget Mihan. Sponsors were Michael Fogarty and Mary Haldeman. On April 17, 1858, he baptized James Rudy, born November 5, 1857, child of Robert Rudy and Sarah Friel. Sponsors were John Gildea and Mary Ann Trasnell. On April 17, 1858, he baptized Elizabeth Gonnor, born March 12, 1858, child of John Gonnor and Joanne Bennet. Sponsors were Joseph Gonnor and Mary Martin. On April 21, 1858, *at Kent County*, he baptized George Willson, born February 23, 1858, son of George Willson and Henrietta Brooke Willson. Sponsors were William Hamilton and Anna M. Young Willson. On April 21, 1858, *at Kent County* he baptized Peter Willson, born December 24, 1857, son of Richard Bennett Willson and Anna M. Young. Sponsor was Ellen Guilland. On April 21, 1858, he baptized Mary McKlosky, born December 9, 1857, daughter of James McKlosky and Margaret Owens. Sponsor was Eleanor B. Willson. On April 30, 1858, Father Villiger baptized James White, born October 2, 1859, child of Daniel White and Mary Jenkins. Sponsors were Dennis McCarty and Anna White. On May 10, 1858, he baptized Edmund Bourke, born February 1, 1858, child of Julius Bourke and Joanna O'Greely. Sponsors were Dennis Meaghen and Catherine Collins. On May 11, 1858, he baptized Elizabeth Horne, born January 30, 1857, child of Richard Horne and Catherine Lions. Sponsors were Dennis

Fungar and Sara Lions. On May 12, 1858, Father Villiger baptized Mary Elizabeth McCalister, born December 23, 1857, child of James McCalister and Catherine Murphy. Sponsors were Patrick Magdy and Mary Larkin. On May 12, 1858, he baptized Margaret Wright, born February 17, 1858, child of Hugh N. Wright and Sara Ann Caldwell. Sponsor was Mary Magdy. On May 12, 1858, he baptized Mary Welsh, born February 18, 1858, child of Robert Welsh and Mary Murphy. Sponsors were Jeremiah Murphy and Margaret Murphy. On May 14, 1858, Father Villiger baptized Joseph Arthur Wilmer, born January 5, 1858, child of Arthur Wilmer and Caroline Carol. Sponsor was Catherine Lusby. On May 17, 1858, he baptized John McShain, born March 24, 1858, child of John McShane and Anna Mears. Sponsors were Patrick Tuite and Mary Mears. On May 17, 1858, he baptized Mary Simons, born January 4, 1858, child of John Simons and Mary McMahon. Sponsors were Patrick McMahon and Mary Simons. On May 17, 1858, Father Villiger baptized Mary Murry, born March 4, 1858, child of John Murry and Catherine Queen. Sponsors were Thomas Corcoran and Margaret Breslin. On May 18, 1858, he baptized Catherine Carroll, born May 10, 1858, child of Patrick Carrol and Bridget Finnigan. Sponsors were Patrick Floid and Mary Clarke. On June 9, 1858, he baptized Theresa Thomas, born, May 1, 1858, child of John Thomas and Sarah Goshen. Sponsor was Mary Frances Thomas. On June 17, 1858, Father Villiger baptized Benedict Bready, born December 15, 1857, child of George Bready and Harriet Johns. Sponsor was Caroline Reilly. On June 17, 1858, he baptized Emma Reily, born January 20, 1858, child of Abraham Reily and Caroline Reily. Sponsor was Anna Brice. On June 20, 1858, he baptized Margaret Hicky, born June 3, 1858, child of Charles Hicky and Anna McBride. Sponsors were Bartholomew Collins and Margaret Quinn. On July 4, 1858, Father Villiger baptized Mary Alice Egan, born June 16, 1858, child of Martin Egan and Mary McDonnell. Sponsors were Thomas Browne and Mary Barrett. On July 6, 1858, he baptized Isabella Barrett, born June 9, 1858, child of John Barrett and Catherine Grant. Sponsors were Patrick and Mary Murphy. On July 25, 1858, he baptized John Carroll, born June 9, 1858, child of Peter M. Carroll and Catherine Kelly. Sponsors were Louis Eberhard and Anne Murphy. On July 27, 1858, Father Villiger baptized Henry Vanbiber Crawford, born June 20, 1858, child of Samuel Crawford and Ann Marie Fogler. Sponsors were Vincent Reynolds and Adeline Morton. On July 31, 1858, he baptized Richard Masse, born July 15, 1858, child of Thomas Masse and Anna I. Verdon. Sponsors were James and Mary Gardiner. On August 1, 1858, he baptized Margaret McGuire, born July 11, 1858, child of Martin McGuire and Margaret Glassy. Sponsors were Patrick and Abigail Deniston. On August 11, 1858, Father Villiger baptized Rachel Rebecca Willis, born July 11, 1858, child of John Willis and Rebecca Killgoar. Sponsor was Nelly Greenwell. On August 12, 1858, he baptized Helen Agnes Reily, born July 9, 1858, child of Michael Reily and Helen McGrath. Sponsors were Patrick Bourke and Catherine Reily. On August 16, 1858, he baptized Patrick McNiclas, born July 5, 1858, child of Patrick McNiclas and Bridget Dayly. Sponsors were Patrick Brown and Mary O'Day. On August 16, 1858, Father Villiger baptized Thomas Foley, born July 4, 1858, child of Patrick Foley and Julia Moloney. Sponsor was Martin Cranstone. On August 20, 1858, he baptized Mary Galigher, born August 16, 1858, child of John Galigher and Mary Mulligan. Sponsor was James Mulligan. On August 24, 1858, he baptized Mary Jane Helpen, born May 4, 1858, child of John Helpen and Elizabeth Vance. Sponsors were Hugh Murphy and Mary Helpen. On September 2, 1858, Father Villiger baptized Elizabeth Brushnaham, born August 17, 1858, child of Patrick Brushnaham and Margaret Sweeny. Sponsor was Catherine Fogarty. On September 4, 1858, he baptized Peter McCormick, child of James McCormick and Alice Breen. Sponsors were Michael McCoy and Ann White. On September 12, 1858, he baptized John Brothers, born March 14, 1858, child of John Brothers and Catherine O'Neal. Sponsors were Thomas Sullivan and Rose Dougherty. On September 12, 1858, Father Villiger baptized Catherine Brothers, born March 14, 1858, (twin) child of John Brothers and Catherine O'Neal. Sponsors were John Lockey and Mary Brothers. On September 12, 1858, he baptized Sarah Elizabeth Remer, born May 24, 1858, child of Joseph Remer and Otilia Higler. Sponsors were Michael Stauband Christine Staub. On September 12, 1858, he baptized Margaret Higler, born July 15, 1858, child of Joseph Higler and Christine Siver. Sponsors were Joseph Remer and Otilia Higler. On September 12, 1858, Father Villiger baptized James Dorsey, born August 11, 1858, child of Patrick Dorsey and Honora Shehan. Sponsors were Thomas Sullivan and Catherine O'Donnel. On September 26, 1858, he baptized John McCloskey, born August 27, 1858, child of James McCloskey and Mary Bradley.

Sponsor was Anna Bradly. On September 26, 1858, he baptized Ellen Donlon, born July 31, 1858, child of Peter Donlon and Bridget Cosgrove. Sponsors were Thomas Cosgrove and Mary Cosgrove. On October 3, 1858, Father Villiger baptized John Gahagen, born September 8, 1858, child of James Gahagen and Mary Glassy. Sponsors were James Farrell and Mary Gahagen. On October 9, 1858, he baptized Ellen Jane Moore, born September 1, 1858, child of John Moore and Mary Hicky. Sponsors were Patrick Hicky and Mary Mullen. On October 9, 1858, he baptized Elsie Loretta Booker, born June 17, 1858, child of Francis Jerome Booker and Susanna Rebecca Booker. Sponsors were Benjamin Green and Mary Thomas. On October 18, 1858 Father Villiger baptized Margaret Ahern, born November 15, 1857, child of Jeremiah Ahern and Catherine Collins. Sponsor was Margaret Ahern. On October 18, 1858, he baptized Thomas Horen, born August 7, 1858, child of Richard Horen and Catherine Brice. Sponsors were Timothy Hartnett and Joan Collins. On November 6, 1858, he baptized Charlotte Congdon, born October 21, 1858, child of William Thomas Congdon and Ellen Farmer. Sponsors were Bartholomew and Catherine Shea. On November 6, 1858, Father Villiger baptized Ellen McCarthy, born October 26, 1858, child of Eugene McCarthy and Ellen Creedon. Sponsors were James Vaughan and Elizabeth McCarthy. On November 7, 1858, he baptized Jeremiah Mahegan, born November 7, 1858, child of Arthur Mahegan and Jane McCarty. Sponsors were Jeremiah Reagan and Ellen McCarty. On November 28, 1858, he baptized Jane Britt, born October 25, 1858, child of John Britt and Jane Baly. Sponsors were John Larkin and Rose Dougherty. On November 29, 1858, Father Villiger baptized James Kilmartin, born October 1, 1857, child of James Kilmartin and Ellen McPartland. Sponsor was Margaret Mara. On November 29, 1858, he baptized Ellen Foly, born September 11, 1858, child of John Foly and Ellen Dee. Sponsor was Jane Donohoe. On November 29, 1858 he baptized Catherine Foly, born August 7, 1858, child of Timothy Foly and Mary Scanlan. Sponsor was Margaret McCarty. On November 29, 1858, he baptized James Hartnett, born September 11, 1858, child of Timothy Hartnett and Margaret Connor. Sponsors were James and Mary Hartnett. On November 29, 1858, Father Villiger baptized David Horan, born November 12, 1858, child of John Horan and Margaret Ahern. Sponsors were William Hartnett and Elizabeth Lions. On December 23, 1858, he baptized Catherine Dilhofer, born November 17, 1858, child of Martin Dilhofer and Dorothy Staffer. Sponsor was Cecelia Haley. On December 24, 1858, he baptized Harriett Gieves, born November 30, 1858, child of Anna Gieves. Sponsor was Mary Wasly. On January 6, 1859, Father Villiger baptized John James Corbaley, born December 27, 1858, child of John Corbaley and Martha Mary Hutchinson. Sponsor was William Hutchinson. On February 20, 1859, Father Villiger baptized Charlotte Rosalie Murray, born December 15, 1858, daughter of Daniel Murray and Catherine Cook. Sponsor was Elizabeth Willson. On February 20, 1859, *at Kent County* he baptized John Thomas Sweeney, born January 15, 1858, son of Bernard Sweeney and Mary McFadden. Sponsors were John and Elizabeth Grady. On March 16, 1859, Father Villiger baptized Anna McAlister, born February 21, 1859, child of Robert McCalister and Mary Dillon. Sponsors were William McGeogan and Mary McAlister. (Father Nota filled in for Father Villiger from April 1859 to September, 1859). On September 10, 1859, Father Villiger baptized Charles Henry Cady, born July 15, 1859, child of Henry Cady and Mary Gibbs. Sponsor was Mary Huston. On September 11, 1859, he baptized Ellen Dayly, born February 1, 1859, child of James Dayly and Mary Broders. Sponsors were Mary and Margaret Broders. On October 15, 1859, Father Villiger baptized John Bohen, born June 3, 1859, child of John Bohen and Jane Katen. Sponsors were Patrick Bohen and Mary Sahan. On October 23, 1859, he baptized Lewis George, born August 6, 1859, child of Nicholas George and Paulina Baby. Sponsors were Lewis Eberhart and Teresa Drake. On October 23, 1859, he baptized Christopher Burns, born September 2, 1859, child of Christopher Burns and Mary Dougherty. Sponsors were John Lockay and Rose Dougherty. On November 12, 1859, he baptized John Collins, born August 24, 1856, child of Thomas Collins and Julia Wigens. Sponsor was Ellen Collins. On December 21, 1859, *at Kent County* he baptized George Frisbey, son of William Frisbey and Margaret Berryman. Sponsor was Elizabeth Willson. On January 12, 1860, Father Villiger baptized Rose Ann Vandegrift, born September 2, 1859, child of George Vandegrift and Maria Cosgriff. Sponsor was Pat Cosgriff. On January 21, 1860, he baptized Haslet Chrysostom Crawford, born December 20, 1859, child of Samuel Crawford and Anna Maria Fogler. Sponsors were J. L. Hickey and Margaret Morton. On January 22, 1860, Father Villiger baptized John Peter Ahern, born December 6, 1859, child of

Dennis Ahern and Ann Alworth. Sponsors were Patrick O'Neal and Mary Desmond. On March 25, 1860, he baptized Margaret Miser, born February 2, 1860, child of Michael Miser and Bridget Dayly. Sponsors were Joseph Miser and Bridget Lary. On April 8, 1860, he baptized Margaret Higler, born December 15, 1859, child of John Higler and Sarah Lambert. Sponsor was Rose Dougherty. On April 16, 1860, he baptized McMahon, born March 4, 1860, child of John McMahon and Ann McConaghy. Sponsor was William Thomas. On April 16, 1860, Father Villiger baptized John Woodlan, born November 15, 1859, child of Joseph Woodlan and Alethy Seul. Sponsor was Jane Thomas. On April 16, 1860, he baptized Catherine Dugan, born March 30, 1860, child of Daniel Dugan and Catherine Mannan. Sponsor was Jane A. Dixon. On April 1, 1860, he baptized Maria Christina Reinhart, born October 23, 1859, child of Lewis Reinhart and Isabella Ertell. Sponsor was Alma Craddock. On April 16, 1860, he baptized William David Bromer, born February 10, 1859, child of David Bromer and Maria Boger. Sponsor was Alma Craddock. On May 1, 1860, Father Villiger baptized Theresia Cecelia Price, born March 31, 1860, child of Thomas L. Price and Mary Corbaley. Sponsor was Ann Price. On May 13, 1860, he baptized Georgia Anna Stant, born April 3, 1860, child of Daniel Stant and July Ann Webb. Sponsor was Mary Houston. On May 15, 1860, he baptized Oliver Baby, born September 22, 1859, child of Rose Baby. Sponsor was Elizabeth Richardson. On May 27, 1860, he baptized Leverine Roberson, born April 17, 1860, child of Sam Roberson and Isabella Gasaney. Sponsor was Maria Houston. On May 27, 1860, Father Villiger baptized Mary Cosgriff, born January 10, 1860, child of Patrick Cosgriff and Margaret Donolan. Sponsor was Margaret Cosgriff. On May 27, 1860, he baptized Maria Victoria Price, born October 5, 1859, child of William H. Price and Mary Richardson. Sponsor was Anne McCafferty. On May 27, 1860, he baptized Mary Cahill, born March 16, 1860, child of Dominic Cahill and Marie Elizabeth Muthrie. Sponsors were Margaret Siber and Constance Lewis. On May 27, 1860, he baptized Margaret Dorsey, born April 27, 1860, child of Patrick Dorsey and Honora Shehan. Sponsor was Catherine Degnan. On June 7, 1860, Father Villiger baptized Robert Bready, born January 2, 1860, child of George Bready and Harriett Jones. Sponsor was Susan Flintham. On June 15, 1860, he baptized Thomas Donelan, born March 10, 1860, child of Peter Donelan and Bridget Cosgriff. Sponsor was Rose Cosgriff. On July 4, 1860, he conditionally baptized Benjamin Walmsly, born February 7, 1819, child of John Walmsly and Margaret Barnsby. No sponsor given. On July 8, 1860, Father Villiger baptized Samuel Waters, colored, born May 24, 1860, child of Emory Waters and Anna E. Hughes. Sponsor was Mary Ann Houston. On July 23, 1860, Father Villiger baptized Hugh Brothers, born January 13, 1860, child of John Brothers and Catherine O'Neal. Sponsor was Charles Burns. On August 13, 1860, he baptized Daniel Amos Canmal, born February 1, 1858, child of Leahy Canmal and Catherine McBride. Sponsors were Dennis Ahern and Ann Ahern. On October 24, 1860, Father Villiger baptized Daniel Murry, born June 15, 1860, child of Daniel Murry and Catherine Cook. Sponsor was Henrietta Willson. On October 28, 1860, he baptized Martin Beehan, born August 30, 1860, child of John Beehan and Jane Katen. Sponsor was John Lockman. On November 5, 1860, he baptized Agnes Evans, born July 28, 1860, child of William Evans and Ellen B. Lynam. On December 3, 1860, Father Villiger baptized John Amery, born March 24, 1859, child of Robert Amery and Priscilla Abbott. Sponsor was Agnes Johnson. On December 3, 1860 he baptized Maria Amery, born June 6, 1860, child of Robert Amery and Priscilla Abbott. Sponsor was Agnes Johnson. On December 18, 1860, Father Villiger baptized *at Kent County* Louisa, born November 12, 1860, daughter of Ann James (colored). Sponsor was Ann Martha Willson. On June 8, 1862, Father Villiger baptized Thomas McCallister, born May 29, 1862, child of Robert McCallister and Mary Dillin. Sponsors were James McCallister and Ellen Dillin. On June 8, 1862, he baptized John Smith, born February 6, 1862, child of William Smith and Mary Gisetling. Sponsors were John Christian and Waldburger Wildman. On June 17, 1862, he baptized Maria Ann Beck, born January 20, 1862, daughter of John beck and Elizabeth Trimble. Sponsors were Thomas B. Willson and Virginia Ewing. On June 17, 1862, Father Villiger baptized Ann Rebecca Murray (colored) born June 16, 1862, child of Adam Murry and Ann James. Sponsor was Ann Marthy Willson. On June 22, 1862, he baptized Joseph Schafer, born May 28, 1861, child of Joseph Schafer and Catherine Huber. Sponsors were Joseph and Mary Kirchner. On June 29, 1862, he baptized Edward Perry Walters (colored), born May 18, 1862, child of Emory Walters and Anna Hughes. Sponsor was Mary Robison. On July 27, 1862, Father Villiger baptized Rosalia Kliiber, born December 15, 1861, child of Lewis Kliiber and Placida Eisele. Sponsor was Francis Kautz. On July 27, 1862, he baptized James Edward Kearns, born June 20, 1862, child of James Kearns and Mary Cosgrave. Sponsors were Hugh Donahue and Anne Corrigan. On July 28, 1862, he baptized William Barr Murphy, born December 28, 1861, child of Thomas Murphy and Rosalie Money. Sponsor was Mary Ann Wigman. On January 10, 1861, Father Villiger baptized George Clemens Reily, born November 2, 1860, child of Abraham Reily and Caroline Jones. Sponsor was Susanna Perkins. On February 5, 1861, he baptized Julia Elizabeth Morton, born December 3, 1860, child of Hamilton Morton and Mary Teresa Durkee. Sponsors were Michael Angelo and Henrietta Catherine Durney. On February 9, 1861, he baptized Robert McCalister, born January 29, 1861, child of Robert McCalister and Mary Dillin. Sponsors were Dennis McCalister and Catherine Derrah. On February 9, 1861, Father Villiger baptized William Lotringer, born December 28, 1860, child of Nicholas Lotringer and Christopher Pfeifer. Sponsors were Lawrence Pina and Mary O'Neal. On February 21, 1861, *at Kent County* he baptized Frederick Francis de Sales Willson, born June 6, 1860, son of George Willson and Henrietta Brooke. Sponsors were Francis and Georgia Willson. On February 24, 1861, Father Villiger baptized Peter James McCarroll, born August 25, 1860, child of Peter McCarroll and Catherine Kelly. Sponsors were Joanne Hamilton and Thomas McPherson. On May 12, 1861, he baptized Mary Britt, born April 29, 1861, child of John Britt and Jane Baby. Sponsors were William Ryan and Catherine Devine. On June 9, 1861, he baptized Edward Harrington, born April 8, 1861, child of Cornelus Harrington and Elizabeth McCarty. Sponsor was Ann McMahon. On June 9, 1861, Father Villiger baptized Carroll Conmeyer, born February 27, 1861, child of Carroll Conmeyer and Teresa Collins. Sponsor was Francis Gallies. On July 13, 1861, he baptized John Dorsey, born June 23, 1861, child of John Dorsey and Honora Shehan. Sponsor was Margaret Cradcock. On July 14, 1861, *at Kent County, Maryland* Father Villiger baptized Thomas Henry Willson, born January 9, 1861, child of Thomas Willson and Matilda Willson. Sponsor was Adelia Morton. On July 29, 1861, he baptized Susan Anne Gibbs, born December 27, 1860, child of George Gibbs and Emma Kenard. Sponsor was Mary Houston. On August 20, 1861, he baptized James McClosky, born May 18, 1861, child of James McClosky and Margaret Owens. Sponsor was Mrs. Nora Blunt. On August 20, 1861, Father Villiger baptized *at Kent County* Clement Joseph Beaeregard Willson, born May 5, 1861, son of Richard Bennett Willson and Anna Martha young. Sponsor was A. E. Willson. On August 27, 1861, he baptized Mary Sophia Willmer (colored) born May 1, 1861, child of Arthur Willmer and Caroline Carol. Sponsor was Augusta Lusby. On September 2, 1861 he baptized Josephine Corbaley, born August 28, 1861, child of Samuel Cerbaley and Elizabeth Craddock. Sponsors were Richard and Agnes R. Johnson. On September 8, 1861, Father Villiger baptized James Reid, born September 27, 1854, child of Ben Reid and Elizabeth Waugh. Sponsor was M. L. Morton. On September 8, 1861, he baptized George Reed, born March 23, 1856, child of Ben Reed and Elizabeth Waugh. Sponsor was Mary L. Morton. On September 8, 1861, he baptized Julius Reed, born March 23, 1856, child of Ben Reed and Elizabeth Waugh. Sponsor was Mary l. Morton. On September 8, 1861, he baptized Joseph Reed, born October 23, 1859, child of Ben Reed and Elizabeth Waugh. Sponsor was Mary L. Morton. On September 22, 1861, Father Villiger baptized George Vandegriff, born June 23, 1861, child of George Vandegriff and Maria Cosgriff. Sponsors were John Cosgriff and Marge Bowles. On September 22, 1861, he baptized Christine Kleiber, born October 20, 1859, child of Alois Kleiber and Blasinda Eisenlab. Sponsor was Christian Stant. On October 10, 1861, he baptized Alice McMahon, born October 6, 1861, child of John McMahon and Amy McLunchan. Sponsor was Mary Bowles. On October 13, 1861, Father Villiger baptized Robert Thomas Doglas, born September 13, 1861, child of Robert Doglas and Sarah Dara. Sponsors were John and Anne McMahon. On October 22, 1861, Father Villiger baptized *at Kent County* William Graffen Blunt, born September 11, 1861, son of Charles B. and Eleanora Willson. Sponsors were Carroll and Ann E. Willson. On October 22, 1861, he baptized Edward Joseph Beauregard Hamilton, born August 27, 1861, son of William Edward Hamilton and Anna Maria Willson. Sponsors were N. Willson and W. J. C. Duhamel. On December 17, 1861, he baptized Fuch, son of Mary Spence, colored. Sponsor was Georgianna Willson. On October 23, 1861, Father Villiger baptized Alexander Reynolds (colored), born September 18, 1861, child of James Reynolds and Henrietta Jones. Sponsor was Jane E. Kennard. On October 23, 1861, he baptized John Ringgold, (colored), born August 30, 1861, child of Reisden Ringgold and Ellen Brown. Sponsor was Jane E. Kennard. On August 23, 1861, he baptized Alphonsa Willmer (colored), born February 28, 1861, child of James Willmer and Ellen Right. Sponsor was Jane E. Kennard. On October 23, 1861, Father Villiger baptized Henrietta Augusta Rason, born September 23, 1860, child of John Rason and Mary Jane Baker. Sponsor was Jane E. Kennard. On November 10, 1861, he baptized Anna Margaret Christian, born June 19, 1860, child of Adam Christian and Anna Maria Yunker. Sponsors were John and Margaret Christian. On November 10, 1861, he baptized John Reily (colored), born August 17, 1861, child of Sam Reily and Rachel Henson. Sponsor was Isabella Robinson. On November 27, 1861, Father Villiger baptized Nolan Thomas Theodore Price, born November 10, 1861, child of Thomas J. Price and Mary Corbaley. Sponsor was Margaret Price. On December 8, 1861, he baptized Emile Elizabeth McKee, born November 27, 1861, child of John McKee and Mary O'Neal. Sponsors were John Loughery and Emilia Elizabeth Smith. On December 17, 1861, Father Villiger baptized Elizabeth Craddock, born September 30, 1861, child of Joseph Craddock and Martha Maslin. Sponsor was Corina Craddock. On December 23, 1861, he baptized Thomas O'Sullivan, born December 7, 1861, child of Thomas O'Sullivan and Catherine Sheehan. Sponsor was Joanna Ahern. On March 19, 1862, he baptized Margaret Maguire, born March 4, 1862, child of Peter Maguire and Sarah Kennedy. Sponsor was Bridget Donelan. On April 22, 1862, Father Villiger baptized Daniel McLane, born February 22, 1862, child of Thomas McLane and Mary McKee. Sponsors were William McKee and Emilia Thomas. On April 22, 1862, he baptized Alfred Francis Dixon, born March 5, 1862, child of Thomas Dixon and Jane Shields. Sponsors were William McKee and Emilia Thomas. On April 22, 1862, he baptized Wilhemina Komorin, born March 25, 1860, child of Isaac Komorin and Anna Becker. Sponsor was Joseph Zeizel. On April 22, 1862, Father Villiger baptized Joseph James Martin, born January 23, 1862, child of John Martin and Mary Bradly. Sponsor was Ann Cook. On April 25, 1862, *at Kent County* Father Villiger baptized Charles James, born April 25, 1860, son of Eliza James, colored. Sponsor was Martha Willson. On April 25, 1862, *at Kent County* he baptized Teresy Ann Murray, born December 18, 1861, child of Henry Murray and Julie Bentley. Sponsor was Martha Willson. On April 25, 1862, he baptized *at Kent County* Catherine Meier, born December 25, 1862, daughter of Joseph Meier and Catherine Connolly. Sponsors were Prosper Sibre and Margaret Sibre. On August 19, 1862, Father Villiger baptized William Joseph Murry (colored), born January 26, 1862, child of Mary Murry. Sponsor was Elizabeth Willson. On August 19, 1862, he baptized *at Kent County* Henrietta Berryman, born April 19, 1862, daughter of Margaret Berryman. Sponsor was Ann Maria Hamilton. On August 19, 1862, Father Villiger baptized *at Kent County* Robert Murray, born August 1, 1862, son of Daniel Murray and Catherine Cook. Sponsor was Henrietta Willson. On September 5, 1862, Father Villiger baptized Henry Johnson (colored), born April 18, 1862, child of John Johnson and Tammy Simms. Sponsor was Mary Robinson. On September 14, 1862, he baptized William Jenkins, born July 17, 1861, child of Jeremiah Jenkins and Ann Williams. Sponsor was Margaret Dunn. On September 14, 1862, he baptized Maria Margarita Sum, born November 18, 1859, child of John Sum and Antonetta Friedenback. Sponsor was Lewis Eberhardt. On September 20, 1862, Father Villiger baptized Mary Caroline Cohee, born September 1, 1862, child of James E. Cohee and Margaret Ellis. Sponsor was Ellen Evans. On September 20, 1862, he baptized Keven Andrew Cohee, born January 17, 1859, child of B. Franklin Cohee and Amanda Jones. Sponsor was Ellen Evans. On September 20, 1862, he baptized Margaret Eveline Cohee, born December 9, 1860, child of B. Franklin Cohee and Amanda Jones. Sponsor was Ellen Evans. On September 20, 1862, Father Villiger baptized Amanda Cohee, born June 6, 1862, child of B. Franklin Cohee and Amanda Jones. Sponsor was Ellen Evans. On October 2, 1862, he baptized Henry Haslett Crawford, born August 17, 1862, child of Samuel L. Crawford and Anna M. Fougler. Sponsors were John A. Durkan and Elizabeth C. Durkan. On October 20, 1862, he baptized Philip Gearing, born July 13, 1862, child of William Gearing and Catherine Flynn. Sponsors were Daniel and Catherine Dugan. On October 20, 1862, he baptized Remigius Felix Zisel, born October 15, 1862, child of Felix Zisel and Josephine Hederer. Sponsors were Gilmer Rime and Maria J. Heier. On October 20, 1862, Father Villiger baptized Thomas Gearing, born September 12, 1860, child of William Gearing and Catherine Flynn. Sponsors were Gottlieb Heier and Josephine Heier. On November 30, 1862, he baptized Christina Stapp, born September 1, 1862, child of Michael Stapp and Christina Koerbel. Sponsors were Nicholas Lutringer and Christina Pfifer.

On November 30, 1862, he baptized Otilia Roemer, born February 12, 1861, child of Joseph Roemer and Otilia Hügler. Sponsors were Michael Stapp and Christina Stapp. On December 14, 1862, he baptized Margaret Ahern, born October 6, 1862, child of Dennis Ahern and Ann Allworth. Sponsors were John Murphy and Catherine Sullivan. On December 14, 1862, Father Villiger baptized Emilia Luisa Ruly (colored), born July 10, 1862, child of George Ruly and Lilla Willson. Sponsor was Mary Roberson. On December 14, 1862, he baptized Mary Lynch, born July 28, 1862, child of Morris Lynch and Mary McGinnis. Sponsors were John McGinnis and Alice McNerhany. On December 14, 1862, he baptized James McNerhany, born November 30, 1862, child of James McNerhany and Alice Magoff. Sponsors were John and Mary McNerhany. On December 15, 1862, he baptized Michael Dorsey, born November 22, 1862, child of Patrick Dorsey and Honora Shehan. Sponsors were Patrick Shehan and Joanna Ahearn. On January 12, 1863, Father Villiger baptized Charles Heart, no date of birth given, child of John Heart and Barbara Pauris. Sponsor was Mary Reily. On February 8, 1863, he baptized John McMahon, born January 29, 1863, child of John McMahon and Anne McConaghy. Sponsors were James and Elizabeth Divine. On March 8, 1863, he baptized Sam Thomas Briscoe (colored), born February 25, 1863, child of Jarvis Briscoe and Cecelia Ann Fountain. Sponsor was Margaret Louisa Queen. On March 23, 1863, he baptized Elizabeth Ganon, born February 2, 1863, child of Joseph Ganon and Margaret Hashen. Sponsors were James Powderly and Mary Dougherty. On March 29, 1863, Father Villiger baptized conditionally Rachael Newsome, born February 28, 1842, daughter of Martin Newsome and Susan Ann Clayton. No sponsors given. On April 21, 1863, he baptized James Thomas James (colored), born on March 30, 1863, child of Catherine James. Sponsor was Carroll Willson. On May 10, 1863, he baptized John Ceile, born April 15, 1863, child of Dominic Ceile and Maria Elise Matier. Sponsors were Thomas and Rose Murry. On April 21, 1863, he baptized Mary Alice James, born 1860, child of Lewisa James. Sponsor was Margaret Wally. On May 10, 1863, Father Villiger baptized Victor Ceile, born April 15, 1863, child of Dominic Ceile and Maria Elisa Matier. Sponsor was Ellen Bowls. On May 10, 1863, he baptized John Kanz, born February 16, 1863, child of Fridolin Kanz and Francesca Burger. Sponsor was Maria Elisa Matier. On May 10, 1863, he baptized Mary Elizabeth Semmes (colored) born June 10, 1841, daughter of Raphael Semmes and Anastasia his wife. Sponsor was Mary Amanda Roberson. On May 18, 1863, he baptized Alice Scott, born July 27, 1862, child of Isaac Scott and Rachael Turner. Sponsor was J. E. Kennard. On May 18, 1863, Father Villiger baptized Henrietta Jones (colored), born January 9, 1863, child of Ben Jones and Margaret Ward. Sponsor were J. E. Kennard. On May 18, 1863, he baptized Wilhelmina Wilmer (colored), born July 4, 1862, child of James Wilmer and Ellen Right. Sponsor was J. E. Kennard. On May 18, 1863, he baptized Isabella Rason, born August 4, 1862, child of John Rason and Mary Rebecca. Sponsor was J. E. Kennard. On May 24, 1863, he baptized Mary Ann Anwill, born September 20, 1862, child of Edward Anwill. Sponsors were Thomas McPherson and Catherine McCarroll. On May 31, 1863, Father Villiger baptized Elizabeth Lutringer, born January 1, 1863, child of Nicolas Lutringer and Christine Pfifer. Sponsors were Michael Staub and Christine Staub. On June 6, 1863, he baptized Francis Wilmer Walmsley, born September 29, 1362, child of Benjamin Franklin Walmsley and Frances Wilmer Briscoe. Sponsor was Mary Agnes Skidmore. On June 28, 1863, he baptized William Kormyer, born March 28, 1863, child of Carroll Kormyer and Theresa Gillis. Sponsor was Gregory Lotringer. On June 28, 1863, Father Villiger baptized Helen Morton, born May 22, 1863, child of Hamilton Morton, and Mary Theresa Durkie. Sponsors were Henry Morton and Virginia Bond. On April 26, 1859, *at East Neck, Kent County* Father Nota baptized Alonzo, about 12 years old, servant of George Willson. Sponsor was Elizabeth Willson. April 26, 1859 *at East Neck, Kent County* he baptized Henrietta, born February 19, 1859, daughter of Louisa, a servant of Carroll Willson. Sponsor was Maria, a servant of Dr. Thomas Willson. On April 26, 1859, *at East Neck, Kent County*, he baptized Louisa, born July 31, 1858, daughter of Andrew, servant of James Wicke and his wife, a servant of Anne Marie Willson. Sponsor was Anne Marie Willson. On April 27, 1859, *at Chestertown, Kent County*, Father Nota baptized James Glen Alvin Greet, born June 25, 1857, son of William Greet and Mary A. Birch. Sponsors were Joseph Craddock and Mrs. Susanna Delenaux. On May 4, 1859, he baptized James Campbell, born September 11, 1858, child of Andrew Campbell and Catherine Byrnes. Sponsors were James Malone and Ellen Bowles. On May 6, 1859, he baptized Craddock Lusby, born November 27, 1858, child of Thomas Lusby and

Mary Ellen Lusby. Sponsor was Margaret Price. On May 6, 1859, he baptized Robert Henry Hensen, born March 9, 1859, child of Rachael Hensen of Mrs. Susanna Perkins. Sponsor was Susanna Perkins. On May 22, 1859, Father Nota baptized Bridget Troy, born April 22, 1859, child of Michael Troy and Hanna Murphy. Sponsors were Charles Byrnes and Sarah Drake. On June 7, 1859, *at Chesapeake City*, Father Nota baptized Mary Ann Ganzeling, born January 22, 1859, daughter of Jacob Ganzeling and Margaret Junker. Sponsor was Mary Anne Christian. On June 7, 1859, *at Chesapeake City*, he baptized Margaret Eliza Christian, born April 28, 1859, daughter of Adam Christian and Mary Ann Junker. Sponsor was Margaret Ganzeling. On June 7, 1859, Father Nota baptized Margaret Eliza Christian, born April 28, 1859, child of Adam Christian and Mary Ann Junker. Sponsor was Margaret Ganzeling. On June 12, 1859, he baptized Nicholas Lutheranger, born February 11, 1858, child of Nicholas Lutheranger and Christine Pfifer. Sponsors were Laurence Peire and Mary McCallister. On June 12, 1859, he baptized Mary Kearne, born April 1, 1859, child of John Kearn and Ellen Leary. Sponsors were Jeremiah Leary and Ellen Kearn. On June 15, 1859, *in East Neck, Kent County*, he baptized Paul Alexander Willson, born June 3, 1859, son of Richard Bennett Willson and Ann Martha Young. Sponsors were Maurice Augustine Willson and Sara Jane Davidson. On June 16, 1859, *in Chestertown, Maryland*, he baptized Thomas Dillon, born March 13, 1859, son of John Dixon and Ellen McGrughan. Sponsors were Thomas and Mary McClane. On June 26, 1859, he baptized Oswell Mann, born April 1, 1859, child of Patrick Mann and Catherine Mannon. Sponsors were Thomas and Mary Jeannette Craddock. On June 26, 1859, Father Nota baptized Ella Frances Othoson, born May 9, 1859, child of John Othoson and Mary Ann Pearson. Sponsors were James Oliver and Virginia Bond. On July 22, 1859, *at Bohemia*, Father Nota baptized William Toomey, born January 14, 1859, son of Jeremiah Toomey and Ellen Flinn (from Delaware). Sponsor was Mary Devine. On July 28, 1859, *in Dover, Delaware*, Father Nota baptized Margaret Elizabeth Daily and Johanna Pierce. Sponsors were Cornelus Harrington and Elizabeth Harrington, his wife. On August 14, 1859, he baptized Maria Schetzely, born April 14, 1859, child of Joseph Schetzely and Sarah Hughes. Sponsor was Mary Teresa Grammenger. On August 17, 1859, *at East Neck, Kent County*, he baptized Margaret McCloskey, born June 22, 1859, daughter of James McCloskey and Margaret Owens. Sponsors were Charles Willson and Mrs. Ann Clarke, On August 17, 1859, he baptized *at East Neck, Kent County* Laurence Murray, born June 27, 1859, son of Henry Murray, servant of James Wickes and Julia, his wife, servant of Martha Willson. Sponsor was Henrietta Maria Willson. *Buried at Bohemia* in 1859 was Catherine Brothers, sixteen months old, daughter of Catherine O'Neil Brothers.

FATHER VILLIGER'S WEDDINGS AT BOHEMIA:
On October 28, 1856, between Patrick Mangern and Sarah Williams. Witnesses were Patrick Walsh and Margaret Walsh. On November 17, 1856, between Patrick Shannon and Bridget Hannah. Witnesses were Philip Cahill and Ellen Reilly. On January 6, 1857, between Francis Sutter and Mary Hicky. Witnesses were John Sullivan and Catharine McBride. On March 7, 1857, between Francis Thomas and Susanna R. Rooker. Witnesses were Casovo B. and Benjamin Thomas. On March 22, 1857, between Joseph Meier and Catherine Conley. Witnesses were John Burchard and Patrick Mackin. On October 15, 1857, between John Horan and Margaret Ahern. Witnesses were Dennis Lyons and Michael Kennedy. On November 8, 1857, between John More and Mary hickey. Witnesses were Daniel Mullen and Patrick Hicky. On January 25, 1858, between John Corbaley and Martha M. Hutchinson. Witnesses were Thomas t. Price and Mary Emily Price. On March 15, 1858, between Michael Burns and Bridget Quinn. No witnesses given. On August 10, 1858, between Dennis Dwyer and Rachael Rebecca Willis. Witnesses were Nelly Greenwell and William Rise. On December 15, 1858, between James Flanigan and Anna Mullen. Witnesses were Patrick Fitzpatrick and Maria Mullen. On December 15, 1858, between James Flanigan and Anne Mullen. Witnesses were Patrick Fitzpatrick and Maria Mullen. On December 15, 1858, between John Haly and Cecelia Stanfer. On January 6, 1859, between Henry Carty and Ellen Gibbs. Witnesses were Thomas John and Eleanora Rhodes. On January 9, 1859, between Dennis Sullyvan and Catherine McCafferty. Witnesses were John Mahan and Catherine Divine. On March 3, 1859, between William Griffin and Margaret O'Mar. Witnesses were John Finn and Catherine O'Reily. On October 29, 1859, between Robert Sullivan and Mary Hartnett. Witnesses were Timothy Hartnett and Jane

Hartnett. On November 12, 1859, between Thomas Collins and Ellen Hahey. Witnesses were Jeremiah Riordan and Richard Johnson. On October 18, 1860, between Ashbary Sappington and Mary Thomas. Witnesses were Samuel Merritt and Albert Corey. On November 27, 1860, between Charles Blunt and Ellen Willson. Witnesses were Carroll Willson and Maria Tilghman. On February 10, 1861, between Thomas O'Sullivan and Catherine O'Donnell. Witnesses were Patrick Dorsey and Hugh McGonigle. On April 5, 1861, between James Powderly and Margaret Dunn. Witness were John Harrigan and June Britt. On February 17, 1862, between Adam H. Murry, colored, and Ann Willson Jones. Witnesses were Marty and Ann E. Willson. On December 22, 1862, between Alexander McNeil and Bridget McClaman. Witnesses were Daniel McClaman and Margaret Mullin. On December 28, 1862, between Thomas Dunn and Bridget Nolan. Witnesses were Patrick Quinn and Catharine Connor. On December 31, 1862, between Isaac Queen and Fedis Ann Cain. Witnesses were Thomas Roberson and Margaret Queen. On April 4, 1863, between George L. Bryan and Mary Hester Willson, both of Queen Anne County. Witnesses were Thomas and Carroll Willson. On August 26, 1863, between John Strokes and Ann Colary. Witnesses were Ellen and Mary Bowls. On October 19, 1863, between William B. Bean and Emily Thomas. Witnesses were William Thomas and Elizabeth T. Hyder. On October 19, 1863, between William Thomas and Elizabeth Hyder. Witnesses were William and Emily Bean. On January 18, 1864, between John C. Scofield and Anna McCafferty. Witnesses were John C. Manlove and Mary E. McCafferty. On January 18, 1865, between Daniel Mullin and Rose Murry. Witnesses were James Mullin and Anna Creeney. On February 2, 1864, between Francis Murry and Ellen Bowls. Witnesses were James Bagly and Mary Bowls. On February 9, 1864, between Henry Fox and Mary Roberson. Witnesses were Thomas A. Queen and Margaret Queen. On April 26, 1864, between F. Adolph Wallis and Georgia Willson. Witnesses were Samuel Roseberry and Philip F. Raisin. On August 5, 1864, between William H. Moffitt and Elizabeth Gready. Witnesses were John Burris and Ann Finn. On November 10, 1864, between George W. Morris, colored, and Emily Queen. Witnesses were William Johnson and Margaret Queen. On January 12, 1865, between Joseph C. Wright and Christy Hinson. Witnesses were James Scott and Terry Wright. On May 23, 1865, between James B. Sappington and Gertrude Craddock. Witnesses were John A. Schmearer and Margaret Sappington. On July 20, 1865, between John C. Manlove and Mary E. McCafferty. Witnesses were John E. Scoffield and Anne Scoffield. On November 9, 1865, between Thomas Guigly and Susan McKee. Witnesses were N. McKee and Roberta McCallister. On January 26, 1866, between L. L. Taylor and E. F. Watkins. Witnesses were John McCallister and Peter Chisholm. On March 22, 1866, between Edward Perkins, colored, and Susan Briscoe. Witnesses were William Smallwood and Susan Perkins. On November 8, 1866, between James S. Asy and Margaret L. Cail. Witnesses were Hugh McGonigle and Edward Robrecht. On June 20, 1866, between Samuel Thomas Robinson, colored, and Caroline Chandler. Witnesses were Robert Gardiner and Mary Ann Gibbs. On October 11, 1866, between George T. Moore, colored, and Josephine Brown. Witnesses were Henry Rimbaugh and Mary Gardener. On February 13, 1867, between John T. Beaston and Mary A. Reilly. Witnesses were James Marley and John Murry. On August 25, 1867, between Thomas W. Dugan and Corinne Helen Craddock. Witnesses were Theodore and May Craddock. On October 14, 1867, between John Gready and Bridget Connor. Witnesses were Patrick Gready and Catharine Connor. On November 3, 1867, between Robert C. Corbaley and Laura Helen Bond. Witnesses were William T. Noble and Jeremiah Reynolds. On January 2, 1868 between Peter McCardle and Bridget Maher. Witnesses were Bernard McCafferty and Jane Cohey. On January 10, 1868, between John Clark and Rosina Gattis. Witnesses were William Spry and Sarah Clarke.

37. "Newtown Manor," *Woodstock Letters* 15 (1886) 28. After leaving Bohemia, Father Nota returned to teach dogmatic theology at Georgetown. In 1861, he became professor of logic, metaphysics, and ethics at the same college. In 1868, he was professor of logic, metaphysics, and ethics at Holy Cross College, Worcester, Massachusetts. On April 5, 1870, he died at Holy Cross College. Devitt, "History of the Province," *Woodstock Letters* 63 (1934) 38

WEDDING BY FATHER NOTA AT BOHEMIA:
On June 12, 1859, between Patrick Fitzpatrick and Mary Mullens. Witnesses were Patrick and Anne Mullens.

38. Baltimore *The Catholic Mirror* August 1, 1885, "Rev. L. S. Malloy;" Clarence V. Joerndt, *St. Ignatius Hickory, Maryland and Its Missions* (Baltimore, Maryland: Publication Press, 1972) 260, 308-309
39. Daniel J. McGlynn, *Celebrating Our Faith, Past, Present, Future: History of Immaculate Conception Parish, Elkton, Maryland, 1849-1999* (Elkton, Maryland: Immaculate Conception Church, 1999) 7
40. Spalding *Premier See* 177-178
41. Thomas W. Spalding, *Martin John Spalding: American Churchman* (Washington, D.C.: The Catholic University of America, 1973) 157-158. On April 3, the pope confirmed his nomination to Baltimore. Spalding received the bulls on June 9, and departed from Louisville on July 10.
42. Spalding, *Premier See* 179: He was born in 1810, attended Urban College in Rome before ordination, became Coadjutor – bishop of Louisville in 1848. He had been earmarked by Archbishop Kenrick to play a leading role at the First Plenary Council of Baltimore in 1852. APF *Acta* 228: 841 – "Pious, zealous, learned, eloquent, amiable, highly regarded in Baltimore, and of Maryland origin."
43. Spalding, *Spalding* 128.; Leo Francis Stock, "Catholic Participation in the Diplomacy of the Southern Confederacy" *Catholic Historical Review* 16 (January, 1930) 1-18
44. On July 26, 1863, Father Villiger baptized Frances Kleiber, born March 4, 1863, child of Aloysius Kleiber and Placida Eisele. Sponsor was E. Bowls. On July 27, 1863, he baptized Joseph Wilmer (colored), born July 16, 1863, child of Arthur Wilmer and Caroline Carwell. Sponsor was Catherine Lusby. On August 18, 1863, *at Kent County* Father Villiger baptized John Charles Beck, born September 29, 1858, son of John Beck and Elizabeth Maslin Trimble. Sponsors were Charles and Elizabeth Willson. On August 18, 1863, *at Kent County*, Father Villiger baptized James Brooke Hamilton, born July 1, 1863, son of William E. Hamilton and Ann Marie Willson, his wife. Sponsors were Francis Willson and Ann Hamilton. On August 30, 1863, Father Villiger baptized Michael Sullivan, born August 7, 1863, child of Thomas Sullivan and Catherine Shehan. Sponsors were Patrick Dorsey and Catherine Dynan. On September 5, 1863, he baptized Rebecca Burns, born November 23, 1862, child of Christopher Burns and Mary Dougherty. Sponsor was Ann Williams. On September 13, 1863, he baptized William Vandergrift, born June 1, 1863, child of George Vandergrift and Maria Cosgriff. Sponsor was Mary Bowles. On October 20, 1863, *at Kent County* he baptized Lydia Murray, colored, born September 1, 1863, daughter of Henry Murray and Aelisa his wife. Sponsor was Anna Willson. On October 20, 1863, he baptized *at Kent County* Samuel Murray, born October 3, 1863, son of Henry Murray and Julie Bentley, his wife. Sponsor was Martha Willson. On October 20, 1863, he baptized Louisa James, born June 15, 1863, child of Elisa James. Sponsor was Henrietta Willson. On October 25, 1863, Father Villiger baptized John Cosgriff, born October 11, 1863, child of Thomas Cosgriff and Catherine Boglen. Sponsors were John Cosgriff and Bridget Boglen. On October 30, 1863, he baptized John Mooney Chrisfield Murphy, born April 9, 1859, child of Hyland Price Thomas Murphy and Rosaline Romuald Mooney. Sponsor was Harriet Mooney. On November 4, 1863, he baptized Francis Wolff Murphy, born October 24, 1863, child of Hyland Price Thomas Murphy and Rosaline Romuald Mooney. Sponsor was Harriet Mooney. On December 23, 1863, Father Villiger baptized John Thomas McLane, born December 4, 1863, child of Thomas McLane and Mary McKee. Sponsors were Daniel and Hannah McKee. On January 28, 1864, he baptized Edward Carroll Lockwood, born June 5, 1863, child of Edward William Lockwood and Sara Elizabeth Alricks. Sponsors were Michael Angelo and Henrietta Durney. On June 28, 1864, he baptized Ada Letitia Lockwood, born August 26, 1859, child of Edward William Lockwood and Elizabeth Alricks. Sponsors were Michael Angelo and Henrietta Durney. On February 25, 1864, Father Villiger *at Kent County* baptized Henrietta Murry, born January 8, 1864, child of Adam Murry and Ann James. Sponsor was Ann M. Willson. On March 21, 1864, he baptized Margaret Emma Morgan (colored), born July 15, 1863, child of Edward Morgan and Elizabeth Pierce. Sponsor was E. J. Kennard. On March 21, 1864, he baptized Adeline Rason, born October 27, 1863, child of John Rason and Mary Jane Baker. Sponsor was E. J. Kennard. On April 18, 1865, Father Villiger baptized James Zisel, born February 25, 1864, child of Felix Zisel and Josephine Hiderer. Sponsors were Theodore Craddock and Mary Gillmore. On April 19, 1864, at Kent County he baptized Margaret Virginia Hurst, born July 14, 1863, child of John A. Hurst and Margaret Scott. Sponsor was Georgia Willson. On April 24, 1864, he baptized Mary Helen Crawford, born March 3,

1864, child of Crawford and Ann M. Fougler. Sponsor was Helen Ford. On May 22, 1864, Father Villiger baptized Charles John McCallister, born April 30, 1864, child of Robert McCallister and Mary Dillon. Sponsors were Hugh Horgan and Mary McGrogan. On May 29, 1864, he baptized Charity Bready, born March 5, 1864, child of George Bready and Harriet Jones. Sponsor was Christy Hinson. On June 20, 1864, *at Kent County* he baptized Murry, (colored), born May 14, 1864, child of Daniel Murry and Catherine Cook. Sponsor was Henrietta Willson. On June 20, 1864, he baptized Emilia Murry, born April 23, 1864, child of Mary Murry. Sponsor was Elizabeth Willson. On June 26, 1864, Father Villiger baptized John Christian Flintham, born April 4, 1862, child of William Flintham and Caroline Elizabeth, his wife. Sponsor was Susan Ann Flintham. On July 8, 1864, he baptized Catherine Dorsey, born June 20, 1864, child of Patrick Dorsey and Mary Honora Shehan. Sponsor was Mary Dorsey. On July 31, 1864, he conditionally baptized Washington Morris, born March, 1841, child of Matthew Morris and Catherine Morris. No sponsors given. On August 2, 1864, Father Villiger baptized Mary Powderly, born May 11, 1864, child of James Powderly and Margaret Dunn. Sponsor was Theresia Druka. On September 1, 1864, he baptized Ann Ganon, born May 22, 1864, child of Joseph Ganon and Margaret Hessiger. Sponsor was John Carroll and Ann A. H. Ahern. On September 7, 1864, he baptized George Callaghan, born August 18, 1864, child of James Callaghan and Margaret Cosgriff. Sponsor was Agnes Stap. On September 7, 1861, Father Villiger baptized Maria Francisca Theresa Bauman, born December 27, 1863, child of Joseph Bauman and Francisca Meier. Sponsor was Agnes Stap. On September 11, 1864, he baptized Anna Maria Remer, born April 6, 1864, child of Joseph Remer and Otilia Hiigler. Sponsor was Agnes Stap. On September 11, 1864, he baptized Anna Maria Sirchler, born February 14, 1864, child of Joseph Sirchler and Seraphia Hiigler. Sponsor was Otilia Hughes. On September 11, 1864, he baptized Anna Elizabeth Hiigler, born January 19, 1864, child of Joseph Hiigler and Christian Sider. Sponsor was Agnes Stap. On September 26, 1864, Father Villiger baptized Charles Augustus Dreka, born August 26, 1864, child of Augustus Dreka and Theresa Schnepf. Sponsor was Eva Hans. On October 5, 1864, he baptized Joseph Humphry Bailey (colored) born May 2, 1864, child of Rose Bailey. Sponsor was Constantine Richardson. On October 5, 1864, he baptized May Jeminy Bailey (colored), born March 25, 1862, child of Rose Bailey. Sponsor was Elisa M. Richardson. On October 7, 1864, Father Villiger baptized Thomas Henry Simons, born April 5, 1853, child of James Willson Simons and Mary Elizabeth, his wife. Sponsor was Mary Houston. On October 7, 1864, he baptized James Willson Simons, born March 10, 1860, child of James Willson Simons and Mary Elizabeth, his wife. Sponsor was Mary Houston. On October 9, 1864, he baptized Samuel Joseph Lemuel Pierson, born August 9, 1864, child of Robert L. Pierson and Elizabeth Wooters. Sponsor was Sarah Wooters. On October 23, 1864, Father Villiger baptized William Bogenshiite, born October 7, 1863, child of Michael Bogenshiite and Waldberga Schumaker. Sponsors were Kasper Schumaker and Crescentia Schumaker. On October 30, 1864, at Kent County he baptized Margaret Indiana Queen (colored), born May 3, 1864, child of Michael Queen and Matilda Willson. Sponsor was Margaret Queen. On November 27, 1864, he baptized Patrick McMichael, born November 1, 1864, child of William McMichael and Rosa Laverty. Sponsors were John and Margaret McMichael. On November 27, 1864, Father Villiger baptized John Sullivan, born October 27, 1864, child of Thomas Sullivan and Catherine Shehan. Sponsors were Cornelius Bowls and Catherine Devine. On December 18, 1864, he baptized Maria Louisa Homen, born November 16, 18564, child of George Homan and Hanna Ann Anderson. Sponsor was Jane Dixon. On December 19, 1864, he baptized Anna Maria Fischer, born September 12, 1864, child of N. Fischer and Catherine Fischer. Sponsor was Gotlieb Hirst. On December 28, 1864, Father Villiger baptized James Mullen, born December 27, 1864, child of Patrick Mullen and Mary McCallister. Sponsors were Archy Mullen and Margaret McCallister. On January 22, 1865, he baptized George Henry Young, born October 28, 1864, child of John Henry Young and Mary Semmes. Sponsor was Emilia Morris. On March 12, 1864, he baptized John Burns, born March 15, 1864, child of Christopher Burns and Mary Dougherty. Sponsors were Daniel McClemens and Bridget McNeil. On March 26, 1865, Father Villiger baptized Rose Ann McMahon, born March 7, 1865, child of John McMahon and Ann McConeghy. Sponsors were Dennis and Elizabeth Kilty. On March 26, 1865, he baptized Ages Fox, born December 15, 1864, child of Henry Fox and Mary Roberson. Sponsors was Margaret Queen. On April 9, 1865, he baptized

Thomas McCarroll, born February 11, 1865, child of Peter McCarroll and Catherine Kelly. Sponsors were Henry Doyle and Joanna Cowey.

BURIAL RECORDS AT BOHEMIA
1854- Brennan, Patrick, Died by accident working on Delaware Railroad, Middletown, Del.; 1855-2-10 Durrand, Mary Bocat, Age 73 of Warwick, Md.; 1855-7-29 Norris, James, Age 25; 1855-10-28 Durraind, Edw J., Age 23; 1855-11-22 Knight, Catherine (Kitty), Age 79 of Georgetown, Md.; 1856-1-10 Corbaley, Wm. J., Age 25; 1856-11-21 Scanlan, Edward, Age 65, native of Tyrone Co., Ireland; 1857-2-28 Conway, Margaret, Age 30; 1857-12-30 Craddock, John B., Age 7 mos.; 1858-8-7 Degnan, Patrick, Age 29 of Warwick, Md.; 1859- Brothers, Catherine, Age 16 mos. Mother Catherine O'Neil Brothers.; 1859-8-3 O'Marow, Anne, Age 17 of Smyrna, Del Born in Waterford, Ireland.; 1859-8-12 Morton, Arthur, Age 1.; 1860-4-2 Riley, John, Age 7; 1861-1-6 Corbaley, Hannah J., Age 6.; 1861-9-17 Dreka, Charles A. Age 7 days; 1862-5-22 Cayot, Lydia Mary, Age 58; 1864-12-20 Mullen, James; Age 22; 1865-3-26 Price, Mary A., Age 35 wife of Wm. H. Price.; 1866- Price, Ann N., Age 68; 1866-1-21 Durkee, Capt. John A., Age 65; 1866-9-9 Bowman, Frances, Age 38; 1867-6-11 Reynolds, Amelia, Age 85; 1867-6-25 Durkee, Elizabeth G., Age 69; 1867-5-15 Hanson, J. Archie B., Age 2

45. Alice E. Miller, *Cecil County, Maryland, A Study in Local History* (Port Deposit, Maryland: Mary E. Miller, 1949) 46, 95, 97

46. AAB 39B-A2, printed circular. After the close of the Civil War, Father Villiger administered the sacrament of Baptism to the following: On April 18, 1865, *at Kent County* Father Villiger baptized Rose Alma Beck, born December 24, 1865, child of John Beck and Elizabeth M. Trimble. Sponsors were Carroll and Martha Willson. On April 18, 1865, he baptized Anna Elizabeth Spalding, born March 30, 1865, child of Samuel S. Spalding and Sarah E. McComas. Sponsor was Henrietta Willson. On April 22, 1865, he baptized Robert E. Price, born August 29, 1864, child of William H. Price and Mary Ann Richardson. Sponsor was Rosina Gates. On April 23, 1865, Father Villiger baptized Ida Virginia Queen (colored), born June 15, 1864, child of Isaac Queen and Felice Ann Cane. Sponsor was Mary Houston. On June 12, 1865, he baptized Mary Catherine Murry, born June 4, 1865, child of Francis Murry and Ellen Bowls. Sponsors were Patrick Murry and Mary Bowls. On June 14, 1865, he conditionally baptized Sara Ann Clayton, born January 7, 1814, child of Isaac Clayton and Rachel Davis. No sponsors given. On June 21, 1865, *at Kent County* Father Villiger baptized Charles John McClosky, born February 22, 1865, child of James McClosky and Margaret Owens. Sponsors were Benjamin Young and Julia M. Willson. On August 1, 1865, he baptized Joseph A. B. Hanson, born May 10, 1865, child of Thomas P. Hanson and Mary Hutaire. Sponsor was Mary E. Broadbent. On August 23, 1865, he baptized Anna J. H. Ziesel, born August 9, 1865, child of Felix Ziesel and Josephina Ziesel. Sponsors were Gottlieb and Joanna Heier. On August 27, 1865, Father Villiger baptized Richard Vandergrift, born May 19, 1865, child of George Vandergrift and Mary Cosgriff. Sponsor was Agnes Stapp. On October 8, 1865, he baptized Rose Ann Cosgriff, born September 12, 1865, child of Thomas Cosgriff and Catherine Bogden. Sponsors were James and Margaret Callahan. On October 8, 1865, he baptized Caroline Barbara Wals, born September 8, 1865, child of Jacob Wals and Barbara Troll. Sponsors were Fridolin Troll and Carolina Buhan. On October 27, 1865, Father Villiger baptized Bridget Nery, born October 27, 1865, child of Thomas Nery and Ann Melvin. Sponsor was Bridget Melvin. On November 11, 1865, he baptized Edward Anwiler, born September 10, 1865, child of Edward Anwill and Mary Kirkin. Sponsors were John Flinn and Catherine Pascault. On November 12, 1865, he baptized Ida Willson, born May 14, 1865, child of Steven Willson and Harriett Abb. Sponsor was Emilia Morris. On November 22, 1865, Father Villiger conditionally baptized Felix Cane (colored) born in 1840, child of Christopher Cane and Rody Green. Sponsor was Emilia Morris. On November 22, 1865, he conditionally baptized Marie Morris, born in 1842, child of Matthew Morris and Catherine Ann Gooddy. Sponsor was Emilia Morris. On November 24, 1865, he conditionally baptized Clarence Walmsley, born March 12, 1855, child of B. F. Walmsly and Frances W. Briscoe. On December 4, 1865, Father Villiger baptized Augustine Bede Walmsly, born October 6, 1865, child of Benjamin Franklin Walmsly and Frances Wilmer Briscoe. Sponsor was Adeline Morton. On January 25, 1866, he baptized Sara Pauline Cohee, born June 28, 1865, child of Benjamin F. Cohee and Amanda Jane Covey. Sponsor was Sara Elizabeth Lockwood. On February 22, 1866,

he baptized Robert Bowie, born July 15, 1863, child of Isaac Bowie and Harriett Scott. Sponsor was Patrick A. Curtis. On March 11, 1866, Father Villiger baptized Dennis Dorsey, born February 7, 1866, child of Patrick Dorsey and Honora Shehan. Sponsor was Mary Dignan. On March 12, 1866, he baptized Rose Ann Price Wright, born February 20, 1866, child of Chandeler J. Wright and Charity Hinson. Sponsors were Henrietta and Philomena Price. On March 22, 1866, he conditionally baptized John M. Flintham, born December 8, 1792, child or Richard Flintham and Christina Meldrum. No sponsors given. On March 26, 1866, Father Villiger baptized Maria Magdalen Bohm, born December 10, 1866, child of William Bohm and Caroline Droll. Sponsors were Fridolin Droll and Barbara Wals. On March 30, 1866, he baptized conditionally James George, born May 10, 1785, child of Hackless George and Matilda Harris. No sponsors given. On April 21, 1866, he baptized Michael Carroll, born March 19, 1866, child of John Carroll and Bridget Barrett. Sponsors were Michael Carroll and Ellen McWilliams. On April 21, 8166, Father Villiger baptized George Edward Dugan, born February 18, 1866, child of Daniel Dugan and Catherine Manning. Sponsors were James and Mary Jane Dixon. On April 21, 1866, he baptized Mary Jane McClean, born March 8, 1866, child of Thomas McClean and Mary McKee. Sponsors were Thomas and Jane Dixon. On April 22, 1866, he baptized Francis Adolphus Wallis, born March 19, 1866, child of Francis Adolphus Wallis and Georgianna Willson. No sponsors given. On April 22, 1866, Father Villiger baptized Margaret Ann Powderly, born December 6, 1865, child of James Powderly and Margaret Dunn. Sponsor was John Bowls. On April 22, 1866, he baptized Mary Manlove, born December 19, 1865, child of John Manlove and Mary E. McCafferty. Sponsor was Anna Scofield. On May 13, 1866, he baptized Francis Charles George, born March 7, 1866, child of Nicolas George Caroline Bay. Sponsors were Nicolas Kieffer and Maria E. Motri. On May 13, 1866, he baptized Ada Denning, born January 25, 1866, child of Michael Denning and Bridget Powell. Sponsors were James Bourke and Mary McCormick. On May 13, 1866, Father Villiger baptized Catherine Gardener, born November 15, 1865, child of Robert Gardener and Maria Morris. Sponsor was Isabella Roberson. On May 26, 1866, he baptized Daniel Dalayney, born November 4, 1865, child of Daniel Dalayney and Joanna Clear. Sponsors were Thomas and Catherine Cosgriff. On June 13, 1866, he baptized John William Gorman, born April 3, 1860, child of Peter Gorman and Mary Jane Kelly. Sponsor was Mary McCallister. On June 13, 1866, Father Villiger baptized Joanna Catherine Gorman, born July 28, 1857, child of Peter Gorman and Mary Jane Kelly. Sponsor was Mary McCallister. On June 13, 1866, he baptized Mary Ellen Gorman, born January 30, 1863, child of Peter Gorman and Mary Jane Kelly. Sponsor was Mary McCallister. On June 13, 1866, he baptized James Edward Gorman, born June 8, 1865, child of Peter Gorman and Mary Jane Kelly. Sponsor was Mary McCallister. On June 18, 1866, Father Villiger baptized Thomas H. H. Sapington, born May 28, 1865, child of William A. Sapington and Mary A. B. Brannock. Sponsor was William Thomas. On June 18, 1866, he baptized Annie E. Sapington, born June 16, 1858, child of William A. Sapington and Mary A. B. Brannock. Sponsor was William Thomas. On June 19, 1866, at Kent County, he baptized Henrietta E. Willson, born April 22,1866, child of George H. Willson and Henrietta E. Brook. Sponsor was Matha Willson. On June 10, 1866, Father Villiger conditionally baptized William Johnson (colored), born October 15, 1845, child of John Johnson and Ann young. Sponsor was Martha Willson. On June 24, 1866, he baptized William Francis Queen (colored), born January 14, 1863, child of Isaac Queen and Felice Cane. Sponsor was William Johnson. On July 8, 1866, he baptized Mary Anne Sullivan, born June 5, 1866, child of Thomas Sullivan and Catherine Shehan. Sponsors were Patrick and Eleanora Dorsey. On August 18, 1866, Father Villiger baptized Justin O. Schofield, born July 13, 1866, child of John C. Schofield and Annie McCafferty. Sponsor was Mary Hanson. On August 20, 1866, he baptized James Lillhofer, born April 5, 1862, child of Martin Lillhofer and Ellen Stuped. Sponsors were William Thomas and Alice McElhenny. On April 21, 1866, he baptized Mary Jane McClean, born Mach 8, 1866, child of Thomas McClean and Mary McKee. Sponsors were Thomas and Jane Dixon. On April 22, 1866, Father Villiger baptized Francis Adolphus Wallis, born march 19, 1866, child of Francis Adolphus Wallis and Georgianna Willson. Sponsors were Thomas and Jane Dixon. On April 22, 1866, he baptized Margaret Ann Powderly, born December 6, 1865, child of James Powderly and Margaret Dunn. Sponsor was John Bowls. On April 22, 1866, he baptized Mary Manlove, born December 19, 1865, child of John Manlove and Mary E. McCafferty. Sponsor was Anna Scofield. On May 13,

1866, Father Villiger baptized Francis Charles George, born March 7, 1866, child of Nicolas George and Caroline Boy. Sponsors were Nicolas Kieffer and Maria E. Motri. On May 13, 1866, he baptized Ada Denning, born January 25, 1866, child of Michael Denning and Bridget Powell. Sponsors were James Bourke and Mary McCormick. On May 13, 1866, he baptized Catherine Gardener (colored), born November 15, 1865, child of Robert Gardener and Maria Morris. Sponsor was Isabella Roberson. On May 26, 1866, Father Villiger baptized Daniel Dalayney, born November 4, 1865, child of Daniel Dalayney and Joanna Clear. Sponsors were Thomas and Catherine Cosgriff. On June 13, 1866, he baptized John William Gorman, born April 3, 1860, child of Peter Gorman and Mary Jane Kelly. Sponsor was Mary McCallister. On June 13, 1866, he baptized Joanne Catherine Gorman, born July 28, 1857, child of Peter Gorman and Mary Jane Kelly. Sponsor was Mary McCallister. On August 22, 1866, Father Villiger baptized William Evans, born November 12, 1865, child of William Evans and Ellen R. Lynam. Sponsor was Henrietta Durney. On September 9, 1866, he baptized Lydia Sterling Flintham, born May 28, 1866, child of William Flintham and E. Caroline King. Sponsors were Christian King and Mary Ann Craddock. On September 27, 1866, he baptized Elizabeth L. Riley, born August 9, 1866, child of Peregrin Riley and Eleanora Benningham. Sponsors were James Timons and Mary Shehy. On October 8, 1866, Father Villiger baptized Mary Chew Pascault, born September 5, 1866, child of Francis Pascault and Catherine H. Lusby. Sponsors were Rev. Thomas Foley and Teresa Roberts. On October 8, 1866, he baptized Ida Clark, born July 4, 1865, child of James Clark and Kesia, his wife. Sponsor was Elizabeth Rotliffe. On October 27, 1866, he baptized Rose Callahan, born August 20, 1866, child of James Callahan and Margaret Cosgriff. Sponsors were Thomas and Catherine Cosgriff. On November 30, 1866, Father Villiger baptized Ellen Catherine McMahon, born October 27, 1866, child of John McMahon and Ann McConaghy. Sponsors were Robert and Mary McCallister. On March 31, 1867, he baptized Thomas Sewell Welch, born February 8, 1867, child of James Welch and Rachael R. Davis. Sponsor was Thomas Craddock,. On March 31, 1867, he baptized Henry Welch, born April 4, 1860, child of James Welch and Rachel R. Davis. Sponsor was Thomas Craddock. On April 28, 1867, Father Villiger baptized George Thomas More (colored), born February 16, 1867, child of George More and Josephine Browne. Sponsor was Catherine Pascault. On May 27, 1867, he baptized Anne Frances Murry, born May 19, 1867, child of Francis Murry and Eleanora Bowles. Sponsors were Thomas Murry and Rose Money. On June 23, 1867, he baptized Benjamin F. Cohee, born October 25, 1833, son of Steven R. Cohee and Margaret Craddock. No sponsors given. On August 6, 1867, Father Villiger baptized Mary Krestle, born July 2, 1867, child of Adam Krestle and Maria A. Yunker. Sponsor was Mary Krestle. On September 27, 1867, he baptized Margaret Virginia Briscoe, born February 8, 1867, child of Jervis Briscoe and Sintri Ann Fountain. Sponsor was Isabella Roberson. On October 13, 1867, he baptized Patrick Dorsey, born September 16, 1867, child of Patrick Dorsey and Honora Shehan. Sponsors were Thomas and Catherine Sullivan. On October 14, 1867, Father Villiger baptized George Willson Wallis, born August 22, 1867, child of Francis R. Wallis and Georgia Willson. Sponsors were Thomas Willson and Annie Hamilton. On October 27, 1867, he baptized Mary Catherine Muller, born September 10, 1867, child of William Muller and Catherine Schwarz. Sponsors were John Willson and Mary McGrath. On November 24, 1867, Father Villiger baptized Rose Ellen O'Hara, born October 25, 1867, child of Patrick O'Hara and Rose McConechy. Sponsors were Alexander McNeil and Briget McClement. On December 28, 1867, he baptized Charles B. Richards, born February 17, 1847, son of Enoch Richards and Rebecca E. Taylor. Sponsor was Hugh McGonagle. On December 28, 1867, he baptized Edwin Oscar Burns, born October 23, 1867, child of Owen Burns and Martha A. Armstrong. Sponsor was Mary Lockwood. On January 29, 1868, Father Villiger baptized Dorthea Eugenia Beaston born December 1, 1867, child of John Beaston and Mary Antonetta Reilly. Sponsors were Jacques Cayot and Virginia Bond. On February 21, 1868, he conditionally baptized Robert Pearson, born August 3, 1825, son of John Pearson and Catherine Clemence. On February 20, 1868, he baptized Eugene Ahern, born December 4, 1867, child of Dennis Ahern and Annie Alworth. Sponsors were Patrick Murphy and Mary Ann Ahern. On April 26, 1868, Father Villiger baptized Edward Stapp, born December 17, 1867, child of Michael Stapp and Christina Korbel. Sponsors were Nicolas and Christina Lotringer. On April 26, 1868, he baptized Laura Wooters, born August 4, 1860, child of Joseph Lemuel Wooters and Rebecca, his wife. No sponsors given.

47. Baltimore *The Catholic Mirror* November 11, 1865; EPISCOPAL VISITATION – Divine Providence permitting, the Most Revered Archbishop will make the visitation and administer Confirmation in the order following:
Monday, November 20 – 9 a.m. at St. John's, Long Green.
Tuesday, November 21 – 11 a.m. at St. Mary's, Harford County.
Wednesday, November 22 – 10 a.m. at St. Ignatius, Hickory P.O., Harford County.
Thursday, November 23 – 9 a.m. at Abbington, Harford County.
Thursday, November 23 – 3 p.m. at St. Stephen's, Baltimore County.
Friday, November 24 – 11 a.m. at St. Patrick's, Havre de Grace, Harford County.
Saturday, November 25 – 12 o'clock at Immaculate Conception, Elkton, Cecil County.
Sunday, November 26 – 10 a.m. at St. Francis Xavier, Bohemia, Cecil County.
Monday, November 27 – 10 a.m. at St. Dennis, Kent County.
Tuesday, November 28 – 1 p.m. Chestertown, Kent County. Lecture
Wednesday, November 29 – Lecture at Reese's Corner, Kent County at 12 noon.
Thursday, November 30 – 10 a.m. at Willson's, Kent County (Trumpington)
Friday, December 1 – 11:30 at St. Peter's, Queenstown, Queen Anne's County.
Friday, December 1 – 7 p.m. Lecture at Centreville, Queen Anne's County.
Sunday, December 3 – 10 a.m. at St. Joseph's, Talbot County
Monday, December 4 – 10 a.m. at St. Elizabeth's, Denton, Caroline County.
Tuesday, December 5 – 9 a.m. at Easton, Talbot County.
Tuesday, December 5 – 7 p.m. Lecture at Easton

48. An anonymous account of his visitation was written to the Editors of *The Catholic Mirror* – "December 9, 1865 – *The Catholic Mirror*, EPISCOPAL VISITATION. November 28, 1865"

49. On November 25, 1865, at Elkton confirmed 41 persons. Baltimore *The Catholic Mirror* December 9, 1865: "This is a stone building – I cannot say what style of architecture it claims to be but it resembles a square box pierced with six windows – three on either side the basement large and unfurnished – the interior is tolerable decent and commodious – on the frontal of this building a tower sprung up a few feet and then abandoned the idea of proceeding further upward. His Grace made the arrangements for a Sunday School on the days on which there would be no service and appointed some gentlemen and ladies for the purpose who willingly promised their services. His Grace has a watchful solicitude for everything and he saw at once that his congregation needed a little stirring up very much. He promised them a resident pastor as soon as they would make arrangements for his support and he would be able to send them one. He also made arrangements to have a Mission for the congregation very soon."

50. Recorded in the Bohemia baptismal register 95. Baltimore *The Catholic Mirror* December 9, 1865: "At 10:30 o'clock Mass was sung by the pastor. Delmonte's Mass was well discoursed by the choir. His Grace preached to a large congregation including many of the most respectable non-Catholics in the surrounding neighborhood. Every available spot in the church was filled and the Archbishop preached for an hour on the Divine Institution of the Holy Church. It was evident from the marked attention of the audience that His Grace's powerful and convincing arguments were not spent in vain. The Church at Bohemia is a neat brick structure and although it was built before the year 1792 it is in a good state of preservation. It is located on one of the farms of the Jesuit fathers and is a very old missionary station, perhaps one of the oldest in this State or in the country. The fathers had a college and long before any of our present literary institutions had existence. There is a tombstone in the adjoining graveyard recording a burial as long ago as A. D. 1750."

51. Baltimore *The Catholic Mirror*, December 9, 1865: "We were no less surprised and delighted when we heard the deep tones of the organ accompanied by Bernard McCauley, Esq., Jr. so well performed. The music and Mass would do credit to any of our city churches. The church of brick is 50x30 feet, has a bell organ and all the conveniences of a well-established church. It cost about $3,000, which was mainly defrayed by Mr. McCauley. The bricks were burnt here, and, as the clay was for this purpose not of the best kind, the edifice is by no means as substantial as it should be. I understand that they are ready at any moment to build a larger and more beautiful church and Mr. McCauley offers the first subscription of $3,000, another gentlemen, a convert to our Holy Religion, $3,000 more, and another gentleman non-catholic $500. They are sanguine of erecting a church with $10,000 or $12,000 and paying for it. Is it not moving in the

right direction and manifesting real and substantial zeal for the good of God in the promotion of the true Church. Verily the grain of mustard seed is expanding here – let others take good example."

52. Baltimore *The Catholic Mirror* December 16, 1865: To The Editors of the Catholic Mirror, December 3, 1865. "A church is to be erected here (at Reese's Corner) early in the spring and I understand an acre of land has been offered to locate it on. Although there are scarcely any Catholics in the immediate neighborhood, yet the location is most desirable, as the place is midway between Chestertown and Willson's – 10 miles from each place. Nearly $2,000 have been subscribed for this purpose by two or three families of the Willson's, who are numerous, highly respectable and zealous Catholics. There is hardly a doubt but a church edifice will be reared here in the spring. His Grace made all the necessary arrangements and appointed a committee to solicit subscriptions and have general care of the work." As we know today, the plans for a church at Reese's corner never materialized. A church was built at Rock Hall in 1890. *Richard Bennett Willson*, child of Dr. Thomas Bennett Willson II and Anna Maria Smythe, was born on December 10, 1817, in Queen Anne County. *He inherited Trumpington in 1859*, and died December 30, 1901. He married Anna Martha Young on October 3, 1842, in St. Thomas Roman Catholic Church. (Rev. James Curley). She was the daughter of Benjamin Young and Ann Manning. She was born November 14, 1819, in Charles County and died September 10, 1900. Children of Richard Bennett Willson and Anna Martha Young were Dr. Thomas Bennett Willson, born September 13, 1843, practised medicine at Reese's Corner, died March 23, 1923; William Macline Willson, born June 24, 1845; Wilford Manning Willson, born September 17, 1847, died November 9, 1902; Richard Bennett Willson, Jr., born July 16, 1849, resided next to Trumpington, died December 10, 1918; Horace Augustine Willson, born January 3, 1857, resided in Edesville, Kent County, died 1897; Notley Oswald Willson, born July 8, 1852; Julia Rena Ringgold Compton Willson, born November 28, 1854; died June 30, 1935; Mary Charlotte Willson, born May 7, 1856; Peter Cazinove Willson, born December 24, 1857, died 1943; Paul Alexander Willson, born June 3, 1859, married Sophia Charlotte Pascal on October 28, 1884; Clement Joseph Beauregard Willson, born May 5, 1861. John Charles Willson, child of Dr. Thomas Bennett Willson II and Anna Maria Smythe, was born on April 5, 1816 and died January 25, 1858. He married Anne Elizabeth Brooke, January 7, 1840, daughter of James Brooke and Mary Brooke. She was born c. 1818 in Kent County, Maryland. Both were Catholic. Their children were Henrietta Maria Willson, born November 10, 1848, in Kent County, died July 25, 1937; Anna M. Brooke Willson, born 1850, died 1930.

53. Baltimore *The Catholic Mirror*, December 16, 1865. Those who were confirmed evere –
54. Baltimore *The Catholic Mirror*, December 16, 1865. The archbishop arrived too late at Gray's Inn Landing to take the first boat down the Chester River. An hour later he took another boat, landing at the Corsica River, a distance seven miles from St. Peter's Church, Queenstown. Mr. Charles J. B. Mitchell in his private carriage conveyed the archbishop to St. Peter's Church. Here an incident occurred during the administration of the Sacrament of Confirmation, which if His Grace had not been detained two hours or more after the appointed time, would in all probability have terminated in the destruction of the church. A fire had been made earlier in the morning in the stove placed in the middle of the church and the pipe passing in through the roof had been placed near one of the timbers which it ignited. As the children were gathered around the railing receiving the Sacrament the middle of the Church was partly vacated, down fell the stovepipe, bricks and plaster – for a few minutes there was considerable consternation. It was now evident that the timbers of the roof were on fire; but soon a few active gentlemen scaled the roof and extinguished the fire. No one was seriously injured, only one man and a small boy received slight flesh wounds from falling bricks. It was evident that the timber had been on fire for a considerable time previous and if His Grace had not been detained the services would have been over and the people dispersed so that it would have been almost impossible to save the building. Delays are often dangerous but they are sometimes fortunate as in the present instance. In a short time the fire was extinguished and His Grace, in the house adjoining, confirmed 31 persons, 10 of whom were converts."
55. Carley, *Queenstown* 88
56. Carley, *Queenstown* 88. Before the archbishop left for Centreville, Mrs. Alfred Bryan (nee Emily Higgins), who lived at Bennett's Point on the Wye River, eight miles from St. Peter's,

Queerstown, provided dinner for the archbishop and his attendants. John Palmer and his family in Centreville were not Catholic. They cordially hosted the archbishop's visit to Centreville. Baltimore *The Catholic Mirror*, December 16, 1865: "The people of Centreville are most anxious to have a church here and although there are very few Catholic in the place, non-catholics are ready to subscribe for this purpose. A splendid lot has already been secured and they will commence building the church early in the spring. All they ask are the services of a priest, and His Grace promised to supply one as soon as a church will be built. There is a liberal and generous disposition in this place among non-catholics, and I am sure the Archbishop's able and appropriate discourse will long be remembered by them. Mr. Palmer, an energetic and influential gentleman, takes much interest in the undertakings. His Grace appointed a committee consisting of the following gentlemen to take charge of the work; viz: Mr. John Palmer, Dr. Thomas S. Willscn, Capt. Augustus McCabe, Capt. John Friel and Daniel Friel. The mission at Centreville and St. Peter's (Queenstown), both in Queen Anne County, will furnish sufficient employment for one pastor for there are a great many respectable old Catholic families scattered throughout the county and, besides, there are many who will join the Church when they have an opportunity to know its doctrines and consolation."

57. Carley, *Queenstown* 88-89
58. AAB 36-G10, George Villiger, S. J., to Archbishop Spalding, Bohemia, January 31, 1866: "Your kind note of the 10th inst. has come to hand in due time, also a copy of the correspondence for which I feel very thankful to your grace."
59. Gerald Shaughnessy, *Has The Immigrant Kept The Faith?* (New York: Macmillan Company, 1925) 81: Prior to the Civil War about 1.5 million Germans came to the United states. Previous to 1871, the Catholic percentage for all German immigrants averaged about 30 to 32 percent.
60. Colman J. Barry, *The Catholic Church and German Americans* (Milwaukee: The Bruce Publishing Company, 1953) 7
61. Paul Dukes, *A History of Europe 1648-1948: The Arrival, The Rise, The Fall* (Hong Kong: Macmillan Company 1985) 228
62. Barry 4; *A Century of Population Growth 1790-1900* (Washington: 1909). Shaughnessy 81 – In the decades previous to the establishment of the Empire (1871) about two and a half million Germans entered the United States. In the German confederation, 1866, militarism became the keynote of the new regime in Germany. Economic conditions put many out of work. An attempt to suppress all religious differences in the confederated states of Germany sent many fleeing to the United States.
63. Russell H. Perkins, *The Seed has Grown To Harvest, Centenary of St. Rose of Lima Mission 1874-1974* (Hackensack, New Jersey: Custom Book, 1974) 16. SCHAEFER FAMILY OF CHESAPEAKE CITY – On January 26, 1897, Catherine (Katrina Huber) Schaefer died in Chesapeake City, Maryland. Born in Baden, Germany in 1822, Katrina married Joseph Schaefer, also born in Baden, Germany on July 29, 1823. They married in Germany in 1851, and had two children, buried in Germany in 1852 and 1853. (Philip was nine months old and Sophia two years old.) They came to America in 1854 and had three children as follows: Charles J. Schaefer, born June 16, 1854 in Buffalo, New York, died in Delaware City, Delaware; Mary Schaefer born in Toledo, Ohio, February 2, 1858, died in Delaware City, Delaware; Joseph Schaefer, born in Chesapeake City, Maryland, February 28, 1861, died in Chesapeake City, September 30, 1923. Joseph married Winifred Smith on May 26, 1887 at Bohemia. Joseph died in Chesapeake City, Maryland, on October 18, 1905. Winifred Smith (Schmidt) was daughter of Wilhelm Schmidt (born August 30, 1827, died April 13, 1907, in Chesapeake City, Maryland) and Mary Gentling (born 1825, died in Chesapeake City, Maryland, April 25, 1893). They changed their name to Smith when they became American citizens. Besides Winifred, their other children were William, Frank, Mary , and Joseph Smith. Winifred and Joseph Schaefer had the following children: William W., Joseph Edward, Franklin, Kathryn, John Francis Schaefer.
64. AAB 36-G10, George Villiger, S. J. to Archbishop Spalding, Bohemia, January 31, 1866 Since most Polish immigrants also spoke German, because of the partition of Poland. Father Villiger was able to communicate with them. Such persons as John Jankowski, Maria Janiszewska, George Rosinski, and Frances, Eva, and Josephine Wachowicz were some of those settling in Kent County at this time. Some German names on the record: Adolphus Wallis, Adolph Hess, Joseph Eising, Elizabeth Fischler, John Ziegler, Felix Ziesel, Gottlieb Heier.

65. Thomas J. Peterman, "From Age to Age," in *Centenary of St. John's Church, Rock Hall, Maryland 1890-1990* (Chestertown, Maryland: printed privately, 1990) 18. There is no record of a letter in the AAB of Villiger's promised report on the proposed church at Reese's Corner.
66. AAB 36-G9, George Villiger, S.J. to Archbishop Spalding, Bohemia, December 1, 1866. Mass was offered continually in the home on Thomas Dixon's farm near Chestertown until 1877, when Father George Bradford completed the Church of the Sacred Heart on High Street. Some of the German families who moved into the neighborhood of Chestertown were the Schauber, Muench, Dilhofer, Schnepf, Gravenstein and Baehser families.
67. Spalding, *Premier See* 191
68. Thomas W. Spalding, *Martin John Spalding American Churchman* (Washington, D.C.: The Catholic University of American, 1973) 173
69. AAB 39A-D4, Minutes of the Plenary Council
70. APF *Scritture originale* 994, 832r-836r, Council Fathers to Propaganda Fide, Baltimore, October, 1866 Thomas Becker was ordained in Rome in 1859 for the Diocese of Richmond. He was pastor of St. Joseph Church in Martinsburg, [now West Virginia] during the Civil War. A Confederate sympathizer and thorough secessionist, he was arrested for omitting prayers for President Lincoln and imprisoned in Washington, D.C. President Lincoln released him to the care of Archbishop Kenrick in 1863. When Archbishop Spalding came to Baltimore he made Thomas Becker, who held a doctorate in theology from Rome, his personal secretary. He accompanied the archbishop on his travels and assisted him in ceremonies. When the war ended, Becker returned to Richmond, and became rector of the Richmond Cathedral, August 20, 1865.
71. APF *Scr. Orig.* 994 765r-766r, Spalding to Prop. Fide, Baltimore, November 8, 1866
72. Spalding, *Spalding* 234
73. Philadelphia *The Catholic Standard*, February 22, 1868, "The New Bishops;" Thomas J. Peterman, *The Cutting Edge: Life of Thomas Andrew Becker, First Bishop of Wilmington, Delaware and Sixth Bishop of Savannah, Georgia* (Devon, Pennsylvania: Cooke Publishers, 1982) 67
74. Baltimore *The Catholic Mirror* August 29, 1868

CHAPTER FIVE

Bohemia Under Jesuit Pastors in the New Diocese of Wilmington
1868-1898

THE EPISCOPATE OF THOMAS A. BECKER

Thomas Andrew Becker was named first Bishop of Wilmington upon its establishment on March 3, 1868. He was consecrated at the Basilica of the Assumption in Baltimore on August 6, 1868. Thirty six years of age, the scholarly and energetic new bishop plunged into the task of evangelizing the vast missionary district of his diocese which comprised the entire Delmarva Peninsula.

Portrait of
Bishop Thomas A. Becker

Three weeks after his installation as first Bishop of Wilmington, Thomas Becker wrote to Archbishop Spalding informing him that the had just traveled through all the Eastern Shore counties except Dorchester.[1] He confided in his Daybook at the time: "There are seven buildings called churches (on the Eastern Shore), all old and wretched... None of these are of any importance. Most are frame chapels, or very plain brick, in a sorry state of decay.[2] The first of these was the mission of St. Francis Xavier in Cecil County. The church Becker referred to was that begun by Father Beeston in 1792 and completed by Father Maréchal in 1797.[3]

On October 11, 1868, Bishop Thomas Becker administered the Sacrament of Confirmation *at Bohemia* to the following persons: James Dorsey, John Kirchner, Edward Rolerecht, Joseph Morin, Thomas Kennedy, Thomas Green, William Gallagher, Aloysius Price, J., Charles Craddock, Edwin Glanson, Thomas M. Hanson, John Strick, and Robert Parsons, a convert; Mary Dorsey, Philomena Price, Delphine Hanson, Gracy Bowman, Agnes Stapp, Mary Stapp, Carolina Strick, Mary

Kleiber, Justina Strids, Elizabeth Coil, Sally Lilly (colored), and Rachel (a colored convert).

Swiss Jesuit George Villiger

After visiting with Father George Villiger in 1868, Becker noted that he found him "advancing in years and broken in health."[4] Villiger was then 60 years of age and had no assistant. He had served at Bohemia as pastor since 1856. Although he was still capable of making the rounds of his mission stations, he appeared no longer vigorous enough to participate in the ambitious building programs envisioned by the new bishop.

One of Becker's first official actions as bishop was to appoint Father Francis Joseph Blake as the first resident pastor of the church in Elkton.[5] Up to the time of the establishment of the Diocese of Wilmington, both Elkton and Newark had been served by the clergy of St. Patrick's Church, Havre de Grace, in Harford County. This arrangement ended in 1868 and the care of these congregations fell back on Father Villiger. With Father Blake's appointment, Father Villiger's obligations were lightened.

Father Villiger had already discussed with Archbishop Spalding some plans for the construction of a church in Chestertown. The matter now became a concern for Bishop Becker. To push forward those plans, the bishop assigned in 1871 Father William Dallard, newly-ordained, to take charge of the church at Galena (Georgetown Crossroads) and the mission station at Chesapeake City.[6]

Unexpectedly, Father Blake left the Elkton-Newark pastorate in the same year, and Father Dallard was given that charge as well.[7] Father John O'Connor was sent to work at Chestertown, but lived at Bohemia during his brief incumbency.[8]

When O'Connor left for Newark, New Jersey, Father Villiger was again alone

Father Emil Stenzel

Photo of Parishioners outside Church at turn of Century

at Bohemia with the charge of the Kent County missions: at St. Dennis (Georgetown Crossroads), at Bennett Willson's (on Eastern Neck), and at Thomas Dixon's (at Chestertown). In 1872 there were about 350 Catholics in his care.[9]

On November 22, 1874, *at Bohemia*, Bishop Thomas Becker administered the Sacrament of Confirmation to the following persons: Edward Lockwood, convert, George Lockwood, convert, Louis Stam, convert, Edward Tomlinson, convert, Thomas Tomlinson, John Dorsey, Michael Dorsey, Michael Finn, Charles M. Corrigan, Gervase Briscoe, Mary Sophia Miller, convert, Teresa Dorsey, Charlotte Tomlinson, Fannie Walmsley, Catherine Tomlinson, Emma Stapp, Frances Maggie Walmsley, Elizabeth Morton, Helen Morton, Indiana Rosalia Ruley, Sarah Ruley, Rose Laura Wooters, Lillia Tronner Wooters, Sara Brady, a convert, and Sophia, colored convert.

With each passing year after the close of the Civil War, Father Villiger's fluency in the German tongue was found to be increasingly useful. In the early 1870's the *Kulturkampf*, a cultural persecution of Catholics in Germany, sent many to the religious freedom of America.[10] Bishop Becker also learned that his fluency in German was extremely helpful in ministering to these latest arrivals.[11]

In May of 1872, Bishop Becker was pleased to accept the services of Father Emil Stenzel, who was also fluent in German. Father Stenzel was assigned to serve the German immigrants in Chestertown where efforts were under way to build a church. He remained there until 1876 when he was replaced by Father George Bradford, who built the new church.[12]

At the same time, a growing German population at Chesapeake City was moving forward on plans to build their own church.[13]

At Chesapeake City Father Villiger was accustomed to leave his horses with the Stapp family, and then to stay with the Schaefer family until Sunday morning when he would celebrate Mass for the growing congregation of mostly German immigrants. At other times the faithful gathered at the home of John August Krastel or of Wilhelm Schmidt (later known as Smith).[14]

When Bishop Becker first visited the largely German congregation in Chesapeake City, he spoke to them in their native tongue, telling them that his own dream was that they should have their own church. He urged them to form a building committee and to secure a suitable site. Before departing the bishop encouraged them with his pledge to help them see the project to completion. He assigned Father William Dallard of Elkton to lead the building project. The building committee located the present site on Cecil Street and negotiated to purchase a little over one acre from Henry H. and Rebecca S. Brady for the sum of four hundred and seventy-five dollars.[15]

The decision was made to construct a brick building of Gothic design on the site in Chesapeake City. The cornerstone was blessed and laid by Bishop Becker at ten o'clock in the morning of August 30, 1874. It was the Feast of St. Rose of Lima, in whose honor the new church was named. At the time she was the only native of the western hemisphere to have been canonized a saint. The bishop was assisted by Father Villiger and Father Dallard, in the presence of a crowd estimated at five hundred people.[16] After the blessing of the stone, Bishop Becker gave a brief account of the meaning of the ceremony and then sprinkled the foundations of the building with holy water. Then in a sermon Bishop Becker

236 *The Bohemia Historical Society*

Church of St. Rose of Lima, Chesapeake City

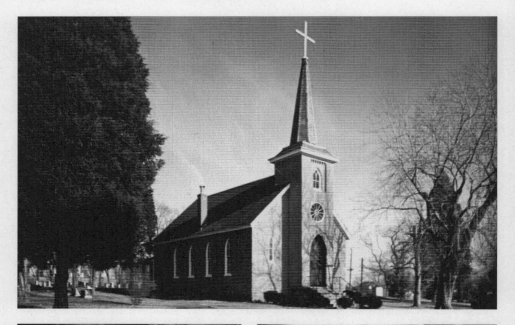

Cornerstone 1874, St. Rose of Lima Church

Monstrance, St. Rose of Lima Church

explained the teaching authority of the church based on the command of Christ to the Apostles: "Go therefore and teach all nations." He continued with remarks on the temporal advantages that would accrue from the building of the church. He then spoke in German, invoked God's blessing, and the ceremony ended.[17] The dedication of the completed building was delayed until June of 1875. Practically all the Catholics of Cecil County were organized for participation in the festivities. Father Villiger suffered a stroke early in the new year and was unable to participate.[18] From April 1, 1875 until August 23, 1875, he recorded no baptisms.[19]

On Saturday, June 12, 1875, the Elkton *Democrat* announced that Bishop Becker would dedicate the new Church of St. Rose of Lima at Chesapeake City on Sunday, June 20, 1875, at ten o'clock. Several of the local clergy would assist him, and it was anticipated that several hundred persons would be present and that dinner would be prepared for all of them. The parishioners of Immaculate Conception Church in Elkton would prepare the dinner in honor of Bishop Becker who would arrive there after the dedication to bless the new bell in their church in the evening.[20]

On the morning of June 20, 125 persons from Port Deposit boarded the steamer "Lancaster," stopped first at an ice house on the way, on to Perryville and Havre de Grace, having taken on 250 more passengers. The ship pulled up to the dock at Schaefer's, on the Canal, and the beautiful church stood prominently before them on the hill.[21] Bishop Becker dedicated the church, and Father Joseph Luke Barry, pastor of St. Patrick's Church, Havre de Grace and of St. Theresa of Avila, Port Deposit, officiated at a Solemn High Mass assisted by Father Patrick J. O'Connell then pastor of St. Rose Church, and by Father William Dallard, pastor of Immaculate Conception in Elkton. The formalities terminated at about noon, and "a long table filled with the substantials of life was spread, where many repaired and did justice to the occasion."[22]

Because of his stroke, Father Villiger was unable physically to participate in the festivities. Only a few weeks before, on April 22, 1875, "Apud Bohemiam," at St. Francis Xavier Church, Father Villiger had assisted Bishop Becker at his first Confirmation ceremony there when 25 persons were confirmed, seven of them adults. On May 9, 1875 Father Villiger had assisted Bishop Becker in his first Confirmation at Chestertown in which 18 children were confirmed.[23]

Mary Rose Krastel Stapp

Father Joseph Luke Barry

Father Dallard continued to attend the mission at Chesapeake City for three years after the dedication of the church.[24] In November, 1878, Father Villiger was transferred to Frederick, Maryland.[25] Recovering a bit, he was assigned on February 15, 1879 to St. Aloysius Church, Littlestown, Pennsylvania. He continued his courageous work for souls until his death on September 20, 1882.[26]

Bavarian Jesuit, Charles H. Heichemer

Father Heichemer, S.J.

A young priest succeeded Father Villiger as pastor at Bohemia. He was Bavarian born Charles H. Heichemer, who at an early age came to America and engaged successfully in business in New York. At age 30 he began studies for the priesthood under Jesuit Father Augustin Bally at Goshenhoppen, Pennsylvania. On July 25, 1867, he was admitted as a Jesuit novice in Frederick, Maryland. Ordained a priest at Woodstock in 1876, he was appointed assistant – procurator of the Province and remained in that position for two years. In 1878, he was temporarily named pastor of Trinity Church in Boston. In November 1878, he was appointed superior at Bohemia in Cecil County, Maryland.[27] Since he was an energetic young priest, Bishop Becker returned the church at Chesapeake City to his pastoral care. Father Heichemer gave it his immediate attention, installing and blessing the Stations of the Cross there on April 20, 1879.[28] He found the church and residence at Bohemia in deplorable condition, and the spiritual condition of the Bohemia congregation in a generally feeble condition. Immediately he set about restoring the buildings and enriching them with new furnishings. By his preaching and visiting families he renewed the spirit of his parishioners. He provided instructions in St. Ignatius' *Spiritual Exercises* and introduced the Sodality of the Blessed Virgin Mary.[29]

At the same time his attention was called to the pressing needs of the growing number of Catholics in the nearby village of Middletown, Delaware. He learned of the need for a church and regular Mass there. A number of Catholics from Middletown would walk the six miles of muddy roads to attend Mass on Sunday at Bohemia. After the arrival of the railroad to Middletown in 1855 the town had taken on more importance.

In the early 1870s Mr. and Mrs. Hamilton Morton who had formerly lived at "Strawberry Hill," the former Matthews' estate, "Vulcan's Rest," adjacent to the Jesuit Mission at Bohemia, moved to Middletown. Soon after moving to town, Mary Morton (nee Durkin) organized a Catholic Sunday School at her home where children were taught the Catechism and Bible History.[30] In 1876 Father George Bradford, new pastor of Chestertown, celebrated the first Sunday Mass for the young congregation at the Morton home. He frequently left his horse at the Morton's as he caught the train to Wilmington. Mass was later celebrated in the Town Hall , a site now occupied by the Everett Theater.[31]

Father Heichemer promoted the goal of building a new church in Middletown. Through the efforts of Mrs. Hamilton Morton and Mrs. Edward Lockwood, a considerable sum was raised toward this end.

But it would not fall to Father Heichemer's lot to fulfill that dream. After twenty one months as pastor of Bohemia, in September 1881, he was transferred. He had shown great zeal for his apostolate. Fourteen funeral Masses were celebrated by him in twelve months, from July 1879 until July 1880, among them Edward W. Lockwood. For many months Father Heichemer travelled to Chesapeake City to give religious instructions to John Lloyd, whom he received into the Church in June 1880. He officiated at the wedding between Charles Pensels and Mary Emma Stapp in March, 1880, and baptized their first child Henry Jacob in April, 1881.[32] Father Heichemer died at an early age in Baltimore on October 21, 1893. In his last years he served as procurator of the Maryland Province of the Jesuits with great success.[33]

American Jesuit, John B. Gaffney

Father
John B. Gaffney, S.J.

A veteran army chaplain of the American Civil War, Father John B. Gaffney was sent to replace Father Heichemer in September, 1881.[34] He immediately espoused the cause of a new church in Middletown. However, the money for the project was slow in coming. After many suppers, bazaars, and seeking donations from family and friends, the congregation finally accumulated three hundred dollars, enough to buy a lot for the building.[35]

On October 19, 1883, a contract for building the church was awarded to Stevens, Miller, and Company.[36] The ceremony of the laying of the cornerstone was celebrated on November 18, 1883. Mass was offered in the old Town Hall on Main Street at ten o'clock in the morning. Then the congregation marched in procession to the site of the new church. After the laying of the cornerstone, a 750 pound bell was blessed by Father John J. Murphy, a Jesuit from Georgetown in Washington, D. C. Later in the evening, Father Murphy gave a sermon in the Town Hall to the congregation and their friends in the community.[37] Father Gaffney wrote his Jesuit superior that "the flock grows daily, not only in numbers, but also in the quality of their faith and morals. There is great cause for enthusiasm.... the foundations have been laid for a large and beautiful church in Middletown...."[38]

Bishop Becker dedicated the completed building on October 5, 1884. He was assisted by Fathers John B. Gaffney, George Bradford, Benjamin Keiley, and Thomas W. Hayes. The choir of St. Peter's Cathedral in Wilmington embellished the occasion with appropriate music.[39] In this way the last Jesuit mission on the Delmarva Peninsula (Middletown) had become a reality.

In the notice of the completion of the Middletown Church, the Jesuit journal commented: "Most likely the Fathers will have their residence after a time in

Middletown instead of Bohemia."[40]

At the same time Father Gaffney completely renovated the church at Bohemia. He added a beautiful spire to the tower constructed by Father Villiger and surmounted it with a golden cross, while further embellishing the interior of the church.[41] He did much to make the old mission flourish again. The sacramental records of Bohemia testify eloquently to his steadfast zeal.[42]

Father Gaffney was over six feet tall, stood always militarily straight, and had a disposition of positive contentment. In his missionary travels he showed undaunted skill on horseback from his days of military service, and regularly entertained people "with stories of his military experiences with a savory sense of humor." He accomplished much in the five years of his Bohemia pastorate in spite of economic hardships caused by a continuing local peach blight called "the yellows" during the 1880s that wiped out the peach trees in the Bohemia orchards. Eight thousand trees at Bohemia were wiped out by the blight. Local farmers were on the verge of bankruptcy, as the peach crop was the principal source of income for a majority of them.[43]

In early 1886, Father Gaffney was transferred to take charge of the Frederick County missions. He lived almost to the completion of his 81st year, never losing his soldierly bearing, his gracious charity, and his attractive sanctity of life.[44]

THE EPISCOPATE OF ALFRED A. CURTIS

News of the transfer of Bishop Becker to Savannah, Georgia, reached Bohemia in the spring of 1886. In the eighteen years of Becker's incumbency the number of clergy in the diocese had tripled, and eighteen churches had been built or rebuilt. The new bishop, Alfred A. Curtis, was a native of the Eastern Shore, a convert from Episcopalianism, and formerly an Episcopal priest. He came with great gifts of eloquence, selfless service, and administrative skill. Curtis was consecrated in Baltimore on November 14, 1886, and was installed in Wilmington by James Cardinal Gibbons, Archbishop of Baltimore, the following Sunday.[45]

French Jesuit, John M. Giraud

Father Gaffney was succeeded on August 4, 1886 by Father John M. Giraud. Born and reared in France, he suffered some lack of fluency in English, but made up for it by his kindly and courtly manner. He was of rugged physique and wore a patriarchal beard. All the years of his priestly work in the United States were marked with a missionary zeal.[46]

Father Giraud was officially assigned as pastor of St. Joseph's in Middletown, with Bohemia and Chesapeake City as missions.

In the spring of 1887, Bishop Curtis visited all three congregations under Father Giraud's charge. On June 24, 1887, at St. Joseph's Church in Middletown, he confirmed twenty children. On June 26, 1887, he was at Bohemia, where he confirmed forty-six children and adults. On June 28, 1887, he was at St. Rose of Lima Church in Chesapeake City, where he confirmed seventeen candidates.[47]

At Bohemia, Father Giraud added a new altar "built entirely by Father Giraud

Bishop Alfred A. Curtis (front left) and Father John M. Giraud, S.J. (bearded)

Bishop Curtis with priests at Elkton, Maryland, 1893

Photo of Altar Built by Father Giraud

Mr. And Mrs. Joseph Shaefer, Circa 1887

himself. Even the brass on the tabernacle door was hammered out by him, in which work he was assisted by a young man of the parish. In the gallery there is a beautiful pipe organ, which was placed there by Father Giraud."[48]

Father Giraud had a Jesuit assistant Father John B. Archambault, who was assigned especially to the congregation of St. Rose of Lima, Chesapeake City.[49] Giraud's sacramental records at Bohemia show evidence of his zeal.[50] In his first annual report to his Jesuit superiors, Father Giraud expressed a concern over the number of Catholics in the area around Odessa who were sending their children to Protestant churches and Sunday schools.[51]

Father Giraud made progress and was not daunted by the local economic depression during his time at Bohemia. Though the peach blight had put many of his congregation on the verge of bankruptcy, he continued to pay off the parish debt, aided by the "Tournament," held on the Peninsula Fair Grounds, just north of Middletown. On the first day of the first tournament in the fall of 1887, the contestants "tastefully clothed in knightly garb.... Formed on Green Street" at about eleven o'clock in the morning, and "led by Chief Marshal, J. P. Hoffecker, the assistant marshalls and pages, and the Diamond State Cornet Bank, marched through Broad, Main, Labe, Catherine, and Wood Streets, and then on to the Fair grounds.[52]

Both Father Giraud and Father Archambault were transferred from Bohemia on November 24, 1890.[53]

Irish Jesuit, Father Daniel F. Haugh

At the beginning of the year 1890 the new pastor, Father Daniel F. Haugh, and his assistant, Father Herman T. Richard, arrived at Middletown, to serve St. Joseph, St. Francis Xavier, and St. Rose congregations.

Father Haugh was born in Ireland on November 27, 1840. When he was nine years old, he came with his family to New York City. He attended local schools there, and then at the age of sixteen enrolled at Georgetown College, with the intention of studying for the priesthood. Upon completion of his studies, he entered the Society of Jesus and taught at Georgetown for the next six years. He was later sent to Woodstock College where he completed his courses and was ordained tot he priesthood. After ordination he was assigned to California, then to Colorado. In 1887, he returned to the East Coast and was appointed to the parishes in Petersville and Libertyville, Maryland. From there he came to Bohemia.[54]

Father Haugh continued the policy of dividing the parish ministry with his associate. He ministered to the families of Bohemia while Father Richard was assigned to the care of the congregations at Middletown and Chesapeake City. Both lived at Bohemia.[55]

Father Richard remained only a brief time, until September, 1891, and was the first of several assistants to care for the congregations of Chesapeake City and Middletown for the next four years.[56]

At Bohemia the Feast of the Assumption of the Blessed Virgin Mary on August 15, was a prominent parish celebration. It was combined with the celebration of Forty Hours, and the annual picnic for the Sunday School children. This event was for the entire parish, at Bohemia, whereas other feasts such as Christmas and Easter were celebrated locally by the individual congregations.

A Solemn High Mass began the Forty Hours, concelebrated by other Jesuits from Fordham, Georgetown and Philadelphia.[57] An eminent preacher was invited for the occasion. The ceremony concluded with a procession of the Blessed Sacrament followed by Benediction. The picnic followed with offerings from the large baskets brought along in the carriages. Then there were games for the youngsters as well as for the adults. Scattered congregations came together to celebrate the event with great joy.

The choir at Bohemia was essential to such a grand celebration and other special events. The pastor occasionally treated the choir to an excursion by boat, a very popular pastime for people of the day. On at least one occasion the choir was taken on a trip to Baltimore and back, leaving from Georgetown on the Sassafras.[58]

Finances were always a problem for the pastor. Father Haugh wrote:

"In these three stations there are about 350 Catholics. The income for the three churches is approximately $850 (per annum), of which about $200 comes from Mass stipends. We received $56 from the parish bookstore and $80 from the cemetery. The income drops about $50 each year...."[59]

On July 23, 1893, *at Bohemia*, Bishop Alfred A. Curtis conferred the Sacrament of Confirmation on the following persons: Henry K. *Joseph* Marsh, Joseph M. *Aloysius* Dorsey, George J. *Alexander* Lockwood, Julia M. *Elizabeth* Lockwood,

Summer Festival in the 1890's

Old Bohemia Church 1885

Elsie May *Cecelia* Marsh, Mary *Agnes* Sullivan, and Eglentine *Mary* Wright.

French Jesuit, Joseph Desribes

On September 5, 1893, Father Haugh was transferred to Providence, Maryland, to serve for one year there as superior. For that one year, September, 1893 to September 1894, Father Joseph Desribes was superior at Bohemia.[60] He was born at Tissoire, Auvergne, France on July 30, 1830. He entered the Society of Jesus at Avignon at age nineteen, and after his novitiate was professor in colleges of the Jesuit Province of Lyons. He came to America in 1857, and was prefect for eleven years at Spring Hill College, Alabama, where he was ordained during the Civil War.

In 1866 he was sent to complete his theological studies in France, and upon return was again at Spring Hill College. In 1889, he became superior at St. Inigo's St. Mary's City, Maryland, where he remained for four years.[61]

When Father Desribes arrived at Bohemia in the late summer of 1893, he was accompanied by an assistant, Jesuit Father Andrew Rapp. Father Rapp was assigned to the congregations at Chesapeake City and Middletown. The first baptism of Father Rapp, on October 15, 1893 was that of Sarah Collins, daughter of Bartholomew Collins and Bertha Morgan. Sponsors were Joseph Schaefer and Agnes T. Emmons. On December 17, 1893, he baptized James Albert Stapp, son of Edward Stapp and Mary Rose Krastel. Sponsors were Andrew Slicher and Lena Slicher. On March 18, 1893, he baptized Francis Clifton, son of George Clifton and Adelinda Plummer. Sponsors were William Molitor and Josephine Robison.

In 1894, Father Desribes was sent from Bohemia to St. Ignatius Residence at St. Laurence, New York.[62]

Irish Jesuit, Daniel F. Haugh

Father Daniel F. Haugh

Father Haugh returned at age 37 in 1894 to serve as the last Jesuit pastor at Bohemia. The parish had diminished to the point that it could no longer support two priests. Bishop Curtis placed the mission of St. Rose in Chesapeake City under the charge of the young pastor of Elkton, Father William J. Bermingham.[63]

By 1896, the last year of Curtis' episcopate, Father Haugh was reporting that his congregation was dwindling in numbers. There remained scarcely two hundred Catholics at the Bohemia and Middletown churches. Father Haugh appointed himself as the collector for the annual Orphans Collection on which Bishop Curtis placed great emphasis.[64]

Sturdy in frame and robust in health, Father Haugh knew no weariness. With ardent love for his vocation he faced every difficulty with courage. He continued at Bohemia beyond Bishop Curtis' departure and into the years of a new Bishop of Wilmington's episcopate.⁶⁵

THE EPISCOPATE OF JOHN J. MONAGHAN

At age 41, on May 9, 1897, John J. Monaghan was consecrated. Third Bishop of Wilmington, in which capacity he would serve for the next 28 years.⁶⁶

Upon his arrival, Bishop Monaghan was confronted with the possibility that the Jesuits were about to withdraw from their last mission in his diocese. In 1897 the Jesuit superiors employed a surveyor to draw up a plot of their properties at Bohemia in preparation for turning the church, cemetery, and the "home farm" over to the Diocese of Wilmington. In the summer of 1898 this came about. The Jesuits transferred ownership of church, cemetery, and 177 acres to the Diocese of Wilmington.⁶⁷

Irish Jesuit, Daniel F. Haugh

The last entry of Father Haugh was the reception of a convert, Sarah E. Crowley, on June 18, 1898. Father Haugh left Bohemia and died at Georgetown University Hospital on January 6, 1902.⁶⁸

NOTES FOR CHAPTER FIVE

1. Associated Archives at St. Mary's Seminary and University, Baltimore, Maryland, Archives of the Archdiocese of Baltimore (hereafter AAB) 33-E-3, Thomas Becker to Martin J. Spalding, Wilmington, Delaware, November 10, 1868. Archives of the Diocese of Wilmington, Old Church Road, Greenville, DE 19807, E-mail donndevine@aol.com (hereafter ADW), *Becker Daybook* 1: Becker's first entry was made on August 23, 1868. On the same page, Becker noted that on October 24, he had visited Father Villiger "in the home of Bennett Willson" at Trumpington on Eastern Neck in Kent County, Maryland. Becker's daily entries in the *Daybook* were made usually in Latin, occasionally in Italian or in Greek. On March 1, 1968, the *Delmarva Dialog*, in anticipation of the centenary celebration of the founding of the Diocese of Wilmington, on March 3, 1968, featured a picture of Bishop Becker, accompanied by an article entitled: "Nine Priests Once Served All Delmarva." Tracing briefly the history of Bohemia, the unidentified author spoke of Father Villiger and the fact that Jesuit priests had been caring for the Eastern Shore Catholics from Old Bohemia since 1704.
2. ADW, *Becker Daybook* 16
3. Edward I. Devitt, S. J., "Bohemia, Cecil County, Maryland," *Woodstock Letters* 15 (1886) 105
4. AAB 33-E-3, Becker to Spalding, Wilmington, Delaware November 10, 1868. He added: "George Villiger, S. J., is very active and energetic in spite of his troublesome cough." ADW, *Becker Daybook* 4: Becker noted on March 4, 1869 that Rev. George Villiger had collected for the Bishop's new house (in Wilmington) and grounds $111.00 from St. Francis Xavier Church, and $65.00 from St. Dennis Church in Galena. Again on April 16, 1869, he noted that Father Villiger had collected $36.00 from Bohemia and $20.00 from Kent County for the Bishop's new house.
5. ADW, *Becker Daybook* 17: September 29, 1868. Only a month after he was installed in Wilmington, Becker was approached for acceptance by an Irish priest, Francis J. Blake, who arrived in Wilmington on September 29, 1868, bearing testimonial letters from his bishop. Becker placed him immediately in charge of Elkton and Newark: Thomas J. Peterman, *The Cutting Edge, The Life of Thomas Andrew Becker, 1831-1899* (Devon, Pennsylvania: Book Publishers, 1982) (hereafter Becker) 166. John K. Sharp, *Priests and Parishes in the Diocese of Brooklyn, 1828-1944* (New York: published privately, 1944) 14
6. AAB-33-E3 Becker to Spalding, Wilmington, Delaware, November 10, 1868. Becker told the archbishop that "Father Villiger thinks that the church of St. Dennis (or St. Mary's as St. Dennis Church was first called) on Mr. Dennis McCauley's estate, should be taken down and a new dry one built near Galena, which seems to be the best place." Thomas J. Peterman, *Priests of A*

Century, 1868-1968, Diocese of Wilmington, Delaware (Devon, Pennsylvania: William T. Cooke Publishing Inc. 1970) 28

7. Thomas J. Peterman, *Catholic Priests of the Diocese of Wilmington, A Jubilee Year 2000 Commemoration* (hereafter *Priests*) (Devon, Pennsylvania: William T. Cooke Publishing Inc., 2000) 36

8. *Sadlier's Catholic Directory Almanac and Ordo, 1872* (New York: D. J. Sadlier and Co., 1872) 313; Peterman, *Priests* 30

9. *Sadlier's Catholic Directory Almanac and Ordo, 1874* (New York: D. J. Sadlier and Co., 1874) 343. BAPTISMS BY FATHER VILLIGER. On May 10, 1868, *at Bohemia* Father Villiger baptized Catherine Sullivan, born March 31, 1868, daughter of Thomas Sullivan and Catherine Shehan. Sponsors were Dennis Mollon and Mary Devine. On May 29, 1868, he baptized Edward Lockwood, born September 9, 1821, son of Richard Lockwood and Mary R. Willson. No sponsors given. On June 4, 1868, he baptized Catherine Teresa Manlove, born January 5, 1868, daughter of John Manlove and Mary Elizabeth McCafferty. Sponsor was Catherine McCafferty. On June 14, 1868, he baptized James Harris Vandergrift, born May 11, 1867, son of George Vandergrift and Mary Cosgriff, Sponsors were James and Margaret Callahan. On June 28, 1868, Father Villiger baptized James Finn, born May 21, 1868, son of John Finn and Catherine Reilly. Sponsors were David Reilly and Catherine Finn. On August 9, 1868, he baptized John Powderly, born May 10, 1868, son of James Powderly and Margaret Dunn. Sponsors were David Powderly and Eva Dreka. On August 30, 1868, he baptized Stephen Charles Ryan, born July 9, 1868, son of Martin Ryan and Jane McMullan. Sponsors were Charles and Ann Mullen. On October 26, 1868, he baptized Michael Kleiber, born September 27, 1868, son of Aloysius Kleiber and Placida Eisele. Sponsors were Nicholas and Christina Lotsinger. On November 20, 1868, Father Villiger baptized James Callahan, born September 21, 1868, son of James T. Callahan and Margaret Cosgriff. Sponsor was Mary Vandegriff. On November 21, 1868, he baptized Elizabeth Joanna Burns, born December 19, 1866, daughter of Christopher Burns and Mary Dougherty. Sponsors were David and Alice Powderly. On November 21, 1865, he baptized Gideon Francis Clark, born October 18, 1868, son of John and Rose Clark. Sponsor was Elizabeth Kedes. On December 17, 1868, he baptized Henrietta Walls, born November 9, 1868, daughter of Francis A. Wallis and Mary Georgia Ann Willson. Sponsors were Frederick and Elizabeth Willson.

On December 17, 1868, Father Villiger baptized George Cecil Cokee, born September 15, 1868, son of Benjamin F. Cokee and Amanda Jane Covey. Sponsor was Mary Lockwood.

On January 30, 1869, Father Villiger baptized Charles Pascault, born January 12, 1869, son of Francis R. Pascault and Catherine H. Lusby. Sponsor was Lily Roberts. On February 12, 1869, he baptized Margaret Jane Lambert, born July 9, 1869, daughter of George Lambert and F. Ann Cully. Sponsor was Martha Burke.

On March 30, 1869, Father Villiger baptized Henrietta Aloysia Murphy, born March 9, 1869, daughter of Thomas H. T. Murphy and Rosaline B. Mooney. Sponsors were Cagot and Mary Beeston. On April 1, 1869, he baptized Amelia Tenser, born June 30, 1869, daughter of John Tenser and Arabella Morgan. Sponsor was Anna O'Neil. On April 1, 1869, he baptized Clara B. Tenser, born February 2, 1866, daughter of John Tenser and Arabella Morgan. Sponsor was Anna O'Neill. On April 1, 1869, he baptized Leonard Tenser, born March 19, 1869, daughter of John Tenser and Arabella Morgan. Sponsor was Anna O'Neill.

On April 28, 1869, Father Villiger baptized Mary Teresia Schofield, born March 19, 1869, daughter of John C. Schofield and Annie McCafferty. Sponsors were Marcell Bogenschultz and Waldaburger Bogenschultz.

On May 23, 1869, he baptized Edward Lerihlie and Sara Hugler. Sponsor was Michael Kapp. Sponsors were Marcell Bogenschultz and Waldaburga Bogenschultz. On May 23, 1869, he baptized Elizabeth Lerihlie, born August 2, 1866, daughter of Joseph M. Lerihlie and Sara Hugler. Sponsors were Marcell Bogenschultz and Waldaburga Bogenschultz.

On July 11, 1869, Father Villiger baptized George William Remer, born June 30, 1868, son of Joseph Remer and Otilia Hugler. Sponsor was Michael Kapp. On July 24, 1869, he baptized William V. Grimminger, born September 18, 1869, son of Michael Grimminger and Sophia Bauman. Sponsors were Stanislaus Wiest and Elizabeth Knott. On July 24, 1869, he baptized Charles Grimminger, born September 6, 1867, son of Michael Grimminger and Sophia Bauman.

Sponsors were Stanislas Wiest and Elizabeth Knott.

On August 4, 1869, Father Villiger baptized Helena Murray, born July 27, 1869, daughter of Francis Murray and Helena Bowls. Sponsors were Henry Foster and Margaret Bowls.

On September 6, 1869, he baptized Agnes Leona Ruley, born August 11, 1869, daughter of Peregrine Ruley and Annaro Bermingham. Sponsor was Franny Walmsley. On November 14, 1869, he baptized Charles Cosgriff, born October 23, 1869, son of Thomas Cosgriff and Catherine Boylan. Sponsor was Bridget Boylan.

On November 26, 1869, Father Villiger baptized William McClemens, born November 1, 1869, son of James McClemens and Elizabeth Gordon. Sponsors were Alexander Steward and Catherine Degnan. On December 12, 1869, he baptized Thomas Dorsey, born November 9, 1869, son of Patrick Dorsey and Honora Sheahan. Sponsors were James and Margaret Dorsey. On January 8, 1879, he baptized George Keiser, born September 19, 1869, son of Stephen and Louise Keiser. Sponsor was Joseph Thalmann.

On January 8, 1870, Father Villiger baptized Joseph Krist, born March 15, 1869, son of Joseph Krist and Mary Keiser. Sponsor was Joseph Thalmann.

On March 13, 1870, he baptized Ralph John Ryan, born January 28, 1870, son of Martin Ryan and Jane McMullan. Sponsor was Patrick Hagan. On April 10, 1870, he baptized Mary L. Asay, born December 13, 1869, daughter of James Asay and Elizabeth Margaret Cail. Sponsor was Anne Craddock.

On April 28, 1870, Father Villiger baptized Jacques Cayot Beaston, born January 18, 1870, son of John Beaston and Mary A. Reilly. Sponsors were George W. Lockwood and Adelaida Morton. On May 17, 1870, he baptized Mary Agnes Clark, born March 30, 1870, daughter of John T. Clark and Rosina Kerdes. Sponsor was Elizabeth Kerdes. On July 26, 1870, he baptized Francis Patrick O'Sullivan, born April 30, 1870, son of Thomas O'Sullivan and Catherine Sheahan. Sponsors were Thomas Devine and Mary Dorsey.

On July 10, 1870, Father Villiger baptized Michael O'Hara, born June 19, 1870, son of Patrick O'Hara and Rose McConeghy. Sponsors were Michael McConeghy and Mary Dignan. On July 24, 1870, he baptized George Edward Starling, born June 13, 1870, son of George Edward Starling and Jane Henrietta Able. Sponsor was Julie Stahl. On July 24, 1870, he baptized Agnes Henrietta Starling, born February 11, 1867, daughter of George Edward Starling and Jane Henrietta Able. Sponsor was Julie Stahl.

On August 20, 1870, Father Villiger baptized Louis D. Hopkins Lea, born June 17, 1869, son of George T. Lea and Martha Cross. Sponsor was Susan T. Lea.

In September, 1870, he baptized Mary Catherine Moore, born April 18, 1870, daughter of George Thomas Moore and Josephine Brown. Sponsor was Catherine Pascault. On October 29, 1870, he baptized Thomas John Callahan, born September 14, 1870, son of James T. Callahan and Margaret Cosgriff. Sponsor was Michael Grimminger.

On October 29, 1870, Father Villiger baptized George Walter Wiest, born August 29, 1870, son of Stanislaus Wiest and Elizabeth B. Knott. Sponsor was Michael Grimminger. On October 29, 1870, he baptized George Louis Grimminger, born Mach 30, 1870, son of Michael Grimminger and Sophia Bauman. Sponsor was Stanislaus Wiest. On October 29, 1870, Father Villiger baptized George Grimminger, born December 30, 1869, son of Jacob Grimminger and Sarah Smith. Sponsor was Stanislaus Wiest.

On February 17, 1871, he baptized Mary Ann Jane McMahon, born January 20, 1871, daughter of Andrew McMahon and Mary O'Connor. Sponsor was David O'Connor and Mary McMahon. On March 13, 1871, he baptized James Ryan, born January 15, 1871, son of Martin Ryan and Jane McMullen. Sponsors were John Carroll and Sara Jane Mullen.

On April 23, 1871, Father Villiger baptized William Dorsey, born March 27, 1871, son of Patrick Dorsey and Honora Shehan. Sponsors were Michael and Catherine Dignan. On May 3, 1871, he baptized John Henry Manlove, born October 8, 1870, son of John Manlove and Mary McCafferty. Sponsor was Anna McNeil. On May 28, 1871, he baptized Mary Margaret Thomlinson, born April 1, 1869, daughter of James F. Thomlinson and Mary Ann Rice. No sponsor given.

On May 28, 1871, Father Villiger baptized John N. Thomlinson, born July 19, 1837, son of Henry Thomlinson and Charlotte McCray. No sponsor given.

On December 2, 1871, he baptized Elizabeth Murray, born November 24, 1871, daughter of

Francis Murray and Ellen Bowls. Sponsors were George Conway and Mary Bowls. On December 9, 1871, he baptized George Thomlinson, born November 11, 1871, son of James Thomlinson and Mary Ann Rice. Sponsor was Charlotte Thomlinson.

On December 9, 1871, Father Villiger baptized Joanna Thomlinson, born December 7, 1866, daughter of James Thomlinson and Mary Ann Rice. Sponsor was Mary M. Thomlinson. On December 10, 1871, he baptized John Scofield, born November 11, 1871, son of John C. Scofield and Annie McCafferty. Sponsor was Catherine Ruby.

On January 17, 1871, he baptized George McBride born November 3, 1870, son of John McBride and Mary Murray. Sponsors were Robert Douglas and Sara Douglas.

On February 18, 1872, Father Villiger baptized Charles Borromeo Cohee, born November 14, 1871, son of Benjamin T. Cohee and Amanda G. Covey. Sponsor was Maggie Walmsley. On March 18, 1871, he baptized Ella Louise Walmsley, born March 11, 1871, daughter of Benjamin Walmsley and Frances G. Briscoe. Sponsor was Elizabeth Justaise. On March 24, 1872, he baptized James Joseph Burns, born February 27, 1872, son of Charles Burns and Elizabeth Dalson. Sponsors were John N. Thomlinson and Catherine Thomlinson.

On April 10, 1872, Father Villiger baptized Mary Theresa Lockwood, born February 28, 1872, daughter of George W. Lockwood and Adelaide Morton. Sponsors were Hamilton Morton and Mary Lockwood. On April 28, 1872, he baptized Mary Ann Rice, born October 10, 1838, daughter of James Gustus Rice and Joanna Doan. Sponsor was Joanna Rice.

On July 10, 1872, he baptized Margaret Brothers born March 1, 1870, daughter of John Brothers and Catherine O'Neil. Sponsors were Richard Murray and Sara Douglas.

On August 25, 1872, Father Villiger baptized Joseph Sullivan, born July 31, 1872, son of Thomas Sullivan and Catherine Sheahan. Sponsors were James Dorsey and Honora White. On September 15, 1872, he baptized Christina Clarke, born August 1, 1872, daughter of James Clarke and Keziah Husfield. Sponsors were James Powderly and Theresa Dreka. On September 28, 1872, he baptized Andrew Lindell Beaston, born August 13, 1872, son of John T. Beaston and Mary A. Reilly. Sponsors were Jaques Cayot and Mary T. Morton.

On October 9, 1872, Father Villiger baptized John Donovan, born October 3, 1873, son of Denis Donovan and Catherine Leary. Sponsor was Frederick Droll. On October 8, 1872, he baptized Frederick Vonace Weist, born July 24, 1872, son of Stanislaus Weist and Elizabeth Knott. Sponsors were Michael Grimminger and Sophia Bauman. On October 8, 1872, he baptized John Grimminger, born December 1, 1871, son of Michael Grimminger and Sophia Bauman. Sponsors were Stanislaus Weist and Elizabeth Knott.

On October 27, 1872, Father Villiger baptized Mary Miller Minta Teuser, born November 21, 1869, daughter of John Teuser and Arabella Morgan. Sponsor was Anne Price. On December 25, 1872, he baptized Martin Brain, born November 10, 1872, son of Martin Brian and Jane McMullen. Sponsors were Patrick O'Neil and Rose O'Neil.

On February 2, 1873, he baptized James Walker, born September 2, 1872, son of David Walker and Annie McMullan. Sponsors were Martin Ryan and Jane McMullan. On April 20, 1873, he baptized George Dorsey, born February 6, 1872, son of Patrick Dorsey and Honora Shehan. Sponsors were Thomas Sullivan and Mary Dorsey.

On April 29, 1873, Father Villiger baptized Henry V. B. Crawford, born September 15, 1833, son of William H. Crawford and Catherine Reading. Sponsor was Fannie Cann. On June 2, 1873, he baptized Laura Virginia Morris, born January 1, 1873, daughter of Bradford Morris and Philis Mary Quinn. Sponsors were Michael Finnan and Sarah Lily. On June 29, 1873, he baptized George Joseph Buchm, born March 1, 1873, son of William Buchm and Carolina Droll. Sponsors were Joseph and Emma Stapp.

On July 13, 1873, Father Villiger baptized Howard Aloysius Temple, born October 1, 1872, son of William G. Temple and Emma V. Roberts. Sponsor was Mollie Craddock. On July 18, 1873, he baptized William Blansville, born October 15, 1868, son of Thomas Blansville and Rebecca G. Corniger. Sponsors were John and Temperance Craddock. On July 27, 1873, he baptized John Neintze born August 4, 1868, son of John Neintze and Victoria Droll. Sponsors were Frederick and Mary Droll.

On July 28, 1873, Father Villiger baptized Sarah Robertson, born October 6, 1870, daughter of Samuel Thomas Robertson and Cardina Chambers. Sponsor was Sally Lilly. On October 1, 1873, he baptized George Benjamin Ruby, born August 27, 1873, son of P. W. Ruby and Eleanor

Birminghan. Sponsor was Margaret Walmsley. On October 19, 1873, he baptized Elizabeth Lockwood, born September 2, 1873, daughter of George W. Lockwood and Adelaide Morton. Sponsors were Edward W. Lockwood and Sara Elizabeth Lockwood.

On November 16, 1873, Father Villiger baptized Ann Powderly, born October 15, 1873, daughter of James Powderly and Mary Gillin. Sponsors were Alexander and Bridget McNeil.

On March 18, 1874, he baptized Joseph Finn, born March 4, 1874, son of John Finn and Catherine Reilly. Sponsor was Eleanor Agnes Reilly. On March 23, 1874, he baptized Francis Mullan, born March 11, 1874, son of Charles Mullan and Margaret McMaikall. Sponsors were Archibald Mullan and Mary McCallister.

On April 19, 1874, Father Villiger baptized Caroline Tershley, born November 30, 1869, son of Joseph Tershley and Sarah Hugler. Sponsors were Marcellus and Waldburga Rogenschultz. On May 26, 1874, he baptized F. Vincent Scofield, born April 12, 1874, son of John C. Scofield and Annie McCafferty. Sponsor was Mary Manlove. On April 19, 1874, he baptized Patrick, Ryan, born April 1, 1874, son of Martin Ryan and Jane McMullan. Sponsors were Abe Mooney and Rose O'Neil.

On May 26, 1874, Father Villiger baptized Margaret Manlove, born December 5, 1872, daughter of John C. Manlove and Mary McCafferty. Sponsor was Ann O'Neil. On May 26, 1874, he baptized John Penser, born December 5, 1872, son of John Penser and Arabella Morgan. Sponsor was Ann O'Neil. On May 27, 1874, he baptized Margaret Murray, born May 18, 1872, daughter of Frank Murray and Ellen Bowls. Sponsors were John Murray and Margaret Bowls.

On August 15, 1874, Father Villiger baptized James Maloney, born July 5, 1874, son of Denis Maloney and Honora White. Sponsors were Dennis and Ellen Maloney. On August 27, 1874, he baptized William A. Briscoe, born July 27, 1874, son of Gervase Briscoe and Tanti Ann Fountain. Sponsor was John Finn. On November 12, 1874, he baptized Francis Callahan, born September 4, 1873, son of James Callahan and Margaret Cosgriff. Sponsor was Mary Walmsley.

On December 12, 1874, Father Villiger Ann Isabella Cohee, born November 1, 1873, daughter of Benjamin F. Cohee and Margaret Cosgriff. Sponsor was Lily Burns. On December 22, 1874, he baptized Mary Teresa Smith, born October 21, 1873, daughter of William Smith and F. Alice Green. Sponsors were Michael Dignam and Margaret Dorsey.

On February 10, 1875, he baptized Andrew Stout, born November 10, 1873, child of Joseph Stout and Araminta Green. Sponsor was John Finn.

On April 1, 1875, Father Villiger baptized Mary Droll, born February 2, 1875, daughter of Frederick Droll and Mary Regan. No sponsors given. On August 23, 1875, he baptized Mary Ann Burns. Born July 22, 1875, child of Charles Burns and Elizabeth Dolton. Sponsor was Ellen Murray.

On September 27, 1875, he baptized Catherine McMullin, born August 31, 1875, daughter of Ryan and Jane McMullin. Sponsors were Michael and Catherine Finn. On September 27, 1875, he baptized Henry Lockwood, born July 27, 1875, son of George W. Lockwood and Adelaide Molton. Sponsors were William Morton and Julia Elizabeth Morton.

On November 4, 1875, Father Villiger baptized Mary Lionore Beaston, born August 15, 1875, daughter of John T. Beaston and Mary Reilly. Sponsors were Benjamin Green and Mary Morton. On January 13, 1876, he baptized Vincent Lily, born October 30, 1874, son of Vincent Lily and Elizabeth Grace. Sponsor was Kate Hennessy. On January 16, 1876, he baptized John James McKee, born January 10, 1876, son of Charles McKee and Mary A. McMullen. Sponsor was Susanna Quigley.

On February 20, 1876, Father Villiger baptized Thomas Edward Smith, born July 23, 1875, son of William Smith and Felis Queen. Sponsor was Gervase Briscoe. On March 27, 1876, he baptized and received into the church William Crawford, born July 17, 1846, son of Benjamin Crawford and Ann S. Naindain. Sponsor was Margaret Crawford. On March 27, 1876, he baptized Mary Ellen Walling, born November 18, 1875, daughter of Dennis Walling and Honora White. Sponsors were Thomas Welch and Mary Walsh.

On April 21, 1876, Father Villiger baptized Mary Ann Gore, born March 9, 1876, daughter of Thomas Gore and Ann E. Wiggins. Sponsor was Catherine Finn. On August 26, 1876, he baptized Thomas Grady, born August 22, 1876, son of John Grady and Bridget Connor. Sponsors were John Donahoe and Mary Connor. On August 26, 1876, he baptized Ann E. Dugan, born March 9, 1876, daughter of Thomas Waters Dugan and Corinne H. Craddock. Sponsors were

Benjamin Green and Virginia Bond.

On October 29, 1876, Father Villiger baptized Emma Theresa Henry, born July 2, 1876, daughter of Nicholas Henry and Pauline Barby. Sponsor was Emma Stapp. On November 13, 1876, he baptized Charles H. Crawford, born November 2, 1876, son of Henry B. Crawford and Margaret Price. Sponsors were Thomas Price and Susan Flintham.

On January 21, 1877, he baptized John F. Murray, born December 13, 1876, son of Francis Murray and Ellen Bowles. Sponsors were John and Margaret Dorsey.

On June 10, 1877, Father Villiger baptized Elizabeth A. Wright, born March 27, 1877, child of Joseph C. Wright and Charity Hymon. Sponsor was Mary P. Price. On July 7, 1877, he baptized Catherine Droll, born June 20, 1877, child of Frederick Droll and Mary Leary. Sponsors were Arthur and Catherine Leary.

On January 6, 1878, he baptized Joseph M. Dorsey, born November 21, 1877, child of Patrick Dorsey and Eleanora Sheahan. Sponsors were Michael Dignan and Mary Dorsey. On January 25, 1878, he baptized Rose E. Green, born January 6, 1878, child of Thomas L. Green and Ann H. Phillips. Sponsors were William and Agnes Green.

On February 29, 1878, Father Villiger baptized Anne Indiana Briscoe, daughter of Gervase Briscoe and Anna Fountain. Sponsor was John Briscoe. On March 24, 1878, he baptized William H. Smith, born August 8, 1877, child of William Smith and Philis Queen. Sponsor was John Briscoe.

On April 24, 1878, Father Villiger baptized William Francis Ryan, born February 17, 1878, child of Martin Ryan and Jane McMullin. Sponsors were Patrick Mullen and Ann McMullen. On April 24, 1878, he baptized Ann Mary Tomlinson, born October 9, 1875, child of James Tomlinson and Mary A. Price. Sponsor was Mary Tomlinson. On May 26, 1878, he baptized Joseph G. Roemer, born October 25, 1875, child of Joseph Roemer and Otilia Hugler. Sponsor was Seraphina Shetzler. On May 26, 1878, he baptized Mary Lambert, born October 25, 1876, child of Anton Lambert and Mary Rausch. Sponsor was Otilia Roemer.

On August 4, 1878, he baptized Walter Clarence Briscoe, born May 9, 1878, child of Gervase Briscoe and Anna Fountain. Sponsor was charity Wright. On August 30, 1878, he baptized Mary Money, born August 21, 1878, child of Alexander Money and Elizabeth Campbell. Sponsors were Patrick O'Neil and Rose O'Neil.

Joseph A. Dickerson, THE DOUBLE LL WILLSONS OF KENT COUNTY, Maryland – (joebeaches@friendly.net) – Dr. Thomas Bennett Willson married Henrietta Maria Willson on January 3, 1872. He was son of Richard Willson and Anna Young, born on September 13, 1843, practised at Reese's Corner and died March 23, 1923. She was daughter of John Willson and Anne Brooke, born November 10, 1848, and died July 25, 1937. Their children were: Thomas Bennett Willson, Jr., born 1873 and died 1938; Maria Regina Willson; Ann E. Willson; Julia Rena Willson born 1896 and died 1898; Charlotte Manning Willson born June 18, 1884, died March 22, 1915; Maude Agnes Willson born September 11, 1888, died November 23, 1952; Julia Rena Willson born April 9, 1882, died July 8, 1970; married Harry Skirven who was born October 31, 1879 and died February 9, 1929.

BURIAL RECORDS OF BOHEMIA:
1869- Burns, Capt. Owens, Age 59, U.S. Navy 1824-1840; 1870-12-27 Dixon, Janie L., Age 10; 1870-4-1 Powderly, Catherine, Age 38, Parish of Herring Town, County of Meath, Ireland; 1870-8-2 Powderly, Margaret, Age 29; 1871-12-28 Price, James, Age 49; 1873- Powderly, Anna, Age 67; 1873-3-21 Bond, James T., Age 63; 1875-6-15 Murray, Henry, Age 25; 1875-10-2 Stam, Antoinette, Age 1; 1876-1-19 Riley, David, Age 48; 1876-7-6 Corbaley, Samuel J., Age 61; 1877- Powderly, Helen M., Age 86; 1877-7-24 Killkoff, August Dreka, Age 2 mos.; 1879-7-22 Dixon, Jane A. Age 60; 1879-10-2 Mahoney, Catherine, Age 70, wife of Andrew; 1879-10-16 Mahoney, Andrews, Age 65; 1879-11-13 Brothers, William; 1879-12-18 McCafferty, Wife of J.C. McCafferty; 1879-12-28 Beaston, Eugenia Dorothy, Age 12; 1880-3-10 Lockwood, Edward W., Age 59; 1880-3-28 Moffett, Wm. Henry, Age 56; 1880-6-27 Cannon, Margaret; 1880-7-27 Green, Mary Agnes, Dau. Of Thomas and Harriet; 1880-8-4 Ryan, Jane Ann, Daughter of Martin and Jane; 1880-10-28 Killkoff, Lewis George, Son of Godfrey & Eva, age 1 mo.; 1880-11-7 Schonerd, Anne Grace; 1180-11-11 Mullen, Amie; 1881- Lockwood, Grace, Age 2; 1881-5-8 Corbaley, Hannah T.; 1881-5-29 Reynolds, George, Age 69; 1881-5-30 Dixon, Thomas P., Age 65; 1881-6-13 Gore, Amie Elizabeth,

Age 30, wife of Thomas Gore; 1881-7-28 Mooney, Alexander, Age 4 mos. Son of Alex & Elizabeth; 1882-1-26 Stam, Mary Nona, of Chestertown, Md.; 1882-1-28 Lockwood, Mary Nona, of Chestertown, Md.; 1882-2-11 Stam, Robert Austin, Age 1; 1882-6-4 Harris, Major; 1882-6-8 Reynolds, Sarah, Age 69; 1882-9-14 Moriarty, Mary DeVine, Age 45 – died at St. Inigo Farm; 1882-11-12 Braughman, Mary; 1822-11-17 Brothers, John, Age 53; 1882-11-27 Craddock, William, 1880-11-30 Powderly, James, Age 4; 1882-12 Lockwood, Grace Alricks, Dau. of George and Adelaide; 1882-12-5 Dreka, Agnes Teresa, Age 4 mos.; 1883-3-20 Flintham, Susan, Age 76, died at Middle Neck, Md.; 1884-10-24 Lockwood, Sarah Elizabeth, Age 60 wife of Edw. Lockwood; 1885-6-26 Douglas, Robert, Age 52; 1885-8-5 Bond, Mary A. Age 76; 1885-5-2 Price, Thomas T. Age 59; 1886-10-25 Curry, Lottie (Tomlinson), of Middletown, Del; 1887-6-22 Perkins, Dr. W. Charles, Age 61, of Philadelphia, Pa.; 1887-11-5 Briscoe, Co. of Warwick, Md.; 1887-11-5 Bowles, James Herbert, of Warwick, Md.; 1887-11-5 Stephens, of Middletown, Del.; 1887-11-6 Penn, James H., Age 5; 1888-7 Harkins, Maggie, of Middletown, Del.; 1888-7-2 Moore, Charles, (Col.) of Warwick, Md.; 1888-8-18 Murray, Lizzy, of Chester, Pa.; 1889 Rhoades, Harriet, Age 44 of Warwick, Md.; 1889-2-5 Caffery, Bernard, of Warwick, Md.; 1888-12-6 Stapp, M. Emma, Age 27 of Warwick, Md.; 1889-2-14 Murray, Robert, of Middletown, Del.; 1890-1-30 Dorsey, Denis, of Bohemia; 1889-2-24 Powderly, David, of Sassafras, Md.; 1889-9-30 Cayot, Jacques, Age 83, born Bessoncourt, France; 1890-3-16 Moss, Jane, of Odessa, Del; 1890-4-26 Carroll, Harry E., Age 9 mos., of Middletown, Del.; 1890-1-11 Saunders, Edward, Native of Germany; 1890-3-5 Heinz, Lizzie, Baby; May 14, 1890 – Benjamin J. Green, age 70; July 10, 1890 – James Daly, age 80; 1891-1-31 Burns, Charles, Age 24, of Warwick, Md.; 1891-8-24 Mullen, Patrick, Age 86 of Middletown, Del.; 1891-11-8 Luthringer, Christine, Age 70; 1892-2-15 Reynolds, Benjamin, 1892-2-25 Burns, Eliza, Age 55; 1892-7-1 Bowles, Charles, Age 53; 1892-11-21 Manlove, John, November 29, 1892 – Morris Devine, age 89, County Kerry, Ireland; 1893-1-14 Miller, Sophia, Age 66; 1893-2-7 Stapp, Joseph, Age 67 of Warwick, Md.; 1893-3-2 Mooney, Thomas; 1893-10-11 Craddock, Infant of Mr. Craddock of Middletown, Del.; 1893-12-26 Reynolds, Agnes; 1894-1-29 McFadden, Leonard, Age 77; 1894-2-15 Marsh, Galdin, S., Infant son of Mr. Marsh of Warwick, Md.; 1894-3-21 Shetzler, Sara, Age 65 of Odessa, Del.; 1894-6-20 Carroll, John, Age 6 mos.; 1894-7-21 Crawford, Dr. J.V.; 1894-11-6 Tomilson, Catherine; 1894-11-21 Morton, Mrs.; November 21, 1894 – Catherine Desmond; 1894- Piser, H. Leonard, Age 27; 1895-4-3 Freeman, Anna M; 1896-9-4 Beaston, Loretta, Age 1; 1896- Mary R. Devine, age 30; September 26, 1896 – Mary Theresa Dreka, age 72; 1897-1-14 Crawford, Henry Van, Age 63, Co. B, 1st Md. Confederate Cavalry; February 18, 1897 – Michael A. Durney, M.D.; 1897-4-17 Powderly, John Co., Age 29; 1897-William C. Degnan; April 24, 1897 – Henrietta C. Durney; 1897-10- Carroll, Michael, of Middletown, Del.; 1898-11-17 Beaston, Cayot, Age 1 mo.

10. Dieter Cunz, *The Maryland Germans* (Princeton, New Jersey: Princeton University Press, 1948) 389. As excellent farmers they soon won the respect of the Eastern Shore population. Dieter Cunz, "The Maryland Germans in the Civil War," *Maryland Historical Magazine* 36 (1941) 394-419
11. Peterman, *Becker* 90; Philadelphia; *The Catholic Standard*, May 25, 1872
12. Peterman, *Priests* 20; *Becker* 94 – In 1876 George Bradford was ordained and assigned to build the new church in Chestertown. Baltimore: *The Catholic Mirror*, August 26, 1876; *Sacred Heart Church, Chestertown, Maryland, 75th Anniversary Booklet, May 31, 1954* (Chestertown: published privately, 1954) n. p.
13. Russell H. Perkins, *The Seed Has Grown To Harvest, Centenary of St. Rose of Lima Mission, 1874-1974* (Hackensack, New Jersey: Custombook, Inc., 1974) 59
14. Perkins 16. One of the mission stations attended by Father Villiger was the home of Jacques Cayot, built in 1846. Father Villiger offered Mass there on a large square piano used as an altar. Catholic families from the surrounding area made up the small congregation among whom there were two Negro families from Towne Point – Perkins 18
15. Perkins 19. The deed was not recorded until December 16, 1876, more than a year after the completion of the church – Land Records of Cecil County, Book AWM, No. 4. Mss Archives of Cecil County, Cecil County Courthouse, Elkton, Maryland, folio 485. As Bishop Becker took steps to complete a new church in Chesapeake City, he was distressed to receive notice from the Jesuits of their withdrawal from St. Joseph's in Talbot County. He wrote a protest to Archbishop Bayley of Baltimore – AAB-41-B-10, Becker to Bayley, Wilmington August 10, 1874: "They wish me to

purchase the farm. I hold that if they abandon the mission they ought to give the farm over to the diocese." He also made a strong plea to the Jesuit provincial on September 4, 1874 – Georgetown University Archives (hereafter GUA) New York – Maryland Province, Society of Jesus, Box 228, folios S-18-23. The mission of St. Joseph's, Talbot County, was surrendered to the Diocese of Wilmington in October, 1874 – Edward B. Carly, *The History of St. Joseph's Mission, Cordova, Maryland, 1765-1965* (Easton, Maryland: Tidewater Publishers, 1965) 23; Peterman, *Becker* 99

16. Elkton, Maryland: *The Cecil Whig*, August 29, 1874: "...the ceremonies .... seemed to be very interesting, if one could judge from the eagerness of the people to see all that could be seen."
17. Elkton, Maryland *The Democrat* August 29, 1874 and September 4, 1874. Mary Rose Krastel, daughter of John August and Mary (Smith) Krastel, was the first to be baptized in the new building. She later married Edward Stapp, and is now buried in the church cemetery – Perkins 19
18. Perkins 21
19. The few that appear in the parish records after that were written in a very shaky handwriting. From January of 1876 until June of 1787, all of Father Villiger's baptisms were recorded by Father Robert Wasson Brady, his Jesuit provincial superior, upon his visitation of the mission. On April 15, 1877, Father Brady himself baptized William Francis Ryan, born February 19, 1877, son of Martin Ryan and Jane McMullen. Sponsors were Patrick and Ann McMullen. On April 24, 1877, he baptized Ann Mary Tomlinson, born October 9, 1876, daughter of James Tomlinson and Mary A. Price. Sponsor was Mary Tomlinson. On May 26, 1877, he baptized Joseph G. Roemer, born October 25, 1876, son of Joseph Roemer and Otilia Hugler. Sponsor was Seraphia Shetler. On May 26, 1877, he baptized Mary Lambert, born November 5, 1876, daughter of Anton Lambert and Mary Rausch. Sponsor was Otilia Roemer.
20. Perkins 20
21. Elkton *The Democrat*, June 20, 1875; Peterman, *Becker* 110
22. Elkton *The Democrat*, June 26, 1875
23. ADW, *Becker Daybook* 23-24: May 2, 1875, Becker noted that he confirmed at St. Mary's (St. Dennis *vulgo* (i.e. commonly called) Church in Galena he confirmed 31 children, 19 boys and 12 girls. 26: October 24, 1875, at St. Rose of Lima, Bishop Becker "preached and heard many confessions." 46: Becker preached "apud Elkton" on March 26, 1878. On April 1, 1878, Becker at Chestertown, on April 7, 1878, at Willson's, on April 28, 1878, Becker noted that money was given him through the hands of Father George Bradford from Josephine Redue at Chestertown. Baltimore *The Catholic Mirror*, May 29, 1875: "First Confirmation at Chestertown."
24. Peterman, *Becker* 94: On October 27, 1878, Father Dallard was transferred tot he pastorate of St. James Church in Wilmington.
25. Devitt, "Bohemia," *RACHS* 23 (1913) 43; *Woodstock Letters* 5 (1876) 185
26. No author given, *Souvenir Book: St. Aloysius Church, Littleston, Pennsylvania, August 26, 1862 – August 26, 1962* (Littlestown, Pennsylvania: published privately 1962) n. p. Devitt, "History of the Province" *Woodstock Letters* 40 (1911) 365: There is "The story of the Conewago Ghost,' which Father George Villiger used to narrate with dramatic gusto. It was said, that the housekeeper of the dwelling in which the priest stayed on his visits to Paradise, punished a small colored boy by locking him in a closet, intending to release him on her return from a short visit; she was delayed beyond the expected time, and the boy was found dead. After that, the house had the reputation of being haunted; mysterious rappings and scratching disturbed the priest's room. Father Villiger determined to probe the matter; he summoned the ghost to appear in his room at midnight; declared in a loud voice that he would be prepared with pen and paper to take down answers to his questions. Midnight came – but no ghost. He explained the disturbing phenomena, – and explained away the *Conewago Ghost*, - by the switching of the branches of a walnut tree on the roof of the house, and the scampering of the squirrels after the fulling nuts. Jesuits at Conewago, Pennsylvania, served Paradise and Littleston nearby. Devitt, "Conewago 1741-1961," *Woodstock Letters* 61 (1932) 335. Conewago was the earliest Catholic settlement in Pennsylvania.
27. *Woodstock Letters* 23 (1894) 153
28. Perkins 22; ADW *Becker Daybook* 57: On April 22, 1878, Becker preached at the Chesapeake City church. On April 28, 1878, Becker dedicated the cornerstone of the new Sacred Heart Church in Chestertown. 58: October 13, 1878 – Becker at Bohemia writes that George Villiger is "of

advanced age and infirmity, a man of greatest zeal and inestimable virtue." ADW, *Becker Daybook* 77: On October 12, 1879 "apud Bohemiam," at Church of St. Francis Xavier, assisted by Father Heichemer, Bishop Becker confirmed 23 children, 12 boys and 11 girls. ADW – On October 12, 1879, Bishop Thomas A. Becker administered the Sacrament of Confirmation to the following persons: Patrick *James* Ahern, Edward Carroll *Joseph* Lockwood, Thomas *Joseph* Sullivan, Michael *Anthony* Sullivan, John *Joseph* Russel, Patrick *Joseph* Russell, John *Joseph* Ahern, Christopher *John* Connor, Robert *Jerome* Lusby, Noel *Joseph* Price, Patrick *Henry* Dorsey, Dennis *Joseph* Dorsey, Catherine *Maria* Dorsey, Emelia *Mary* Piser, Clara *Mary* Piser, Alice Mary *Anna* Powderly, Margaret *Mary* Powderly, Anna *Mary* George, Alice *Mary* Welsh, Anna M. L. Marlove, Catherine *Agnes* Manlove, Anna *Mary* Murray, Ellen *Mary* Murray.

29. Georgetown University Archives (hereafter GUA) Special Collections Division, Box 571174, Washington, D. C. 20057. The searchable index to these Georgetown University Library Special Collections is found at this web address:: http://www.library.georgetown. edu/dept/spec-coll/index1st.htm. And for the Jesuit Complex at Bohemia, this web address: http://www.library.georgetown.edu/dept/speccoll/mi/mi}176.htm. And the Bohemia Records are continued at: http://www.library.georgetown.edu/dept/speccoll/mi/mi}177.htm. GUA – *Litterae Annae*, Archives of the Maryland – New York Province, Society of Jesus, Baltimore, Box 335, Folio 7. BOHEMIA – LIST OF JESUIT FARM (1876)
30. Edward B. Carley, "St. Joseph's Church, Middletown, Delaware" (unpublished manuscript, archives of St. Joseph's Church, Middletown, Delaware, n. d.) n. p.
31. Thomas Scharf, *History of Delaware 1609-1888* (Philadelphia: L. J. Richards and Co., 1888) 2:998. Archives of St. Joseph Church, Middletown: "Burial Instructions in the Will of Mrs. Hamilton Morton, March 31, 1884" – Mrs. Morton is emphatic that Father Bradford said the first Mass in their home.
32. BAPTISMS BY FATHER HEICHEMER

    On November 10, 1878, Father Heichemer baptized Jane Anna Ryan, born October 16, 1878, child of Martin Ryan and Jane McMullen. Sponsors were Patrick O'Mullen and Rose Ann Cosgriff. On December 12, 1878, he baptized Sara Elizabeth Gore, born December 31, 1871, of Thomas Gore and Ann Elizabeth Wiggins. Sponsor was Elizabeth Devine. On February 8, 1879, he baptized Paulina Peuser, born May 15, 1876, child of John Peuser and Arabella Morgan. Sponsor was Ann O'Neil. On March 30, 1879, he baptized Adelaide Grace Lockwood, born February 23, 1879, child of George W. Lockwood and Adelaide Morton. Sponsors were Jacques Cayot and Mary R. Beaston.

    On April 13, 1879, Father Heichemer baptized Martha Elizabeth Sterling, born May 15, 1878, child of George Sterling and Harriett Abel. Sponsor was Elizabeth Devine. On May 25, 1879, he baptized John Williams King, born January 5, 1879, child of William King and Mary Fahey. Sponsors were Denis and Elizabeth Devine. On May 25, 1879, he baptized *at Chesapeake City* Francis Moore, born February 16, 1876, child of George Thomas Moore and Josephine Brown. Sponsor was Mrs. Mary Schmidt. On September 21, 1879, he baptized *at Chesapeake City* William M. Kirk, born May 15, 1876, child of William A. Kirk and Anna Quillan. Sponsors were John Miller and Mary Stapp.

    On February 1, 1880, Father Heichemer baptized *at Middletown, Delaware* Mary Elizabeth Price, born January 15, 1880, child of Patrick F. Price and Mary E. Moffett. Sponsor was John F. Connor and Charlotte E. Tomlinson. On February 8, 1880, he baptized Charles B. Warren, born February 8, 1859, son of Samuel R. Warren and Emma N. Porter. Sponsor was John J. Dorsey. On March 23, 1880, he baptized George Rupert Reynolds, born February 29, 1880, child of Jeremiah C. Reynolds and Anna A. Green. Sponsor was Virginia F. Bond.

    On March 28, 1880, Father Heichemer baptized Christopher Joseph Connor, born March 2, 1880. child of John Francis Connor and Margaret Roston. Sponsors were Thomas Augustus Connor and Mary L. Donohue. On May 17, 1880, he baptized Madeline R. Flintham, born February 12, 1880, child of William Flintham and Caroline Elizabeth King. Sponsor was Varina Josephine Corbaley. On May 30, 880, he baptized Ann Elizabeth Wright, born March 27, 1880, child of John Chandler Wright and Charity Henson. Sponsor was Theresa Cecelia Price.

    On June 28, 1880, Father Heichemer baptized John Paul Daily born November 28, 1874, child of John Daily and Cora Davis. On June 28, 1880, he baptized Elizabeth Daily, born September 25, 1876, child of John Daily and Cora Davis. On June 28, 1880, he baptized Mary

Daily, born August 1, 1878, child of John Daily and Cora Davis. Sponsor was Charles Burns.

On August 20, 1880, Father John J. Ryan baptized Catherine Josephine Powderly, born June 26, 1880, child of James Powderly and Mary Gillan. Sponsors were Thomas and Mary Welsh. On August 23, 1880, he baptized conditionally and received into the church Thomas Gore, born September 18, 1850, son of James Gore and Sara Baggs. Sponsor was Thomas Sullivan, Jr.

On August 29, 1880, Father Heichemer baptized Cecelia Ethel Green, born May 17, 1880, child of Thomas F. Green and Harriet Anna Philips. Sponsor was Varina J. Corbaley. On September 24, 1880, he baptized Agnes Gore, born May 10, 1880, child of Thomas Gore and Anne E. Wiggins. Sponsor was Maggie Dorsey. On September 26, 1880, he baptized Caroline Droll, born August 20, 1880, child of Frederick Droll and May Leary. Sponsors were Charles Burns and Ellen Murray. On October 3, 1880, he baptized George Ignatius Lockwood, born August 28, 1880, son of George W. Lockwood and Adelaide Morton. Sponsors were Edward C. Lockwood and Helen Morton.

On January 2, 1881, Father Heichemer baptized Alexander Mooney, born December 19, 1880, son of Alexander Mooney and Elizabeth Campbell. Sponsors were James and Mary Campbell. On January 21, 1881, he baptized Theresa Ryan, born November 24, 1880, child of Martin Ryan and Jane McMullen. Sponsors were Alexander Mooney and Rose Herkens. On March 22, 1881, he baptized Margaret King, born November 24, 1880, child of William King and Mary Fahey. Sponsor was Margaret Theresa Dorsey. On March 27, 1881, he baptized James Murray, born February 26, 1881, son of Francis Murray and Ellen Bowles. Sponsors were Mary Agnes and Patrick Dorsey, Jr.

On April 17, 1881, Father Heichemer baptized Henry Jacob Pensel, born January 15, 1881, son of Charles Pensel and Mary Emma Stapp. Sponsors were Michael Paul and Margaret Stapp. On June 12, 1881, he baptized Mary Ethel Warren, born May 2, 1881, child of Charles Warren and Kathie J. Lambe. Sponsors were Thomas Francis and Virginia F. Lambe. On July 28, 1881, he baptized Charles Robert Joseph, born June 7, 1881, son of John Martin Joseph and Ellen Douglas. Sponsors were Patrick O'Neil and Sara Douglas. On August 21, 1881, *at Chesapeake City* he baptized John Joseph Paul, born July 25, 1881, son of Michael Paul and Felicitas Rohlader. Sponsors were Joseph Schaefer and Maria Genslinger. GUA – The Maryland Province Collection – A BOHEMIA PEW RENT BOOK (1880s).

33. "Obituary – Charles H. Heichemer" *Woodstock Letters* 23 (1894) 153-4; Edward I. Devitt, "Bohemia," *RACHS* 24: 137; GUA – Last Will and Testament of Charles H. Heichemer, of Loyola College, Baltimore, November 4, 1893. GUA – April 20, 1883, C. H. Heichemer, Agent of Corporation of Catholic Clergy. Agreement, February 23, 1892, purchase of Chapel Point in Charles County.

34. Born June 21, 1827, John B. Gaffney entered the Society of Jesus on August 14, 1850 – *Catalogue of the Maryland – New York Province of the Society of Jesus* (New York: The Meany Printing Company, 1909) 70. He entered the Jesuit novitiate at St. Andrew-on-the-Hudson, Poughkeepsie, New York – *Catalogue of the Maryland – New York Province of the Society of Jesus* (Baltimore: John Murphy Associate, 1903) 19. In September, 1878, he became professor of rhetoric at Boston College – "Our Fathers at Providence, R. I.," *Woodstock Letters* 29 (1900) 234. He succeeded Father Michael Tuffer at St. John's Church, Frederick, Maryland, "St. John's Church and Residence Fredrick, Md., *Woodstock Letters* 5 (1876) 186

35. New Castle County, Delaware, County Courthouse, *Land Records* Deed Y-13-381: Recorded may 5, 1887. Conveyed to George W. Lockwood, Thomas W. Hayes, and John M. Giraud, S. J., Trustees. Purchased from Edwin R. Cochran.

36. Frank R. Zebley, *The Churches of Delaware* (Wilmington, Delaware: William N. Cann Co., 1947) 184

37. Scharf, *History of Delaware* 2:998; Perkins 24

38. GUA, Maryland – New York Province Society of Jesus, *Litterae Annae 1803*, Box 335, folio 7

39. Zebley 184; Scharf 2:998 – The writer described the new church in the following way: "The church is a neat frame structure, Gothic in style, sixty-two by thirty-two feet, with spire and bell, and has a seating capacity for three hundred persons."

40. *Woodstock Letters* 13 (1184) 415, Perkins 25 – Mrs. Edward Lockwood purchased the adjoining lot from E. R. Cochran with the intention of donating it to the parish. However, she died before conveying the title and it was purchased by the trustees for three hundred dollars at an auction conducted by her executor at the Middletown Hotel on April 3, 1886. Land Records, New

Castle County Courthouse, Wilmington, Delaware, Deed P-13-522. The new mission was incorporated in the State of Delaware on February 3, 18874. – New Castle County Courthouse, Wilmington, Delaware, *Paper of Incorporation*, X-12-273, dated February 3, 1884.

41. L. Sterling, "An Old Jesuit Mission, A Charming Picture of Bohemia And Its Pastors, A Pretty Spot in Cecil County, Maryland, Where Archbishop Carroll and Charles Carroll of Carrolton Attended School," *Philadelphia Times*, September 22, 1894. The spire atop the bell tower built by Father Gaffney was lost in the fire of 1912 – Devitt, "Bohemia," *RACHS* 24:137

42. BAPTISMS BY FATHER GAFFNEY

On August 21, 1881, *at Chesapeake City* Father Gaffney baptized Catherine Rosalia Lloyd, born July 17, 1881, daughter of John Lloyd and Susanna Molitor. Sponsor was Catherine Anton. On August 21, 1881, *at Chesapeake City* he baptized Ignatius Hume Craig, born July 3, 1881, son of George W. Hume Craig and Clementina E. Barton. Sponsors were David Duncan and Rose Barton. On October 20, 1881, he baptized Anna Boarman, born October 28, 1870, daughter of Joseph Boarman and Anna Seigle. Sponsor was Margaret Dorsey.

On October 20, 1881, Father Gaffney baptized Margaret Boarman, born October 26, 1872, child of Joseph Boarman and Anna Seigle. Also Laura Boarman (no date of birth given), William (no date of birth given) and Joseph (no date of birth given), children of Joseph Boarman and Anna Seigle. Sponsors were Margaret Dorsey, Barbara Seigle, and Anna Weidemier. On November 20, 1881, he baptized William Andrew Krastel, no date of birth given, son of John Krastel and Mary Smith. Sponsors were Andrew Fox and Mary A. Genslinger. On November 21, 1881, he baptized Lydia Collins, no date of birth given, child of Bartholomew Collins and Elmira Davis. Sponsors were James Dorsey and Ellen Maloney.

On April 9, 1882, Father Gaffney baptized Julia E. Morton Lockwood, born February 9, 1882, daughter of George W. Lockwood and Adelaide Morton. Sponsors were George Stephens and Mollie Stephens. On May 4, 1882, he baptized Joseph E. Briscoe, born April 19, 1872, son of Gervase Briscoe and Ann Fountain. No sponsors given. On May 14, 1882, he baptized Thomas Briscoe, born December 20, 1875, son of Gervase Briscoe and Ann Fountain. No sponsors given. On June 1, 1882, he baptized Elizabeth Clark, born January 16, 1876, child of John C. Clark and Rosina Gaddess. Sponsor was Blanche Lockwood.

On June 1, 1882, Father Gaffney baptized Walter R. Sterling, born January 3, 1882, son of George Sterling and Harriet Abel. Sponsor was Emma Price. On June 1, 1882, he baptized Margaret Clark, born November 27, 1881, child of John C. Clark and Rosina Gaddess. Sponsor was Catherine Shehan. On June 4, 1882, he baptized Mary Connor, born September 9, 1881, child of John F. Connor and Margaret Roslin. Sponsors were P. F. Pierce and Eugenia Lamb.

On June 7, 1882, Father Gaffney baptized Mary N. G. Reynolds born march 19, 1882, child Jeremiah C. Reynolds and Agnes Green. Sponsors were W. O. Green and Verina Corbaley. On June 7, 1882, he baptized Charles Wright, born October 16, 1867, child of Chandler Wright and Charity Henson. Sponsor was Emma Price. On June 7, 1882, he baptized Mary E. Wright, born June 29, 1869, child of Chandler Wright and Charity Henson. Sponsor was Agnes Green.

On June 24, 1882, Father Gaffney baptized Joseph F. Maloney, born May 16, 1882, child of Dennis Maloney and Catherine White. Sponsors were Henry Bake and Mary Bake. On June 24, 1882 he baptized Anna V. Smith, born March 21, 1882, child of William Smith and Philis Queen. Sponsors were Frank William Watts and Chandler Wright. On July 24, 1882, he baptized Howard B. Craddock, born September 8, 1872, Charles A. Craddock, born October 15, 1874, Sara H. Craddock, born March 26, 1876, Anna G. Cradock, born June 23, 1878, and Henry B. Craddock, born September 9, 1881, all children of Theodore Craddock and Frances Kates. Sponsors were M. Morton and m Tomlinson.

On August 4, 1882, Father Gaffney baptized Mary A. Dugan, born May 3, 1881, child of Thomas A. Dugan and Corrine Craddock. Sponsor was m. Morton. On August 11, 1882, the Jesuit P. H. Reuman baptized Sara Theresa Green, born April 7, 1882, child of Thomas L. Green and Harriett Anne Philips. Sponsor was Mary A. Clapburn. On August 13, 1882, the Jesuit P. H. Reuman baptized Mary Barbara Bucher, born June 17, 1882, child of William Bucher and Caroline Droll. Sponsors were Joseph Stapp and Margaret Stapp.

On September 4, 1882, Father Gaffney baptized Agnes Teresa Dreka, born August 16, 1882, child of Louis H. Dreka and Mary E. Malsberger. Sponsors were Richard C. Johnson and Teresa Dreka. On November 4, 1882, he baptized Henry Harrison, born September 7, 1882, son of

Henry Harrison and Catherine Elizabeth Quinn. Sponsor was Catherine Conway. On November 4, 1882, Father Gaffney baptized Gertrude Harrison, born April 22, 1881, child of Henry Harrison and Catherine Elizabeth Quinn. Sponsor was Rosa Brothers. On November 8, 182, he baptized Laura R. Manlove, born September 3, 1882, child of John C. Manlove and Mary McCafferty. Sponsor was Clara B. Puser. On November 20, 1882, he baptized Rose Mooney, born September 6, 1882, daughter of Alexander Mooney and Elizabeth Campbell. Sponsors were George and Sarah O'Neil. On December 25, 1882, Father Gaffney baptized Irvin Henry Pierce, born May 4, 1879, Irene H. Pierce, born April 1, 1877, and Thomas Edwin Pierce, born July 10, 1881, all children of James Pierce and Harriet Moore. Sponsor was Indiana Briscoe.

On January 12, 1883, Father Gaffney baptized Harold Jacob Krastel, born December 29, 1883, and Edith May Krastel, born December 29, 1883, twin children of John F. Krastel and Jane R. Elmer. Sponsors were Jacob Krastel and Mary A. Genslinger. On January 13, 1883, he baptized James Abbott Stephens, born December 7, 1882, child of Samuel Stephens and Sarah F. Brady. No sponsors given. On February 4, 1883, he baptized Hamilton Morton Joseph Stephens, born January 6, 1883, child of George W. Stephens and Mollie Morton. Sponsors were George H. and Addie Lockwood.

On March 3, 1883, Father Gaffney baptized Adeline Jones, born March 2, 1882, child of Edmond Jones and Mary A. Ryan. Sponsors were John Tomlinson and Catherine Ford. On March 25, 1883, he baptized Pearl F. Lloyd, born January 1, 1883, child of John Lloyd and Susanna Molitor. Sponsor was Fannie Myers. On March 25, 1883, he baptized Charles Antoine, born February 11, 1883, son of Nicholas Antoine and Catherine Molitor. Sponsors were Washington Montgomery and Frances Molitor.

On June 3, 1883, Father Gaffney baptized Mary D. Workman, born May 1, 1880, child of George Workman and Mary N. Desmond. Sponsor was F. Dugan. On June 24, 1883, Jesuit W. F. Hamilton baptized Eugene Briscoe, born May 22, 1883, and Emeline Virginia Briscoe, born May 22, 1883, twin children of Jervis Briscoe and Sandy Ann Fountain. Sponsors were Henny Ann Horsey and Sarah Watts. On August 3,1 883, Jesuit W. F. Hamilton baptized William Andrew Ayres, born July 9, 1883, child of Peter Ayres and Indiana Briscoe. Sponsor was Sarah Watts.

On August 25, 1883, Father Gaffney baptized Thomas Mooney, born August 21, 1883, son of Alexander Mooney and Elizabeth Campbell. Sponsor was Catherine Bowles. On August 25, 1883, he baptized Anna Mooney, born August 21, 1883, twin daughter of Alexander Mooney and Elizabeth Campbell. Sponsor was Rosa Harkins. On October 14, 1883, he baptized Leo Leslie Reynolds, born August 22, 1883, son of Jeremiah Reynolds and Agnes A. Greene. Sponsors were Louis Dreka and Mary E. Dreka.

On October 21, 1883, Father Gaffney baptized Charles Edward Clifton, born June 18, 1883, child of George W. Clifton and Adelaide Plummer. Sponsors were John Krastel and Mary Krastel. On June 1, 1883, he baptized Eugene Jacob Heintz, born April 8,1 883, son of Jacob Heintz and Solina Berman. Sponsors were John Heintz and Mary Leary. On October 28, 1883, he baptized William C. Dean, born September 30, child of William Dean and Mary Quinlan. Sponsor was M. Morton.

On January 26, 1884, Father Gaffney baptized Carrie Walston, age twenty years, daughter of Wiley Walston and Mary Walston. Sponsor was Anna Flintham. On March 16, 1884, he baptized John Thompson Lyle, born December 29, 1883, child of William Lyle and Teresa Barr. Sponsors were Charles and Mary Shaefer. On April 16, 1884, he baptized John Grimes, born April 1, 1884, child of John Grimes and Mary Campbell. Sponsor was Elizabeth Campbell.

On April 20, 1884, Father Gaffney baptized John Patrick Maloney, born November 4, 1883, son of Dennis Maloney and Catherine White. Sponsors were James Maloney and Anna Whelan. On May 1, 1884, he baptized William H. Lucas, born April 13, 1884, son of George Lucas and Anna George. Sponsors were Nicholas George and Maggie Stapp. On May 4, 1884, he baptized Nellie Whitlock, born April 20, 1884, daughter of Eugene Whitlock and Maggie Harkins. Sponsor was Saddie Walker. On July 6, 1884, he baptized Otto Hohmann, born June 30, 1884, child of Martin Hohmann and Bridget Grimminger. Sponsor was Matilda Romer

On July 6, 1884, Father Gaffney baptized Emma Elizabeth Craddock, born September 10, 1883, daughter of Theodore Craddock and Frances Kates. Sponsor was Mary Stephens. On July 19, 1884, Jesuit John Harper baptized Caroline Paul, born June 21, 1884, daughter of Michael and Louse Paul *from Chesapeake City*. Sponsors were Charles Shaefer and Mary Pensel. On July

21, 1884, Jesuit Father John Harper baptized Charles H. Brown, born May 25, 1884, son of John Brown and Ida Queen. Sponsor was Mary Briscoe. On September 30, 1884, Father Gaffney baptized John K. Krastel, born August 4, 1884, son of John Krastel and Mary Smith. Sponsors were John Krastel and Margaret Grimminger.

On November 16, 1884, Father Gaffney baptized Catherine Lilly Montgomery, born October 15, 1884, child of Washington Montgomery and Frances Molitor. Sponsor was Frances Antoine. On November 30, 1884, he baptized Maggie Krastel, born October 27, 1884, child of John Krastel and Jane Elmer. Sponsors were Henry Krastel and Annie Krastel.

On January 4, 1885, he baptized George McIlhenny Stephens, born December 11, 1884, son of George Stephens and Mollie Morton. Sponsors were Hamilton Morton and Helen Morton.

On March 26, 1885, Father Gaffney baptized H. Emerson Water, born December 11, 1884, son of Henry Water and Henny Horsey. Sponsor was Maggie Penn. On March 26, 1885, he baptized Joseph Chandler Heyer, born December 13, 1884, child of Peter Heyer and Indiana Briscoe. Sponsor was Mary Briscoe. On April 9, 1885, he baptized Ellen Green, born November 30, 1884, daughter of Thomas L. Green and Anna Phillips. Sponsor was Mary Camac. On May 5, 1885, he baptized Elias E. Marsh, age 35, and Elsie M. Marsh, age 4. Sponsors were Benjamin Green and Emma Stapp.

On June 20, 1885, Father Gaffney baptized Charles Robert Lyle, born June 19, 1885, son of William Lyle and Theresa Barr. Sponsors were Joseph Shaefer and Mary Shaefer. On June 20, 1885, he baptized Ella Molitor, 21 years of age. On August 15, 1885, he baptized Mary Ann Lloyd, born January 14, 1885, child of John Lloyd and Susan Molitor. Sponsors were Washington Montgomery and Frances Molitor. On August 30, 1885, he baptized Eva Joseph, born May 19, 1885, daughter of John m. Joseph and Ella Douglas. Sponsors were Joseph Douglas and Rose Cosgrove.

On September 6, 1885, Father Gaffney baptized Mary Eliza Bignear, born August 7, 1885, child of John Bignar and Mollie Shetzlar. Sponsor was Fredrick Droll and Mary O'Leary. On September 13, 1885, he baptized Amelia Boahm, born July 17, 1885, daughter of William Boahm and Catherine Droll. Sponsors were Frederick Droll and Mary O'Leary. On September 13, 1885, he baptized Elsie Garner, born July 29, 1885, daughter of George W. Garner and Ella Daly. Sponsors were John Delaney and Rose Brothers.

On October 18, 1885, Father Gaffney baptized Edwin J. Molitor, born September 15, 1885, child of Edward Molitor and Fannie Myers. Sponsors were Charles Ostenrider and Marsalina Myer. On October 25, 1885, he baptized Mary Pauline Lucas, born October 6, 1885, child of George Lucas and Anne George. Sponsors were Nicholas George and Margaret George. On March 1, 1885, he baptized Royden Marsh, born November 30, 1882, son of H. E. Marsh and Estelle Hayes. Sponsors were H. P. Weber and Virginia Bond.

On November 20, 1885, Father Gaffney baptized John Heintz, born November 1, 1885, son of Jacob Heintz and Sophia Berman. Sponsor was Rose Cosgrove. On December 1, 1885, he baptized Michael Angelo Oldham, born November 7, 1885, son of George W. Oldham and Mary V. Durney. Sponsors were Francis F. Finney and M. Durney. On December 6, 1885, he baptized Elizabeth Joy Mooney, born October 29, 1885, child of Alexander Mooney and Elizabeth Campbell. Sponsors were Charles Breslin and Anna Walker.

On December 6, 1885, Father Gaffney baptized Charles Flinthan, 16 years of age. On December 23, 1885, he baptized Mary Alice Dreka, born December 6, 1885, child of Louis Dreka and Mary Maulsburger. Sponsors were R. C. Johnson and Mary P. Clark. O

On August 4, 1886, *at Bohemia* Father John Gaffney baptized Ada Rose Marsh, born July 24, 1885, child of E.E. Marsh and Alice Estella Hayes, his wife. Sponsors were Aloysius Price and Esta Price.

BAPTISM BY FATHER PATRICK NEALE

On October 10, 1886, Father Patrick Neale baptized Eliza Stephens, born October 8, 1886, child of George W. Stephens and Mary Morton. Sponsors were Henry Weber by proxy and Bessie Morton.

43. Joseph C. Cann, *History of Saint Francis Xavier Church and Bohemia Plantation Now Known As Old Bohemia, Warwick, Maryland* (Warwick, Maryland: Old Bohemia Historical Society, 1976) 259:
Failure of peach crop, 1873-1874
C.C. Lancaster, Esq.

Frederick, Md.
September 21st, 1874

Dear Sir:

"Having made no money during the last year, I am unable to meet the settlement notes due October 3, and therefore ask your indulgence for another year… the past year has been a very trying one for business in this section, and the failure of the peach crop following the failure last year has added to the difficulties, so that the income from my business will not permit an attempt to pay off these notes at this time…."

Very truly yours,
E. T. Evans, per Jn. Jolls

A disease called the "yellows" attacked the peach trees on the upper Peninsula and many farmers who had planted thousands upon thousands of trees in the years between 1850 and 1875 were ruined. Bohemia plantation had a diversified harvest, with only a few acres planted in peach trees, and the blight had no lasting effect on the income from the plantation.

44. "Jubilarian Review," *Woodstock Letters* 76 (1947) 63. He died at St. Andrew's-on-the-Hudson Jesuit novitiate on January 14, 1908. GUA – Last Will and Testament of J. B. Gaffney, City of Bowie, Maryland, Frederick County.

45. ADW *Becker Daybook* 158 – August 26, 1885: newspaper clipping with headlines "A New Bishop Is Coming – Bishop Becker To Be Transferred o See of Savannah" Becker noted on April 20, 1886, that he had received the apostolic letters of appointment. Sisters of the Visitation, *Life and Characteristics of Right Reverend Alfred A. Curtis, D. D., Second Bishop of Wilmington*, (New York: P. J. Kenedy and Sons, 1913) 3 – Alfred A. Curtis was born on July 4, 1831, converted to the Roman Catholic Church on April 18, 1872, was ordained a priest on December 19, 1874, elected to the See of Wilmington on August 3, 1886, and consecrated on November 14, 1886. Thomas J. Peterman, *Catholic Priests of The Diocese of Wilmington, A Jubilee Year 2000 Commemoration* (Devon, Pennsylvania: Cooke Publishing Company, 2000) 41, 42; ADW *Becker Daybook* 169: Last entry by Bishop Becker was on May 10, 1886 – "Retrospect." 170: First entry by Bishop Curtis was on November 14, 1886.

46. "Father John M. Giraud," *Woodstock Letters* 42 (1913) 238-239. John Giraud was born in Caton de St. Antheme, France, on September 29, 1817. He was ordained as a diocesan priest in early 1863 at Tarare, France. He came to Louisiana and entered the Jesuit novitiate as a diocesan priest. His first assignment was to Galveston, Texas, where he built the first church in what is now the Diocese of Dallas, where he spent five years in missionary work. In August of 1882, he was stationed at St. John's Church in Frederick, Maryland. In 1886 he came to Middletown as pastor in charge of Bohemia and Chesapeake City as missions.

47. ADW *Curtis Daybook* 171: On December 16, 1886, Curtis notes that he said Mass at Galena and Chestertown. 175: June 26, 1887, at Bohemia he confirmed 49. On June 26, 1887, Bishop Alfred A. Curtis, in the Church of St. Francis Xavier, Bohemia, confirmed the following converts: Elias Eccleston Marsh, William Thomas Lucas, William Frederick Knott, Charles Henry Warren, James Joseph Moriarity, Henry Charles Dugan, Charles Anthony Flintham, Francis Patrick Sullivan, Thomas Paul Dorsey, and Leonard Joseph Piser. In addition one adult was confirmed: Edward John Stapp. The following boys were confirmed: Francis Clemens Dorsey, Joseph Aloysius Sullivan, George Joseph Dignan, Raphael Joseph Newman, Cosmas Augustine Price, Frederick Knott, Joseph Angelus George, Henry Edward Lockwood, Charles Aloysius Crawford, George Ignatius Dorsey, William Leo Dorsey, Henry Alphonsus Stapp, Joseph Ignatius Crawford, John Francis Devine, George Henry O'Neil, John Joseph Piser, William Allen Briscoe (colored), Thomas Howard Wright (colored). Sponsor for all the above was Henry Weber. The following convert was confirmed: Stella Teresa Marsh, and the following adults were confirmed: Julia Paulina George, Sarah Ayres O'Neil, Mary Millimenta Piser, Lydia Mary Flintham. The following girls were confirmed: Stella Rose Marsh, Teresa Emma George, Mary Margaret Devine, Blanche Josephine Lockwood, Marie Agatha Lockwood, Mary Ellen Powderly, Emma Augusta Knott, Mary Ann Burns, Rose Ann Powderly, Margaret Block Manlove, and Anna Teresa Powderly. Mary Agnes Briscoe, adult, colored was confirmed. Sponsor for all the above was Virginia Bond. On June 28, 887, at St. Rose of Lima in Chesapeake City he confirmed 17: Liona Beaston, Mary Paul, Sarah Lyle, Caroline Wright, Mary Connor, Mary Myers, Mary Rose Krastel, Margaret Krastel, Sarah Ciscoe, Alexander Ciscoe, Joseph Stout, Josephine Stork, Francis Moore, William Emmons, Ellen Molitor, Julia Stork, and Helen Myers. The sponsors for the group were Joseph Schaefer and Mary Krastel.

48. L. Sterling, "An Old Jesuit Mission," *Philadelphia Times*, September 22, 1894. A photo of the altar built by Father Giraud is framed and is leaning against the altar rail on display in 2004 at the Bohemia church. It is Romanesque in style and has two Gothic side altars. Behind the right altar you can see the frame of the original window. It was destroyed by fire in 1912.

49. BAPTISMS BY FATHER ARCHAMBAULT

On December 28, 1886, Father Archambault baptized William Thomas Lucas, age 28 years. Witness was William Powderly.

On January 16, 1887, Father Archambault baptized Mary Frances Molitor, born January 4, 1887, daughter of George Molitor and Ellen Manning, his wife. Sponsors were John Krastel and Mary Krastel. On January 16, 1887, he baptized Viola Montgomery, born January 6, 1887, child of Washington Montgomery and Frances Molitor. Sponsors were John Krastel and Agnes Emmons.

On June 19, 1887, Father J.B. Archambault baptized Sarah Catherine Stout (colored), age ten years, and Daniel Stout, age about five years, children of Joseph Stout and Araminta Green, his wife. Sponsors were Gervase Briscoe and Sarah Ciscoe.

On June 22, 1887, Father Archambault baptized Peter Lyle, six months old, son of William Lyle and Teresa Barry, his wife. Sponsors were Mich. Mulligan and Sarah Lyle. On June 21, 1887, he baptized William Carroll, born May 22, 1887, child of Michael Carroll and Sarah L. Connor, his wife. Sponsors were William Carroll and Rosy Pope. On June 28, 1887, he baptized Joseph Stout, colored, conditional baptism aged 50 years. Witness was Joseph' Schaefer.

On July 10, 1887, he baptized John Edward Hohmann, three months old, child of Martin Hohmann and Brigit Grimminger, his wife. Sponsors were Edward and Lizzie Shetzle.

On July 20, 1887, Father Archambault baptized John Michael Grimminger, about two years old, and Margaret Grimminger, about four years old, children of Michael Grimminger and Sophia Baumann, his wife. Sponsors were John and Mary Bingman.

On August 9, 1887, he baptized Joseph Phelan, two years nine months old, child of Daniel Phelan and Mary Wall, his wife. Sponsor was Maggie Pearce.

On September 9, 1887, Father Archambault baptized Henry Joseph Bingnear and Annie Shetzle, his wife. Sponsors were Joseph Bingnear and his wife, Mary. On April 1, 1888, he baptized Thomas Shannon, born March 13, 1888, son of James Shannon and Rose Harkins, his wife. Sponsors were George O'Neil and Sarah Shannon. On April 22, 1888, he baptized George Records, born December 28, 1887, son of Grishammer Records and Margaret Ellet, his lawful wife. Sponsors were James Ellet and Rose Cosgriff.

On June 10, 1888, Father Archambault baptized Florentine Wilhelmina Blome, born May 10, 1888, daughter of Fred Blome and Florentine Karsinen Gievix, his wife. Sponsor was Mollie Droll. On July 16, 1888, he baptized William Taylor, born October 16, 1885, son of Fred Michael Hagenmeyer and Annie E. Magilly, his wife. Sponsors were William Smith and Mary Fox.

On August 12, 1888, Father Archambault baptized Paul Durkey, Stephens, born July 27, 1888, son of George W. Stephens and Mollie Morton, his wife. Sponsors were Harry and Marie Lockwood. On September 16, 1888, he baptized John Molitor, born August 15, 1888, son of Edward Molitor and Frances Magee. Sponsors were John and Sarah Magee. On October 27, 1888, he baptized Mary Virgie Henry, born September 29, 1888, daughter of Clement Henry and Mary Collins, his wife. Sponsor was Mary Stock.

On August 4, 1889, Father Archambault baptized Rachel Barnett Mifflin, born July 1, 1889, child of Edward L. Mifflin and Helen Morton, his wife. Sponsors were John L. Durkee and Mary L. Morton. On August 8, 1889, he baptized Henry Clarence Lilly, about ten years old, and Mary Cora Lilly, about six years old, children of Vincent Lilly and Elizabeth William, his wife. Sponsor was Lydia Flintham.

On August 11, 1889, Father Archambault baptized Dorothy Kennedy, born July 12, 1889, daughter of William F. Kennedy and Rose Ennis, his wife. Sponsors were Percy and Bernice Ennis

Sacramental Records of Bohemia were examined and signed on December 10, 1889 by Thomas Hamphull, S.J. "on visitation."

On May 24, 1890, Father Archambault baptized Alexia Mary Goff, born May 9, 1890, daughter of Thomas Goff and Margaret Moran, his wife. Sponsors were Francis Droka and Mary Droll.

Father Archambault had only one marriage at St. Rose of Lima Church – that between

Patrick J. Mulligan and Mary L. Schaffer. He had seven baptisms there between 1888 and 1889: George Clifton, John Molitor, Marie Collins, Joseph Leo Krastel, Mary Schaefer, George Lyle, and William W. Schaefer. Devitt, "History of the Province," *Woodstock Letters* 40 (1911) 363. Father Archambault attended Paradise near Conewago in Pennsylvania from 1881 to 1884 and returned there as pastor one year before his death, at St. Francis Xavier Church, New York City on December 23, 1910. He had labored at St. Lawrence Church, New York, and at St. Peter's Church, Jersey City. He was born near Montreal, Canada, on October 16, 1825. He was ordained in 1861 in Brooklyn, New York. "Obituary John Baptist Archambault," *Woodstock Letters* 40 (1911) 236

50. BAPTISMS BY FATHER J.M. GIRAUD

On December 3, 1886, *at Bohemia* Father Giraud baptized Charles Arthur Culley, born September 1, 1885, son of Charles Buddy Culley and Henrietta Starling (colored). Sponsor was Emma Price. On December 3, 1886, he baptized John Ernest Starling, born May 12, 1886, son of George Starling and Henrietta Jane Abell his wife. Sponsor was Emma Price.

On December 29, 1886, Father Giraud baptized George Washington Oldham, born November 29, 1886, son of George W. Oldham and Mary V. Durney, his wife. Sponsors were Michael Angelo Durney and Henrietta Durney. On January 2, 1887, he baptized Charles Heintz, born November 2, 1886, son of Jacob Heintz and Salvina Bergman, his wife. Sponsors were Frederick Droll and Mary A. Jones.

On February 20, 1887, Father Giraud baptized John Edward Lloyd, born January 2, 1887, son of John Lloyd and Suzanna Molitor, his wife. Sponsors were Edward Molitor and Madeline Morris. On May 14, 1887, he baptized Joanna Heaney, born December 14, 1886, daughter of Claymen Heaney and Mary Collins, his wife. Sponsors were Bartholomew Collins and Elmira Collins.

On June 17, 1887, Father Giraud baptized George Ambrose Stephen, colored, born April 19, 1887, son of Samuel Stephens and Sarah F. Brady, his wife. Sponsor was Addie Lockwood.

On January 20, 1887, Bishop Curtis confirmed Paulina Agatha Piser. Signed J. M. Giraud, S.J.

On August 2, 1887, Father Giraud baptized Margaret Johnson, born December 3, 1883, son of George Johnson and Rose Flanigan, his wife. Sponsors by proxy were Daniel Flanigan and Kate, his wife. On August 2, 1887, he baptized Elizabeth Johnson, born July 17, 1886, child of George Johnson and Rose Flanigan, his wife. Sponsors by proxy were Michael Carroll and Sarah, his wife.

On August 2, 1887, Father Giraud baptized William Nicholas Lutheringer, born July 3, 1887, son of William Lutheringer and Sarah V. Lesciere, his wife. Sponsors were Nicholas and Lizzie Lutheringer. On August 9, 1887, he baptized, conditionally, Rose Turner, born October 13, 1882, and Elizabeth Turner, born February 13, 1886, daughter of John Turner and Margaret Flanigan, his wife. Baptismal Book examined and signed August 11, 1887, by Rev. Robert Fulton, S.J., "on visitation."

On September 27, 1888, Father Giraud baptized Lily May Pope, born August 29, 1888, child of Charles L. Pope, not Catholic, and Rosemarie Hener, his wife.

On November 4, 1888, Father Giraud baptized Lilly Agnes Turner, born August 13, 1887, child of John Turner and Margaret Finigan, his wife. Sponsor was Annie E. Price. On December 30, 1888, he baptized James Thomas Warren, born November 16, 1888, child of Charles B. Warren and Kate J. Lamb, his wife. Sponsors were George H. and Sadie O'Neal.

BAPTISMS BY FATHER ROBERT WATSON BRADY

On February 26, 1888, Father Robert Watson Brady baptized conditionally Ollie Mary Leveridge, daughter of Benjamin and Elma, born June 15, 1877. Sponsor was Lizzie Moriarty. On September 20, 1887, Father Robert Watson Brady, S.J., baptized Alban John Giraud Marsh, born September 3, 1887, child of Elias Eccleston Marsh and his wife Alice Estella Hayes. Sponsors were Timothy P. Devine and Lizzie Moriarty. On October 30, 1887, he baptized Caroline Mary Wylie, age about 60 years, formerly a slave in the Lusby family. Sponsor was Miss Lusby. On December 25, 1887, he baptized Edward Lawrie Mifflin, born November 17, 1887, son of Edward Lawrie Mifflin and his wife Ellen Morton. Sponsors were George and Millie Stephens.

On January 22, 1888, Father R.W. Brady baptized conditionally Cinthia Ann Briscoe (colored), wife of Gervase Briscoe. She had been a Methodist, seems to be about thirty years old.

Sponsor was Eleanora Dorsey. On February 19, 1888, he baptized Benjamin Joseph Leveridge, aged about 58 years. He had been a Methodist. Sponsor was Maurice Divine. On February 19, 1888, he baptized conditionally Emma Mary Leveridge, wife of Benjamin J. Leveridge, born October 17, 1859. She had been a Methodist. Sponsors were Mr. and Mrs. Maurice Divine. Father Fulton, S.J. examined and signed Bohemia sacramental records on May 12, 1888. On May 30, 1888, Father Brady baptized John Gaffney Smith, colored, born October 2, 1884, child of William Smith and Phillis Quinn, on Grove Neck the farm of Mr. Rowan. I find from Fr. Gaffney's last baptism.

On July 8, 1888, Father R.W. Brady baptized John C. Manlove, born May 11, 1834, a convert never baptized before. Sponsor was James Clark. On July 22, 1888, he baptized Eugene Clyde Reynolds, born June 15, 1888, son of Jeremiah Reynolds and his wife Agnes Green. Sponsors were Michael and Mary Sullivan.

On January 20, 1889, in the Church of St. Francis Xavier, Bishop Curtis confirmed Paulina Agatha Piser. Recorded and signed by Father Giraud.

BAPTISMS BY FATHER GIRAUD

On January 8, 1889, Father Giraud baptized William John Lucas, born of William Thomas Lucas and Alice Walsh, his wife. Sponsors were Michael Dignan and Alice Mary Powderly.

On January 29, 1889, Father Giraud baptized Cecelia Agnes Ayers, born December 13, 1888, child of Peter Ayers and Annie Briscoe, his wife. Sponsor was Mary Briscoe. On February 25, 1889, he baptized Teresa Catherine Dreka, born February 18, 1889, child of Louis H. Dreka and Mary Walsberger, his wife. Sponsor was Teresa Dreka.

On February 27, 1889, Father Giraud baptized conditionally Mary C. Sudler, convert from the Society of Friends. She was born May 16, 1868, of Joshua Sudler and his wife Alice Callister. Sponsor was Maggie Paron.

On September 20, 1891, Father Giraud baptized Joseph Schaefer, born September 18, 1891, son of Joseph P. Schaefer and Winnie Smith, his wife. Sponsors were Charles J. Schaefer and Mary L. Mulligan. On September 21, 1891, he baptized Joseph R. Douglas, born April 26, 1889, son of Joseph Douglas and Odilia Roemer, his wife. Sponsor was May Roemer.

On October 11, 1891, Father Giraud baptized Maurice Joseph Donaghue, born September 13, 1891, son of Richard Donaghue and Georgia Pucker, not-Catholic, his wife. Sponsor was Alice Burns. On November 1, 1891, he baptized Eva Robinson, born September 5, 1891, daughter of Isaac Robinson and Anna Powell, his wife. Sponsors were Harry J. Krastel and Lena Powell.

On January 22, 1892, Father Giraud baptized John and Emma Jarrell, born January 18, 1892, twins, son and daughter of Alexander Jarrell and Lucinda Rose, his wife. Sponsors were George and Mary Jarrell.

On January 26, 1892, Father Giraud baptized James Polke Lyle, born February 4, 1890, son of William Lyle and Teresa M. Barr, his wife. Sponsor was Bridget Curran. On January 26, 1892, he baptized Anna Lyle, born August 20, 1891, child of William Lyle and Teresa M. Barr, his wife. Sponsor was Sarah M. Lyle.

On May 22, 1892, Father Giraud baptized Adelaide Morton Mifflin, born April 24, 1892, daughter of Edward Mifflin and Helen Morton, his wife. Sponsors were George W. Lockwood and Adelaide, his wife.

On January 31, 1892, Father Giraud baptized Magdalena Molitor, born January 10, 1892, daughter of Edward Molitor and Frances Myers, his wife. Sponsor was Michael Stephenson and Suzanne Meyers.'

BAPTISMS BY FATHER ANDREAS RAPP

On October 8, 1893, *at Bohemia* Father Rapp baptized William Hollingsworth, born October 13, 1891, son of William Sanders Hollingsworth and Lucia Briscoe. Sponsor was Walter Briscoe. On October 15, 1893, he baptized Sarah Collins, born August 28, 1893, daughter of Bartholomew Collins and Bertha May, his wife. Sponsors were Joseph Schaefer, Jr. and Agnes T. Edwards.

On December 17, 1893, Father Rapp baptized Gayle Albert Stapp born October 30, 1893, son of Edward Stapp and Mary Rose Crossdel. Sponsors were Andrew Schleicher and Lena Schleicher. On January 9, 1894, he baptized Martha Douglas, born December 10, 1893, daughter of Joseph Douglas and Ethel Roemer. Sponsor was Anna McClain.

On March 18, 1894, Father Andreas Rapp baptized Francis Clifton, born December 1, 1893, son of George Clifton and Adelaide Plummer. Sponsors were Joseph Schaefer and Linda Crandel. On March 18, 1894, he baptized Josephine Robison, born on February 6, 1894, child of Isaac Robison and Anna Powell. Sponsors were John Schleicher and Josephine Powell.

On March 18, 1894, Father Rapp baptized William Molitor at Chesapeake City, born January 23, 1894, child of Edward Molitor and Frances Meyers. Sponsors were John Fagan and Mary Meyers.

On August 22, 1900, Father Giraud returned to baptize Ellen M. Mifflin, born July 13, 1900, daughter of Edward Mifflin and Helen Morton, his wife. Sponsors were Edward and Rachel B. Mifflin.

BAPTISMS BY FATHER JAMES SMITH

On January 20, 1889, *at Bohemia* Father James L. Smith baptized Joseph Leo Krastle (sic), born December 23, 1888, son of John Krastle and Mary Smith, his wife. Sponsors were Frederick Feastin and Mary Feastin. On January 30, 1889, he baptized Mary Schaefer, born December 25, 1888, child of Charles Schaefer and Ellen Mulligan, his wife. Sponsors were John Lang and Mary Mulligan.

BAPTISMS BY FATHER JOSEPH M. STADELMAN

On July 5, 1890, *at Bohemia* Father Stadelman baptized John Eccleston Marsh, born May 20, 1890, daughter of Elva Eccleston Marsh and Maria Stella Hayes. Sponsors were John Piser and Emilia R. Piser. On July 26, 1891, he baptized Emma Joanna Pope, born March 4, 1891, daughter of Charles Pope and Rose Hover. Sponsor was Margarita Penn.

BAPTISMS BY FATHER A. DUFOUR

On July 13, 1890, *at Bohemia* Father A. Dufour baptized Henry Mark Bingnear, born May 28, 1890, son of John Bingnear and Mary Shetzler. Sponsors were Edward Shetzler and Anna Bingnear. On September 3, 1893, he baptized Catherine Henrietta Goff, born August 18, 1893, daughter of Goff and Maggie Goff. Sponsors were Timothy Devine and Catharina Connor.

BAPTISM BY FATHER W.H. WALSH

On September 2, 1891, Father Walsh baptized Mary Anne Grzeszezak, born July 20, 1891, daughter of Matthias and Johanna Grzeszezak. Sponsors by proxy were George and Mary Lockwood.

BAPTISM BY FATHER J.J. ROVOCK

On September 25, 1892, Father Rovock baptized Ruth Craddock, born February 27, 1892, daughter of B. J. Craddock and Francis Krastel. Sponsors were Sebastian Harges and Catherine Droll. On September 25, 1892, he baptized Edward Shetzler, born August 23, 1892, at Odessa, son of Edward F. Shetzler and Lucida Carpenter. Sponsor was Mary Bingnear.

BAPTISM BY FATHER D.J. GARDINER

On December 18, 1892, Father Gardiner baptized Grace Marie Bingnear, born October 29, 1892, daughter of Henry Bingnear and Anne Shetzler. Sponsor was Rose Cosgriff.

BAPTISM BY FATHER PATRICK J. O'CONNELL

On April 25, 1893, he baptized Gildon S. Marsh, born February 8, 1893, son of Elias E. Marsh and Alice E. Hayes. Sponsors were Michael A. and Mary A. Sullivan. On May 21, 1893, he baptized Regina L. Devine, bon May 7, 1893, daughter of Thomas H. Devine and Mary R. Sheehan. Sponsors were Frank Shanahan and Mary Scully. On June 11, 1893, he baptized Sandanella Anna Arras, born February 5, 1893, daughter of Peter Arras and Indiana Briscoe. Sponsor was Louisa Hollingsworth.

On March 26, 1893, Father O'Connell baptized Grace Elizabeth Stephens, born February 23, 1893, daughter of George W. Stephens and Mary M. Morton. Sponsors were Hamilton M.J. Stephens and Julia E. Morton. On September 12, 1893, he conditionally baptized Bertha Morgan, born November 18, 1875, daughter of Charles Morgan and Sapora Morgan. Sponsor was Mrs. Schaefer.

On July 3, 1893, Father O'Connell baptized Annie Rosa, aged about 16 years, daughter of Silvester Rose and Annie Toll. Sponsor was Silvester Rose, Jr. On July 23, 1893, he baptized Joseph Craddock, born June 17, 1890, son of Benjamin V. Craddock and Frances S. Kates. Sponsor was Frederick Droll. On July 23, 1893, he baptized Alexander B. Craddock, born March 2, 1893, child of Benjamin J. Craddock and Frances S. Kates. Sponsors were Frederick Droll and Alice S. Adams.

BAPTISMS BY FATHER WILLIAM F. CLARK

On October 20, 1895, *at Bohemia* Father William F. Clark baptized Francis Bingnear, son of John Bingnear and Mary Shetzler of Odessa. Sponsors were Edward Shetler and Kate Croll. On October 20, 1895, Father Clark baptized Anne Carolina Shetzler, born July 10, 1895, child of Edward Shetzler and Lucinda Carpenter. Sponsors were John Bingnear and Mary Bingnear.

51. GUA Archives of Maryland – New York Province, Society of Jesus, Baltimore, *Litterae Annae 1886*. Box 336
52. Perkins 27
53. "Jubilarean Review," *Woodstock Letters* 76 (1947) 32. Father Giraud later served at Frederick, White Marsh, and Newtown in Maryland, before becoming chaplain to institutions in New York City from 1901 to 1906. After service at St. Mary's Church in Boston, he retired at St. Andrew's-on-the-Hudson novitiate Poughkeepsie, New York, where he died on March 31, 1913, in his 76th year.
54. No author given, *Portrait and Biographical Record of Harford and Cecil Counties, Maryland, Containing Portraits and Biographical Sketches of Prominent and Representative Citizens of the Counties, Together with Biographies and Portraits of All the Presidents of the Untied States* (New York: Chapman Publishing Company, 1897) 489. He is described as "given to the details of his work as a priest, and he guards well the spiritual interests of his parishioners...a pronounced Republican ... he considers himself a thorough American."
55. GUA – Archives of the Maryland – New York Province of the society of Jesus, *Litterae Annae* 1892, Box 54 Folios T-1, T-2. BOHEMIA BOOK TO 1897, HOUSE HISTORY 1892-1894, HOUSE FINANCES 1884 TO 1900.

BAPTISMS BY FATHER DANIEL F. HAUGH

On September 28, 1890, Father Haugh baptized Charles Frederick Dreka, born September 5, 1890, son of George Augustus Dreka and Katherine E. Malsberger. Sponsors were Louis H. Dreka and Mary E. Dreka. On January 7, 1891, he baptized James Connor, born December 2, 1890, son of Christopher Connor and Mary Laden. Sponsors were John Dorsey and Mary Connor.

On March 29, 1891, Father Haugh baptized John H. Reynolds, son of Jerome Reynolds and Agnes Greene. Sponsors were John and Kate Sullivan. On April 26, 1891, he baptized Mary Loretta Devine, born March 21, 1891, daughter of Thomas Devine and Mary R. Sheehan. Sponsors were Timothy Devine and Nora Sheehan. On May 17, 1891, he baptized George Lucas, born June 16, 1890, son of George Lucas and Annie V. George. Sponsors were E. Marsh and Margaret Parson.

On March 10, 1890, Father Haugh Ida Eugenia Turner, born February 5, 1890, daughter of John Turner and Margaret Flanigan, his wife. Sponsor was Annie Price. On May 27, 1890, he baptized Paul Hayes Marsh, born March 31, 1890, son of E. Marsh and Alice E. Hayes. Sponsors were John and Maggie Dorsey. On June 1, 1891, he baptized Samuel Joseph Cox, born January 25, 1891, son of Samuel Cox and Julia P. George. Sponsor was Teresa Dreka.

On August 25, 1891, Father Haugh baptized Henrietta Mary Oldham, born July 17, 1891, daughter of George and Mary V. Oldham. Sponsors were Henry and Mrs. Crawford.

On September 27, 1891, Father Haugh baptized Lydia Ann Stephens, born August 17, 1891, daughter of Samuel Stephens and Fanny Brady, his wife. Sponsor was Mary Lockwood.

On January 17, 1892, he baptized Henry V. Ayers, born July 14, 1891, son of Peter Ayers and Indiana Briscoe. Sponsor was John Briscoe.

On February 14, 1892, Father Haugh baptized Eva Maria Dreka, born January 15, 1892, child of Louis H. Dreka and Mary E. Malsberger. Sponsors were Henry Crawford and Elva H. Crawford.

On May 24, 1892, he baptized Benjamin Green, born May 23, 1892, son of Lilly Green. Ceremonies supplied. No sponsor given. On May 29, 1892, he conditionally baptized James Hollingsworth, born May 12, 1868, son of Jonathan Hollingsworth and Eliza Ann Perkins. Sponsor was John Briscoe.

On October 23, 1892, Father Haugh baptized Clara May Cox, born on July 21, 1892, daughter of Samuel Cox and Julia George. Sponsors were Fred Grissert and Teresa George.

On March 26, 1893, he baptized Louis D. George, born November 27, 1892, son of George Lucas George and Anne George. Sponsors were Mr. and Mrs. Louis Dreka.

BAPTISMS BY FATHER H.F. RICHARD

On March 2, 1890, *at Bohemia* Father H.F. Richard baptized Ethelberta Ennis, daughter of Thomas Ennis and Sarah Shaetzler. Sponsors were Eddie Shaetzler and Anna, Bergencer. On May 3, 1890, he baptized Marianne Scanlan conditionally, wife of James Francis Fortier. Sponsors were Francis and Mary Krastel. On May 24, 1890, he baptized conditionally Sarah Elizabeth Gerald, born July 12, 1873, daughter of Henry Gerald and Louise Rosa. Sponsor was Alexia Adams.

On June 4, 1890, Father Richard baptized Sarah Mary Johnson, born Dagvitky, a convert, age about 68 years, wife of Alfred Johnson. Sponsor was Patrick Dorsey. On June 8, 1890, he baptized at Middletown Thomas Francis Lucas, son of William Lucas and Alexia Welsh. Sponsors were Henry Williams and Mary Powderly.

On August 6, 1890, Father Richard baptized Alex Victor Moody, born April 29, 1890, child of Wallace Moody, not Catholic, and Caroline Schaetzler, his wife. Sponsors were Edward Kraetzler and Anna Bingnear. On August 31, 1890, he baptized Henry Edward Molitor, born June 9, 1890, child of Edward Molitor and Frances Meyer, his wife. Sponsors were Henry and Josephine Meyer.

On September 21, 1890, Father Richard baptized Charles James Schaefer, born September 8, 1890, child of Charles Schaefer and Helen Mulligan, his wife. Sponsors were James and Emma Mulligan. On September 21, 1890, he baptized Cecelia Catherine Saram, born August 16, 1890, daughter of Alex Mooney and Elizabeth Campbell. Sponsors were James Walker and Sarah O'Niel.

On September 28, 1890, Father Richard baptized in Middletown Mary Theresa Stephens, born September 8, 1890, child of George M. Stephens and Mary Stephens. Sponsors were George and Blanche Lockwood. On January 1, 1891, he baptized in Odessa Joseph Douglass born September 20, 1890, child of Robert Douglass and his wife. Sponsors were John and Sarah Douglass.

On January 1, 1891, Father Richard baptized in Odessa Anna Maria Grimiger, born May 11, 1890, child of John and Bridget Grimiger. Sponsors were John and Mary Bingnear. On April 26, 1891, he baptized in Chesapeake City Caroline Pensel, born February 24, 1891, child of Charles Pensel and May Stapp. Sponsors were Edward Stapp and Agnes Emmons.

On May 17, 1891, Father Richard baptized in Middletown Sophie Elizabeth Bloom, born May 3, 1891, child of Frederick Bloom and Florence Hammergilder. Sponsor was Mary Elizabeth Bloom. On June 27, 1891, he baptized in Chesapeake City Francis Aloysius Clifton, born March 7, 1891, child of George W. Clifton and Alexia Plummer. Sponsor was Mary Egan.

56. Perkins 29. Father Giraud returned as associate to Father Haugh from September, 1891 until May, 1892. Father John B. Meuer followed him for only a short time. Then Father John J. Rodock until September, 1892, where he was assigned to St. John's College at Fordham. He was followed by Father James Gardiner, who remained until February, 1893, when he was made superior at St. Thomas, Bel Alton, Maryland. The same month he was replaced by Father Patrick J. O'Connell, who was transferred to Washington during July of the same year.
57. Perkins 30. The Jesuits visiting would usually stay a while for a summer vacation. Those from Philadelphia were usually members of the staff of the *Messenger of the Sacred Heart* magazine.
58. GUA, Archives of the Maryland New York Province of the Society of Jesus *Litterae Annae 1892*, Box 336, Folio 72
59. GUA – NOTES ON MEN AT BOHEMIA, BY DEVITT (1898), NOTES ON BOHEMIA (1894-1898). Devitt, "Bohemia," *RACHS* 24:137
60. Cann 10:

BAPTISMS BY FATHER JOSEPH DESRIBES

On March 29, 1894, *at Bohemia* Father Joseph Desribes baptized Lucinda Boyles, born September 8, 1874, child of James and Annie Boyles. Sponsors were John and Maggie Dorsey.

On June 10, 1894, he baptized at Bohemia Marianne Cox, born February 15, 1894, child of Samuel Cox and Julia Georges. Sponsors were Frederick Grussert and Annie Lucas.

On June 10, 1894, Father Desribes baptized Martha Frances Stevens, born February 10, 1894, daughter of Samuel E. Stevens and Sarah Francis Brady. Sponsors were James B. Lockwood and Julia Elizabeth Morton Lockwood.

BAPTISMS BY FATHER EDWARD I. DEVITT
On December 29, 1895, at Bohemia Father Edward I. Devitt baptized Mary Agnes Neale, born November 21, 1895, daughter of Clarence Neale and Theresa George. Sponsors were Fred Greissert and Theresa Drohan.

On June 11, 1899, Father Edward I. Devitt baptized Nora Jeannette Stephens, born April 29, 1898, daughter of Samuel Stephens and Frances Brady, colored, with all ceremonies. Sponsor was Mary Dorsey.

BAPTISM BY FATHER EDWARD CONNOLLY
On July 18, 1896, Father Connolly baptized Margaret Mary Walker, born May 4, 1896, child of Sarah Walker. Sponsor was Anna Walker.

61. "Obituary – Father Joseph Desribes," *Woodstock Letters* 33 (1904) 94. He died there on January 19, 1903, in his seventy-third year – "Obituary" 95
62. Canon 10
63. "William J. Birmingham," Peterman, *Priests 2000* 58
64. GUA, Archives of the Maryland – New York Province, Society of Jesus, *Litterae Annae 1896*, Folios 117, 163, 196.

BAPTISMS BY FATHER DANIEL F. HAUGH
On February 18, 1895, *at Bohemia* Father Haugh baptized Francis D. Marsh, born December 13, 1894, son of E.E. Marsh and Alice E. Hayes. Sponsors were Royden and Hilda Marsh. On April 7, 1895, he baptized Charles Joseph Bingnear, born January 22, 1895, son of Henry Bingnear and Annie Shetzler. Sponsors were John Bingnear and Mary Shetzler.

On April 21, 1895, Father Haugh baptized John Joseph Dignan, born January 5, 1895, son of Michael Dignan and Louisa Boyles. Sponsors were Joseph and Mary Dorsey. On June 23, 1895, he baptized Magdalen Lucas, born January 21, 1895, daughter of George Lucas and Anna George, his wife. Sponsors were Fred Grussert and his wife.

On September 15, 1895, Father Haugh baptized Ethel C. Lucas, daughter of William Lucas and Alice Walsh. Sponsors were George and Sadie O'Neil.

On October 27, 1895, Father Haugh baptized Thomas E. Cox, born June 30, 1895, son of Samuel Cox and Julia George. Sponsors were Thomas Devine and Margaret George.

On November 17, 1895, Father Haugh baptized John Francis Carroll, born on September 26, 1895, child of Michael Carroll and Sarah Haver. Sponsor was Mary Droll. On November 19, 1895, he baptized Loretta W. Beaston, born July 7, 1895, child of Cajot Beaston and Bessie Parks Wooters. Sponsor was Mary Beeston.

On November 24, 1895, Father Haugh baptized Bessie Collins, born September 20, 1895, child of Bartholomew Collins and Bertha Morgan. Sponsors were Michael Sullivan and Reba Collins.

On January 5, 1896, he baptized Claude B. Goff, born December 13, 1895, child of John B. Goff and Margaret Moran. Sponsors were Michael Sullivan and Rose Shannon.

On January 26, 1896, Father Haugh baptized James Alfree, born August 15, 1895, son of James and Emma Alfree. Sponsors were Michael Carroll and Elizabeth Haaga. On May 29, 1896, he baptized conditionally Maria Stephens, born November 1, 1880. On May 10, 1896, he baptized Margaret Eliza Marsh, born March 22, 1896, daughter of E.E. Marsh and Alice E. Hayes his wife. Sponsors were Royden and Stella Marsh.

On July 5, 1896, Father Haugh baptized Thomas Kennedy, born May 26, 1896, child of William J. Kennedy and Rose Evans. Sponsors were Leo Evans and Elizabeth McMahon.

On April 4, 1897, Father Haugh baptized Michael Carroll, born February 15, 1897, child of Michael Carroll and Sarah Hoover. Sponsor was Margaret Keegan. On May 16, 1897, he baptized Wilhelmina Ennis, born September 26, 1896, child of Thomas Ennis and Sarah Shetzler. Sponsors were Edward Shetzler and Maria Bingnear.

On May 16, 1897, Father Haugh baptized Maria F. Shetzler, born February 20, 1897, child of Edward Shetzler and Lucinda Carpenter. Sponsor was Maria Bingnear. On June 5, 1897, he baptized John J. Sullivan, son of John Sullivan and Lilly Moriarity. Sponsors were Francis Sullivan and his wife.

On July 25, 1897, Father Haugh baptized Agnes Marsh, born July 4, 1897, daughter of E.E. Marsh and Alice Hayes. Sponsors were Royden and Elsie Marsh. On August 8, 1897, he baptized William R. Goff, born July 21, 1897, son of John B. Goff and Margaret Moran. Sponsor was

Michael Sullivan and Josephine Collins. On October 10, 1897, he baptized conditionally Joseph Wilson Merritt, born December 10, 1874, child of Richard Merritt and Jane Wilson Merritt. Sponsor was John J. Dorsey.

On January 9, 1899, Father Haugh baptized Charles and Augustus Lucas, born on August 16, 1897, sons of George Lucas and Anne Lucas. Sponsor was Mrs. G. Lockwood. On January 23, 1899, he baptized John W. Cox, born September 30, 1897, son of Samuel and Julia Cox. Sponsor was Mrs. G. Lockwood.

BURIALS AT BOHEMIA CEMETERY (1868-1898):

Burial Register of Old Bohemia, St. Francis Xavier Church, Warwick, Maryland:

1871-1- Walmsley, Oliver P.H., Age 34; 1878- 4-16 Walmsley, B.F., Age 59; 1879-10-28 Welsh, John Joseph, Age 38; 1880-10-18 Wright, Charity, Age 39, wife of Chandler; 1882-10-7 Williams, Frank; 1885-1-25 Williams, George; 1886-10-25 Walsh, Mary, of Sassafras, Md.; 1890-6-1 Warren, Charles B., Age 31; 1890-6-1- Warren, Katie J., Age 36, wife of Charles Warren; 1890-7-2 Wright, Mrs.; 1894-7-2 Workman, Mary Desmond, Age 49; 1898-11 Wright, Chandler, Age 54. Published in *The Genealogist's Post* Volume 3, No. 2 (February, 1966) 3-14; Cann 116-142

65. ADW, *Curtis Daybook* 202: Curtis' last entry was on April 11, 1897. After his resignation in 1896, Curtis was appointed apostolic administrator for the diocese of Wilmington, *sede vacante*, pending the arrival of the new bishop. *Sadlier's Catholic Directory 1897* (New York: D. J. Sadlier Co., 1897) 485

67. Peterman, *Priests Jubilee 2000* 52-53

68. If Bishop Monaghan objected to the Jesuits' withdrawal we have no record of it. GUA has no correspondence from Bishop Monaghan. ADW, "Land Map of Old Bohemia – Surveyor's Report, April 29, 1898"; Devitt, "Bohemia," *RACHS* 24:137. As of 2004, the Jesuits continue to own some 900 acres, adjoining the church and cemetery which they lease to local farmers.

69. At the time of Father Haugh's death Bishop Curtis said of Father Haugh that when he was pastor at Bohemia: "The late Father Haugh had the high esteem and thorough good will of every one in Wilmington. To the Bishop he was always much more than simply loyal. For he was ready to go far beyond what would seem simple loyalty. He interested himself genuinely in all concerning the diocese at large no less than in everything gratifying the bishop personally. No one ever desired his aid without finding him willing and glad to render it to the uttermost. It is needless to add after this that his life and character in private won everybody's highest respect not unaccompanied by any means with that which does not always go with respect, namely, affection. May he rest in peace, and when called to follow him, may we leave behind us an odor as good." – "Obituary – Father Daniel F. Haugh," *Woodstock Letters* 31 (1902) 134-140

CHAPTER SIX

Bohemia Under Diocesan Pastors
1898-2004

THE EPISCOPATE OF JOHN J. MONAGHAN

Bishop Monaghan had been Bishop of Wilmington only two years when the Jesuits withdrew completely from the diocese. He would serve as bishop and would assign pastors to Bohemia for another twenty seven years.

On Sunday, October 22, 1899, *at Bohemia*, Bishop John J. Monaghan conferred the Sacrament of Confirmation on the following persons: Joseph Wilson Merritt, convert, James *John* Lockwood, Thomas *Paul* Carroll, William *Edward* Carroll, Alban *James* Marsh, Paul *Joseph* Marsh, J. Eccleston *Matthew* Marsh, Clarence Leveridge, Joseph Phelan, Louis Dreka, Joanna *Josephine* Maloney, Mary Elizabeth Leveridge, Catherine Agnes Carroll, Alice Dreka, and Teresa Dreka. All the above are listed by Father Daly as from St. Francis Xavier Parish, Bohemia.

In the same ceremony at Bohemia, Bishop Monaghan confirmed the following from St. Joseph's Church, Middletown, Delaware: John *Francis* Bignear, Henry Knotts, John Campbell, Thomas Mooney, John *Joseph* Goff, Elizabeth Dugan, convert, Marcella *Catherine* Owens, Elizabeth *Philomena* Mooney, Anna *Mary* Mooney and Mary *Madeline* Bignear. Sponsors for the entire group were Thomas Devine, Thomas Dorsey, Elizabeth Price and Margaret Dugan.

Diocesan Pastor, John Aloysius Daly

Father John A. Daly

In the summer of 1898, Father John A. Daly was assigned as the first diocesan priest to serve as pastor of Bohemia. He took charge of St. Francis Xavier Church with Middletown as its mission. Father Daly had been the first priest to apply for acceptance in the new Diocese of Wilmington in 1868, and upon acceptance had served first at New Castle and Delaware City in Delaware. He lived at Bohemia and served as pastor there for a little more than two years.[1]

Diocesan Pastor, Charles P. McGoldrick

Father Charles P. McGoldrick succeeded Father Daly in June, 1901. He had been ordained the year before. He was in charge of Bohemia and the Middletown mission for a year and a half.[2]

Diocesan Pastor, Charles A. Crowley

Father and later, Monsignor, Charles Crowley was assigned to the residence at Bohemia on January 15, 1904, and was the third diocesan priest in charge of the parish since the departure of the Jesuits.[3] With the growth of the parish in Elkton, Bishop Monaghan was persuaded to return the mission at Chesapeake City to the care of Father Crowley in 1905.[4]

On June 1, 1905, *at Bohemia*, Bishop John J. Monaghan conferred the Sacrament of Confirmation on the following persons: Mary Teresa Shetzler, Eva May Dreka, Emily Jane Pope, Grace Mary Bignear, Lucida Viola Ayers, Margaret Mary Walker, Margaret Elizabeth Marsh, Edward Thomas Shetzler, William Paul Schaefer, Joseph Edward Schaefer, Anna Caroline Shetzler, Francis Pennington Bignear, Michael Francis Carroll, Alice Aquina Marsh, Henry Marcelle Bignear, Charles James Schaefer, John Joseph Sullivan, Lidia Anna Stevens, Francis Haugh Marsh, Lillia May Pope, Mary Veronica Devine, Charles Joseph Bignear, Joseph Marcelle Shetzler, Joseph Paul Carroll, and Lillian Maria Devine. Sponsors were C. Crawford and M. Lockwood.

The Schaefers were from Chesapeake City. The Popes and Dreka were from Cecilton, Sassafras. The Shetzlers and Bignears were from "The Rocks" near Odessa. The Marshes, Carrolls, Devines and Sullivans were from Warwick.

This was the last time Father Crowley gathered all the candidates from the

Portrait of Bishop
John J. Monaghan

Father
Charles P. McGoldrick

Reverend Charles A. Crowley, Pastor at Old Bohemia, 1904–1929

parish for Confirmation at Bohemia.

The winter of 1893-4 was the coldest in over twenty-five years. Father Crowley became well acquainted with the discomfort of the residence at Bohemia in the open country fields. The pastor began to think in terms of moving to Middletown as soon as it would be financially feasible. The people in Middletown were anxious to have their pastor in their midst, and began to contribute liberally to the construction of a house next to St. Joseph's Church.[5]

In 1905 Father Crowley set up a schedule for Mass at Bohemia, Middletown, and Chesapeake City on alternating Sundays.[6] Four years after his arrival in the parish, he moved to a new house built at 15 West Cochran Street in Middletown. He then (in 1908) changed the schedule to arrange for Mass every Sunday at St. Joseph's, Middletown, and a later Mass each Sunday alternating one week in Chesapeake City and the next at Bohemia.[7] It took two hours each way by horse and wagon to travel from Middletown to Chesapeake City.[8]

Beginning around 1910, Father Crowley began to welcome to the area of Chesapeake City members of an immigrant Ukrainian community. These devout, hard-working people were deprived of the regular celebration of their liturgy for many years. Father Crowley over the years welcomed them to the sacraments and provided some pastoral care.[9]

On May 25, 1910, *at Bohemia*, Bishop John J. Monaghan bestowed the Sacrament of Confirmation on the following persons: Maurice Joseph Francis Devine (born February 26, 1899), Edward George Joseph Moffitt (born October 28, 1900), Ellen Aloysia Moffitt (born August 3, 1903), William Joseph Moffitt (born May 22, 1900), William Charles James Dignan (born October 1, 1897), Mary Anne Gertrude Dignan (born June 11, 1899), Lawrence Aloysius Devine (born June 8, 1900), Marie Gertrude Devine (born February 26, 1899), Katherine Cecelia Sullivan (born August 11, 1902), John Devine, John Dignan, Anna Moffitt, Louise Dignan, Francis Sullivan, Bradford Sullivan, and Mrs. Louise Dignan.

The low point came in 1912, when fire gutted St. Francis Xavier Church. Only the walls remained. By then shifting population trends had bypassed the Warwick area and Bohemia's parishioners had dwindled sharply.

On the morning of New Year's Day, 1912. Father Crowley was saying the early Mass at St. Joseph's in Middletown when he received the alarming news that St. Francis Xavier Church was on fire. Father Crowley and all at the Mass that morning rushed to help save the ancient edifice, but when they arrived the entire roof was on fire.[10] A bucket-brigade was quickly formed, and men stationed themselves on the roof of the old pastoral residence now unoccupied, and by pouring water on it, saved that building.[11]

The only part of the church left standing were the walls erected by Father Beeston one hundred and twenty years before. The altar rail made by Ambrose Maréchal, the ancient painting which hung behind the altar, the altar itself and the pipe-organ installed by Father Giraud, the frescoes added by Father Gaffney and the bell installed by Father Villiger were all lost.[12] The bell tower remained. In the early moments of the conflagration some person or persons rescued all but one of the framed Stations of the Cross.[13]

Bishop Monaghan was determined that this cradle of Catholicity in the diocese should be rebuilt. With his encouragement, Father Crowley pushed for its restora-

St. Joseph's Church and Rectory 1908

Photo of pew rents 1909 and pew collection 1909

tion even though the congregation had been gradually dwindling in numbers for some time.

St. Francis Xavier Church arose from its ashes and was rededicated by Bishop Monaghan on Thursday, October 24, 1912, at a 10:30 a.m. Mass. The sermon was preached by Rev. Charles W. Lyons, S. J., rector of St. Joseph's College, Philadelphia. The reconstructed church occupies the site of the one destroyed. The foundations and greater part of the walls remained intact, and the general exterior outline of the ancient church has been preserved. The altar, roof, floor and pews had to be replaced. The ancient sacramental registers and sacred vessels were saved in the residence which also was saved.[14]

On November 16, 1913, *at Bohemia* Bishop John J. Monaghan confirmed the following persons: Agnes Liliana Moffitt, George Brady Bingnear (15 years old), William Joseph Shetzler (14 years old), John Patrick Moffitt, Henry Rowan Pope, Remona Jane Baptista Newman, Anna Seraphina Bingnear, Joseph Henry Murray, Corbit David Bignear, Joseph Aloysius Sullivan, John Francis Joseph Murry, James Joseph Murry, Henry Vaughn Bingnear (13 years old), Lucinda Cecelia Shetzler (12 years old), Thomas Michael Brothers (about 40), Rachel Agnes Brothers (12 years old), and Biola Brothers (convert).

On December 19, 1914, Bishop Monaghan confirmed the following persons: Catherine Theresa Schaefer (age 14), Gertrude Elizabeth Pope (age 12), Mabel Cecelia Money (age 12), Adelaide Mary Cliften Dutton (an adult), Henry Joseph Clifton Dutton (age 14), Edwin Thomas Stapp (age 12), Blair John McCormick

Church at Bohemia After Fire of 1912

Church at Bohemia Before Fire of 1912

(age 10), Harry George McCormick (age 13), Grace Frances McCormick (age 18), John Francis Schaefer (age 18), William Lawrence Clifton Dutton (age 16), Blanche Loretta McCormick (age 20).

At the end of World War I in 1918, the Federal Government was convinced of the vital importance of the Chesapeake and Delaware Canal for national welfare. The canal was purchased by the government from private stockholders in 1919, and by 1927 it had been widened to 90 feet and made 12 feet deep, bringing it to sea level and allowing the stocks to be removed. This was not good, however, for the local economy as Chesapeake City ceased to serve as a stop-over for ships. Local fortunes diminished and more parishioners moved away to seek employment.[15]

With the advent of the automobile just prior to 1920 and better paving of the roads, Father Crowley was able to reach the far-distanced parts of his parish with less effort.

Father Crowley continued to celebrate Mass at Bohemia until 1923, when finally the site was no longer used for the regular celebration of Mass.[16]

THE EPISCOPATE OF EDMOND J. FITZ MAURICE

Pleading failing health, Bishop Monaghan forwarded his resignation to Rome on August 1, 1925. He was succeeded by Bishop Edmond J. Fitz Maurice, a native of Tarbert, County Kerry, Ireland, who recently had been rector of St. Charles Seminary, Overbrook, Pennsylvania. He arrived in Wilmington on December 9, 1925.[17]

Diocesan Pastor, Charles A. Crowley

Father Crowley continued to serve as pastor of Bohemia for four more years under Bishop Fitz Maurice. To keep alive the cultural and religious significance of the first permanent Catholic foundation on the Delmarva Peninsula, Father Crowley initiated the first of the Field Masses at Bohemia on October 10, 1926. Bishop Fitz Maurice presided. About two thousand persons are reported to have attended.[18] Father Crowley promoted fundraising through various parish projects, such as the Bazaar, and kept up maintenance of the properties in a rather sound economy.[19] He was transferred in April, 1929, only months before the Stock Market Crash of October, 1929. He had served at Bohemia for a productive 25 years.[20]

Diocesan Pastor, John Howard Walsh

Born in Newark, New Jersey, John H. Walsh was ordained in Wilmington, Delaware on April 6, 1927. After serving for brief periods in Wilmington, Milford, and Galena, he was assigned to the care of Middletown, Chesapeake City, and Bohemia, where he would serve for the next 27 years.[21] Only a few months before, Herbert Hoover had taken the oath of office as President of the United States after a bitter campaign against the Catholic Democrat from New York, Alfred E. Smith. Cecil County was southern in sentiment enough to be the scene of Ku Klux Klan marches, rallies, and cross-burnings. Anti-Catholic and racist manifestations were evident for a number of years to come in the Cecil County area. A greater disaster accompanied Father Walsh's arrival at Bohemia when on October 29, 1929, the crash of the stock market brought about an economic depression that would plague the country for the next decade. One after another, local Cecil County farms were forfeited to banks for failure to pay on their mortgages. One such farm to be lost was St. Xaverins Farm, the "home farm" deeded to the diocese by the Jesuits in 1898. Money had been borrowed with the farm for collateral, and as income from the faithful dwindled, the diocese was unable to

Father John H. Walsh

Bishop
Edmond J. FitzMaurice

repay the loan. The property was put up for sale in 1931 by the bank, and it was purchased by a local farmer. Only the buildings and four acres including the cemetery remained in church hands. With the help of his parishioners, Father Walsh struggled to defray the expense of operating the parish. Card parties, and bingos were held in different homes, offering attractive prizes and delicious refreshments. One of the great events of the summer was a picnic at Deemer's Beach near New Castle.[22]

When the annual Field Masses at Bohemia were scheduled, Father Walsh would arrange for the Chesapeake City school bus to transport parishioners to that event. In those days the Field Mass at Bohemia was celebrated on the front porch of the old rectory building with chairs arranged on the lawn. The musical highlight was the Army Band from Fort Delaware. Hundreds of people would come from far and wide. After Mass refreshments were served, and tombstones in the cemetery served as good places to sit down.[23]

After a rainfall the as yet unpaved road out to Bohemia from Middletown turned to mud. Travelers could easily get bogged down. Father Walsh later recalled an occasion when Bishop Fitz Maurice arrived at the rectory in Middletown with several clergymen, some of them domestic prelates, or monsignori. Father Walsh urged them to ride with him in his own car, rather than in the large vehicle in which they had arrived. They rejected the idea, and Father Walsh with a twinkle in his eye rescued them from the mud into which their car had sunk. After that Father Walsh sought to have the road paved. He personally traveled to Annapolis many times to request Governor Lane to do something about the road. His efforts were successful.

However, with gasoline rationing during the Second World War, the Field Masses had to be discontinued.[24] With the discontinuance of the annual Field Mass, the grounds at Bohemia fell into disrepair. The buildings were abandoned and continued to deteriorate with the passing of time. The cemetery was overgrown and cows were grazing between the tombstones. Trees had fallen over, knocking down some of the grave markers with them. Access

Bishop's House
1301 Delaware Avenue
Wilmington, Delaware

March 4, 1959

My fellow Americans:

St. Francis Xavier Church, or Old Bohemia, as it is more familiarly called, is a well known and historic landmark. Founded in 1704, it was the earliest permanent Catholic foundation in the English Colonies outside of the Jesuit establishments in Southern Maryland, where Lord Baltimore's colonists settled in 1634. While it stands somewhat isolated but majestic on a hill near the little village of Warwick in Cecil County, Maryland, its influence down through the years has extended far beyond its geographical location. It is truly the "Mother Church" of the Diocese of Wilmington and surrounding areas.

The Bohemia Academy, founded there in 1745, was the immediate predecessor of Georgetown University in Washington, D. C. It was attended by such personages as John Carroll, who became the first Catholic Bishop of our country, and his well known cousin, who is identified in history as Charles Carroll of Carrollton and a signer of the Declaration of Independence. Bohemia Academy thus played an important role in the early education of boys destined to be outstanding in their service to God and country.

Old Bohemia truly symbolizes the faith of our forefathers. It stands as a monument to the memory of the men who labored there so long ago and to those who started life's journey from the Academy.

These facts alone merit its restoration and preservation; and as Bishop of the Diocese of Wilmington, in which geographical area Old Bohemia is located, I sincerely and prayerfully endorse The Old Bohemia Historical Society's plans to restore and preserve this truly meaningful and historic shrine.

Yours sincerely in Christ,

+ Edmond J. FitzMaurice
Bishop of Wilmington

Bishop FitzMaurice's Letter to the Old Bohemia Society

to the cemetery was virtually impassable. Father Walsh began a series of annual carnivals in Warwick, with John Maloney as general chairman. These efforts resulted in the development of a new section of the cemetery complete with an entrance of brick pillars and a paved road.

During the Second World War, attention was brought to the importance of Old Bohemia and its maintenance in a feature article in a Cecil County newspaper. The writer gives an account of Bohemia's history and concludes: "In fact this is the most interesting church in this community considering its history in the olden times and the sentiment it arouses among the descendants of those who years ago helped to establish it."[25]

After the war, further attention was focused on the importance of Bohemia to the Diocese of Wilmington by a radio program broadcast on the Catholic Forum of the Air on November 2, 1947.[26]

An interested layman, Frank Krastel wrote first to the top officials of Georgetown University in Washington, D.C., the Catholic Diocese of Wilmington and the Archdiocese of Baltimore, as well as to prominent laymen, but with no tangible results.[27] On June 18, 1952, Mrs. Krastel received a letter from Miss Carrie Wright, a retired school teacher living in Chesapeake City, Maryland, in which she wrote: "Father Walsh tells me that the historic church is doomed to fall down. What a pity!"[28]

From all this persistent effort, mostly on the part of Frank Krastel, and co-founder a Presbyterian, Alfred N. Philips, came the establishment of the Old Bohemia Historical Society. Mr. Krastel wrote Father John H. Walsh pastor, seeking permission to organize a program to save the ancient church. A reply from Father Walsh soon announced that he had discussed the matter with Bishop Fitz Maurice and they both gave it their wholehearted support.[29]

In the meantime Frank Krastel wrote Mrs. John P. Corcoran seeking help from the Raskob Foundation for Catholic Activities. Mrs. Corcoran, formerly Helen Green, was the widow of John J. Raskob, a financier who built The Empire State Building. She was a native of the Bohemia church area. As a result of the request, the Society was granted $25,000, with the requirement to form a corporation in the State of Maryland.[30]

On September 6, 1952, Frank Krastel sent a letter to fourteen persons inviting them to attend a meeting on September 12, 1952, at St. Joseph's rectory in Middletown, Delaware, to discuss plans for the organization. Present at the meeting were Francis X. Donahue, Francis W. Krastel, Sr., Francis W. Krastel, Jr. (then a student at St. Mary's Seminary, Baltimore, Maryland), Rev. John H. Walsh, Mrs. Josephine Padley, Mr. and Mrs. James A. Quinn, Mrs. Francis Sullivan, Joseph Whitlock, J. Bradford Sullivan, Mr. and Mrs. John A. Maloney, John J. Ward, Jr., Michael F. Carroll and James Mullen. Francis W. Krastel was elected temporary chairman.[31]

Peter J. Nolan, Esquire, a lawyer in the DuPont Company's legal department, agreed to volunteer guidance in the preparation of by-laws and procedures for incorporation of the society as a non-profit tax exempt organization.

It was agreed that the group should organize under the name of *The Old Bohemia Historical Society*. Frank Krastel was delegated to work on a tentative set of by-laws. He was asked to invite the following other persons to serve on the

Board of Directors: Stanchfield Wright, I. Frank Huey, John F. Hynes, M.D., John Stokes, Mrs. Frank Dick, Mrs. Alice Crawford, and Frank Zaffers.

The Old Bohemia Historical Society came into being on February 3, 1953, with the signing of the Articles of Incorporation by Francis W. Krastel, John J. Ward, Jr., Francis X. Donahue, Alfred N. Phillips, J. Bradford Sullivan, Michael F. Carroll, James A. Quinn, Edward D.E. Rollins, Sr., John F. Hynes, M.D., John H. Herndon and William C. Brothers.

Rt. Rev. Monsignor Joseph D. Sweeney, chancellor of the Catholic Diocese of Wilmington and Reverend John H. Walsh met with the incorporators in the living room at Worsell Manor, then owned by Alfred N. Philips, on February 28, 1953, to formally organize the society. The officers elected were: Francis W. Krastel, president; Alfred N. Phillips, vice-president; Francis X. Donahue, secretary; Rev. John H. Walsh, treasurer, with John J. Ward, Jr., chairman of finance committee and co-signer of checks.[32] The first religious service sponsored by The Old Bohemia Historical Society was called 'Old Bohemia Day' and was held on Sunday, August 16, 1953 at 4:30 p.m. An altar was erected under the large hemlock tree near the gateway to the old section of the cemetery at the beech tree. Benediction of the Most Blessed Sacrament was sung by the Rev. John H. Walsh. Father Joseph Durkin, S. J., Professor of History at Georgetown University, talked on the heritage of Old Bohemia. Copies of the historical pamphlets were distributed. The Oblates of St. Francis de Sales Novitiate, Childs, Maryland, led the singing. Fathers Eric McDermott, S. J., Neil Gargan, S. J., John M. Daley, S. J. and John J. Conny, OSFS were also present.

The original Board of Directors included the incorporators: G. Reynolds Ash, John A. Maloney, James Mullen, Jesse D. Otley and John Stokes. Jesse D. Otley was named director of the restoration in 1953.[33]

Cleanup and repair work started immediately. Truckloads of debris and trash were hauled away. With the $25,000 grant from the Raskob Foundation sent by check on March 5, 1953, Frank Krastel and 14 other pioneers jumped into action

Photo of Original Board of the Old Bohemia Historical Society

Photo of Jesse D. Otley   Field Mass at Bohemia's 250th Anniversary

as soon as the rigors of the 1953 winter subsided. An eyewitness recorded the following description of the deplorable state of the buildings and grounds in 1953 before the Society began its work:

> The roof leaked causing major damage to plaster and woodwork. Windows were broken, evidently by thrown stones and bullets from small caliber rifles. Birds were nesting on the altar structure with dead grass strewn about the floor, evidently having been blown in by the wind through the open doorways. The grounds were overgrown with tall grass and weeds and littered with branches broken from the trees, the teetering front porch on the rectory, the cobwebs on the boxwood across the brick walkway leading to the front of the church, the farmer's chickens roosting in the boxwood and cows wandering around the cemetery presented a scene of such abandonment and desolation as to make one wonder whether or not the damage that had been caused by time, the elements and vandalism could be corrected.[34]

The major repairs to the church undertaken at that time included checking the foundations and pointing the brick walls, and as necessity dictated replacement of floor joists in the sanctuary that had been ruined by termites and rot, strengthening the roof structure and repairs to the slate roof, repairs to plaster and the shutters that were hanging askew with some of the louvers missing.

The major repairs on the rectory building consisted of a new wood shingle roof, removal of the dilapidated front porch, repairs to the brick wall at the back end of center hall and the kitchen walls which in several places were in a near state of collapse, rebuilding center hall rear door retaining panels from the original door, major repairs to plaster throughout the house shoring-up the floor joists supporting the dining room floor, replacing timbers supporting the floor of small rear bed room and renewing the flooring ruined by termites, closing-up the doorway from the room next to the sacristy to closet under stairway, installing brick

"Old Bohemia" showing rear of Church, Jesuit burial lot, connecting Sacristy, rear of Rectory and Kitchen.

Excavations by Pope and Kruse in 1955

floor in kitchen and railing platform with seats outside the front door (later replaced with brick), replacing missing door locks and latches that had been carried away. Sometime in the past the mullions had been cut from the second floor window sash on the front of the rectory so that one large pane of glass could be used instead of the original six. This sash was replaced. The outside woodwork and interior walls were cleaned of years of accumulated paint and whitewash, and were repainted. Both buildings were treated for the extermination of termites and a contract signed for yearly checkup. Copper rain gutters and downpipes were installed on the rectory.[35]

The farm on which Old Bohemia is located had been sold in 1931. Possession of it was regained by purchase in 1953, and progress in paying off the mortgage was reported then. The farm was needed because it was here that the Jesuits had their Plantation headquarters, their water-powered grist and saw mills, the kiln for making bricks, the carpenter and blacksmith shops, the ice house and the various farm buildings used in such a large operation.

The Old Bohemia Historical Society, founded as a non-sectarian non-profit corporation in the State of Maryland, operated the site in behalf of the Foundation Income from the lease of 200 plus acres of farmland and leased hunting rights in the woodland cover the expense of insurance, taxes and operating costs.

Religious services were resumed in the summer of 1953 with an outdoor Mass celebrated under the large hemlock at the gateway to the old section of the cemetery. In 1953 visitors could join the Society for $15 a year or $40 for three years.

In March 1954, the Catholic Television Guild, over channel WDEL-TV, presented a program on "Old Bohemia." The program, conducted by Richard Connolly, featured Reverend David Burke, S. J., Reverend Robert Parsons, S. J., and Frank W. Krastel, president of the Old Bohemia Historical Society. Father Parsons was just completing a book on the Maryland Province of the Jesuits. Father Burke was a member of the Jesuit Mission Bureau.

Later in 1954 the Society sponsored a Mass to observe the 250th Anniversary of the founding of St. Francis Xavier Mission at Bohemia. Nearly 1000 persons attended the Mass celebrated on August 29, 1954. The sermon was given by Reverend Neil Gargan, S. J., from Georgetown University. During the Mass a guard of honor formed by the fourth-degree Knights of Columbus stood at attention in front of the altar.[36]

In 1955 the firm of Pope and Kruse was engaged to conduct an archeological dig to identify brick foundations. This was done by Miss Jeannette Eckman, whose findings were detailed in a report submitted by Pope and Kruse in 1956. Excavations made by Pope and Kruse, supervised by Harry L. Lindsey, uncovered old brick foundations in front of the 1825 rectory. These foundations uncovered in front of the old rectory were accepted as the remains of the building that had served as the house-chapel-school between 1720 and 1745.[37]

The first annual Mass inside the church, following the organization of The Old Bohemia Historical Society, was held on September 11, 1955 at 2:00 p.m. The Mass was celebrated by the Rev. Philip J. Tarallo of St. Joseph's Orphanage School, Clayton, Delaware assisted by Rev. Paul F. Huber, OSB, pastor of Sacred Heart Church in Wilmington, Delaware and Rev. John H. Walsh. Father Huber preached the sermon using a public address system so that the people who could not get inside the church could hear the proceedings. The choir was from Wilmington under the direction of Mr. George Finnan.

At a Board of Directors meeting on February 23, 1956, it was agreed to have Mass celebrated in St. Francis Xavier or Old Bohemia Shrine annually on the third Sunday of June, July, August and September, at 4:00 p.m. The time was changed to 3:00 p.m. in 1957 and in 1958 the Mass again celebrated at 4:00 p.m. and has been so conducted since at that time. Members of the clergy who have generously volunteered their time to celebrate these services have come from Georgetown University, Loyola College in Baltimore and parishes in the Archdiocese of Baltimore, Washington and Philadelphia, Dioceses of Wilmington and Camden, N.J., St. Mary's Seminary, Baltimore, Maryland, St. Charles Seminary, Philadelphia and The Oblates of St. Francis de Sales Novitiate.[38]

The next annual meeting of The Old Bohemia Historical Society was held on February 25, 1956. The business to be transacted at this meeting at St. Joseph's Hall, Middletown was the election of a board of directors and officers, as well as revisions of certain by-laws. Frank Krastel was reelected president. Alfred N. Phillips was renamed vice-president, as were Rev. John H. Walsh, treasurer, and Miss Selma Borgstrom, secretary.

At this meeting in 1956, plans were announced to increase the public worship at Old Bohemia Church, with Mass offered at 4 p.m. on the fourth Sundays of June, July, August, and September. The board of directors also agreed on an all-out effort to collect the various articles which once belonged to the Old Bohemia Church which had been scattered among friends and neighbors for safekeeping after the church became inactive.[39]

Diocesan Pastor, Herbert T. Rimlinger

The new pastor assigned to the care of Bohemia was Reverend Herbert

Father Herbert Rimlinger

Theodore Rimlinger, born in Wilmington, Delaware, and ordained a priest on June 12, 1930.[40] On June 28, 1956, he was sent to replace Father Walsh, who left to become pastor of St. Paul's Church in Wilmington.[41]

During the weeks of October 7, 1956, Father Rimlinger and The Old Bohemia Historical Society provided an exhibit at the International Eucharistic Congress Exhibit at Convention Hall Philadelphia. Fifty thousand copies of a leaflet on the history of Old Bohemia were distributed from the booth sponsored by the Catholic Diocese of Wilmington.[42]

In 1956 the facts uncovered by the exploratory excavations were detailed in drawings submitted by Pope and Kruse. On April 25, 1957, at the seventeenth regular meeting of the Old Bohemia Historical Society's Board of Directors, the Research and Restoration Committee made the following recommendations based on the Pope and Kruse findings: (1) That Pope and Kruse be asked to prepare for The Old Bohemia Historical Society sketches showing the high spots of the work inside and out, that would have to be done to put the present church in conformity with what it was in the 1792-97 period. (2) That the drawings referred to in #1 be made with one showing the steeple essentially as it exists today and one showing the exterior as it may have looked before the existing steeple was erected. (3) That Pope and Kruse give the Society an order of magnitude estimate of the cost of the foregoing plans. (4) That the work involved in the making of these drawings be done by Pope and Kruse on an hourly basis as per our understanding of our contract with them. It was regularly moved, seconded and carried that these recommendations be accepted and that a prompt contact be made with Pope and Kruse by the Research and Restoration Committees. The President thanked the members of these committees for having worked so hard and patiently in bringing the basic research work to a conclusion.[43]

Membership in the Society was increasing.[44] A pilgrimage was planned for May 10, 1957, to Old Bohemia, focusing upon it as one of the historically important spots in Cecil County.[45] Summer Masses in 1957 were to be held at 3 p.m. on the third Sundays of June, July, August, and September.[46]

Following the adjournment of the April 25, 1957 meeting, one of the members described a bell reputed to have been in use at Old Bohemia a hundred years before. The history of the bell seemed substantial enough to warrant trying to purchase it for return to Old Bohemia. Mrs. Dunn received a substantial amount in contributions from those present and contacted the present owner relative to its purchase for $40.00, the amount paid for it at a recent sale in Cecil County. The need of a typewriter for the Society's Secretary was brought up for consideration and following an open discussion, it was moved, seconded and carried that a typewriter be purchased with the choice of make and price to be made by the President.[47]

In October, 1957, Frank Krastel issued a typewritten promotional letter entitled: "A Shrine to 'Inspire' All Americans – Old Bohemia."[48]

Portrait of Alfred N. Phillips

Portrait of Frank W. Krastel

Historical Marker in Warwick

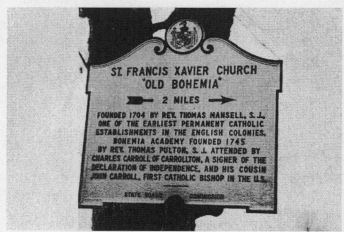

Bohemia Church and Rectory in 1954, 250th Anniversary

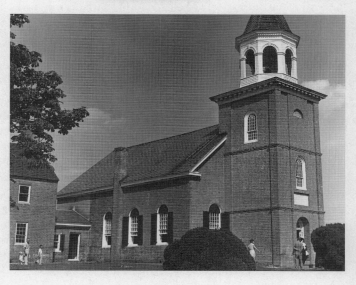

In 1958, a historical marker was placed in Warwick at the road leading to Old Bohemia Church and grounds. It was set up by the State Roads Commission through the efforts of G. Reynolds Ash and John H. Scarff, director of historic markers for the commission.[49]

On Sunday, July 20, 1958, Very Reverend John J. Conny, OSFS, master of novices at the Oblates of St. Francis de Sales Novitiate, Childs, Maryland, celebrated the second of the four summer Masses at Bohemia. The historic iron cross brought by Rev. Thomas Mansell, S. J., when he founded Bohemia in 1704, was placed on display. It had remained at Bohemia nearly two centuries until it was transferred to the Georgetown University museum.[50]

In 1959, five thousand brochures and mailing envelops were printed for free distribution and twenty-five hundred copies of a single folded page leaflet on Old Bohemia were distributed to people who would spend summers along the nearby rivers or visit them on weekends.[51]

On August 24, 1959, a special reburial took place at the Bohemia cemetery, that of the remains of James Heath, one of the early settlers and large land owner in the area of the Old Bohemia Church. Because of his association with the church and ownership of nearby historic Worsell Mannor it was considered advisable to move his mortal remains from an obscure and almost forgotten grave on the Warren Farm, owned by Mrs. Thomas Lattomus of Townsend, Delaware and tenanted by Mr. Colin Walter, in Appoquinimink Hundred, New Castle, County Delaware to the St. Francis Xavier or Old Bohemia cemetery. The transfer was done under the supervision of Mr. Robert T. Jones, Newark, Delaware undertaker, by Mr. Tyson F. Sartin of St. Georges, Delaware. The exhumation and reburial were witnessed by Mr. George Jones, Mr. Sartin, Mr. Charles White, Mr. Michael F. Carroll, Miss Lillian deVine, Mrs. Joseph P. Dunn, Mr. Francis W. Krastel and three of Mr. Sartin's men. The original slab marker over Mr. Heath's grave bears the following inscription:

> Here lyes the body of James Heath who was born at Warwick, on the 27th day of July 1658 and died the 27th day of November 1731 in the seventy-fourth year of his age. Requiescat in Pace.[52]

In 1959, his last year before retirement as Ordinary, Bishop Fitz Maurice wrote an eloquent testimony to his veneration of Old Bohemia and his support of its restoration in a letter which we have published earlier in its entirety.

Bishop Fitz Maurice died at St. Francis Hospital in Wilmington on July 25, 1962.[53]

THE EPISCOPATE OF MICHAEL W. HYLE

With the untimely death of Coadjutor-bishop Hubert Cartwright in early 1958, Michael William Hyle was appointed Coadjutor – bishop of Wilmington on July 3, 1958, and assumed duties in that capacity on October 8, 1958. He succeeded to the position of Ordinary as the Fifth Bishop of Wilmington on March 2, 1960.[54]

In 1961 an agreement was signed by Bishop Hyle designating the Old Bohemia Historical Society as caretaker and steward of the buildings and property, except

Bishop Michael W. Hyle

Bishop Hyle's Letter to the Old Bohemia Historical Society

My fellow Americans:

As Bishop of the Wilmington Diocese since March, 1960, I subscribe to what my predecessor, Archbishop FitzMaurice, had to say in his letter of March 4, 1959, which is reproduced on the inside of the front cover of The Old Bohemia Historical Society's brochure.

Old Bohemia, as the friends of this historic shrine fondly call it, is a monument to early Catholicity and to early Catholic education in Colonial America. While this hallowed spot happens to be in the geographical confines of the Wilmington Diocese (Eastern Shore of Maryland, Virginia and the State of Delaware), its early influence and importance had national significance, as you will find out by reading this brochure. Truly, therefore, Old Bohemia belongs to the people of America and not just to those who happen to be living in the Wilmington Diocese.

I, therefore, commend the work of The Old Bohemia Historical Society and extend my personal thanks and blessing to all who assist this organization in any way to restore and maintain this historic shrine.

Sincerely yours in Christ,

Most Reverend Michael W. Hyle, D. D.
Bishop of Wilmington

for the cemetery, which is owned and maintained by St. Joseph Parish, Middletown, Delaware.[55] At the same time Bishop Hyle published a letter for the Old Bohemia brochure, which we produce above here in its entirety.

Diocesan Pastor, Herbert T. Rimlinger

Father Rimlinger continued to serve as pastor of St. Joseph Church, Middletown, for two more years under Bishop Hyle. On August 8, 1960, lightning struck the steeple at Bohemia and badly damaged it. The Society had it repaired, and lightning protection along with lead coated copper sheeting was provided for the steeple. At that time running water and electricity were installed in the rectory building. Fences were erected to keep out wandering cattle. Expert attention was given the centuries-old boxwood. Several trees in danger of falling were removed. Twenty-four trees donated by Mr. Henry duPont of Longwood Gardens, Longwood, Pennsylvania were planted.[56] In June, 1962 a flagpole donated by Mrs. Lewis Straughan, of Penns Grove, New Jersey, was erected on the Bohemia grounds.[57] The Society raised a substantial sum from the sale of historical memory plates in 1961 and 1962.[58]

In 1962, Father Rimlinger was transferred as pastor to St. Patrick Church, Wilmington, Delaware.

Diocesan Pastor, John H. Dewson

In June 1962 John Henry Dewson was appointed to succeed Father Rimlinger as pastor of St. Joseph Parish, Middletown. In 1963 he conducted a census of the parish.[59]

Father Dewson was an enthusiastic student of Catholic history and showed great interest in Old Bohemia. Liturgical celebrations were held regularly on the fourth Sundays of June, July, August, and September. He encouraged the work of the Society and attended meetings. The first newsletter of the Society was issued in

Father John H. Dewson

1963, now published on a quarterly basis.[60]

On August 16, 1963, The Old Bohemia Historical Society displayed articles from the Bohemia church and museum at the National Liturgical Conference in Philadelphia. The articles displayed drew major attention, especially the Old Bohemia host mold. A picture of Old Bohemia was featured on the 1963 calendars produced by the Doherty Funeral Home in Wilmington.[61]

On August 26, 1963, John J. Ward, chairman of the "Plans for the Future" Committee of The Old Bohemia Historical Society asked Father Dewson, G. Reynolds Ash, and Frank W. Krastel to serve as a sub-committee to re-negotiate the re-acquisition of the 177 acre St. Xaverius Farm, the original patrimony purchased by Father Mansell in 1704, from Mr. and Mrs. Richard D. Aitken. An eighteen – month option specifying the monthly payment of $100. to Mr. and Mrs. Richard D. Aitken was signed on September 14, 1963. The Society, however, raised $40,000 and borrowed another $15,000 from the Catholic Diocese Foundation to buy back the farmland owned by the Aitkens since its sale in 1931. The farm was purchased at $65,000 on December 17, 1964, in the name of The Catholic Diocese Foundation of the Diocese of Wilmington, Inc.[62]

In 1963 measured drawings were submitted by Pope and Kruse of the church and rectory. These drawings, with mylar reproducibles and azalid prints, and a photo data book (including twelve photographic negatives with prints and three data pages for St. Francis Xavier Church), are on file in the library of Congress.[63] In 1964 a wrought iron cross, which is a replica of the Maryland colonists' wrought iron cross of 1634 and which was used at Bohemia until 1898, was erected at the corner of the south foundation wall of the original house – chapel – academy building (circa 1720-1745). The cross monument and the plaque attached to it were dedicated following the July 19, 1964 Mass. Five thousand more folder type brochures on Old Bohemia church and museum were purchased for free distribution by the Society in 1964.[64]

On September 6, 1963, when Bishop Hyle returned from the second session of the Second Vatican Council, he asked Father Dewson to assist in the founding of a new diocesan newspaper to be called *The Delmarva Dialog*. Father, later Monsignor, Dewson was transferred to Wilmington, Delaware to serve as pastor of St. Mary's Church, on May 29, 1964, where he also served as director of the Catholic Press of Wilmington.

Diocesan Pastor, John P. McLaughlin

Father John Patrick McLaughlin became pastor of St. Joseph's while the Second Vatican Council was in progress and the Third Session was about to begin.[65] In October, 1965, the priest celebrating Mass was turned around at the altar to face the people, and in March, 1966, a new order of the Mass in the vernacular was

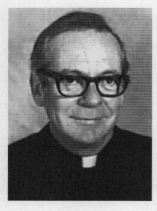

Father
John P. McLaughlin

promulgated.

With these and many other similar significant changes taking place in the church and in the diocese at this time, Old Bohemia was featured in the press as its history was told and its need for preservation reasserted. Rev. Msgr. Roderick B. Dwyer, Vicar General of the Wilmington Diocese, represented Bishop Hyle, who was again in attendance at the Second Vatican Council, at a Sunday afternoon celebration at Old Bohemia on September 22, 1965.[66] Another article updated the public on the work of the Old Bohemia Historical Society at that time: "When funds become adequate it is planned to rebuild the water wheel and grist mill, the carpenter shop, forge, slave quarters, and other plantation buildings as they stood in the late 1700s and this site will someday be a showplace for Maryland and the Nation."[67] *The Delmarva Dialog*, was first published by the Diocese of Wilmington in 1965. Its first issue on September 3, 1965, included an article entitled "A Shack, A Priest, and 200 years," commemorating the institution of St. Joseph's Church in Talbot County by Father Joseph Mosley in 1765. No mention is made of the Jesuits at Bohemia in that first issue. But in the issue of October 1, 1965, shortly thereafter, there was a full page feature of "Old Bohemia," consisting mostly of pictures, and a short article on its founding and the statement that the last services for the season had been celebrated there on the previous Sunday.[68] Two articles were published on Old Bohemia in 1966 which featured its clergy and the burial register.[69] In 1967 Colonel A. M. Musgrove of Newark, Delaware mounted the old bell, which tradition says predates the bell in the tower, on a hand-hewn post at the rear of the kitchen near the spot where the old well was located.[70] On March 31, 1967, an article announced the forthcoming observance of the Centenary of the Diocese of Wilmington on March 3, 1968. The article traced the growth of the faith on the peninsula which originated at St. Francis Xavier.[71]

The summer series of Masses at Bohemia in 1967 brought out good numbers. Father Francis J. Tierney, pastor of St. Joseph's Church, Clayton, Delaware, was celebrant and homilist at the Mass in July. The choir from the Oblates of St. Francis de Sales, Childs, Maryland, provided the music.[72] The Mass in August was celebrated by Monsignor John H. Dewson, pastor

Father John McLaughlin and Father Joseph Dunn, O.S.F.S.

of St. Mary's of the Immaculate Conception Church in Wilmington. The choir from the Immaculate Conception Church in Elkton provided the music.[73]

Bishop Michael Hyle accepted the invitation to celebrate Mass and to speak at St. Francis Xavier Church at Bohemia on June 4, 1967. He died at age 66 on December 26, 1967.

THE EPISCOPATE OF THOMAS J. MARDAGA

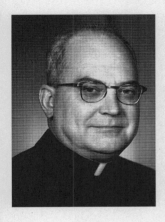

Bishop
Thomas J. Mardaga

The appointment of a new bishop was announced on March 13, 1968, and on April 6, 1968, Bishop Thomas J. Mardaga was installed as the Sixth Bishop of Wilmington.[74]

The celebration of the Diocesan centennial was already in progress. In anticipation of its observance, *The Delmarva Dialog* had published at the beginning of the year a full page historical article, entitled: "Our Diocese Began With Mass Offered Mainly In Colonial Homes." The article told of Jesuit missionaries centered at Bohemia, such as Father Thomas Mansell and Father John Lewis and featured a picture of Trumpington in Kent County, Maryland, one of the homes where Jesuits from Bohemia offered Mass in colonial times.[75] On April 5, 1968, again in anticipation of the diocesan Centennial, the diocesan newspaper featured articles entitled: "Old Bohemia – First Church in the Diocese" and "First Bishop Was A Pennsylvanian."[76] The official Diocesan Centennial Celebration was presided over by Bishop Mardaga in Wilmington on October 25, 1968.

Diocesan Pastor, John P. McLaughlin

Father McLaughlin continued to serve at Middletown under Bishop Mardaga. On June 6, 1968, the diocesan newspaper announced: "Old Bohemia To Have Summer Masses." The first Mass on June 16 was celebrated by Monsignor Paul J. Taggart, Vicar General. The second Mass was celebrated on July 21 by Monsignor Henri I. Foltz, Chancellor. The Mass on August 18 was celebrated by Reverend Paul J. Schierse, Assistant Chancellor. The final Mass of the season celebrated in September by the new Bishop of Wilmington, Thomas J. Mardaga. The choir from the Oblates of St. Francis de Sales Seminary at Childs, Maryland, provided music for each Mass.[77]

On September 6, 1968, Bishop Mardaga appointed Father McLaughlin rector of The Cathedral of St. Peter in Wilmington.

Diocesan Pastor, Russell H. Perkins

Father Russell Hedley Perkins followed Father McLaughlin as pastor in September, 1968.[78] An article in the diocesan newspaper shortly after his arrival featured Old Bohemia and the iron cross brought there by Father Mansell in 1704. Father Perkins celebrated the first Mass of the new season at Old Bohemia on June 5, 1969. The same issue of the diocesan paper chronicled that Bishop Mardaga would celebrate the Mass there in September.[79] Another article in the summer of 1969 featured "Middletown, Once A Mission Of Historic Old Bohemia" and focused on several Jesuit pastors of Bohemia who served the congregation at Middletown.[80] A month later an article in the same paper featured the church in Elkton and its founding by a Jesuit pastor from Bohemia.[81] The Old Bohemia Historical Society was greatly encouraged by Father Perkins. In his time as pastor the society was making great strides in promoting the church and museum. The grounds there were kept in beautiful condition by Edward J. Ludwig III, chairman of the grounds committee. Frank Krastel and Morton Taylor were making great progress in developing the museum at Bohemia.[82] In 1970 the society's brochure on Old Bohemia was revised and seven thousand copies of it were printed for free distribution. Picture postcards and note paper with the image of the church on it were also sold as a source of revenue and publicity.[83] Frank W. Krastel, of Penns Grove, New Jersey, president of the Old Bohemia Historical Society since its founding, was responsible for most of these significant accomplishments.[84]

The Mass at Bohemia in July 1970, was celebrated by Reverend William M. J. Driscoll, S. J., of Loyola College, Baltimore. The church and adjacent museum were open to visitors from 1 to 5 p.m. at the time of the monthly Mass. Krastel reported that the average attendance at the monthly summer Masses was from 125 to 150.[85] In August of 1970, the *Cecil Whig* of Elkton ran a feature article on Bohemia, its history, its restoration, and its museum.[86]

On March 26, 1971, the Old Bohemia Historical Society received a bequest of ten thousand dollars.[87] The four summer monthly Masses were celebrated at Bohemia in 1971.[88]

On September 17, 1972, Bishop Thomas Mardaga celebrated the final Mass of the season. The Cathedral Choir of St. Peter's Cathedral, Wilmington, sang under the direction of Carmen Consiglio. A personal electronic organ donated to St. Francis Xavier Church by Firmin Swinnen, was used for the first time on this occasion.[89]

In 1973 work at Bohemia included roof reinforcement of the church and rectory, weatherproofing the walls, adding gutters and downpipes, and installation of a heating system.[90]

On February 4, 1974, the Old Bohemia Council (Ms. 6543) of the Knights of Columbus was organized. Father Perkins was the first chaplain to the Order which numbered 33 charter members. David Shebock was the first Grand Knight. Today the council numbers 160 members and meets at Price Hall at St. Joseph's in Middletown.

In August, 1974, the office of Archeology and Historic Preservation, United States Department of the Interior, announced that St. Francis Xavier Church had been recorded by the Historic American Buildings Survey, a program of the National Park Service, as having such significant historic value as to warrant its preservation.[91]

The diocesan newspaper announced that Father Perkins, pastor, would be cel-

Picnic at Bohemia in 1973

> **OLD BOHEMIA**
>
> The hills were splashed with beauty
>   In the light of early morn'
> And, as they raised their chapel...
>   Old Bohemia was born.
>
> Good priests gathered at the well,
>   Its waters sweet and cool,
> Would pause awhile – to hear the drone
>   Of latin from the school.
>
> The seeds they placed in Mother Earth
>   Have long since passed away...
> But seeds they placed in human hearts
>   Are bearing fruit today.
>
> List' awhile... and hear the bell...
>   It rings for you and me,
> Blending with the other bell
>   That rang for Liberty.
>
> Your prayers, good friend, are needed
>   To ease the load we bear.
> And he... who loves his fellow man...
>   A golden crown will wear.
>
> *Edward J. Ludwig III*
> 9/18/61

Poem "Old Bohemia" by Edward Ludwig III in 1961

Bohemia Brochure Cover, 1970

Father Russell H. Perkins

Bishop Mardaga's Letter to the Old Bohemia Historical Society

> Diocese of Wilmington
> Post Office Box 2030
> Wilmington, Delaware 19899
>
> Office of the Bishop   August 5, 1976
>
> My dear friends:
>
> As Bishop of the Diocese of Wilmington, I am pleased to reaffirm the sentiments expressed by my predecessors with regard to St. Francis Xavier Shrine at Warwick, affectionately known as Old Bohemia.
>
> The history and traditions of this Jesuit mission establishment are far too well-known to be recounted here. Suffice it to say that due to the deep interest and sustained labors of the members of the Old Bohemia Historical Society, Inc., the entire St. Francis Xavier complex of church, rectory, grounds, cemetery and farm museum has not only been restored, but continues to be maintained in excellent condition.
>
> In this Bicentennial Year of our nation's founding, places like Old Bohemia vividly remind us of our Catholic heritage and provide us with greater incentives to value, live and spread the Faith.
>
> Consequently, I highly commend the efforts of the Old Bohemia Historical Society as they continue the work of renovation and preservation. I am pleased to invoke God's blessing on them and all who aid their work.
>
> Cordially in Christ,
>
> + Thomas J. Mardaga
> Most Reverend Thomas J. Mardaga, D.D.
> Bishop of Wilmington
>
> TJM/r

ebrant and homilist on Sunday, June 15, 1975, with music provided by St. Rose of Lima Choir under the direction of Thomas J. Ortt. The same announcement included the information that a U.S. Bicentennial Committee had been formed under the Old Bohemia Historical Society. Officers were Mrs. Argus Robinson of Elkton, assisted by Edward Ludwig III of Elkton and Morton Taylor of Perryville.[92]

In March, 1975, St. Francis Xavier Church was listed on the National Register of Historic Places.[93]

As part of the preparation for the 1976 American Bicentennial Observance, 13 oak trees were planted at Bohemia in 1965, the number to represent each of the original thirteen colonies.[94] Also in preparation for the U.S. Bicentennial Observance, Bishop Mardaga wrote a letter to the whole diocese pointing out the significant part that Old Bohemia had played in the history of the diocese.[95]

Bishop Mardaga celebrated the final Mass of the season at Bohemia on September 21, 1975. Music was provided by the Choir of St. Peter Cathedral, Wilmington under the direction of Carmen Consiglio.[96]

The diocesan U.S. Bicentennial Historical Exhibit was held in Wilmington in February, 1976. Members of the Old Bohemia Historical Society provided for it a prominent display of vestments, candelabra, sacred vessels, and various items to tell of the great contribution Bohemia had made to the development of the faith in the colonies. Frank Krastel, Sr. and Edward Ludwig III were present at the exhibit to give information and to distribute brochures.[97] In conjunction with the

Celebration of the U. S. Bicentennial at Bohemia (*Dialog*, Wilmington, Delaware)

U.S. Bicentennial Observance, a history was published in book form in 1976, compiled and edited by Joseph C. Cann. Numbering 271 pages it gives an account of the various aspects of the founding and operation of the church and plantation at Old Bohemia up to the year 1976.[98]

Father Russell Perkins celebrated the Field Mass at Bohemia in August, 1977. Music for the Mass was provided by the folk music group at St. Joseph's Church in Middletown.[99] In September, 1977, Father Eugene Clarahan, pastor of St. Peter's Church in New Castle was celebrant of the Field Mass at Bohemia. Music was provided by the choir of St. Peter's, led by Rev. David Shaum, of Mt. St. Mary's College, Emmitsburg, Maryland.[100] Father David Shaum was celebrant at Old Bohemia on June 18, 1978. The choir of St. Peter's, New Castle, provided the music.[101]

Father Perkins was transferred as pastor to Sacred Heart Church in Chestertown, Maryland, in 1978.

Diocesan Pastor, Patrick A. Brady

The next pastor of St. Joseph's Parish, Middletown, was Patrick Anthony Brady.[102] As he was entering into his new assignment, the Old Bohemia Historical Society was announcing a new fundraising drive. The president Frank Krastel, and vice-president Joseph Cann, along with the board of directors were attempting to raise $100,000 in order to accomplish two goals: finance necessary renovations expected to cost $50,000, and to establish a fund to finance future needs, repairs, maintenance. The drive was to last over two years.[103]

Father Brady himself was celebrant of the Field Mass on July 16, 1978. The choir of St. Rose of Lima Church, Chesapeake City provided the music under the direction of Thomas Ortt.[104]

The following year Father Brady celebrated the 275th Anniversary of the Old

Father Patrick A. Brady

Bohemia establishment.[105] The Mass on July 15 was offered by Reverend Henry J. Butler, director of the Jesuit Seminary, Maryland Province, Baltimore. Father Brady assisted. The choir of St. Rose of Lima Church, Chesapeake City, Maryland, provided music under the direction of Thomas Ortt.[106]

The first of the traditional summer Masses in 1980 was held on June 15. Monsignor Paul J. Schierse, pastor of St. Joseph on the Brandywine Church in Wilmington, was celebrant and homilist. Father Brady concelebrated. The choir and altar servers were from St. Joseph on the Brandywine Church.[107]

The diocesan newspaper on July 4, 1980, published a large portrait of Charles Carroll of Carrollton, the single Roman Catholic signer of the Declaration of Independence, who, according to tradition, had attended the academy at Bohemia in his youth.[108]

In 1981, Father Edward Carley told his history of the Jesuits' missionary work on the Eastern Shore of Maryland in a feature article in *The Dialog*.[109]

Bishop Mardaga was celebrant and homilist at the last Mass at Bohemia on September 20, 1981. Music was provided by the Cathedral Choir of St. Peter's, Wilmington.[110] The first of the Masses at Bohemia in 1982 was celebrated by Father William Driscoll, director of the radio Mass in Baltimore. Music was provided by the choir of St. Rose of Lima Church, Chesapeake City, Maryland.[111] On September 17, 1983, Bishop Mardaga again celebrated the Mass at Bohemia. The Cathedral Choir of St. Peter's, Wilmington provided the music under the direction of Carmen Consiglio.[112] The last Mass at Bohemia for 1983 was celebrated on October 16, by Father Bernard Dudek, chaplain of the Alcoha in Baltimore. Music was provided by the Alcoha Chanters of Baltimore and by the choir of St. Rose of Lima Church, Chesapeake City, Maryland under the direction of J. Thomas Ortt.[113] On May 20, 1984, the first Mass of the season at Bohemia was celebrated by Father George P. Schneider, pastor of Our Lady of Consolation, Church, Parkersburg, Pennsylvania, with music provided by the choir of that church. Other Masses were set for September 16 and October 21.[114]

Bishop Mardaga died on May 24, 1984, after sixteen years as Bishop of Wilmington and forty-four years a priest. Father, later Monsignor, Brady was transferred as pastor to St. Ann Church in Wilmington in 1984.

THE EPISCOPATE OF ROBERT E. MULVEE

On February 19, 1985, Bishop Robert Edward Mulvee was appointed seventh Bishop of Wilmington. He was installed on April 11, 1985.[115]

Diocesan Pastor, Carmen D. Vignola

Father Carmen Daniel Vignola was appointed administrator of St. Joseph's

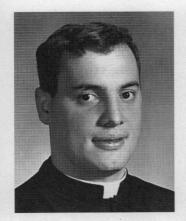

Father Carmen Vignola

Church, Middletown, in 1984 and pastor in 1985.[116] Father Vignola was celebrant of the first Mass of the season at Bohemia on April 21, 1985. The combined choirs of St. Joseph's Church, Middletown, and of St. Rose of Lima Church, Chesapeake City, provided the music.[117]

On April 15, 1985, the president of the Old Bohemia Historical Society for 31 years, Francis William Krastel, Sr., died. His Funeral Mass was offered on April 19 at his home parish, Corpus Christi Church, at Carney's Point, New Jersey. His son, Reverend Francis W. Krastel, Jr., officiated, with concelebrants: Monsignor Joseph Rebman, chancellor of the diocese, Monsignor John Dewson, Father Russell Perkins, and Father Carmen Vignola. Frank Krastel, Sr. was buried at Old Bohemia.[118]

James Garrigan was elected to take his place as president of the Old Bohemia Historical Society. He had previously served as vice-president of the Society for a number of years. He served as president for ten years. As president he arranged all the Masses at Bohemia, inviting visiting priests and choirs and sending out notices to the newspapers. He made application to have five acres and the farm buildings and new Visitors' Center taken off the taxable part of the estate and put on a non-taxable basis with the Church complex. He designed, built, and installed the layout for the Stations of the Cross. Tony Starr, Jim Quinn, Dave Dorman, and Father Vignola assisted in this project. He designed and supervised the construction of the Visitors' Center. The Old Bohemia Council of the Knights of Columbus helped in the project. When the Society was running out of money he applied to the Catholic Diocese Foundation and was granted $7,500. for plumbing purposes. Another donation of $2500. from an unnamed company enabled the Society to pay for an inspection of the condition and structural strength of the church roof, framing, and drainage plans. The cradle that supports the church bell was

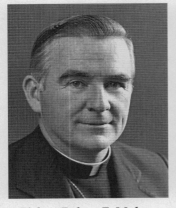

Bishop Robert E. Mulvee

Bishop Mulvee celebrating Mass at St. Francis Xavier Church, 1988 (*Cecil Whig*)

Picture of Frank Krastel, Restorer, in 1970   Photo of James Garrigan

replaced with treated lumber.[119]

Bishop Mulvee greeted a congregation of more than 250 persons who attended the first Mass he celebrated as Bishop of Wilmington at Bohemia on Sunday, September 15, 1985. In an eloquent homily Bishop Mulvee praised the zeal of St. Francis Xavier, after whom the church was named, and pointed out that years after the saint's death when priests again returned to the areas he converted they often found the faith flourishing where for years there had been no priest. He traced the work of the Jesuits at Bohemia who followed the example of St. Francis Xavier in taking up the cross of Christ in missionary work. The bishop went on to say: "The people of God here in this Chapel today have said 'I want to follow you.'"[120]

In 1986 the first Mass for the season at Bohemia was celebrated in memory of Frank Krastel, Sr. The Mass was celebrated by his son, Father Frank W. Krastel, Jr., pastor of St. Bernadette Church in Silver Springs, Maryland. The music was provided by the choir of St. Rose of Lima Church, Chesapeake City, Maryland.[121]

The Visitors Center at Old Bohemia had been under construction for some time and was completed in time for its dedication by Bishop Mulvee on September 21, 1986. He was assisted by Father Vignola who on the occasion expressed the hope that the new center would draw folks, young and old alike, to the 282 year old landmark. Father Vignola continued to say: "We pray that indeed the shrine which houses the memories and ghosts of Jesuits past can become a viable place of worship and celebration for the Catholic Church present. That, as a result, the shrine won't settle into a collection of cobwebs."[122] Father Vignola was transferred as pastor to Holy Cross Church in Dover, Delaware in June, 1987.

Diocesan Pastor, Philip L. Siry

Father Philip Siry

The next pastor of St. Joseph's Church, Middletown, was Father Philip Lawrence Siry, who replaced Father Vignola in 1987.[123] Father Siry worked with James Garrigan to complete the Visitors' Center at Bohemia, and promoted greater attendance at the summer Masses.

Bishop James Burke, O. P. was celebrant of the Mass at Bohemia in September, 1987. The music was provided by the Cathedral Choir of St. Peter's, Wilmington under the direction of Carmen Consiglio.[124] The last Mass of the season was celebrated by Monsignor John Dewson, pastor of St. Paul's Church, Delaware City. Music was provided by the choir of St. Rose of Lima Church, Chesapeake City.[125]

Bishop Mulvee celebrated the 35th Anniversary of the Old Bohemia Historical Society at St. Francis Xavier Church on September 18, 1988, with Monsignor Rebman, chancellor, and Father Siry, pastor, assisting.[126]

In 1992, Father Siry was appointed pastor of St. Paul's Church in Delaware City.

Diocesan Pastor, Thomas A. Flowers

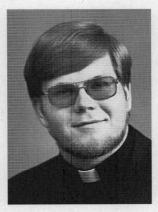

Father Thomas Flowers

In June, 1992, Father Thomas Anthony Flowers was appointed pastor of St. Joseph's Parish, Middletown. Himself a historian, Father Flowers showed great interest in Bohemia and its preservation. He was elected president of the Old Bohemia Historical Society in the spring of 1992.[127] During his presidency he gave frequent lectures at St. Francis Xavier Church, promoted pilgrimages and days of recollection there, and with enthusiastic determination moved the development of Old Bohemia forward. In his first year as president, a large bequest was made to the Old Bohemia Historical Society by the will of Marie Price of Cecilton, Maryland.[128]

Father Flowers scheduled seven Masses at Bohemia in 1993, on the third Sundays of April, May, September, October, Memorial Day, All Souls Day, and Feast of St. Francis Xavier (December 3). At his invitation, on May 6, 1993, Reverend Edward B. Carley, pastor of St. Dennis Church, Galena, Maryland, was celebrant of the Mass and homilist at Bohemia.[129] On September 19, 1993, Reverend Leonard Kempski, pastor of Christ Our King Church in Wilmington, was celebrant and homilist.[130] On April 17, 1994, Reverend Richard Reissmann, pastor of St. John's – Holy Angels Parish in Newark, Delaware, was celebrant and homilist. The choir from his parish provided the music.[131] On June 20, 1994, Reverend Thomas Peterman celebrated the monthly Mass at Bohemia, and talked on the foundation on St. Francis

Bishop Basil Losten

Scaffolding in 1995

Xavier Church by the Jesuits.

In September, 1994, Bishop Basil Losten of the Ukrainian Rite, a native of Chesapeake City, Maryland, returned to Cecil County to celebrate a Divine Liturgy (Mass) at Old Bohemia. Some 200 faithful filled the church. Bishop Losten was assisted by Father Flowers.[132]

On October 16, 1994, Bishop Mulvee dedicated and blessed a large stone cross at the cemetery adjoining St. Francis Xavier Church. The 8 foot cross monument was carved of Carnelian granite in Minnesota and the four foot *Corpus* in bronze imported from Italy. Bishop Mulvee was assisted by Father Flowers, pastor, and by John Merlini and Mark Christian of the Catholic Cemetery Office of the Diocese of Wilmington. Mrs. Bernice Dill of St. Joseph's Church, Middletown, was appointed as director of the cemetery and the Bohemia Center.[133]

On Saturday, May 14, 1994, the Rosary and Altar Society of St. Catherine of Siena Parish, Wilmington, held a mini-retreat, given by Father Flowers. On Sunday, May 15, 1994, Father John Klevence, pastor of Immaculate Conception Church, Marydel, Maryland, was celebrant and homilist at the 4 p.m. Mass. His parish choir provided the music.[134]

Since the church roof was then in danger of caving in the Society embarked on a $400,000 project to replace the ceiling and roof, and to reattach the bell tower to the main structure, to repoint the bricks, and to install new lighting. In 1994, Father Flowers engaged the services of Peter Newlin, an historic architect from Chestertown, Maryland, recommended by the National Trust for Historic Preservation. St. Francis Xavier Church was closed to visitors from November, 1994, through spring 1995.[135]

The Old Bohemia Historical Society had undertaken the structural stabilization

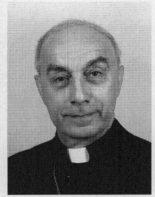

Bishop
Michael A. Saltarelli

and preservation programs in 1994. However, once the work began, architects and engineers realized that a greater scope of need existed, costing over $100,000 more than anticipated.

By the end of May, 1995, the construction work on the preservation phrase would be roughly 75% completed, but the Society would run out of funds. Since the Catholic Diocese Foundation was owner of the property, the Old Bohemia Historical Society requested a grant of $100,000 to enable them to complete the on-going work on the church. A review of the materials by the Board of the Catholic Diocese Foundation indicated that the Society ran out of money before providing the church with electrical service and lighting as well as heating and air conditioning. Funds were also needed to complete the ceiling and other interior finishes.[136] The church was renovated in 1995. A special Mass for benefactors was scheduled to be celebrated inside the newly-renovated shrine church at Old Bohemia.[137] After a year-long closure for repairs and renovations, the church was opened for the monthly summer Masses and in the fall was included in a tour of historic churches on Delmarva on October 15, 1995. Monsignor Joseph Rebman, Vicar General of the Diocese of Wilmington, was celebrant of the Mass on October 15, 1995. Monsignor Rebman had been involved in expansion plans for the Old Bohemia cemetery.[138]

Early in 1995, the diocesan newspaper announced that on February 7, 1995, Bishop Robert E. Mulvee had been named Coadjutor Bishop of Providence, Rhode Island.[139]

THE EPISCOPATE OF MICHAEL A. SALTARELLI

On November 21, 1995, Bishop Michael A. Saltarelli was appointed Eighth Bishop of the Diocese of Wilmington. He was installed on January 23, 1996. Michael Saltarelli was born in Jersey City, New Jersey on January 17, 1933. He was ordained a priest on May 28, 1960.[140]

Diocesan Pastor, Thomas A. Flowers

Restorative work continued at Bohemia, although the church was opened in the spring of 1996 for the summer monthly Masses. In May of 1996, the Old Bohemia Historical Society announced the discovery of the antique stations of the cross images that had been saved from the fire of 1912. Father Flowers noted at the time that "The lithographs are among the finest works of art housed in the (Bohemia) church, vestry, and adjoining parish house." He added that the society hoped to continue restoration work in preparation for the bicentennial of the church (completed in 1797 by Father Maréchal) in October, 1997.[141]

The celebration of the bicentennial of St. Francis Xavier Church began on April 20, 1997, with Father James F. Salmon, S.J., treasurer of the Jesuit Province of Maryland presiding and preaching. He was assisted by Father Flowers and Father William K. McGroarty, S. J., manager of the Jesuit properties in Cecil County. The handbell choir of Holy Cross Church, Dover, Delaware, enhanced the liturgy.[142]

The interior restoration of the church was still in progress when a small fire occurred on May 7, 1997. A rapid response by the local fire companies prevented any extensive damage.[143] Work continued on repair of the windows, and painting the walls and woodwork of the interior of the church. The fire did not cause the cancellation of any events. Masses were celebrated on the third Sundays of May, September and October, 1997. A day of prayer starting with Mass was celebrated by Father Flowers on Saturday, May 17. The Schola Cantorum, a men's choir from Wilmington specializing in Latin harmony, sang at the Mass celebrated by Father Flowers on May 18. A Memorial Day Mass was celebrated by Father Joseph Cocucci on May 27, 1997. The Mass was attended by the Chesapeake City Veterans of Foreign Wars. For the third year a history trail and open house was planned for persons visiting historic churches of Maryland and Delaware.[144]

In May, 1997, twenty-eight prints of a rare photograph of St. Francis Xavier Church on a snowy winter day in 1960 by James Warner had been donated to the Old Bohemia Historical Society by his daughter after his death in 1990. The prints that now remained were put up for sale in an effort to raise funds for the restoration projects.[145]

On October 19, 1997, the bicentennial celebration of St. Francis Xavier Church reached it high point and conclusion with Mass celebrated by Bishop Michael Saltarelli. It was his first Mass at Bohemia, celebrated in an outdoor gazebo located next to the church and near the graves of those clergy who served at Bohemia and who are buried there. The *Schola Cantorum* from Wilmington provided the music. In conjunction with the diocesan observance of Jubilee 2000, fifteen churches in the diocese were presented with scrolls designating them as official pilgrimage sites to offer the Jubilee special indulgence.[146]

With the anticipation of an influx of Jubilee pilgrims, Margaret Matyniak on behalf of the Old Bohemia Historical Society advertised for donation of "new and used religious articles of all kinds for the gift shop at St. Francis Xavier. All proceeds benefit the restoration fund for the Old Bohemia Shrine."[147]

In October, 1998, Father Flowers, who headed the pilgrimage committee of Jubilee 2000, through the diocesan newspaper announced that all pilgrimage sites in the diocese would be open on Sunday, October 18, 1998. St. Francis Xavier would open with a talk by Father Flowers at 2 p.m., followed by an outdoor rosary at the Memorial

Old Bohemia Council, Knights of Columbus 1997

To Unborn Children at 3 p.m. Father William Gore, O.S.F.S., pastor of St. Nicholas Church in Wilmington and of St. Basil the Great in Chesapeake City, would offer Mass in the Ukrainian Rite at 4 p.m.[148]

Some of the rectory's rooms have become period displays. Other rooms feature museum display cases to show relics of three centuries of Catholicism-elaborately embroidered processional cloaks, an iron used to make Communion hosts, and candleholders for Mass.

In the spring of 1999, a gift from Jane Krastel Williams, daughter of Frank Krastel, helped the Society replace window sashes on the north side of the rectory. Later that year a modern HVAC system was installed. A $85,000 bequest in late 1999 from Maurice Adelman, Jr., allowed the Society to continue restoration.[149]

Open House was held at Bohemia on October 17, 1999, beginning with a lecture by Father Flowers at 2 p.m., followed by a living rosary led by the Old Bohemia Council of the Knights of Columbus at the Monument For Unborn Children in the cemetery. Bishop Michael Saltarelli celebrated Mass at 4 p.m.[150]

The Shrine opened the Jubilee Year 2000 series of Masses on the third Sunday of April, with outdoor Stations of the Cross and Mass, led by Father Flowers.[151] The final Mass at Bohemia for the Jubilee Year 2000 was celebrated in September by Father Paul Calamari, associate pastor of Our Lady of Fatima Parish in New Castle, Delaware. Music was provided by the choir of St. Joseph's Church, Middletown, under the direction of Thomas McKenna.[152]

On September 28, 2000, the main event of the diocesan observance of Jubilee Year 2000 was celebrated at Convention Hall, Ocean City, Maryland. At the well attended gathering, Old Bohemia took a featured spot in a historical display called "Twenty Centuries of Catholic History," a walk-through exhibit, which included diocesan along with the universal history of the Catholic Church.[153] In 2001 the main altar was cut back and all the altars repainted. In 2002 Father Flowers was delegated by Bishop Saltarelli to consecrate a new altar of sacrifice in St. Francis Xavier Church at which the priest would face the congregation.[154] Father Flowers was transferred as pastor to St. Polycarp Church in Smyrna, Delaware in June, 2002.

Diocesan Pastor, Steven B. Giuliano

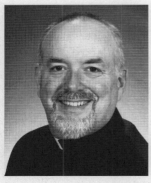

Father Steven Giuliano

Father Steven Bruce Giuliano succeeded Father Flowers on June 24, 2002.[155] He has continued efforts to improve Bohemia and to prepare for the 300th anniversary. In the spring of 2002, Margaret M. Matyniak was elected the 4th president of the Society. She was born on June 10, 1941 in Wilmington, Delaware, attended St. Hedwig's Grade School, Ursuline Academy, Thompson's Private Business School, and the University of Delaware. She was married for thirty five years to Bernard Matyniak, now deceased. Her association with Old Bohemia dates back to 1961. After serving as a member of the board, she was elected president in April, 2002. She has been

Margaret Matyniak, President of the Old Bohemia Historical Society

busily engaged in redoing the rectory and museum. Some of the rectory rooms have become period rooms. A new museum room has been setup with new glass display cases to exhibit relics of Old Bohemia. The rectory bricks have been repointed and the interior walls repaired and painted, and heat and air conditioning have been installed. The membership of the society has increased to 200. In addition, she has been the organizer of the Tercentenary Celebrations and chairwoman of the book committee.

On October 18, 2003, an inaugural Farm Show was presented at Bohemia. Bernard Matyniak, Jr. displayed antique farm equipment, tractors, engines, an antique fire truck and vintage military equipment. Visitors enjoyed demonstrations and rides on the fire truck. The newly restored rectory building was open.[156] The Tercentenary Year was officially opened on October 26, 2003, by Bishop Saltarelli with the celebration of mass. The American flag and the Tercentenary Banner were raised together to signal the commencement of the celebration.[157] Father Steven Giuliano was the homilist. On April 18, 2004, Reverend Joseph Rossi, a Jesuit historian at Loyola College in Baltimore, celebrated Mass and gave the homily. After Mass, Kevin Moulton, an Irish tenor from New Jersey, gave a concert.[158]

On May 16, 2004, Bishop Basil Losten, Ukrainian Bishop of Stamford, Connecticut and a native of Chesapeake City, Maryland, celebrated a Liturgy of the Byzantine Rite. This "Ukrainian Day" at Bohemia commemorated the strong connection between the Ukrainian community in Chesapeake City and Old Bohemia.[159]

On Sunday, October 24, 2004, Bishop Michael Saltarelli celebrated a Mass which brought the tercentennial observance to a conclusion. Reverend David Collins, S.J. of Georgetown University gave the homily. Bishop Saltarelli was assisted by Father Steven Giuliano, pastor, and Father Paul Campbell, associate-pastor. Other concelebrants were Monsignor Patrick Brady, Rev. Philip Siry and Rev. Thomas Peterman. The Master of Ceremonies was Rev. William Cocoa. A contingent of the Fourth Degree Assembly Knights of Columbus was present at the ceremony, as were members of the Knights of Malta and Knights of the Holy Sepulchre.

Sister Genevieve Kotyk and Sister Bernarda Arkatin represented the religious of the Order of St. Basil the Great. There were 200 hundred in attendance at the Mass. The Old Bohemia Historical Society hosted a banquet at the Kitty Knight House after the Mass.

The Old Bohemia Historical Society has succeeded in restoring and perpetuating the entire complex of church, rectory, grounds, cemetery and farm museum. Up to the present moment the board and members of the Society continue to support and promote interest in this hallowed spot, and to guarantee that the beacon of St. Xavier Shrine will shine on into a bright and certain future.

Old Bohemia is the cradle of Catholicity in the Delmarva Peninsula and the mother church of the Catholic Diocese of Wilmington. It is, therefore, of prime interest to us locally and nationally, especially for the critical role it played in the formation of the colonial American Catholic Church. In spite of fire, neglect, and occasional disarray, Old Bohemia stands proudly today as a testament to three centuries of Catholic faith.

ANNIVERSARY YEAR

(Tercentenary photographs compliments of
Edward Macchione, Marji Matyniak, Eileen Edelin, Lilia Chaika, and Joy Getty)

Bernard Matyniak, Jr. demonstrates the grinding of corn in a burr mill to Evan, Nathan, Ellen, and Jenna Stewart at the Farm Show on October 18, 2003.

Raising the American flag and the "Old Bohemia" Tercentenary flag on October 26, 2003 officially signals the beginning of the Tercentenary Year.

Interior of St. Francis Xavier Shrine "Old Bohemia" for the opening of the Tercentenary Year.

Reception in newly restored rectory dinning room after mass celebrating the beginning of the Tercentenary.

Rev. Steven Giuliano and Rev. James Rossi, SJ, guest homilist concelebrate mass on April 18, 2004.

Mary Maloney and Joy Getty are hostesses ready to show off the newly restored rectory to visitors from the Maryland House and Garden Tour.

Bohemia Under Diocesan Pastors 303

Tina Farrow, Marji Matyniak, Tracey Farrow, and Pat Panacek prepare to welcome visitors to "Old Bohemia" for the Maryland House and Garden Tour on April 25, 2004.

Kevin Moulton, Irish tenor performs at "Old Bohemia" April 18, 2004.

Bishop Basil Losten of the Ukrainian Diocese of Stamford (Conn.) concelebrates a Byzantine Divine Rite liturgy with Rev. Steven Giuliano, Rev. Bondon Danylo, Stamford, Msgr. John Bura, pastor St. Basil Ukrainian Church, Chesapeake City, Md, and Rev. Thomas Peterman, St. Dennis, Galena, Md at the Ukrainian Day celebration on May 16, 2004. Deacon Volodymyr Sybirny is pictured at extreme left.

Bishop Basil Losten, who grew up in Chesapeake City, gives the homily for the Divine Liturgy for Ukrainian Day which commemorates the close ties of the Ukrainian people to "Old Bohemia."

Msgr. John Bura, Bishop Basil Losten, Deacon Volodymyr Sybirny, and Father Bondon Danylo at the Ukrainian Dinner at St. Basil Hall in Chesapeake City, MD.

Bishop Basil Losten and Marji Matyniak, President of the Old Bohemia Historical Society at the Ukrainian Dinner.

Members of St. Basil Parish and guests stand for the blessing.

Dinner guests enjoy a Ukrainian feast.

Mary Luike, Postmaster Warwick, MD cancels mail at the special 300th Anniversary Station on Sept 19, 2004. The US Postal Service made a special cancellation stamp to commemorate the Tercentenary.

Exposition of Blessed Sacrament on the Feast of Coysus Christi, June 13, 2004.

The St. Agnes Woodwind Ensemble of Good Shepherd Parish, Perryville, MD perform on Sept 19, 2004. Note Tercentenary painting of "Old Bohemia" painted and donated by Stephanie Gillies in background.

Richard Konrad and Bernard Matyniak, Jr. fold the American flag while Donn Devine, Mary Maloney, and Richard Kwasizur look on. The flags will be placed in the museum.

Richard Konrad raises a new flag which signals the beginning of the a New Century for Old Bohemia.

President. Marji Matyniak and Bernard Matyniak, Jr. lower the flags that have flown during the past year signaling the end of the Tercentenary Year on Oct 24, 2004.

Knights of Columbus Father Lutz Assembly 2702, Knights of Holy Sepulchre, and Knights of Malta at Tercentenary Celebration October 24, 2004.

Officers and board members of the Old Bohemia Historical Society with Rev. Steven Giuliano and Bishop Michael Saltarelli, 2004, left to right, Rev. Steven Giuliano, Dorcas Gamble, Marla Dill-Palmer, Bernice Dill, vice-president, Geoffrey Gamble, Margaret (MARJI) Matyniak, president, James Quinn, Bishop Saltarelli, Richard Konrad Mary Maloney, treasurer, Eileen Edelin, secretary, Carl Edelin, Donn Devine, Richard Kwasizur, Lilia and Joseph Chaika, and George Barczewski.

Rev. David J. Collins S.J. guest homilist, Bishop Michael A. Saltarelli and Rev. Steven Giuliano at closing of Tercentenary Mass.

Bernice Dill, George Barczewski and Jim Quinn enjoying dinner.

Bernard Matyniak, Jr., Helen Dugan, Msgr. Joseph Rebman, Mary Maloney, Marji Matyniak, and Geofrey and Dorcas Gamble are all smiles at the end of the a successful Tercentenary Year.

Rev. William Cocco, Bishop Saltarelli, Rev. John Campbell and Rev. Steven Giuliano at the Tercentenary dinner at the Kitty Knight House.

Tanya and Joseph Chaika, Sr. Bernarda, Sr. Genevieve, Veronica Tokash, Lilia Chaika, and Anne Losten at the Tercentenary dinner.

Friends of Old Bohemia at the Tercentenary dinner.

Rev. Thomas Peterman and Rev. Philip Sciry enjoy a conversation at the Tercentenary Dinner.

Ellyn and Don Lapointe, Katherine Gregg, Clarice Kwasnieski, Eileen Edelin, Denis Kwasnieski, Carl Edelin, and Dick and Valerie McAloon.

Rev. Steven Giuliano and Marji Matyniak cut "Old Bohemia" 300th birthday cake.

President Marji Matyniak gives her final speech of the Tercentenary Year.

Marji Matyniak Presents a plaque to Rev. Thomas Peterman for all his outstanding dedication and contributions to "Old Bohemia" including the book "Bohemia 1704-2004."

Tercentenary boxwoods planted alongside the old boxwood ensures there will always be "Old Bohemia" boxwood.

New show cases display artifacts in the rectory museum.

Bohemia Under Diocesan Pastors 309

New shutters installed on church windows for the Tercentenary.

Old Bohemia Vestments date back to 1700's.

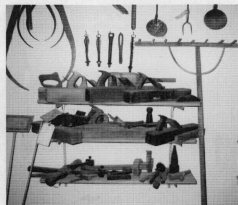

Old tool display in the Farm Museum.

A Portrait of John and Helena Greene Raskob hangs in the showroom in grateful remembrance of the first grant to restore the shrine.

The Rectory dinning room was restored for the Tercentenary.

The Old Kitchen building was restored for the Tercentenary.

NOTES FOR CHAPTER SIX
1. Thomas J. Peterman, *Priests Of A Century, 1868-1968, Diocese of Wilmington* (Devon, Pennsylvania: Cooke Publishers, Inc., 1970) 54: Father John Aloysius Daly was born in County Donegal, Ireland in 1841, he was ordained to the priesthood in Baltimore on June 21, 1888. In 1900 he was appointed pastor of St. Dennis Church, Galena, where he served the next twenty seven years. He died on May 13, 1933, at age 92 and 45 years a priest. Joseph Horgan, *History of St. Dennis Church, Galena, Maryland 1855-1970* (Devon, Pennsylvania: Cooke Publishers, 1970) 43, Joseph C. Cann, *Old Bohemia 1704-1976* (Wilmington, Delaware: Cann Publishing Co., 1976) 10. He is not to be confused with Father John James Daly, who built the present church of St. Peter's in New Castle, Delaware, and lies buried within its walls.

BAPTISMS BY FATHER DALY –

On August 20, 1899, *at Bohemia*, Father John Daly baptized Francis Thomas Sullivan, born July 12, 1899, son of John Sullivan and Lilly Moriarty. Sponsors were Michael Sullivan and Mary Sullivan. On September 3, 1899, *at Bohemia*, he baptized Donald Lee Ross, born July 28, 1898, son of James A. Ross and Helen Evans, his wife. Sponsors were John B. Lee and Mary E. Lee. On September 13, 1899, he baptized John Robert Ennis, born May 8, 1899, son of Thomas J. Ennis and Sarah Elizabeth Shetzler, his wife. Sponsor was John Edward Bingnear.

On September 15, 1899, *at Bohemia*, Father Daly baptized Anna Victoria Pierce born March 29, 1899, child of Julia Virginia Pierce. Sponsor was Philis, colored. On July 1, 1900, *at Bohemia*, he baptized Lawrence Aloysius Divine, born June 8, 1900, child of Timothy P. Divine and Mary Agnes Scully, his wife. Sponsors were Thomas Divine and Catherine T. Sullivan.

On September 9, 1900, Father Daly baptized Francis Edward Lucas, born May 19, 1900, son of George Henry Lucas and Anna V. George, his wife. Sponsors were William Carroll and Mary Balina Lucas. On October 28, 1900, he baptized James Bradford Sullivan born September 16, 1900, son of John J. Sullivan and Lilly Moriarty, his wife. Sponsors were Joseph A. Sullivan and Catherine L. Sullivan.

On January 23, 1901, Father Daly baptized William Dignan, born October 1, 1897, child of Michael Dignan and Lilly Boyles, his wife. Sponsor was William Baker. On January 23, 1901, he baptized Mary Anna Dignan, born June 11, 1898, child of Michael Dignan and Lilly Boyles, his wife. Sponsor was Mary Dorsey. On February 27, 1901, he baptized Henry Vaughn Bingnear, born October 28, 1900, child of Henry Bignear and Anna Shetzler, his wife. Sponsors were John Daly and Maria Bignear.

On February 27, 1901, Father Daly baptized Lucinda Viola Shetzler, born January 23, 1900, child of Edward Shetzler and Lucinda Carpenter. Sponsor was Anna Bingnear. On April 11, 1901, he baptized Roseann Helen Shannon Goff, born March 24, 1901, daughter of John B. Goff and Margaret Moran, his wife. Sponsor was Rose A. Money. On June 23, 1901, he baptized John Paul Devine, born May 30, 1901, child of Timothy P. Devine and Mary Agnes Scully, his wife. Sponsors were John and Lily Sullivan.

MARRIAGE PERFORMED BY FATHER DALY AT BOHEMIA:

February 27, 1900 – between Michael A. Sullivan and Reba Collins. Witnesses were Bartholomew Collins and Mary Davis.

Burial Register of Old Bohemia, St. Xavier Church, Warwick, Maryland:

September 4, 1898 – Infant child of Mr. Deggs; September 11, 1898 – Infant child of Mr. Sullivan; June 1899 – Mary Bowler, age 90; November 2, 1899 – James Clark, age 75; November 2, 1899 – Francis Murry, age 64; November 16, 1899 – Nowland T. Price, age 30; January 1, 1900 – Thomas Murry, age 70; February 25, 1900 – Infant child of Thomas Sullivan, April 11, 1900 – John Piser, age 63; June 20, 1900 – John Stout; March 12, 1901 – Andrew Hutchinson, age 78, of Warwick, Maryland; February 21, 1901 – Bridget Eberhard, age 75 of Sassafras, Maryland; February 25, 1901 – Mary Devine, age 12 of County Kerry, Ireland; July 2, 1901 – Catherine Boyle, age 69; March 25, 1902 – Charles Braceland, of Middletown, Delaware; April 3, 1902 – George Washington Lockwood, age 56; July 26, 1902 – William T. Lusby, age 82; May 17, 1903, Paul Olway Burns, of New York, died in Council Bluff, Iowa; June 6, 1903 – Hugh McAleer, Jr., age 60, of Fredericktown, Maryland; July 1, 1903 – Mary Morris, age 80 of Middletown, Delaware; February 5, 1904 – Francis Lucas, age 4, son of Mr. and Mrs. William Lucas of Cecilton, Maryland.

Burial Records of St. Dennis Church, Galena, Maryland:

Buried at Bohemia Cemetery, July, 1902 – William T. Lusby, 82, born in Maryland; Blanche Ottingen, 16, born in Pennsylvania – Recorded by Father Daly.

2. Peterman, *Priests of A Century* 76: Charles P. McGoldrick was born in Wilmington, Delaware on December 19, 1874. He was ordained on October 14, 1900, and first assigned to assist Father William Temple at Easton. In January, 1904, he replaced Father Temple as pastor of Easton. In 1905 he was appointed pastor of Centreville, and was in charge of the Queen Anne County missions for the next 23 years. He died on May 10, 1928, at 54 years of age and 28 years as a priest.

BAPTISMS BY FATHER McGOLDRICK:

On February 9, 1902, Father Charles P. McGoldrick baptized *at Middletown*, Delaware, Mildred Cecelia Holten. On March 23, 1902, he baptized at Middletown, William Joseph Krastel of Summit Bridge, Delaware. On June 1, 1902, he baptized Daniel Corbett Bignear *of Odessa*, Delaware, born May 16, 1902, child of John Bignear and Mary Shetzler. Sponsors were Henry and Anna Bignear.

On September 7, 1902, *at St. Francis Xavier Church*, Father McGoldrick baptized Cátherine Rebecca Sullivan, born August 11, 1902, child of Michael Sullivan and Rebecca Collins, his wife. They lived at Earleville, Maryland. Sponsors were Francis Sullivan and Josephine Collins.

On April 24, 1903, he baptized conditionally Joshua Johnson, about 58 years of age, a negro supposed to have been baptized previously by Father Villiger but had not lived as one. He was baptized *in articulo mortis*. Witness was Mrs. Frank Sullivan.

On May 10, 1903, Father McGoldrick *at St. Francis Xavier Church* baptized Joseph Aloysius Sullivan, born April 6, 1903, son of John Sullivan and Lillian Moriarty, his wife. Sponsors were Thomas Devine and Agnes Sullivan. On June 21, 1903, he baptized *at St. Francis Xavier Church* Sarah Maria Swartz of Middletown, Delaware, twenty-three years old, daughter of John Swartz and Rachael Johnson who live near Mt. Pleasant, Delaware. Sponsors were John Dorsey and Mary Dorsey.

On June 28, 1903, *at Bohemia* Father McGoldrick baptized Gertrude Pope, infant daughter of Charles Pope and his wife, of Warwick. Sponsors were William and Mrs. Carroll.

Burial Register of Old Bohemia:

January 9, 1904 – Henry V. Ayers, age 13, son of Mr. and Mrs. Peter Ayers of Warwick, Maryland. Peter Ayers and Mrs. Peter Ayers of Warwick, Maryland.

MARRIAGE PERFORMED BY FATHER McGOLDRICK AT BOHEMIA:

November 18, 1902 – between William Andrew Ayers and Cora Wright. Witness was Peter Ayers.

3. Cann 10; Peterman, *Priests Of A Century* 80: Born in Glenn Falls, New York, on July 29, 1873. He was ordained in Baltimore in 1903, and appointed at once to Bohemia and its mission at Middletown. When the newly ordained priest moved into the rectory at Bohemia, he was accompanied by his mother and his sister Agnes.

BAPTISMS BY FATHER CROWLEY

On March 12, 1902, *at Bohemia* Father Charles A. Crowley baptized John Briscoe, born February 12, 1902, child of John Briscoe and Ida Queen. Sponsors were John and Margaret Dorsey. On May 1, 1904, at St. Joseph's Church, Middletown, he baptized conditionally Helen Elizabeth McClary, daughter of Mr. McClary, non-Catholic, and Mrs. McClary, Catholic. Sponsors were James Mullen and Sadie O'Neill.

On June 21, 1904, Father Crowley baptized Charles Andrew Shetzler, born May 9, 1904, child of Edward Shetzler and Lucinda Carpenter, his wife. Sponsors were Paul Marsh of Warwick and Mary Bartholomew of Philadelphia. On July 31, 1904, he baptized Dorsey Louis Ennis, son of Thomas and Elizabeth Ennis. Sponsors were E. Marsh and Mary Dorsey.

On November 6, 1904, Father Crowley baptized James Murry, born October 18, 1904, child of James Murry and Mary Crowley. Sponsors were John Dorsey and Anna Crowley. On December 11, 1904, he baptized Anna Bignear, born October 17, 1904, child of John Bignear and Mary Shetzler. Sponsors were John Devenny and Eva Franks. On January 8, 1905, he baptized John Edwards Fahey, born December 31, 1904, child of E. J. Fahey and Anna Holleran. Sponsors were Margaret E. Fahey and Frank Holleran.

On February 26, 1905, Father Crowley baptized Leo Devine, born February 4, 1905, son of Timothy P. Devine and Mary A. Scully. Sponsors were John J. Dorsey and Mary Dorsey.

On October 1, 1905, Father Crowley baptized Laura Dutton, born August 11, 1905, child of

George Clifton Dutton (non-Catholic) and Annie Plummer, both of Chesapeake City. Sponsors were Ed Stapp and Mrs. B. N. Buchelle.

On October 15, 1905, Father Crowley baptized George Scott (colored) an old man. Witnesses were John Sullivan and William Sullivan.

On October 17, Father Crowley baptized Eva Cecelia Shetzler, born October 6, 1905, child of Ed Shetzler (Catholic) and Lucinda Carpenter (non-Catholic). Sponsors were John Bignear and Eva Cecelia Franks. On September 6, 1905 he baptized Catherine Louise Dignan, about four years old, daughter of Michael Dignan and Louise Boyles. Sponsors were Thomas Dorsey and Margaret Dorsey.

On January 21, 1906, Father Crowley baptized at Middletown Joseph Lucas, son of William Lucas and Alice Welsh. Sponsors were Mr. and Mrs. George O'Neil. On April 7, 1906, he baptized Margrete Murray, born March 11, 1906, daughter of John Francis Murray and Margrete Connelly. Sponsors were Ellen Murrey and John J. Dorsey.

On April 26, 1906 Father Crowley baptized Anna Elizabeth Ryan, two weeks old, daughter of James Ryan and Katherine Leybold, at Chesapeake City. Sponsors were Rose Dufendorf and William Schaefer. On April 26, 1906, he baptized Harry Joseph Krastel, son of Harry Krastel and Beckie Libold. Sponsors were Ed Stapp and his wife. On June 24, 1906, he baptized and received into the church Elizabeth Jones Hopkins, born September 3, 1882, daughter of George S. Hopkins and Elizabeth Jones. Sponsors were John J. Dorsey and Elizabeth Price.

On June 26, 1906, Father Crawley baptized Florence Pauline McClary, six months old, child of Mr. McClary, not-Catholic, and Mrs. McClary, Catholic, maiden name Bloom. Sponsors were James Keegan and Florence Bloom. On November 10, 1906, he baptized Frances Pearson Maloney, born September 8, 1906, daughter of Patrick Maloney and Rhodie Ennis. Sponsors were John and Margaret Dorsey.

On January 27, 1907, Father Crowley baptized Mary Elizabeth Carroll, born November 7, 1906, daughter of Arthur Carroll and Elizabeth Money. Sponsors were George and Sophie O'Neil. On March 17, 1907, he baptized and received into the church Mrs. Lucinda Shetzler. Sponsors were Charles Carpenter and Mrs. John Bignear. On March 17, 907, he baptized and received into the church Charles Carpenter. Sponsors were Ed Shetzler and Mrs. John Bignear.

On June 16, 1907, Father Crowley baptized Cornelius Murray, born June 6, 1907, child of John F. Murray and Margaret Connelly. Sponsors were Cornelius Brooks and Mrs. Penn (at Chesapeake City). On August 11, 1907, he baptized Robert Bryan Burchell, born July 31, 1907, son of Byron N. Burchell and Elizabeth Taylor. Sponsors were William S. Taylor and Mary R. Beaston.

On July 28, 1907, Father Crowley baptized Mary Magdalene Paul, born March 10, 1907, daughter of John J. Paul and Mamie Preston. Sponsors were Mr. and Mrs. Slicher. On November 9, 1907, he baptized Margaret Moffett, born November 4, 1907, daughter of John P. Moffett and Ellen Penn. Baptized privately by Father Crowley and ceremonies supplied by Father John A. Daly. Sponsors were Jacob McCrea and Ellen Murray.

On November 12, 1907, Father Crowley baptized at Chesapeake City Mary Rebecka Collins, born October 28, 1907, daughter of Bart Collins and Bertha Morgan, his wife. Sponsors were Ed Molitor and Catherine McCloskey. On February 10, 1908, he baptized Charles Pope, born September 27, 1907, child of Alexander Pope and Rose Hoover, his wife. Sponsors were William and Sarah Carroll.

On October 11, 1908, at Middletown Bishop John J. Monaghan confirmed the following persons: Mrs. Lucinda Shetzler, Charles Thomas Carpenter, Florence Wilhelmina Bloome and Sophie Bloome, adults.

MARRIAGES PERFORMED BY FATHER CROWLEY AT BOHEMIA:

October 11, 1904 – between Louis M. Haas and Sarah M. Swartz. Witnesses were John Dorsey and Mary Dorsey; December 20, 1904 – between John C. Lucas and India Walker. Witnesses were Mr. Ryan and Mrs. Ryan; December 30, 1904 – Charles Brown (non-Catholic) and Cecelia Ayers (Catholic). Witnesses were Agnes F. Crowley and Elsie Marsh; May 11, 1905 – between George Ayers and Clara Wright (non-Catholic). Witnesses were Timothy Moynihan and A.B. Crowley; September 27, 1905 – between Louis Augustus Dreka and Elsie Eccleston Marsh. Witnesses were Earle Davis and Estella A. Marsh, by John J. Monaghan, bishop of Wilmington; November 2, 1905 – Benjamin F. Lamborn and Helena C. Blome. Witnesses Mr.

Blome, Jr. and Miss Blome; September 15, 1906 – between Charles C. Miller, Catholic, of Philadelphia and Beatrice F. Whitlock, not Catholic, of Middletown, Delaware. Witnesses were Mr. Taylor and Miss Jones; September 15, 1906 – between Eugene Briscoe, Catholic, and Elizabeth Brown, not Catholic. Witnesses were Dr. Wright and Agnes Crowley; April 27, 1909 – between John C. Green and Julia Elizabeth Morton Lockwood. Witnesses were Harry W. Lockwood and Marie T. Lockwood. Performed by John J. Monaghan, Bishop of Wilmington; April 28, 1909 – between Thomas H. Devine and Honora Sheahan. Witnesses were Mary Dunn and Joseph Dunn; June 1, 1909 – between A. Lindell Beaston and Anna B. Buckworth. Witnesses were Thomas F. Burke, C.A.P. and Agnes Crowley; August 7, 1909 – between Charles Carpenter and Mary Bignear. Witnesses were Henry Bignear and Grace Bignear; November 17, 1909 – between Charles Mullen and Mary A. Spear. Witnesses were Daniel Mullen and Annie Spear; January 11, 1910 – between Joseph P. Dunn and Mary L. Devine. Witnesses were Paul Dunn and Lillian Devine; April 4, 1910 – between Harry Bowman and Lillian May Pope. Witnesses were William and Emily Pope; January 25, 1911 – between Edward E. Woodall, Jr. and Anna Geneva Cochran. Witnesses were Woodall Cochran and Elizabeth Woodall; January 22, 1913 – between John Piser and Mary F. Carpenter. Witnesses were Leslie Naylor and Mrs. Naylor; May 12, 1916 – between James Connor and Emelia Smith. Witnesses were John Garner and Johanna Connor;

BURIAL REGISTERS OF OLD BOHEMIA, ST. XAVIER CHURCH, WARWICK, MARYLAND March 17, 1904 – Alice E. Marsh, age 47; April 20, 1904 – Ellen Henry Price, age 75, died at Atlantic City, New Jersey; June 4, 1904 – Margaret Stapp, age 74, of Mount Hope Retreat, near Warwick, Maryland; December 3, 1904 – Mary Price, of Middletown, Delaware; January 18, 1905 – James T. Moriarity, age 33, of Middle Neck; January 24, 1905 – Rosie O'Neil, age 67 of Middletown, Delaware; September 20, 1905 – William Hutchinson, of Warwick, Maryland; October 11, 1906 – Francis Wilmer Walmsley, age 75; July 10, 1906 – Nicholas Luthringer, age 88; August 25, 1906 – Gott, of Camden, New Jersey; September 24, 1906 – Margaret Dunn, age 68, of Middletown, Delaware; November 22, 1907 – Elsie Marsh Dreka, age 28; August 23, 1909 – Frank Sullivan; May 4, 1910 – September, 1910 – George Bryan November 21, 1910 – Dennis Boyle; December 30, 1910 – Lucendia Briscoe, of Warwick; Mary Daisey McAleer; 1910 – Alexander Mooney; September 16, 1910 – Charles Mullen; December 21, 1910 – M. Millie Piser, age 41; February 7, 1911 – Katherine Sullivan; March 22, 1911 – Mary Z. Dreka, age 34; October 16, 1911 – Alice Powderly, age 53, at Philadelphia; October 21, 1911 – Anna O'Neil, of Cecilton, Maryland; November 24, 1911 – Annie Manlove; December 23, 1911 – Carrie T. McAleer; August 18, 1912 – Katherine Hoppe; 1912 – Honora Dorsey, age 77; January, 1912 – James Mullen, age 40 of Middletown, Delaware; October 18, 1912 – Emily Theresa Walmsley; October 23, 1912 – Patrick Dorsey; November 21, 1912 – Mrs. Walmsley, wife of Clarence Walmsley; January 14, 1913 – Arabella Piser, age 80; March 29, 1913 – Catherine C. Moore, age 53; September 24, 1913 – Thomas O. Sullivan, age 52 of Girardville, Pennsylvania; July 4, 1914 – Margaret Penn; July 8, 1914 – Margaret Moffett; November 2, 1914 – Susanna Perkins, age 76, of Philadelphia; January 4, 1915 – Elias Eccleston Marsh, age 62; 1915 – Patrick Dorsey, age 87; Michael A. Dorsey, Dennis J. Dorsey – children of Patrick Dorsey – Markees only – no dates. 1915 – Elizabeth Mooney; October 1915 – George Moffett, Jr., age 9; March, 1916 – Oyde Reynolds; April 23, 1916 – John T. Sullivan, age 19; 1916 – Catherine Tyson Devine, age 72; April, 1916 – Alice Mooney; March 30, 1916 – Nora Sheahan Devine, August 18, 1916 – John Dunn, age 71; August 16, 1916 – Clarence Walmsley; August 28, 1916 – Mary A. Scully, age 77, Philadelphia, Pennsylvania; September, 1916 – Mrs. Walker; February 27, 1917 – Elizabeth Devine, age 76; March 6, 1917 – James W. Devine age 66; March 19, 1918 – Leslie Reynold's; October 9, 1918 – Antoneo Lourenso, age 38, of Warwick, Maryland, born in Portugal; July 1, 1920 – Ellen Murry, age 74; November 25, 1920 – C. Theresa Dreka, age 31; September 17, 1920 – Mollie McAleer Craddock of Fredericktown; April 12, 1921 – Michael Sullivan, age 55 Earleville, Maryland; August 11, 1921 – Patrick O'Neil, age 85; October 19, 1924 – Louis H. Dreka, age 71; April 13, 1925 – Margaret Mullen; June 22, 1925 – Amy Piser, age 61; May 30, 1926 – Anna Theresa Zeffere, of Middletown, Delaware; June 2, 1926 – Charles H. Crawford, age 49; May 1, 1913 – Martha Ann Burns Armstrong, age 79; August 24, 1913 – Katherine Louise Koreman Gregg; October 1, 1913 – Mary Ann Brown; December 2, 1913 – Eugene Briscoe; October 7, 1914 – Mary Beaston, age 72; November 2, 1914 – Lerna Grissert of Middletown, Delaware; July 9, 1915 – Margaret Price Crawford, age 77; March 22, 1917 – Rose Goff, of

Camden, New Jersey; July 2, 1920 – Cornelius Bowles; 1924 – Charles Owens Burns, age 60; July 1, 1924 – Lillian Barns Grant, wife of Jesse Root Grant, and daughter-in-law of President Ulysses S. Grant, age 63; January 13, 1925 – Francis Virginia Bond; March 14, 1925 – John Cayot Beaston, age 55; May 31, 1926 – Ann Theresa Gaffere, age 11 months; July 18, 1927 – Indiana Briscoe Garnet. November 15, 1928 – Henrietta C. Price, age 75; January 8, 1929 – George Murray; January 31, 1929 – Catherine Johnson.

4. Russell H. Perkins, *The Seed Has Grown To Harvest, Centenary of St. Rose of Lima Mission, 1874-1974, Chesapeake City, Maryland* (Hackensack, New Jersey: Custombook, Inc., 1974) 41
5. Perkins 42: The McCloskey family who operated the "Buck Tavern" at Summit Bridge were particularly generous. Mr. George Garner was employed as the carpenter to bring the project to completion. Before the rectory was built, an addition on the rear of St. Joseph's Church was used as an overnight residence for the priest when travel to and from Bohemia was difficult.
6. Perkins 45
7. ADW – *Bohemia Receipts 1908-1909* (bound register) p.51 – Plate Collections, Bohemia 1909, and p.52 – Pew Rents, Bohemia 1909; *Financial Records of St. Joseph's Parish 1908-1914*, Archives of St. Joseph Church, Middletown, Delaware. Perkins 45 – Father Crowley made every effort to provide Mass at each church on Christmas. Staying overnight in Chesapeake City the evening before he would celebrate the Christmas liturgy there at seven in the morning, leaving immediately for Middletown to repeat the ceremony, and then say the final Mass at Bohemia. In 1910 Bishop Monaghan began a diocesan newspaper, which was entitled: *The Delmarvia Catholic*, to be published every two weeks. Reverend James McSweeney, of Hockessin, Delaware, was the first editor. The publisher was The Catholic Publishing Company, 124 West Fourth Street, Wilmington, Delaware. The office was at the Bishop's Residence, 301 North Jackson Street, Wilmington, Delaware. The first issue was dated February 10, 1910. The only known copies still preserved are kept at the Philadelphia Archdiocesan Historical Research Center, Overbrook, Pennsylvania, where all of the semi-monthly 1910 issues and seven issues (January to April) 1911 are available for examination. The author examined each of these and found no mention of St. Francis Xavier Church at Bohemia. A single issue of *The Delmarvia Catholic* (April, 1928) is preserved in ADW, Bohemia file.
8. Perkins 44: The Schreibers would watch to see the priest and his horse "Star" (a beautiful bay with white hoofs and a white star on his forehead) heading down St. Augustine Road toward town at about four in the afternoon on the Saturday before "Church Sunday." He would stay overnight with Joseph Schaefer and his family. Early on Sunday morning Mr. Schaefer would start the fires in the church before the priest and the congregation would arrive.
9. Perkins 46. The first Ukrainian – Byzantine Rite bishop in the United States Soter Stephen Ortynsky, O.S.B.M., arrived in 1907. He purchased about seven hundred acres of land near Chesapeake City to encourage and help his people settle as farmers in the area. Plans consisted of a church, a school, a convent, and an auxiliary orphanage. *Golden Jubilee 1920-1970, St. Basil's Ukrainian Catholic Church, Chesapeake City, Maryland* (published privately, 1970). Only in October, 1930, did St. Basil's Church receive its first full-time pastor, although the church was constructed at the end of World War I.
10. Cann 227: As the sacristan Gervase Briscoe was starting the fires in the church stoves to heat the church for Mass at eleven o'clock, the stove-pipes which extended through the roof had become red hot up to the timbers causing them to burst into flame.
11. Edward I. Devitt, "Bohemia Church Destroyed By Fire" *Records of the American Catholic Historical Society (hereafter RACHS)* 24 (1913) 97, 138 and note. If one looks at the outside of the church today, one can see the damaged brick near the top of the walls.
12. Devitt, *RACHS* 24 (1913) 97
13. Wendy Hiester Gilbert, "Bohemia Society Notes Discovery of Antique Icons," Elkton, Maryland *The Cecil Whig*, May 24, 1996: The Old Bohemia Historical Society announced the discovery of antique framed stations of the cross icons, rescued during a 1912 fire which gutted the St. Francis Xavier Church near Warwick. The lithographs were produced in the studios of Lith. De L. Turgis of Paris and New York. They are probably early 19th century in origin.
14. Devitt, "Bohemia," *Woodstock Letters* 63 (1934) 1: Having received thirty-five hundred dollars from the insurance company and another thirty eight hundred and fifty dollars from donors far and wide, Father Crowley employed John J. Kennedy as the architect to plan the restoration.

Charles J. Dougherty was engaged for the carpentry work and B. T. Vinyard to do the painting. Reverend Brother Gratian was commissioned to construct the altars, pews, and altar rails – Archives of St. Joseph Church, Middletown, Delaware, *Receipt and Expense Book 1908-1914*, 138, 155 Many priests attended the dedication ceremony on October 24, 1912. However, of former Jesuit pastors only Father Giraud was alive – he died in April 1913. Father Haugh died in 1902, Father Gaffney died in 1908, Father Villiger died on September 20, 1997. Invitations were mailed out which read:

<blockquote>
St. Joseph's Rectory
Box 58
Middletown, Delaware
You are cordially invited to be present at
the dedication of
St. Francis Xavier Church
Old Bohemia, near Warwick, Md.
On Thursday, October twenty-fourth, 1912
At 10:30 o'clock
Rev. C. A. Crowley
</blockquote>

BAPTISMS BY FATHER CROWLEY

On July 26, 1908, *at Bohemia* Father Crowley baptized Mary Moffitt, born July 6, 1908, daughter of George Moffitt and Mary McDowell, his wife. Sponsors were John Moffitt and Ellen Moffitt. On May 14, 1909 Father Crowley baptized Reba Brothers, born October 8, 1908, daughter of Thomas M. Brothers and his wife, Biola G. Latta. Sponsors were Henry Bingnear and Katherine Mullin. On May 14, 1909, he baptized John Brothers, born August 8, 1906, son of Thomas M. Brothers and his wife Biola G. Latta. Sponsors were John Maloney and Mrs. Mary Bingnear.

On June 11, 1913, Father Crowley baptized Mary Caroline Bingnear, born May 2, 1911. Sponsors were Frank Bingnear and Anna Shetzler.

On March 5, 1914, he baptized Marcella Mary Shetzler, born January 7, 1914, daughter of Edward Shetzler and Mary Shockley, his wife. Sponsors were Edward Shetzler and Ann Shetzler.

On March 5, 1914, Father Crowley baptized Marcella Mary Shetzler, born January 7, 1914, child of Edward Shetzler and Mary D. Shockley, his wife. Sponsors were Edward and Anna Shetzler.

On December 19, 1914, he baptized Helen Catherine Bingnear, born December 14, 1914, daughter of John Bingnear and Amelia Mulburger, his wife. Sponsors were Corbit Bingnear and Anna Bingnear. This was the last baptism recorded in the first Bohemia register.

15. Edward J. Ludwig III, *The Chesapeake And Delaware Canal, 1829-1979* (Elkton, Maryland: The Cecil County Bicentennial Committee, 1979) 26-27. Robert Hazel, *The Chesapeake and Delaware Canal, Chronicles of Early Life in Towns Along the Historic Waterway* (Chesapeake City, Maryland: Rare Harmony Publishing Co., 2004) 29

16. Archives of St. Joseph Church, Middletown, Delaware *Receipt and Expense Book 1919-1926*; no author given, unpublished historical notes of Old Bohemia Historical Society, no date given, 1- C. Georgetown University Archives (hereafter GUA) Special Collections Division, Box 571174, Washington, D.C. 20057. The searchable index to these Georgetown University Library Special Collections is found at this web address:: http://www.library.georgetown.edu/dept/speccoll/index1st.htm For the Jesuit Complex at Bohemia, this web address: http://www.library.georgetown.edu/dept/speccoll/mi/mi}176.htm - The Maryland Province Collection BOHEMIA – ARTICLE ON MISSIONS OF – 1913 Box: 1 Folder: 5; BOHEMIA CHURCH – GUIDEBOOKS TO – 1930-1960 Box: 1 Folder; BOHEMIA CHURCH CROSS – PHOTOS OF Box: 1 Folder: 6

17. "Bishop John J. Monaghan," Thomas J. Peterman, *Catholic Priests of the Diocese of Wilmington, - A Jubilee Year 2000 Commemoration* (Devon, Pennsylvania: William T. Cooke Publishers, Inc., 2000) 90 (hereafter *Priests Jubilee 2000*) 90 As Titular Bishop of Lydda, he lived until his 79th year and died on January 7, 1955. "Bishop Edmond J. Fitz Maurice," Peterman, *Priests Jubilee 2000*) 53

18. "First Field Mass at Bohemia on October 26," *Woodstock Letters* 55 (1926) 383. Reverend Francis X. Delang of Georgetown College gave the sermon. "Field Mass At Old Bohemia," Elkton,

Maryland Cecil Democrat, September 24, 1927 – "Another Field Mass will be sung at Old Bohemia at 11 o'clock on the Second Sunday of October (October 9, 1927). All who attended last year were well pleased...." The article goes on to give a brief sketch of the history of St. Francis Xavier's Church. Bishop Fitz Maurice would officiate, assisted by Very Rev. Charles P. McGoldrick, V. F., of Centreville, and Rev. James McGiveney, S. J. of New York. The Reverend Patrick Brennan, of Newark, Delaware, will be celebrant. Reverend Peter J. Dolan, S. J. will preach the sermon. "Catholic Parish of St. Joseph's, Middletown, Delaware," Wilmington *The Delmarvia Catholic* April, 1928: gives an outline history of Old Bohemia Church, Father Charles Crowley, Pastor.

19. Perkins 48. Michael Sullivan helped Father Crowley with generous personal donations at Bohemia.
20. Peterman, *Priests Jubilee 2000* 88. He would serve as pastor of St. Peter's Church, New Castle, Delaware, for the next 22 years. He died on November 11, 1951, at 78 years of age and 48 years as a priest.
21. Peterman, *Priests Jubilee 2000* 131 BURIAL RECORDS OF OLD BOHEMIA, ST. XAVIER CHURCH, WARWICK, MARYLAND Father Walsh's burial records begin with May 22, 1929 - February 20, 1930 – Mary Philips; October 17, 1930 – Emma Price, age 77; November 3, 1931 – James Wilson Merritt, age 57; December 5, 1931 – Michael Degnan, age 75, of Warwick, Maryland; May 18, 1932 – Alex Karmiescuk; March 16, 1933 – Frederick Grissert of Philadelphia and Middletown; August 4, 1933 – Fanny Stevens; 1933 – Thomas H. Devine, age 82; October 16, 1933 – Mary A. Dorsey; October 16, 1935 – March 19, 1934 – Jervis Briscoe; 1935 – John Maloney, age 74; July 8, 1935 – Mrs. John Sullivan; July 24, 1935 – Mary R. Sullivan, age 70, of Girardville, Pennsylvania; January 10, 1936 – Timothy P. DeVine; November 3, 1936 – Hannah Maloney; November 30, 1936 – Edna Moffett; December 3, 1936 – John Sullivan; March 24, 1937 – Aloysius B. Price, age 82; February 9, 1938 – Catherine Sullivan; June 22, 1939 – Katherine Price, age 71; No date – J. H. Manlove, buried in Price lot; February 7, 1940 – Mary Powderly, Philadelphia, March 25, 1940 – Frank Mullen, age 63; May 9, 1940 – John Mullen; March 14, 1941 – Elizabeth P. Price, age 83; October 13, 1940 – John Murray, age 63; October 28, 1939 – Kathryn Denver, age 56, wife of John; November 4, 1940 – Elizabeth Briscoe; August 9, 1941 – Margaret Mullen, age 67; September 4, 1941 – Joseph Sullivan, November 22, 1941 – John Price, age 74; December 24, 1941 – George O'Neil, age 66; June 6, 1942 – Walter Briscoe; August 25, 1952 – Thomas T. Dorsey; November 30, 1943 – Samuel Pierson; September 18, 1944 – John Workman of Middle Neck; October 4, 1944 – Marcia McAleer Baldwin, age 18 months; October 9, 1944 – Margaret A. Powderly, age 78; April 21, 1943 – Sarah Hover Carroll of Warwick, Maryland; June 13, 1945 – Joseph Stackley, age 56 of Middletown, Delaware; 1945 – Robert A. Kirk, age 75; September 28, 1945 – Thomas Carroll; February 17, 1947 – Mary Sullivan; April 17, 1947 – John Briscoe; October 11, 1947 – Mary E. Moffett; 1947 – Gervase Briscoe, age 87; April 25, 1949 – Rebecca Sullivan, age 72 of Earleville, Maryland; April 25, 1949 – Pauline Merritt, age 73; January 3, 1950 – Francis Scully Holton, age 76; April 22, 1950 – John Dorsey; September 23, 1950 – Elizabeth T. Ruthlinger; November 4, 1950 – Margaret M. Dorsey; March 27, 1951 – Lena Grissert, of Philadelphia and Middletown; November 7, 1951 – Catherine C. Dorsey of Warwick; November 25, 1952 – Margaret O'Neal; January 24, 1953 – William L. Dorsey, of Philadelphia; September 24, 1953 – Delia K. O'Grady, age 69; October 10, 1953 – George Degnan; December 16, 1954 – Elsie May Garner; January 28, 1955 – Cecelia Brown; March 19, 1955 – John Henry Manlove; September 1, 1955 – Paul P. Potocki, age 69, U.S. Coast Guard, WW II; January 10, 1956 – Teresa Ann Naylor, age 10; Father Walsh burial records at Bohemia end with February 6, 1956 – Marie G. Quinn, age 57, of Warwick, Maryland.
22. Perkins 49-50. In 1932 fire destroyed the farm house inhabited by the Aikens. They built the existing tenant house.
23. "Annual Event Near Warwick, Cecil County, Recalls Events Connected With Early Center of Catholicity on Eastern Shore," Elkton, Maryland *Cecil Democrat* October 2, 1929. Woodstock, Maryland: *Jesuit Seminary News*, October 2, 1930, - "Bishop Fitz Maurice to Preside at Field Mass – October 5, 1930." *Middletown Transcript*, October 9, 1930: On Sunday, October 5, 1930, Bishop Fitz Maurice addressed 700 persons at the conclusion of the Annual Field Mass at Bohemia October 5, 1930. Joseph T. Murphy, S. J., a Wilmington, boy stationed at St. Joseph College, Philadelphia preached. The celebrant of the Mass was Rev. John J. Bolen, chancellor of the dio-

cese. He was assisted by Rev. John M. Walsh of Galena, Rev. John A. Lynch of Christ Our King, Wilmington, Rev. Peter Brennan, pastor of Newark, and Rev. John H. Walsh, pastor of Middletown. October 8, 1932: "More Than 1000 Attend Military Mass, Warwick – Held in Commemoration of The Two Hundredth Anniversary of General George Washington." Bishop Fitz Maurice was present and Traced the History of Old Bohemia. "With perfect weather for an outdoor service, more than a thousand persons attended the Military Mass held last Sunday morning at Old Bohemia." The Rt. Rev. Edmond J. Fitz Maurice, Bishop of the Diocese of Wilmington, made a short address in which he traced the history of the old church and stressed the need of great patience and patriotism in these days of economic distres: "Friends and lovers of Old Bohemia greatly desire to make this hallowed place a shrine sacred to the memory of pioneering priests and their sturdy parishioners and to those ideals of liberty, justice and freedom of conscience which they and we cherish," he said. "This mass is a part of the nationwide celebration of the Bicentennial of the birth of George Washington, the great citizen, soldier and patriot, who will always hold the first place in every American heart," he continued. "Washington often viewed this old church as he passed north and south on his journeys through the colonies and among the men who worshipped there, notably Charles Carrol of Carrolton, were some of the sturdiest supports of his cause. Let us pledge his country and ours your undivided allegiance and unswerving fidelity. In this period of economic distress, grant us patience like unto that of Washington, Oh God, and deliver us from the evils, pain and perils of our present situation." The Rev. Martin M. Ryan, pastor of St. Joseph's-on-the-Brandywine, delivered the sermon in which he stressed that the church, morality and hope are the foundation of all happiness.

The services started shortly before 11 o'clock Sunday morning when a detachment of soldiers from the First Engineers Regiment, Fort duPont, under the command of Lieut. Philip R. Gargas, formed two lines from the church to the place where the field mass was held. As they came to a "present arms" the procession comprising the Rev. John J. Bolen, chancellor of the diocese and celebrant of the Mass; the Rev. John W. Walsh, pastor of St. Dennis Church, Galena, and the Very Rev. Ralph M. Fontaine, superior of the Salvatorian Mission House at Elkton, subdeacons of the Mass; the Rev. William Shevland, assistant pastor of St. Peter's Pro-Cathedral, Wilmington, master of ceremonies; the Very Rev. J. Francis Tucker, pastor of St. Anthony's Church Wilmington, and Bishop Fitz Maurice moved slowly through the lines of soldiers toward the improvised altar. During the Mass a squad of soldiers under the command of Sgt. C. J. DeSheine fired three volleys over the old graveyard in which lie buried Revolutionary patriots, veterans of both the Union and Confederate armies and a number of soldiers of the World War. The music at the Mass was rendered by a choir of forty voices from Wilmington under the direction of Miss Agnes Curley. Mozart's "Twelfth Mass" was sung. The choruses, "Praise Ye the Father" and "Unfold Ye the Portals" were sung at the close of the solemn benediction of the Most Blessed Sacrament. At the close of the service the congregation joined in singing the "Star Spangled Banner." Instrumental music throughout the program was furnished by the band from St. Joseph's Catholic school for Colored Boys at Clayton, Del. The scene already made impressive by the vari-colored robes of the priests and the uniforms of the soldiers was made doubly colorful by the regimental American Legion post and national flags placed in the church yard.

Lieut. Col. L. W. Watkins, commanding officer at Fort duPont, was among the many visitors to the old church which is considered the cradle of Catholicism on the Eastern Shore of Maryland. Several hundred persons motored down from Wilmington, Philadelphia and other nearby cities and spent the day on the church grounds visiting the ancient graveyard, strolling through the lanes of boxwood and inspecting the old brick buildings.

Woodstock College, Woodstock, Maryland: *The Jesuit Seminary News*, May, 1934 – "Where Bishop Carroll was Educated – Bohemia On The Eastern Shore of Maryland." Newark, Delaware: *Evening News*, February 8, 1934: "Church of St. Francis Xavier Near Warwick, Founded 229 Years Ago." This article featuring a picture of the church and rectory states that St. Francis Xavier church was built on an old Indian trail of the Choptank Indians that was there hundreds of years before the coming of the white man. George Washington passed Old Bohemia many times, travelling between Philadelphia and Mount Vernon. Also Colonel Tilghman passed Old Bohemia while announcing the patriot victory at Yorktown over the

British. The article also mentions that Father Walsh, pastor of Old Bohemia at that time, was once an employee of the *Newark Evening News* when he was a resident of Newark before entering the seminary. *Wilmington Morning News*, June 13, 1936: "Old Bohemia Has Military Field Mass." "Bishop To Preside At Military Field Mass Near Warwick Sunday" – Sunday, June 15, 1941, at 11 a.m., *"in commemoration of the 237th anniversary of this venerable edifice"* celebrant of the Mass was Very Reverend Ethelred Mai, Prior of the Salvatorian Mission House in Elkton. He was assisted by Very Rev. Daniel Hurley, O. Praem., headmaster of Archmere Academy, and Reverend George A. O'Gorman, chaplain of the 12th Battalion at Fort duPont Delaware. Mr. Thomas Reese, student at St. Charles College, Catonsville, Maryland acted as master of ceremonies. The sermon was given by Reverend John A. McGee, assistant rector of St. Theresa of Avila Church, Port Deposit, Maryland. A detachment of soldiers from the 122nd Battalion, consisting mostly of men from New Jersey and New York, participated in the ceremonies. The Catholic Choristers of Wilmington under Mr. George Finnan provided the musical program.
24. Perkins 50
25. Elktor, Maryland *Cecil Whig*, 1942: "The History of St. Francis Xavier Church Near Warwick," by Lorraine Cox of Cecilton, D. A. R. Contest Winner For 1942.
26. ADW, Bohemia File, Text of Program, Catholic Forum of the Air, November 2, 1947.
27. ADW, Bohemia File, letter Frank Krastel to Bishop Thomas J. Mardaga, November 11, 1968, in which Mr. Krastel outlined the origins of the Old Bohemia Historical Society. The Krastels were natives of Cecil County. Frank Krastel's parents, John F. and Jane Rodney Krastel, were married in St. Francis Xavier Church at Bohemia. A letter to Rev. Clifford M. Lewis, S. J., brought a copy of the Edward I. Devitt, S. J.'s article on "Bohemia" in the *Woodstock Letters* 63, No. 1. This article on Bohemia's history increased the desire in many to see the ancient church restored.
28. ADW, Bohemia File, notes refer to letter from Carrie Wright to Mrs. Krastel.
29. ADW, Bohemia File, Krastel notes.
30. A letter dated October 23, 1952, from the Raskob Foundation for Catholic Activities stated that the board had approved the grant, and a check was sent to the Elkton Banking and Trust Company, March 5, 1953, for deposit to the credit of the Old Bohemia Historical Society, Inc. Helena Springer Green Raskob Corcoran lived in the area of Bohemia as a young girl. The Corbaly – Green family members are buried in the St. Francis Xavier cemetery.
31. ADW, Bohemia File, Notes, Minutes Of The First Meeting of the Old Bohemia Historical Society.
32. The Phillips, who were not Catholic but who hosted this meeting at Worsall Manor, had become interested in the restoration of Old Bohemia when someone suggested razing the rectory and selling the bricks. The Phillips joined in the effort to prevent this from happening.
MINUTES OF MEETING – February 28, 1953 The first or organization meeting of the incorporators of THE OLD BOHEMIA HISTORICAL SOCIETY, INCORPORATED, was held on the above date at WORSELL MANNOR, the estate of Mr. Alfred N. Phillips, with the following present: Rt. Reverend Monsignor Jos. D. Sweeney, Reverend Father John H. Walsh, Frank W. Krastel, John J. Ward, Jr., Alfred N. Phillips, J. Bradford Sullivan, Michael F. Carroll, James A. Quinn, Edward D. E. Rollins, John F. Hynes, M. D., John M. Herndon, Ph.D., Francis X. Donahue, and Stanley M. Kaplow, Maryland State Trooper, Guest. Mr. W. C. Brothers was unable to be present, having so advised the Chairman prior to the meeting. Prior to calling the meeting to order, the guests were invited to a very interesting tour of the Mannor House by our host, Mr. Phillips. The meeting was called to order by the temporary chairman, Frank W. Krastel. Motion was made, seconded and carried that Mr. Krastel be elected President. Mr. Krastel then took the chair, thanked the group for the honor and asked for their cooperation. Motion was made, seconded and carried that Mr. Alfred N. Phillips be elected Vice President. Motion was made, seconded and carried that Mr. F. X. Donahue be elected Secretary, with the proviso that this would be on a temporary basis. Motion was made, seconded and carried that Reverend Father John H. Walsh be elected Treasurer, with John J. Ward, Jr., as Chairman of the Finance Committee. Motion was made, seconded and carried that the Elkton Banking and Trust Company of Maryland, Elkton, Maryland, be the depository for the funds of the Society. The Chairman of the Finance Committee, Mr. John J. Ward, Jr., and the Treasurer, Rev. Father Walsh, were authorized to open this account. The By-Laws, as recommended by the

Incorporators, were reviewed in complete detail by all present and motions were made, seconded and carried adopting each Article, with amendments as deemed necessary. These By Laws, as revised and amended, have been rewritten and are submitted herewith. As noted in these By-Laws, the Ordinary of the Diocese of Wilmington will be Honorary President of the Society. The Reverend Pastor of St. Joseph's Church in Middletown, Delaware, along with the President of the Society, will be Ex-Officio members of all committees. Motion was made, seconded and carried, that the Treasurer, and the Chairman of the Finance Committee, be authorized to pay the expenses of the incorporation of this Society, amounting to approximately $45. Motion was made, seconded and carried that the Secretary be empowered to purchase necessary stationery, stamps and record books. Temporary adjournment followed so that all could make a personal inspection of the St. Francis Xavier Church and grounds, the restoration and preservation of which historic shrine is our immediate goal. Return to Worsell Mannor was followed by a delightful social get-together, climaxed by a buffet dinner, all of which was provided by our Host and Hostess, Mr. and Mrs. Phillips, to whom the sincere thanks of all were offered. Final adjournment was made at 8 P.M. Francis X. Donahue, Secretary.

33. "To The Rescue of the 18th Century," *The Philadelphia Inquirer Magazine* October 18, 1853: In 1937 Otley bought a house a few miles from his birth place in Cecil County. While restoring this home he explored along the Bohemia River where he likes to hunt and fish. He says he stumbled on a partly abandoned old church and learned it was the first Catholic Church on the Eastern Shore dating back to 1704. He started the ball rolling until the recently formed Old Bohemia Historical Society made him director of the church's restoration. He was a partner in the John B. Kelly contracting firm in Philadelphia.
34. ADW – The Old Bohemia Historical Society Folder 3-C, typewritten notes
35. ADW – The Old Bohemia Historical Society, 4-C, typewritten notes.
36. Elkton, Maryland: *Cecil Whig* August 30, 1954. A telegram of good wishes from President Dwight D. Eisenhower was read before the Mass. Assistants at the Mass were: the Rev. Edward M. Leinheiser, pastor of St. Dennis' Church, Galena; the Rev. Frank W. Krastel, Washington, D. C., and the Rev. John Gausch, Phoenixville, Pa. Father Krastel is the son of the president of the Old Bohemia Historical Society. The Rev. John H. Walsh, pastor of St. Joseph's Parish, Middletown, read a letter from the Most Rev. Dr. A. G. Cicognani, apostolic delegate from the Holy See to the United States, conferring the apostolic blessing of Pope Pius XII upon all those present at he mass. Frank W. Krastel, Sr., Penns Grove president, announced the objectives of the historical society and Col. Alfred Phillips of Worsell Manor, Warwick, a director of the society, introduced the representatives of local and state governments attending the celebration. Among those there were U. S. Marshal Richard C. O'Connell, Baltimore, representing Gov. Theodore R. McKeldin of Maryland and Mayor Thomas Newman, Middletown, representing Gov. J. Caleb Boggs of Delaware. Solemn High Mass was celebrated at an altar set up under the large hemlock tree, (destroyed by Hurricane Hazel in October 1954), was sung by the Rt. Rev. Joseph D. Sweeney, Chancellor of the Diocese of Wilmington. Rev. Paul Gausch was Master of Ceremonies. Father John H. Walsh, local pastor, was in the sanctuary as were the Very Rev. Thomas Lawless, OSFS, Principal of Salesianum High School and superintendent of schools in the Diocese of Wilmington; Rev. John A. Corrigan, pastor of St. John's Church, Milford, Delaware; Rev. William R. Couming, pastor of Good Shepherd Church, Perryville, Maryland; Rev. Gervase Glaser, OSB, assistant pastor Sacred Heart Church, Wilmington; Rev. Victor Pospieshil, pastor of the Church of St. Basil, Chesapeake City, Maryland and Rev. James McDonald, assistant pastor of Immaculate Conception Church, Elkton, Maryland. Rev. Neil J. Gargan, S. J., Georgetown University, was the speaker. He traced the history of Old Bohemia in his talk. The Oblates of St. Francis de Sales Novitiate Choir, Childs, Maryland sang appropriate selections during the Mass.
37. Pope and Kruse, a well known and competent architectural firm was engaged to conduct research work and offer recommendations for a restoration program. Their studies under the guidance of M. J. Otley and John A. H. Sweeney, chairman and vice-chairman of the Research Committee, consisted of careful studies of old documents and included extensive excavation. Fred Krastel wrote on March 20th, 1954: "Mr. John B. DeLancey, North East, Maryland I understand that you were engaged to make a survey of the Church Farm located near Warwick in Cecil County when it was sold by the Catholic Diocese of Wilmington to Mr. Richard D. Aiken

some years ago and that this survey clearly established the boundaries of the property that was retained, i. e., the Old Bohemia or St. Francis Xavier Church yard and cemetery. If I have been informed correctly, could you supply The Old Bohemia Historical Society, Inc. with a copy of the map which records this survey and what would be the charge? I shall appreciate any information you can make available to the Society which has been organized to restore and maintain this historic old church." Mr. John B. DeLancey responded on March 25, 1954: "Dear. Mr. Krastel – I have received your letter of the 20th instant. I made a survey of the farm and Church Property of the Old Bohemia Church a number of years ago but I have not been able to locate the record this instant. I have so many records that it is rather hard some times to locate the particular record just at the time when wanted. The charge for supplying you with a good durable copy of the land now owned by the Church would hardly cost more than $10.00 or $15.00 at the most. I will be glad to supply you with this information." Mr. J. D. Otley of 1720 Cherry Street, Philadelphia, 3, PA wrote to Frank Krastel on April 28th, 1954: "Just to report to you that I am making out very well with the architects and research authorities. I am waiting for just one letter from Mr. Hepburn of Perry, Shaw and Hepburn, Architects of Boston. When I have all this information complete, I will have a meeting with Dr. Hines and John Sweeney and we will then prepare a report for the Board of Directors. Possibly you forgot one little thing you were going to do for me. That is to send me a photostatic copy of the old map that you and John Sweeney had of the entire property." Again on June 9th, 1954, Mr. Otley wrote Krastel: "Your Architectural and Research Committee had a meeting. Those present were Mr. John Sweeney, Dr. John F. Hynes, and Mr. J. D. Otley. We had an interesting discussion on the subject of research and architecture. The letters were read and we made the final decision that the architectural work should be awarded to the architectural firm of Pope and Kruse of Wilmington, Del. with Perry, Shaw and Hepburn as Associates. We discussed the question of selecting the research expert and decided to let that matter in abeyance until the architects were finally assigned so that they could have some authority on this important subject as the research expert must work in harmony with the architect. Various letters and papers were given to Mr. Sweeney for further reading and checking and the suggestion was made that we would like to hasten the assignment of the architect so it could be announced at the field service this Summer. This, as mentioned by John Sweeney, would have great effect. At this particular time, I suggest you get your Publicity Committee working so everything can be timed properly. We will not do anything of a positive nature with the architects until our actions have been approved by you and the Board of Directors. We would appreciate your consideration and call upon us for any advice or help in this matter." On January 14, 1955, Mr. Albert Kruse wrote J. B. Otley: "Enclosed are the three contracts, which are now all signed, except for the approval signature of the Bishop. I will be in touch with Miss Eckman and John Sweeney in the next few days and after we get a few things in mind we will be calling you for a meeting so that we all can get better acquainted and do some planning. As I said last night, I think Miss Eckman and I should get a little more information absorbed before we can proceed very far. I enjoyed your company last night and the meeting with your group. Thank you again." On January 25, 1955, Fred Krastel wrote to Rev. Mr. J. Walsh, S. J., Woodstock College, Woodstock, Maryland: "The Wilmington, Delaware architectural firm of Pope and Kruse has been engaged to handle the research and restoration work on St. Francis Xavier or Old Bohemia Church at Warwick, Cecil County, Maryland. This will introduce their research specialist, Miss Jeannette Eckman, about whom we recently wrote you. We shall appreciate anything that you can to do facilitate Miss Eckman's study of the records in connection with the Old Bohemia Church, school and plantation which may be available in the Woodstock archives. We are interested in the overall subject of Old Bohemia from the time of its founding in 1704 by Thomas Mansell, S. J. to the time the church farm was turned over to the Wilmington Diocese. We are particularly interested in information relative to the Bohemia School which Bishop John Carroll and others, who later became prominent in church and United States history, attended in the 1740's. Thanking you for your cooperation in the historic cause and with kindest personal wishes, I am." On January 29th, 1955, Krastel wrote Otley: "The following quoted letter just received from the Diocese of Wilmington Chancery Office is self explanatory: `Dear Mr. Krastel, "You will find here the contracts you left with me the other night. Since the Most Rev. Bishop is not a party to the contract, I have cut off the place left for his approval. If you look over the papers carefully, you will find that while the carbons are properly put together, the original has one page out of place. I am making no change for fear of spoiling the appearance. "With every best wish, I am Sincerely yours in Christ', (signed) Joseph D. Sweeney, Chancellor." I have changed the page in the original copy of the contract referred to by Monsignor Sweeney. I believe the proper execution of the contract between the firm of Pope and Kruse and The Old Bohemia Historical Society, Inc. can now be considered complete. I am, therefore, keeping the original for filing in the Society's lock box in The Elkton Banking & Trust Company of Maryland at Elkton, Maryland; and am enclosing the two carbon copies – one for Pope & Kruse and one for use by your Research Committee. The following quoted letter from Woodstock College was received yesterday: `Dear Mr. Krastel, Father Ryan has asked me to answer your letter which was sent to Hyattsville by mistake. Hence the delay. Your research specialist will be welcome any Thursday or Sunday you choose. Kindly let us know what day you will be coming an about what time you will arrive. Since our archives are cloistered, we shall take any material on Old Bohemia to the front parlor where Miss Eckman may see them. If you come on a Sunday, I may not be here. In that event Mr. James Hennessy, S. J. will take care of you." On February 3rd, 1955, J. D. Otley wrote to Pope & Kruse, 1108 Washington St., Wilmington, Del., "Attention Mr. Albert Kruse: I am enclosing executed contract accompanied with a copy of a letter addressed to me by Mr. Frank W. Krastel, President , Old Bohemia Historical Society. I am also enclosing a letter addressed to Rev. William J. Walsh, S. J., for the use of Miss Eckman. In the meantime we will try to obtain for you a letter of introduction to St. Mary's or Georgetown or any other source that would be required in accordance with Miss Eckman's findings. Will you arrange a meeting with Miss Eckman at some mutual time satisfactory to Mr. Krastel, Mr. Sweeney and Dr. Hynes." JDO/k Enc. CC: Mr. F. Krastel, "Dear Frank: I received your note and appreciate all your help. I will let Mr. Kruse establish the time for the meeting with Miss Eckman before she goes to Woodstock. John Sweeney's handling of the organ situation and your handling of the Garden Club situation would be very sensible." On February 18, 1955, Rev. Edward Brown, S. J. wrote Frank Krastel: "I received your letter relative to the Old Bohemia Historical Society's work. We shall be happy to welcome Miss Eckman to Georgetown and to cooperate with her in every way we can. I would suggest that Miss Eckman write directly to Reverend William C. Repetti, S. J., our Archivist, and make an appointment which will be mutually convenient. Father will be happy to see her any day except Saturday or Sunday. Assuring you of my thanks for the very interesting pamphlet and with all good wishes, etc." On February 24, 1955, Father William O'Shea, Librarian at St. Mary's Seminary in Baltimore, wrote Fred Krastel: "You must excuse my delay in answering your letter, which came at a particularly busy time for me, and I could not immediately check the archives to see what we have. I have to do that myself whenever anyone comes seeking information because I am not allowed to let any one in; I must get all the material and bring it to the library where it is to be studied. I find that we do have some material on Bohemia and whenever you wish to send the lady you mentioned she may examine it at her leisure. Just let me know when she will be coming. I do remember your son of course. He is a very nice person and I am sure that he is an excellent priest. He told me about your "project" last year. I hope this answers your question. Sincerely yours in Christ William O'Shea." Cecil County Historical Society, Bohemia File: Historical Search At Various Sources Made In 1955 For The Study Of Old Bohemia Church Warwick, Maryland, Pope & Kruse, Architects, 911 Washington Street, Wilmington, Delaware, Miss Jeanette Eckman, Historian.

38. Wilmington, *Morning News*, February 28, 1956
39. The home of James D. Quinn, North Main Street, Warwick, Md. was the central collection point. Persons preserving any of the original furnishings, particularly the chair used by John Carroll when he attended the Bohemia Academy, books, pictures, antique hardware from the doors, and similar articles are to be deposited with Mr. Quinn. Elected at the meeting were the following members of the board of directors: C. Reynolds Ash, John J. Ward, Jr., E. D. E. Rollins and John J. Denver of Elkton, William C. Brothers, Kentin Park, Md.: M. F. Carroll, James A. Quinn, J. B. Sullivan, James D. Quinn, Warwick, Md., Alfred N. Phillips, Warsall Manor; Rev. John H. Walsh, John P. Maloney and James Mullen, Middletown, John F. Stokes, Sudlersville, Md.; Miss A. Dorothy Arthur, Dr. John P. Hynes and John A. H. Sweeney, Wilmington; Jesse D. Otley and John H. McClatchy, Philadelphia; F. X. Donahue and Frank W. Krastel, Penns Grove, N. J.
40. Peterman, *Priests Jubilee 2000* 141

41. Perkins 55
42. ADW – Bohemia File, Notes: This cost the Society $275. Old Bohemia got considerable publicity from this effort.
43. *Minutes of the Seventeenth Regular Meeting of the Old Bohemia Historical Society, Inc. Board of Directors, Thursday, April 25, 1957* The seventeenth regular meeting of The Old Bohemia Historical Society's Board of Directors was called to order and opened with prayer by Father Rimlinger in St. Joseph's Hall, Middletown, Del., April 25, 1957 at 9:10 p.m., with the following present: W. C. Brothers, S. A. Borgstrom, J. B. Sullivan, M. F. Carroll, J. P. Maloney, J. A. H. Sweeney, J. J. Denver, J. D. Otley, J. J. Ward, Jr., F. X. Donahue, A. N. Phillips, O. P. Gentile, J. A. Quinn, F. W. Krastel, J. D. Quinn, Rev. Dr. Herbert T. Rimlinger, Visitors: Mrs. Mary Dunn, Miss L. deVine, Mrs. J. Maloney, Mrs. J. Ward, Jr. Motion was made, seconded and carried that minutes of the last meeting be approved as sent out acknowledging the inadvertent omission on page 6 of the names of Messrs. John B. McClatchy, John A. H. Sweeney and J. Bradford Sullivan. Treasurer's Report Motion was made, seconded and carried that the Treasurer reimburse J. D. Quinn and F. W. Krastel for amounts expended in connection with Old Bohemia activities, as follows: J. D. Quinn - $38.10 for labor and material in back filling trenches and erecting guard rail around house-chapel foundation. F. W. Krastel - $50.69 for printing of minutes, reports, purchase of stencils, paper, envelopes (1,000), stamps and copies of Old Bohemia pictures used for publicity purposes during the past fourteen months. James Quinn's *Report on Data of Restoration for Old Bohemia* April, 1957 Information contained in the historical search (1955) by Miss Jeanette Eckman and submitted by Pope & Kruse, Architects, includes dates that various buildings at Old Bohemia were erected and dates that some were subsequently dismantled. Presently it can be considered that three units remain that were constructed at different times. The west end of the rectory, the 1? story kitchen unit is early, the rectory date is 1825 and the church, based on the dedication date is 1797, the vestibule and belfry of the church was added sometime between 1856 and 1876, possibly 1865. There appear to be three plans for restoration that should be considered. 1. Early Restoration 1797. This plan suggests that a. The present rectory be dismantled with the exception of the kitchen section. b. The belfry and vestibule be removed from the church. c. That the original house-chapel be erected on the foundations recently uncovered. d. That two small out-buildings be erected northwest of the rectory kitchen. e. That the church be restored to conform with details of the 1797 period. 2. Considering various points of the 1797 plan: 1. At present there are only the church and the rectory, including the kitchen wing. The plan would require the removal of the rectory proper which could be restored to the date of 1825. The rectory is approximately 50' x 20' without the kitchen or sacistry wing. 2. It would require the erection of the house-chapel 35'4" x 15'8" according to prototypes in the Chesapeake Bay Area. The value of a chapel in addition to the church is questionable. 3. The outbuildings could be erected at a moderate cost and would add considerably to the group. 4. The removal of the vestibule and belfry would result in a considerable change in the appearance of the church, but would result in "colonial appearance" if that is the criteria. An estimate of cost for the 1797 restoration is not available but it does seem reasonable to assume that the cost could be high, but regardless of the cost the group of buildings would not have utility for any purpose except occasional masses. This should be considered when the long range objective of the restoration is discussed. *1825 Plan* This plan would consider restoration of existing buildings to their original date, with the exception of the church vestibule and belfry. Considering the 1825 plan: 1. This approach would eliminate the dismantling of the rectory and erection of the house-chapel. 2. The plan would include the restoration of the kitchen wing and erection of the out buildings northwest of the kitchen. 3. The plan would include restoration of the church to the 1797 date, but would require the removal of the vestibule and belfry. This restoration could result in the rectory having utility as a residence in the event that the project is later extended. *1865 (1876) Plan* This plan is essentially the same as the 1825 plan with the exception that the belfry and vestibule added to the church about 1865 would remain. As an initial plan this could be considered with the possibility of reverting to the 1825 plan at an appropriate time. This could result in additional expenditure if either improvement or maintenance of the present belfry were required. After considering the three possible dates, the concensus of the special committee is that the 1825 Plan is the most logical approach, for the following reasons. 1. As this is an historical project, it is important that the restoration reflect not only the early days, but the development to the extent that the principal buildings are considered. The date of 1825 or 1865 are considered to

be a reasonable point because it would permit us to take advantage of known things rather than to consider erection of a prototype as a principal building. In the 1797 plan we cannot expect to duplicate the original building but are limited to what is known about similar buildings in other areas. The utility of this building would be limited because of the church facilities that now exist. Apparently in the development of Old Bohemia it was not the intent to have both a chapel and church – one followed the other. The restoration of the rectory kitchen wing would also be the same in either the 1797 or 1825 Plan. The rectory proper is a well proportioned and arranged building, essentially in it's original state from the standpoint of design. The structural restoration will require replacement of some floor beams, flooring, roofing, caulking, pointing and painting. Heating, plumbing and lighting systems are also required. Following this plaster patching wood work, painting, sanding of floors, etc. The indicated cost is considerably below the cost of erecting a building having equivalent floor area. Conditions indicate a cost of $15,000 - $20,000 or $10,000 - $15,000 without heating and plumbing. The cost of the church restoration cannot be estimated as there are insufficient data available regarding the original state and extent of restoration. The rectory can be, though, as the conditions and requirements are known. In the event that a proposal to proceed according to the 1825 or 1865 plan is considered, the committee suggests the following plan of action. 1. That the possibility of purchasing the farm, originally church property, for a reasonable market value be investigated. 2. That Pope & Kruse, or an independent architect, be retained on a consulting basis to develop a detailed plan, to assist in developing scope of work and estimates and negotiations with local contractors or individual craftsmen. 3. That consideration be given to the possibility of having the project "alive" either as a parochial or trade school, home, or for other purposes that may be proposed. This plan could require the erection of temporary buildings in addition to the permanent buildings (or the farm dwelling might be utilized) until additional funds and income allows improvement of the temporary facilities. There are two considerations that appear to be important concerning an inactive or active restoration: a. When the facilities are improved they must be maintained. b. Having the location active would not add and could possibly reduce the base maintenance cost. Operation of the farm could also provide income. Reference has been made to a Williamsburg type of restoration and while the Bohemia restoration can be of considerable interest it must be recognized that we are not condemning a restoration of the Williamsburg scope, neither do we have access to unlimited funds for action. Therefore, it could be necessary to develop attention and interest through having a project of historical interest that is not only a shrine, but that it also has as an objective activity that will contribute to betterment of conditions. This report of the Special Committee is respectfully submitted for consideration on behalf of the committee by James D. Quinn, Chairman, (typed August 11, 1957). Copies sent to: Rev. H. T. Rimlinger, John J. Ward, Jr., W. C. Brothers, Michael F. Carroll. Michael and Joseph Carroll of Warwick were most zealous workers at Bohemia. They kept the buildings in good shape with hammer, saw, and paint brush.

44. ADW – Bohemia File, Minutes of Board of Directors, April 25, 1957: *Membership* It was reported that since the February 28th, 1957 meeting, memberships and contributions had been received, as follows:

Annual	Contribution	Name
$1.00	-	James Mullen
1.00	-	James A. Quinn in memory of Mrs. James A. Quinn
1.00	-	Joseph Carroll
1.00	-	Dr. and Mrs. Arthur T. Keefe
1.00	-	James Kincaid
2.00	-	John A. Beers
1.00	-	Mrs. R. Melson
1.00	-	George E. Springer
-	$ 3.00	H. Geiger Omwake
-	10.00	E. Churchill Murray
$9.00	$13.00	

45. ADW – Bohemia File, Minutes April 25, 1957: *Maryland Pilgrimage* – Mr. Phillips reported in detail on this project, the high spots being as follows: The Pilgrimage, May 10 from 10 a.m. to

6 p.m., will include the following Cecil County places of interest – Worsell Manor, Old Bohemia Church, Quinn House, Rose Hill, St. Stephen's Church, Greenfields, St. Mary Anne's Church, Perry Point Mansion, Rodgers Tavern, Art of Mt. Ararat. Tickets for the entire Pilgrimage ($3.50) will be sold only on grounds of the places to be visited. Admission to any one individual place will be $1.00. The Restoration and Grounds Committees agreed to take care of keeping the church cleaned, the outside toilet repaired and cleaned as well as handling the parking of cars in the church yard. Mrs. Dunn and Messrs. Donahue, Carroll, James A. Quinn, J. B. Sullivan, John Denver and F. W. Krastel agreed to be on hand to help handle the visitors from 10 a.m. to 6 p.m.

46. ADW – Old Bohemia Historical Society, "Notes" 4 – Summer Masses – Following considerable discussion it was moved, seconded and carried that the 1957 Summer Masses be held at 3 p.m. on the third Sunday of June, July, August and September. Father Conmy of Childs Novitiate has kindly agreed to again handle these summer services. Mr. and Mrs. Maloney agreed to handle such matters as flowers for the altar and the transportation of vestments, candles and other items needed for Mass from Middletown to Old Bohemia. *Business* Mrs. Dunn and her sister, Miss Lilliam deVine, have donated six lovely lathe turned wood candle sticks that can be kept on the altar during the summer. Mrs. Dunn also exhibited the following items which are to be returned to the Old Bohemia Church: two Victorian candlesticks, two cedar candlesticks, one monstrance, two satin glass vases, one poor box, one collection box, one crucifix, one after Mass prayer card, one book of gospels, two vestment hangers (home made), a hook for pulling down old style sanctuary lamp and one walnut gauge used for holding door open.

47. ADW – Bohemia File, Notes: The meeting was adjourned at 10:45 p.m., followed by delicious refreshments through the kindness of Mrs. Dunn and Miss deVine. Selma A. Borgstrom, Secretary.

48. A copy is at the Cecil County Historical Society, Bohemia File, October, 1957. Five pages.

49. At the Board meeting in April, 1957, J. D. Quinn had reported that Mr. Leon DeValinger, Delaware Archivist, had not as yet been in the neighborhood to inspect the location to determine whether or not it would be permissible to erect an Old Bohemia historical marker in Delaware at the junction of the Bay Bridge and Warwick-Middletown Roads. "Historical Marker Placed at Old Bohemia Church," Maryland – *Cecil Whig*, February 2, 1958. The annual meeting of the Society was announced for February 23, in St. Joseph's Hall, Middletown, Delaware.

50. Elkton, Maryland *Cecil Whig*, July 1958: "Historical Cross Will Be Shown At Old Bohemia." The traditional history of the cross which is mentioned in Johnson's *History of Cecil County* is that it was brought from England when the colonists came to Maryland in the *Ark and Dove* in 1634.

51. ADW – Bohemia File, Notes, 9-C. Elkton, Maryland: *Cecil Whig*, August 6, 1959: "Mass Set At Old Bohemia Church" – The Reverend Ferdinand C. Wheeler, S. J., of Loyola High School, Towson, Maryland, will celebrate the third in a series of four summer Masses on August 16 at 4 p.m. at Old Bohemia Church. The choir of the Oblates of St. Francis de Sales Seminary, Childs, Maryland, will render selections during the Mass and Benediction.

52. ADW – Bohemia File, Notes 8-C. The Warwick mentioned on the marker was Warwick, England.

53. Peterman, *Priests Jubilee 2000* 90

54. "Michael William Hyle," Peterman, *Priests Jubilee 2000* 125: Born in Baltimore on October 13, 1901, he was ordained a priest on March 12, 1927.

55. ADW – Bohemia File, correspondence and Notes 5-C. the contract gave the Society the right to veto sale or development of any parcel of the property.

56. ADW – Bohemia File, Notes 5-C. The trees were later supplemented by six hemlock trees which were donated and set out by the family of Bryan Field, in his memory. Bryan field was a member of the Old Bohemia Historical Society's Board of Directors at the time of his death on December 14, 1968.

57. ADW – Bohemia File, Notes 9-C

58. ADW – Notes 9-C. Three hundred and sixty plates were purchased in 1961 and another two hundred and forty in 1962. These were sold at $2.50 each.
BURIAL REGISTERS OF OLD BOHEMIA, ST. XAVIER CHURCH, WARWICK, MARYLAND: August 11, 1956 – Mary Catherine Schapf, age 51, native of Germany; November 25, 1957 – Jean

V. Soha, age 47; February 25, 1958 – Mary A. DeVine, age 87; August 9, 1958 – Mary Green; 1959 – Leonard C. Gesulfo, Jr., age 18; March 16, 1959 – Wiley I. North, age 77, Texas; July 27, 1959 – Charles Mullen, age 81; 1959 – Margaret Murray, age 85; 1959 – George R. Moffett, of Earleville, Maryland. October 24, 1959 – Catherine G. O'Connor, age 77 of Penns Grove, New Jersey; June 30, 1960 – Louise Mary Degnan, age 82, of Warwick, Maryland; 1960 – George H. Harrison, age 64, of Penns Grove, New Jersey; 1960 – John Rehfuss; January 28, 1961 – Bessie Beaston, age 86; April 15, 1961 – Kenneth Grabrowski; May 15, 1961 – William Carroll; May 30, 1961 – Carrie Reynolds.

59. Peterman, *Priests Jubilee 2000* 185: Born in Wilmington, Delaware on July 6, 1921, John Dewson was ordained a priest on May 31, 1947.
BURIAL REGISTERS OF OLD BOHEMIA, ST. XAVIER CHURCH, WARWICK, MARYLAND: October 9, 1961 – Michael P. O'Grady, age 74; September 20, 1961 – Katherine J. Powderly, age 81; 1962 – John G. Denver, age 80; November 19, 1962 – Lucinda Ayers Truitt, age 69, of Mt. Pleasant, Delaware; June 9, 1963 – James Bundy, age 72; June 15, 1963 – Thomas J. Moffett, of Warwick, Maryland; August 10, 1963 – Edward J. Counters, of Middletown, Delaware; 1963 – Maurice J. DeVine, age 64; 1963 – Rose M. Mullen; September 11, 1963 – Francis J. O'Connor, age 86, classmate of President Franklin Delano Roosevelt

The first burial register ends November 19, 1962.

60. Subsequent newsletters have not been preserved in any collection.
61. ADW – Bohemia File, Notes 10-C
62. ADW – Bohemia File, Notes 6-C
63. These drawings are preserved at the Library of Congress, Washington, D. C. – (MD-241) – Old Bohemia, Cecil County, Maryland
64. ADW – Bohemia File, Notes 6-C; Mary deVine Dunn, "Old Bohemia," *Upper Shoreman* 1 (January, 1963) no. 8, n.p.; Mary deVine Dunn, "History of St. Xavier Church, Warwick, Maryland," *Genealogist's Post* (February, 1964) published by Richard T. and Mildred C. Williams, Miami, Florida 33142 ADW – Bohemia File, Notes 6-C: The field-stone based monument was suggested by Mrs. Joseph P. Dunn, and was donated by Mrs. Robert E. Mackey of Elkton, Maryland in memory of her husband. It was designed and constructed as a volunteer project by Edward J. Ludwig III and by Frank W. Krastel, members of the Board of Directors.
65. Peterman, *Priests Jubilee 2000* 183: He was born in Wilmington, Delaware on June 26, 1920, and ordained a priest on June 29, 1946.
66. Eileen Spraker, "A Reporter Goes To Church – Old Bohemia Was Mission in 1703," Wilmington, Delaware *Every Journal*, September 25, 1965. Monsignor Dwyer's message praised the work of the Jesuits, especially that of Father Joseph Greaton and Father Matthias Manners. At that time St. Francis Xavier Church was open for Mass on the third Sundays of June, July, August, and September.
67. Elkton, Maryland *The Cecil Democrat*, September 15, 1965
68. Wilmington, Delaware *The Delmarva Dialog*, October 1, 1965
69. Mary Devine Dunn, "Priests And Brothers Who Were At Old Bohemia, 1704-1962" and "The Burial Register of Old Bohemia," in *The Genealogist's Post* (volume 3, No. 2, February, 1966), published by Richard T. and Mildred C. Williams, 3374 N. W. 35th Street, Miami, Florida 33142 ADW – Bohemia File, Notes.
70. Wilmington, Delaware *The Delmarva Dialog*, January 10, 1967
BURIAL REGISTERS OF OLD BOHEMIA, ST. XAVIER CHURCH, WARWICK, MARYLAND: September 26, 1964 – Minnie Thomas, age 77; 1964 – Margaret C. Atkinson, age 46; August 6, 1965 – Charles Brown, age 84; 1965 – Amelia B. Moffett, age 80; October, 1965 – Deborah Lynne Gesullo; 1966 – Albert M. Rehfuss; March 29, 1966 – John B. Hobson, age 72, of Middletown, Delaware; 1966 – Laurette M. Stockley, age 82, of Smyrna, Delaware; 1967 – James A. Quinn, age 73, of Warwick, Maryland; 1967 – Daniel J. Quinn, Jr., age 68, of Galena, Maryland; March 11, 1967 – Elizabeth A. Isaacs, age 63, of Odessa, Delaware; May 23, 1967 – Jesse Woodall; November 27, 1967 – Robert E. Simpson, age 65, Pennsylvania Private N. S. A. W.W. II; 1967 – Eva P. Soha; 1968 – Catherine E. Moffett, age 80
71. Wilmington, Delaware *The Delmarva Dialog*, March 31, 1967

72. Wilmington, Delaware *Evening Journal*, July 8, 1967
73. Wilmington, Delaware *Morning News*, August 19, 1967
74. Wilmington, Delaware *The Delmarva Dialog*, March 15, 1968; Peterman, *Priests Jubilee 2000* 170: born in Baltimore on May 14, 1913, he was ordained a priest on May 14, 1940. In 1967 he was consecrated auxiliary bishop of Baltimore, a capacity in which he served only fourteen months before he was named Bishop of Wilmington.
75. Wilmington, Delaware *The Delmarva Dialog*, January 26, 1968 Joseph Dickerson, *The Double LL Willsons of Kent County, Maryland* (joebeagles@friendly.net) Seventh and Eighth Generations from John Willson, Dr. Thomas Bennett Willson I, Dr. Thomas Bennett Willson II, Dr. Thomas Willson III, Alexander Hoskins Willson, Alexander Carroll Willson, and James Ernest "Tot" Willson) James Ernest "Tot" Willson was born November 16, 1889, *purchased Trumpington*, and died March 2, 1976. He married Mary Ann Isabel Ringgold on January 11, 1911, daughter of James Ringgold and Julia Willson. She was born December 11, 1885 and died February 19, 1977, in Trumpington Farm. Their children were: James Ringgold Willson, born June 10, 1913 and died October 8, 1950; Ernest Carroll Willson, born May 19, 1917 and died December 21, 1931; Julia Ringgold Willson; Mildred Neale Willson; Marian Casanove Willson. Mildred Neale Willson married Robert Henry Srong. Their children are: Gail Louise Strong, married Gregory Romain; Mary Carroll Strong, married George Richard Walbert; Robert Henry Strong, married Donna Larraine Newcomb , Julia Ringgold Strong, married James Richard Strong; James Ringgold Strong, married Ann Zotos; James Ernest Willson Strong, married Mildred Louise Johnson, Rose Marie Strong, married Mark Epperson.

    Julia Ringgold Willson married Joseph G. Ridgely, Eugene Parker, Frank Engler. Children of Eugene Parker and Julia Willson are Eugene Parker and Anne Parker.

    Marian Casanave Willson was born May 15, 1924, in Trumpington Farm, and died January 25, 2003. She married Jesse Taggart. There were nine children.
76. Wilmington, Delaware *The Delmarva Dialog*, April 5, 1968
77. Wilmington, Delaware *The Delmarva Dialog*, June 6, 1968
78. Peterman, *Priests Jubilee 2000* 231: born in Rome, New York, on May 15, 1926, he was ordained a priest on May 31, 1958.
    BURIAL REGISTERS OF OLD BOHEMIA, ST. XAVIER CHURCH, WARWICK, MARYLAND: 1968 – P. Bryan Fields, of Wilmington, Delaware; 1968 – Lydia Sterling Flintham; 1968 – Pauline Price Kirk, age 73; October 11, 1968 – Kathleen Kabis, age 49, of Odessa, Delaware; December 23, 1968 – Arleta M. O'Shea, of Middletown, Delaware; February 1, 1969 – Emma P. Williams; February 5, 1969 – Emma Walters of Warwick, February 17, 1969 – Josephine Padley Nickeson, of Middletown, Delaware; 1969 – Roy Bryan Davis; April 2, 1969 – Lui Bevilacqua of Newark, Delaware; April 12, 1969 – Helena P. Walmsley, age 4 months; July 26, 1969 – Joseph Pajerowski, of Port Penn, Delaware; December 17, 1969 – Michael O'Grady, of Chester, Pennsylvania; 1970 – Marie L. Harreson, age 70, of Penns Grove, New Jersey; 1970 – John P. DeVine, Sr., age 69 of Darby, Pennsylvania; 1970 – Robert Douglas, Co. A., 116th Pa. Inf. February 6, 1970 – Hugh I. Dugan, age 74 of Townsend, Delaware; 1970 – Mary M. Compton, age 82; December 24, 1970 – Margaret E. Hobson, age 71; September 14, 1971 – Francis Sullivan, age 72, of Middletown, Delaware; April 25, 1972 – Mary Eileen Bice, of Middletown, Delaware; August 14, 1972 – James E. Mullen, of Middletown, Delaware; September 9, 1972 – James Murray, Middletown, Delaware; 1972 – Mary L. Toomey, age 38; April 7, 1973 0 Edward T. Shetzer, of Odessa, Delaware; November 22, 1973 – E. Verna Giles Krastel, of Penns Grove, New Jersey; December 21, 1973 – Jimmy John Biddle, age 1 day A. D. Condon, R. P. Condon, buried in Price Lot; March 30, 1974 – Joseph P. Carroll, of Warwick, Maryland; March 30, 1974 – Frank O'Linenski, of Port Penn, Delaware; August 19, 1974 – William Muller, age 67, of Townsend, Delaware; October 26, 1974 – James Noland Bice, of Middletown, Delaware; November 7, 1975 – Joseph Hibbert of Middletown, Delaware; November 10, 1975 – Mary R. Pochuvat, age 56, of Middletown, Delaware; December 5, 1975 – J. Bradford Sullivan, age 75, of Warwick, Maryland; April 10, 1976 – Elizabeth M. Sparks, age 75, of Penns Grove, New Jersey; July 5, 1976 – Edward D. E. Rollins, age 76, died at Elkton, Maryland; November 2, 1976 – Sara V. Cann, of New Castle, Delaware
79. "Iron Cross Marks Beginning of Faith in Area," Wilmington, Delaware *The Delaware Dialog*

October 17, 1968
80. Wilmington, Delaware *The Delaware Dialog*, June 5, 1969
81. Wilmington, Delaware *The Delaware Dialog*, July 21, 1969
82. Wilmington, Delaware *The Delmarva Dialog*, August 28, 1969
83. Cecil County Historical Society, Elkton, Maryland – Bohemia File. Letter from Fred Krastel to Morton Taylor, July 21, 1969: "In the Farm Museum Shed we have two new saddles hanging – an English and an Army saddle. We also have a potato planter, a beet-cutter and a fire-hose reel from St. Joseph's School from 1898.... Two wheel-barrows and a one-hole corn sheller which we just obtained last Sunday while you were there. We also have another old grindstone and the date on the metal brackets is Oct, 1866. Upstairs we have obtained (AND I KEEP BEGGING AND BEGGING AND THIS IS THE ONLY WAY TO BUILD A MUSEUM)..... Old rakes – hoes – bale hook – ice tongs – sickle – ice pole – saws – planes – augers – corn knife – iron wedges – wagon tongue – hewing axe – spirit level – corn husker – draw knife – 4 large wooden clamps – old (150 years) wooden mallet – 37 horse shoes – beading planes – blacksmith tongs – wagon jack – two man saw – bridles & hames – double trees - .etc. I forgot to mention our new buggy (how could I forget this?) in the Farm Museum. In the barn I have a few odds & ends and just last week I obtained the biggest doggone blacksmith vice you ever did see... I had to drag it into the cow-barn. I had my eye on this for over a year and did finally get my paws on it. Oh Brother – how you must keep asking and asking and asking if you really have your heart set on a good museum. We have another regular size blacksmith vice in the barn. OUR NEED IS FOR BLACKSMITH TONGS AND HAMMERS AND OLD CARPENTER TOOLS... AND IF YOU EVER SEE AN OLD METAL FORGE LIKE THE ONES USED ON FARMS FOR SMALL BLACKSMITH JOBS —– GRAB IT"'" I have been after a propeller (or fan) from on old wind-mill – and think we are going to have one donated in the near future."
84. ADW – Bohemia File, copy of brochure features the objectives of the Old Bohemia Society at the time: 1 – The restoration of the church and house to the period of 1792-1797 to include heating, electricity and modern sanitary facilities. Estimated cost: $150,000. 2 – The replacement of trees and shrubbery that have been lost due to old age and storms. Estimated cost: $1500. 3 – The erection of adequate fencing and gates to keep wandering cattle from entering the yard and cemetery. Estimated cost: $2000. 4 – Repairing, where necessary, and recutting some of the eroded names, dates and epitaphs on the old grave markers. Estimated cost: $1200. 5 – The reconstruction of the academy building and working toward the establishment of a permanent and sustaining activity at this historic site. 6 – The continued research in connection with the old plantation buildings, such as the living quarters, the water powered saw and grist mills, kiln for making bricks, blacksmith shop and barns with the idea of reconstructing these units. The brochure then presented pages of a broader historical background to further support the justification for this restoration. Frank Krastel was quoted in the Wilmington, Delaware *Evening Journal*, July 18, 1870, as saying: "I am a native of Cecil County, and my wife and I saw what was happening to the church. We got permission to do a little work around it, and eventually more people became interested. Besides the obvious historical value of preserving this church, my parents were married here and I hated to see it destroyed."
85. Susan Sterberger, "Mother Church of Diocese 266 years old" Wilmington, Delaware *Evening Journal*, July 18, 1970: The grounds at Bohemia had been replanted to replace original trees which died or had been destroyed by storms. One of the first of the new trees was a fig planted on the south side of the church. Krastel said that the tree came from a branch of the original one planted at the church. He said tradition called for Jesuits to plant fig trees next to the churches. Longwood Gardens at Kennett Square, Pennsylvania also donated trees to help restore the area.
86. Ben Herman, "Old Bohemia, Cradle of American Catholicism," Elkton, Maryland *Cecil Whig*, August 30, 1970. The article called attention to items of interest in the museum, such as the "Willcox Chalice," made in London in the 1690s, and a missal printed in 1645 on display in the museum.
87. ADW – Bohemia File, copy of the will of Cecelia E. Baker, with a letter from Msgr. Paul J. Schierse, chancellor, to James P. Collins, Esq., Wilmington, Delaware, forwarded to Treasurer Edward Ludwig III by Frank W. Krastel, president, on May 12, 1971. On May 24, 1971, a bronze memorial plaque was ordered through the Oblates of St. Francis de Sales, Childs, Maryland,

	costing $79, to commemorate Cecelia E. Beste Baker and her husband Scott Samuel Baker.
88.	Notable among celebrants was Father Edward Brown, S. J., celebrant and homilist at the Mass in July, 1971 – Wilmington, Delaware *The Delmarva Dialog*, July 9, 1971
89.	Wilmington, Delaware *The Delmarva Dialog*, September 8, 1972. At his death in 1972 the designer of the pipe organ at Longwood Gardens and organist there for thirty-two years, Firmin Swinnen, bequeathed his personal Allen electronic organ to St. Francis Xavier Church. Firmin Swinnen was born in Montaigne, Belgium. He graduated from the Royal Conservatory of Music in Antwerp. During the World War I he came to the United States. He died in April, 1972. The organ was installed at Bohemia under the supervision of Arthur Bernicker of the Allen Organ Company and M. D. Benwick of "Your Home Inc." of Wilmington, Delaware.
90.	ADW – Bohemia File, typewritten lecture notes of Reverend Thomas Flowers. At this time, Father Flowers notes, the rectory flooring damaged by termites was repaired, a new wood shingle roof was added, and doorlocks and latches removed by "souvenir hunters" were replaced by the Society.
91.	ADW – Bohemia File, Notes 10-C
92.	Wilmington, Delaware *The Dialog*, June 13, 1975. (The diocesan paper's name was shortened on August 16, 1974).
93.	ADW – Bohemia File, Correspondence. On August 5, 1962, Alfred N. Phillips on behalf of the Old Bohemia Historical Society, had written Wayne N. Aspinall, Chairman of the Committee on Interior and Insular Affairs, House of Representatives, Washington, D. C., when the first request had been denied. Alfred Phillips a Presbyterian, was a former member of the United States Congress. He told the chairman: "Your committee must have been armed with very poor information indeed to the end that the Assistant Secretary of the Interior made this faulty decision based thereon. I ask your reconsideration." Phillips wrote the Assistant Secretary of the Interior himself on October 9, 1962: "Now you tell me…that Old Bohemia can not be considered a National Historic Site because it is a church, etc., as it is not the policy of the U. S. government to signalize churches as National Historic Sites because of the separation of Church and State in the United States. To lift this whole thing out of the cloud of error into which it has fallen, please allow me to restate the case all over again. The request has been made that the whole establishment at Old Bohemia be named a National Historic Site, etc. Trusting that this letter will serve to set at rest some of the misunderstanding concerning the Old Bohemia Colonial restoration enterprise, I am …" This correspondence brought no action until thirteen years later.
94.	Attention was paid to the grounds, especially the ancient boxwoods. The thirteen oak trees were donated by the Salem County (New Jersey) Sportsmen's Club and were named the Old Bohemia Bicentennial Oaks. Henry DuPont donated 24 trees from Longwood. The Bryan Field Family donated 6 hemlocks.
95.	At Bishop Mardaga's request, a series of historical articles were produced and published by *The Dialog* in preparation for the U. S. Bicentennial Observance: Thomas J. Peterman, "Harried On All Sides, Catholics In The Colonies," *The Dialog*, July 18, 1975; "Catholic Involvement, Coming Of The Revolution," *The Dialog*, July 25, 1975; "Looking Back 200 Years, Jesuits in Maryland and Delaware, *The Dialog* October 17, 1975; "John Carroll, First Bishop of America," *The Dialog* October 24, 1975. GUA – The Maryland Province Collection BOHEMIA – CLIPPINGS ABOUT 1895-1970 Box 1 Folder 7, BOHEMIA – PHOTOS OF –CA 1960S Box: 1 Folder: 6
96.	Wilmington, Delaware *The Dialog* September 16, 1975
97.	"Bicentennial Exhibit To Open Sunday" Wilmington, Delaware *The Dialog*, February 20, 1976; "A Time To Remember – Diocesan Bicentennial Exhibit," *The Dialog*, February 27, 1976. Edward Ludwig III, "Old Bohemia Church – Maryland's Showplace," Elkton, Maryland *Cecil Whig*, March 10, 1976
98.	Joseph C. Cann, *History of Saint Francis Xavier Church and Bohemia Plantation, Now Known As Old Bohemia, Warwick, Maryland* (Wilmington, Delaware: Old Bohemia Historical Society, 1976). The book was researched by the Old Bohemia Historical Society's History Committee: Joseph C. Cann, chairman, Anne M. Barczewski, Rev. Edward B. Carley, S. T. L., Michael F. Carroll, Mary deVine Dunn, Francis W. Krastel, Edward J. Ludwig III, Rev. Russell H. Perkins, S. T. L., Dorothy D. Robinson and Morton F. Taylor. Joseph C. Cann was vice-president of the Old Bohemia Historical Society and a member of the Cecil County Historical Society. He died on

June 7, 1986 in New Castle, Delaware. A Mass of Christian Burial was offered at St. Francis Xavier Church, at Bohemia and burial was in the adjoining cemetery – Wilmington, Delaware *Morning News*, June 11, 1986. Edward J. Ludwig III died at the age of 79, on May 13, 1982. Services were held at Old Bohemia Church, and burial was in Holy Sepulchre Cemetery, Philadelphia. Mr. Ludwig was treasurer of the Old Bohemia Historical Society, and member of the Historical Society of Cecil County. He belonged to St. Rose of Lima Catholic Church, Chesapeake City, Maryland – Elkton, Maryland *Cecil Whig*, May 19, 1982. Morton F. Taylor died at age 82 on November 3, 1998. He was born in Perryville, Maryland on March 24, 1916. Burial was at West Nottingham Cemetery, Olora, Maryland. Mr. Taylor belonged to the Perryville United Methodist Church... - Elkton, Maryland *Cecil Whig*, March 5, 1998. Mary deVine Dunn died at age 98 on November 29, 1989. She was a charter member of the Old Bohemia Historical Society. She was buried at the Immaculate Conception Cemetery, Elkton, Maryland. Her son, Reverend Joseph T. Dunn, of the Oblates of St. Francis de Sales in Childs, died at age 85 on September 6, 1998. Burial was at the Oblate Cemetery, Childs, Maryland. Wilmington, Delaware *Evening Journal*, November 30, 1989. Elkton, Maryland *Cecil Whig*, September 10, 1998. Michael W. Carroll died February 25, 1996. He was born in Elkton on August 10, 1959. He was a self-employed carpenter. Mr. Carroll was buried in Immaculate Conception Cemetery, Cherry Hill, Elkton, Maryland – Elkton, Maryland *Cecil Whig*, February 27, 1996. Rev. Edward B. Carley was born in New York City on July 19, 1917. He was ordained in Wilmington, Delaware on May 22, 1948. He was well known for his historical research and writing about the Catholic Diocese of Wilmington. He died on January 25, 1998. Mass of Christian Burial and interment were at St. Peter's Church, Queenstown, Maryland. Peterman, *Priests Jubilee 2000* 988 Wilmington, Delaware *The Dialog*, September 17, 1998: Death of Rev. Joseph T. Dunn, U.S.F.S., Elkton native, died September 6, at Annecy Hall at Childs. He was 85. Dorothy B. Robinson was born May 18, 1909. Her family's ancestry in Cecil County started in the 1760s. (the Denver family). One of her life long interests was the Cecil County Historical Society of which she served as the first female president from 1965 to 1973. She was a life-long member of Immaculate Conception Church, Elkton, the Old Bohemia Historical Society and Head of Elk Chapter of the Daughters of the American Revolution. She died at age 91 on April 1, 2001. She is buried in Elkton Cemetery – Elkton, Maryland *The Cecil Whig*, April 3, 2001. Anne Martha Barczewski was an early member of the Old Bohemia Historical Society joining shortly after its founding. She was born on a farm near Hockessin Delaware and Coffee Run on November 29, 1910. She attended a one room school with her 4 sisters and 4 brothers and assisted her parents John and Mary Napolski on the farm and going to Wilmington to sell farm produce. Anne married Steve Barczewski in 1930 and helped establish West End Dairy in Wilmington. Anne and Steve purchased a farm in Glasgow Delaware in 1942, restored the home built in 1815 and raised Guernsey cows. Anne's 3 children Steven, JoAnne and George grew up on the farm. Anne collected antiques, grew hybrid roses and managed the business after Steve's passing in 1958. The furnishings in the rectory were selected with Anne's guidance. She purchased items for the rectory and donated them. She arranged the altar flowers for masses over many years with flowers from her garden. Anne now resides in a nursing home a few miles from Coffee Run and the farm she was raised on.
BURIAL RECORDS OF BOHEMIA CEMETERY: There were no burials in Bohemia Cemetery during 1976 and 1977. On March 14, 1978 – William Moffitt, Sr., died March 8, 1978, age 77; December 13, 1978 – Edward N. Meyer, born May 21, 1906, died December 10, 1978, age 72; January 27, 1979 – Laurence Devine, (wife Margaret) born January 1901, died January 23, 1979, age 78; January 30, 1979 – Marianna S. Mullen, born October 7, 1886, died January 27, 1979, age 92; February 13, 1979 – Elizabeth Nini (Mrs. Edwin) Jones, born January 15, 1897, died February 10, 1979, age 82; February 11, 1979 – Walter Williams (wife Emma) born May 20, 1886, died February 11, 1979, age 92; March 25, 1979 – Frances Whitlock (husband Richard) Mozcieski, died March 25, 1979, age 54; April 20, 1979 – Elizabeth Andrews Rollins, born May 19, 1899, died April 17, 1979, age 79; April 27, 1979 – Alice T. Crawford, born 1884, died April 23, 1979, age 95; July 30, 1979 – John Briscoe, Jr. (wife Rose), died July 23, 1979, age 77; July 30, 1979 – Matilda H. Potocki, born January 28, 1898, died July 7, 1979, age 81; Mary C. Quinn (Daniel's wife), born June 25, 1902, died July 22, 1979, age 77; August 20, 1979 – Sophia B. Skomorucha, born December 4, 1916, died August 16, 1979, age 62; August 27, 1979 – Nora (Mrs. Henry, Sr.)

Haywood, born July 16, 1914, died August 23, 1979, age 65; September 3, 1979 – Frank J. Muller (wife Frances), born July 12, 1912, died August 31, 1979, age 67; October 28, 1979 – Paul Sparks, died October 23, 1979, age 81; December 24, 1979 – Emily M. (Mrs. Peter) Weber, born November 8, 1909, died December 15, 1979, age 70; December 24, 1979 – Wing Harry Lee, born September 9, 1909, died December 20, 1979, age 69; March 6, 1980 – Domenico Carchedi (wife Maria) born December 18, 1908, died February 8, 1980, age 70; April 1, 1980 – Charles Andrew Shetzler (wife Emma) born May 9, 1904, died March 30, 1980, age 75; July 19, 1980 – Gladys Pearson (Mrs. Thomas I.) Greer, born October 6, 1897, died July 16, 1980, age 82; July 20, 1980 – James J. McCaffery, born July 19, 1980, age 3 hours; July 5, 1980 – John Patrick O'Grady (wife Mary), born February 15, 1913, died July 1, 1980, age 67; October 11, 1980 – Jean and Jan Getty, still born on October 7, 1980; October 30, 1980 – Frank A. Skomorucha, born March 19, 1916, died October 27, 1930, age 64; November 24, 1980 – Josephine (Mrs. Anthony) Burger, born April 14, 1910, died November 20, 1980 , age 70; January 20, 1981 – Donald Ames, born May 1, 1926, died January 17, 1981, age 54; February 13, 1981 – Catherine O'Connor, born July 2, 1892, died February 10, 1981, age 88; April 30, 1981 – Richard M. Hamilton, died April 26, 1980, age 37; June 16, 1981 – John Paraskiewicz, born February 13, 1913 , died June 12, 1981, age 68; August 24, 1981 – Myrtle M. Reynolds, born March 1, 1910, died August 20, 1981, age 71; August 26, 1981 – Frances Marie Curtes, born December 3, 1896, died August 22, 1981, age 84; November 11, 1981 – Henry J. Kwiesniuski, born December 20, 1924, died November 8, 1981, age 56; December 31, 1981 – Theodore J. O'Tanyi, born May 1, 1914, died December 28, 1981, age 61; March 6, 1982 – Peter G. Weber, Sr., born June 3, 1909, died March 6, 1982 – Peter G. Weber, Sr., born June 3, 1909, died March 3, 1982, age 72; April 29, 1982 – Hazel Willey, born September 17, 1907, died April 27, 1982, age 74; June 26, 1982 – Walter Stanley Soha, born June 2, 1915, died June 23, 1982, age 67; July 16, 1982 – Modesta M. Poterowski, born September 29, 1912, died July 13, 1982, age 69; September 18, 1982 – Joseph A. Stackley, born October 24, 1913, died September 12, 1982, age 68; 1983 – James Meyer, born 1963, died February, 1983, age 20; April 9, 1983 – John J. Lobacewicz, born February 6, 1919, died April 6, 1983, age 64; July 4, 1983 – John A. Kurzeja, born September 9, 1916, died June 30, 1983, age 66; July 22, 1983, Michael F. Carroll, born February 1, 1897, died June 19, 1983, age 86; September 1, 1983 – Joseph P. Graham, born January 1, 1917 died August 29, 1983, age 66; September 19, 1983 – Joseph A. Sullivan, born April 6, 1903, died September 15, 1983, age 80.

99. "Mass Slated August 21 at Old Bohemia," Wilmington, Delaware *The Dialog*, August 19, 1977
100. "Old Bohemia Mass September 18," Wilmington, Delaware *The Dialog*, September 9, 1977
101. "Old Bohemia Mass, June 8," Wilmington, Delaware *The Dialog* June 9, 1978
102. Peterman, *Priests Jubilee 2000* 239: Father Brady was born in Ireland on February 12, 1921 and was ordained a priest on May 27, 1961.
103. "Old Bohemia Society Opens Fundraising Drive," Wilmington, Delaware *The Dialog*, June 23, 1978; "Old Bohemia Opens Drive," Wilmington, Delaware *The Dialog*, November 17, 1978: "The program is to undertake important repair work. The property is owned by the Diocese of Wilmington and is supported by fees and donations."
104. Wilmington, Delaware *The Dialog*, July 7, 1978
105. "Old Bohemia Shrine Commemorates 275 Years," Elkton, Maryland *Cecil Whig*, July 11, 1979. Masses at Bohemia for 1979 were scheduled to be celebrated on July 15, August 19, September 16, and October 21. National recognition was given to the 275th Anniversary by a large picture and article: "Cradle of Eastern Shore Catholicism," South Bend, Indiana *Our Sunday Visitor*, April 20, 1979
106. Eileen Spraker, "Old Bohemia, Site of Celebration," Wilmington, Delaware *News Journal*, July 7, 1979; "Old Bohemia Hosts Masses," Wilmington, Delaware *The Dialog*, July 13, 1979
107. Wilmington, Delaware *The Dialog*, June 13, 1980. The article told of the recent replacement of 33 deteriorated window sills by the Old Bohemia Historical Society, and mentioned that Jack Kyle of Wilmington was doing the work. General repairs to broken plaster and the restoration of the Stations of the Cross and two statues were being undertaken but the Old Bohemia Council 6543 of the Knights of Columbus and the Old Bohemia Historical Society. Mrs. Jane Farbizi of Elkton, Maryland, did the restoration work on the statues as a gift. Repairs needed in the interior of the rectory building were to be completed during the summer.
108. Wilmington, Delaware *The Dialog*, July 4, 1980

109. "Father Edward Carley – Exploring The Eastern Shore," *The Dialog* August 14, 1981
110. Wilmington, Delaware *The Dialog*, September 11, 1981
111. Wilmington, Delaware *The Dialog*, April 9, 1982
112. Wilmington, Delaware *The Dialog*, September 9, 1983
113. Wilmington, Delaware *The Dialog*, October 7, 1983
114. Wilmington, Delaware *The Dialog*, May 11, 1984
115. Peterman, *Priests Jubilee 2000*, 221
116. Peterman, *Priests Jubilee 2000*, 295
117. "Old Bohemia Masses Resume," Wilmington, Delaware *The Dialog*, April 5, 1985
118. "Old Bohemia Society President Dies," Wilmington, Delaware *The Dialog*, April 19, 1985: Francis W. Krastel, 88, of Penns Grove, New Jersey, was killed when his car struck a tree on the north side of the Delaware Memorial Bridge. Wilmington, Delaware *The Dialog*, April 2, 1985: The son was pastor of St. Bernadette's Parish, Silver Springs, Maryland. Frank Krastel, Sr. was born February 17, 1897. He had retired on January 1, 1962, after a 44 year career at E. I. duPont Company, Carneys Point, New Jersey. His wife Verna Giles Krastel had preceded him in death by nearly twelve years. Her death was on November 22, 1973. Their daughter Jane E. Williams lives in Buckhammon, West Virginia.
BURIAL RECORDS OF BOHEMIA CEMETERY: March 9, 1984 – Mildred A. Meyer, born February 16, 1909, died March 6, 1984, age 75; July 16, 1984 – Joseph Schmidt, born July 22, 1893, died July 13, 1984, age 90; August 16, 1984 – Marge M. King, born August 26, 1908, died August 12, 1984, age 70; November 20, 1984 – Arthur Boulden, born October 27, 1935, died November 16, 1984, age 49; April 19, 1985 – *Francis W. Krastel, Sr.*, born February 17, 1897, died April 15, 1985, age 88; May 31, 1985 – Kathryn Austin, born August 11, 1902; died April 30, 1985, age 82; August 19, 1985 – Jason Anton Verheggen, born December 17, 1918, died September 14, 1985, age 66; October 26, 1985 – Anne C. Norton, born February 4, 1900, died October 22, 1985, age 85; January 8, 1986 – A. Marshall Whitlock, born September 11, 1902, died January 5, 1986, age 83; March 8, 986 – Josephine M. Simpson, born September 18, 1914, died March 4, 1986, age 71; April 2, 1986 – Margaret J. Devine, born July 31, 1907, died March 29, 1986, age 78; May 6, 1986 – William Edgar Powers, born August 26, 1932, died May 2, 1986, age 53; June 12, 1986 – Joseph C. Cann, born March 30, 1904, died June 7, 1986, age 82; June 27, 1986 – Louis Edward Ford, born November 10, 1912, died June 24, 1986, age 73; July 26, 1986 – Joseph Stephen O'Grady, Sr., born July 14, 1915, age 71; August 26, 1986 – Ann B. Devine, born November 9, 1907, died August 22, 1986, age 78; September 8, 1986 – Catherine Cruchley, born October 1, 1913, died September 2, 1986; September 19, 1986 – Joseph Whitlock, born August 21, 1927, died September 16, 1986, age 59; November 10, 1986 - Helen Mary Hibbert, born November 10, 1904, died November 6, 1986, age 81; December 30, 1986 – Katie Briscoe Harris, born April 4, 1896, died December 28, 1986, age 90; January 24, 1987 – Leo F. Maloney, born May 1, 1923, died January 20, 1987, age 63; January 29, 1987 – Daniel M. Toomey, born July 24, 1899, died January 24, 1987, age 88; February 4, 1987 – Rebecca Schlatter, born August 20, 1926, died January 31, 1987, age 60
119. Born in Harrison, New Jersey, on February 16, 1919, James Garrigan was a member of the Old Bohemia Historical Society for years before he became an officer. Early on he built and installed the entrance sign to the Shrine, and planted thirty-two holly trees along the road leading from mill point to the entrance sign. He served on the liturgy committee from the beginning of his membership. As president he worked with Father Vignola in maintaining the Shrine, installing aluminum screens for the church windows, filling the letters on the weathered stone slab above the church entrance to make its message readable, applied to have the Shrine listed on national historic building sites, installed a bronze plague in the church entrance. He began the layout of lights and fans in the church, sacristy, and meeting room. He laid out a stairway to the second floor of the barn, and with the help of Dave Dorman, Tony Starr, and Jim Quinn, installed plywood on the floor and walls and moved all of the antiques from the first floor to the new second floor Farm Museum Room A little gift shop was opened on the first floor along with a classroom for visiting school children. Along with Bud Dill and Jim Quinn, he built the gazebo designed for outdoor Masses and other large crowd affairs. The Pioneer Priest grave enclosure was completed with the donation of $3000 to the Society by the Jesuit Province of Baltimore. ADW – Bohemia File – President Jim Garrigan, "December 16, 1992 – Summary of

Bohemia Under Diocesan Pastors 333

My Stewardship of the Shrine St. Frances Xavier, Historically Known As Old Bohemia."
120. Wilmington, Delaware *The Dialog*, September 20, 1985. Father Vignola and Father Frank Krastel, Jr. assisted Bishop Mulvee.
121. "Old Bohemia Mass April 20 Memorial Mass," Wilmington, Delaware *The Dialog*, April 18, 1986
122. Mar.elena Zuniga, "Shrine is 'Lost Jewel: Spiritual, Historical Treasures At New Center," Wilmington, Delaware, *The Dialog*, August 15, 1986: Father Vignola's words continued: "It's nice that it's a shrine, but if it doesn't become a viable part of the Catholic Church, what's the sense of having it? It's just a church in the middle of a field."
123. Peterman, *Priests Jubilee 2000*, 251. Father Siry was born at Woodlawn, New York on December 4, 1934, and was ordained on May 26, 1962. ADW – Bohemia File, President Jim Garrigan, "Summary of Stewardship" – A replica of the leverage wheel that rings the church bell was raised up into the tower and installed on the bell by Jim Garrigan, Father Siry, Bud Dill, and Jim Quinn. In his business life, Mr. Garrigan had been an industrial piping contractor. A drainage system along the east wall and part of the west wall was designed and a four inch roof drainage pipe system from roof down spouts installed to a large dry well. The stone placed on the Bohemia grounds by Father Mansell, marking the beginning of St. Francis Xavier Church, was buried in tree growth and was uncovered by a fifty-foot exposure area. Cinder block and a cement floor was installed for the farm wagon and equipment barn.
124. Wilmington, Delaware *The Dialog*, September 11, 1987. Bishop James C. Burke died May 28, 1994. Peterman, *Priests Jubilee 2000*, 213.
BURIAL RECORDS OF BOHEMIA: April 27, 1987 – Anna May Zeh, born May 2, 1928, died April 23, 1987, age 8; May 29, 1987 – Paul Allen Angeline, born October 16, 1965, died May 25, 1987, age 21; August 27, 1987 – James B. McAlpin, born November 5, 1964, died August 18, 1987, age 22; October 9, 1987 – Georgiana R. Fields, born October 5, 1897, died October 7, 1987, age 90; October 27, 1987 – Franklin G. Douglas, born January 2, 1919, died October 18, 1987, age 68; November 3, 1987 – Helen B. Rutkowski, born October 13, 1960, died October 8, 1987, age 27; November 16, 1987 – Bernard G. Fisher, born August 11, 1914, died November 12, 1987, age 71; December 30, 1987 – Morgan John Rowan, Sr., born January 3, 1901, died December 25, 1987, age 85; January 30, 1988 – Madelyn H. Quinn, born May 25, 1902, died January 27, 1988, age 85; February 1, 1988 – Earl B. Bowman, Jr., born February 2, 1953, died January 28, 1988, age 34; February 20, 1988 – Marion E. Kwasniewski, born April 13, 1988 – Edward T. Shetzler III, born February 24, 1925, died April 10, 1988, age 63; May 6, 1988 – Stanley Irving Karlow, born April 30, 1919, died May 4, 1988, age 69; September 24, 1988 – Leo Charles Murray, born April 9, 1910, died September 21, 1988, age 78; December 2, 1988 – William C. Shetzler, born April 10, 1899, died November 29, 1988, age 89; July, 1988 – Earl Bowman, Sr., died July 1988; January 9, 1989 – Herbert G. Sparks, died January 6, 1989, age 80; January 21, 1989 – Cecelia M. Sullivan, died January 18, 1989; age 82; July 8, 1989 – Agnes Louise Rehfuss, born May 02, 1904, died July 3, 1989, age 85; July 18, 1989 – Patricia Ann Whitlock, born November 29, 1965, died July 14, 1989, age 23; August 25, 1989 – Matthew John Jack, stillborn August 23, 1985; August 22, 1989 – Roy Willey, born February 6, 1904, died August 18, 1989, age 85; November 11, 1989 – Esther K. Muller, born My 21, 1906, died November 8, 1989, age 83; December 18, 1989 – Marie Moffett, born April 15, 1907, died December 13, 1989, age 82; January 27, 1990 – Viola Bundy, born May 19, 1904, died January 19, 1990, age 85; March 17, 1990 – Margaret Carmen Price, born July 27, 1896, died March 14, 1990, age 93; May 24, 1990 – Rudolph Schlatter, born September 16, 1924, died May 1, 1990, age 65; July 31, 1990 – Frances Johanna Panciroli, born January 19, 1914, died July 25, 1990, age 76; September 7, 1990 – Mary H. Davis, born May 20, 1916, died September 2, 1990, age 74; November 6, 1990 – Bryan Field; November 26, 1990 – Clementine A. Janucik, born March 4, 1923, died November 21, 1990, age 67; December 26, 1990 – Rupert Reynolds, born June 27, 1906, died December 20, 1990, age 84; January 4, 1991 – Jewell M. Ames, born July 9, 1923, died December 31, 1990, age 67; January 19, 1991 – Louis P. Janucik, Sr., born January 27, 1917, died January 15, 1991, age 73; January 12, 1991 – Anna Elizabeth Shetzler, born December 1, 1902, died January 8, 1991, age 88; April 15, 1991 – Lorraine Keefe, born March 29, 1923, died April 13, 1991, age 68; June 4, 1991 – Helen Quinn Dugan, born January 2, 1899, died June 1, 1991, age 92; June 28, 1991–Joseph Kwasniewski, Jr., born August 27, 1951, died June 26, 1991, age 39; August 30, 1991 – Edwin J. Jones, born January 27, 1904, died August 25, 1991, age

87; August 23, 1991 – David J. Moody, born March 14, 1966, died August 20, 1991, age 25; October 22, 1991 – Dominick Paul Gentile, born March 1, 1913, died October 18, 1991, age 78; January 5, 1992 – Leo Michael Maloney, born June 25, 1949, died January 2, 1992, age 42; January 11, 1992 – Frances Helen Smith, born December 25, 1912, died January 8, 1992, age 79; February 1, 1992 – Robert Charles Meyers, born September 29, 1965, died January 29, 1992, age 26; March 16, 1992 – Stanley Ignatius Karlon, born February 4, 1958, died March 13, 1992, age 34; April 15, 1992 – Richard David Mozeleski, born September 4, 1923, died April 12, 1992, age 68; May 12, 1992 – Charles Hamilton Johnson, born November 2, 1910, died May 8, 1992, age 82.

125. Wilmington, Delaware *The Dialog*, October 16, 1987
126. Elkton, Maryland *Cecil Whig*, October 1, 1988
127. Peterman, *Priests Jubilee 2000*, 316: Father Flowers was born in Wilmington, Delaware on January 2, 1951, and ordained a priest on October 1, 1977. ADW – Bohemia File, Jim Garrigan, "December 16, 1992, Summary of My Stewardship." Jim Garrigan started a program for a Field Day at Bohemia and a one-day retreat for school children. Also he started a Candlelight Christmas Concert to take place on the first Sunday of December. The newsletter of the Society was revived and membership was increased. A sacristy fund was established and new robes for altar servers purchased. Jim Garrigan retired from the presidency in 1992. He now lives in Cape May, New Jersey.
128. Elkton, Maryland: Cecil County *Register of Wills*, Will of Marie Price, dated March 27, 1991 (RST 001-450, Estate 7308): Marie Price left $314,000 each to the Oblates of St. Francis de Sales, St. Joseph Parish in Middletown, and the Old Bohemia Historical Society. Miss Catherine Marie Price passed away June 23, 1992.
BURIAL RECORDS OF BOHEMIA CEMETERY: June 25, 1992 – *Catherine Marie Price*, born July 26, 1893, died June 23, 1992, age 93; July 24, 1992 – Anna Fisher, born October 15, 1914, age 77; December 15, 1992 – Lewis D. Stiles III, died December 12, 1992, age 40; December 15, 1992 – Henry Clement Haywood, Sr., born December 31, 1904, died December 11, 1992, age 87; January 7, 1993 – Annette Ott, born March 1, 1919, died January 6, 1993, age 73; April 5, 1993 – George H. Clegg, born June 23, 1917, died March 31, 1993, age 75; May 10, 1993 – George E. Dunn, born January 18, 1930, died May 7, 1993, age 63; October 14, 1993 – Corenne Allen, born October 24, 1916, died October 15, 1993, age 77; March, 1994 – Walter Pochwat, born October 28, 1916, died March 8, 1994, age 78; July 2, 1994 – Paul Raymond Kramer, born August 14, 1927, died June 30, 1994, age 66; January 3, 1995 – Rebecca Ann Woodrow, born September 10, 1908, died January 1, 1995, age 86; July 7, 1995 – Samuel Hugh Brooks, born March 26, 1914, died July 4, 1995, age 81; December 2, 1995 – Woodrow McDonald, born June 2, 1916, died November 28, 1995, age 77; January 17, 1996 – Margaret E. Toomey, born March 11, 1906, died January 8, 1996, age 89; February 23, 1996 – Affan R. Cruchley, born February 18, 1903, died February 18, 1996, age 93; May 8, 1996 – Horst E. Blanke, born September 6, 1938, died May 4, 1996, age 57; May 21, 1996 – William S. Foley, born June 17, 1953, died May 17, 1996, age 40; May 28, 1996 – Lawrence David Moffett, born November 9, 1949, died May 23, 1996, age 46; February 8, 1997 – Anton Burger, born 1908, died February 3, 1997, age 89; June 26, 1997 – Michael Joseph Rossi, born March 28, 1962, died June 21, 1997, age 35; September 1, 1997 – Anne E. Rutkowski, born October 20, 1934, died August 27, 1997, age 62; September 6, 1997 – Margaret Y. Schmidt, born June 7, 1901, died September 2, 1997, age 96; September 11, 1997 – Josephine L. Bagnoli, born November 20, 1923, died September 4, 1997, age 73; September 23, 1997 – Michael Stephen Maghan, born February 4, 1992, died September 17, 1997, age 5; October 3, 1997 – John T. Green, born February 15, 1913, died September 26, 1997, age 84; November 29, 1997 – Donald R. Willey, born April 16, 1939, died September 26, 1997, age 58; March 29, 1998 – Bernard C. Carbine, born May 17, 1936, died March 15, 1998, age 61; June 8, 1998 – Baby Boy McKee, stillborn June 5, 1998; September 4, 1998 – Ellen Morray Whitlock, born December 28, 1911, died August 28, 1998, age 86; September 24, 1998 – Charles L. Panciroli, born April 8, 1906, died September 20, 1998, age 92; October 19, 1998 – William C. Ward, born July 11, 1927, died October 13, 1998, age 71; March 9, 1999 – Constance Marie Pierce, born August 3, 1944, died March 4, 1999, age 54; March 24, 1999 – Maurice Adelman, Jr., died March 17, 19999; April 6, 1999 – Edward F. Kwasnieski, born September 3, 1911, died April 2, 1999, age 87; September 20, 1999 – Samuel Joseph McAlpin, Jr., born December 24, 1924, died September 18, 1999, age 64; September 30, 1999 – William J. H. Ryan, II, born June 18, 1925, died September 27, 1999, age 74; October 9,

1999 – Charles Bernard Johnson, born February 18, 1935, died October 6, 1999, age 64; November 20, 1999 – Bernard J. Matyniak, born August 5, 1931, died November 17, 1999, age 68; December 14, 1999 – Margaret Augusta Moffett, born October 12, 1999, died December 11, 1999, age 100; March 31, 2000 – Edith I. Gesullo, born June 19, 1921, died March 27, 2000, age 78; June 5, 2000 – Vernon Hinze Diers, born October 7, 1913, died June 1, 2000, age 86; June 26, 2000 – Helen Virginia Wolfe, born August 24, 1942, died June 20, 2000, age 57; July 17, 2000 – Rev. Francis W. Krastel, died July 3, 2000, age 72; August 3, 2000 – John Danko, born July 17, 1919, died July 30, 2000, age 81; George Fry (no information); September 22, 2000 – Margaret T. Gentile, born March 9, 1925, died September 18, 2000, age 75; October 14, 2000 – Robert Allan Cahall, born October 23, 1935, died October 11, 2000, age 64; November 9, 2000 – Doris Kelly Johnson, born November 28, 1913, died November 6, 2000, age 86; December 7, 2000 – Margaret V. Ford, born February 26, 1919, died December 4, 2000, age 81; December, 2000 – James D. Quinn, born November 11, 1919, died December 1, 2000, age 93; April 20, 2001 – Agnes J. Sparks, born March 19, 1911, died April 17, 2001, age 90; June 1, 2001 – Audrey Lee Davis, born Mary 27, 1982, died May 27, 2001, age 19; June 19, 2001 – Arthur Thomas Keefe, Jr., born April 29, 1920, died June 15, 2001, age 81; August 31, 2001 – William R. Love, born January 25, 2001, died August 28, 2001, age 86; October 25, 2001 – Richard Armen Amirikian, Jr., born January 2, 1960, died October 21, 2001, age 41; January 3, 2002 – Marie Verhaggen, born April 22, 1922, died December, 2002; February 18, 2002 – Edwin Allen Dill, born March 23, 1924, died February 13, 2002, age 77; April 12, 2002 – Emma Elizabeth Shetzler Barcus, born February 15, 1917, died April 9, 2002, age 85; May 10, 2002 – Betty Sue England, born May 3, 1935, died May 8, 2002, age 67; May 17, 2002 – Juliet Rawlings Du Ross, born May 5, 2002, died same day; May 30, 2002 – Nellie Garrigan, born August 7, 1919, died May 25, 2002, age 82:

129. "Old Bohemia Revisited," *Newsletter of the American Catholic Historical Society* Washington, D. C. (March, 1993). Eighty six persons attended.
130. Wilmington, Delaware *The Dialog*, September 9, 1993
131. Wilmington, Delaware *The Dialog*, April 4, 1994
132. "Bishop's Back Home," Wilmington, Delaware *The Dialog*, September 22, 1994. In 1971 Father Basil Losten was named auxiliary to the Ukrainian Archeparch of Philadelphia. In 1977 he was appointed Eparch of Stamford, Connecticut.
133. "Bishop To Bless Old Bohemia Cross," Wilmington, Delaware *The Dialog*, October 6, 1994. The base for the cross was donated by Mumford and Miller Concrete of Odessa, Delaware. The image of Christ was hand cast in Italy and imported by Conrad Pinkel Studio of Viero Beach, Florida. A memorial book with the names of benefactors of the monument was placed on permanent display in the vestibule of the church. The blessing by Bishop Mulvee was twice postponed after it was first announced in the diocesan newspaper: "Old Bohemia Monument Blessing Set," Wilmington, Delaware *The Dialog*, October 21, 1993.
134. "Old Bohemia Shrine Hosts Parish Events," Wilmington, Delaware *The Dialog*, May 12, 1994
135. ADW – Bohemia File, copy of minutes of meeting May 18, 1995 of board of the Catholic Diocese Foundation. It was noted that in a review of documents on file, an agreement dated February 11, 1965, placed restrictions on the Foundations ability to alienate real estate. Although the deed from the Aikens farm to the foundation conveys a fee simple title, the agreement with the Historical Society stated that no sale can occur without the agreement of both the Society and the Foundation. In a quid pro quo move, the Foundation requested that the Society remove the restrictions in return for the grant. The positive unanimous vote of the board was given on the condition that the Society relinquish the right to agree to alienation of real estate. A barn and silo separate from the church – rectory structures house historical society offices and gift shop. They also contain various carriages, sleds and farm equipment that give insights into rural life. In July, 1995, Father Flowers, responding for the Old Bohemia Historical Society, indicated that the condition to be imposed was not acceptable. He suggested that members of the Catholic Diocese Foundation meet with members of the Old Bohemia Historical Society in September to discuss the matter. It was agreed that certain members of the Foundation would travel to Bohemia to review the site with a possible view of segregating part of the farmland and permanently attaching it to the Old Bohemia Church (minutes of meeting, September, 1995). Foundation members met with officers of the Society on October 7, 1995. The meeting was reported as valuable but it had not resulted in any meeting of the minds. Members of the

Society were reported strong in their position not to give up the Society's right to block the sale of any property. On-going discussions were in order. The Foundation needed to secure from the Society its actual plan regarding the restoration of the whole site. The Foundation should return to Bohemia to lay the groundwork for an improved relationship. The request for the Society to surrender its right to approve any proposed sale of property was to be taken off the table. Some type of "limited involvement of the CDF" should be negotiated. Foundation members agreed to leave alone the issue of the right to object to sale of property by the Society. A full discovery should be undertaken to review legal and canonical issues. (minutes of meeting, November, 1995). ADW – Bohemia File: On April 15, 1997, Monsignor Cini, on behalf of the Catholic Diocese Foundation, wrote Mrs. Bernice Dill, who had called him on behalf of the Old Bohemia Historical Society. Msgr. Cini reviewed the whole matter from the May 1995 minutes through the minutes of the November 1995 meeting, and advised that the Society consider developing a written response to the Foundation members' request that "some attempt should be made to secure from the Old Bohemia Society its intentions (actual plan) regarding the continued improvement and restoration to the whole site." If that were submitted, the Foundation would take up the question again at that time.

136. "Old Bohemia Shrine Makes A Comeback," Wilmington, Delaware *The Dialog*, April 20, 1995. Repairs to the Mission Complex, declared unsafe by local authorities, will now enhance tricentennial celebrations.
137. "Old Bohemia Hosts Tour of Four Historic Delmarva Churches," Wilmington, Delaware *The Dialog*, September 28, 1995
138. "Old Bohemia's New Look on Tour – Historic Churches Open Sunday," Elkton, Maryland *Cecil Whig*, October 13, 1995
139. Wilmington, Delaware *The Dialog*, February 9, 1995. Bishop Mulvee became the Seventh Bishop of Providence, Rhode Island on June 11, 1997
140. "Welcome Bishop Saltarelli – Newark Auxiliary Bishop Named Chief Shepherd of the Wilmington, Diocese," Wilmington, Delaware *The Dialog*, November 23, 1995 Peterman, *Priests Jubilee 2000* 238: In 1984 Father Saltarelli was named a Prelate of Honor with the title of Monsignor by Pope John Paul II. On June 12, 1990 he was appointed Auxiliary bishop of Newark, New Jersey.
141. Wendy Hiester Gilbert, "Bohemia Society Notes Discovery of Antique Icons," Elkton, Maryland *Cecil Whig*, May 24, 1996. All but one of the fourteen stations had been preserved.
142. "Old Bohemia Bicentennial Starts April 20," Wilmington, Delaware *The Dialog*, April 10, 1997
143. "Fire Can't Stop Plans for Church Activities," Wilmington, Delaware *The Dialog*, May 15, 1997. When a painter's heat gun caught fire, a wooden window frame was ignited. The damage did not exceed $5000.
144. Wilmington, Delaware *The Dialog*, May 30, 1997
145. "Prints of Rare Photograph of Historic Church on Sale," Wilmington, Delaware *The Dialog*, May 15, 1997. The photograph was part of Warner's 1982 book, "Chesapeake A Portrait of the Bay Country." The price for each print was $100.
146. "Bishop Celebrates His First Mass at Old Bohemia This Sunday," Middletown, Delaware *The Transcript*, October 16, 1997. "Old Bohemia Bicentennial To Close with October 19 Mass," Wilmington, Delaware *The Dialog*, October 16, 1997. "Old Bohemia Celebration Recalls Persecutions of Early Maryland," Wilmington, Delaware *The Dialog*, October 23, 1997. "Once a Jesuit Plantation, Warwick, Site Has A Rich History," Middletown, Delaware *The Transcript*, October 16, 1997
147. "Religious Articles Sought For Old Bohemia Gift Shop," Wilmington, Delaware *The Dialog*, April 16, 1998
148. "Diocesan Pilgrimmage Sites To Be Open Sunday October 18," Wilmington, Delaware *The Dialog*, October 15, 1998
149. ADW – Bohemia File: Father Flowers' Lecture Notes
150. Wilmington, Delaware *The Dialog*, October 7, 1999
151. "Old Bohemia Opens Sunday For Outdoor Stations and Mass," Wilmington, Delaware *The Dialog*, April 6, 2000. It was stressed that St. Francis Xavier Shrine was a "pilgrimmage church" so designated by Bishop Saltarelli.
152. "Old Bohemia Open For Mass This Sunday," Wilmington, Delaware *The Dialog*, September 14,

2000
153. "Twenty Centuries of Catholic History" Wilmington, Delaware, *The Dialog*, March 4, 2000. "Art Exhibit of Catholic History To Be Displayed at St. Dennis, Galena," Wilmington, Delaware *The Dialog*, May 25, 2000. "A Diocese Celebrates – Complete 'Sonrise 2000' Schedule," Wilmington, Delaware The Dialog, September 28, 2000
154. ADW – Bohemia File, Father Flowers' Lecture Notes Peterman, *Priests Jubilee 2000* 326: "Old Bohemia Will Host Memorial Day Mass," Wilmington, Delaware *The Dialog*, May 24, 2001: Father Flowers pastor, will be celebrant at 9 a.m. After Mass there will be a procession to the cemetery and a 21-gun salute and the playing of taps by the Chesapeake City Veterans of Foreign Wars.
155. Peterman, *Priests Jubilee 2000* 326; Wilmington, Delaware *The Dialog* May 30, 2002. Effective on June 24, 2002 Father Steven Giuliano became pastor of St. Joseph's parish, Middletown.
BURIAL RECORDS OF BOHEMIA CEMETERY: June 24, 2002 – Marie B. Rowan, born December 4, 1922, died June 19, 2002, age 79; October 15, 2002 – Katherine E. Allen, born October 23, 1916, died October 8, 2002, age 85; October 15, 2002 – James T. Allen, born November 11, 1939, died September 28, 2002, age 62; October 15, 2002 – Theresa Miller, born June 17, 1942, died September 28, 2002, age 60; December 2, 2002 – Charles William Harwell, Jr., born April 22, 1927, died November 27, 2002, age 76; December 28, 2002 – Elizabeth Oakes Ward. born June 24, 1924, died December 22, 2002, age 78; March 11, 2002 – William A. Cross, born August 1, 1931, died March 7, 2003, age 71; May 19, 2003 – Vera Lee Burger, born December 27, 1941, died May 15, 2003, age 61; May 24, 2003 – Earl Hugh Martin, born July 2, 1920, died May 20, 2003, age 82; July 12, 2003 – Arthur Ralph Woodrow, born January 22, 1909, died July 8, 2003, age 94; August 22, 2003 – Robert Adam Meninger, born November 22, 1915, died August 19, 2003, age 87; September 5, 2003 – Edward L. Kuberski, born August 27, 1947, died September 2, 2003, age 56; September 22, 2003 – Eleanor S. O'Conner, born April 26, 1915, died September 19, 2003, age 87. Ellen Coleman O'Grady, born April 1,1905, died July 20, 2004; Charlotte M. O'Tanyi, died January 15, buried in Soha crypt January 29, 2002; Gertrude Degan Stearns, born September 4, 1912, died October 1, 2003.
156. Wilmington, Delaware *The Dialog*, October 19, 2003
157. Wilmington, Delaware *The Dialog*, October 30, 2003
158. Wilmington, Delaware *The Dialog*, April 22, 2004
Wilmington, Delaware *The Dialog*, May 20, 2004
160. Wilmington, Delaware *The Dialog*, October 28, 2004

Index Of Persons

A

ABEL
   Harriett Jane 224, 253, 260
ABLE
   Jane Henrietta 247
ABBOTT
   Priscilla 216
ADAMS
   Alice S. 262
   Alexia 264
ADELMAN
   Maurice 325
   Maurice Jr. 299
ADHEARNE
   Michael 205
AHEARNE
   James 207
   Joanna 219
   John 207
   Michael 207
AHERN
   Ann 216, 263
   Anne 211, 216
   Catherine 202, 212
   Dennis Robert 211
   Dennis 211, 216, 219, 226
   Eleanore 216
   Eugene 226
   Joanna 216
   Jeremiah 215
   John 202, 213, 253
   John Peter 215
   Margaret 215, 219, 220
   Mary 202, 213
   Mary Ann 224
   Michael 213
   Patrick 253
AITKEN
   Richard D. 285
ALFREE
   Emna 265
   James 265
   William 14
ALLEN
   Catherine 328
   Corinne 325
   Elizabeth 181
   James 131
   James T. 328
ALLWORTH
   Ann 219
   Anna 211, 216, 226
ALRICKS
   Sara Elizabeth 222
AMERY
   John 216
   Mary 216
   Robert 216

AMES
   Donald 322
   Jewell M. 324
AMIRIKIAN
   Richard Armen 326
ANDERSON
   Anna 153
   Hannah Ann 223
   Henry 158
   Jane 142
   Matilda 153
   Rebecca 142
ANGELINE
   Mary 205, 206
   Paul Allen 324
ANGELO
   Michael 217, 222
ANGLIN
   Mary 203
ANNE, QUEEN OF ENGLAND
   19
ANTOINE
   Charles 256
   Francis 257
   Nicholas 256
ANTON
   Catherine 255
ANINILL
   Mary Ann 219
   Edward 219, 224
APPLEGARTH
   John E. 157
ARCHIBOLD
   Richard, S.J. 56
ARCHIMBAULT
   John B. S.J. 242, 259, 260
ARJOIN
   Thomas 92
ARMSTRONG
   Ann 105
   Martha Ann 226, 305
ARRAS
   Sandanella Anna 262
   Peter 262
ARRATIN
   Sr. Bernarda, OSBM 301
ARTHUR
   A. Dorothy 313
AS
   Peter 213
   William 213
ASAY
   Mary 247
   James 247
ASH
   G. Reynold 277, 283, 285, 303
ASHBY
   James, S.J. 36

ASPINALL
   Wayne N. 320
ASY
   James 221
ATKINSON
   Dennis 207
   John 208
   Margaret 317
ATTWOOD
   Peter, S.J. 21, 22, 52
ATWELL
   John 144
   Lucinda 144
AUSTIN
   Kathryn 323
AYERS
   Andrew 203
   Cecelia 304
   Cecelia Agnes 261
   George 304
   Henry V. 263, 303
   Peter 261, 265, 303

B

BABY
   Jane 217
   Oliver 216
   Pauline 215
   Rose 216
BACCHUS
   Clara 157
BACKES
   John 210
BADIN
   Stephen, Rev. 85
BAGGS
   Sarah 254
BAGGUS
   Mary Adeline 174, 182
BAGLY
   James 221
BAGNOLI
   Josephine L. 325
BAHAN
   Ann 159
BAILEY
   Jane 207
   Joseph Humphrey 223
   Margaret 205
   Rosalie 223
BAKER
   Cecelia 321
   Henry 255
   Mary 255
   Mary Jane 218
   Samuel 320
   Scott 320
BALDWIN

Index of Persons 339

Maria McAleer 308
BALTIMORE
  Third Lord 15, 19
BARBY
  Pauline 250
BARCZEWSKI
  Anna M. 321
BARDIS
  Elizabeth 166
BARNEY
  James 93, 144
BARR
  Teresa 256, 257
BARRETT
  Isabella 214
  James 144
  John 214
  Mary 214
BARRY
  Joseph Luke, Rev. 237
  Mary 139
  Theresa 259
BARTON
  Clementina 255
  Rose 255
BAEMAN
  Catherine 201
BATES
  Henry 213
  Mary Ann 213
BAUMAN
  Joseph 223
  Maria Francisca 223
  Sophia 246, 248, 259
BAXTER
  Ann 142
  Mary 174
BAYARD
  James 145
  Martha 145
  Mary 145
BAYARDS
  Elizabeth 100
BEADNALL
  James, S.J. 36, 37, 40, 60, 64
BEAN
  Emily 221
  William B. 221
BEAR
  Henry 211
  James 211
BEARD
  Rebecca 174
BEARDS
  Gorge 204
BEARS
  George 156, 174, 182
  James 156
BEASTON
  Bessie 317
  Cayot 251
  Dorothea Eugenia 226, 250

John 226
John T. 221
Liona 258
Mary Lionore 249
Mary R. 253
Robert T. 249
BECK
  Amelia 101, 103
  John 216, 222, 224
  John Charles 222
  Maria Ann 216
  Rose Alma 224
  Samuel 27, 103
BECKER
  Anna 218
  Thomas A., Bishop 198, 229, 230, 233, 258
BECKS
  Alma 204
  Ben 204
  John 204
BEDINI
  Gaetano, Archbishop 188
BEEHAN
  John 216
  Martin 216
BEERS
  Catherine 157
  James 127, 211
  John A. 315
  Mary 159
  Mary G. 157
  Thomas 157, 208
BEESTON
  Francis, S.J. 12, 80-85, 88, 103, 105
BEIRS
  James 208
BELTON
  Thomas 158
BENNETT
  Joanne 213
  John, S.J. 21
  Richard III 33
BENNINGHAM
  Eleanora 226
BENTLEY
  Julie 222
BERGER
  Frances 207
BERGMAN
  Salvina 260
BERGSTROM
  S.A. 314
BERMAN
  Solina 256
  Sophia 257
BERMINGHAM
  Amaro 247
  William J. Rev. 244
  Eleanora 226, 249
BERRY

William 203, 213
BERRIMAN
  Mary 212
  Joseph 212
BERRYMAN
  Henrietta 218
  Margaret 215
BIRCH
  Mary A 219
BIRD
  Catherine 211
BIGGERS
  Daniel 100
BIGNEAR (BINGNEAR)
  Henry Joseph 259
  John 257
  Joseph 259
  Mary Elizabeth 257
BLACK
  Rebecca Burns 174
BLADEN
  Thomas 28
BLAKE
  Family 169
  Alphonsa 135, 139, 182
  Charles 18
  Eleanore 155
  Ellen 182
  Germana 144
  Henrietta 155
  Henry E. 157, 159
  James 130, 174, 158, 182
  James Joseph, Rev. 234
  Jane 130, 155, 182
  John Sayer 34, 40
  Martha 18
  Philemon Charles 34
  Samuel 157
  Susan 182
  William A. 158
BLANKE
  Horst E. 325
BLANSVILLE
  Thomas 248
  William 248
BLOME
  Florentine Wilhelmina 259
  Fred 259
BLOUNT
  James 157
  Martha 157
BLUNT
  Billy 195
  Charles 221
  Joe 193
  Nora 217
  William Graffen 217
BOARMAN
  Anna 255
  Joseph 255
  Laura 255
  Margaret 255

William 253
BOGDEN
  Bridget 222
  Catherine 222, 224
BOGENSCHIITE
  Michael 223
  William 223
BOGENSCHULTZ
  Maldeburger 246
  Marcell 246
BOGER
  Marcia 157, 216
BOGGS
  J. Caleb, Gov. 311
  Sarah 105
BOGLE
  Robert 201
BOHM
  Maria Magdalen 225
  William 225
BOILE
  James 102
  Marianna 152
  Mary 152
BOILES
  Eleanor 118
  Robert 118
BOILS
  Eleanor 99
  Mary Jemina 174
  Robert 99, 182
BOILT
  James 152, 157
  Marianna 152
  Mary 152
BOLAND
  Jeremiah M. 138, 174
BOLDEN
  William 200
BOLEN
  John J., Msgr. 308
BOLLS
BOND
  Gracey 208
  James T. 250
  Jane Frances 192
  Laura Helen 221
  Mary A. 251
  Virginia 219, 220, 226, 257, 258
  William G. 17
BOOKER
  Elsie Loretta 215
  Francis Jerome 215
  Susannah Rebecca 215
BOOTH
  Sara 138, 139
BOSKIN
  Belinda 203
BOURKE
  Edmund 213
  Elizabeth 102, 103

Jacob 102
James 226
Julius 213
Patrick 214
Thomas 102
William 102
BOWIE
  Isaac 225
  Robert 225
BOWING
  Levy 133
  Lewis 133
  Rebecca 133
BOWLES
  Benita 207
  Ellen 219, 250, 254
  Catherine 256
  Charles 251
  James Herbert 251
  Marge 217
BOWLING
  Anna 119
  Mary 100
BOWLS
  Cornelius 223
  Charles 192
  Ellen 221, 222, 224, 247, 249
  Elizabeth 192
  Francesca 192
  Helena 247, 250
  John 192
  Maggie 195
  Margaret 247, 249
BOWMAN
  Charles 103
  Earl B. Jr. 324
  Earl B. Sr. 324
  Frances 224
  Gracey 233
  Sara 102
BOY
  Carolina 226
BOYLAN
  Bridget 247
  Catherine 247
BOYLE
  Jane 145
  Margaret 145
  Sarah Ann 145
  St. 157
BRACKIN
  Catherine 205
  Isabella 205
BRACKON
  Catherine 208
BRADSHAW
  Elizabeth 204
BRADFORD
  George, Rev. 251, 252
BRADLEY
  Catherine 206
  Edward 212

James Franklin 212
John 145, 203, 206
Mary 206, 211, 213, 214
BRADLY
  Anna 215
  Bartholomew 208
  Catherine 209
  James 99, 202, 208
  John 213
  Peter John 202
BRADY
  Anthony 147
  Bartholomew 159
  Bernard 174
  Catherine 201
  Christopher 211
  Felix 165
  George 159, 201, 206
  Henrietta 201
  Henry 235
  Isabella 174
  Jane 174, 182
  John 174, 182
  Letitia 151, 156, 166
  Louise 119, 137, 206
  Martin 182
  Mary 124, 137, 147, 153, 201, 207
  Patrick A., Msgr. 12, 291, 292
  Perry 157
  Rebecca 235
  Robert 174, 182
  Robert Watson, S.J. 260
  Sarah 102, 174, 182, 235, 256, 260
BRANNON
  Frances 144
BRASHLER
  Michael 144
  Timothy 144
BRASKELL
  Helen 144
  Marshal 144
  Timothy 144
BRAUGHMAN
  Mary 250
BRAY
  Ellen 159
BRAZIL
  Isabella 138
  Mary 138, 174
BREADY
  Benedict 214
  Catherine 212
  Charity 223
  George 214, 216, 223
  Robert 216
BREEN
  Alice 214
  Catherine 212
BRENNAN
  Patrick 201, 224

Index of Persons 341

Peter, Msgr. 308
BRENT
  Robert 34
BRESLIN
  Charles 257
  Margaret 214
BREY
  Jacob 144
BRIAN
  Michael 208
BRICE
  Anna 214
  Catherine 215
BRICKLEY
  Mary 138
BRIER
  Isaac 133
  Levy 133
  Patricia 133
BRINNAN
  Monica 209
  Patrick 202
  William 202
BRISCOE
  Cinthia Ann 260
  Elizabeth 308
  Emeline Virginia 256
  Eugenia 256
  Frances Wilmer 219, 224, 248
  Gervase 155, 235, 237, 249, 259, 260, 308
  Indiana 250, 256
  Jervis 219, 226, 256, 308
  John 250, 321
  Joseph E. 255
  Margaret 226
  Mary 257, 258
  Sam Thomas 219, 255
  Susan 221
  Walter 308
  William A. 249, 258
BRITT
  Catherine 207
  Jane 215, 221
  John 207, 215, 217
  Mary 215
BROAD BENT
  Mary E. 224
BRODERS
  Margaret 215
  Mary 215
BROMER
  David 216
  William David 216
BROOKE
  Family 169
  Amy Elizabeth 156
  Elizabeth 203
  Ignatia 90
  John B. 124
  Robert, S.J. 14, 19
BROOKS

Samuel Hugh 325
BROPHEY
  Ann 204
BROPHY
  Thomas 211
BROTHERS
  Catherine 214, 220, 224
  Catherine O'Neil 220, 224
  Dorothy 250
  Eugenia 250
  Hugh 216
  Jane 203
  John 214, 248, 250
  Margaret 216, 248
  Rosa 256, 257
  William C. 250, 313, 314, 315
BROWN
  Ann 139, 142
  Cecelia 308
  Charles 157, 257, 317
  Edward, S.J. 320
  Ellen 204
  Jean 164
  John R. 158, 205, 206, 208, 257
  Josephine 221, 247
  Letitia 153
  Margaret 206
  Martha 157, 158
  Mary E. 161, 205, 212
  Mike 202
  Patrick 214
  Robert 156
BROWNE
  Josephine 226
  Martha L. 156, 159
  Mary E. 156, 159
  R. V. 159
  Thomas 214
BROWNING
  Thomas 40
BRUSHNAHAM
  Elizabeth 214
  Patrick 214
BRYAN
  Arthur 157
  Charles 158, 159
  Edward 157, 158
  Elizabeth 154
  Ellen 206
  Francis 157
  George L. 221
  John 157
  Thomas A. 159
  Valentine 155, 158, 159
BRYSON
  Sarah 207, 208
  Stanley 195
BUCHER
  Mary Barbara 255
  William 255
BUCHIM

George Joseph 248
  William 248
BUCHLIN
  Jeremiah 139
  Mary 139
BUCKLEY
  Mary 174
BUHAN
  Carolina 224
BUNDY
  James 317
  Viola 324
BURCHARD
  John 220
BURGER
  Anton 325
  Francesca 219
  Josephine 322
  Vera Lee 328
BURK
  Family 46
  William 100
BURKE
  Christopher 246
  Edward 141
  Jacob 40, 141
  John 91
  Leroy 207
  Martha 207, 246
  Susanna 141
  William 120
BURNS
  Anna 199
  Bernard 174
  Catherine 205, 207, 209
  Christopher 159, 199, 205, 207, 209, 210, 215, 223
  Charles 192, 216, 248, 249, 254
  Daniel 144
  Elizabeth 144, 251
  Elizabeth Joanna 246
  James 209
  John 144, 223
  Joseph 248
  Martha T. 161
  Mary 199
  Mary Ann 209, 249, 258
  Maurice 208
  Michael 158, 200
  Owens 250
  Rebecca 222
  Susan 200
  Thomas 100
  Virginia 253
  Walter Clarence 250
BURRES
  Mary 201
BURRIS
  John 221
BUTLER
  Edward 174
  Margaret 182

Michael 174
BUTTER
BYRNE
    Christopher 204, 208
    Edward 204
    Mary 201, 208
    Patrick 208
BYRNES
    Catherine 219

C

CADY
    Charles Henry 215
    Henry 215
CAFFERY
    Bernard 251
CAHALL
    Robert Allan 326
CAHILL
    Alexis Victor 211
    Dominic 211, 216
    Mary 216
    Michael 205
    Philip 220
    Thomas 212
    Thomas Edward 212
CAIJO
    Josephine 202
CAIL
    Elizabeth Margaret 247
    Margaret 221
CAIN
    Ann 105
    Daniel 105
    Fedis Ann 221
    Jeremiah 100
    Johanna 144
    John 32, 116, 144
    Joseph 116
    Manassey 32
    Rachel 105
    Roger 99, 118
CALBY
    Mary 100
CALDWELL
    Sarah 211
    Sarah Ann 214
CALIMAN
    Catherine 195
CALL
    Elizabeth 247
    Margaret 247
CALLAGHAN
    Jeremiah 212
    Richard 212
CALLAHAN
    Ann 175
    Francis 249
    George 223
    James 223
    James T. 224, 226, 246, 247, 249

John 105
Joseph 158
Margaret 224, 246
Mary 175
Robert 158
Rose 226
Thomas 166
Thomas John 247
William 166
CALLAN
    Roseann 204
CALLIMER
    Margaret 211
CALVERT
    Benedict Leonard 19
    Charles 19, 24, 39, 40
CAMAC
    Mary 257
CAMEL
    Joseph 201
CAMPBELL
    Andrew 208, 219
    Catherine 207
    Elizabeth 207, 250, 254, 256, 257
    Levi 207
    Martin 207
    Thomas 116, 174
    James 219, 254
    Mary 254, 256
CANE
    Christopher 224
    Falice Ann 224
    Felix 224
CANN
    Ann Reynolds 156
    Fannie 248
    Joseph C. 300, 321, 323
CANNAL
    Daniel Amos 216
    Leahy 216
CANNON
    Jane 157
    Margaret 250
CARAL
    Catherine Ellen 200
    John 200
    Mary 213
    Rosey 200, 201
CARBINE
    Bernard C. 325
CARBERRY
    Charles 158
CARDICKI
    Domenico 321
CAREY
    Helen 141, 144
    Jeremiah 116
    John 41
    John, S.J. 175
    John Baptiste, Rev. 154, 164
    Matthew 82, 140

CARLAND
    Philip 147
CARLEY
    Edward B. Rev. 321
    Margaret 203
CARLIN
    Anna 203
    Joseph 202, 203
    Roseanna 208
CARNEY
    Daniel 102
    Sarah 102
CARTHY
    Bill 204
    Catherine 206
CAROL
    Caroline 214, 217
    Catherine Ellen 200
    John 200
    Rosey 200, 201
CARR
    Walter 213
CARRELL
    Charles 14, 41
CARROLL
    Charles of Annapolis 34
    Charles of Carrollton 14, 34, 42, 48, 81
    Daniel II 32
    Harry E. 251
    John 214, 223
    John 225, 251
    John Abp. 34, 35, 49, 79, 81, 85, 92, 94-96, 123, 129
    Michael 225
    Michael 164, 251, 259, 260
    Peter M. 214
    Sarah 260
    Sarah Hover 308
    William 259
CARSON
    Mary 145
CARTY
    Edward 200
    Elizabeth 165
    Elizabeth 213
    Henry 220
    Isaiah 165
    Jeremiah 119
    John 102
    Mary 116, 120, 137-38, 139
    Mary Agnes 165
CASEY
    John 208
    Mary 100, 120, 207, 208
CASHMAN
    Bridget 147
    Maurice 147
CATENER
    Joseph 205
    Mary Elizabeth 205
CAUGHLEN

Index of Persons

Jeremiah 145
CAULK
  W. 164
CAVANAUGH
  Anthony 174
  Catherine 205
  Martin 200, 202, 207
  Mary 202
  Sarah 205
CAVENDER
  Catherine 139, 142
CAYOT
  Jacques 226, 248, 251, 253
  Lydia 224
  Mary 192
CEILE
  Dominic 219
  John 219
  Victor 219
CHAIRA
  Anne 208
CHAMBERS
  Cardina 248
CHANCE
  Elijah 157, 195
CHANCY
  Susan 157
CHANDLER
  Caroline 221
CHICOISNEAU
  John B. S.S. 85
CHIFFENS
  William Henry 166
CHISOLM
  Peter 221
CHRISTIAN
  Adam 205, 218, 220
  Ann Margaret 218
  John 212, 216
  Margaret Eliza 218, 220
  Mary 205
  Mary Ann 220
  Rachel 205
CHARLEY
  Mary 205
CIETY
  Sylvester 100
CILLER
  Charles 174
CISCOE
  Alexander 258
  James Henry 201
  Sarah 258, 259
CLANCY
  James 100
CLAPBURN
  Mary B. 255
CLARCK
  James 201, 204
  John 204
CLARK
  Benjamin 119

Elizabeth 255
John C. 255
John T. 247
Margaret 255
Mary 257
Mary Agnes 247
Michael 174
Teresia 119
Sara 119
CLARKE
  Ann 220
  Christina 248
  Isaac 110
  Jacob 27
  James 248
  Joseph 27
  Sarah 221
  William F., S.J. 165, 183
CLAYTON
  Isaac 224
  Sara Ann 224
  Susan Ann 219
CLEAR
  Joanna 226
CLEARY
  Mary Ann 213
CLEFFARO
  Timothy 174
CLEGG
  George H. 325
CLEMENCE
  Catherine 226
CLEMENTS
  Elizabeth 157
CLERCK
  Sarah 100
CLIFTON
  Charles Edward 256
  George W. 256, 260
COALMAN
  Charles 133
  Henrietta 133
  Henry 133
  Sarah 133
COFFIN
  Araminta 212
COGAN
  John 174
COGHLAN
  Bridget 204
  James 208
COGLAN
  Bedelia 205
  Helen 174
  James 205
COHEE
  Amanda G. 248
  Benjamin F. 224, 226, 246
  Benjamin T. 248
  Bergman F. 249
  Charles Borromeo 248
  Franklin 208

George Cecil 246
Isabella 249
James E. 218
Kevin Andrew 218
Mary Caroline 218
Sara Pauline 224
Steven 226
COHEY
  Jane 221
COIL
  Elizabeth 234
COILE
  Edward 204
  James 204
COINISH
  Sylvia 147
COKLAN
  Jeremiah 145
  Mary 145
COLARY
  Ann 221
COLE
  Anna 110
  Elizabeth 23
  John 27
  Mary 109
  Peregrine 26, 102, 103, 109, 114, 135
  Sarah 42, 101, 109, 138, 151, 182
  Solomon 102
  Zebulon 42
COLLINS
  Bartholomew 214, 244, 255, 260
  Catherine 213, 215
  Charles 205
  Daniel 211
  Denis 208
  Edward 211
  Elizabeth 211
  Ellen 215
  Elmira 260
  Joan 215
  Joanna 212
  Joanne 205
  John 211, 212, 215
  Lydia 255
  Marie 260
  Mary 259, 260
  Michael 211
  Patrick 205, 208
  Sarah 244
  Teresa 217
  Thomas 215, 221
COMEGYS
  Peggy 157
COMETELE
  James 116
  Liger 116
COMPTON
  Julia 155, 203

CON
  Margaret 213
CONGDON
  Charlotte 215
  William Thomas 215
CONGRAY
  Margaret 203
  Mary 203
  Patrick 203
CONLAN
  Ellen 202
  John 155
  Martin 202
  Mary 155
CONLEY
  Anne 204
  Catherine 211
  Elizabeth 204,
  Maria 140
  Martin 211
  Patrick 142, 211
  Peter 139
  Sarah 207
CONLIN
  Elizabeth 175
  Martin 205
CONLON
  OM 205
  Thomas 206
CONMEYER
  Carroll 217
  Cornelius 217
CONMY
  John, O.S.F.S. 316
CONNELLY
  Eliza 199
  Laurence 204
  Patrick 208
  Sarah 201
CONNOLLEY
  Mary 206
CONNOLLY
  Catherine 218
  Lawrence 202
CONNOR
  Adam 212
  Agnes Elizabeth 212
  Anne Honora 212
  Bridget 206, 249
  Christopher Joseph 253
  Cornelius 210
  Dennis 203
  Elizabeth 213
  Ellen 206
  John 145, 159, 255
  John Francis 207, 253
  Margaret 212
  Mary 203, 206, 249, 255, 259
  Michael 203
  Patrick 203
  Richard 212
  Rose Ann 209

  Sarah 259
  Susanna 114
  Thomas Augustus 253
  Timothy 203
  William 114
CONNORSE
  Margaret 147
CONVERY
  Bridget 204
CONWAY
  Catherine 256
  George 247
  Margaret 224
CONWELL
  Sarah 208
COOK
  Ann 218
  Catherine 215, 216, 223
  John 103, 218
  Mary 103
  Temperance 103
COONEY
  Amy 205
COOPER
  Elizabeth 158
  Hannah 212
  Henry 165
  Jacob 159
  John Frisby 165
CORBALEY
  Family 170
  Ann 142
  Hannah 131, 133, 135, 137, 224, 250
  Henrietta 135
  Henrica Emerentia 139
  John 120, 124, 133, 137, 175, 201, 205, 208, 212, 213, 215, 220
  John James 215
  Josephine 217, 253
  Mary 205, 216, 218
  Mary Emely 142
  Richard 142
  Robert C. 221
  Samuel 131, 217, 250
  Varina 255
  Varina Josephine 253
CORBIT
  Anne 200
  Bridget 202
  Hannah M. 165
  Henrietta 174
  John 166, 174, 203, 206
  Margarete 202
  Mary 166, 206
  Michael 205
  Patrick 200, 201, 203, 205
  Richard 174
  Robert 200
  Roger 202
  T.T. 174

CORBY
  Henrietta 175
CORCORAN
  Thomas 214
CORESKY
  John 159
COREY
  Albert 221
CORNIGER
  Rebecca 248
CORRIGAN
  Anne 217
  Charles M. 255
  John A. Msgr. 311
COSGRAVE
  Bridget 202, 206
  Margaret 206
  Maria 159
  Mary 217
  Thomas 206
COSGRAY
  John 209
  Margaret 209
  Maria 203, 209
  Marie, 203
  Mary 212, 215, 224, 246
  Patrick 203
  Rose Ellen 203
COSGRIF
  John 222
  Margaret 223
  Maria 222
  Thomas 222
COSGRIFF
  Bridget 216
  Catherine 226
  Charles 247
  Jon 213, 217
  Margaret 216, 246, 247, 249
  Maria 215, 217
  Pat 215
  Patrick 213, 216
  Rose 213, 259
  Rose Anna 216, 224, 253
  Thomas 213, 224, 226, 247
COSGROVE
  Jane 200
  Mary 215
  Patrick 200
  Rose 257
  Thomas 200, 215
COTTER
  Cornelius 203, 209
  Mary 203
COUNCELL
  Family 106-107
  Ann Marie 195
  Carey 119
  Edward 102
  E.C. 116
  James 90, 102, 132 133
  John 158

Samuel 110
COUNCILL
  Bernard 208
  John 40
COOMING
  William, Rev. 311
COUNTERS
  Edward J. 317
COURSEY
  Gerard 157
COUSINNE
  Michael J. S.J. 11, 12, 135, 136, 174
COVEY
  Amanda Jane 224, 246
COWEY
  Joanna 224
CRAIG
  Elizabeth 90
  George 90
  George W. Hume 255
  Ignatius Hume 255
  Levi 90
CRADDOCK
  Family 46-47
  Alma 211. 216
  Anna 195
  Anna Elizabeth 100, 142
  Anna G. 255
  Anne 247
  Arthur 175
  Benedict 96, 110, 137, 151, 153, 156, 157, 159, 175, 192
  Benjamin 165
  Charles 233
  Charles Augustine 165, 255
  Corinne 218, 249, 255
  Corinne Helen 254
  Daniel 116, 137, 138, 174
  David 100, 102, 119, 120, 121
  Don 116
  Edward 102
  Elizabeth 120, 137, 156, 165, 217
  Emma Elizabeth 256
  Francis 100, 116, 119
  Gertrude 202, 221
  Henry B. 255
  James 133
  Jane 195
  John 157, 165, 195, 248
  John B. 224
  John Daniel 205
  Joseph 148, 156, 157, 165, 202, 218, 219
  Joseph Taylor 137
  Mary 100, 110, 221
  Mary Ann 226
  Mary Jeannette 212, 222
  Margaret 96, 110, 137, 175, 217, 226
  Margaret Ryland 151

Mollie 248
Netty 205
Rebecca 165
Richard 137, 138, 142
Sara 255
Susan 156, 165, 166, 175
Susan Ann 165
Temperance 157, 166, 248
Theodore 195, 221, 222
Thomas 137, 151, 153, 157, 165, 174, 201, 205, 208, 220, 226, 255, 256
Thomas Mooney 251
William 110, 116, 131, 148, 174, 250
William Alfred 137
William Alfonso 139, 174
CRANSTONE
  Martin 214
CRAWFORD
  Anna Marie 213
  Benjamin 249
  Charles 258
  Haslet Chrysostom 215
  Henry B. 250
  Henry Haslet 218
  Henry Vanbicher 214, 251
  Joseph 258
  J.V. 251
  Margaret 249
  Mary Helen 222
  Olive T. 321
  Samuel 214, 215, 218
  Samuel I. 211
  William 249
  William Emile 211
CREEDON
  Ellen 215
CREENY
  Anna 221
CREIGHTON
  Dorothy 157
  Mary 158
  Robert 158
  Sara 175
CRIMNEY
  Neil 207
CROAT
  Uriah 116
CRUMMY
  Francis 203
  James 203
  Neil 203
CROMDIGGING
  Michael Keenan 202
  Sarah Conwell 202
CROSS
  Martha 247
  William A. 328
CROSSGROVE
  Sarah 142
CROUCH

Benjamin 108, 109
Daniel 110
Elisha 109, 138, 182
George 109
John 124
Sarah 97, 124
Theresia 102, 109
CROUT
  Benjamin 120
  Bernice 100
  Theresia 120
CROWLEY
  Charles A. 12
CRUCHLEY
  Allan R. 325
  Catherine 323
CRUZE
  Elizabeth 105, 112
CULLY
  Elizabeth 101
  F. Ann 246
  Henry A. 36
CULLEY
  Charles Arthur 260
  Charles Buddy 260
CUNNINGHAM
  Francis 92
CURLEY
  Agnes 309
  Margaret 211
CURRAN
  Mary 200
CURTES
  Frances Marie 322
CURTIS
  Alfred A., Bishop 240, 241, 244, 258
CUSACK
  James 203

D

DADDS
  William 158
DAGUIN
  Daniel 175
DAILY
  John Paul 253
  Margaret Elizabeth 220
DALEY
  James 102
  Mary 105
DALSON
  Elizabeth 248
DALY
  Bridget 214
  David 141, 144
  Ella 257
  Gertrude 141, 144
  James 211, 251
  Joanne 211
  John 303
  John A., Rev. 302

Laurence 141, 144
Winifred 141
DALLARD
    William, Rev. 234
DANKO
    John 326
DANSKIN
    Mary 105
DARA
    Sarah 217
DARCY
    John 165
DARNALL
    Henry 20
DARRAH
    Catherine 217
DARROW
    Harriet 136
    James 136
DAUGHERTY
    John 175
DAVID
    Jacob 204
    Samuel Scott Graham 204
DAVIDSON
    Sara Jane 220
DAVIS
    Audrey Lee 326
    Earle 304
    Lydia 213
    John 110
    Mary H. 302, 324
    Rachel R. 224, 226
    Robert 212
    Tabiltra 157
    Thomas P. 157
DAVY
    John 120
DAY
    Ellen 206
DAYLY
    Bridget 216
    Ellen 215
    James 215
DAZELMAN
    John 175
DEAN
    William C. 256
    William E. 256
DE BARTH
    Louis, Rev. 81, 1777
DE COURCEY
    Henrietta M. 158
    William 158
DEE
    Ellen 215
DE GEE
    Henry, S.J. 56
DEGNAN
    Catherine 216, 247
    Daniel 216
    George 308

Michael 308
Patrick 224
William C. 251
DELAHAND
    Casey 120
    Samuel 120
    Thomas 120
DELANEY
    John 257
    Maurice 91, 100
DELAPOOLEE
    Clandimore 100
DELAYNAY
    Daniel 226
DELAVAN
    Louis Caesar, S.S. 85
DELENAUX
    Susanna 219
DELUOL
    Louis Regiol, S.S. 85
DENISTON
    Abigail 214
    James 213
    Patrick 213, 214
DENNING
    Ada 226
    Michael 226
DENNISTON
    James 213
    Patrick 213
DENVER
    John G. 317
    John J. 313, 314
    Kathryn 308
    William 203
DERAN
    Ann 144
DERMOTT
    Anna 100, 120
    Charles 120
DE ROSEY
    Sebastian, Rev. 88
DESHANE
    John 159
DESMOND
    Catherine 251
    Mary 216, 256
DESRIBES
    Joseph, S.J. 12, 244
DEUR
    Peter 201
DEVENNY
    John 303
DEVINE
    Ann B. 323
    Catherine 204, 217, 223, 305
    Denis 253
    Elizabeth 219, 253, 305
    Ellen 203
    James 200, 203, 207, 219, 305
    John 258
    John Paul 302

Lawrence 314, 321
Leo 303
Lillian 305
Margaret J. 323
Michael 205
Maurice J. 31
Morris 201
Mrs. 198
Nora Sheehan 305
Thomas 201, 211, 247, 303, 305, 308
William 208
DEWARD
    L.V. 208
DEWSON
    John Henry, Msgr. 12, 284, 285
DIERS
    Vernon 326
DIFFENDORF
    Rose 304
DIGGES
    John, S.J. 31, 56
DIGNEY
    Patrick 212
DIGNAN
    Catherine Louise 304
    George 258
    Mary 225, 247
    Mary Anna 302
    Michael 195, 206, 302, 304
    Patrick 206
DIGNAM
    Michael 200, 249
DILHOFER
    Catherine 215
    Martin 215
DILL
    Edwin Allen 326
DILLAN
    Mary 206
DILLIN
    Mary 217
DILLON
    Mary 215, 223
DIVINE
    Catherine 220
    James 195
    John 209
    Joseph 200
    Laurence A. 302
    Maurice 261
    Thomas 302
    Timothy 302, 303
DIXON
    Alfred Francis 218
    James 225
    Jane 202, 216, 223, 225, 250
    Jane Lavinia 202, 250
    John 220
    Mary Jane 225
    Margaret Jane 204
    Thomas 102, 202, 203, 208,

Index of Persons 347

212, 218, 220, 225
Thomas P. 212, 250
DOAN
  Joanna 248
DOGLAS
  Robert 217
  Robert Thomas 217
DOLAN
  Catherine 195
DOLTON
  Elizabeth 249
DONAHAN
  Peter 173
DONAHOE
  John 249
DONAHUE
  F.X. 313, 314
DONELAN
  Bridget 218
  Hugh 217
  Margarate 203
  Peter 216
  Thomas 216
DONIGAN
  Julia 212
DONLAN
  Margaret 213
DONLON
  Bridget 199
  Ellen 215
  Margaret 215
  Peter 199, 215
  William 199
DONNEL
  Eliza 206
  Peter 206
DONNELAN
  John 202
  Peter 202
DONOHO
  Benjamin 26, 43, 156
DONOHOE
  Honora 213
  James 202
  Jane 215
  Matthew 213
DONOHUE
  May L. 253
DONOVAN
  David 248
  Ellen 175
  James 175
  John 218
  Patrick 147
  Richard 175
DOODEY
  David 205
  Eugene 205
  Mary Anne 205
DORETY
  Daniel 200
  Edward 200

Mary 200
Patrick 200
DORETHY
  Ellen 199
  Margaret 199
DORN
  Elizabeth 206
DORR
  Charles 203
  Peter 203
DORSEY
  Catherine 206, 223, 250, 253, 308
  Dennis 225, 250, 251, 253, 305
  Eleanora 261
  Elia 205
  Francis 258
  Frederick 249
  George 208, 258
  Honora 305
  James 214, 233, 247, 248, 253
  John 217, 250, 303, 304, 308
  John J. 235, 253, 304
  Joseph M. 243, 250
  Maggie 254
  Margaret 195, 216, 304
  Margaret M. 247, 249, 250, 308
  Margaret Theresa 235, 254, 258
  Mary 212, 215, 247, 248, 249, 250, 302, 303, 304, 308
  Michael 219, 235, 305
  Patrick 201, 203, 204, 206, 208, 212, 216, 219, 225, 226, 235, 247, 248, 254, 305
  Thomas T. 247, 258, 304, 308
  William L. 258, 308
DOUGHERTY
  Ann 139
  Anne 142
  Bridget 147
  Charles 145
  Daniel 203
  Edmond 204
  Frances 204, 205
  Helen 145
  James 203, 208
  Michael 145
  Rose 210, 212, 213, 214, 215
  Thomas 200
DOUGLAS
  Ella 257
  Ellen 254
  Franklin C. 324
  Joseph 257
  Robert 248, 251
  Sara 248, 254
DOUGLASS
  William 16
DOWELL
  Henry 213

Thomas 192, 213
DOWLING
  Laurence 141
DOWNING
  Thomas 141, 144
DOWNY
  Owen 156
  Sarah 156
DOWELL
  Henry 213
  Thomas 192, 213
DOWLING
  Laurence 141
DOWNING
  Thomas 141, 144
DOWNY
  Owen 156
  Sarah 156
DOYLE
  Bridget 203, 213
  Henry 224
  James 140, 175
  Julia 205
  Thomas 140
DRAKE
  Sarah 226
  Teresa 215
DREKA
  Agnes Theresa 251, 255
  August 213
  Augustus 223
  Catherine 223
  Charles 224
  Charles Augustine 223
  C. Theresa 305
  Elsie Marsh 305
  Eva 246
  John George Augustine 213
  Louis 256, 257
  Louis Augustine 304
  Louis H. 255
  Mary Alice 257
  Mary E. 256
  Mary Theresa 251
  Mary Z. 305
  Theresa 223, 248
DREW
  Patrick 212
DRISKEL
  Catherine 213
  John 213
  Driver Joanne 156
  John 156
DROLL
  Catherine 251
  Carolina 245, 248
  Frederick 248, 254, 257, 260
  Friedolin 225
  Mary 259
  Mollie 259
DRUGGER
  Mr. 175

DRUKA
  Eva 195
  Louis 195
DUBOURG
  William, S.S. Archbp. 121
DUFFENDORF
  Rose 304
DUFFY
  Isabella 201, 202, 208
DUGAN
  Ann E. 249
  Bridget 212
  Catherine 218
  Daniel 144, 208, 218, 225
  Eleanor 135
  George Edward 225
  Helen Quinn 325
  Henry 258
  Hughey 135
  Mary A. 255
  Matthew 144
  Thomas A. 255
  Thomas W. 221
  Thomas Watson 249
DUHAMEL
  W.J.C. 217
DULANY
  Daniel 25
DULIN
  Adele 166, 198
  Ellen 216
DUN
  Eliza 202
  Kate 203
DUNCAN
  David 255
DUNGAN
  James 202, 208
DUNIVAN
  Patrick 147
DUNN
  Catherine Tyson 305
  Francis 175
  George E. 325
  John 140, 305
  Joseph 305, 317
  Mary 305, 314
  Mary Devine 311, 321
  Margaret 218, 221, 225, 305
  Patrick 175
  Thomas 221
DUNNOCK
  Isaac 157, 175
  James 157
  John 157
  Margaret 157
DURAIND
  F.J. 175
DURAND
  J.G.E. 91, 100
  Theresa 91, 100
DURKAN
  Elizabeth C. 218
  Elizabeth E. 165
  John A. 218
  John L. 207
  Mary 207
DURKEE
  Elizabeth 224
  Mary Theresa 213, 217, 219
  John A. 218
  John L. 259
DURKEY
  John 200
DURKIE
  Henrietta Catherine 217
  Hugh 212
  Mary V. 257, 260
  Michael Angelo 260
DURNEY
  Ann Marie 175
  Henrietta 222, 226, 251, 260
  Henrietta Catherine 217
  Hugh 212
  John 175
  Mary V. 257, 260
  Margaret 165
  Michael A. 251
  Paul J. 158
DU ROSS
  Juliet Rawlings 326
DURRAND
  Edward J. 224
  Mary Bocat 224
DUTTON
  George Clifton 303
  Laura 303
DWYER
  Dennis 220
  Roderick B. Msgr. 317
DYNAN
  Ann 165
  Catherine 222
  Mary 192

E

EBERHARD
  Bridget 302
  John Sebastian 213
  Lewis 215, 218
  Louis 214
EBERHART
  Lewis 215, 218
ECCLESTON
  Samuel, Archbp. 152, 159, 160, 161, 167
ECKMAN
  Jeannette 280
EDELIN
  Leonard, S.J.
EDGAR
  Ann 157
  Henry 157
EDWARDS
  Agnes J. 261
  Ruth 103
Egan
  Mary 264
  Mary Alice 214
  Martin 214
EISELE
  Francis Xavier 204, 211
  Huber 207, 210
  John 207
  Mary 213
  Mathias 264
  Matthew 213
  Placida 217, 222, 246
EISENLAB
  Blasinda 217
EISLY
  Anna Maria 212
  Elizabeth 212
ELLET
  James 259
  Margaret 259
ELLIS
  Margaret 218
  William 102
ELMER
  Jane 256, 257
EMMONS
  Agnes T. 244, 259, 264
  William 258
ENNIES
  Ellen 201
ENNIS
  Anna 175
  Bernice 209
  Catherine 139
  Charles 175
  Dorsey Louis 303
  Eleanora 164
  Elizabeth 175
  Ellen 159
  Ethelberta 264
  John 139
  John Robert 302
  Patrick 139
  Perry 259
  Rose 259
  Thomas 264, 265, 303
  Thomas J. 302
ENGLAND
  Betty Sue 326
EPINETTE
  Peter, S.J. 11, 12, 136, 140, 141, 142, 144, 145, 175, 177
ERTELL
  Isabella 216
ERWIN
  Family 47
  Catherine 199
  Charles 100
  James C. 119
  Robert 119

Index of Persons 349

EVANS
  Agnes 216
  Elizabeth 165
  Ellen 218
  George 42
  Helen 302
  Jonathan 105
  Lee 265
  Rose 265
  William 216, 226
EWEN
  Anaetasia 105
EWING
  Virginia 216
EWINGS
  David 164
  James 105
  Jane 164

F

FAGAN
  John 262
FAHEY
  Edward J. 303
  John Edward 303
  Mary 253, 254
  Margaret 206
FAIRBARN
  Elizabeth 158
  Elizabeth Ann 161
FANNIE
  Nicholas 175
FARMER
  Elizabeth 102
  Ellen 215
  Ferdinand, Rev. 801
FARRAGHER
  David 141
  Lawrence 141
FARRAR
  James, S.J. 23, 31, 53
FARRELL
  Edward 175
  Elizabeth 133, 139
  Ignatius O. 156
  James 137, 205
  Jane 144
  John 175
  Mary 144
  Mary Ann 213
  Matthew 175
  Michael 175
  William 137
FATIN
  Hannah 136
FAULKNER
  Marie 110
FAURE
  Stephen, Rev. 11, 100, 121
FAY
  Mary 201
FEASTIN
  Frederick 262
  Mary 262
FEEHELEY
  John 206, 208
  Rodger 206, 208
  William 206
FENEMAN
  Lawrence 175
FENLON
  Ann 137
FERRAL
  Ellen 202
FERRIS
  John 175
FERRIT
  Henry 133
FIELD
  Bryan 316, 318, 320, 324
FIELDS
  Georgianna 324
FIETER
  Catherine 102
FIFE
  Elizabeth 102
  Grace 102
  James 102
FILINGHAM
  Flora 80
  George 93
FIN
  Anna 210
  Eliza 209
  Ellen 213
  Richard 213
FINE
  John 145
FINEY
  Helen 145
  John 145
FINLEY
  Francis F. 257
  John 212
  Joseph 212
FINN
  Ann 221
  Catherine 246, 249
  Elizabeth 211
  James 246
  John 201, 211, 220, 246, 249
  Joseph 249
  Michael 235, 249
FINNEGAN
  Dennis 203
  Thomas 205
FINNEY
  Ellen 147
  John 147
  Mary 147
FINNIGAN
  Dennis 211, 212
FINY
  Ann 144

  John 145
FISCHER
  Anna Marie 223
  Catherine 223
  N. 223
FISHER
  Anna 325
  Bernard G. 324
  John 164
  Mary 164
FITZGERALD
  Catherine 203
  Dennis 200
  Dennise 200
  Edward 102
  James 92, 200, 203, 206
  Mary 200
  Rose Ann 206
FITZ MAURICE
  Edmond J. Bishop 273, 276, 283, 309
FITZPATRICK
  Patrick 220, 221
FITZSIMMONS
  Matthew 175
FLANAGAN
  James 208, 220
FLANARY
  Amelia 141, 144
FLANERY
  Henry 144
FLANIGAN
  Daniel 260
  Katie 260
  Margaret 260, 263
  Rose 260
FLANNAGAN
  James 204
FLANT
  Joseph 156, 159
FLEMING
  Francis, Rev. 109
FLEMMING
  Johanna 159
FLIMING
  James 147
FLIN
  Alia 203
  Bridget 202
  Helen 141
FLING
  Alexis 212
  Alice 205
  Bridget 204, 206
FLINN
  Ellen 220
  Florence 147
  John 224
  Maurice 139
FLINTHAM
  Anna 256
  Caroline Elizabeth 223

Charles 251, 258
John Christian 223
John 166, 175
John M. 225
John W. 159
Lydia 258, 259
Lydia Sterling 226, 318
Madeline R. 253
Richard 225
Sarah 116
Susan 216, 250
Susan Ann 223
William 159, 223, 226, 253
FLORA
　Susanna 211
FLOWER
　Henry 212
　Joseph L. 212
FLOWERS
　Thomas, Rev. 215, 297, 320, 325, 327
FLYNN
　Catherine 147, 218
FOGERTY
　Catherine 214
　Michael 213
FOGLER
　Ann 214
　Anna Maria 215
FOHEY
　Mary 208
FOLEY
　Ann 139, 142
　Catherine 201, 21
　Ellen 215
　Joanna 212
　John 215
　Thomas 226
　Thomas, Rev. 189
　Timothy 215
　Patrick 214
　William S. 325
FOOT
　Abigail 125
FORAN
　Robert 201
　Thomas 201
FORD
　Anna Theresa 166, 212
　Catherine 256
　Ellen 200, 323
　Francis Wheeler 200
　Helen 223
　Leonard George 212
　Louis Edward 200
　Marie 192
　Mary Susan 203
　Thomas 158, 166, 200, 212
　Walter 175
FORTIER
　James Francis 264
FOSTER

Henry 247
FOUGLER
　Ann M. 218, 223
FOULTING
　Anne 139
FOUNTAIN
　Ann 140, 255
　Anna 250
　Cecelia Ann 219
　Sandy Ann 226, 256
　Tanti Ann 249
FONTAINE
　Ralph W., Rev. 309
FOWLER
　Ann 138
FOX
　Agnes 223
　Andrew 255
　Henry 221, 223
　John 202
　Mark 212
　Mary 259
FRAIL
　Catherine 207, 312
FRANCE
　Jack 175
FRANCIS
　John 158
　Samuel 110
FRANKLIN
　John 158
FRANKS
　Eva 303, 304
FREEBERY
　John 200
　Mary 200
FREMONT
　Clementine 206
FRIEDENBACK
　Antoinetta 218
FRIEL
　Bernard 195
　Catherine 195
　Daniel 195
　John 195
　Mary 195
FRISBEY
　Ann 205
　George 215
　Thomas 205
　William 215
FROMONT
　Anne 203
　Clementine 203
FRY
　George 326
FULLAM
　M. 116
　Walter 120
FULLS
　Dennis 175
FULTON

Robert, S.J. 260
FUNGAR
　Dennis 214
FURLY
　Patrick 140
FURY
　Ann 145
　John 145

G

GODDESS
　Rosina 255
GAFFERE
　Ann Theresa 306
GAFFNEY
　Biddy 208
　James 140, 144
　Jane 140, 144
　John B., S.J. 12, 239, 246, 255
GAFFORD
　Alma 46
　Anna 112
　Benjamin 105
　Edward 112
　Jacob 102, 105, 112, 119
　John 116
　Juliana 116
　Levy 105, 112
　Mary 102, 112
　Nelly 116
　Rachel 116, 120
　Sally 112, 116
　Samuel 102, 105, 112
　Sarah 116
　Sophia 116
　Thomas 105
GAHAGEN
　James 215
　John 215
　Mary 215
GAINLEY
　Anne 205
GALLAGHER
　John 214
　Mary 214
　William 223
GALLIBRANDE
　Richard, S.J. 36, 37, 64
GALLIES
　Francis 217
GAMMON
　John 110
GANLY
　Bridget 140, 144, 175
　Brigid 141
　Catherine 140
　James 141
　Jane 140
　John 140
　John Charles 140
　Patrick 142
　Thomas 140, 144

Index of Persons

GANNON
  Elizabeth 219
  Joseph 219
GANZELING
  Jacob 220
  Margaret 220
  Mary Ann 220
GARDENER
  Catherine 226
  Mary 221
  Robert 226
GARDINER
  D.J., S.J. 262
  James, S.J. 264
  James 214
  Mary 214
  Robert 221
GARGAN
  Neil, S.J. 227, 280, 311
GARNER
  Elsie 257
  George 254, 257
GARNET
  Indiana Briscoe 306
GARNIER
  Antoine, S.S. 12, 85, 88
  Elsie May 308
  John 305
GARRIGAN
  James 293, 294, 295, 323, 324, 325
  Nellie 326
GARTLENAY
  Margaret 203
GASANAY
  Isabella 216
GASAWAY
  Isabel 212
GATES
  Rosina 224
GATTIS
  Rosina 229
GEARING
  Philip 218
  Thomas 218
  William 218
GUNSLINGER
  Maria 254
  Mary A. 255, 256
GENTILE
  Dominick Paul 325
  Margaret I. 326
  O.P. 314
GEORGE
  Anna 253, 256, 302
  Francis Charles 226
  Hackles 225
  Lewis 215
  James 225
  Joseph 21, 258
  Nicolaus 215, 226
GEORGES
  Ann 263
  Annie V. 263
  George Lucas 263
  Julia 258, 263
  Louis D. 263
  Julia 258
  Margaret 251
  Nicholas 257
  Theresa 263, 265
GERALD
  Henry 264
  Sara Elizabeth 264
GERARDIN
  Charles 211
GERBER
  Christopher 211
  Thomas 211
GERRY
  Lydia 212
GESULLO
  Deborah Lynn 317
  Edith 325
  Leonard 317
GETTY
  Jan 321
  Jean 321
GIBB
  Henry 204
  John Anthony 204
  Sissie 204
GIBBEN
  Richard 99
GIBBIN
  Henry 110
  Rachel 118
  Sarah 120
GIBBS
  Charles Andrew 166, 198
  Ellen 220
  Gorge 217
  Henry 151, 153, 166, 198, 201
  Laura Virginia 165
  Letitia 166, 198, 201
  Susan Ann 217
  William 201
GIBSON
  Ann 157
  Ann Louisa 157
  Dorrington 157
GIESETLING
  Mary 216
GIEVES
  Anna 215
  Harriett 215
GIEVIX
  Florentine 259
GIFFORD
  John 211
GIL
  John 135
  Magdalen 135
  Rebecca 135
GILDEA
  John 213
GILFOYLE
  Maria 207
GILKISON
  David 147
GILLAN
  Mary 254
GILLESPIE
  J.B. 166
  Mary 212
GILLIN
  Mary 249
GILLIS
  Theresa 219
GILMORE
  Mary 222
GILZE
  Fanny 133
  Mary Ann 133
  John 133
GINLEY
  Mary 203
GIRAVD
  John M., S.J. 240, 258, 260
GIULIANO
  Steven B., Rev. 291, 300, 328
GIVEY
  James 203
GLANSON
  Edwin 233
GLASER
  Gervase, O.S.B. 311
GLASSY
  Margaret 214
  Mary 215
GLEASON
  Mary 140
GLISSON
  Honora 145
GLENN
  John 206, 207
GOFF
  Alma Mary 259
  Catherine Henrietta 202, 265, 269
  Claude 265
  John B. 302
  Maggie 262
  Rose Ann 265
  Thomas 265
  William R. 265
GOGAN
  Edward 147
GOLDSBOROUGH
  Benjamin 158, 166
  Esther 155
  Esther A. Pascault 155
  Howes 158
  John 161
  Mary 166
  Robert 158

William 195
William L. 158
GOLT
  Ann 158
GOOD
  John 211
GOODDY
  Catherine Ann 224
GOODHAM
  Harriett 175
GORAM
  Sarah 204, 208
GORDON
  Elizabeth 247
GORE
  Anne Elizabeth 250
  James 254
  Mary Ann 249
  Sara Elizabeth 253
  Thomas 249, 253, 254
  William, O.S.F.S. 299
GORMAN
  Owen 147
  Peter 226
  William 226
GOSHEN
  Sarah 214
GOVIN
  Henry 145
  Rebecca 145
GRABOWSKI
  Kenneth 317
GRACE
  Elizabeth 249
GRADY
  Anne 135
  Eleanor 135
  Elizabeth 135, 215
  George 142
  John 215, 249
  Thomas 249
GRAESSEL
  Lawrence, Rev. 109
GRAHAM
  Joseph P. 322
GRAMMENGER
  Mary Theresa 220
GRANT
  Catherine 214
  Hugh 102, 103
  Jesse 306
  Mary 102
  Ulipses S., Pres. 306
  William Barnes 306
GRASON
  Richard 157
GRAY
  Anne 203, 204
  Michael 203
  Peter 203
GREADY
  Elizabeth 221

Patrick 221
GREATON
  Joseph, S.J. 11, 12, 22, 31, 64
GREEN
  Agnes 250, 261
  Anna 253
  Araminta 249, 259
  Ben 208, 257
  Benjamin 166, 204, 215, 249, 250, 263
  Benjamin J, 251
  Cecelia Ethel 254
  Elizabeth 165
  Ellen 175, 257
  F. Alice 249
  Frances 201, 202
  Francis 207
  Gladys Pearson 321
  Harriett 250
  Helen Raskob Corcoran 276
  Helena 156, 165
  Henry 112
  John 305
  Lilly 203
  Mary 137, 138, 166
  Mary Agnes 250
  Peirry 112
  Philip 201
  Rody 224
  Rose 250
  Thomas 233, 250
  Thomas F. 254
  Thomas J. 250
  William 250
  William P. 156, 165
  W.O. 255
GREENE
  Agnes 263
GREENWELL
  Ellen 165, 166, 204
  Helena 212
  Mary 204
  Mollie 207
  Nelly 214, 220
GREENWOOD
  Henrietta 119
  Jonathan 119
  Perry 119
GREET
  Alvin 219
  James Glenn 219
  William 219
GREGG
  Katherine Louise 305
GREIAS
  Helen 145
GRIBBIN
  Henry 100
  Matthew 100
GRIBBING
  Henry 119
  James 119

Sala 119
GRIBBINS
  Jane 151, 182
GRIEVES
  Anna 215
  Harriett 215
GRIFFIN
  John K. 157, 182, 195
  Margaret 200
  William 220
  William K. 157
GRIMES
  John 256, 257
GRIMIGER
  Anna Maria 264
  Bridget 264
  John 264
GRIMMINGER
  Bridget 256, 259
  Charles 246
  George Louis 247
  John 248
  John Michael 259
  Margaret 257
  Michael 246, 247, 248, 259
  William V. 246
GRISLEY
  Frances 205
GRISSERT
  Frederick 264, 265
GRZESCZAK
  Johanna 262
  Mary Anna 262
  Mathias 262
GUIGLY
  Thomas 221
GUILFORD
  Marie 205
GUILLARD
  Ellen 213
GULICK
  Nicholas, S.J. 21
GUMER
  Joseph 208
GUNNER
  Joseph 206
GUNNERE
  Robert 206
GUTLEY
  Winnie 205

H

HAAGA
  Elizabeth 265
HAAS
  Louis M. 304
HADDER
  Mary 105
HADDOCK
  James 19, 20
HAGAN
  Athanasius Gregory 212

Bernard 212
David 156
Michael 140
Patrick 247
HAGENMEYER
  Fred Michael 259
HAGERTY
  Alfred 175
  Catherine 175
  Mary 175
HAGGARD
  Peter 110, 116
HAGGERT
  Peter 116
HAHEY
  Ellen 221
HAJDN
  Mary 140
HALDEMAN
  Mary 213
HALEY
  Anna 212
  Cecelia 215
  Michael 147
  Richard 212
HALL
  Edward 211
  John 155
  Richard 159
  Susanna 110, 141
HALY
  John 220
HAMILTON
  Ann 105
  Ann Marie 218
  Annie 222, 226
  Charles 201
  Edward Joseph Beauregard 217
  James Brooke 222
  Joanne 217
  Richard 322
  William 213
  William Edward 217, 222
  W.F., S.J. 256
HAMMERGILDER
  Florence 264
HAMMERSLY
  Ann 159
HAMMON
  Bridget 205
HAMPHILL
  Thomas, S.J. 259
HAMPTON
  Anne 195
  James 195
  Susan 195
HANDLEY
  Charles 38
HANLON
  Cornelius 166
HANNAH

Bridget 220
Hannon Mary 145
HANS
  Eva 223
HANSON
  Archie 224
  Delphine 233
  Edwin Slater 166, 198
  John 91
  Joseph 224
  Mary 166, 198
  Thomas M. 233
  Thomas P. 166, 198, 224
HARDEY
  Richard B., S.J. 146
HARDIN
  Martha 189
HARDING
  Edward 109
  George, S.J. 37, 60, 64
  Mary 109
  Robert, S.J. 37, 60, 64
  Sarah 109
HARES
  Andrew 142
  Eliza 142
  Elizabeth 142
  James 142
HARGES
  Sebastian 262
HARKINS
  Hugh 111
  Maggie 251, 256
  Rosa 256, 259
HARLAND
  Beth 152
HARNETT
  Ellen 208
  David 204
  Michael 204
HAROLD
  Robert 203
  William B. 203
HARPER
  John, S.J. 256
HARRIGAN
  John 147, 221
  Michael 147
HARRINGTON
  Cornelius 217, 220
  Edward 217
  Elizabeth 200
  William 165
HARRIS
  Eliza 142
  Isaac 165
  James 142, 176
  Jane 144, 145, 162
  Kate Briscoe 323
  Lydia Ann 165
  Major 250
  Mary 147

Matilda 176, 225
Molly 175
Rachel 164
Sapien 43
HARRISON
  Albert 145
  George H. 317
  Gertrude 256
  James 145
HARROGAN
  Nancy 205
HARTNETT
  Edward 201
  Ellen 211
  James 215
  Jane 220
  Joanna 205
  John 201
  John Henry 211
  Laurence 201
  Mary 215, 220
  Michael 208, 211
  Timothy 205, 215, 220
  William 215
HARWELL
  Charles William 328
HARWOOD
  Martha 157
HASELTON
  Jeremiah 155
  Susanna 155
HASHEN
  Margaret 219
HASKINS
  Charles 146, 147
HASSETT
  Mary 200
HAUGH
  Daniel F., S.J. 12, 242, 244, 263, 265, 266
HAUSELMAN
  Barbara 207
HAVER
  Sarah 265
HAYES
  Alice Estella 247, 262, 263, 265
  James 175
  Maria Stella 262
  Thomas W., Rev. 239
HAYS
  Ann 211
  David 203
HAYWOOD
  Henry Clement 325
  Nora 321
HEALEY
  Daniel 205
HEALY
  Ellen 211
  Frederica 211
HEANEY

Claymen 200
Joanna 260
HEANILOW
    Anne Sabina 200
    John 200
HEARD
    Joseph, S.J. 147, 148
HEARLY
    James 211
HEART
    Charles 219
    John 219
HEATH
    Daniel Charles 33, 44, 83
    Hannah 110
    James 18, 20, 25, 38, 283
    James Paul 113
    Richard 119
    Richard Key 83
HEDE
    James 175
HEDERER
    Josephine 218
HEDEVEL
    Margaret Henry 202
    Thomas 202
HEDEVELT
    Mary Ellen 200
    Thomas 200
HEDLEY
    Catherine 205
HEICHEMER
    Charles H., S.J. 12, 238, 239, 253
HEIER
    Gottlieb 224
    Joanna 224
    Martha J. 218
HENRY
    Clement 259
    Elizabeth 163
    Emma Theresa 250
    John, S.J. 12, 132
    Mary Virginia 259
    Nicholas 250
HENSON
    Charity 253, 255
    Joseph Cephas 165
    Mary 165, 166
    Rachel 218, 219
    Robert Henry 219
HERMAN
    Augustine 89
    Ephraim 21
HERNDON
    John H. 277
HERON
    Elizabeth 112
    John 112
    Susanna 112
    Thomas 112
HERRENS
    Rosa 254
HERRIGAN
    Thomas 212
HERRING
    Abraham 109
    Charles 110
HESSEY
    Elizabeth 175
    Ellen 211
HEINTZ
    Charles 257, 260
    Eugene Jacob 256
    Jacob 256, 257, 260
    John 257
HEINZ
    Lizzie 257
HEINZELMAN
    Barbara 213
HELPEN
    John 214
    Mary 214
    Mary Jane 214
HELPERN
    Francis 212
    William 212
HENER
    Rose Marie 260
HENNESSY
    John 146
    Kate 249
    William 211
HENNISLEY
    John 205
HESSIGER
    Margaret 223
HESSY
    Ellen 159
    Susan 153
HEVELOW
    John Roderick 142
    Roderick 142
HEVERIN
    Abraham 102
    Alice 107
    Alize 102, 103
    Barbara 103, 110, 116
    Charles 100, 102, 107, 116, 119, 120
    David 151, 175
    Elizabeth 102, 103, 133
    Esther 137
    George 132, 137
    Hannah 100, 119
    Isaac 103, 109, 138
    James 153
    James Morgan 153
    Jan 153
    John 109, 182
    Margaret 116, 156
    Polly 109, 110
    Rebecca 132, 137
    Rebecca Ann 137
    Samson 102
    Sara Jane 141, 142
    Sarah 100, 102, 109, 120
    Stephen Hill 137, 138, 156
    Steven 103
    Susan 119, 151, 175
    Thomas 23
    William 23, 24, 26, 27, 43, 100
HEYER
    Estelle 257
    Joseph Chandler 257
    Peter 257
HICKEY
    Charles 208
    John, S.J. 176
    John Francis 136
    J.L. 215
    Mary 220
    Patrick 211, 220, 286
HICKY
    Charles 211, 214
    Honora 213
    Mary 215, 220
    Michael 213
    Patrick 215
HIDERER
    Josephine 222
HIGGINS
    Patrick 92
HIGLER
    Francis Xavier 211
    Joanne 211
    John 215
    Joseph 214
    Margaret 214, 216
    Otilia 214
HILBERT
    Helen May 323
HILL
    Ann 199, 200
    Betsy 205
    Mary 175
    William 43, 195
HILSEN
    Isaac 153
HINSON
    Christy 223, 225
    Henry 142
    Jane 142
    John 142
    Peter 157
HIRONS
    John S., S.J. 135
HIRST
    Gotlieb 223
HISSORY
    Mary 200
HOBBS
    Laura Jane 156
    W.G. 159
    William 159
HOBSON

Index of Persons

John B. 317
HODGSON
  Thomas, S.J. 12, 19, 20, 21, 52
HODEN
  James 213
  Thomas 213
HOECKEN
  Anthony 205
HOECKEY
  Catherine 208
HOGAN
  Daniel 140
  Jeremiah 100, 121
HOHEY
  Margaret 164
HOHMAN
  Martin 256, 259
  Otto 256
HOLDEN
  James 201
  Michael 201
HOLDIN
  James 208
  Michael 199, 208
HOLFER
  John 157
HOLIDAY
  Mary 166, 198
  Richard 166, 198, 210
  Sarah Joanne 210
  Thomas 166, 198
HOLLAHAN
  Cornelius 23, 37, 44, 49
  John 43
HOLLAND
  Bridget 204
  Winnie 204
HOLLERAN
  Frank 203
HOLLINGSWORTH
  Henry 42
  James 263
  Jonathan 263
  Louisa 262
  William 261
  William Sanders 261
HOLMES
  Celia 103
  Robert 103
HOLTEN
  Mildred 303
HOLTON
  Francis Scully 308
HOLTZ
  George 207
  John 207
HOLZ
  Emmanuel 212
HOMEN
  George 223
  Maria Louisa 223
HOOKEY

Anthony 204
HOOVER
  Herbert, Pres. 214
  Rose 304
  Sarah 265
HOPKINS
  Ann 142
  Charles 142
  Edward Jones 136, 138, 140, 142
  Edward George 138
  Elizabeth 136
  Elizabeth Jones 305
  Esther Ann 140
  George 5, 304
  Mary 144, 145
HOPPE
  Katherina 305
HORAN
  David 215
  John 215, 220
  Mary 213
HOREN
  Richard 215
  Thomas 215
HORGAN
  Hugh 223
  John 147
  Michael 147
HORN
  John 205
  Margarate 205
  Mary 205
  Richard 205
HORNE
  Elizabeth 213
  Richard 213
HORNING
  Polly 116
HORSEY
  Henny Ann 256, 257
  Outerbridge 172
HOUGHTON
  Anne 206
HOUSTON
  Maria 216
  Mary 213, 216, 217, 223, 224
  Mary Ann 216
HOVER
  Rose 262
HORST
  Catherine 261
  Mary Catherine 211
HUBER
  Paul F. O.S.B. 280
HUCHARDSON
  Andrew 164
  Mary Johanna 164
HUCHESON
  Anthony 164
HUD
  Mary 204

Sam 204
HUEY
  I. Frank 277
HUGH
  Mole 119
HUGHES
  Ann 211, 216
  Ann Elizabeth 211
  Mary 157
  Sarah 320
HUGHSTON
  Anne 204
HUGLER
  Ann Elizabeth 223
  Joseph 223
  Otilia 219, 246, 250, 252
  Sara 246, 249
  Sophia 213
HUNT
  Ellen 157
  James 157
HUNTER
  Francis Xavier ß
  George, S.J. 36
  Susan 212
  William, S.J. 14, 21
HURLEY
  Daniel, O. Praem. 310
  John 208
  Margaret 208, 213
  Mary 208
HURST
  John A. 222
  Margaret Virginia 222
HUSFIELD
  Keziah 248
HUSSEY
  Edward 205
HUSTON
  Ellen 205
  Mary 211, 212, 215
HUTCHING
  Barnabas 157
HUTCHINSON
  Andrew 201, 206, 302
  Martha 220
  Martha Mary 215
  Mary Ellen 201
  Rachel 201, 206
  Thomas 206
  William 215, 305
HYDEN
  Elizabeth 221
HYLAND
  Nicholas 39
HYLE
  Michael W. Bishop 283, 287
HYMON
  Charity 250
HYNES
  John F. 277
  John P. 313

I

INNES
 Mary 211
IRVIN
 James 100
 Robert 102
ISAACS
 Elizabeth 318
ISLEY
 Mary 207

J

JACK
 Matthew John 324
JACKSON
 Elizabeth 100
 Isaac 105
 James 91
 Joseph 105
 Tilphman 110
JAMARY
 William 153
JAMES
 Ann 216, 222
 Catherine 219
 Charles 204, 218
 Eliza 218, 222
 James T. 219
 Lewisa 219
 Louisa 222
 Mary Alice 214
 William Henry 204
JANNICK
 Clementine A. 324
 Louis P. 324
JARRELL
 Alexander 261
 George 261
 Mary 261
JEFFERSON
 Henrietta 144, 145
JENKINS
 Jeremiah 218
 Mary 213
 William 218
JEROME
 William 147
JOHN
 John Paul II, Pope 5
 Thomas 220
JOHNS
 Harriet 214
 Molly 100, 121
JOHNSON
 Alfred 264
 Catherine 202, 306
 Charles Bernard 325
 Charles Hamilton 325
 Doris Kelly 326
 Elizabeth 260
 George 260
 Hannah 157
 Henry 218
 John 218
 Margaret 260
 Rachel 303
 Richard 184, 217, 221, 255
 Samuel 157
 Sarah Mary 157, 264
 William 221
JOHNSTON
 Agnes R. 165
JOICE
 Ellen 205
 Martin 205
JONES
 Adeline 256
 Ann Willson 221
 Anna 139
 Amanda 218
 Araminta 141
 Caroline 217
 Catherine Jane 144
 Clara Elizabeth 147
 David 37, 40
 Edmond 256
 Edwin 321, 325
 Elizabeth 144, 304, 321
 George 283
 Harriett 147, 159, 165, 216, 223
 Henrietta 217
 Hugh 27, 29, 35, 40
 John 144, 157
 John Hiram 159
 Richard 155, 157, 159
 Robert T. 283
 Solomon 43, 102, 103, 110
 Stephen 144
 Suzanna 141
 Tom 147
 William 144
JORDAN
 Michael 211
 Patrick 211
JOSEPH
 Charles Robert 254
 Eva 257
 John Martin 254, 257
JOYCE
 Michael 213
JUNKER
 Margaret 220
 Mary Ann 220
JUSTAISCE
 Elizabeth 248

K

KABERSKI
 Edward L. 328
KANE
 Ellen 205
 Francis 92
 Lawrence 147
KANTHING
 Mary Simmons 205
KANTZ
 Catherine 205
 Fred 205
 Petronella 213
 Sylvester 205
KANZ
 Fridolin 207, 219
 John 219
 Mary 207
 Manelille 204
 Sylvester 204
KAPP
 Michael 246
KARKITE
 James 175
KARLON
 Stanley Ignatius 324, 325
KARMIESCHUK
 Alex 308
KATEN
 Amy 202
 James 204
 Jane 215, 216
 Mary 204
 Winnie 208
KATES
 Frances 255, 256, 262
KATLEY
 D. 158
KAUTZ
 Francis 217
KAVANAUGH
 Catherine 140
KEAN
 Margaret 105
KEARNE
 Ellen 220
 John 220
KEARNS
 James 217
 James Edward 217
KEARNEY
 Francis 202
 Thomas 202
KEATH
 Edward 147
KEATING
 Elizabeth 154
 Margaret Ann 154
 Michael 154
KEDES
 Elizabeth 246
KEEFE
 Arthur T. 315, 326
 Lorraine 325
KEEGAN
 James 304
 Margaret 265
KEELEY
 Anne 206

Index of Persons

Bridget 206
John 206
Thomas 206
KEELY
  Bridget 211
  James 211
  Margaret 211
  Michael 211
KEENAN
  Catherine 211
  Matilda Mary 202
  Michael 202, 208
KEENE
  Ann 157
  John R. 159
  Priscilla 158
  Richard 157
  Thomas H. 159
KEHELER
  Catherine 208
KEILEY
  Benjamin, Bishop 239
  Michael 202, 209
KEISER
  George 247
  Louise 247
  Stephen 247
KEITH
  John 105
KELEGAN
  Morris 119
KELEGOM
  Morris 100
KELL
  Anne 203
  James 175
KELLEY
  Anne 203
  James 175
  John 147
  Mary 208
KELLY
  Anne 204, 208
  Catherine 211, 212, 214, 224
  Hugh 144
  Mary Jane 226
KEMPSKI
  Leonard, Rev. 295
KENARDLY
  Ann 175
  John 175
  Margaret 175
KENNARD
  Emma 217
  E.J. 222
  Jane E. 217, 218, 219
KENNEDY
  Catherine 205, 206
  Daniel 202
  David 205
  Dorothy 259
  Henrietta J. Hill 156

Joannah 202
John 206
Michael 206, 220
Sarah 218
Thomas 233, 265
William F. 259, 265
KENNEY
  Hugh 144, 175
  Margaret 144, 175
KENNY
  Dorothy 212
  Michael 144
  Patrick, Rev. 91, 92, 130, 134, 135
  Peter, S.J. 136, 147, 148, 150, 174, 177
KENRICK
  Francis Patrick, Abp. 187, 188, 190, 191, 193, 208
KERDES
  Elizabeth 247
  Rosina 247
KERNAN
  Mary 207
KERRIGAN
  Bridget 142
KERTZ
  Manilla 207
KEY
  Bridget 201
  Richard 44
KIDD
  Agnes 145
KIEFFER
  Nicholas 226
KILKOFF
  August Dreka 250
  Eva 250
  Geoffrey 250
  Lewis George 250
KILLEN
  Catherine 144
KILLGOAR
  Rebecca 214
KILMARTIN
  James 215
KILT
  Susan 208
KILTY
  Dennis 223
  Elizabeth 223
KIMLIN
  Mary 212
KINCAID
  James 315
KINDLE
  Horace James 156
  Stephen 156
KING
  Ann Elizabeth 141, 144
  Bridget 200
  Caroline Elizabeth 226, 253

Charles, S.J. 153, 180, 181, 184
Christian 226
George, S.J. 12, 141, 144, 153, 154, 159, 160, 163, 167, 180, 181
KINGDOM
  John S.J. 12
KINZ
  Manilla 207
KIPP
  Catherine 165
KIRCHMAN
  Joseph 212
  Maria 212
KIRCHNER
  John 233
  Joseph 215
  Mary 216
KIRIVAN
  John 203
KIRK
  Mary 200
  Pauline Price 318
  Robert A. 308
  William A. 253
  William M. 253
KIRKIN
  Mary 224
KLEIBER
  Alois 217
  Aloysius 222, 246
  Christine 217
  Francis 222
  Mary 234
  Michael 246
KLEVENCE
  John, Rev. 296
KLIBER
  Lewis 217
  Rosalia 216
KNIGHT
  Family 112-113
  Catherine (Kitty) 25, 46, 86, 87, 224
  John Leach 46, 86, 87
  William 25, 46, 87, 100
KNOELL
  Cusies 204
KNOTT
  Catherine 99, 102, 118
  Edward 99, 118
  Elizabeth 247
  Emma 258
  Frederick 258
  William 258
KNOTS
  Henry 269
KOERBEL
  Christina 218
KOLEGAN
  Nelly 119
KOMORA

Isaac 218
Wilhelmina 218
KORBEL
　Christina 226
KORMYER
　Carroll 219
　William 219
KOTYK
　Genevieve, O.S.B.M. 301
KRAETZLER
　Edward 264
KRAMER
　Paul Raymond 325
KRASTEL
　Annie 257
　Edith May 256
　Francis W., Sr. 262, 264, 276, 280, 282, 283, 285, 288, 290, 293, 294, 312, 313, 314, 318, 321, 322
　Francis W., Jr., Rev. 213, 294, 326
　Harold Jacob 256
　Harry 304
　Harry Joseph 261, 304
　Henry 257
　Jacob 256
　John 255, 256, 257, 262
　John F. 256
　John K. 257
　Maggie 257, 258, 259
　Margaret 258
　Mary Rose 244, 258
　William Andrew 255
　William J. 303
KRESTLE
　Adam 226
　Mary 226
KRISS
　Catherine 212
　Henry 212
KUTSZEJA
　John A. 322
KWASNIEWSKI
　Edward F. 325
　Henry J. 322
　Marion E. 324

L

LADEN
　Mary 263
LAFAYETTE
　Marquis de 47
LAFFERTY
　Dorothy 175
　Thomas 208
LAIDEN
　Mary 204
LA LUZERNE
　Chevalier 80
LAMB
　Eleanor 105

Eugenia 255
Kate J. 260
LAMBE
　Virginia F. 254
LAMBERT
　Anton 250, 252
　George 246
　Margaret Jane 246
　Mary 250, 252
　Sarah 216
LAMBORN
　Benjamin F. 304
LANCASTER
　Charles 166
　Ignatius 158
　Sara Jane 165
LANE
　Ines 212
　Joanne 211
　Timothy 212
LANG
　John 261
LANGLER
　Ann Marie 211
LAPAIRE
　Marguerite 158
　Rainé 158
LAPIRI
　Victor 200
LAREY
　Lawrence 116
　Mary 116
　Thomas 116
LARKIN
　Alexander 175
　Catherine 175
　Henry 206
　John 140, 213
　Margaret 207
　Mary 214
　Michael 140, 175
　Patrick 206
LARRIMORE
　Debora 157, 158
　Mary 158
LARY
　Bridget 216
LATROBE
　Benjamin 89, 121
LATTA
　Biola G. 307
LATTOMUS
　Thomas 283
LAUFTIS
　Bridget 206
LAVERTY
　Rosa 223
LAVERY
　Eliza 203
LAWLER
　Bridget 212
LAWLESS

Thomas, O.S.F.S. 311
LEA
　George T. 247
　Louis D. Hopkins 247
　Susan T. 247
LEAHY
　Amelia 137
　Jeremiah 220
LEARNER
　Bridget 204
　Thomas 204
LEARY
　Arthur 250
　Catherine 248, 250
　Elizabeth 105
　Ellen 205, 220
　John 206
　Lawrence 165
　Leonard 112
　Mary 112, 250, 254, 256
LEE
　Family 171
　Barbara 100, 111, 119
　David 133, 135
　Eliza 172
　Elizabeth 133
　George T. 247
　Harry 321
　Helen 172
　John B. 302
　Louis D. Hopkins 247
　Mary 138
　Mary 302
　Patty 133, 308
　Rachel 90, 110
　Richard 110
　Sala 120
　Sarah 99
　Thomas Sims 112
　William 110, 133, 172
LEEK
　Anna 145
　Elizabeth 145
　John 145
LEICH
　Ann 107
LEINHEISER
　Edward M. Rev. 311
LEONARD
　Edward 175
LEPIERE
　Generosa 246
LERIHILE
　Edward 246
　Elizabeth 246
　Joseph 246
LESCHIERE
　Sara V. 260
LESTRANGE
　Michael 175
LEVERIDGE
　Benjamin 260

Benjamin Joseph 261
Clarence 269
Elma 260
Emma Mary 261
Mary Elizabeth 269
Ollie Mary 260
LEWIS
Constance 216
Deborah 165
John, S.J. 11, 12, 35, 41, 44, 47, 49, 58, 67, 80
Sara Jane 158, 166
LEYBOLD
Katherine 304
LIBOLD
Becky 304
LIBRE
Francis Victor Prosper 200
Prosper 158, 207
LIDDY
Richard 157
LIGHT
Anne 200
John 200
John Thomas 200
Nicholas 200
LILLY
Amelia 202
Dick 202
Henry C. 259
Mary Cora 259
Mary Ellen 158
Richard J. 158, 166
Sally 243
Sam 202
Sarah 199
LILY
Sara 248
LINCH
Hugh 37
Peregrinus 175
LINCOLN
Abraham, Pres. 188, 192, 199, 229
LINDSEY
Harry L. 280
LINKHORN
Mary 100
LIONS
Abby 206
Elizabeth 213
Joanna 201, 211
Mary 201
Sara 212
LITTLE
John 110
Prudence 110
Temperance 110
LIVERS
Arnold, S.J. 64
LLOYD
Catherine Rosalia 255

Henrietta Maria 27
Henrietta Maria II 25
John 239, 255, 256, 257, 260
John Edward 260
Mary Ellen 257
Pearl F. 256
LOBASEWICZ
John J. 322
LOCKAY
John 214, 215
LOCKMAN
John 204, 207, 216
LOCKWOOD
Addie 256, 260
Adelaide 261
Adelaide Grace 253
Blanche 255, 258
Blanche 261, 262, 264
Edward 235, 246
Edward William 222, 250, 251, 254
George 113, 256
George H. 256
George Ignatius 254
George J. 243
George W. 249, 253, 254, 255
George Washington 302
Grace Alrichs 251
Grace 250
Harry 259
Harry W. 305
James 269
James B. 264
Julia E. Morton 255
Julia Elizabeth Morton 264
M. 270
Mary 195, 246
Mary 262, 263
Mary Nora 226, 243, 250
Mary T. 305
Mary Theresa 248
Richard 246
Sara Elizabeth 224
LONDEY
John 27
LONGAN
James 146
LONGFELLOWS
E.A. 157
LOOBY
Andrew 102
Elizabeth 102
Patrick 102
LOSTEN
Basil Bishop 296, 300, 326
LOTRINGER
Caroline 195
Christina 226
Gregory 219
Nicholas 217, 218, 226
William 217
LOTSINGER

Christina 246
Nicholas 246
LOUGHERY
John 218
LOUGHLAN
Ann Marie 201
LOURENSO
Antoneo 305
LOVE
William R. 320
LOWBER
Daniel 75
Matthew 32
Peter 32
LOWE
Milcah 156
LOWNEY
Catherine 200
LUBER
Margaret 211
LUCAS
Anna 265
Annie 266
Augustus 266
Charles 266
Ethel C. 265
Francis 302
Francis E. 302
George 251, 256, 257
George H. 263, 265, 302
James F.M., S.J. 163
John C. 304
Joseph 304
Magdalen 265
Mary Pauline 257
Sara 261
Thomas 259
Thomas 261
Thomas Francis 264
William 258
William 302, 304
William H. 256
LUCEY
John 200
LUDWIG
Edward J. III 289, 290, 321
LUPILL
Ellen B. 159
James P. 159
LUSBIE
Augusta 206
Laura 199
Robert 201
Virginia 201
LUSBY
Anne 119, 212, 214
Augusta 217
Catherine 222, 226, 246
Craddock 199
John 133, 137, 138, 141
Mary Elinore 165
Mary Ellen 156, 165, 219

Thomas 156, 165, 219
William T. 302, 303
LUTHERANGER
  Nicholas 220
LUTHERINGER
  Lizzie 260
  Nicholas 260
  William 260
  William Nicholas 260
LUTRINGER
  Elizabeth 219
  Nicholas 219
  Nicholas 305
LYLE
  Anna 261
  Charles Robert 257
  George 260
  James Polke 261
  John Thompson 256
  Mary Paul 258
  Peter 259
  Sara M. 261
  Sarah 258, 259
  William 256, 259
  William 261
LYMAN
  Edward Dwight, Rev. 190, 209
LYNAM
  Ellen B. 216, 226
LYNCH
  Anna 110
  Edward 175
  John, Msgr. 308
  Mary 140, 142, 219
  Morris 219
LYONS
  Anne 204
  Bartholomew 110
  Charles W. S.J. 212
  Catherine 205
  Daniel 205
  Dennis 220
  James 100
  Margaret Butler 159
  Mary 145
  Patrick 26, 43, 205
  Sarah 205

M

MACKEY
  David 148
  Robert E. 317
MACKIN
  Patrick 220
MADDEN
  George 213
  Henry 213
  Rebecca 213
MAGDY
  Mary 214
  Patrick 214

MAGEE
  Arthur 141
  Frances 259
  James 147
  John 259
  Patrick 200
  Sara 259
MAGHAN
  Michael Stephen 325
MAGILLY
  Annie E. 259
MAGINN
  Martha 91
  Paul 92
MAGINNIS
  Ellen 201, 203
  Margaret 203
  Peter 201
  William 201
MAGOFF
  Alice 219
MAGRA
  Martin 199, 201
  Mary 199, 201
MAGRAK
  Ellen 205
MAGRAW
  Martin 202
MAGUINNEGAN
  Mary 205
MAGUINNEY
  Edward 200
  Mary 200
MAGUIRE
  Elizabeth 202
  George 99, 118
  Margaret 218
  Peter 218
  Thomas 92
MAGUNNIGER
  Dennis 200, 203
  Margaret 200
MAHAN
  Arthur 144
  John 220
MAHEGAN
  Arthur 215
  Jeremiah 215
MAHER
  Bridget 221
MAHONEY
  Catherine 226
  Francis 206
MAIR
  Michael 175
MAITLAND
  John F. 158
  Thomas 165
MAKEFALL
  Stephen 119
MAKIN
  John 202

Patrick 151-159, 166, 199, 207, 208
MALLAIX
  Bridget 175
MALLON
  Henry 142
MALLOY
  Frances 203, 204
  Lawrence, Rev. 192
MALONE
  James 219
MALONEY
  Andrew 250
  Catherine 201, 250
  Dennis 249, 255, 256
  Ellen 205, 249
  Frances Pearson 304
  James 249, 256
  Joanna 269
  John 307, 308, 313, 314
  John Patrick 256
  Joseph F. 255
  Leo F. 323
  Leo Michael 325
  Patrick 304
MALONY
  John 213
  Michael 213
MALSBERGER
  Augustine 208
  Katherine E. 263
  Margaret 263
  Mary E. 255
MALSBURGER
  Augustine 205, 212
  Joseph 175
  Mary Emma 212
  Thomas 205
MAN
  Lydia Mary 213
  Thomas 213
MANAGAN
  Patrick 146
MANES
  Anne 205
MANEY
  Catherine 208
  James 206
  Patrick 206
MANGERN
  Patrick 220
MANLOVE
  Amelia B. 317
  Anna 253, 305
  Catherine 253
  Catherine Theresa 246
  John 246
  John C. 221, 225, 256, 257, 261
  John Henry 246, 308
  Laura 256
  Margaret 208, 209
  Mary 225, 249

Index of Persons **361**

MANLY
  John James 175
MANN
  Oswell 220
  Patrick 220
MANNAN
  Catherine 216
MANNERS
  Matthew, S.J. 11, 12, 23, 41, 44, 60
MANNING
  Catherine 208, 225
  Ellen 259
MANNON
  Catherine 220
MANRY
  James 175
MANSELL
  Thomas, S.J. 12, 16, 19, 20, 23, 51, 283
MARA
  Margaret 215
MARDAGA
  Thomas J., Bishop 287, 288, 290, 292
MARÉCHAL
  Ambrose, S.S., Archbp. 12, 81, 84-89, 109, 133, 135, 137, 139, 143
MARLEY
  James 221
MARLIN
  Henry 142
MARLSBURGER
  Augustine 202
  Catherine 202
  Elizabeth 204
MARSH
  Ada Rose 257
  Agnes 2265
  Alban 269
  Alice E. 305
  E. 265, 303
  Elias Eccleston 257, 258, 305, 262, 263, 266
  Ellen M. 257
  Elsie 244, 265, 304
  Elva Eccleston 262
  Estella A. 304
  Francis D. 265-7, 270
  Goldin 251
  H.E. 257
  Henry K. 243
  Hilda 265
  John J. Eccleston 262, 269
  Margaret Eliza 265, 270
  Paul 263, 269, 303
  Royden 257, 265
  Stella 258, 265
MARSHALL
  John 145
  Mary 102

MARTIN
  Alexander 201
  Bridget 205
  Clara 201
  Earl Hugh 328
  Edward 158
  Elva 147
  Henry 139
  James 120
  John 151, 153, 201, 202, 204, 206, 218
  John James 204
  Joseph James 100, 218
  Margarita Laura 201
  Martha 218
  Mary 207, 208, 211, 213
  Mary Ann 213
  Mary Elizabeth 226
  Mary Theresa 212
  Patrick 153
  Peter Philip 201
  Thomas 139
MASLIN
  Martha 218
MASSE
  Richard 214
  Thomas 214
MASSEY
  Anne 156
MATIER
  Maria Elise 219
MATTHEWS
  Family 97, 98
  Catherine 46, 86
  Hugh 33, 45, 46
  James 46, 83, 84, 99, 118
  James V. 83, 84
  Lizzy 195
  William 45, 80, 83, 86, 118
MATYNIAK
  Bernard 299
  Bernard J. 300, 326
  Margaret 298, 299, 300
MAULSBURGER
  Mary 257
MAY
  Bertha 262
  Charles 209
  Ellen 209
  Henry 158
  Milton 151
MAYARD
  Anna 139
  Margaret 139
  Samuel 139
MEAGHER
  Dennis 213
  Martin 157
MEARS
  Anna 214
  Mary 214
MEEKIN

Matthew 182
MEEKINS
  Margaret 175
  Matthew 158, 159
  Priscilla 159
  Sara 158
MEGHAN
  James 144
MEGINNIS
  Margaret 202
MEIER
  Catherine 218
  Francisca 223
  Joseph 218, 220
MEIGAN
  James 144
MELDRUM
  Christina 225
MELSON
  R. 315
MELVIN
  Ann 224
  Bridget 224
MENINGER
  Robert Adam 328
MEREDITH
  Anastasia 105
  James 105
MERLINI
  John 216
MERRITT
  James Wilson 308
  Jane Wilson 266
  Joseph Wilson 266, 269
  Pauline 308
  Richard 266
  Samuel 221
MERRYCROFT
  Elizabeth 145
  William 145
MESSER
  Josephine 213
  Michael 213
METZINGER
  Adeline 213
MEURER
  John B., S.J. 264
MEYER
  Edward N. 321
  Frances 264
  Henry 264
  James 322
  Josephine 264
  Mildred A. 323
MEYERS
  Frances 262
  Robert Charles 325
  Suzan 145
  Suzanne 261
MIDDIFIELD
  Louisa 204
MIFFLIN

Adelaide Morton 261
Edward L. 259, 260, 261, 262
Ellen M. 262
Rachel 259
MILLEGAN
　Maria 139, 142
MILLER
　Catherine C. 211
　Charles C. 305
　Christian 211
　Edward 175
　John 158, 253
　Sophia 251
MILNAN
　Bridget 213
MILON
　James 142
MILTON
　Isaac 151
MISER
　Joseph 216
　Margaret 216
　Michael 216
MITCHELL
　Ann 90, 124
　Bennett 156, 157, 158
　Caroline 155
　Charles B. 159, 161
　Charles J. 154, 155
　Henry S. 157, 161
　James 90, 124
　Joseph 90, 121, 124, 135
　Laura Anna 135
　Maria L. 159
　Martha Louise 155
　Mary Anna 135
　Mary Horsey 154
　Sara Maria 90, 124
　Sophia 90, 124
MITTON
　Isaac 147
MOBBERLY
　Joseph, S.J. 133
MOCKEN
　William 202
MOFFETT
　Catherine 308
　Edna 308
　George R. 317
　John P. 304
　Lawrence David 325
　Margaret 304
　Margaret Augusta 325
　Marie 324
　Mary 253
　Mary E. 308
　Thomas J. 317
　William 321
　William Henry 250
MOFFITT
　Agnes 212
　Anna 211

Edward 271
Ellen 271
Ellen 307
George 141, 305, 307
John 307
Margaret 305
Mary 307
William H. 221, 271
MOGURN
　Catherine 145
MOLEN
　James 146
MOLITOR
　Catherine 256
　Edward 257, 259, 260, 261, 264, 304
　Edwin J. 257
　Ella 257
　Ellen 258
　Francis 256, 257, 259
　Genevieve 211
　George 259
　Henry Edward 264
　John 259, 260
　Magdalena 261
　Mary Frances 259
　Susan 257
　Susannah 255, 256, 257, 260
　William 244, 262
MOLLEN
　William 202
MOLLON
　Dennis 246
MOLONEY
　Dennis 200
　Ellen 201
　Francis 201, 220
　John A. 276, 277
　Julia 214
　Mary 200
MOLONY
　Catherine 207
　Hannah 144
　Frank 207
　John 207
　Mary 207
　Thomas 207
MOLTON
　Adelaide 249
MOLYNEUX
　Richard, S.J. 28, 31, 56
　Robert, S.J. 12, 49, 79, 80, 81, 102
MONAGHAN
　John J., Bishop 245, 269, 270, 271, 272, 304
MONEY
　Alexander 250
　Honored 139, 142, 143
　Mabel 272
　Mary 250
　Rosalie 217

Rose 226
MONNELLY
　James, Rev. 154, 165
MONSIEUR
　Christina 105, 119
MONTGOMERY
　Catherine Lilly 257
　Viola 259
　Washington 256, 257, 259
MOODY
　Alex Victor 264
　Charles 158, 159
　David J. 325
　Wallace 264
MOONEY
　Abe 249
　Alexander 250, 254, 257, 264, 305
　Alice 305
　Anna 256, 269
　Daniel 201
　Elizabeth Joy 257, 269, 305
　Harriett 222
　John 222
　Michael 145
　Rosalind 222
　Rose 195, 256
　Rose Ann 201, 246
　Thomas 256, 269
MOORE
　Catherine 247, 305
　Charles 251
　Ellen Jane 215
　Francis 253, 258
　George Thomas 221, 247, 253
　Harriet 256
　John Henry 247
　Maria 213
　Mary Catherine 247
MORAN
　Margaret 259, 265
MORE
　George 226
　George Thomas 226
　John 220
MORGAN
　Arabella 246, 248, 249, 253
　Bertha 244, 262, 265
　Charles 262
　Patrick 206
　Sapora 262
MORIARITY
　Charles 258
　James 258
　Lily 265
　Lizzie 260
　Mary Devine 250
MORIN
　Joseph 233
MORKEN
　Daniel 208
　William 208

Index of Persons

MORRIS
  Ann 114
  Bradford 248
  Catherine 223
  David 144
  Devine 251
  Emilia 223, 224
  George W. 195, 221
  James 141
  Laura Virginia 248
  Madeline 260
  Maria 195, 224, 226
  Mary 302
  Matthew 223, 224
  Peter, S.J. 44
  Washington 223
MOLONEY
  Dennis 200
  Ellen 201
  Francis 201, 220
  Julia 214
  Mary 200
MOLONY
  Catherine 207
  Frank 207
  Hannah 144
  John 207
  Mary 207
  Thomas 207
MOLTON
  Adelaide 249
MOLYNEUX
  Richard, S.J. 28, 31, 56
  Robert, S.J. 12, 49, 79, 80, 81, 102
MONAGHAN
  John J., Bishop 245
MONEY
  Alexander 250
  Elizabeth 304
  Honored 139, 142, 143
  Mary 250
  Rosalie 217
  Rose 226, 302
MONNELLY
  Rev. 154
MONSIEUR
  Christina 105, 119
MONTGOMERY
  Catherine Lilly 257
  Viola 259
  Washington 256, 257, 259
MOODY
  Charles 158, 159
MORAN
  Margaret 302
MORGAN
  Bertha 304
  Edward 222
  Margaret E. 222
MORIARITY
  James T. 305
  Lily 302, 303
MORTLAND
  Cecelia 135
  John 135
  Maria Helene 135
MOSLEY
  Joseph, S.J. 37, 43, 45, 76, 286
MORTON
  Adelaide 209, 211, 224, 247, 253, 254, 255
  Adelia 217
  Adeline 214
  Arthur 213, 224
  Bessie 257
  Edward C. 254
  Ellen 260
  Frank 175
  Helen 219, 235, 254, 255, 257, 259, 261
  Henry 213, 219, 261, 262
  Henry Clement 209
  Julia Elizabeth 217, 235, 249, 262, 305
  Margaret 213
  Mary 158, 204, 207, 217, 238, 248, 249, 256, 262
  May L. 257, 259
  Mrs. Hamilton 253
  William 195, 249
  Wilson 165
MORTON
  Hamilton 113, 158, 165, 175, 204, 207, 213, 217, 239, 248, 257, 279
MOSS
  Charles 212
  Jane 251
  Joanne 212
MOTRI
  Mary E. 226
MOULTON
  Kevin 300
MOUTHRIE
  Elizabeth 211
MOYNIHAN
  James, Rev. 12, 130, 135, 140
  Timothy 304
MOZELESKI
  Richard David 325
MOZCIESKI
  Frances Whitlock 321
MRATZ
  John 212
  Margaret Crescentia 212
MULBERGER
  Amelia 307
MULCHANOCK
  Patrick 210
MULHERINE
  Mary Jane 163
MULHRIE
  Marie Elizabeth 216
MULHULRANE
  James 157
MULLAN
  Archibald 249
  Charles 249
  Francis 249
  Margaret 207
MULLEN
  Ann 204, 246
  Anna 220
  Archy 223
  Charles 246, 305, 317
  Charles Glen 206
  Daniel 206, 220, 305
  Frank 308
  James 175, 223, 313, 315
  John 276, 277, 303, 305, 308
  Margaret 305, 308
  Mary 206, 215, 220
  Marianna 321
  Patrick 223
  Rose M. 317
  Thomas 100, 120
MULLENS
  Anne 221
  Mary 221
MULLER
  Esther K. 324
  Frank J. 321
  Mary Catherine 226
  Mary Sophia 236
  Theresa 328
  William 226
MULLIGAN
  Eva 261
  Emma 264
  Helen 264
  James 214, 264
  Mary 214, 261, 262
  Michael 259
  Patrick J. 260
  Peter 175
  Rose Ann 140
  Theresa 262
MULLIN
  Daniel 221
  James 221
  Margaret 221
MULNIGERIE
  Sara 175
MULVEE
  Robert E., Bishop 292, 293, 294, 296, 297, 326, 327
MURPHY
  Anne 203, 206, 214
  Catherine 144
  Chrisfield 222
  Elizabeth 208
  Ellen 204
  Francis Wolf 222
  Hannah 220

Henrietta Aloysia 246
Hugh 214
James 43
Jeremiah 214
Joanna 203, 212
John 219
John J., S.J. 239
Joseph P., S.J. 308
Julia 203, 204, 208, 211
Margaret 206, 213, 214
Mary 163, 208, 211, 213
Mary Ann 206, 208
Patrick 139, 142, 206, 213, 214, 226
Stephen 92
Thomas H.T. 217, 222, 246
William Barr 217
MURPHEY
 Elizabeth Jane 202
 William 202
MURRAY
 Abraham 162
 Adam 216
 Alias 222
 Andrew 163, 206
 Anna 253
 Ann Rebecca 216
 Charlotte Ann 163
 Charlotte Rosalie 215, 216
 Cornelius 304
 Daniel 162, 215, 218
 Ellen 249, 253, 304, 305
 Francis 249, 250, 254
 George 306
 James 254
 John 249, 250, 308
 John Francis 304
 Joseph 272
 Lawrence 220
 Leo Charles 324
 Lydia 222
 Margaret 249, 304, 317
 Mary Ann 155
 Richard 218
 Teresa Ann 218
 Thomas 205
MURRY
 Adam 221
 Anne Frances 226
 Catherine 211
 Daniel 216, 223
 Emilia 223
 Frances 221, 224, 226
 Francis 302
 Henrietta 222
 Henry 211
 James 303
 John 211, 214, 221
 Mary 214, 218, 223
 Mary Catherine 224
 Rose 219
 Thomas 159, 219, 226, 302

William Joseph 218
MURTHER
 Mary 206
MUSGROVE
 A.M. 286
MYER
 Marselina 257
MYERS
 Fannie 256
 Frances 261, 262
 Helen 258
 Mary 258
MC ALEER
 Carrie T. 305
 Hugh 302
 Mary Daisey 305
MC ALFEE
 Mary 211
MC ALISTER
 Anna 215
 Mary 215
 Robert 215
MC ALPIN
 James A. 324
 Joseph 325
MC AVOY
 Mary 213
MC BRIDE
 Amy 208
 Anna 211, 214, 216
 Catherine 220
 Daniel 201
 George 248
 Jane 206
 John 248
 William 92
MC CAFFERTY
 Anne 216, 221, 246, 248, 249
 Bernard 175, 221
 Catherine 175, 220, 246
 Francis 175
 J.C. 250
 Mary 221, 225, 246, 249, 256
MC CAFFERY
 Bernard 159
 James J. 314, 321
 John 157
MC CAFFREY
 Alice Marie 202
 Margaret 202
 Mary 201
 Patrick 202
MC CAFFRY
 Philip 144
 Thomas 175
MC CAIN
 Andrew 175
MC CAKE
 John 146
MC CALLISTER
 Charles John 223
 Dennis 217

James 206, 214, 216
Joseph 195
Joseph Henry 206
Margaret 195, 223
Mary 220, 223, 226, 249
Mary Elizabeth 214
Robert 206, 217, 223, 226
Roberta 221
MC CARDLE
 Catherine 110
 Peter 221
MC CARICK
 Richard 212
 William 212
MC CARTNEY
 John 202
MC CARTY
 Ann 211
 Dennis 213
 Elizabeth 217
 Ellen 215
 James 211, 215
 Margaret 215
MC CARTHY
 Elizabeth 215
 Ellen 215
 Eugene 215
 John 203, 205, 206
MC CARROLL
 Catherine 219
 Peter 217, 224
 Peter James 217
 Thomas 224
MC CAULEY
 Bernard 227
 Dennis 189, 195
MC CLAIN
 Agnes 261
 Louis 201
MC CLAMAN
 Bridget 221
 Daniel 221
MC CLANE
 Mary 220
 Thomas 220
MC CLARY
 Florence Pauline 304
 Helen E. 303
MC CLATCHY
 John H. 313
MC CLEAN
 Mary Jane 225
 Thomas 225
MC CLEESE
 Simon 147
MC CLELAND
 Jane 137, 138, 141, 142
MC CLEMENS
 Daniel 223
MC CLEMENT
 Bridget 226
MC CLEMENTS

Index of Persons

James 247
William 247
MC CLOCKLAN
  Bridget 202
MC CLOCKLIN
  Bridget 208
MC CLOGHLIN
  Sally 205
MC CLONE
  Arthur 146
MC CLOSKEY
  Anna Joanna 211
  Catherine 304
  James 211, 214, 220
  John 214
  Margaret 220
MC CLOSKY
  Charles John 217, 224
  James 224
MC COLT
  John 110
MC COMAS
  Sarah E. 224
MC CONAGHY
  Ann 216, 219, 226
MC CONECHY
  Rose 226
MC CONEGHY
  Ann 223
  Michael 247
  Rose 247
MC CORKLIN
  Bridget 200
MC CORMICK
  Anne 199
  Blair 272
  Blanche 273
  Catherine 145
  Catherine Elizabeth 202
  Grace 273
  Harry 273
  James 214
  John 142, 199
  Patrick 140, 202
  Peter 214
MC COY
  Harriett 156
  Michael 214
MC CRAY
  Charlotte 247
  Elizabeth 247
MC CREA
  Jacob 304
MC CREADY
  Bridget 100
  Dennis 92
MC CREEDY
  Elizabeth 131
  Francis 131
MC CUBBIN
  George 159
MC DERMOTT

Ann Catherine 212
Catherine 212
Charles 102
Eric 277
Hannah 102, 103
Patrick 212, 213
MC DONALD
  Hannah 102
  James, Rev. 311
  Woodrow 325
MC DONNAL
  Edward 203
  Ellen Agnes 203
MC DONNEL
  Edward 211
  Elizabeth 211
MC DONNELL
  Mary 214
MC DOWELL
  Mary 306
MC ENEMY
  Bernard 92
MC ENESTRY
  John 139, 142
MC ENTIRE
  Jane 204
MC EVENY
  Constantine 156
  Mary 156
MC FADDEN
  Hannah 201
  Leonard 251
  Mary 215
MC FALL
  Anna 100
MC FARLAND
  Ellen 215
MC GAINLEY
  George 213
  Mary 213
MC GAN
  John 175
MC GAW
  John 175
MC GEE
  Hugh 147
  John A., Msgr. 310
  William 140
MC GEOGAN
  William 215
MC GILLIS
  Bridget 155
MC GINNES
  Ellen 208
MC GINNIS
  Catherine 205
  John 219
  Mary 219
MC GIRR
  Ann 155
MC GLONIGAN
  Elizabeth 140

James 140
Mary 140
MC GOLDRICK
  Charles P., Rev. 12, 270, 303
MC GONAGLE
  Hugh 226
MC GONIGLE
  Hugh 221
MC GOVERN
  James 147
  Jane 204
  Patrick 146
MC GRIFF
  John 175
MC GRATH
  Ellen 210
  Helen 209, 214
  James 209
  Martin 210
  Mary 210
  Michael 210
  Mr. 166
MC GROARTY
  William 298
MC GROGAN
  Mary 223
MC GRUGAN
  Ellen 220
MC GUIRE
  James 141, 199
  Margaret 214
  Martin 214
  Patrick 175
  Robert Alexander 141
MC GUNNIGAN
  Dennis 211
  Edward 211
MC GUNNIGER
  Edward 202
MC HALE
  Mary 141
MC HUGH
  Susan 144
MC INTIRE
  John 139, 142, 143
MC KAN
  Margaret 145
MC KANN
  John 175
MC KATIN
  Veronica 211
MC KAY
  Bridget 203
MC KEE
  Charles 249
  Daniel 222
  Elizabeth 218
  Hannah 222
  John 200, 218
  John James 249
  Mary 218, 222, 226
  Susan 221

William 218
MC KENNA
   Thomas 299
MC KEROB
   Eliza 200
MC KERVAN
   Mick 116
MC KIM
   Patrick 164, 165, 166
MC KING
   Matthew 175
MC KINSEY
   Charlotte 105
   Kennard 105
MC KLOSKY
   James 213
   Mary 213
MC KULLY
   Jane 200
MC LAIN
   Mary 211
MC LANE
   David 218
   John 175
   Thomas 218, 222
MC LAUGHLAN
   Sarah 207
MC LAUGHLIN
   John 175
   John P. Rev. 12, 285, 286, 287
   Thomas 102
MC LEAN
   Mary Ann Marsh 161
   William 161
MC LUNCHAN
   Amy 217
MC MAHON
   Alice 217
   Ann 217
   Ellen Catherine 226
   Elizabeth 265
   John 216, 217, 219, 223, 226
   Mary 205, 214, 242
   Patrick 214
   Rose Ann 223
MC MAIKALL
   Margaret 249
MC MANUS
   Bernard J., Rev. 189, 190
   Daniel 146, 147
MC MICHAEL
   John 223
   Margaret 223
   Patrick 223
   William 223
MC MULLAN
   Anne 248, 250
   Jane 248, 249
MC MULLEN
   Jane 203, 248, 254
   Mary A. 249
MC MULLIN
   Anne 252
   Catherine 249
   Jane 249, 250, 252
   Ryan 249
MC NAMEE
   John 141
MC NARY
   Mary 145
MC NEAL
   Bridget 195
MC NEIL
   Alexander 221, 226, 241, 249
   Bridget 223, 249
MC NELTY
   Mary 145
MC NERHANY
   Alice 219
   James 219
   John 219
   Mary 219
MC NICLAS
   Patrick 214
MC NULTY
   Elizabeth 140
   John 140
   Margaret 140
MC PHELAN
   Catherine 175
MC PHERSON
   Thomas 217, 219
MC SHANE
   John 205, 214
   Mary Anne 205
MC SHERRY
   William, S.J. 147
MC WILLIAMS
   Anna 212
   Ellen 225

N

NAINDAIN
   Ann S. 249
NAUDAIN
   Andrew 156
   Mary 156
NAUGHTEN
   Mary 175
NAYLOR
   Leslie 305
NEA
   Thomas 208
NEAL
   Pierce 102
NEALE
   Benedict, S.J. 64
   Bennett 83
   Charles 34
   Clarence 265
   Edward 33
   Eliza 145
   Francis, S.J. 92, 131
   Henry, S.J. 31, 57
   Leonard, Archbp. 34, 129, 132, 133
   Martha 34
   Mary Agnes 265
   Patrick, Rev. 257
   Philip 145
   Richard 145
NEIDE
   John 102
   Michael 102
NEIL
   Hugh 37
NEILL
   Ann 103
NEINTZE
   John 248
NERY
   Bridget 224
   Jacob 145
   Thomas 224
NEWLIN
   Peter 296
NEWMAN
   Christopher 211
   John 211
   Raphael 258
   Remona 272
NEWSOME
   A. 195
   Martin 219
   Rachel 219
   S.A. 195
NEWTON
   John 203
NEY
   Thomas 206, 209
NICHOL
   Mary 211
NICHOLAS
   Margaret 145
NICHOLSON
   Anna 110
   Charles 110
   Mary 110
   Richard 110
   William 110, 111, 116
NIORDEN
   William 201
NOBLE
   William T. 221
NOLAN
   Bridget 221
NORRES
   James 200
   Thomas 200, 202
NORRIS
   Bridget 208
   James 208, 224
   Jeffrey 207
   Jeremiah Michael 207, 208
   Mary 208
   Thomas 207, 208

Index of Persons

NORTH
  Wiley J. 317
NORTON
  Anne C. 323
NOTA
  Leonard, S.J. 192, 221
NOWLAND
  Family 46
  Ann 91, 94, 96, 137, 138, 139, 142
  Bridget 100, 116, 119
  Catherine 103
  Desmond 46
  Elias 46
  Elizabeth 102, 115
  Gilbert 46
  James 140, 175
  Jesse 110, 116, 119
  John 46
  Margaret 140
  Mary 90, 116, 120, 132, 138, 139
  Mary Brady 175
  Michael 175
  Sally 116
  Stephen 100, 116
  Sylvester 100, 105, 110, 120, 136, 137, 175
  Thomas 116, 120, 138, 139, 175
  William 175
NUGENT
  Catherine 102
  Hannah 102
  Margaret 116
  Mary 102, 175
  Mola 100
  Peter 103, 119

O

O'BRIEN
  Darby 213
  Dennis 164
  Ellen 199, 201, 213
  Margaret 213
  William 199
O'CALNON
  Margarate 203
O'CONAR
  William 100
O'CONNELL
  Catherine 160
  Patrick J., S.J. 262, 264
O'CONNOR
  Catherine G. 317, 322
  Eleanor S. 328
  Francis J. 317
  Margaret 144, 145
  Martin 110
  John, Rev. 234
O'CONOR
  Beet 206
  Cornelius 203
  Denis 203
  Jeremiah 206
  John 204
  Martin 205
  Mary 205
  Mary Ellen 204
  Richard 204
  William Henry 119
O'DANIELL
  Margaret 15
  Marian 16
  Mary 211, 214
  Morris 16
O'DAY
  Biddy 204
  Edward 204
  John 202
  Mary 204
  Neal 202
O'DONALD
  Family 47
  Alice 100, 116, 119
  Barbara 100
  Biddy 110, 116
  Catherine 100, 121
  Daniel 175
  Elizabeth 90, 102, 116, 119, 176
  Emily 200
  James 90, 102, 110, 124
  John 102, 175
O'DONNEL
  Mary 204
O'DONNELL
  Alice 80, 144,1 45
  Catherine 214, 221
  Ellen 200, 202
  Juliana 142
  Mary 211
  Patrick 202
  Thomas 207, 208
O'DONOHO
  James 102
O'FLIN
  Thomas 175
O'FLINN
  Maurice 133
OGLE
  Samuel 39
O'GORMAN
  George A., Rev. 310
O'GRADY
  Delia K. 308
  Ellen Coleman 328
  John Patrick 321
  Joseph Stephen 323
  Michael P. 317
O'GREELY
  Joanne 213
OH
  Annette 325
O'HARA
  Michael 247
  Patrick 226, 247
  Rose Ellen 226
OLDHAM
  George Washington 260
  George W. 257, 260, 263
  Henrietta Mary 263
  Mary Ann 212
  Mary V. 263
  Michael Angelo 257
O'LEARY
  Mary 257
  Michael 206
  Timothy 206
OLIVER
  James 220
  Maurice 105
O'MAR
  Margaret 220, 224
O'MARROW
  Anne 224
OMWAKE
  H. Geiger 315
O'MULLEN
  Patrick 253
O'NEAL
  Benedict 164
  Catherine 214
  Charles 164
  Elizabeth 164
  George H. 260
  John Bernard 175, 176
  Margaret 308
  Mary 216, 217, 218
  Patrick 216
  Sadie 260
  Sara Jane 176
O'NEALE
  Ann 142
  Bernard 132, 138, 141, 142
  Charles 141
  Edward 142
  Elizabeth 138
  Jane 132
  John Bernard 138
  Mary 132
  Susan Augusta 141
O'NEIL
  Anna 253, 305
  Bernard 137
  Catherine 205, 248
  Charles 90
  George 256, 259, 265, 304, 308
  Helen 212
  Hugh 206
  James 208
  Jane 90
  Joseph 208
  Mary 206
  Patrick 248, 250, 254, 305
  Rose 206, 248, 249, 250

Rosie 305
Sadie 265
Sara Jane 137
Sophie 304
O'NEILL
  Anna 246, 249
  Charles 176
  David 224
  George 258
  Margaret 176
  Sadie 303
  Susan 176
  Thomas 175
O'REILLY
  Catherine 220
  James 175
ORTT
  Thomas J. 290, 291, 292
O'ROURICK
  May 200
  James 200
  John 200
O'ROURKE
  Bartholomew 204
  Bridget 204
  Catherine 205
  James 203, 204
  John 204
  Margaret 204
  Patrick 206
  Timothy 205
  William 204
OSBORN
  Ann 105
  John 105
O'SHEA
  William, S.S. 313
OSTENRIDGER
  Charles 257
O'SULLIVAN
  Francis Patrick 247
  James 166
  John, S.J. 166
  Thomas 166, 218, 221, 247, 305
O'TANYI
  Charlotte M. 328
  Theodore 322
OTHOSON
  John 203
OTLEY
  Jesse D. 277, 278, 311, 313, 314
O'TOUL
  Lawrence 206
  James 195
  Marie 206
OTTINGEN
  Blanche 303
OTWELL
  Lucinda 145
OWENS
  Marcella 269
  Margaret 213, 217, 220, 224
  Philip 175
OZENON
  Mary Ann Woolisby 155

P

PACA
  Edward 158
  William 158
PADLEY
  Josephine 276
PALMER
  John 157, 196
PANCIROLI
  Charles L. 324
  Frances Johanna 324
PARASKIEWICZ
  John 322
PARKER
  Peter, Capt. 90
PARON
  Maggie 261
PARSON
  Margaret 203
PARSONS
  Robert, S.J. 233, 279
PARTRIDGE
  William 158
PASCAULT
  Catherine 224, 226, 247
  Charles 246
  Daniel 195
  Francis 195, 226
  Francis R. 158, 246
  Lewis 156
  Mary Cheev 226
  Mary G. 155
PASCO
  Rebecca 158
PASQUET DE LEYDE
  William, Rev. 12, 89, 91, 92, 94, 96, 118
PATRICK
  George 140
PATTERSON
  Alexander 102, 124
  Catherine 102
  James 102
PAUL
  Catherine 256
  John Joseph 254, 304
  Louise 256
  Mary Magdalene 304
  Michael 254
PAURIS
  Barbara 219
PEARCE
  Maggie 259
PEARSON
  John 226
  Mary Ann 220
  Rebecca 154
  Robert 199, 220
PEIRE
  Laurence 220
PENN
  Ellen 304
  James H. 251
  Letitia 23
  Margaret 305
  Margarita 262
  William 19
PENNINGTON
  Abraham 133, 139
  Ann Rebecca 176
  Catherine 109, 116
  Elizabeth Ann 139
  James H. 251
  John 100, 137, 141
  Joseph 176
  Katy 90, 109, 133
  Mary Jane 137
  Otho 109
  Sarah 130
  Sylvester 130
PENSEL
  Caroline 264
  Charles 254, 264
  Henry Jacob 254
  Mary 256
PENSELS
  Charles 239
  Henry Jacob 239
PENSER
  John 249, 251, 253
  Paulina 253
PENSIL
  Louise Philomena 211
PERKINS
  Charles 195
  Edward 162, 164, 221
  Elizabeth Ann 263
  John D. 204
  Margaret Ann 164
  Mary Ann 162
  Russell H., Rev. 12, 287, 288, 290, 291, 293, 321
  Sarah 103
  Susan 202, 221
  Susanna 217, 220, 305
  William Charles 204, 251
PETER
  George 211
PETERMAN
  Thomas J., Rev. 8, 295, 300
PETERS
  Thomas 212
PFEIFER
  Christina 218
  Christopher 217
PFIFER
  Christine 219, 220
PFITZER

Barbara 211
PHALAN
  James 211
  Margaret Ann 211
  Patrick 213
PHELAN
  Daniel 259
  Joseph 259, 269
  Lawrence S., O.F.M. Cap. 12, 88, 89, 117, 118
PHELZ
  Timothy 212
PHILIPS
  Alfred N. 276, 277, 280, 282, 310, 313, 314
  Catherine 210
  Mary 308
  Thomas 151
  Vincent, S.J. 23
PHILLIPS
  Ann H. 250
  Harriet Anne 255, 257
PIERCE
  Anna Victoria 302
  Constance Marie 325
  Edwin 255
  Elizabeth 222
  Henry 256
  Irene H. 256
  Irwin 256
  James 256
  Johanna 220
  Julia Virginia 302
  Leonard 258
PIERSON
  Mary Ann 208
  Robert L. 223
  Samuel Joseph Lemuel 223, 308
PINA
  Lawrence 217
PINKIND
  Henrietta 158, 159
  John 158
PISER
  Clara 253, 256
  Emelia 253
  Emma R. 262
  H. Leonard 251
  John 258, 262, 302, 305
  Mary 258
  M. Millie 305
  Paulina 260, 261
PIUS
  VI, Pope 79
  VII, Pope 80
PLATER
  Alice 259
PLOWDEN
  Charles, Rev. 81
PLUMER
  Samuel E. 158

PLUMMER
  Adelaide 256, 262
  Adelinda Alice 246
  Alexia 264
  Annie 304
  Lena Adelinda 244
PLUNKET
  John 201
  Mary Jane 201
  Patrick 201
PLUNKETT
  Patrick 204
  Thomas 204
  Thomas James 204
POCHWAT
  Walter 325
POPE
  Alexander 304
  Charles 203, 260, 262, 304
  Emily 270, 305
  Emma Johanna 262
  Gertrude 272, 303
  Henry 272
  Lillian May 260, 270, 305
  Rosy 259
  William 305
PORTER
  Emma N. 253
POTEROWSKI
  Modesta 322
POTTER
  Catherine 147
  Lucy 147
  Zebediah W. 147, 158
POTOCKI
  Matilda 321
  Paul 308
POULTON
  Thomas, S.J. 8, 12, 31, 56, 75
POWDERLY
  Alice 253, 305
  Alice Mary 261
  Ann 249
  Anna 250, 258
  Anna Theresa 258
  Catherine 258
  David 251
  Helen M. 250
  James 219, 221, 225, 249, 250, 254
  Margaret 253, 308
  Margaret Ann 223, 225
  Mary 223, 264
  Mary Ellen 258
  Rose Ann 258
  William 259
POWELL
  Bridget 226
POWER
  Bridget 261
  James 205
  James, S.J. 12, 166, 187

POWERS
  James 207
  William Edgar 323
PRENDERGAST
  Anne 203
  James 204
  John 203
  Marge 206
PRESTON
  Mamie 304
PRICE
  Aloysius 233, 257, 308
  Ann 216, 224
  Annie E. 260, 263
  Araminta 195
  Caroline 166
  Catherine Marie 308, 325
  Cosmas 258
  Edward 164
  Elizabeth 110, 162, 164, 269, 304, 308
  Ellen 200
  Elsie 195
  Emmas 204, 255, 260, 308
  Esta 257
  George Robert 212
  George T. 157
  Henrietta 201, 225, 258, 306
  Hyland 222, 224
  James 204, 211, 250
  John 90, 308
  John M. 156
  John V. 139, 142, 144, 153, 159, 166
  John Veasey 166
  Margaret E.C. 213, 218, 220, 258
  Margaret Carmen 324
  Maria Victoria 216
  Marie 295
  Mary 200, 202
  Mary A. 250, 252, 305
  Mary Elizabeth Philomena 213, 253
  Mary Ellen 164
  Mary Emily 220
  Mary P. 250
  Mary Laura 200
  Mary Rebecca 144, 176
  Nolan Thomas Theodore 218
  Nowland T. 302
  Patrick F. 253
  Robert 212, 224
  Sara Jane 199
  Teresa Cecilia 216, 253
  Thomas 202
  Thomas J. 218, 220, 250, 251
  Thomas L. 216
  Thomas Theodore 142
  Vincent Hamilton Flintham 211
  William 137

William H. 216, 224
PRINDALL
  Elizabeth 204
PRIOR
  Alice 212
PROCTOR
  Anne Rebecca 140
  James 140
  Rebecca 140
PRYOR
  Joseph 42
  Martha 182
  Mary 151
  William 42, 137, 138, 151, 182
PURCELL
  Judith 142

Q

QUEEN
  Catherine 214
  Charles 195
  Emily 221
  Felice 195, 249
  Hugh 206
  Ida 257
  Isaac 221, 224
  Margaret 208, 219, 221
  Margaret Indiana 223
  Mary 207, 250
  Melvina 195
  Michael 223
  Philis 255
  Thomas 221
  Virginia 224
QUIGLEY
  Susanna 249
QUILLEN
  Anna 253
QUINBY
  John 37
QUINLAN
  Mary 256
QUINN
  Bridget 220
  Catherine Elizabeth 256
  Daniel J. 318
  Ida 303
  James 23, 24, 26, 53
  James A. 276, 277, 293, 313, 314, 315, 317
  James D. 314, 315, 320
  Joseph 176
  Madelyn H. 324
  Margaret 214, 223, 326
  Marie G 308
  Mary C. 321

R

RADICK
  Mary Anne 204
RAFFERTY
  Andrew 201
  Anne 203
  Ellen 159
  John R. 159, 201
  Martin 204
  Patrick 203
  Thomas 204
RAGAN
  Hannah 200
  Hugh 175
RAISIN
  Philip F. 221
RAMBO
  George 160
RAPP
  Andrew, S.J. 244, 262
RASKOB
  Helena Green 276
  John J. 276
RASON
  Henrietta Augusta 218
  John 218, 219, 222
RATLIFFE
  Elizabeth 226
  Lily 246
RATTY
  Hugh 176
RAUSCH
  Mary 250, 252
READ
  Amelia 90
  Ann 90, 133, 142
  Benjamin 90, 133
READING
  Catherine 248
  Philip 32, 45
READY
  Charles 203
  Mary 208
REAGAN
  Jeremiah 215
REARDON
  Mary 205
REBECCA
  Mary 219
REBMAN
  Joseph, Msgr. 293, 295, 297
RECORDS
  George 259
  Grishammer 259
REED
  Ann 136, 138, 139, 156, 165
  Benjamin 133
  Catherine 110
  Eliza 136
  Elizabeth 133
  George 217
  Jacob 107
  John Waugh 165
  Joseph 217
  Julius 217
REEDY
  Robert 209
REESE
  Thomas J., Msgr. 310
REGAN
  Mary 249
REGISTER
  Ann 166
REHFUSS
  Agnes Louise 324
  Albert M. 317
  John 317
REID
  Ben 217
  James 217
REIDY
  Margaret 201
  Mary 201
  Robert 201
REILLY
  Abraham 205, 214, 217
  Agnes 249
  Caroline 205, 214
  Catherine 246, 249
  Charles Abraham 202
  David 246
  Ellen 203, 220
  Frances Benedicta 205
  George Clemens 217
  Helen Agnes 214
  James Gustas 248
  Kate 203
  Mary A. 221, 247, 248, 249
  Mary Antoinetta 224
  Michael 203, 214
  Patrick, Rev. 153
REILY
  Catherine 211, 214
  Elizabeth 201
  Emma 214
  John 218
  Sam 218
REINHART
  Lewis 216
  Maria Christina 216
REISSMANN
  Richard, Rev. 295
REMER
  Anna Melia 223
  Elizabeth 214
  George William 246
  Joseph 214, 223, 246
RENTZ
  Petronella 211
REUMAN
  P.H., S.J. 255
REYNOLDS
  Family 170
  Agnes 251
  Alexander 217
  Amelia 136, 138, 139, 176, 229

Araminta Maria 139, 176
Benjamin 42, 102, 103, 192, 251
Carrie 317
Catherine Ann 133, 135
Cecelia Carmella 176
Clyde 305
Edward 142.
Eleanor 137
Elizabeth 103, 119
Eugene Clyde 261
George 153, 165, 250
George Rupert 253
Hannah 101
Jacob 130
James 32, 42, 102, 110, 137, 138, 151, 182, 217
Janet 176
Janet Boyce 137, 138
Jared 176
Jeannette 153, 176
Jeremiah 42, 100, 130, 133, 139, 176, 211, 221, 253
Jeremiah Camillus 152
Jerome 263
John 23, 24, 37, 42, 103, 109, 110, 116, 120, 137
John H. 263
Leslie 256, 305
Margaret 116
Martha 151
Mary 99, 100, 102, 103, 118, 120, 212, 255
Myrtle M. 322
Nancy 110, 116
Nicholas 23, 24, 37, 42, 102, 137
Parmela 138
Polly 116
Rachel 102, 103
Robert 324
Rupert 324
Sara C. 90, 102, 103, 109, 142, 182, 250
Sarah 109, 116, 130, 133, 138
Tally 116
Vincent 214
William 116
William Peregrine 100, 102, 103, 151
RHODES
  Eleanora 220
  Emily M. 158
  Harriett 251
RICE
  Mary Ann 247, 248
RICHARD
  Herman T., S.J. 242, 264
RICHARDS
  Charles B. 226
  Elira M. 220
  Enoch 226

RICHARDSON
  Constantine Augustine 147
  Elizabeth 216
  Joseph 147
  Joseph Philip 147
  Mary 216
  Mary Ann 224
  Sallie L. 158
RIEN
  Mary 210
RIGGS
  Althea 120
  Daniel 100, 120
  Sarah 110
RIGS
  Eleanor 119
  John 119
RIGHT
  Ellen 218, 219
RIGNEY
  Anne 209
  John 205
  Mary 205
RILEY
  Abraham 166
  Caroline 199
  David 250
  Dennis 176
  Elizabeth L. 226
  John 224
  Mary 166, 198, 213
  Michael 205
  Peregrine 226
  Sara Edna 199
  Thomas 147
  Thornton 147
RIMBAUGH
  Henry 221
RIME
  Gilmer 218
RIMLINGER
  Elizabeth T. 308
  Herbert T., Rev. 12, 280, 281, 284, 314, 315
RINGGOLD
  Edward 158
  John 217
  Martha 90
  Risden 217
  William 90
RIORDEN
  Jeremiah 221
RISE
  William 220
ROACH
  Amy 203
  Ellen 211
ROBERSON
  George Edward 212
  Isabella 226
  Leverine 216
  Mary 192, 221, 223

Peggy 120
Samuel 212, 216
Thomas 192, 221
ROBERT
  Charles 199
ROBERTS
  Emma V. 248
  Teresa 226
  William 164
ROBINSON
  Dorothy D. 321
  Edward 100, 119
  Emily 164
  Eva 261
  Isaac 261
  Mary 218
  Peggy 100
  Samuel Thomas 221
ROBISON
  Agnes 290
  Isaac 262
  Josephine 244, 262
  Mary 216
ROBRECHT
  Edward 221
ROCHE
  Winifred 212
ROCHER
  Benjamin 212
  Reuben 212
  Samuel 212
RODERICK
  Mary 204
RODGERS
  Joseph 147
RODRICK
  Francis 199
  James 199
  Mary 199
ROE
  Ann Maria 154
  Thomas 154
ROEMER
  Ethel 261
  Joseph 219, 250, 252
  Joseph G. 250, 252
  Mary 261
  Otilia 219, 250, 252, 261
ROGENSCHULTZ
  Marcellus 249
  Waldeburga 249
ROGERS
  John 47
ROHLADDER
  Felicitas 254
ROHN
  Apollonian 138
  Simon 138
ROLERECHT
  Edward 233
  Elizabeth 321
ROLLINS

Edward D. 217
D.E. 313
ROMER
  Matilda 256
ROMUALD
  Rosalind 222
ROOKER
  Susanna B. 220
ROOSEVELT
  Franklin D., Pres. 317
ROSA
  Annie 262
  Louise 264
  Silvester 262
ROSEBERRY
  Samuel 221
ROSEWICK
  Bridget 199, 201
ROSINE
  Charles David 206
ROSLIN
  Margaret 255
ROSNY
  Bartholomew 176
ROSS
  Donald 302
  James A. 302
ROSSI
  Joseph, S.J. 300
  Michael Joseph 325
ROSTON
  Margaret 253
ROURKE
  Margarate 203
  Mary 166, 198, 212
  Thomas 166
  Timothy 166, 203, 212
ROVOCK
  John J., S.J. 262, 264
ROW
  Margaret 142
  Patrick 142
ROWAN
  John Morgan 324
  Marie B. 328
ROWIK
  Alice 200
  Bartholomew 200
  Bridget 201
  James 200, 201
  Jane 200
  John 200, 201
  Timothy 200, 201
RUBY
  Catherine 248
  F.W. 248
  George Benjamin 248
RUDDEN
  Letitia 145
  William 145
RULEY
  Agnes Leona 247

Caroline 201
Elizabeth 202
Emilia Louisa 219
Indiana Rosalia 235
Peregrine 247
Sarah 235
RULY
  George 219
  Henry 201
  William Henry 201
RUSSELL
  John 253
  Patrick 253
RUTKOWSKI
  Ann E. 325
  Helen B. 324
RYAN
  Anna Elizabeth 304
  Ellen 204
  James 304
  Jane Anna 250, 253
  John 147
  John Baptist 140
  John Francis 140
  John J., Rev. 254
  Margaret 203, 208
  Martin 247, 248, 249, 253, 254
  Martin M., Rev. 308
  Mary 203, 208
  Mary A. 256
  Matthew 145
  Patrick 203, 249
  Peter 208
  Theresa 254
  William 217
  William Francis 250, 252

S

SABINA
  Anne 142
SALMON
  James F., S.J. 298
SALTARELLI
  Michael A., Bishop 6, 7, 297, 299, 300
SANDERS
  Matthew F., S.J. 12, 188, 198, 199
SAPPINGTON
  Ashbary 221
  James 221
  John 19
  Margaret 221
  Maria 119
SARAM
  Cecelia Catherine 264
SARTIN
  Tyson 283
SASTRE
  Margaret 145
SAUNDERS
  Edward 251

SAVAGE
  Hannah 145
SAVIN
  Susan Fullum 176
  Thomas 176
  William Morris 176
SAXTON
  Catherine 152
  Elizabeth 53
  Joann 153
SAYER
  Peter 18, 34
SCANLAN
  Ann 99
  Bartholomew 141, 144
  Daniel 212
  Ellen 212
  Margaret 202, 208, 212
  Marianne 264
  Mary 141, 144, 203, 215
SCANLON
  Family 170-171
  Ann 118
  Arthur 176
  Catherine 138
  Edward 135, 156, 157
  James 135, 137, 176
  Margaret Vance 155
  Mary Amanda 156, 176
  Rebecca 176
  Rose 176
  Thomas 176
SCANNAL
  Mary 210
SCARF
  John H. 283
SCHAEFFER
  Family 229
  Catherine 229, 272
  Charles 256, 264, 270
  Charles James 261, 262, 264
  John 273
  Joseph 216, 229, 241, 244, 254, 258, 259, 261, 262, 270
  Joseph P. 261
  Mary 229, 260, 262
  William 260, 270, 304
SCHAFFER
  Mary L. 260
SCHAPF
  Catherine 317
SCHAUM
  David, Rev. Dr. 291
SCHETZELY
  Maria 220
SCHETZLER
  Caroline 264
  Edward 265
  Mollie 257
  Sarah 251, 265
  Seraphina 250, 252
SCHIERSE

Paul J., Msgr. 292
SCHLATTER
   Rebecca 323
   Rudolph 324
SCHLEICHER
   Andrea 261
   John 262
   Lena 261
SCHMEARER
   John A. 221
SCHMID
   William 212
SCHMIDT
   John 211
   Mary 253
   Joseph 212, 323
SEIGLE
   Anna 255
   Barbara 255
SELOOQUIN
   James 176
SEMMES
   Anastasia 219
   Mary 223
   Mary Elizabeth 219
   Raphael 219
SETH
   Charles 105, 116
   Elizabeth 105
   George Washington 105
   Jacqueline 140
   Nancy 116
SEUL
   Alethy 216
SEVERE
   Peter M. 116, 120
SEVERS
   Francis 103
   Margaret 103
   Peter 100, 103
SEWALL
   Charles, Rev. 85
   Jane 20
SEYMOUR
   John, Gov. 13, 14, 15
SHAEFER
   Charles 256
   Joseph 251
   Mary 256, 257
SHAHAN
   Anne 200, 206
   Catherine 200, 207
   Patrick 201, 206
SHANAHAN
   Frank 262
SHANE
   John 144
   Robert 144
SHANNON
   James 259
   Patrick 200
   Rose 265
   Sarah 259
   Thomas 259
SHARPE
   Horatio 41
SHARTER
   John 164
   Michael 164
SHEA
   Bartholomew 215
   Catherine 215
   James 159
SHEAHAN
   Catherine 247, 248
SHEARIN
   Hanna 202
SHEBOCK
   David 288
SHEEHAN
   Anne 208
   Catherine 218
   Honora 305
   Patrick 208
SHEHAN
   Catherine 222, 223, 246, 255
   Eleanora 250
   Honora 212, 214, 216, 217, 219, 226, 247, 248
   Mary 215, 262, 263
   Mary Honora 223
   Nora 263
   Patrick 219
SHEHY
   Mary 226
SHELDON
   Catherine 141
SHENTON
   John 158
SHERIDAN
   Catherine 141
   John 141, 144
   Lawrence 211
   Margaret 211
   Philip 146
   Suzanne 141, 144
SCHETZLE
   Annie 259
   Edward 259
   Lizzie 259
SCHETZLER
   Anna 302
   Anna Elizabeth 307, 324
   Anne 265
   Anne Caroline 263
   Bradford 271
   Charles Andrew 303, 321
   Edward 252, 263, 265, 270, 302
   Edward T. 303, 304, 324
   Elizabeth 302
   Eva Cecelia 304
   Francis 265, 271
   Gladys 321
   John 265, 270
   John J. 265
   Joseph 210
   Katherine 271
   Lucinda 272
   Lucinda Viola 302
   Marcella 307
   Mary 262, 263, 265, 303
   Mary Teresa 270
   Michael 265, 266
   Sara 264
   Sarah Elizabeth 302
   William C. 324
SHEVLAND
   William, Rev. 309
SHIELDS
   Jane 156, 218
   Joanna 212
   Margaret 156, 157, 201
SHIFFLEY
   Suzanne 139, 142
SHIRDEN
   Ellen 211
SHOCKLEY
   Mary 307
SHY
   Bridget 145
SIBER
   Margaret 216
SIBRE
   Frances Thibaud 202
   George 207
   Jenny 207
   Margaret 218
   Mary Susannah 207
   Prosper 202, 218
SILK
   Roseanna 151
SILTE
   Roseanna 153
SIMMS
   John 20, 214
   Mary 214
   Tammy 218
SIMMONS
   John 202, 204, 205
   Willi Ann 205
SIMONS
   James Willson 223
   Mary Elizabeth 223
   Thomas Henry 223
SIMPKINS
   Jerry 204
   Sarah 204
SIMPSON
   Isaac 103
   James 103
   Josephine M. 323
   Margaret 103
   Robert E. 318
SIRCHLER
   Anna Maria 223

Joseph 223
SIRY
   Philip, Rev. 12, 295, 300, 324
SITTENSBERGER
   Mathias, S.J. 11
SIVER
   Christine 214
SKELLEN
   Sara Ann 176
SKELLY
   Catherine 213
   William 213
SKIDMORE
   Agres 219
SKIRVEN
   Harry 250
SKOMORUCHA
   Francis A. 321
   Sophia B. 321
SLATTERY
   Dennis 147
   John 147
SLAUGHTER
   Amelia 195
   Mary 195
   Theodore 195
SLEIGH
   Joseph 201
SLEVEN
   Helen 145
SLICKER
   Andrew 244
SMALLWOOD
   William 221
SMITH
   Alfred E. 274
   Anna V. 201, 255
   Carolina 176
   Catherine 141
   Charles Stephen 156
   Edward 158
   Eliza Ann Stephens 156
   Elizabeth 176, 201
   Ellen Theresa 201
   Emelia Elizabeth 218, 305
   Frances Helen 325
   James, S.J. 262
   James 200
   John 176, 205, 216
   John Gaffney 261
   Margaret 145, 200, 201, 202, 211
   Martha 203
   Mary 192, 200, 202, 205, 253, 255, 257, 262
   Mary Theresa 249
   Matthew 201, 203, 208, 211
   Nicholas 139, 140, 142
   Thomas 145, 159
   William 156, 158, 205, 249, 250, 255, 259
SMYTH

James 155
William Reilly 155
SOHA
   Jean 317
   Walter Stanley 322
SPALDING
   Anna Elizabeth 224
   Martin J., Archbp. 193, 194, 196, 198, 222, 227
   Samuel E. 224
SPARKS
   Agnes J. 326
   Paul 321
SPEAR
   Annie 305
   Mary A. 305
SPEARMAN
   Alfred 158
   Elizabeth 158
SPENCE
   Mary 217
SPRIG
   Rebecca 142, 145
SPRIGS
   James 176
SPRINGER
   Anne 137, 142
   George E. 315
SPRY
   William 221
STACKS
   Thomas 206
STADELMAN
   Joseph M., S.J. 262
STAFFER
   Dorothy 215
STAHL
   Julie 247
STAM
   Louis 235
   Robert Austin 250
STAMM
   Antoinette 250
STANLEY
   Elizabeth 137, 141, 142, 153, 156
STANT
   Christina 217
   Daniel 216
   Georgia Anna 216
STAP
   Agnes 223
STAPP
   Agnes 224, 233
   Christina 218, 219
   Ed 304
   Edward 264
   Edward John 226, 244, 258, 261
   Edwin 272
   Emma 254
   Gayle Albert 261

Henry 258
James Albert 244
Joseph 255
Maggie 256
Margaret 254, 255, 305
Mary 233
Mary Rose Krastel 237
May 235, 239, 264
Michael 218, 219
STERLING
   George 260
   Henrietta 260
   John Ernest 260
STARR
   Tony 293
STAUB
   Christine 219
   Michael 219
STAUFFER
   Cecelia 220
STAUNTON
   George, O.S.A. 88, 89, 117
STEARNS
   Gertrude Degan 328
STEINBACHER
   Nicholas, S.J. 164
STEINHEISER
   George, Rev. 193
STENSON
   William 152
STENZEL
   Emil, Rev. 234, 235
STEPHEN
   Mary 138
STEPHENS
   Eliza 158, 257
   George 255, 256, 257, 264
   George Ambrose 260
   George W. 262
   Grace Elizabeth 262
   Hamilton Morton 256, 262
   James A. 256
   Lydia Ann 263
   Maria 265
   Martha Frances 256, 264
   Mary 256, 264
   Mary Theresa 264
   Mollie 255, 260
   Mr. 207
   Nora Jeannette 265
   Samuel 256, 260, 263, 264, 265
STEPHENSON
   Michael 261
STERLING
   Agnes Henrietta 247
   George 247, 253, 255
   Martina Elizabeth 253
   Walter R. 255, 256
STEVENS
   Fannie 308
   Lidia 270

Index of Persons 375

Priscilla 124
STEWARD
  Alexander 247
  Stewart Henry 158
STILES
  Lewis D. 325
STOCK
  Mary 259
STOCKLEY
  Laurette M. 317
  Joseph A. 308, 322
STOKES
  John F. 313
STORK
  Josephine 258
  Julia 258
STORY
  Elizabeth 144
  William Henry 144
STOUT
  Andrew 249
  Catherine 255
  Daniel 259
  John 302
  Joseph 249, 258
STRANE
  John 141
  Robert 141
STRANGE
  Michael 176
STRASSNER
  Mary 213
STRAUGHAN
  Lewis 284
STRICK
  Carolina 233
  John 233
STRIDS
  Justina 233
STROKES
  John 221, 277
STRONG
  Millie 318
STUART
  Charles Edward 20, 28
  James Edward 20
  James II, King 14, 15
SUDLER
  Joshua 261
  Mary C. 261
SULLIVAN
  Agnes 303
  Catherine 207, 213, 219, 226, 246, 302, 305, 308
  Catherine Rebecca 323
  Cecelia 324
  Ellen 203
  Francis Patrick 258, 276, 305
  Francis T. 302
  James 203, 206, 209
  James Bradford 276, 277, 302, 313, 314
  Jeremiah 144
  John 209, 213, 220, 222, 263, 302, 303, 304, 308
  John T. 305
  Joseph 258, 302, 308, 322
  Joseph Aloysius 308
  Kate 263
  Lily 302
  Mary 159, 244, 261, 302, 308
  Mary A. 262
  Mary Ann 199
  Michael 194, 222, 261, 302, 303, 305
  Michael A. 262
  Rebecca 308
  Robert 200
  Simon 203, 207, 302
  Thomas 166, 198, 206, 207, 214, 222, 223, 226, 246, 302
  Timothy 157
  William 304
SULLYVAN
  Dennis 220
SUM
  John 218
  Maria Margarita 218
SUTTER
  Francis 211
SUTTER
  Francis 220
SWEENEY
  Bernard 215
  Edward 176
  John 211
  John A.H. 313, 314
  John Edward 211
  John Thomas 215
  Joseph D., Msgr. 277, 311, 313
SWEENY
  Edward 212
  Eugene Owen 212
  James 105, 112, 116
  John 208
  Margaret 214
SWEETMAN
  Daniel 109
  Martha 109, 182
SWINNEN
  Firmin 288
SYLVAN
  Elizabeth 140

T

TAGGART
  Paul J., Msgr. 116
TAILOR
  Rebecca 121
TASSEL
  Catherine Butler 176
TATE
  Hannah 105

Rachel 158, 159
Richard 105
Robert 158
William 105
TATTLER
  Robena 100
TAYLOR
  Ann 42
  David 159
  Harriet M. 159
  Rebecca 42, 226
  Richard 42
  Vincent J. 156
  William 259
  William H. 158, 159
TEMPLE
  Howard Aloysius 248
  William G. 248
TENSER
  Amelia 246
  Clara B. 246
  John 246
  Leonard 246
TERRY
  John 176
TERSHLEY
  Caroline 249
  Joseph 249
TESSIER
  Jean, S.S., Rev. 12, 87
TEUSER
  John 248
  Mary Miller 248
THALMANN
  Joseph 247
THOMAS
  Alfred B. 144, 145, 156, 157, 176
  Alice 153
  Alice Mary 204
  Anthony 147
  Benjamin 201, 220
  Casovo B. 220
  Emilia 218
  Emily 209, 221
  Francis 220
  Jane 204, 208, 216
  John 96, 157, 175, 204, 214
  John T. 208
  Mary 202, 204, 212, 215, 221
  Mary Frances 214
  Richard 155
  Theresa 214
  William 202, 204, 212, 216, 221
THOMLINSON
  Ann Mary 250, 252
  Catherine 248, 251
  Charlotte 248, 253
  George 248
  Henry 247
  James 248, 250, 252

Joanna 248
John N. 227, 248, 252
Lattie Curry 251
Mary M. 248, 250
TIERNEY
   Francis J. Rev. 286
   Margaret 159, 202
TIGHE
   Peter 202
TILGHMAN
   Anna M. 157
   Anna R. 161
   Maria 158, 221
   Mary E. 161
   Mary Fairbarn 161
   Ogle 158
   R.C. 159
   Robert 161
   Samuel 157, 161
   Samuel Ogle 161, 195
   William G. 161
TIMONS
   James 226
TIPPENS
   John 105
TOM
   David 176
   James 145, 176
   Margaret 145, 176
TOMAN
   John 145
TOMLINSON
   Catherine 235
   Charlotte 235
   Edward 235
   Thomas 235
TOOMEY
   Catherine 156
   Jeremiah 220
   William 156, 220
TRACY
   Thomas 147
TRACEY
   James 195
TRAINOR
   Patrick 92
TRASNELL
   Mary Ann 213
TRIMBLE
   Elizabeth 216, 222, 224
TROEL
   Barbara 224
   Fridolin 224
TROY
   Arthur 203
   Bridget 220
   Mary Ann 212
   Michael 203, 220, 212
TRUITT
   Baker 138
TUBMAN
   John 158, 159
   John Augustine 157
   Mary 157
   Mary G. 157
   Robert 157
TUCKER
   Catherine 204
TUFFER
   Michael, S.J. 164
TUITE
   Patrick 214
   Robert 105
TULLY
   Ann 105
   Margaret 105
   Michael 105
TURNER
   Ann 213
   Nancy 144
   Rachel 219
TWEED
   Mary 176
TYGARD
   Mary 124

U V

UNGLE
   Frances 37
USHER
   John 176
VANCE
   Elizabeth 214
   Mary 156
VAN DE GRIFF
   George 212
   Maria 303
   Perry 203, 212
   Thomas 212
VANDEGRIFT
   George 215, 217, 222, 224
   James H. 296
   Mary 246
   Richard 224
   Rose Ann 215
   William 222
VARIN
   Francis, Rev. 12, 151, 152
VAUGHAN
   James 215
VERDON
   Anna I. 214
VERHEGGEN
   Jason Anton 323
   Marie 326
VIGNOLA
   Carmen D., Rev. 12, 292, 293, 294
VILLIGER
   George, S.J. 12, 163, 184, 190, 193, 196, 234, 237, 238, 252
VINCUM
   Joseph 100
VIZEY
   George 144
VOSH
   Nicholas 103

W

WADE
   Francis 42
WALINSKY
   Clarence 195
WALKER
   Anne 257, 262,
   David 248
   India 304
   James 248, 264
   Rose 137
   Sadie 256
   Sarah 265
WALL
   John 199
   Mary 201, 204, 259
WALLING
   Dennis 249
   Mary Ellen 249
WALLIS
   Francis Adolphus 221, 225, 226, 246
   George Willson 226
WALLS
   Caroline Barbara 224, 225
   Henrietta 246
   Jacob 224
WALLY
   Margaret 219
WALMSLEY
   Ann Theresa 305
   Augustine Bede 224
   Benjamin 216, 248
   Benjamin Franklin 219, 224, 266
   Clarence 224, 305
   Elia Louisa 248
   Emily Theresa 305
   Frannie 195, 235, 247
   Frances Maggie 235
   Francis Wilmer 219, 305
   John 216
   Maggie 248
   Margaret 249
   Mary 195, 249
   Oliver 266
   R.L. 195
WALSBERGER
   Mary 261
WALSH
   Alice 253, 261, 265
   Clara 304
   Elizabeth 156
   James 147
   John H., Rev. 12, 121, 274, 276, 277, 280, 308
   John M., Rev. 308
   Margaret 220

Index of Persons 377

Mary 249, 266
Patrick 200
WALSTON
  Mary 256
WALT
  Ricio 182
WALTER
  Colin 283
WALTERS
  Henry 211
  William Henry 211
WARD
  Elizabeth 328
  John 199, 203
  John J. 313, 314, 315
  John J., Jr. 276, 277, 285
  Margarate 203
  Mary 195
  Rachel 99. 118
  William 99, 118, 325
WARNER
  James 298
WARREN
  Charles 253, 254, 248, 260, 266
  James 260
  Jeremiah 140
  Kate 266
  Mary Ethel 254
  Samuel R. 253
WARTER
  James 139
WASLY
  Mary 215
WATER
  Henry 257
  H. Emerson 257
WATERS
  Emory 216
  Jacob 112
  Perry 216
  Sally 112
  Samuel 216
WATKINS
  E.F. 221
  Margaret 116
  Samuel 42, 120
WATKINSON
  Mary 103
  Peter 100, 102, 103
  Samuel 43
  Samuel Peter 102
WATSON
  Carrie 256
  Wiley 256
WATTS
  Abraham 102
  Ann 102
  Frank William 255
  James 102
  Samuel 102
  Sarah 256

WAUGH
  Elizabeth 165, 217
WAY
  Phoebe 44
WEBB
  Ann 102
  Benjamin 102
  Cornelia 102
  Holland 102, 103, 109, 120
  Juley Ann 216
  Nehemiah 102
WEBER
  Emily M. 321
  Henry 257, 258
  H.P. 257
  Peter G. 322
WEEKS
  Antoinette 163
  Catherine 155
  Eliza 163
  James 155, 162
WEIDEMIER
  Anna 255
WEIST
  Frederick V. 248
  Stanilaus 248
WELCH
  Ann 204
  Henry 226
  James 226
  Martin 176, 182
  Mary 254
  Mary Margaret 203
  Robert 208
  Robert Edward 211
  Thomas 249, 254
  Thomas Sewall 226
WELD
  Family 79
WELDON
  Abraham 26, 138
  Elizabeth 138
  Isaac 26
  Jacob 42
  Jane 102
  John 26, 212
  Joseph 23, 42
  Millie 138
  Peter 213
  Raworth 42
  Richard Bennett 213
  William 26
WELLS
  Ann 159
  Edward 206
  Jane 176, 182
  Joseph 176, 182, 185
  Patrick 206
WELSH
  Alexia 264
  Alice 304
  Anne 199

John 176
John Joseph 266
Patrick 147
Robert 214
WERING
  James 133
  Mary 133
WEVER
  Lizzie 195
WHALEN
  Ellen 203
  John D. 203
WHEELAN
  Sarah 114
WHEELER
  Helen 158, 166, 212
  Nancy 209
WHELAHAN
  James 147
WHELAN
  Anna 256
  Charles, O.F.M. Cap. 11, 91, 100
WHISTLER
  Edward 145
WHITE
  Ann 214
  Anna 213
  Catherine 209, 255, 25
  Charles 283
  Daniel 213
  Honora 248, 249
  James 213
  Joanna 209, 211
  John 201
  Lizzie 207
  Mary 201, 206
  Michael 207, 208
  Sarah 144
WHITFIELD
  James, Archbp. 143, 151
WHITLOCK
  A. Marshall 323
  Beatrice F. 305
  Ellen Morray 325
  Eugene 256
  Joseph 276, 323
  Nellie E. 256
  Patricia Ann 323
WHITTINGTON
  Mary 102
WICKE
  James 219, 220
  Julia 220
WIGENS
  Julia 215
WIGGINS
  Ann Elizabeth 249, 253, 254
WIGMAN
  Mary Ann 217
WILCOX
  Thomas 23

WILDHAM
  Wildeburer 216
WILLEY
  Donald R. 325
  Roy 324
WILLIAM
  Elizabeth 249
WILLIAMS
  Ann 204, 218, 222
  Betsy 153
  Biddy 116
  Elizabeth 116
  Frank 266
  George 266
  Henry 264
  Jane Krastel 299
  John 158
  Sarah 220
  Walter 321
WILLIS
  Rachel Rebecca 214, 220
  John 214
WILLMER
  Alphonsa 218
  Arthur 217
  James 218
  Mary Sophia 217
WILLOUGHBY
  Catherine 157
WILLSON
  Family 75, 171, 181, 182, 207, 250, 318
  Agusta Smith 199
  Alexander 203
  Alexander H. 155, 162, 163
  Alice Elizabeth Brooke 201
  Alice Josephine 213
  Ambrose 203
  Ann 200
  Ann Marie Smythe 163
  Ann M. Young 26, 162, 213
  Ann S. 163, 221
  Anna 181, 212
  Anna Maria 163, 217
  Anna Young 155
  Anne Elizabeth Brooke 155, 156, 163, 213, 216, 217
  Anne Marie 219, 222
  Beauregard 228
  Bennett 195, 204
  Carroll 207, 219, 221, 224
  Cecelia 205
  Charles 155, 219, 220
  Charles B. 217
  Charlotte Manning 250
  Clement Joseph Beauregard 217
  Daniel C. 155
  Eleanor B. 213
  Eleanore 155, 217
  Elizabeth 199, 202, 204, 215, 218, 222, 246
  Elizabeth H. 163
  Ellen 221
  Ellen Emily Brown 155, 181
  Francis 217, 262
  Frederick 246
  Frederick Francis de Sales 217
  George 199, 200, 203, 205, 213, 217, 219
  George H. 155, 163
  Georgia 206, 217, 221, 222, 223, 226
  Georgianna 217, 225
  Georgina 203
  Henrietta Eleanora Brooke 155, 156, 199, 213, 216, 217, 218, 222, 224
  Henrietta Maria 156, 220
  Henry 156, 203
  Henry Hayward 155
  Ida 224
  James 171
  Julia Rena Compton 203, 250, 260
  Julia M. 224
  John 201, 205, 213, 226
  John Charles 155, 156
  John M. 163
  Leonard 200
  Lilla 219
  Martha 201, 213, 218, 220, 224
  Martha Elizabeth 201
  Martha H. 162
  Marty 221
  Mary 202, 204, 205, 206
  Mary Ann Held 155
  Mary Ann Hoskins 176, 182
  Mary Charlotte 206
  Mary Esther 203
  Mary Georgia Ann 246
  Mary Hester 221
  Mary R. 246
  Matilda 217, 223
  Maude Agnes 250
  Maurice Augustine 220
  Notley Oswald 199, 200, 217
  Richard 158, 162, 199, 200, 206, 213
  Richard Bennett 217
  Richard E. 155
  Thomas 155, 203, 205, 213
  Thomas B. 199, 200, 216
  Thomas Henry 217
  Thomas Smythe 155, 156, 157, 158, 159
  Wilfred Manning 155
  William Griffen Blunt 217
  William Peter 213
WILLY
  Hazel 322
WILMER
  Arthur 214, 222
  Benjamin 159
  Caroline 206
  James 219
  Joseph Arthur 214
  Mary Catherine 206
  Wilhelmina 219
WILSON
  Robert 195
WISE
  Frederick 100
WITHERSPOON
  David 32
WOLFE
  Helen Virginia 326
WOOD
  Patrick 176
WOODALL
  Edward E. 305
  Elizabeth 305
  Emily 205, 208, 212
  Jesse B. 318
WOODLAN
  John 216
  Joseph 216
WOODLE
  Edward 202, 204
  Frances Anne 204
  Joseph Henry 202
WOODROW
  Arthur Ralph 328
  Rebecca Ann 325
WOODWARD
  Mrs. 199
WOOTERS
  Bessie Parks 265
  Joseph Lemuel 226
  Laura 226
  Lilia Trommer 235
  Rebecca 226
  Rose Laura 235
  Samuel 176, 182
  Sarah 223
WOOTIS
  Sarah 165
WORKMAN
  John 308
  Mary Desmond 266
WORTEY
  James 142
WRERY
  Ann 176
WRIGHT
  Ann Elizabeth 253
  B.F. 266
  Caroline 258
  Carrie 276
  Chandler 266
  Charity 250, 266
  Charles 255
  Cora 303
  Eglentine 246
  Elizabeth A. 250

Index of Places and Topics 379

George 99, 118
Hugh N. 214
John 100, 103, 116, 119, 120
John Chandler 225, 253, 255
Joseph C. 221, 250
Margaret 214
Maria 199
Marie 176
Mary 116, 203
Nathan 105
Rachel 103
Roseann Price 225
Stanchfield 277
Terry 221
Thomas 258, 260
WUEST
  George Robert 247
  Stanislaus 247

WYLIE
  Caroline Mary 260

X Y Z

XAVIER
  St. Francis, S.J. 7, 9
YOUNG
  Ann M. 156, 213, 220, 228
  Benjamin 110, 224
  George Henry 223
  John Henry 223
  Martha 110, 199, 200, 206
  Martha Ann 200, 206, 217
  Notley 110
YOUNGER
  Anne Marie 212
  Mary 205
YOUTH

Grace 144
YUNKER
  Anna Maria 218
ZAFFERS
  Frank 277
ZAFFERE
  Anna Theresa 305
ZEH
  Anna May 324
ZEIZEL
  Joseph 218
ZISEL
  Anna 224
  Felix 218, 222, 224
  James 222
  Josephine 224
  Remigius Felix 218

INDEX OF PLACES AND TOPICS

Act To Prevent The Growth of Popery 35
American Revolutionary War 44
American Civil War 187, 191, 193, 239
Anglicanism 13, 41, 88
Annual Orphans Collection 244
Annual Church Picnic 242
Anti-Catholic Bigotry 167, 187
Anti-slavery 188
Appomatox Courthouse 194
Appoquinimink Forest 19, 22, 24, 25, 26, 37, 42, 82, 83, 85, 87, 129, 137, 191
Ark and Dove 7, 16
Askmore Tract 22
Assembly of Maryland 146
Assumption B.V.M., Feast of 242
Baltimore,
  First Plenary Council of 187
  Ninth Provincial Council of 191
  The Catholic Mirror 227
Bible Reading in Public Schools 188
Bohemia Anniversaries
  200th of George Washington 309
  250th of 280, 282
  275th of 291, 322
  300th of 300
  Excavations at 1955 279
  Field Masses at 274, 275, 280, 284
  Fire of 1912 271, 272, 273, 306
  Forty Horns Devstroy at 242
  Home Farm 274, 279, 285
  House Finances 263
  House History 263
  Farm Show 300
  Land Map (1898) 266

Mill at 31
Museum at 319
Monument for the Unborn at 299
Pilgimmages 281
Pillage and Destruction 173
Road Case 198
Visitors' Center 294
Cambridge, Maryland 188
Caroline County 83
Cavil Ridge 32, 44
Catholic Diocese Foundation 285, 293, 297
Catholic Forum of the Air 275
Catholic Television Guild 279
Cecil County 15, 75, 233
Cecil Whig 288
Charlestown, Massachusetts 152
Childs, Maryland 160, 277
Chesapeake and Delaware Canal 89, 91, 139, 140, 144, 145, 159, 196, 273
Chesapeake Bay 121
Chesapeake City 196, 235, 236, 240, 242, 244, 270
Choir of Oblates of St. Francis de Sales 277, 280, 283, 286
Choir of St. Joseph's Church, Middletown 299
Choir of St. Joseph's-on-the-Brandywine 292
Choir of St. Peter's Cathedral 288, 290, . 295
Choir of St. Peter's, New Castle 291
Choir of St. Rose of Lima Church 291, 292
Coffee Run 12, 135
Concord, Pennsylvania 23

Continental Congress 79
Corporation of the Clergy 85, 88, 92, 93, 132, 177
Crispin's Ramble 43
Cuba Rock 44
Culloden, Battle of 28
Currency Act 41
Delaware Assembly 146
Delaware City 270
Delaware, State of 22, 158
Delmarvia Catholic, The 306
Denton, Maryland 147, 196
Department of the Interior, U.S. 288
Dialog, The 292
The Delmarva Dialog 285, 286, 287
Diocese of Wilmington 245, 269
  Centenary of 286, 287
Doherty Funeral Home 285
Dorchester County 157, 165
Dorsey House, 167
Dover, Delaware 22, 41
Dred Scott Decision 191
Eastern Shore of Maryland 129, 143, 196, 198, 233
Edict of Nantes 27
Eleanor's Delight 24, 32, 41, 138
Elk River 146
Elkton, Maryland 83, 89, 159, 160, 161, 194, 234, 287
Episcopal Visitation 227
Essex Lodge 87
Everett Theater 238
Fort Sumter 197
France 27, 29
Frederica, Delaware 32
French Catholics 36, 39
French Forces 79

Frenchtown, Maryland 91, 160
Galena, Maryland 189, 245
Georgetown, Maryland 85
Georgetown University 80, 81, 129, 136, 147, 152, 163, 168
Georgetown Visitation 129
German Immigrants 22, 36, 40, 80, 151, 196, 235
Glasgow, Delaware 146
Golden Hill, Maryland 130
Grande Seminaire, Montreal 85
Greenfields 316
Grove Point 133, 141, 172
Havre de Grace, Maryland 192, 194, 234
Head of Elk (Elkton), Maryland 47, 85, 287
Historical Society of Old Bohemia 7, 84, 276, 277, 301, 326
  Articles of Incorporation 277
  Bequest of Marie Price to 295
  Foundation of 279
  Newsletter of 284
  Original Board of 277
  Thirty Fifth Anniversary of 295
Historic American Buildings Survey 288
International Encharistic Congress 281
Irish Hill 36
Irish Immigrants 15, 25, 39, 151, 167, 187
Irish Laborers 89, 91, 139, 140, 146, 153, 159
Irish Papists 13, 24, 36
Italy 143
Ivy Mills 22, 37
Jesuit Academy 30
Jesuits (see Society of Jesus)
Jubilee year 2000 298, 299
Kansas-Nebraska Act 188
Kent County, Maryland 152
Kent County Free School 31, 48, 189
King George's War 27, 30
Kingstown, Maryland 36, 83
Knights of Columbus 280, 288, 298, 299, 300
Kulturkampf 236
Ku Klux Klan 274
Lambson's Station 189, 190, 195
Laurel, Delaware 130, 153
Leghorn, Italy 143
Letitia Manor 44
Lewes, Delaware 22
Little Elk Creek 159
Loyola College, Baltimore 163
Lulworth Castle, England 79
Manumission of slaves 172
Martinsburg, Virginia 230
Maryland Assembly 13, 15, 19, 30, 35, 49
Maryland Gazette 28, 29, 38, 48

Mason-Dixon Line 25, 41, 193
Meekins Neck, Maryland 23, 88, 129
Middletown, Delaware 201, 224, 270, 293
Mill Creek Hundred, Delaware 23, 37
Mitchell House 90
Mount Harmon 19, 25, 113
Mount Pleasant, Delaware 159, 317
Mt. Arrarat 316
Mt. Cuba 23
National Liturgical Conference 285
National Register of Historic Places 290
National Trust for Historic Preservation 296
Newark, Delaware 234
New Castle County, Delaware 129
New Castle, Delaware 22, 41, 91, 270
  New Castle-Frenchtown Railroad 146, 147, 153
  New Castle-Frenchtown Turnpike 146
Oath of Fidelity 44
Oblates of St. Francis de Sales 277, 280, 283, 286
Oxford, Maryland 29
Peach Blight 240, 258
Pennsylvania 15, 22
Perry Point, Maryland 194, 316
Perryville, Maryland 193
Petersburg, Delaware 130
Philadelphia, Pennsylvania 12, 22, 40, 53, 79, 82, 129, 140, 151
Pilottown, Maryland 49
Polish Immigrants 196
Pope and Kruse Firm 279, 280, 281, 285
Port Deposit, Maryland 146, 192, 193, 207, 208
Presbyterians 13
Price Hall, Middletown 208
Priests Landing 18
Primrose Cemetery 37
Propaganda Fide 177, 198, 230
Quakers 13, 22, 23, 24
Queen Anne County, Maryland 157
Queen Anne's Law 13
Queenstown, Maryland 195
Raskob Foundation 276, 277
Reconstruction, U.S. Era of 187
Recusant Chalice 37
Reese's Corner 195, 228
Rock Hall, Maryland 195, 196, 229
Rogers Tavern 316
Rose Hill 171, 316
Saint Domingue 58
Sassafras, Maryland 25
Sassafras Neck 83, 85, 91
Sassafras River 86
Schola Cantorum 298

Second Vatican Council 286
Seven Years War 30, 35, 39
Slavery Issue 20, 35, 36, 63, 64, 80, 86
Slaves at Bohemia 81, 83, 88, 93, 94, 95, 101, 102, 107, 110, 113, 117, 124, 130, 131, 134, 139, 142, 148, 150, 151, 153, 172, 176, 179, 180, 182, 191, 192, 194, 199, 209
Smyrna, Delaware 22, 224
Society of Jesus 80, 164
Society of St. Sulpice 84, 152
Spain 24, 27, 30
St. Dennis Church 190
St. Ignatius Tract 19, 20, 45
St. John's Church, Rock Hall 196
St. Joseph's Church, Philadelphia 8
St. Mary Ann Church 316
St. Mary's City 14
St. Mary's Seminary 85, 88
St. Patrick Cemetery 49
St. Stephen's Church 316
St. Xaverius Mission 16, 18
Stamp Act 41
Stock Market 274
Sugar Act 41
Sulpician Archives 88
Summer Festival 243
Summit, Delaware 140
Susquehanna River 140
Talbot County, Maryland 150, 163, 188, 196
Tounament at Bohemia 242
Treaty of Paris 39
Trumpington 195, 209, 228, 287
Tuckahoe (later Cerdova) 129
Tully's Neck 83
Twenty Centuries of Catholic History 299
Ukrainian Community 271, 296, 299, 300
United States Census 81
U.S. Bicentennial 290, 320
U.S. Bicentennial Exhibit 290, 320
Vulcan's Rest 238
War of 1812, 86
War of Jemkin's Ear 27
Warren Farm 283
Warrington 196
Warwick, Maryland 9, 17, 83, 276, 282, 283
Washington College 48
White Clay Creek 91
Whitemarsh 85
Wilna Place 159
World War I 273
World War II 275, 276
Woodbridge 45, 46
Worsell Manor 18, 45, 83, 84, 86, 99, 316
Yorktown, Battle of 80

THE BOARD OF DIRECTORS
OF THE OLD BOHEMIA HISTORICAL SOCIETY

extends sincere thanks and appreciation to the individuals and organizations listed on the following pages for their generosity in making possible the publication of this history of Saint Francis Xavier Shrine, "Old Bohemia."

PATRONS

Joanne Moffett Alfree
Richard and Mary Ann Amirikian
Rev. Msgr. John O. Barres, S.T.D., J.C.L.
Mary Brady
Rev. Msgr. Patrick A. Brady
Bob and Virginia Briccotto
Msgr. John Bura
Richard and Bernice Byrne
Rev. Paul J. Campbell
Catholic Cemeteries Incorporated
Joseph and Lilia Chaika
Kelly and James Coughlin
Daniels and Hutchison Funeral Homes
Declan and Emma Doheny
Donn Devine
Helen A. Dugan
Allaire C. DuPont
Carl and Eileen Edelin
Ann and Ray Filasky
Rev. Thomas A. Flowers
Margaret R. and Mary E. Foley
Geoffrey and Dorcas Gamble
Rev. Thomas F. Gardocki, Psy.D.
Agnes Cochran Garton
Joseph and Joyce Stone Gibson and Family
Joseph A. Gillies and Family

Rev. Steven B. Giuliano
Laura P. Gosnay
Anna Gutosky Hargrove
Roseann H. Harkins
Holy Cross Parish, Dover, Delaware
Holy Family Church
Donald and Patricia Honig
Immaculate Conception Church
Pamela Dill Kartachek and Thomas Kartachek
Mr. and Mrs. Arthur T. Keefe III
Knights of Columbus, Father George Villiger Council
Knights of Columbus, Maryland State Council
Rev. Frederick A. Kochan, Ret.
Richard and Dolores Konrad
Tish and Richard Kwasizur
Mr. and Mrs. Denis J. Kwasnieski
The Lapointe-Madden Families
Msgr. Clement P. Lemon
Louise Truesdale Loening
Anne A. Losten
Most Rev. Basil H. Losten, D.D.
E. Edward Losten
Mary A. Maloney
Margaret M. Matyniak
Marilyn Mc Govern
Thomas and Rosalinda McWilliams

Oblate Sisters of St. Francis de Sales
Marla Dill-Palmer and Roger Palmer
Mr. and Mrs. Herman Panacek, Jr.
Dr. and Mrs. William Paré
Rev. Thomas J. Peterman
Frances and John Quinn
Mr. and Mrs. James R. Quinn
John Timothy Quinn and Mary Moynihan Quinn
George and Lora Rayner
Rev. Msgr. Joseph F. Rebman V.G.
Rev. George V. Rhodes Ret.
Mr. and Mrs. Dana P. Robinson
Susan K. Ross MD
Mr. and Mrs. John Adam Roslan, Sr.
Most Rev. Michael A. Saltarelli, D.D.
Dr. Margaret J. Seitz
Patricia Moffett Seitzer
Mr. and Mrs. Jack Sentman
St. Patrick Historical Society - Pilottown
Rev. Msgr. Paul J. Taggart
The Order of Malta
Prof. and Mrs. A. Julian Valbuena
John P. Walsh
Mr. and Mrs. David Dreka Widner
Amy C. and Frank E. Williams III
Jane and Frank Williams

IN MEMORY OF...

Steven Barczewski
 by Susan L. Arday
 by George A. Barczewski
 by Steven & Patsy Barczewski
 by Chester J. Lewis
 by Joanne B. Lewis
Catherine Diers, Mary A. Johnston & Josephine Simpson
 by Ann Theresa (Dunn) Clegg
Edwin A. Dill
 by A. Bernice Dill
George E. Dunn
 by Mrs. Terri Dunn
Foley – Graham Family
 by Mary Foley Graham Perry
Elizabeth A. Getty, Emma Mae Holton, & Frances Holton North
 by Kenneth R. & Joy (Holton) Getty

William Heverin 1714-1782
 by Charles A. Heavrin
Robert M. Huhn & Robert M. Huhn, Jr.
 by Joan M. Huhn
Eloise K. Johnson
 by Bob, Phyllis, & Edwin Johnson
Margaret A. Kaplow
 by Mary A. Maloney
Alex Luzetsky
 by Bette B. Luzetsky
Thomas Francis Murray
 by JoAnne Murray Caira
Elizabeth S. & Wm. Price 3rd
 by Louisa P. Zeh.
Helena S. Green Raskob
 by Mrs. William Duffy
Marion C. Walsh
 by John P. Walsh

ABOUT THE AUTHOR

Thomas Joseph Peterman was born in Dover, Delaware, on April 28, 1931, the son of Albert and Catherine Peterman. After completing eight grades at Milford Public Elementary School, he attended high school at St. Charles' Seminary, Catonsville, Maryland. While in Baltimore, he studied piano at Peabody Conservatory of Music. Graduating from St. Mary's College, he went on for theological studies at Catholic University of America, Washington, D.C. He was ordained to the priesthood at St. John's Church, Milford, Delaware, on June 1, 1957, by Bishop Hubert J. Cartwright. He received a Master's Degree in Education Administration from Villanova University in 1962 and was appointed principal of Holy Cross High School, Dover, the same year. In 1966 he was appointed principal of St. Elizabeth's High School, Wilmington, Delaware. In May 1970, he was appointed pastor, Perryville, Maryland.

In 1974 he was appointed pastor of St. Mary Magdalen Church, Sharpley. He completed studies for a doctorate in American history at Catholic University of America in November 1981. After a term as pastor of Holy Cross Church in Dover (1983-1987), he served as pastor of Sacred Heart Church in Chestertown, Maryland (1987-1994). In 1994 he was appointed Dean of the Eastern Shore Deanery and was elected to the Diocesan Priests' Council. In June, 1994, Father Peterman became pastor of St. Dennis Church in Galena, Maryland, where he continues to serve the people of the Diocese of Wilmington, Delaware.

MISSION STATEMENT

The Old Bohemia Society, Inc. is a non-profit, non-denominational organization. It was formed for the sole purpose of restoring and maintaining the historic St. Francis Xavier "Old Bohemia" Shrine (the Mother Church of the Catholic Diocese of Wilmington), the out-buildings, grounds and museum, and to preserve and keep them as authentically near the original designs as possible.